1 MONTH OF
FREE
READING

at

www.ForgottenBooks.com

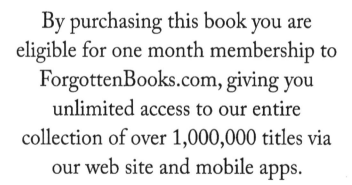

By purchasing this book you are eligible for one month membership to ForgottenBooks.com, giving you unlimited access to our entire collection of over 1,000,000 titles via our web site and mobile apps.

To claim your free month visit: www.forgottenbooks.com/free634859

ISBN 978-0-483-30822-0
PIBN 10634859

For support please visit www.forgottenbooks.com

THE
ECCLESIASTICAL REVIEW

A MONTHLY PUBLICATION FOR THE CLERGY

Vol. XLII

" Ut Ecclesia aedificationem accipiat."

I COR. 14 : 5.

CONTENTS—VOL. XLI.

JANUARY.

FEBRUARY.

CONTENTS.

MARCH.

APRIL.

MAY.

CONTENTS.

JUNE.

THE
ECCLESIASTICAL REVIEW

Fifth Series.—Vol. II.—(XLII).—January, 1910.—No. 1.

THE NEWEST PHILOSOPHY.[1]

I.

THE heyday of Positivism as the ultimate philosophy of the universe is past. The mere heaping-up of scientific facts no longer satisfies us. Our age begins to feel anew that the true riddles of the Universe are after all not those which the naturalist declared to be such, and that we do not understand the world we live in by simply decomposing it into its physical and psychical elements. We have come to feel that life is not the more worth living by the mere accumulation of scientific facts.

Accordingly, Prof. Munsterberg discovers a new demand for a more comprehensive interpretation of the Universe through the understanding of its ultimate ends and causes. And in presence of the prevailing Pragmatism, many thinking minds are all the more insistent in this demand. According to pragmatic tenets " truth is nothing but that which helps us to fulfil our purposes; beauty is nothing but that which appeals agreeably to our senses; morality is nothing but useful prescriptions which secure comfort for our particular social group; religion is nothing but suggestions which give us hope. In short, our so-called values seem to be merely means of personal gratification, changing from age to age, from people to people, from group to group, from man to man." [2]

Outspoken or not, that is the philosophical creed of the overwhelming majority of thinking persons to-day. The faithful believer, to be sure, feels that his religion really brings him in contact with something which is absolutely valuable. The moral man who sacrifices his life to follow the call of duty, believes in his deepest heart that the moral deed is of absolute value. The artist who creates a thing of beauty, imagines that his inspiration, too, opens to him a world of absolute value. The social reformer and the statesman, the pioneer and the captain of industry, when they work and fight for the progress of mankind, feel that the human advance is something absolutely valuable. The judge, when he serves on the bench, is filled with the belief that it is absolutely valuable to have justice prevail among men. And in the midst of his scholarly research the seeker for truth is indeed uplifted by the conviction that the full truth is something eternally valuable. But all these convictions and beliefs, these faiths and inspirations must fade away, it seems, as soon as the philosopher begins to examine them. He shows that they are nothing but illusions which pleasantly deceive the striving man, and that in reality no absolute values can exist. Everything is relative; everything is good only for a certain purpose, for a certain time, for a certain social group, for a certain individual. Goodness and beauty and progress and peace and religion and truth have merely pragmatic value. They help us to our personal ends. Our ideals and our lives have no value in themselves. What we dream of eternal values should simply be explained psychologically, like the fancies of a fairy-tale. " Philosophical scepticism and rela_tivism are thus the last word, and their answer harmonizes with a thousand disorganizing tendencies of our time " (p. 2).

Our time, no doubt, welcomes every achievement of the sciences, physical and mental, and does not want to lose any of their conquests; but it begins to reject the superficiality with which such physical and psychological knowledge is raised to the dignity of a philosophy. The sciences themselves begin to urge a critical examination of their foundations, and that means that they ask about the real value of truth. And in practical life, also, everywhere an uncanny feeling prevails that our hasty, busy life has lost its aim; that our efficiency · has grown, but that the meaning of our life is in danger; that everything is scattered, and that we need a new unity. Clearer and clearer shine the values through the world of facts. More and more do we come to realize that the individual man is not the measure of all things.

We need therefore a philosophy which will do justice to all the knowledge and all the inspirations of the twentieth century, and yet avoid the shallowness of modern scepticism. And it is certain, if our time is to have a new philosophy which may give meaning to life and reality, and liberate us from the pseudo-philosophic doubt of our ideals, that the problem of values must stand in the center of the inquiry. The meaning of what is valuable must decide our view of the world. Of course, others may have their full share in the study of what mankind accredits as valuable. Sociologists and psychologists, historians and biologists, economists and theologians may and must approach the problem of values from new and ever new sides. They have to describe and classify and especially to explain the whole manifoldness of that which men value in the world. They have to make us understand how this endless variety of valuations has grown and how it originated. But the fundamental problem remains untouched by all of them; the philosopher alone is called to answer it: how far have we a right to give to our values an objective character? What does it mean to have values? In what sense can they really be valuable? In what sense are they dependent upon our personal standpoint? Is there anything in the world valuable except our personal likings and pleasures, anything worthless but the sources of our personal discomfort? Is there any moral or logical or esthetic or religious sin which we ought to reject without reference to our personal dislikes? (p. 6).

II

Are there any absolute values? The study of physical nature does not reveal to us anything of real absolute value. For, according to Prof. Munsterberg, the physical sciences, as such, have no relation to men, to his everlasting will; they busy themselves merely with descriptions of phenomena, their causes and effects, and the laws that rule them.

To be sure, that does not exclude the fact that their relations to man play an important rôle also in natural science; but in that case man is himself considered as such a part of nature. For instance, the chemist may consider certain chemical substances in their effects on the human organism, and classify them as food or as drugs or as poison. From that point of view he is justified in calling the food valuable and the poison harmful. But if we take it rigorously, we must say that in the chemical system as such the substances which feed man and the substances which kill man are equally neutral, inasmuch as man is in that system only a chemical substance.

The conception of nature, however, cannot be narrowed down to include only the objects of physical nature. A description of all the objects of experience which we find in the world, must also include the mental contents, the ideas and thoughts, the feelings and emotions. The naturalist may interpret them as products of the organism, and the psychophysicist may consider their occurrence as determined by processes in the brain; but in every case they remain after all something different from the space-filling material object. A sensation is never a nerve-cell and is never mechanical energy; and yet no one denies that such sensations have just as much real existence in the world as the nerves, and that psychology therefore has the right to exist as well as physics. But from a distinctly psychological point of view thoughts and emotions and feelings are as indifferent as the molecules of the universe are indifferent in the system of physics. No atom is more valuable than another atom for the physicist; no feeling is more valuable than another feeling for the psychologist.

But this double series of experiences, this artificial division of nature into physical and mental objects, has been artificially created for scientific purposes; and in my immediate life-experience, unbroken by the division into subject and object, I am always a self for which the things are means and ends, objects of fear and hope, of desire and dislike; they become aims and means of a purposive will; they become values.

We apply the term value to certain human interests, for instance to the things that are desired. But since individuals as such desire and prefer for themselves certain things, because they give them personal satisfaction, we can call these

absolute value from the world of individual desires. There exists no bridge from the individual pleasure and displeasure to the absolute value (p. 28).

If we try to determine absolute values by taking as criterion their desirability or pleasantness, we may arrive at some climax-value, one which I prefer to all others, such as, for instance, the mild peace of a soul without desires, or the completeness of a harmonious active life. Or we may consider as absolutely valuable that which gives the greatest pleasure to the greatest number. But in both cases the standard of evaluation remains personal, because there is no essential difference between those pleasures and the pleasures of those who enjoy a feast; there is only the striving after a larger amount of individual happiness.

At all times the effort has been made to suit the demand for a general philosophy with such individualistic conceptions of value. Modern relativism in all its forms, the American Pragmatism, like the German Empirico-Criticism, glories in its nakedness. Its followers are satisfied in its poverty of thought as soon as it is demonstrated that the tastes and norms are different at various times, and among various peoples, and that even the most important evaluations are frequently changing. They triumphantly show that even in the highest sphere of human valuation everything changes and fluctuates: grotesque contradictions appear in the values of wisdom; that which is true to one generation may be error to the next; alarming contrasts appear in the religious valuations which are so often praised as over-personal, while science shows that in every part they have the stamp of passing civilizations. Chaos is found in the moral valuations of the peoples: the one places as the highest of values what another tribe may condemn as heinous (p. 34). Yet, the truth which I seek in my search for knowledge is an unconditional one, and such truth has lost its meaning as goal for my inquiry as soon as I suppose that the contrary may possibly have the same truth-value. I demand of any truth that its value be independent of the feelings of any majorities and temporal currents, and I subordinate myself to the truth in a way which excludes every relation to individuals, however much they agree in their needs (p. 37). Our moral consciousness affirms immediately that, when we are carried by moral will, we do not aim at goals whose value is determined by our personal like or dislike. Whoever says " duty ", means a value which is not founded on individual pleasures.

The human mind and will, then, are bound by absolute and necessary values: we cannot affirm a judgment in accordance with our caprice; we are bound by the truth, by something of which the opposite is impossible. We cannot act in accordance with every desire: we are bound by duties, the fulfilment of which is independent of any practical effects.

Yet, it would be misunderstanding Prof. Munsterberg, to think that truth and duty are objective realities, that the ultimate ground on which we admit their reality is to be found in the existence of a world independent of the thinking mind. Following in the wake of Kant, he admits that the existence of reality is given to us in judgments, and that their affirmation ultimately has no other reason than the fact that our thought faces a rule, an " ought ". Such an " ought ", he goes on to explain, does not belong to the existing object, but belongs to the will of the subject as its deepest significance.

Again, this ought or obligation should not be understood as if it meant submission to certain crystallized norms, the following of which, as experience has taught us, leads to certain effects which are most frequent, most typical or most beneficial to us. " Not to be obedient to the obligation means to play a risky game." But such a conception of obligation cannot bring us nearer to our goal, the attainment of absolute values; for that which we ought to do is here again ultimately that which we wish to do in the interest of our pleasure. It would bring us back to an individualistic conception of values. This appears more clearly in the consideration of the ethical values. For the idea of an ought lies before us most clearly and comes first to the mind of everyone in the field of moral obligation.

" Moral obligation " means a manifoldness of possibilities of action. Some are tempting and promise pleasure; but only one action may be demanded by our duty. The obligation faces us here in the choice of our action. We feel that we can do that which our duty forbids; this is evidently the commonplace meaning of obligation, and we should not speak of an obligation at all if there were no opportunity for a choice, no possibility to will that which we ought not to will. But does this every-day idea of duty hold for the value of truth or beauty or justice? When I want to judge, do I really stand before a decision whether I want the true judgment or its opposite? Is it not rather the case that if I will to judge at all, I never desire to choose anything but the true valuable judgment? Often an error may tempt me, but it can tempt me only as long as I take it for truth. I never want the error as such.

This is equally true in the moral sphere. The moral value is in reality a value which we always will, and which is never fought by any not-willing. The moral value never stands in contradiction to our own true will. Thus in the case of the thief, if there were only the choice between the two actions as such, stealing and not-stealing, he would never hesitate; he would always prefer the valuable honest action. His difficulty is only that, while he wills of the two achievements only the one, the honest one, he wills at the same time the booty, and to get it, he has to steal. Stealing does not become desirable by it, but he must do it if he is to reach a desired pleasurable result.

The starting-point for a moral decision is therefore always that there are in view two possible actions, of which the one is desired only as a means to an effect, while the other is desired " as action itself, and for itself," and therefore without reference to any pleasurable effect. Such action is willed then as an expression of the will, as a realization of the personality. He alone thinks morally who performs the action which he wants to perform, not for any result, but only as an expression of his whole real will. Moral merit belongs only to the one who brings to realization that particular action which he himself really wants as action. Hence moral value comes in question only where a man chooses what he really wants himself, and what expresses his own deepest will; in short, when he is loyal to himself. This self-consistency is the only thing in the world which is morally valuable. And it needs no outside obligation, but is thoroughly based on one's own will. No one cannot will it. Even the criminal, if he is a criminal and not an insane person, values this loyalty, and feels sharply that he has lost in worth when, under the temptation of a pleasure, he realized that action which as action

other words, he never did not will the moral. But here too it must be acknowledged that this will is a will which is ultimately overpersonal, necessary, and general. I want to be consistent with myself in my actions and thus want to be myself, not for the purpose of getting a personal pleasure from this consistency, but to satisfy a will in me which has no reference to my individual advantage. It is a will which, however much it concerns my personality, is ultimately not referring to myself, but serving an eternal cause. The ought, the obligation in the accepted sense of the word, loses all meaning when a decision between different desires is excluded, and "the will which finds its satisfaction in truth and beauty and morality and religion" is "a pure will," a will not touched by personal pleasure and displeasure.

The first question therefore is answered: we seek a truth which is meant as something absolutely valuable, something of which the opposite is impossible; we believe in the absolute value of our duty, which in our submission to it we conceive as independent of any practical effects. Every doubt of absolute values ultimately destroys itself; as thought it contradicts itself; as doubt it denies itself; as belief it despairs of itself. Absolute values must therefore be presumed by us as real, must have validity for us as superior to the relativistic values which historical individuals create. They are objects of pure will, and are to be fulfilled not in the interest of individuals, but on account of their absolute value; and their realization gives meaning to individual life.

It is in this sense that "we make the world". That does not mean that we construct it arbitrarily like the game of chess. It does not mean that we shape a world in order that we may have new problems about which to think while the true world goes on not caring about our constructions. It means that out of the experience of every-day life we build up, through philosophical investigation, the only world which has any absolute value at all.

Now another question presents itself: what are these absolute values? According to Prof. Munsterberg, they are already vaguely given in our every-day life; and out of these naive evaluations of life arise the purposive efforts which serve the systematic upbuilding of an absolutely valuable

we call the "labor of civilization". Consequently we have the "life values" and the "culture values"; and the history of knowledge is the great effort to elaborate the spontaneous values and to discover them where naive life would not recognize them.

The field of values is divided into four large compartments, each of which is subdivided again, according to whether they are spontaneously created or scientifically developed: we have thus the "logical values" of "existence" and of "connexion", *i. e.,* scientific connexion by the law of causality. Then we have the "esthetic values" of "unity" and of "beauty". Then the "ethical values" of "development" and of "achievement". Finally the "metaphysical values" of "holiness" or religion and of "absoluteness" or philosophy.

It does not come within the scope of this paper to follow Prof. Munsterberg in his analysis of the "logical" and "esthetic" values. We confine ourselves to the examination of the ethical and metaphysical values.

III.—THE ETHICAL VALUES.

The values of existence complete themselves in the scientific values of connexions; the values of unity demand their elaboration in the values of artistic beauty; so the values of development lead on to the values of achievement.

Morality is "that achievement by which the self-development of the personality, its self-realization, becomes a conscious deliberate task." We have seen already that, according to Prof. Munsterberg, moral obligation, in the common acceptance of the term, does not exist, for the pure will always and everywhere necessarily wills that which is good or valuable, and wills it as action itself and for itself. Whenever the action which we will as such comes in conflict with another action which we do not will as such, but which promises a result desirable for us as individuals, the first action, the one which constitutes the value, must be enforced. This can be done by a perfectly new, perfectly unique valuation: we learn to consider ourselves as an absolute valid value, which real-

selves as valuable or worthless. But as soon as we will ourselves in a particular activity, the fulfilment of such a will, that is, the realization of the valued activity, makes ourselves valuable. And when the self is willed in such a way, a pure, over-personal demand is fulfilled. A man is immoral if he does not perform the action which he wills as action, and therefore does not realize himself; but prefers instead an action which is performed only to secure some desired result.

THE RELIGIOUS VALUES.

We feel that this world is not an inner chaos, and the soul yearns for identity, for unity. Religion is the "life-value" which secures this unity of the various worlds of values, viz., of the logical, esthetic and ethical values. The conscious purposive work toward this end is philosophy.

Religion and philosophy have the same task. Both aim to apprehend the worlds of values as ultimately identical with each other, and to show that the world totality is absolutely valuable. Both religion and philosophy must transcend the life-experience for that end. "But while philosophy reaches this end by conscious purposive efforts of thought, religion reaches it by following the feelings and emotions, without a conscious knowledge of the ultimate purpose."

In the system of values the holy represents the last value, coördinated with the true, the beautiful and the good. The world which is penetrated by the belief in God, no longer knows the opposition between the true connexions, the beauty of happiness and the moral realization. "And this world of God is real, because our conviction, which in the sphere of religion we call belief, realizes it; it is real because it offers us a hold for action, and thus dominates our life."

And how does religion bring about this unity in our worldview? "The lowest tribe in Ceylon indulges in wild nocturnal dances in the depths of the forest. They dance around the large arrow with rhythmical shoutings. No spirit and no god is in the arrow for them, but the arrow is the centre of their existence, the chief means of their preservation. Their whole thinking turns around the arrow. In all important events, in disease and need, the arrow is worshipped. In these mid-

his longing for happiness, and all his willing for action are now held together. The arrow helps and will help. The arrow triumphs over the hostile nature. The world now exists to serve their will and desire; all opposites are overcome. From the ecstasies of such savages who have not even reached a real belief in the spirits, up to the solemn worship of a church community, leads a continuous way. The immediate opposites are overcome in purer and purer form, and the highest religion must arise, where the purest union of the purest values is given " (p. 357).

The religious values manifest themselves through belief in creation, revelation and salvation.

With regard to Creation, Prof. Munsterberg thinks that "it remains a question of secondary importance whether God stands above the things or lives in the things themselves, whether there is one God or many " (p. 362). Only one question is always fundamental: whether the same God who orders the things in their natural connexion, at the same time transforms our experiences to beautiful inner agreement and realizes our ideals in the development of the world. The religious feeling must be certain that the world in which the things were in accordance with God's will is a world in which the connexions are controlled by natural law, in which everything unites itself in inner harmony, and in which the good deed brings with it the victory. To believe in God the Creator means therefore to be convinced in our innermost mind that through the agency of an over-experienceable power the opposition between natural order, happiness and morality is removed from the world. And such a creator stands at the central point of every great historical system. Thus for instance, "the original Chinese consciousness found its deepest emotional expression in Laotse, who proclaimed: 'Man comes from the earth and the earth from the sky, and the sky from the Tao, and the Tao comes from itself. The whole created nature with its product is only a manifestation of the Tao. While Tao is a spiritual and immaterial being, it embraces every visible thing, and in it are all beings. A supreme spirit lives in it in an incomprehensible way. This spirit is the highest and most perfect being, because in it there is truth and belief and confidence. From eternity to eternity his glory

good and the beautiful in the highest degree of perfection.'
That is the fundamental tone which sounds through the religions of all nations and all ages. The order of nature, the pure happiness, and the moral striving must somehow be combined in something which is beyond experience, which we cannot understand, but in which we must believe" (p. 364).

As for revelation, "through it the holy spirit pervades the whole fabric of human society as religious doctrine, as cult, as church and clergy, and gives to the life of the community its overpersonal value. If our valuations are to be without contradiction in themselves, it is not sufficient to believe that the world of things is more than mere nature. We must also feel that the claims of men which approach us as historical reality are more than merely demands of historical men. Our social life is not only filled with social strifes, but it is the battle-ground of opposing valuations. The consciousness of our duties and of our rights, the dignity and power of the historical traditions, the over-personal hopes and appreciations, may oppose one another. All these contrasts can and must disappear only when we are certain that the historical connexion ultimately points back to God. We must feel that the demand of men is ultimately sanctioned by God Himself, in whom all order and all bliss and all morality become a unity" (pp. 370-371).

Finally, Prof. Munsterberg's new doctrine of salvation is thus explained: "the soul of every man is filled with contradictions. Through our own power this inner strife of our volitions cannot be subdued, and the soul seeks a beyond in which this inner play comes to silence. And the longing for this absolute value of unity in our soul is the demand for salvation. It arises wherever in the world mankind exists, because the necessary, the moral and the happy never have completely unified themselves in the life-experience of any one."

The thought of life after death is not at all necessarily in the foreground; and on the other hand, just this thought has been often developed without reference to the idea of salvation. In short, "salvation does not result as the effect of a divine action, but by our own aiming towards a higher, purer life. It is therefore an ideal, but this ideal can be believed as real because our conviction maintains it" (p. 383).

IV.

Thus far the exposé of Prof. Munsterberg's philosophy. We have tried to give a faithful, connected outline of it, mostly in his own words. A few critical remarks seem called for.

It cannot be denied that, in sharp contrast with the Naturalism and Pragmatism of the day, this new philosophy brings to the fore the existence of absolute values lying beyond this physical world; values which make for a spiritual and teleological view of the universe. These values, however, as pointed out already, have no objective reality. Prof. Munsterberg is a thoroughgoing follower of Kant and Fichte. We have no room here however to go into further details about that aspect of his system.

We would rather examine briefly some other logical consequences of his system, in as far as it is destined to exercise its influence on thinking minds and on the youth of the University that come under its sway, and for whom it will become a fundamental view of life and the world and a rule of personal conduct.

For that in the mind of the author it is intended to exercise such influence, he confesses himself. Although not writing for the intelligent amateur; although deprecating a tendency often apparent in our time to write philosophy in brilliant epigrams and clever discussions; and although on the other side not pleading for " a philosophical art for art's sake ", yet he asserts with a very good reason: " everybody's life is controlled by some kind of philosophy, however haphazard and fragmentary it may be. And every true philosopher aims finally to reach the conviction of the masses. And if serious thought has distilled some truth, it will be distributed quickly enough through thousands of popular channels."

Such being the case, what does Prof. Munsterberg's theory on Ethics and Religion hold in store for us?

Morality, it will be remembered, is one of the values of achievement, one of the values developed by civilization.

If we ask for " a norm of morality," for a criterion by which to distinguish right from wrong, we are confronted by the assertion that conscience is our light and guide, and that we must follow its dictates. If we ask further why we should follow the dictates of our conscience, whether because there

is an objective difference between right and wrong, which difference we apprehend in our judgment; or whether it is
merely a subjective feeling, something akin to the "moral
sense" of a certain school, we receive no further enlightenment. This last alternative, however, seems to chime in best
with the system of which Prof. Munsterberg is the protagonist.
At any rate it is made perfectly clear that the ultimate foundation of right and wrong is to be sought in man, and not in God.

As for "moral obligation," after having reduced it to a
mere norm, summarizing the good or evil effects of a generally followed line of conduct, that is binding only on the individual, he concludes that there is strictly speaking but one
moral obligation, consisting in this "categoric imperative":
realize the action which you will on its own account, as action.
"There exists no moral law: you ought not to lie, you ought
not to steal, you ought not to kill. Whether your speaking the
truth is that kind of action which you really will as action of
your personality, depends on the height of your development.
But if you will this action, you ought to perform it, and you
ought not to be tempted by pleasure or displeasure to actions
which you do not at all will as actions. Self-faithfulness,
self-loyalty is accordingly the only moral obligation" (p.
342).

And the "sanction of this moral obligation" is the complete
harmonious self-development of nature, in accordance with
the over-personal demands of reason. It is hard, nay impossible to admit, that a moral obligation, the last foundation
and the ultimate sanction of which are found in man himself,
can be really binding on him, as all agree the moral law is
binding. Yet Prof. Munsterberg insists: "the only thing
which is valuable in actions, namely the self-consistency, needs
no outside obligation, but is thoroughly based on the own
will" (p. 64).

But it is plain that when he further explains that a criminal
never wavers between the will to moral self-consistency and
the will to inconsistency; that he never does not will the consistency, he makes an inadmissible confusion between moral
judgment and moral action. The criminal, if he is a criminal
and not an idiot, always knows, perceives, apprehends the
distinction between right and wrong. But by an act of his

And here lies the fundamental weakness of Prof. Munsterberg's elaborate moral synthesis: unless there be an outside obligation which the perverted human will cannot break; unless especially there be an outside sanction, a reward for those who keep and a punishment for those who break the moral law, no morality can hold out against the assaults of human passion. History is there to prove this contention, and every-day life around us forces it upon the most unwilling of men.

The moral law, such as we have it at present, is the outcome of centuries of " Christian " civilization, whose influence all of us undergo unwittingly, and whose ideals even the most inveterate enemies of Christianity cannot altogether put aside. But if with Prof. Munsterberg we admit that morality is only the product of civilization, of the natural evolution of the human mind, what guarantee is there that such a morality is of more than relative value; that a higher degree of culture is not destined to change its laws and ideals? Does his assumption not allow of the wildest speculations in the field of morality, speculations against which Prof. Munsterberg would protest in vain?

In the last analysis his ethics are reduced to the code of the *morale laïque;* they bring the world back to pagan morality. Unless ethics be ultimately founded on God and religious dogma; unless they admit an objective distinction between right and wrong, a moral obligation independent of man and a moral sanction that it is beyond man's power to escape or destroy, they can never contribute to the advancement of the human race. Such a morality may indeed be sufficient to keep a small intellectual elite within the bounds of reason and common decency; but it can never become a light to guide the masses.

A somewhat identical criticism must be made of Prof. Munsterberg's system of religious values.

He is careful indeed to assert that religion and philosophy, " each in its own sphere, are to coördinate the disjointed values into a harmonious whole." But this assertion notwith-

and must be so broad that " inside its boundaries there is room
for Buddhism and the cult of the Greeks, and Christianity and
Islam " (p. 388).

In other words, all religions as such stand on the same level,
since their value does not consist in the truth of their tenets,
but in their power to unify the contradictory values that sur-
round us on all sides. We can therefore also have peace with
all the opposing views that have been advanced in the name
of Christianity. " Since the days of the first Christian communities all the particular views have passed through incessant changes. The order of nature is very unequally conceived if sometimes every change in the world is understood
as always a new action of the Creator and at other times there
is a sure belief that God has given to nature the laws for all
time. Still more, morality is very unequally conceived.
Sometimes it is a presupposition that every human soul has
the free power to decide between good and bad; at other
times it has been a fixed belief that God had decided beforehand who is to have the power for good and bad; at other
times it has been a fixed belief that God has decided beforehand who is to have the power for good and who may vic-
toriously carry through the struggle. And not less different
is the way in which happiness has been conceived, if it is
sometimes promised for the resurrection at the last day, and
sometimes sought in the trustful belief itself in the heart of
the fighter in the hour of the fight. But in the fundamental
demand, these contradictions do not change anything " (p.
368).

Christianity itself, although Prof. Munsterberg grants it
to be a superior form of civilization, when looked upon in the
light of the ultimate purpose it is destined to fulfil, stands no
higher than the religion of the South Sea Islander or the
savage Congolese: all religions are equally supernatural inasmuch as they are considered thus by their adherents; all are
equally true for those who believe in them.

What such doctrines, following logically from Prof. Munsterberg's system, and scrupulously consistent with it, must
lead to, we need not point out. Suffice it to note in conclusion
that his philosophical doctrine of the absolute values leads to
a dreary pantheism: " Religion is philosophy for the I who
maintains its self-hood, also in the face of the all; philosophy

is religion for the I which in its own deed finally grasps the all, and through the all gives up the self-hood " (p. 413).

We do not pretend that Prof. Munsterberg is a deliberate and inveterate foe of Christian morality and religion, and is seeking for cheap notoriety in propounding his doctrine. He is no doubt perfectly sincere in his convictions, and never does he indulge in vulgar attacks on what we hold in sacred reverence. But the danger is all the greater on that score.

In the beginning of this article we quoted Prof. Munsterberg as saying that we need a philosophy that will do justice to all the aspirations of the twentieth century, and yet avoid the shallowness of modern scepticism; that in such a philosophy the problem of values must stand in the center of the inquiry; that the meaning of what is valuable must decide our view of the world. True enough; but when the values have been inverted, when the higher values of revelation are made subservient to the fluctuating values of human reason, our view of the world becomes decidedly faulty. " Next to religion, rigid philosophical systems which the man in the street hardly understood in their original form, have been the most powerful factors in the history of the last two thousand years; they have made revolutions and they have brought reforms," Prof. Munsterberg tells us very rightly. Yet the adoption of his principles would speedily bring the world back to the "splendid paganism" of Greece and Rome, to which, indeed outside of the Catholic Church, it is speedily drifting. In confirmation of this view, we have Prof. Munsterberg's own testimony. Writing in *The Atlantic Monthly* for October, he again outlines his new philosophy, and proceeds: " to give it at once a historical background, we have only to look . . . to the underlying world-views of the German nation . . . during the eighteenth century, the period of Schiller and Goethe, of Kant and Fichte and Hegel. . . . In such a philosophy the moral deed is not valuable because it adds to the pleasure of the neighbor, but because it is eternally good; the work of art is valuable, not because it pleases the senses, but because it realizes the ideal of beauty; the world of the market is valuable, not because it satisfies individual needs, but because it means a realization of the ideal of progress; the life of the state is valuable, not because it secures the

tion of the ideals of right and as such of eternal value; and knowledge too is valuable, not because it is a serviceable tool for the pleasures of individuals, but because it is a fulfillment of the ideal of truth " (pp. 458-459). It is rather remarkable that religion, as a life-shaping force and factor, should be left out of this enumeration; although from a historical stand-point our surprise is lessened when we remember that atheism was predominant in the life of the eighteenth century, and that its greatest thinkers were religion's sworn antagonists.

It is not hard to tell what the influence of such a system of philosophy must be on immature minds that imbibe it from the master's lips. And the study of this newest philosophy certainly gives point to the contentions of those who never cease repeating that many of our Universities are " blasting at the Rock of Ages." [3]

J. B. CEULEMANS.

Moline, Illinois.

EXTREME UNCTION.

" It is also declared that this unction is to be applied to the sick, especially those who are so dangerously ill as to seem to be about to depart this life; whence also it is called the sacrament of the de-parting. And if the sick should recover after having received this unction, they may again get the succor of this sacrament, when they fall into another like danger of death."—Council of Trent, Sess. 14, On the Sacrament of Extreme Unction. Chap. 3.

THIS is the doctrine of the Church as defined at Trent. The words embody a definition, as is plain on the face of them, and from the intention expressed in the preamble: " It hath also seemed good to the Holy Synod to subjoin to the preceding doctrine on Penance the following on the sac-rament of Extreme Unction." We have here, therefore, a law and norm for all time, to which the teaching of theologians

[3] Writing in *The Harvard Theological Review* for October, Prof. Josiah Royce expresses much the same views as Prof. Munsterberg: " The doctrine of the incarnation is the doctrine which teaches that the world-will desires our unity with the universal purpose, that God will be born in us and through our consent, that the whole meaning of our life is that it shall transmute transient and temporal values into eternal meanings. Humanity becomes conscious God

and the practice of priests in the administration of this sacrament should conform.

The Council touches here on two points, the subject or recipient of the sacrament, and the iteration of it. As regards the former of the two, it is declared that this unction is to be applied to the sick, especially to those who are so dangerously ill as to seem to be on the point of death—" in exitu vitae constituti." The first part of the statement, taken by itself, might be construed to mean that the sacrament may be given to any sick person, even though not in danger of death. We have it on the authority of Simeon, Archbishop of Thessalonica in the 15th century, that this was the practice of the Orthodox Greek Church.[1] The tradition of the Latin Church is clean against this, and the context shows that such was not the meaning the Council intended to convey. For in the preamble " it declares and teaches that our most gracious Redeemer, who would have His servants at all times provided with salutary remedies against all the assaults of all their enemies, while in the other sacraments He prepared the greatest aids whereby Christians may preserve themselves whole during life from the more grievous spiritual evils, did, by the sacrament of extreme unction, guard the close of life as with a most firm defense "; also, as we see, in the more immediate context, Extreme Unction is spoken of by the Council as " the sacrament of the departing ". When therefore it declares that this unction is to be applied to the sick, especially those who are so dangerously ill as to seem to be on the point of quitting this life, it does but signify that the sacrament may be administered even when there is no immediate danger of death, or when the sickness is such that a man, though likely to die, has still some chance of recovery.

Touching the iteration of the sacrament the teaching of the Council is precise. " If the sick recover after having received this unction, they may again be anointed when they fall into a like danger of death." The word translated " recover " is " convaluerint " from " convalescere," which properly means to begin to be strong again—to get better rather

---

[1] He inveighs against the Latins who "say it is not to be given to the sick but to the d in ," and affirms that if one were to fall into " a sickness of the soul only " one should call in the priests of the Church, presumably to administer extreme unction. P. G. Tom. CLV, cols. 515-518.

than to get well or be completely restored to health. As often, therefore, as the sick person rallies and is judged to be on the road to recovery, then suffers a relapse and is again considered to be in danger, he may again be anointed, according to the teaching of the Council. Mark the word " may ", for the Council does not say that he should, but that he may— " iterum hujus sacramenti subsidio juvari poterunt." Observe also that the Council does not lay down a time-limit; it is not at all a question of time, but a question of growing better and then again getting worse—of being pronounced out of danger and then falling back into a like danger again. A person may be anointed again even after a few days, if in the meantime he has so far recovered as to be pronounced out of danger and afterwards has a relapse. On the other hand, suppose a person has been anointed and lingers on for two or three months, or even longer, without getting better, sinking slowly all the time, he is not again to be anointed. Such I take to be a plain and necessary inference from the teaching of the Council. The same may be gathered also from the nature of the sacrament and from its effects.

Extreme Unction, as the Council of Trent declares and as the name itself implies, is the sacrament that prepares the Christian for his passage out of this world into the next. And because a man passes out of this world but once, this sacrament, of itself and in the nature of things, should be given but once. As a matter of fact, however, men cannot tell in many cases whether death is going to ensue from an illness or not. Hence the sacrament is often given when death does not follow, or at any rate does not follow without convalescence and subsequent relapse. But once a person dangerously ill has been anointed, he is not to be anointed a second time in the same sickness unless he becomes convalescent, that is, unless he at least gets so much better as to appear to be out of danger. The reason is that whenever the sacrament is both validly and fruitfully administered it at once begets its proper effects, which are, in general, to prepare a person for his passage out of this world. Now these effects endure until death, if death really is to follow from the sickness without

a day as long as the danger lasts. Since, therefore, they do endure, to repeat the sacrament in such a case is to expose it to the manifest risk of being null and void, which would be sacrilege.

Again, the primary end of this sacrament is the spiritual healing of the soul with a view to its entrance into glory. A secondary end is the healing of the body, when God sees this to be for the good of the soul. Now the healing of the body, as being but a secondary end, would not by itself warrant the repetition of the sacrament in the same sickness. In any case, since the sacrament does not operate naturally for the healing of the body, after the manner of corporal medicine, but supernaturally, in such a way that its efficacy depends simply and wholly on the will of God, one administration of it is as effectual in this point of view as half a dozen. But what of the primary end? Would not this warrant the repetition of the sacrament in the same sickness even when there is no convalescence? It does not appear that it would, for the reason that the sacrament, being a divine ordinance, does its work effectually, given the proper dispositions in the recipient— and we are assuming the proper dispositions. It takes away sin, if sin there be; it takes away the remains of sin; it soothes the soul and strengthens it for the last struggle. And all this, as I have said, it does effectually, so that nothing more remains to be done if the sickness is really unto death and the sick person is going to face the last struggle at the end of it without convalescence. This will become clearer if we consider these effects in detail.

The taking away of sin is not itself the proper effect of this sacrament. St. James says: " If he be in sins they shall be forgiven him." The Apostle would not have made his statement conditional if the remission of sin were the proper effect of the sacrament, for no man is to be deemed so perfect as to be wholly free from sin. To remit sin is the proper effect of the sacrament of penance, and what is the proper effect of one sacrament cannot be the proper effect of another. Moreover, all are agreed that Extreme Unction is primarily a sacrament of the living. Hence we understand St. James to mean that if a person is not able, for some reason or other, to confess any grievous sins that may be on his conscience, the sacrament of Extreme Unction will take them away, provided of course, he has at least attrition for them. If, then, one should fall into sin after having been anointed, the proper remedy is the sacrament of Penance, not Extreme Unction.

The other effects are the taking away of the remains of sin, and the healing and strengthening of the soul. By the remains of sin some have understood the temporal punishment due to sin—an unlikely opinion, for the Council of Trent declares that extreme unction "wipes out the remains of sin—peccati reliquias abstergit," and if the temporal punishment were thus wiped out there would be no purgatory for any one who devoutly receives this sacrament. This does not mean that the sacrament may not lessen the temporal punishment, but only that the latter is not to be identified with what is known as "the remains of sin". By this then, we rightly understand the weakness or infirmity of the soul which is consequent on sin. And so these two effects coalesce into one, for the same unction of grace which heals the infirmity of the soul also comforts and strengthens it for the final struggle.

But may not this proper effect of the sacrament, which is the spiritual healing of the soul, be increased by repetition, as in the case of Penance and Holy Communion and so the anointing of the sick over and over again in the same sickness be warranted, even when there is no sign of convalescence? There is no parity between this sacrament and the other two. Holy Communion is the food of the soul, and may be given daily. It might even be given oftener, validly though not lawfully. Penance may be given both validly and lawfully as often as there is matter for absolution. And because sins already confessed are matter for absolution, inasmuch as the acts of the penitent are the matter of this sacrament and one may confess over again sins already confessed, be sorry for them, and be willing to do penance for them if need be, therefore the sacrament of Penance may, both validly and lawfully, be repeated over and over again as often as the penitent presents himself for confession.

On the other hand, it is quite certain that Extreme Unction cannot lawfully be given more than once in the same sickness, except in case of convalescence and relapse. So much is clearly implied by the Council of Trent and expressly affirmed in the Roman Ritual. But would not the repetition of it be at least valid? There does not seem to be any good reason for affirming that it would. In the first place, the very fact that the repetition of it is not lawful goes to show that it would not be valid. Why forbid its being administered again and again if the sacramental effect were increased and added grace were given every time? Moreover, this sacrament is the spiritual medicine of the sick man, and has for its proper effect the spiritual healing of the soul. Now, as a sacrament, as God's own medicine, it does its work effectually, it does heal the soul, and therefore to repeat it would be as void of effect and as senseless as the giving of medicine to a well man, unless there be a recrudescence of the evil and a new crisis to be met. Which is to say, that if a sick person is prepared by the anointing with oil to meet death, he is prepared, and it is absurd to speak of his being further prepared, unless he gets better, then gets worse, and is face to face with death once more. In this case it is a new danger, and he may properly be prepared anew to meet it.

Against this may be urged the practice existing in certain parts of the West, from the ninth to the twelfth century, of repeating the unction seven days, or even while the sickness lasted.[2] But this practice was never widespread, and was never recognized or sanctioned by the Church. Such a rubric is found, indeed, in the rituals of local Churches, but no writer of the time, so far at least as I have been able to find, ever as much as mentions the practice. On the contrary, several writers of that period, who treat of Extreme Unction, either affirm the existence of the very opposite practice, or discuss the repetition of the sacrament in such a way as to imply that the practice in question was unknown to them. Thus Bandinus, in the 12th century, tells us that, "this unction, according to the various use of the Churches, is repeated, or given only once."[3] So also Abelard testifies to the diversity of use in this matter in divers Churches—"De iteratione secundum diversas consuetudines fiat Ecclesiarum."[4]

In the early part of the 12th century, Godfried, Abbot of Vendôme and St. Yves, Bishop of Chartres, both declare against the iteration of the sacrament under any circumstances.[5] Hugo of St. Victor says that " It is the practice in some Churches to repeat this sacrament," and he argues that this may be done.[6] In like manner the Master of the Sentences says: " Some inquire whether this sacrament can be repeated, since baptism and certain other sacraments, once received, are not repeated," and he, too, maintains that it may.[7] In the 9th century, we have, in the " Excerpta e Pontificali S. Prudentii," a detailed account of the way Extreme Unction was adminis- tered, in which there is no trace of the practice of repeating the unction.[8] Once more, some writers maintained that it could be repeated only after three years, others after one year.[9] All this serves to show that the practice was not wide- spread and had not the sanction of the Church. Had it been widespread, had it had the sanction of the Church, it would never have been a moot point whether the sacrament could be repeated. For, to the question whether Extreme Unction could be given a second time, the obvious answer of such writers as Peter Lombard and Hugo of St. Victor would have been that it was a practice sanctioned by the Church to repeat the unction over and over again in the same sickness.

Simeon, of Thessalonica, already cited, testifies that, in the Greek Orthodox Church it was in the 15th century " an an- cient custom " to call in several priests, seven or at least three, each of whom in turn anointed the sick person.[10] This custom he considers to have been founded on the words of St. James, and intimates that one priest alone is not competent to admin- ister the sacrament: " Let him call in [says St. James] the priests of the Church (and not one priest), and let them pray over him, anointing with oil." Whether this custom was an- cient in the sense that it could be traced, in the East, to the early centuries, I am unable to say. In any case, the idea that one priest alone cannot administer Extreme Unction seems

[5] Ib., Tom. CLVII, col. 83.

[6] Ib., Tom. CLXXVI, col. 154.

[7] Tom. CXCII, cols. 899, 900.

[8] Tom. CXV, cols. 1442, 1444.

[9] De Synod. Dioec. lib. 8, cap. 8, n. 3.

[10] Loc. cit. A similar custom of old existed in the West, and there can be no doubt as to the validity of such administration.

to have had its origin in a mistaken, because too rigidly literal, interpretation of the words of St. James. Besides, the seven-fold anointing, or three-fold, as the case may have been, was not regarded as a seven-fold, or three-fold, repetition of the sacrament, for the objection against one priest administering Extreme Unction is grounded on the text of St. James, who seems to say that several priests are required—not to repeat the unction, for this one priest could do—but to administer the sacrament.

It is plain that in the middle age, between the eighth century and the twelfth, there was great diversity of teaching and practice regarding the repetition of Extreme Unction, some maintaining that it should not at all be repeated, others that it might, while others still appeared to think that it was to be repeated, or at any rate might be repeated, daily in the same sickness. The doctrine regarding this point was then in course of development. Those who would have us go back of the Council of Trent, by the path of literary and historical research, for fuller light upon it, permit themselves to forget this.

Among the writers who helped in the following century to free the question from doubt, and bring it to a stage ripe for definition, St. Thomas of Aquin holds a foremost place. His treatment of it is so lucid and so thorough that no writer who has come after him can be said to have bettered it. " In the case of this sacrament," he writes, " regard must be had not only to the sickness but to its state, for it is not to be given except to sick persons who are, as far as men can judge, drawing near to death. Now there are certain kinds of sickness that are not chronic, and if in these this sacrament is given, when the person reaches the stage in which he is in danger of death he does not get over it unless he is cured, and so he is not to be anointed again. But if he suffers a relapse, it will be another [attack of the] sickness, and he may again be anointed. There are, on the other hand, certain chronic diseases, such as consumption and dropsy, and in these the sacrament is not to be administered until the sickness verges to the point where there is real danger of death. If the person escapes the danger, and falls again into a like danger from the same dis-

lutely another illness, it is another crisis of the same." [11]   For
such light on this and kindred points we shall look in vain
to the Schismatical Churches of the East during the same
or any later period.   With their going into schism, the light
seems to have gone out from them.   Development of doctrine
was stayed; tradition handed on truth and error alike.   In
all this time there is not heard among them a magisterial voice
defining what the truth is and what is error.   They are cut
off, though now by no fault of their own, from those to whom
is the divine promise, " Lo! I am with you always even to the
end of the world."   They must bear the curse of stationari-
ness and sterility in consequence.   To advance is to run the
risk of straying from the way and losing what they have so
long held fast.

✝ ALEXANDER MACDONALD,
Bishop of Victoria.

THOMAS AQUINAS AS PREACHER.

THE thirteenth was a century of stupendous intellectual
activity.   It may even be doubted whether the world
has seen another in which the desire for learning rose to so
high a pitch.   History must ever look on it as an age of
schools, students, and universities.   Sacred eloquence or effective preaching was one of the sciences that attained to a
high degree of perfection.   It was, furthermore, an era of
combat, intellectual as well as political, against the violence
and errors of rising heresies.   The very force of circumstances, the very nature of the stirring times, caused and demanded earnest men to speak with vigor and force against
prevailing and threatening evils.   No other century can boast
of greater gifts of thought, of speech, of stronger or deeper
faith or love of God and religion.   An age it was that called
for the best efforts of strenuous and effective preaching.   The
great religious revival called into existence by the newly-
founded religious orders of St. Dominic and St. Francis contributed much to bring the noble science and art of preaching

---

[11] Additiones ad Tertiam Partem, q. 33, a. 2.   For the rest, the Council
took almost word for word from St. Thomas its statement about the repetition
of the sacrament.   Cf. Contra Gentes, lib. 4, c. 73.

to a high degree of perfection. The days of Basil and Gregory, of Chrysostom and Augustine, seemed to have returned; the celebrated preachers of the Crusades, with the famous monk of Clairvaux at their head, appeared to live again in their worthy successors, the sons of the gentle and gentlemanly Guzman and the humble man of Assisi. The new orders, as they were then called, were born in the early glow and glory of Bernard's memory; and they rekindled it anew into full-blown blaze.

We take it for granted that the reader will kindly overlook the bit of honest pride and pardonable warmth with which we here cite unquestioned history in saying that the Dominicans were the great preachers of the thirteenth century. Faithfully adhering to the plan of their saintly and illustrious Founder, they energetically followed the special spirit and calling of their Order, as interpreted by its first head. Preaching the Word of God with the thoroughness of learning, and the fire of zeal and eloquence, was the prime object and purpose of their institute. We may judge of the manner in which they acquitted themselves in their task by the results which history tells us in unmistakable terms they achieved. The black *cappa* over the white habit to this day suggests the sermon. Thomas Aquinas was in the forefront of the battle. He was a leader in this band of leaders.

The university world should attract attention by its great preachers. It did in the age with which we are dealing. Much moral corruption prevailed then, as it has prevailed in all times. But withal it was an era of strong faith. There was need of good, strong preaching; and it exerted a wholesome influence over the students of the universities, as well as over the rest of the world. The success of Bernard proves this; so does the success of Blessed Jordan, the General of the Dominicans, who peopled his numerous monasteries with university men. Albert the Great and his illustrious disciple, Thomas Aquinas, exerted a similar influence. The Dominicans of the thirteenth century introduced a strongly intellectual element into their sermons. The scriptures and the Fathers were given the most important place, somewhat at the expense of rhetoric. They spoke to the people, instructing them in true Catholic doctrine, and waging war against the evils of the day. Their style was earnest, simple and natural. Thomas followed this same method, which was classic among the brethren in his day.

We may form some conception of the great schoolman as a preacher, of his sermons and the manner of their delivery, from the history of their influence over his audiences, from his short sermon-schemata, and from the rules for the guidance of preachers which he lays down in more than one place in his voluminous writings—notably in his commentary on the Gospel of St. Matthew, in his work *Contra Impugnantes Religionem,* and in the *Responsio ad Lectorem Bisuntinum de sex Articulis.*

The Saint's earliest biographers are unanimous in telling us that he was a preacher of great power and acceptance; that, whenever and wherever he preached, the people gathered in crowds eager to hear the truth of salvation spoken by the holy man of God. They received his words, as Tocco, a contemporary biographer, informs us, " as coming from the Holy Ghost." From the same source we learn that on Good Friday, during a Lenten course of sermons he preached, at the request of Urban IV, in the Basilica of St. Peter, Rome, speaking on the Passion of our Lord, he brought the sufferings of our Blessed Saviour so vividly before his hearers, and dwelt so touchingly on His compassion, mercy, love, goodness toward man, that every one in the vast church burst into lamentation. It was almost impossible, for some time, for him to continue his discourse. Then on the Easter Sunday following, his sermon on the Resurrection infused such hope, joy, and happiness into the hearts of his audience that it was with difficulty they were prevented from breaking out into applause.

The Angelic Doctor's reputation was of itself sufficient to draw immense crowds to hear him. And if we are to credit the description his early biographers give of him—a description that has every characteristic of true history—his physical appearance was a sermon in itself. We speak of this, because in forming an estimate of a preacher we must not commit the error of separating the man from his work. The spoken discourse, in no small measure, has its life in that of the man who speaks it. The Saint's tall and commanding figure, his countenance, pale from fasting and mortification, his calm self-possession, his strong and persuasive voice, his extraordinary learning and gifts, his nobility of birth and character, his personal magnetism, and withal his great humility, his gentle, unassuming amiability, and known sanctity,—all these must have made a deep and lasting impression on those who heard him. The eloquent speaker, the learned man, the zealous priest of God, the saint and apostle were all combined in the preacher before them. He was a man, too, whose deeds and life spoke no less tellingly than his tongue. Like St. Paul, whose writings he knew and loved so well, the Angel of the Schools belonged wholly to Christ; like Paul again, he "became all things to all men in order to gain all to Christ," "bringing into captivity every understanding unto the obedience of Christ." His charity knew no bounds, embracing all in his unbounded love of the Master. His look, his manner, his word and action, clearly bespoke his one intent and purpose to draw to God.

Paris, Cologne, Rome, Viterbo, Orvieto, Fondi, Perugia, Bologna, Naples, every city, in short, where he taught, had the good fortune to witness the Angelic Doctor's triumphs as a preacher; for it seems to have been his custom to preach to both people and students wherever he was located. Naples, however, appears to have been the city especially favored with his presence; and justly so, as she may rightfully claim him as her most illustrious son. For ten years, we are told, he occupied the pulpit there, drawing the eyes of the world upon him as one of its foremost preachers. There he discoursed one whole Lent on the words of the Angelic Salutation: *Ave Maria, gratia plena, Dominus tecum;* and Tocco tells us that throughout this course of sermons he spoke as one inspired. As the beautiful thoughts flowed forth in crystal streams from his lips, " he stood with eyes and head uplifted as if lost in vision ". All the city came to the great Dominican church to hear him. It is then no matter for surprise that " his word was received as coming from the Holy Ghost ", or that " the fruits of his preaching were scarcely less than those of his writings ".

It is needless to say that Aquinas never descended to empty

under the cover of pompous and showy language; never sought to make ostentatious display of the figures and devices of rhetoric; never affected the wit, instead of speaking as an apostle and man of God; never aimed at gaining a name rather than souls, or confounding rather than instructing and converting his hearers. There was nothing of the sensational in him. The preëminent schoolman gave out to the people, not studied and high-flown phraseology, but the simple, fascinating, life-giving Word of God; and he did it with a guileless simplicity, charm, and directness that won hearts. His aim was to please, to draw, to gain with the charm of the divine truth which he sought to put before the people in its full spiritual beauty. No preacher of the Gospel ever realized more keenly than did our Saint that his task was not one of marshaling words, of making phrases, or of rounding periods, but that of the grave, serious, instructive, and persuasive discourse.

Yet, so we are told, " he spoke with much animation, and great variety of manner;" his sermons were really eloquent. He himself insists on the necessity of eloquence and learning on the part of those who preach, that they may be able to present the Word of God in a way that will win souls. But the eloquence of which he speaks is that which befits so sacred a place as the Christian pulpit, not the vain display which is sometimes made. Beauty of diction he loved, but that of lucid exposition of Catholic doctrine more. Following the golden rule of sacred oratory, Thomas spoke from the fulness of his heart, and touched the hearts of those who heard him. He felt what he said, and made his audience feel it too.

It is indeed profoundly to be regretted that probably not one of St. Thomas's sermons is extant to-day as it was spoken. Especially is it a pity that we have not the complete discourse on the Blessed Sacrament, which history tells us he preached at the command of Urban IV, in the presence of that pontiff and his cardinals. Thomas's devotion to the august Sacrament of the Altar was boundless. It was under the influence of this consuming love for the Holy Eucharist that he composed, at the request of the same pontiff, the most exquisite of our divine offices—that of Corpus Christi. One cannot

effort of his life in the composition and delivery of this sermon on the subject of his heart's fondest devotion. The conviction that this was his masterpiece forces itself upon us.

The sense of this loss grows with the consideration of the exquisite and sublime poetry in the hymns of the Mass and office of Corpus Christi. Here the Saint gives us the happiest expression of the deepest theology in poetry of the highest order. Never has the poet reasoned so like the philosopher and theologian, or the philosopher and theologian written so like the poet, as has the Angel of the Schools in these compositions. Nowhere else has the profoundest theological thought so aptly clothed itself at once in the garb of clear, clean-cut philosophic language, and in the form and color, the charm and warmth of rhythmic measure.

That we have none of the Saint's sermons as they were delivered by him, is most likely because he did not write them out fully before preaching. To the writer it seems almost certain that the famous schoolman, after the manner of many great preachers of all ages, confined his written preparation to a mere plan or skeleton of what he intended to say. Unfortunately, these sermon-outlines are generally preserved in a rather imperfect shape. In many instances, as we have them, they form nothing more than a naked sketch, giving simply the substance or groundwork of the discourse, as it was reported by some pupil or listener. In truth, we have now no means of ascertaining whether those discourses of which we have only the reports or notes of hearers, were ever written in any manner by Thomas himself. Tocco tells us that he preached not only in Latin, but also in his native tongue, Italian; but it seems more than probable that he likewise preached in French. Instead, however, of the original French or Italian in which they were spoken to the people, even this class of his sermons have survived only in a Latin garb.

And here the reader's attention may be called to a distinction we should make in the sermons of St. Thomas. Some of them were for the faithful generally; some again for university students; and yet others for the brethren of his Order, as was a custom in the early days. The first were always, or

audience; the second sometimes in their native language, sometimes in the Latin. Those to his brethren, it appears certain, were all spoken in Latin; and we take it for granted that these at least we have in the original language, though not in the original form, in which they were delivered.

Despite the grave defect of the imperfect dress in which they have come down to us, the greater number of these outline discourses of the Angelic Doctor's—at least those that are certainly his—are rich in their possibility of moral and doctrinal development. Although at first sight they are of no great importance, on further study they are seen to fairly bristle with deep, vigorous, condensed thought; to abound in a wealth of truth, Scriptural, doctrinal, moral, spiritual, aptly brought together. Bareille[1] remarks that these notes or outlines of St. Thomas may, in a sense, be likened to the recapitulations that Bossuet was accustomed to make of his discourse just before descending from the pulpit. Vaughan,[2] speaking in a similar strain, says that our Saint in his drafts of sermons " divides the meaning of his text into three of four grand divisions; and each of these he subdivides into three of four portions. These divisions are expressed with exceeding brevity, and yet with so good a choice of words that the whole becomes evident at a glance. To each division is attached a text to the point from Holy Scripture, with the proper reference. The skeleton is so well organized that, when once fixed in the mind, there is no difficulty in diversifying each portion into one very clear and consecutive discourse."

The sermon-plans of the noted schoolman that have been preserved to posterity are thus an invaluable index to his method, giving us, as they do, a rather clear insight into the manner in which he treated his subject. They, furthermore, plainly show that even in the pulpit St. Thomas never ceased to be the theologian; for they literally abound in theological thought. Still his sermons did not, for this reason, suffer either in merit or efficacy. Because of his peculiar genius it was rather a quality that lent them an additional charm; certainly it gave them a thoroughness that otherwise had nec-

[1] *Histoire de Saint Thomas d'Aquin*, Chap. XV, p. 163.
[2] *Life and Labors of St. Thomas of Aquin*, Vol. I, p. 446.

essarily been wanting. He preached, too, according to the requirements of the times—Thomas himself was a product of the times. It was an age when men thought, and thought deeply, despite all that has been said to the contrary. It was an age both of great universities and of strong faith; and the world generally was given to no superficial study of philosophy and theology. At the pulpit and at the professor's chair alike it sought instruction and enlightenment rather than an outpouring of merely sonorous and pleasing words. The first Dominicans had introduced into their sermons a strongly intellectual element. Thomas, seeing that this system was best suited to the day, followed in their footsteps, and developed their method along sane lines.

In the learned Friar Preacher's short or minor treatises on theological subjects, known as his *Opuscula Theologica,* we find some two hundred and twenty-five of these skeleton discourses. The greater number of them are on the Epistles and Gospels of the Sundays of the Christian year; many are for the different feasts as they existed in his day, and others are panegyrics of saints. While several of these are of doubtful authorship, most of them are certainly his work; and the evidence in favor of the others has been deemed sufficiently strong to justify their incorporation in the Parma and other splendid later editions of his writings. Nor does this collection, significant as it is, represent all the Saint's apostolical activity. There are various other sermons not found in this list that are admittedly his. Some certainly from his pen have been discovered at a comparatively recent date in the different libraries of Europe; a circumstance which gives strong hope that others still will some day be brought to light. Uccelli and the learned Father Da Fanna have made important finds of this kind.

Again, the *Opuscula* on the Lord's Prayer, the Angelic Salutation, the Creed, and the Sacraments are in reality the groundwork of discourses and conferences pronounced before the brethren of his Order. The one on the Angelic Salutation is one of the most beautiful and striking of St. Thomas's short sermons that has come down to us. It is likewise probably one of the most complete, and most nearly approaching the original form in which it was delivered. Adding this list to that mentioned above, we have a great number of sermons of which the Saint is known to be the author. Assuredly they make a collection showing the Angelic Doctor's great activity in the apostolical labors of his day.

For priests versed in scholastic theology these sermon-schemata of our celebrated Friar Preacher are a treasury of sketches and plans, of superb ideas, for orderly and instructive discourses on the Epistles and Gospels of the Sundays, on feasts of our Lord and the saints; a real mine of instruction, of crisp, vigorous thoughts. All that is needed to fill them out and round them into masterpieces is a masterhand like that which framed them. Clearly do they bear the impress of keen thought and penetration, profound erudition, a broad and comprehensive view of his subject, a marvelous knowledge and command of the Scriptures and the Fathers, along with a marked felicity of adapting these to the moral or doctrine to be inculcated. Whether St. Thomas gives us a homily on the Epistle or Gospel of the Sunday, or a discourse on some mystery of our Blessed Lord, or a panegyric of some saint, we always find the strictly methodical treatment of his subject; a splendid exposition of Catholic doctrine, an earnest effort to stem the evils that prevailed in his day; an ardent longing to enkindle the love of God in the hearts of men. His purpose is ever and always the same—to aid all who hear him: to convert the sinner, to make the good better, and the holy holier, to lead the saintly farther along the way of sanctity; to combat error; to serve God and His Church.

In the course of his numerous works, the Angelic Doctor lays down three general rules which in his mind are of the first importance for all preachers of the Word of God. First, he should seek to instill true, solid Christian doctrine into the minds of his audience, preaching Jesus Christ, and Him alone; for He is the Way, the Truth, and the Life. In all he says the preacher must seek to draw his hearers to God; he should seek souls, not himself; it should be his aim to convert them, or to make them better. The speaker of the Word whose purpose is vain glory, rather than the good fruit of the Word, is an abomination in the eyes of the Lord. His work cannot be productive of any great and lasting good. One

eloquence should be called into requisition for the glory of God and the welfare of souls; not for one's own glory and reputation. This is the gist of what is to be found here and there in the works of St. Thomas—notably in the *Contra Impugnantes Dei Cultum et Religionem*—on the office and duties of a preacher of the Word. This rule is truly golden.

Next the preacher of the Gospel should eschew vain, frivolous, unseemly worldly topics, adhering faithfully and strictly to Christian doctrine (*Responsio ad Lectorem Bisuntinum*). In the opinion of the Angelic Doctor the field of Catholic doctrine is, or should be, wide enough for any preacher of the Word. Certainly this principle needs no comment.

And thirdly, the preacher should practice what he teaches from the pulpit. In short, he should preach not less eloquently by his actions than by his words. Little avails the sermon of him whose life and deeds tell a story far different from that which his lips proclaim from the pulpit.[3] Nor is there need of comment here.

These principles are surely cardinal. They are for all preachers of the Word, and for all time. He who wishes his ministry of "shepherdizing" souls to be of fruitful harvest, cannot lay them aside. To do so brings failure; it means that one's ministry must prove unprofitable. It is not without significance that Pope Pius X has found it advisable to remind our modern preachers of the real duties of their high calling. The Encyclical, *Acerbo nimis,* runs along lines identical with St. Thomas's cardinal principles.

Modern preachers of the Word may learn not a little from the precepts and example of Thomas Aquinas. He has given us a splendid lesson, and this lesson is further emphasized by the words of another Pope. It can hardly have gone out of the remembrance of scholars how the late Pope Leo XIII exhorted the Italian clergy to adopt the very same *modus praedicandi* upon which his saintly successor so strongly insists. Leo's words, it is true, were addressed to the pastors of Italy; but would it not be well and profitable, if they struck a responsive chord in other parts of the world? A law of wisdom is a law for all; it is equally applicable the world over. May we not surmise that the illustrious Pontiff in-

---

[3] Summa, IIIa, q. XLI, a. 3 ad 1m.

tended that his words should go home to the rest of Christendom? No one better understood the needs of the Catholic world than did Leo.

Although it seems almost, if not quite, certain that the Angelic Doctor, in preparing his sermons, confined his writing to notes or sketches, and extemporized the words as he developed and filled in the plan from the pulpit, it were wholly untrue to say that he spoke offhand. No wise man would so tempt God. He was always prepared, because always preparing. Thomas's earliest biographers all tell us that prayer, study, meditation were habitual with him. Thought on the mysteries and life of our Blessed Saviour formed no small part of his life. Schooled by continual reading of Holy Scripture, the Fathers, theology, history, philosophy, and the sciences of the day; practised in speaking, writing, and teaching; possessing a genius of the highest order, he was certainly not obliged to go out of himself in search of ideas, and found no difficulty in readily clothing his thoughts in appropriate words. Thoughts deep, original, and luminous, welled up unbidden from his full mind; and the habit of speaking brought spontaneously to his lips clear and accurate language wherewith to give them suitable expression. He spoke with a heart that was aflame with charity. Hence his words went straight to the hearts of his audience.

The world knows Thomas Aquinas as a great saint and a great scholar, as one of our first theologians and most profound philosophers; as a man, in fact, of many-sided erudition. It is remarkable how he did so many things, and did them so well. But in his transcendent reputation as a scholar his fame as one of the Church's really great preachers has been forgotten even by scholars.

V. F. O'Daniel, O.P.

Washington, D. C.

TRIBUNALS OF THE ROMAN CURIA.

I. The Sacred Penitentiary.

IN the first article of this series upon the Roman Curia [1] it was stated that there were three departments, viz., the Congregations, the Tribunals, and the Offices. We have considered the Congregations in as far as they have been reorganized under the Constitution, *Sapienti Consilio,* and we have seen what are the chief functions assigned to each Congregation. In the present article I propose to deal with the second department of the Curia, which comprises three Tribunals, the *Sacred Penitentiary,* the *Sacred Rota,* and the *Apostolic Segnatura.* I follow the order observed in the New Constitution.

ORIGIN OF THE S. PENITENTIARY.

At a very early date a priest was appointed in the Eastern Church, and somewhat later, one in the Western Church, who received special authority in the sacrament of Penance (*Penitentiarius*), and who was placed over those obliged to perform public penances. In the beginning of the thirteenth century there were special *penitentiarii* appointed for the City of Rome, one of them being St. Raymund of Pennafort. In the same century a cardinal was selected to direct those *penitentiarii* and to take charge of the Apostolic Penitentiary. Somewhat later, viz., in the beginning of the fourteenth century, the cardinal who was appointed Prefect received the title of *Penitentiarius major,* a title which has continued down to the present day in the possession of the Chief Officer of the Tribunal. Originally the Sacred Penitentiary took cognizance of questions of the *forum internum* alone; but during a considerable portion of the fifteenth century a controversy was carried on regarding the proper province of its functions, some contending that it was to be confined to the *forum internum,* others defending its competence to deal with the *forum externum* also. Accordingly a Constitution, *Quoniam nonnulli,* was issued by Sixtus IV, 9 May, 1484, declaring that the Apostolic Penitentiary possessed authority to settle questions of the *forum externum* and could delegate this authority to others. Upon this point according to different circumstances a diversity of discipline has existed. Thus we find that nearly a century later St. Pius V, in order to obviate certain inconveniences, ordained in two constitutions issued together, 18 May, 1567, *In Omnibus* and *Ut bonis,* that the Apostolic Penitentiary should be altogether limited to the *forum internum.* However, during the reign of this Sovereign Pontiff a modification was introduced and was afterwards confirmed by other Roman Pontiffs, such as Urban VIII and Innocent XII.

LEGISLATION OF BENEDICT XIV ON THE S. PENITENTIARY.

Finally, Benedict XIV issued two Constitutions of the same date, 13 April, 1744, *Pastor bonus* and *In Apostolicae.* When one examines these two documents as they are found in the Bullarium of Benedict XIV, he perceives that in the former (*Pastor bonus*) the Pontiff ordained with much minuteness of detail the faculties committed to the S. Penitentiary; while in the other (*In Apostolicae*) he laid down the various classes of offices for the Tribunal as well as the requirements for the incumbents of these several offices. When it is remembered that the enactments contained in these two constitutions have remained substantially in force until the legislation of the *Sapienti consilio* became effective in Nov., 1908, and that even now to a large extent the same faculties are continued, as well as the same classes of offices, it may be easily inferred that these documents are deserving of careful perusal. Yet, as they are of notable length, we can refer here to only a few general headings, and this with a view to a better understanding of the new legislation of our present Sovereign Pontiff.

By the Constitution, *Pastor bonus,* Benedict XIV conferred authority upon the Sacred Penitentiary to absolve from all sins and censures in whatsoever manner reserved, whether to the Roman Pontiff, or to the Ordinaries, or to the Superiors of Regulars. This power should be exercised by the Major Penitentiary or by some one delegated by him in favor of regulars or seculars, ecclesiastics or laics. There was, however, a distinction made, viz., that in the case of regulars the absolution given through this Tribunal was effectual not only for the forum of conscience, but likewise in *foro externo.* The same authority was also available for seculars, whether ecclesiastics or laics, in *foro externo,* when the censures were inflicted *a jure;* not, however, when inflicted *ab homine,* until the jurisdiction of the delegate or judge inflicting the censure had ceased.[2] The S. Penitentiary besides received authority to dispense in occult irregularities for the forum of conscience not only laics, but also clerics, both secular and regular (N. 15). It possessed the authority to validate the titles of benefices obtained with an occult inhability; the power of condoning a portion of the simoniacal price given for a benefice; it received certain faculties of remitting the obligation of restitution under particular conditions; relaxing the obligation of oaths in the forum of conscience, when no injury would arise therefrom; dispensing by commutation from vows, even those reserved to the Pope; dispensing from the obligation of reciting the Divine Office by commuting it into some other prayers.[3] Power was given to the S. Penitentiary of dispensing regulars from any irregularity, whether *ex delicto* or *ex defectu,* in the forum of conscience; even in *foro externo* for public cases, after consultation with the superiors; authority of absolving apostate or fugitive regulars under certain conditions was also conferred.[4] In Matrimony the S. Penitentiary could dispense with occult impedient impediments for the forum of conscience; but not from diriment impediments of consanguinity, affinity, or spiritual relationship, even when the impediment was occult, if there were question of a marriage to be contracted (*contrahendum*). In marriages already contracted (invalidly), the S. Penitentiary should abstain from dispensing in the first and second degree of consanguinity (mixed), or in the second only of consanguinity, or affinity from *copula licita,* even in occult cases; but in the third and fourth degrees (occult) for marriages invalidly contracted it might dispense. It could dispense from the impediment of *crimen* arising out of adultery. It also possessed authority to solve all doubts in the matter of sins or regarding the penitential forum. It was declared, too, by Benedict XIV that whenever the S. Penitentiary would exercise any authority in granting dispensations, absolutions, etc., for the *forum externum,* such exercise should be considered valid, since the Major Penitentiary ought to be held as having received from the Roman Pontiff the requisite jurisdiction in particular cases.[5]

[2] Cf. *Pastor Bonus,* N. 7.
[4] NN. 31, 32, 33.
[3] NN. 20, 23, 25, 28, 29, 30.
[5] NN. 39, 40, 44, 48.

Since the time of Benedict XIV, until the Constitution, *Sapienti consilio,* became effective, the Apostolic Penitentiary lost none of its faculties; rather they were increased, especially in regard to the power of granting matrimonial dispensations. At one period, namely, at the end of the eighteenth century when the French Revolution broke out, the S. Penitentiary was the chief organ through which dispensations in matrimony were procured, even in *foro externo,* the other Tribunal (Dataria) being impeded in the exercise of its functions.

FACULTIES ACCORDING TO THE NEW CONSTITUTION.

In order to understand the change effected in the authority of the Sacred Penitentiary by the Constitution, *Sapienti consilio,* it is well to quote the words in which its present authority is conveyed. " The jurisdiction of this sacred court or tribunal is limited entirely to those things which regard the *forum internum,* non-sacramental as well as sacramental. Hence, matrimonial dispensations of the *forum externum* being assigned to the Congregation for the Discipline of the Sacraments, this tribunal for the *forum internum* concedes favors, absolutions, dispensations, commutations, sanations, condonations; moreover, it examines questions of conscience and decides them."

The foregoing are the only words found in the New Constitution regarding the Sacred Penitentiary; they are, however, sufficient to enable one to perceive the difference between the new legislation and the legislation already existing. The competence of the Sacred Penitentiary is now brought back to the condition in which it was placed by St. Pius V; it may be even said that at present its scope is the same as when this tribunal was originally constituted. The S. Penitentiary is now confined to the *forum internum,* and therefore no longer possesses any jurisdiction in the *forum externum.* To many readers of the REVIEW this distinction between the *forum internum* and the *forum externum* is very well known; still it may not be amiss for a more correct understanding of the competence of the S. Penitentiary to say a few words concerning the meaning of this old distinction.

There is a twofold power existing in the Church; there is the power of the Sacrament of Orders, and there is the power of jurisdiction. This latter power relates to two different kinds of questions. There are some causes which refer chiefly to the private benefit of the individual, and the jurisdiction or authority required to deal with them is termed jurisdiction of the *forum internum,* or of the forum of conscience. This jurisdiction may be immediately connected with the Sacrament of Penance and is called sacramental. Thus the jurisdiction necessary for the absolution from sin is sacramental; and even when the Sacrament of Penance is not actually received, provided that there be confession, the term sacramental jurisdiction in *foro interno* is employed. But jurisdiction in *foro interno* may also be exercised outside the administration of the Sacrament of Penance, and even without any confession; it is then called non-sacramental. For instance, the act of dispensing from a private vow, or of dispensing from a secret irregularity, or of absolving from a secret censure may be performed without reference to Confession or the Sacrament of Penance, and yet be an act of jurisdiction in *foro interno.*

Then there are other causes which proximately relate to the social good of the Church; they regard the relation of the individual to ecclesiastical society. The authority necessary to deal with these causes is called jurisdiction in *foro externo.* Thus if two persons wishing to be married are related by consanguinity within the prohibited degrees, there is required the exercise of jurisdiction in *foro externo* for the granting of the dispensation. Now the radical difference touching the S. Penitentiary·between the new legislation and that immediately preceding is that all jurisdiction in *foro externo* is now taken from it. The chief practical application of this change will be found in matrimonial dispensations. Heretofore the Dataria was the customary channel through which dispensations from matrimonial impediments were granted for those countries not subject to the authority of the Propaganda. But it was not the only channel; the S. Penitentiary was empowered to grant dispensations from diriment impediments, even when these impediments were not occult. I do not mean to say that there was no limitation placed upon the S. Penitentiary in its authority to dispense from matrimonial impedi-

for the matrimonial dispensations were such as could be designated *pauperes* or *fere pauperes,* the dispensations could be obtained from the S. Penitentiary, even though the impediments in the given cases were of their own nature public; while the Dataria was competent to grant matrimonial dispensations in *foro externo,* whether the application came from those who were *pauperes* or not. The main distinction between these two tribunals has been that the Dataria granted dispensations in *utroque foro,* and the S. Penitentiary in *foro interno.* Accordingly, when the impediment was public, either from its own nature, as consanguinity, although it was not commonly known to exist, or when it was foreseen to become public, or when it was actually public, though of its own nature secret, in each of these suppositions the Dataria was the proper tribunal for granting the dispensation. On the other hand, the S. Penitentiary having authority for the *forum internum* could grant a dispensation when the impediment was of its own nature occult and at the same time *de facto* occult, but as was said above, it acquired additional authority to dispense in *utroque foro* those petitioners who could be considered at least *fere pauperes.*

It was noticed before when treating of the Congregation of the Sacraments,[6] that according to the new legislation this Congregation possesses authority to grant matrimonial dispensations instead of the Dataria which is no longer competent to grant them. Thus the Congregation of the Sacraments is empowered to take the place of the Dataria for dispensations in matrimony. It is however to be noted that when there is question of the impediment of *disparitas cultus,* or of *mixta religio,* or the application of the Pauline Privilege, it is the Congregation of the Holy Office which is competent, since matters of this kind pertain to doctrine and therefore belong exclusively to this Congregation. The S. Penitentiary according to the new legislation possesses no authority to dispense in *foro externo,* so that when an impediment of matrimony is of its nature public, or, though secret at present, is likely to become public, it is useless to have recourse to the S. Penitentiary, which is no longer competent in such cases; reference must be made to the Congregation of the Sacraments or, when a dogmatic question is involved, to the Holy Office. It is not however to be inferred that the S. Penitentiary is now deprived of all authority in the matter of matrimonial dispensations. Whatever authority of jurisdiction it hitherto possessed in *foro interno* to grant these dispensations, it retains the same authority under the new legislation. When the impediment is of its nature occult and at the same time actually secret without danger of becoming public, this tribunal has authority to dispense. Thus if A. have illicet copula with B., there rises a diriment impediment to the marriage of A. and the sister of B. which impediment is considered *ex natura sua* occult, and if there be no danger of this impediment becoming public *de facto,* the S. Penitentiary is still the competent tribunal for granting the dispensation. It is scarcely necessary to observe that in sending a petition for such a dispensation to the S. Penitentiary fictitious names should be employed, so that no infamy may arise to any of the parties concerned from the granting of the dispensation. If from any cause it should become publicly known that such illicit copula occurred, the S. Penitentiary would not be competent to grant the dispensation; the case should be referred to the Congregation of the Sacraments. What has been said of the impediment of affinity from illicit copula should be extended to the impediment of *crimen,* in which under similar conditions the S. Penitentiary can dispense. Regarding other ecclesiastical impediments which from their character are public such as consanguinity, spiritual relationship, or affinity from licit copula, a dispensation can no longer be procured from the S. Penitentiary, no matter what be the circumstances of the applicants.

Whether or not the S. Penitentiary still retains authority to dispense when there is question of a marriage invalidly contracted on account of an impediment of its nature public, while *de facto* occult, e. g. spiritual relationship which is secret, the present writer prefers to refrain from offering an opinion,

tains to the Consistorial Congregation alone to give an authoritative decision upon this question.

In matrimonial cases it may happen that two impediments occur, one occult, the other public. In this contingency a rule similar to what was formerly followed should still be observed, viz. application should be made to the S. Penitentiary for a dispensation from the occult impediment with mention that a petition has been or is to be sent to the Congregation of the Sacraments for a dispensation from the public impediment; while in the petition to the Congregation of the Sacraments for a dispensation from the public impediment no allusion is to be made to the presence of an occult impediment. If however the two impediments (one occult, the other public) be of such a character that on account of the presence of one the dispensation for the other would not be rendered more difficult, it is held to be unnecessary to make reference to the existence of the second impediment in the petition to the S. Penitentiary.[7]   Others, e. g. De Becker,[8] and Noldin (N. 133) omit the distinction between impediments *disparata* and *non-disparata,* laying down the rule just given, viz. that mention should be made of the public impediment in the petition addressed to the S. Penitentiary.

"NORMAE PECULIARES" CONCERNING THE S. PENITENTIARY.

After the publication of the Constitution, *Sapienti consilio,* the Holy See issued certain regulations referring to the departments of the Curia. A few of these relate to the S. Penitentiary and should be here noticed. One touching the personnel of this tribunal sets down that, besides the Cardinal Penitentiary who is the Prefect of the tribunal, the Regent, five Prelates of the Segnatura, a Procurator, a Substitute and some inferior officials shall continue in the respective duties assigned them under the previous arrangement. These different offices were created for the proper management of this tribunal by Benedict XIV in his Constitution *In Apostolicae,* above referred to. A second regulation of the *Normae* lays down that all the rules given in that Constitution of Benedict XIV are to be observed by the S. Penitentiary except in those particulars which were subsequently introduced by legitimate use; and changes so introduced are to be in writing and to be submitted by the Cardinal Penitentiary for the approval of the Roman Pontiff. The only remaining regulation of the *Normae peculiares* concerning the S. Penitentiary is that all business transacted by this tribunal should be conducted secretly and gratuitously.[9] When however dispensations in matrimony are required from the S. Penitentiary the taxes which were hitherto imposed will for the present be continued, since one of the *Dispositiones temporariae* (N. 12) is the following: " Pro dispensationibus Matrimonii vigere quoque pergent in praesens taxationes pendi solitae penes Datariam Apostolicam et S. Penitentiariam. In causis vero matrimonialibus dispensationis super rato, et in aliis quae a S. Congregatione de Sacramentis judicantur, standum normis a S. Congregatione Concilii hucusque servatis."[10]

It is unnecessary to explain in detail more than is set forth in the Constitution already quoted, the various powers conferred upon the S. Penitentiary. It should be noticed however that many of these may be subdelegated to Bishops and in some degree to priests also. In this respect no change has been effected in the authority of this tribunal to subdelegate its faculties, keeping within the province assigned to it. *Pagellae* have sometimes been issued by the S. Penitentiary to Bishops, and to some priests on the recommendation of their respective Ordinaries. In the interpretation of such faculties attention should be paid to particular clauses which may be found in the formulas issued by this tribunal in order that the extent of the faculties may be accurately ascertained without either undue amplification or undue limitation.

In conclusion it may be observed that it belongs to the S. Penitentiary to examine cases of conscience and to decide them. Thus a practical question may arise as to what is lawful or unlawful in given circumstances. The person concerned may send a *quaesitum* to this tribunal and from the answer determine the course of conduct he should pursue. In presenting such quaesita it is not necessary to express the real name of the petitioner, but of course the address to which the answer is to be directed is to be given. In order to expedite matters through this Tribunal it is advisable to have the *quae-sita* authenticated by the Ordinary of the petitioner, whenever the latter has no sufficient reason to conceal from him the fact of his *quaesitum.*

M. MARTIN, S.J.

St. Louis University.

THE BLINDNESS OF THE REVEREND DR. GRAY;*

OR

THE FINAL LAW.

CHAPTER XLVI.

THE TRIAL.

DICK DUGGAN had been formally committed for trial and it came off at the summer assizes at Cork in that year. It was not a sensational case. No element of romance entered into it. It was simply a trial for a very vulgar murder, wrought through hate and revenge. But, as the case had an agrarian aspect, the Crown attached some importance to it; and the Solicitor-General was sent down from Dublin to prosecute. The court was crowded, although the one element that could excite public curiosity was absent. There appeared to be no doubt about the prisoner's guilt; and therefore, there was no room for forensic displays. There was a foregone conclusion as to the prisoner's conviction. Nevertheless, as no loophole of escape can be left on such occasions, but every web must be tightened around the doomed man, the Solicitor-General made a most elaborate opening statement, showing that from the beginning that deadly hate, which was the final cause of the dread tragedy, was not only entertained, but publicly avowed by the prisoner. The first element, therefore, of conviction, the establishment of a motive, was evident. Disappointment about the land,

on his supposed enemy in the one way that such natures seek revenge—that is, by the commission of wilful and deliberate murder.

The wretched prisoner stood in the dock with bowed head. Streaks of gray showed themselves in his black hair, signs of the terrible conflict he had waged with himself down there in the narrow cell where he had been confined. He never looked up at judge or jury, but with head bent down he seemed the very embodiment of despair, or sullen hate. With the greatest difficulty, his solicitor coerced him to plead: *Not guilty!* His own wish was to say *Guilty,* and to be hanged without delay. The court was crowded with witnesses and police. The aged mother sat back amongst the audience—the only person in that assembly, who felt no fear, nor pity, because she had perfect faith in God and in His priest.

The first witness called was the Sergeant of Police. He testified that he received information of the murder about seven o'clock on the evening of 7 February. His informant was a servant of Dr. Wycherly's. He proceeded at once to the place which was about two miles from the town of M——. There in a recess in the road, the cob or pony was still quietly grazing. The form of a man lay down over the dashboard, his head almost touching the animal. He raised him up, and saw at once that he was dead. There was a blot of blood on his coat. The pike, one prong stained with blood, lay at the bottom of the cart. He at once with the aid of the constable arranged the dead body in the cart, and drove back to town, where the body was deposited at the barracks. From information received, he proceeded at once to take out a warrant for the arrest of Dick Duggan.

Cross-examined, he testified that the time in which he got notice of the murder could not have been earlier than seven o'clock; and that he was at the scene of the murder at half-past seven o'clock.

Further cross-examined, he declined to give the name of his informant; but it was a well-known fact that there was deep hostility—

But here he was peremptorily called to order by counsel for defense, who was supported by the presiding judge.

Again, examined by the Solicitor-General, he testified that he had proceeded with the warrant to Duggan's house; but having ascertained that he was absent all the evening, he and his men hid themselves in the cow-house, and waited till Duggan arrived.

"At what hour did he arrive?"

"At half-past ten."

" No, he came into the barn."

" What did he do there?"

" He commenced washing away streaks of blood from his face and hands, in a huge boiler or cauldron of water that was there."

" And then?"

" Then I arrested him for wilful murder, and had him handcuffed."

" Did he resist?"

" No, he submitted quietly."

" Did you warn him?"

" Yes, I warned him that every word he uttered might be used in evidence against him."

" Did he make any remark then?"

" Yes! His first remark was: ' My God! did I kill him?' He then said: ' I suppose I'll swing for it; but I deserve it.' He wanted to go in and see his mother; but this wasn't allowed."

Dr. Dalton was called and testified that he saw the deceased in the police office. He had the body stripped. There was a slight accumulation of blood on the inner and outer garments of the dead man. On washing the surface of the body he discovered a wound over the heart, such as would be made by a sharp, keen instrument. He then, aided by another surgeon, Dr. Willis, opened the body and traced the wound through the left ventricle of the heart, severing many vessels, and terminating in the apex, or first lobe of the lung behind. Death must have been instantaneous.

The pike was produced, still blood-stained. Yes, that pike was an instrument that would cause such a wound.

Dr. Willis called, corroborated the testimony of Dr. Dalton. There could be no doubt as to the cause of death.

Cross-examined, he admitted that it was perfectly possible the sad tragedy might have been the result of an accident. Such accidents are extremely common; and if the deceased had had a pike with him in the trap, and if that pike had been placed carelessly, with the points upwards, it is quite possible that the deceased, if thrown forward by a sudden lurch, might have fallen on the prongs of the pike, and met his death. The wound was lateral and upward. Examined by the Solicitor-General, as to whether the deceased, if he had sustained such an accident, could deliberately withdraw the weapon from his side, and place it in the bottom of the trap, witness declared such a thing impossible, as death must have been instan-

prisoner say in his own and Mr. Edward Wycherly's presence, " By
the Lord God, I'll make such an example of Kerins and all belonging to him, and all that has anything to say or do with him,
that it will be remembered in the parish, as long as the old castle
stands." Mr. Wycherly said: " Take care, Duggan, he carries
his six-shooter always about him; and a bullet goes faster than a
shillalagh." Duggan replied: "And there's something that goes
faster than a bullet, *and it makes no noise."* On another occasion,
somewhere about the New Year, he heard Duggan say, in allusion
to Kerins' marriage: " If I thought that Martha Sullivan would
have him, I'd think no more of blowing out his brains than shooting
a dog." And, on another occasion he, the prisoner, asked witness:
" Couldn't the ould woman give the girl something to drab, that is,
to poison her?" And he replied: " We have a bad name enough,
but we've always kept our hands from blood."

Cross-examined, Pete admitted that the gipsies had a bad name
in the parish; but it was not justified. He was a hard-working
tradesman, a tinker if you like; but his mother told fortunes, and
the people were afraid of her.

Cora, the gipsy-girl, came on the table with the same self-assur-
ance that always characterized her. She tossed back her black gipsy
locks, and sitting down, she placed her elbow on her knee, and
supported her head on her hand in the old attitude. She testified
that on the 29th day of January, she was present at the festivities
in Kerins' house; that in the course of the evening she was called
out of the kitchen by Mrs. Kerins, and bade to go over to Duggan's
and tell Dick that she wished to see him in the screen of firs behind
the house; that she went to Duggan's, beckoned Dick from the
kitchen, and in the yard told him the message Mrs. Kerins had
sent; that she hid herself in the screen, and heard the conversation
between Dick Duggan and Mrs. Kerins; that the latter begged and
implored him to let bygones be bygones; that he replied, " Take
this from me, that neither here nor hereafter will I forgive the
man that wronged me and mine." Mrs. Kerins said: " The black
hatred is in your heart, and all for nothing." He replied: " How
can. I forgive the man that first took away from me the place I
wanted to bring you; and then took you from me in the bargain?
I'll not lie to you nor God. I've an account to settle with Kerins;
and when it is settled, there will be no arrears."

in the screen, she coolly answered: "It was her business to know everything;" and then she added: "You have just reminded me that Duggan before he left the kitchen, said in answer to some question about the jollification going on at Crossfields: 'I guess their *ceol* [music] will be changed into keening soon enough.'" The counsel asked no further questions.

Then came one of the sensations of the trial. The gipsy-girl, on being ordered to go down from the witness-table, said solemnly, "I have sworn the truth. But *it wasn't Dicky Duggan that murdered Kerins.*"

She was instantly ordered back, examined and cross-examined; but she gave no information, beyond repeating her assertion: "Dicky Duggan is a bad fellow enough; but he never murdered Kerins."

Dan Goggin, a sturdy farmer, testified that he was in the public-house at the Cross the day of the murder. He was returning from the fair at M———. A lot of farmers were drinking and chaffing Dick Duggan, who had drink taken; but wasn't drunk. He heard Duggan saying: "There may be another dance at Crossfields soon; and the feet won't touch the ground either." He also spoke of a Banshee and a *Caoine*.

The bar-girl at the public-house testified that Duggan had come to the house the day before the murder, had remained there talking and drinking all day. He had several times uttered terrible threats against Kerins and his family. He was too drunk to go home that night; and he slept at the public-house. Next day, he drank again, but not much. The farmers coming home from the fair at M——— were chaffing him about the dance at Kerins'. He again grew furious and threatening, and demanded more drink. This she refused, and bade him go home. At length, he demanded whiskey peremptorily, saying: "Give it to me. I have work to do to-night!" He then left the house.

Cross-examined, the girl said, it could not have been earlier then half-past six when Duggan left the house, because she had heard the Angelus-bell ring some time before. Questioned as to where he went, she declared she had no idea. A second question as to what was her interpretation of Duggan's words: "I have work to do to-night!" was peremptorily challenged by counsel for defense, and the challenge was allowed.

The sergeant of police, recalled, gave evidence that Duggan said something about the parish priest on his way to prison; but seemed to think it a matter of no consequence that Kerins was killed.

the murder, he had taken the pike to Duggan's house, when it was too dusk to notice the blood-stains on the prong; and that old Duggan had admitted that the pike was their property; and that he had seen it last in Dick's hands the morning of the day previous to the murder, when Dick had been cutting soil from a rick of hay near the road.

And thus a terrible chain of circumstantial evidence had been drawn around the unhappy criminal, for whom there seemed no loophole of escape. The statement of Cora, the gipsy girl, affected the sympathies of the audience; but had no effect on the legal progress of the case.

The counsel for defence called no witnesses. He had none to call. The case against the prisoner was overwhelming; and the prisoner positively refused to give the least assistance towards establishing his innocence. His solicitor begged, prayed, implored him to say where he had spent the evening, or to give some evidence that would establish an *alibi;* or even to declare his innocence. No! He maintained a stubborn and sullen silence; and neither the appeals of his lawyer, nor the tearful expostulations of his friends had any effect upon him. It was quite clear to lawyer and counsel, to warder and jailer, that Dicky Duggan would die a felon's death.

Half-ashamed of the wretched defence he had to make, knowing its inutility, and conscious of its hollowness, the senior barrister arose, and after a few words, he rested the entire case for the defence on the evidence of the barmaid, and the untrustworthiness of the witnesses. He seemed to score a point by showing how utterly impossible it was for the prisoner to reach the scene of the murder, which it was averred had taken place before seven o'clock that night, for the barmaid had sworn that he could not have left the public-house before half-past six; and there were four miles at least between the public-house and the scene of the murder. He then raked up in that strong, vituperative manner which characterizes

The bar-maid, recalled again, swore that Duggan could not have left the house before half-past six o'clock that evening, because the Angelus-bell had rung out a considerable time before he had departed.

The learned judge asked rather demurely what was the Angelus-bell to which reference had been made so often during the trial.

The counsel for defence, who was a Roman Catholic, explained that it was a continuation amongst a conservative people, and one tenacious of tradition, of the old Curfew-bell, of which his Lordship had read.

"And at what hour does the curfew-bell ring?" asked the judge. "Does it not change with the seasons?"

But someone had mercifully passed on a slip of paper to counsel, who now declared with evident consciousness of superior intelligence:

"No! my Lord!" he said. "In *this* country, it is always rung at six o'clock in the evening!"

The sergeant, recalled, stated that the gipsies were utterly disreputable characters; and that charges of stealing fowl, fortune-telling, and other such nefarious practices were often alleged against them.

"Alleged?" said the Solicitor-General. "Were they ever proved, sergeant?"

And the sergeant shook his head mournfully. He had never secured a conviction against them.

He was again interrogated about the prisoner's language when he was arrested; and he admitted that the prisoner seemed surprised that it was Kerins, and not the parish priest, who had been killed.

Again interrogated, he said he had taken measurements of the distance between the public-house and the scene of the murder; and found the distance to be three miles, seven furlongs, three yards, and two feet.

"Could the prisoner have possibly reached on foot the scene of the murder, if he had not left the public-house before half-past six?"

"No!" said the sergeant. "That is, if the murder was actually committed in the spot where we found the dead man."

At which remark, the Solicitor-General smiled.

The prisoner's father testified that the gipsies were regarded as dishonest and disreputable characters in the parish; and Pete and his daughter had been driven by the old woman from the house for

And the old man had to answer, " No."

" One more question," said counsel. " I did not intend to ask you to give evidence against your son; but as the opposing counsel, my learned friend opposite, has put you in the chair, perhaps you would answer. Is that pike," pointing to the weapon lying on the table, the one prong still rusty from its ghastly work, " your property?"

" It is," said the old man.

" In whose hands did you last see it?"

" In my son's!" was the reply.

The old man turned around and paused for a few seconds, looking wistfully at his son. Then, brushing aside a tear, he descended the steps.

This closed the evidence; and the junior counsel for defence rose up, and pulled his gown over his shoulders. He was a young man, and therefore eloquent; and as he drew on the vast resources of his oratory, a smile rippled over the faces of the older and more prosaic men. He addressed himself to one point only—the danger of convicting on circumstantial evidence, and the awful responsibility entailed on the consciences of the jurors by reason of the fact that only circumstantial evidence had been adduced in support of the case. He insisted strongly that there was some grave mystery hidden behind the apparent certainties that had been brought under their notice; and he quoted the saying of Cora, and her evident conviction that, notwithstanding her own evidence, the prisoner was innocent of the crime. He tried to torture the minds of the jurors by the suggestion that, if they sent the prisoner to the gallows, the time would come, when, under the light of fresh revelations, they would look back with remorse and horror on the terrible miscarriage of justice that would be perpetrated that day, if they brought in a verdict of " Guilty!"

Then the Solicitor-General arose, and in a few words tore into tatters the little web of oratory which his " very young but learned friend " had spun before their eyes. And with a brevity that was more alarming, because more assured than the lengthiest speech, he marshalled facts and motives, so as to leave no room for doubt of Dick Duggan's guilt in the mind of the vast audience that filled the courthouse.

CHAPTER XLVII.

An Apparition.

DURING the terrible tragedy, the old woman sat back amongst the benches behind the dock. Her face was nearly covered by the hood of the black cloak that she had worn since her marriage. Her white cap, frilled and ironed, shone beneath it; but her face was shrouded as if with the shame and pain of the ordeal through which she was passing. She was rolling her beads through her fingers during the trial; and seemed, in her communion with God, to be oblivious of all around her. But when the final crisis was approaching, she raised her head, and looked ever and again anxiously toward the door of the court. But her heart fell, when the crowd seemed to thicken, as the trial progressed, and no messenger from God appeared to rekindle her hopes, or reassure her faith. Yet these hopes smouldered on, until the final appeal, absolute and convincing, was made; and the judge, with all the solemnity of his high office increased by the gravity of the case, proceeded to recapitulate and sift the evidence before him.

He commenced at once by laying down the law about circumstantial evidence, endorsing the remarks of the prosecuting counsel, that in very few cases was a murderer caught red-handed in his guilt, and that thus justice would be completely frustrated, if convictions could not be obtained on circumstantial evidence. That evidence, however, should be of a nature that would make guilt a moral certainty—a clear, logical deduction from facts and motives converging toward a final issue. If this chain of facts and motives lacked even one link, the presumption should be in the prisoner's favor. If the chain were complete, it was equivalent to direct evidence; and the presumption of guilt became a certainty. It was for the jury to consider and weigh the evidence in the present case, with a view of determining whether, in their judgment, the alleged conversations and facts tended to produce not only a *prima facie* case against the prisoner at the bar; but also an absolute conviction that this brutal murder, by which an innocent man lost his life in a violent and savage manner, was perpetrated by the unhappy man at the dock, and by no one else.

He then went into the evidence, word by word, and fact by fact, referring to his notes, which he had carefully taken down. On the question of motive and the repeated declarations of the prisoner that he would seek to be revenged on the murdered man, there appeared to be no room for doubt; for if the evidence of the

gipsies were discredited, there was still supplementary evidence that
the prisoner did threaten violence, or rather a violent death, against
the murdered man repeatedly. The evidence again as to the owner-
ship of the pike, the instrument of the murder, was unassailable.
But there were two points that needed clearing up. These were the
strange expressions used by prisoner to the sergeant of police, who
arrested him, and in which he seemed to have expected the death
of his parish priest, and not Kerins; and the evidence of the bar-
maid that he could not have left the public-house before half-past
six on the night of the murder; and the evidence of the police
that it was about seven o'clock the intimation of the tragedy
reached them. It was for the jury to determine whether it was
possible for the prisoner to cover four miles of ground and per-
petrate an atrocious crime within that interval; or whether they
would accept the theory of the crown that the murder was committed much nearer the public-house, and the body driven towards
the town with a view of screening the murderer. It was most unfortunate the judge added, that no evidence was adduced by the
defence to show the whereabouts of the prisoner that night; but the
jury would now have to determine whether these varied circumstances
brought home guilt to the prisoner in the dock, or whether there
was still a grave doubt as to his connexion with the murder. The
responsibility of determining his guilt or innocence was probably
the greatest that could be laid on the consciences of men; and he
conjured them to bring to their consideration of the case an unbiased and unprejudiced judgment, not leaning to the side of justice
by any presumptions of guilt, nor to the side of mercy by any false
notions of pity; but examining patiently and minutely the evidence
and arguments on both sides, and bringing in their verdict, fearless
of any consequences, but the violation of their solemn oaths.

Here the jury retired, and the judge also arose. It was noticed
that as he did so, he leaned down, and seemed to be searching for
something, or placing something near his hand; and the whisper ran
around the court:

"He's lookin' for the black cap!"

But all public interest was now more keenly aroused, when the
prisoner's mother, suddenly standing up in her place in the court,
and flinging back the quilted hood of her black cloak, shouted passionately as she stretched her right-hand toward the door:

"Make way, there: make way there, I say, for the minister of
God, who is come to save my child!"

She stood rigid as a statue, her right-hand extended toward the door, where now was distinctly seen above the heads of the multitude the pale face darkened by the deep-blue spectacles of Dr. William Gray. He was pushing his way slowly through the dense mass of people, who surged around him and helped to block his way in their new excitement. The judge paused, and sat down. The crier yelled: " Silence !" which the police repeated from man to man, till it died away in an echo at the door; and at length by dint of pushing and elbowing, the tall figure of the great priest came around the dock, and approached the place where the counsel and solicitors for the defence were sitting. Here there was a hurried conference, pens and pencils flying furiously over sheets of paper, while the deepest silence reigned in court, and the judge looked down interested and curious, and the counsel for the Crown looked anxious and amazed.

At length, the leading barrister for the defence arose, and said:

" An unexpected circumstance has arisen in the case, my Lord ; and I request permission to have the jury recalled for a few moments."

The Solicitor-General at once protested vigorously.

" The case is closed, my Lord," he said. " The fullest time was given to the gentlemen in charge of the defence to summon witnesses in the prisoner's favor. I presume the reverend gentleman, who has just appeared in court, is about to give evidence as to character. That can be done when the jury have brought in their verdict. I totally object to have the case opened again."

" It is certainly unusual and irregular, Mr. ――," said the judge, addressing the counsel for the defence, " to have the case reopened when the jury are consulting about their verdict. But, perhaps, you would acquaint the court with the nature of the circumstance to which you have alluded, and its bearing on the case?"

" Certainly, my Lord," said the lawyer. " This gentleman, Dr. William Gray, late parish priest of the place where the murder was committed, has come hither at great inconvenience to testify that on the night of the murder, the prisoner was at his house at seven o'clock, and this proves so complete an *alibi*, that I demand the prisoner's immediate discharge."

" Why was not the reverend gentleman here at the earlier stages of the trial?" demanded the judge.

" He was fully prepared to come," was the answer, " but he lost his train, and hastened hither by car. The evidence is so important that it cannot be overlooked."

It was quite true the old priest had missed his train; and in an agony of remorse had hurried hither, driving his horse furiously the thirty miles that lay between his house and the City. Ever since the murder, or rather since the committal of Duggan, his mind had been the prey of unusual emotions. The sense of shame and personal dishonor for having used physical violence toward an illiterate peasant, gradually developed into a feeling of compassion for his victim; and when the latter lay under the frightful charge of murder, this sentiment of pity was deepened and intensified, until it almost took on the aspect of the pity of great love. Duggan's demeanor, too, since the blow fell upon him—his total change of manner, his silence, and, above all, his intense remorse and despair for having struck a priest, touched the old man deeply. His was one of those dispositions that are as hard as granite toward the proud and the obstinate, but are instantly melted into compassion at the first indication of sorrow or remorse. Hence, as reports daily reached his ears of Duggan's manifest contrition and horror at his conduct, he grew more deeply interested in his case, and what he had originally determined to do through a mere sense of justice, he now determined to accomplish thoroughly through a new-born and affectionate interest in the unhappy man. Perhaps, too, the revelation was opening up wider and wider to his view, that he had badly blundered during life by mistaking the lower laws, which serve to bind society together, for the higher law that sweetens and strengthens all human life; and looking back on his ministry of a quarter of a century, he began to see that its fruits would have been greater, if he had taken more deeply to heart the Divine Words: "A *new* commandment I give you."

It is easy, therefore, to conjecture his agitation and terror, when, on the morning of the trial, having dressed with unusual care, he drove to the railway station to find that the only train that would reach Cork for hours, had already departed. He had an idea of going to the City the night before; but the dread of meeting people, and sleeping in a strange room, deterred him. Now, half-mad with the terror of thinking that the life of his unhappy parishioner might be lost through his neglect, for he felt, with a pang of reproach, how inexorable was the law, he determined to drive straight to the City, taking his chances of being in time.

"She'll never do it, yer reverence," said the jarvey, whose horse he had hired, and who did not relish the idea of driving thirty miles at a furious rate of speed.

"If she is killed, I'll pay you," was the answer. And so he reached the courthouse as the jury retired; and the big beads of perspiration on his forehead, and the tremulous motions of his hands, showed the tremendous agony through which he had passed.

After a good deal of forensic sparring, the judge recalled the jury; and the aged priest was helped into the witness-box. He was sworn, and gave his name as Dr. William Gray, late parish priest of the united parishes of Doonvarragh, Lackagh, and Athboy; but now retired.

"Do you remember the evening of February the seventh in the present year?" he was asked.

"Yes!" he replied.

"Would you detail the circumstances that brought you into connexion with the prisoner that night?"

"I was in my room that night, the room which serves me as library and sitting-room, when a single knock was heard at the door. My housekeeper announced that Duggan wished to see me, adding that he seemed under the influence of drink. I went into the hall; and he at once made a most insulting observation—"

"Would you be good enough to tell the jury what it was?"

"Is it necessary?" the priest asked, in a pleading manner.

"Yes! It is necessary!"

The priest waited for a moment, as if summoning up courage to bear this latest trial; and then said:

"He said: 'I want to ask you a question. Why didn't you denounce from the altar your niece for eloping with young Wycherly, when you never spared any poor girl before?' These might not have been his exact words, but they were the equivalent."

"Very good. And then?"

"Then I am sorry to say that I lost temper and caught hold of him violently by the neckcloth, and pushed him against the wall, or the door of the opposite room. In an agony of rage, or perhaps to defend himself, he struck me with his left-hand full on the forehead, breaking my glasses. These are the marks."

And he raised his blue spectacles to show the faint scars where the steel of the broken one had penetrated.

There was some sensation in court here; and the old woman muttered aloud:

"The blagard! Hanging is too good for him now!"

"I then swung him round and round the hall," continued the priest, "and finally flung him out through the open door, where he lay face down on the gravel. I locked and bolted the door; and gave the matter no further heed. It was only when I was retiring to rest at ten o'clock, that I heard him raise himself from the gravel before the hall-door, and go away."

"Can you state exactly the hour when all this occurred?" asked

"Yes! The clock on my mantlepiece was just chiming seven when I returned to my room."

"Is your clock correct?" asked the judge.

"Absolutely," said the priest.

"Did you read the dial; for perhaps it might occur that the hours are not struck according to the figures."

"No! I'm blind!" was the mournful admission; and a murmur of sympathy seemed to run through the court. "But there can be no doubt of the hour. The clock is absolutely correct."

"And presuming that this is so, what is the exact distance between the presbytery and the public-house?"

"A little over two miles!" he said.

"And would it be humanly possible for a man to traverse the road to M——, a distance of four miles, commit a murder with all its ghastly details, return to the Cross, and walk two miles towards your house in the space of less than half an hour?"

"That question answers itself," said the priest.

He was then cross-examined.

"You are no longer parish priest of Doonvarragh, and the other unnamable places?"

"No! I'm retired!"

"And you came here to do a good turn for your old friends?"

"I came to testify the truth. Duggan was my worst enemy."

"And a thoroughly and essentially bad character, I presume?"

"No! He is hot-headed and turbulent, especially in drink; and he is a loud boaster. But he is incapable of committing a great crime."

"Now, sir, you have said that the clock was chiming 'seven' when you returned to your room?"

"Yes!"

"Now, don't you think it very unlikely that in the state of high excitement in which you were after your alleged rencontre with the prisoner, you would count the strokes of a clock?"

"I didn't count them," said the priest.

"Then why did you swear the clock was chiming 'seven'?"

"Because the clock had struck six, quarter after six, half-past six, the three-quarters; and I knew I was in the hall only a few minutes."

"I see. And you also allege that the prisoner remained on your gravel walk prostrate for three hours. Do you think that credible; or were you not deceived?"

"I have no more to ask," said counsel. "It is for your lord-ship to say to the jury, how far•they can accept such evidence against the overwhelming case against the prisoner."

"One question more," said the judge. "You aver that the prisoner fell face downwards on the gravel, and remained there?"

"Yes!"

"And that he was flung with much violence?"

"I'm sorry to say, Yes!"

"There can be no doubt, gentlemen," said the judge, turning toward the jury, "that the evidence of the reverend gentleman puts this case in a different aspect. It supplies the information, sullenly withheld by the prisoner, as to his movements after leaving the public-house. It also goes far toward explaining the nature of the blood-stains which the prisoner was striving to wash away when arrested in the cowhouse; and it also seems to explain the strange language used by the prisoner when arrested, when he expressed his horror on supposing that his parish-priest had been murdered, and his subsequent unconcern when he found it was Kerins. When he said: 'Is he dead? I suppose I'll swing for it,' it was clearly un-der the conviction that the blow which he had struck in the hall of the presbytery had had fatal consequences. And when he said sub-sequently: 'Kerins? Is that all?' it may have expressed his sense of relief that the death of his priest was not upon his soul. Of course, it is for you to determine the value you place on the rever-end gentleman's testimony, which, as you have perceived, involved revelations personal to himself, which must have been very humilia-ting. You will also notice the trouble and inconvenience to which an old, infirm, and blind clergyman has put himself voluntarily in order to save the life of one who was persistently and cruelly hostile to him. Yet, sympathy with such heroism must not blind you to the other facts put into evidence by the Crown. The ad-mission that the weapon that caused death was the property of the prisoner, and seen last in his possession by his own father, tells terribly against him—"

"Maybe the pike was stolen for the purpose?" said a shrill voice from the place where the witnesses of the Crown were mar-shalled behind the Crown counsel.

All eyes turned in that direction and saw Cora, the gipsy girl, in her favorite attitude, elbow on knee, and her chin resting on her hand, and her great black eyes calmly surveying the vast multitude that filled the court.

"Remove that girl instantly!" shouted the judge; and Cora was hustled ignominiously out of court. But the judge was disconcerted, and wound up his address to the jury by briefly saying:

"All these things are now subjects for your deliberation, gentlemen. You will please retire again; and may the God of Truth and Justice guide your decision."

The judge descended from the bench; the jury retired; but in less than ten minutes returned with their verdict. The judge was recalled, and resumed his seat; and the stillness and silence of death fell upon the court.

"Have you agreed to your verdict, gentlemen?" said the clerk of the court.

"Yes!" replied the foreman, handing down his paper.

"You find that the prisoner, Richard, alias Dick, Duggan, is NOT GUILTY of the murder of Edward Kerins?"

"Yes!" was the reply.

A sigh of relief was whispered through the court. The judge said:

"I thoroughly agree with your verdict, although the case lies enshrouded in mystery. The prisoner is discharged!"

A roar of triumph shook the building, and, caught up by the multitude waiting outside, was carried down along the street.

Dazed and stupid, Dick Duggan was led from the dock; and his arms were half torn from their sockets by handshakings and congratulations. Then it was remembered that his mother had the first right to see him and embrace him, and he was led through the crowd to where she was sitting. She had been crying with delight and happiness; but when her son was brought to her, she looked at him sternly, instead of embracing him on his rescue from a horrible and shameful death, and sternly said:

"Is it thrue what the priesht said, that you struck him, that you dar lay hands on the ministher of God?"

"Lave the poor fellow alone, Mrs. Duggan," said the more compassionate neighbors. "He has gone through enough already."

But this would not do. She pushed the poor fellow before her rudely, and forced him on his knees before the priest, who was still communing with the lawyers.

"Go down on your two knees," she said, "and ask pardon of God and the minister of God for what you done."

The old priest turned around; and groping in the air, he laid his

" Oh, vo, vo, vo, vo ! And to think the people never knew you till they lost you !"

And the priest heard the echo in his own heart:

" Oh woe, woe ! And I never knew the people till I lost them !"

He would gladly have escaped now from the crowd that still filled the street, but he had to make his way slowly through them ; and he had an ovation a king might envy, as he forged his way with difficulty to the car that was to bear him to the railway station. And as he went, he saw through his blindness the dark ramparts and sullen fortifications with which society seeks to save itself from itself, slowly crumble and fall, and above in the empyrean, the Eternal Star of Love shine liquid and resplendent.

CHAPTER XLVIII.

IT IS THE LAW.

THE murder of Ned Kerins, as the judge said, remained shrouded in mystery. Not the slighest suspicion attached to the gipsy, although it was commonly surmised from the remarks of the gipsy girl, that the tribe knew more than they cared to reveal. And one morning, Dunkerrin Castle, the old keep down by the sea, was untenanted again. In the midnight a strange hulk loomed up over the waters far out at sea ; and a couple of boats containing the gipsy family and all their belongings shot alongside. The boats were rowed homewards empty by one man, who soon after disappeared ; and a few rags of wretched bedding, and some broken tins alone marked the place where the uncanny people had dwelt. They carried their secret with them.

One alone seemed to divine what had happened. That was Dick Duggan, and he held his peace. He was now a changed man. All the fierce violence of his nature had culminated and broken out on that night when he had committed the unpardonable crime of laying hands on a priest ; and he was smitten, as we have seen, with a sudden remorse, that seemed to have opened up the dark gulf of his life, and shown him all its horrors. It was no passing contrition, therefore, that made him wish for death, when death stared him in the face ; but a desire to make atonement

many years of his life, his character underwent one of those sudden transformations that may be witnessed in strong and turbulent natures under the visitation of great trial. Dick Duggan became a model man. All the riotous fun and fierceness of his disposition gave way under a subdued and solemn melancholy, which would have been a subject for Celtic jests and laughter, but that the tragedy of his life was so well known. He worked late and early at the farm; was assiduous in the performance of his religious duties; was respectful and helpful to the priests. And gradually, the old-time intimacy with Martha Kerins began to be resumed. For she was young and a widow, and inexperienced; and she needed advice about the buying and selling of cattle, the rotation of crops, etc.; and her people were far away, and Dick Duggan was so often only on the other side of the ditch, and it became so easy to consult him. And Dick was very obliging and courteous, and had forsworn drink, and therefore had a clear head; and so things went on, until one day it suddenly dawned on him that he might become master of the coveted Crossfields for the asking. And he did ask, and was accepted. There was some reclamation on the part of her friends, not because of Dick's antecedents, but because he had no means or money; but Martha, like every good woman, had a will of her own, and she duly asserted it. Her first husband, by the marriage settlement, had left everything to her; and she used her own discretion in disposing of it.

So peace settled down on the united parishes of Doonvarragh, Lackagh, and Athboy—peace after a turbulent and trying time. But their priests were gone—and there was shame in the hearts of the people for many a long day.

Henry Liston, who was in thorough touch and sympathy with his pastor during all the troublous time, could not remain in the parish after him. He argued, If one so great and good, one, too, who loved so his people that he would have died for them, found yet but disappointment in life and ingratitude in human hearts, what could a weakling, like himself, expect? No. He felt he was not made for the rough play and tumble of life, and he sought peace. Besides, certain letters emanating from the far-off convent, where the sisters, when they were hungry, pulled the convent bell for food, and sat on the bare floor while eating it, began to reveal to him many things. And amongst the rest! this, That, amidst all the "storm and stress" of modern life, the cries and creaking of the chariots of Progress on their way toward some final goal, which no man sees or foresees, and the frantic appeals to the Church and her priests to come out of the sanctuary, and put their shoulders to the chariot-wheels that are forever sinking into the ruts of revolution, perhaps there might be a few souls, who, unpossessed of the physical or intellectual strength that is the first factor in modern progress, might go aside, and help a little by lifting their hands in prayer to the Unseen Powers, that have more to say in the direction of human events than the progressivists and utilitarians of the age will allow. And so, he sought peace for himself and power for many in a quiet little monastery, where there was no activity, no machinery, no economic problems to solve; only the old-fashioned and completely out of date routine, day by day, and night by night, of fasting, contemplation, prayer. And there, under the name of Father Alexis, he lived as unknown and unnoticed as the Saint whose name he was elected to bear.

But the shame on the hearts of the people was greatest for their pastor, whom they felt they had expelled and driven forth from amongst them. He had taken a long, low-roofed cottage in another parish, about a mile to the west of the place where he had ministered for a quarter of a century. A little suite of three rooms ran in front of the house; beyond was a potato-patch badly cultivated and showing but dockweeds and thistles. Beyond the fence of the potato-patch were great sand-dunes, where the sea-thistles grew in profusion; and these sloped down in a firm, glistening, sandy beach, where the waves thundered at high-tide, and the sea-swallows perched at the ebb of the waters to watch and capture their living food. All the rooms faced the sea; and there he fell asleep on wintry nights, lulled by the soft splash of the waves, or rejoicing in their thunder-voices; and on the long summer days he sat outside on a rude bench, fanned by the sea-breezes, or warmed by the sun. And here one day, there stole across the sands, and across the potato-patch, and into the kitchen that very Annie who, he almost swore in his wrath, should never come under his roof-tree again.

It was the autumn time, and she and Dion had been at home for a few days only, when the terrible aching at her heart to see her suffering and abandoned uncle compelled her to set aside every feeling of dread, and brave the chances of rejection. For she did not know, how could she? of the mighty change that had been wrought in his heart; and she pictured in her girlish imagination her uncle as she had first seen him, tall and powerful and impos-

were echoing (they never ceased to echo) the sharp and bitter words with which he pronounced the sentence of her expulsion, and bade her never dream of seeing him again. How could she know that his heart, too, was aching after her? How could she hear him call "Annie!" in the midnight, when no voice came in response save the soft or hoarse whispers of the deep?

She stood at the kitchen door, and the old housekeeper almost fainted when she saw her. Then there were greetings and questions in hushed tones; and there were tears over a past that was sombre enough to the eyes of both women.

A hundred times Annie asked the old housekeeper, "How is he? Had he everything he required? Was there any lack of the little comforts he would require in his old age? Did the people remember him? Who came to see him?"

And the old woman could answer that he was well; but changed, sadly changed to her eyes.

"He's almost like a child now, Miss, or, perhaps I should say, Ma'am. He sits all day, thinking and praying, but never talking. But, whin any of the prieshts comes, he sees 'em, and talks to 'em in the ould way. The people? Ah, the people! They sees now their mistake, and the crachures are doing their besht. See here, Miss, or maybe, I should say, Ma'am!"

And she took Annie out and showed her a whole aviary of young turkeys, geese, and hens, cackling melodiously in the yard, or straying for food across the potato-patch.

"And sure ould Mrs. Duggan comes down every week,—ah! she's the dacent ould shtock, althou' her son was a blagard; but he's all right now; and she doesn't know what she can do for the priesht. But still he's lonesome, Miss, or maybe I should say, Ma'am; lonesome for somethin'; and I do be sometimes afeard that maybe the death is comin' on him."

"I wonder if I could see him, Anne, without his knowing it?'

"Yerra, sure I'll tell him, Miss, that you're here."

"Oh, no! not for the world, Anne," she said, in a great fright. "I mean not now, some other time; and don't tell him for your life that I've been here."

"Faix, I won't, Miss, for he'd kill me if he knew it, and knew I didn't tell him."

"But I'll come again. Tell me now, when you go in or out of his room, does he know you, or speak to you?"

"Yerra, no, Miss. Sure he never opens his lips to me. I takes him in his breakfast and dinner; and I removes the things; and he never says, 'Iss, aye, or no,' no more than if I wor never there at all."

"And do you think now, if I—that is, supposing that I took your place some day, and went in with dinner, do you think he would know that it wasn't you that was there?"

"Yerra, how could he, Miss—Ma'am, I should say? That is, onless you spoke to him."

"Well, now, I'll come some other day, perhaps to-morrow, and try. You know, Anne, that he is old, and that it would never do to give him a great surprise."

"I suppose so, Miss," said Anne, somewhat incredulously.

"You know old people have sometimes died suddenly from sudden surprises like that. We must go gently, Anne. I wonder could I see his bedroom now? Is there any danger he would know?"

"Not the laste, Miss," said Anne. "He won't know but you're one of the neighbours come in wid a few chickens."

They entered the old man's bedroom. It was not too bad. But the heart of the girl sank as her quick eyes noticed the stains on the pillow covers and the counterpane; and some other aspects of things that showed that the skill of the washerwoman was not often called into requisition.

But she said nothing, fearing to hurt the feelings of the old domestic. But, as she was going away, she said gaily:

"There are a lot of linens and things up at the house of which there is no use. I think I'll bring them down to you. And tell me, what does uncle eat?"

"Oh, wisha, Miss, he doesn't ate as much as a sparrow. He haves a cup of tea in the morning, and a bit of toast about the size of a sixpenny bit. And thin I gets him a chop or a chicken for his dinner; but the finest lady in the land couldn't ate less of it. I don't know, I'm sure, how he lives, at all, at all."

"Very well, Anne. Now we'll put our heads together, you and I, as we did long ago—do you remember my cooking, Anne?"

"Ah, wisha, Miss, don't I? Sure 'twas you had the light hand—"

"Very good! Now, we'll commence again; and I'll engage I'll make uncle eat something. Goodbye now! Did I tell you I was married, Anne?"

"You didn't, Miss; but sure I guessed it. And there was me, like an old fool, callin' you 'Miss" all the time. But sure you looks as young, Miss, as the night you stepped off the car in the rain, and gev us all the fright."

"Ah me! I was young then. I am older now, Anne, because I have seen a great deal."

"Wisha thin, Miss, I wish you luck, and may your ondhertakin' thrive wid you. Sure won't the priesht be glad whin he hears it?"

" Of course," said Annie, dubiously. " But not a word, Anne, not a word that I was here. Remember, I'll come to-morrow again."

She came, and brought a complete change of linen, etc., for his bedroom; and glided away again without a word with him. The old housekeeper again urged her to go in and speak to her uncle; but her heart failed her. But his quick senses noticed a change in his bedroom.

"Anne," said he, half jocularly, "you're becoming quite fashionable. Where did you get the lavender that is in my pillow-covers and bed-linen?"

Anne coughed behind her hand; and, this seemed to irritate all her bronchial tubes, because she was seized with a sudden paroxysm of coughing and wheezing. When she recovered her breath, she said faintly:

" I suppose somethin' quare got into the wather; or maybe, 'twas the new soap."

" Maybe so," he said, and he relapsed into silence again.

Then one day, Annie summoned up courage, and with a white face and a beating heart, she took the dinner into the old man's room. She nearly fell at the threshold; but calling on all her strength, she entered the room, and softly laid the plates and dishes on the table. If he should speak now, she thought, as her hands trembled! But not a word. And she was able to observe him, as he sat bolt upright in an arm-chair near the window. But her self-possession was near giving way, when she saw the change, which was greater than even she dreaded. For the tall form, though erect, seemed dwarfed and shrunken; the pale face was paler, and she noticed with a gasp of pity that he, who had been so fastidious and particular about his personal appearance, was unshaven, and that his clothes were discolored and soiled. A little rent in the sleeve spoke volumes to her, and the seam of his coat was opened where it fell over his fingers. He held a book in his hand—one of his old calf-bound volumes, and his fingers were feeling one of the pages, as if he were striving by the sense of touch to read what was written therein. He made no movement, when she entered the room, and seemed not to notice her presence; but, as she was leaving, he gave a little start forward, and seemed to be listening intently. She glided softly from the room, and fell into a chair quite faint and weak with emotion.

the swift intelligence and observation of her uncle were gathering
clue after clue from her movements.

She had now become so accustomed to enter his room unnoticed,
that she had become almost reckless, and probably betrayed herself
in many little ways. And one day, as she busied herself around the
dinner-table, arranging cloths and napkins, she heard her name
called softly, and as if by question:

"Annie?"

She stood silent, watching him intently. He was leaning forward,
as if eager to catch fresh indications of her presence, and yet not
quite sure that he was right. But he said again in a louder tone:

"Annie, I know 'tis you. Come here!"

And she went over, and knelt humbly at his feet, placing her
clasped hands on his knees. He stretched forth his withered hand,
and passed it gently and affectionately over her hair, and then more
tenderly and reverently over the soft lines of her face. She looked
up, and saw the tears streaming down the furrowed cheeks, and she
knew all.

" Oh, uncle, uncle! and have you quite forgiven me?"

He said nothing, but drew her more closely to him. Then he
found words to say:

" I knew you'd come. I knew *you* wouldn't desert me!"

And that was all. For now in the sunset of his life the clouds
had lifted, and were now wreathing themselves in all lovely forms
around the little remnant of his life. Annie came every day, and
remained with him from luncheon time to dinner. Every day Dion
drove her down the four or five miles from Rohira to the home of
the lonely priest. At first, he drove back when his young wife had
alighted; and came for her again in the evening. But when the
great revelation was made he too had to come and stay. When
Annie broke to her uncle the fact of her marriage with Dion, he
started, and just one flash of the old spirit broke out again.

" Wycherly? Why, he's a Protestant!"

But she was able to assure him that she had been faithful to her
principles, and then she opened up before him, as only a devoted
wife could, all the splendors of Dion's character, his fearlessness,
his honor, his manliness, his freedom above all from the passion of
gain. And many an afternoon was whiled away by Dion's recital of
his many adventures by sea and land. And then his voice became
softer, as he remembered with just a little touch of conscience, the
devotion of his black dependents; and softer still, when he spoke
of that grave beneath the African skies, where the stricken brother
had found rest.

"It was poor Jack, sir," he said, "that proposed for me to Annie. I was too much afraid of her to say all that was in my mind. But Jack, poor fellow, knew it all. And one day, he clasped our hands together above his hammock, and 'twas all done. Of course, Annie told me at once that it could never be, never, never, never! Then I began to find that never meant until—. And then she began to explain to me all about the mysteries of faith; but I had no head for these things. I could box the compass, or shoot a flying fish, or horsewhip a coward; but I couldn't get hold of such slippery things as mysteries and doctrines. So Annie explained to me all about explicit faith. And then the good Padre came; and he said to me, ' Do you believe all the Catholic Church teaches?' And I said, ' If Annie believes all the Church teaches, and I believe all that Annie believes, isn't that the same thing?' And, by Jove, he was puzzled; but, of course, he had to say ' Yes!' And I was baptized; and we were spliced. And, by Jove, sir, I hope the Angels will put off my call to glory for some time. I don't want any other heaven just yet."

At another time in earlier life, the stern old theologian would hardly accept this kind of explicit faith as a preliminary to entering the Church; but now he saw by the illumination of sorrow great hidden depths beneath the apparent frivolity of this strong character, and he said nothing. But he asked, with some hesitation, how Dion's father had taken the news of his son's conversion and marriage.

"Dad? Ah, if you were to see dad. He's twenty years younger since we came home; and when he puts on his velvet jacket, and brushes down his hair on his shoulders, he's quite a beau. One day, we had a funny little scene which explains matters. We were talking about old times, and Jack's terrible illness, and Annie's great tenderness and kindness, and dad said: ' I remember I once expressed a wish that I had a daughter like you, Annie.' And Annie blushed, and said, ' I heard you, sir!' And that's the reason, I suppose," Dion continued, as Annie entered the room, "that Annie set the trap for me; and, I, an innocent fellow, fell into it."

And one day, Annie proposed to her uncle, very modestly and gently, that she would read to him some hours each day, at intervals, from his old favorite books, the classics, or the theologians, whom he had never parted with. His face lighted up with pleasure. She took down a Horace, and began to read one of the Odes. The Latin was beyond her own comprehension, for old Horace had a dainty way of saying things. But she had not proceeded far, when he stopped her:

"Do you think you understand the meaning of that Ode, Annie?"

"No!" she said. "I recognize a word here and there; and that is all."

"And 'tis enough," he said. "I think I've had enough of Horace."

"Well, then, we'll try the magician, Virgil," she said, replacing the Horace, and taking down a Delphin Virgil.

She read on for some time, opening the pages here and there; but he seemed to be weary of it also.

"Well, then, here's St. Thomas," she said. "Of course, 'tis all Greek to me; but I shall be able to read so that you, uncle, can follow."

And she commenced to read slowly and with difficulty from the *Summa*. He listened more patiently now, and apparently with some pleasure. But, the brain was now less elastic than in former times; and he again showed signs of weariness.

"I'll tell you what, uncle," she said gaily, although her heart misgave her, "I'll bring on to-morrow what Dion calls a good rousing novel—lots of fighting and love-making, and thunder and lightning; and I'll put you through a course of them."

He smiled. He had never read a novel in the whole course of life.

She kept her word. She brought down not what she had suggested; but a tender and gentle tale; but alas! it was full of the tragedy and sorrow of the world. He grew almost angry.

"Is there not sorrow and trouble enough in real life," he said, "without wringing our hearts with pictured misery and desolation?"

And Annie desisted; and looked around her in a hopeless manner.

There was an old Greek Testament, hidden among his books; and she took it out, and dusted it.

"Well," she said, "I must keep up my Greek, uncle. I wonder can I translate this?"

And she opened the Fourteenth Chapter of the Gospel of St. John, and began to read.

This time he did not interrupt her. The soft, sweet music of the Greek, in which are enshrined the solemn messages of the "new commandment", sank into his soul; and he allowed his niece to read on to the very end of that sublime discourse and prayer for his disciples which the Divine Master uttered under the most solemn circumstances of His life.

"Take the Douay Testament, and read it for me again, if you are not tired," he said.

" That will do !" he said. " That is now my poetry, philosophy, and theology, unto the end. We need no more !"

And every day, even unto the end, that was his mental food and medicine. He saw at last that the " new commandment " was the " final law " of the universe, although everything in Nature and in Man seems to disprove it ; or as that sad poet interpreted it, who, had he lived, would have been the fervent disciple of Him whom he railed against during life:

" Love is celebrated everywhere as the sole law which should govern the moral world."

It is a doctrine difficult to believe, as the " law " is a difficult one to practise ; but the law is final. It is the last word that has been uttered by Divine and human philosophy.

[FINIS.]

P. A. SHEEHAN.

Doneraile, Ireland.

Analecta.

INDULGENTIAE SS. NOMINIS JESU CONFRATERNITATI CONCEDUNTUR.

Beatissime Pater,

In America Septentrionali, curis et zelo Fratrum Praedicatorum, celebris est SSmi Nominis Jesu Confraternitas, cui plus quam 500,000 virorum nomen dederunt; eorum major pars semel in mense Sacris Sacramentis participat; pluries insuper in anno solemnes per vias publicas instituunt processiones (quae *Holy Name Rallies* dicuntur), in professionem Fidei erga Divinitatem D. N. Jesu Christi, et in reparationem blasphemiarum. Hujusmodi processiones in magnis civitatibus, 50,000 virorum aliquando constant; et quotidie augentur.

Ut autem haec adeo salutaris erga SS. Dei et Jesu nomen devotio magis ac magis foveatur, crescat et dilatetur, Fratres Praedicatores qui Confraternitati SS. Nominis Jesu praesunt

2. Indulgentiam 300 dierum semel in die lucrandam ab iisdem Confratribus, qui modo visibili habitualiter idem insigne deferunt, dum in publicum prodeunt, si devote dixerint: *Sit Nomen Domini benedictum!*

3. Benedictionem Apostolicam pro Redactoribus et Lectoribus Ephemeridis ejusdem Confraternitatis cui titulus: *The Holy Name Journal,* et pro omnibus illis qui Confraternitatis SS. Nominis Jesu propagationi dant operam.

Et Deus . . .

Juxta preces perlibenter Indulgentias in Domino concedimus, et cunctis dilectis Patribus Praedicatoribus, Confraternitatis a SS. Nomine nuncupatae Sociis, et Scriptoribus, Redactoribus Lectoribusque Ephemeridis ejusdem Confraternitatis Apostolicam Benedictionem peramanter impertimus.

PIUS PP. X.

Die 4 Novembris 1909.

S. CONGREGATIO RITUUM.

I.

Addenda in Breviario Romano.

DIE 27 IANUARII

In Festo S. Ioannis Chrysostomi, Episcopi Confessoris et Ecclesiae Doctoris.

Ad calcem lectionis VI, post verba dictasse videatur, *addatur:*

Hunc vero praeclarissimum universae Ecclesiae Doctorem Pius decimus Pontifex maximus coelestem oratorum sacrorum patronum declaravit atque constituit.

DOMINICA I IULII

In Festo Pretiosissimi Sanguinis D.N.I.C.

Lectio IX.

Serm. 31, alias 344.

Habuit ille sanguinem, unde nos redimeret; et ad hoc accepit sanguinem, ut esset quem pro nobis redimendis effunderet. Sanguis Domini enim tui, si vis, datus est pro te; si nolueris esse, non est datus pro te. Forte enim dicis: Habuit sanguinem Deus meus, quo me redimeret; sed iam, cum passus est, totum dedit. Quid illi remansit, quod det et pro me? Hoc est magnum, quia semel dedit, et pro omnibus dedit. Sanguis Christi volenti est salus, nolenti supplicium. Quid ergo dubitas qui mori non vis, a secunda potius morte liberari? Qua liberaris, si vis tollere crucem tuam, et sequi Dominum; quia ille tulit suam, et quaesivit servum.

Te Deum laudamus.

DOMINICA INFRA OCTAVAM NATIVITATIS B. MARIAE V.

In Festo Sanctissimi Nominis Mariae

Si hoc festum extra Dominicam recolatur, deficiente alia lectione IX, Officii utcumque simplicis, erit sequens

Lectio IX.

Beata, quae inter homines audire sola meruit prae omnibus: Invenisti gratiam. Quantam? Quantam superius dixerat: plenam. Et vero plenam, quae largo imbre totam funderet et infunderet creaturam: Invenisti enim gratiam apud Deum. Haec cum dicit, et ipse angelus miratur, aut feminam tantum, aut omnes homines vitam meruisse per feminam: stupet angelus totum Deum venire intra virginalis uteri angustias, cui tota simul angusta est creatura. Hinc est quod remoratur angelus, hinc est quod virginem vocat de merito, de gratia compellat, vix causam prodit audienti, sane ut sensum promoveat, vix longa trepidatione componit.

Te Deum laudamus.

DOMINICA III SEPTEMBRIS

In Festo Septem Dolorum B. M. V.

Si hoc festum extra Dominicam reponatur, deficiente alia

cruce Christus, et inter matrem atque discipulum dividebat pietatis officia. Condebat Dominus non solum publicum, sed etiam domesticum testamentum; et hoc eius testamentum signabat Ioannes, dignus tanto testatore testis. Bonum testamentum non pecuniae, sed vitae aeternae; quod non atramento scriptum est, sed Spiritu Dei vivi, qui ait: Lingua mea calamus scribae, velociter scribentis.

Te Deum laudamus.

DIE 3 DECEMBRIS

In Festo S. Francisci Xaverii Confessoris
Ad calcem lectionis VI, post verba Sanctis adscripsit, *addatur:*

Pius autem decimus ipsum sodalitati et operi Propagandae Fidei coelestem patronum elegit atque constituit.

DECRETUM

Sanctissimus Dominus noster Pius Papa X, referente infrascripto Cardinali sacrorum Rituum Congregationi Praefecto, suprascriptas additiones, respectivis suis locis Breviarii Romani inserendas, suprema auctoritate Sua approbavit. Die 10 Novembris 1909.

Fr. S. Card. MARTINELLI, *Praefectus.*

L. ✠ S.

PHILIPPUS CAN. DI FAVA, *Substitutus.*

MONITUM.—*In festo sancti Paulini Episcopi et confessoris, sub finem lectionis VII, dictatur:* QUIDQUID de suis donis, *atque sub initium lectionis VIII dicatur* in die MALO ab ira, *et infra* in die MALO liberabit.

II.

ADDENDA IN MARTYROLOGIO ROMANO

DIE 27 IANUARII

DIE 6 MARTII

Primo loco legitur:
Sanctarum Perpetuae et Felicitatis martyrum, quae nonis Martii gloriosam martyrii coronam a Domino receperunt.

DIE 7 MARTII

Ad calcem elogii sanctorum Perpetuae et Felicitatis, post verba sub Severo principe, *addatur:*
Sanctarum vero Perpetuae et Felicitatis festum pridie huius diei recolitur.

DIE 15 MARTII

Ultimo loco legitur:
Vindobonae in Austria, sancti Clementis Mariae Hofbauer, sacerdotis professi congregationis sanctissimi Redemptoris, plurimis in Dei gloria et animarum salute promovenda ac dilatanda ipsa congregatione exantlatis laboribus insignis; quem virtutibus et miraculis clarum Pius decimus Pontifex maximus in Sanctorum canonem retulit.

DIE 23 MARTII

Ultimo loco legitur:
Barcinone in Hispania, sancti Iosephi Oriol presbyteri, ecclesiae S. Mariae Regum beneficiarii, omnigena virtute, ac praesertim corporis afflictatione, paupertatis vultu, atque in egenos et infirmos caritate celebris; quem in vita et post mortem miraculis gloriosum Pius Papa decimus Sanctorum numero accensuit.

DIE 3 DECEMBRIS

Ad calcem elogii sancti Francisci Xaverii, post verba hac die celebratur, *addatur:*
Pius vero Papa decimus ipsum beatum virum sodalitati et operi Propagandae Fidei coelestem patronum elegit atque constituit.

DECRETUM

mano suis locis respective inseri iussit. Die 10 Novembris 1909.

Fr. S. Card. MARTINELLI, *Praefectus.*

L. ✠ S.

PHILIPPUS CAN. DI FAVA, *Substitutus.*

III.

CIRCA CONSECRATIONEM ECCLESIAE " COEMENTO ARMATO" CONSTRUCTAE.

A Rmo Dno Iuliano Conan, Archiepiscopo Portus Principis sacrorum Rituum Congregatione nuper propositum fuit, pro opportuna solutione, sequens dubium: An ecclesia, constructa vel construenda ex materia quae *coementum armatum* nuncupatur, consecrari valeat, adhibita forma ac ritu Pontificalis Romani?

Et sacra Rituum Congregatio, exquisito Commissionis liturgicae suffragio, ita respondendum sensuit: *Affirmative,* dummodo duodecim crucium loca, et postes ianuae principalis, sint ex lapide.

Atque ita rescripsit, die 12 Novembris 1909.

Fr. S. Card. MARTINELLI, *Praefectus.*

L. ✠ S.

PHILIPPUS CAN. DI FAVA, *Substitutus.*

S. CONGREGAZIONE DEL CONCILIO.

CONCORSO

Per ordine superiore, e in conformità al Regolamento annesso alla Costituzione Apostolica *Sapienti consilio,* parte I, capo 2, si dichiara aperto un concorso per due posti di scrittore nella Segreteria della S. C. del Concilio. I sacerdoti che vol-

SACRA PENITENZIERIA.

Concorso

Indicitur omnibus et singulis in ordine sacro constitutis, concurrere volentibus ad munus officialis sacrae Poenitentiariae, ut, intra spatium triginta dierum a data praesentium computandum, documenta de nomine, cognomine, patria, consensu Emi Cardinalis Urbis Vicarii, bono proprii Ordinarii testimonio, aetate, requisitis, studiis, conditione, exercitio ceterisque qualitatibus et gradibus R. P. D. Oresti Giorgi Regenti, vel R. P. D. Iosepho Latini Correctori exhibeant; quibus probatis, admittentur ad concursum, qui habebitur in Secretaria S. Poenitentiariae die 24 Novembris hora octava ante meridiem, pro examine in scriptis; die vero 30 Novembris hora nona ante meridiem in aedibus nostris, pro examine orali.

Datum Romae, ex nostris aedibus, die 22 Octobris 1909.

S. Card. VANNUTELLI, *Poenitentiarius maior.*

L. ✝ S.

VINCENTIUS CAN. ROSETTI, *S. P. Capellanus.*

ROMAN CURIA.

Official announcement is made of the following honors:

4 November: The Rev James Anesagasti, Canon of the Metropolitan Church of Guadalaxara, nominated to the Cathedral See of Campeche in Mexico.

The Rev. Right Rev. John Stariha, formerly Bishop of Lead, appointed to the titular See of Antipatris in Palestine.

12 November: The Rev. Joseph of Jesus Guzman, Canon of the Metropolitan Church of Durango, nominated to the Cathedral See of Taumalipas in Mexico.

21 September: The Rev. Victor Deby, of the Diocese of Nicaragua, for Honorary Chamberlain *in abito paonazzo.*

8 October: The Rev. Augustine Piaggio, of the Archdiocese of Buenos Ayres, for the same honor.

Studies and Conferences.

OUR ANALECTA.

The Roman documents for the month are:

SOVEREIGN PONTIFF grants to the members of the Holy Name Society (a) Plenary Indulgence for wearing the Society badge in procession (i. e. at their " Rallies "), on condition that they go to confession and receive Communion; (b) Indulgence of 300 days, once a day, for saying " Blessed be the Name of God," to those members who regularly wear the badge in public; and (c) the Apostolic Benediction to the editors and readers of the *Holy Name Journal,* and to all who work for the spread of the Society.

S. CONGREGATION OF RITES: 1. Publishes some corrections and additions to the Roman Breviary—viz. for the feast of St. John Chrysostom (27 January); the feast of the Most Precious Blood (first Sunday of July); the feast of the Holy Name of Mary (Sunday within the octave of the Nativity of the B. V. M.); the feast of the Seven Dolors B. V. M. (third Sunday in September); the feast of St. Francis Xavier (3 December); and for the feast of St. Paulinus (24 June).

2. Additions and changes are indicated for the Roman Martyrology—27 January, 6 March, 7 March, 15 March, 23 March, 3 December.

3. Sanctions the consecration of church edifices built of cement or concrete (*coementum armatum*).

SS. CONGREGATIONS OF THE COUNCIL AND OF THE PENITENTIARY issue announcements for the concursus of officials for their respective departments, as prescribed by the Decree *Sapienti consilio.*

ROMAN CURIA announces recent appointments.

FREQUENT COMMUNION AND THE EUCHARISTIC FAST.

In replying to a suggestion of a correspondent in the December issue of the REVIEW, advocating the modification of the present law of fasting for those who wish to communicate frequently, we stated that, in order to open the way practically toward obtaining such modification it would be necessary before all to. point out definitely the reasons, social, ecclesiastical, and hygienic, the existence of which our correspondent had estimated in a general way. The following letter is the answer, which we submit to our clerical readers with a view to further discussion:

To the Editor, The Ecclesiastical Review.

Ever since the appearance of the Decree on Frequent Communion a constant stream of books, pamphlets and articles has issued from the Catholic press, in which the several writers have exhorted the faithful to avail themselves of the privileges which the Decree extends to them. Priests in their pulpits have everywhere zealously urged the Holy Father's fervent appeal. The results have been most gratifying, as every pastor of souls can happily testify. Communions have been multiplied and the spiritual life of our people has been wonderfully benefited. While, however, writers and preachers have thus earnestly exhorted the faithful to the practice of frequent Communion, not a word has been said or written (so far as I am aware) in behalf of large classes of our people who are practically prevented from receiving Holy Communion frequently by the severe requirements of the law of fasting. As examples of these classes I may instance the following:

1. In our country churches Masses are usually fixed at a late hour to accommodate the scattered population of the parishes. This is especially true of mission churches, in which the priests may be saying a second Mass. The people come to these churches from long distances and, if they propose to receive Holy Communion, they are obliged, besides, to fast until 10 o'clock, or 11, or even later. Experience shows that the few who do receive Holy Communion at these Masses receive but rarely. Were it not for the necessity of fasting till nearly mid-day, there is every reason to believe that very many more of such people would approach the altar. Catholics living in country districts are necessarily deprived of many of the spiritual advantages which are within reach of their more fortunate brethren who live in cities and towns. This is an additional reason why their reception of Holy Communion should be facilitated rather than hindered. Exhortations to frequent Communion can mean nothing to the large number of Catholics who fall under this class, as long as the law obliging them to a rigorous fast remains in force.

2. A large number of our girls are employed as night operators in telephone offices. A midnight luncheon is usually provided for

such operators. Many of them would, doubtless, gladly receive Holy Communion on their way home from duty at 6 or 7 o'clock were it not for the law of fasting. To take their luncheon before midnight would mean an impossible fast of six or seven hours while working. The law operates similarly against other night workers, such as nurses, who would be unable to fast from midnight until the time of the first available Mass.

3. There is every reason to believe that a great many working people (who should receive every encouragement in this matter) would receive Holy Communion on week days as well as on Sundays if some mitigation were allowed in the law of fasting. As it is, it is simply impossible for them to go to church, return home for breakfast, and then hurry to their several places of work. The comparatively few who do attempt it are usually obliged to cut short their prayers and thanksgiving, much to the detriment of their spirit of piety. And there are many housekeepers who would be glad to go to Mass and receive Holy Communion after their early morning work is finished, if they could do so without being obliged to an absolute fast.

4. In most parish churches there is an "after breakfast" Mass at 9 or half past 9 o'clock during Lent. The attendance at this Mass is always very large; Communions, however, are few. It seems certain that a very considerable proportion of those who attend this Mass could be brought to receive daily Communion during this season of devotion, if they were allowed to take their cup of coffee before Mass instead of after it.

THE BISHOP'S RIGHT TO FIX.AN AGE LIMIT FOR ADMISSION TO FIRST COMMUNION.

We have been asked whether a diocesan statute determining a fixed age before which children are not to be admitted to First Communion has any binding force, since it appears to contradict the general law of the Church which gives to the individual, if properly instructed, the right of receiving Communion as soon as he or she has arrived at the age of discretion. Since the development of the natural intelligence of children is not confined to a fixed age, it would seem that to prevent a child from receiving Communion when its intelligent appreciation of the graces of the Blessed Eucharist fits it for the same, is depriving the individual of a right beyond the reach of episcopal or parish legislation.

The answer to this difficulty is that a bishop may fix by diocesan statute a certain age before which children are not to be admitted to the solemn and public celebration of First Communion in the parish church. For many reasons a uniform method of admission to a sort of parochial incorporation through the solemn act of First Communion may be desirable and useful. Thus the retention of children in the parish school, their introduction to the sodality, or to certain other organizations connected with the church, may be more readily secured for the benefit of the parochial body; above all, the instruction in the rudiments and practices of faith will have a better chance of becoming a vital matter of conscientious observance the longer children are kept under the surveillance

minence of a greater evil to the community. As a matter of fact this contingency is not included in such legislation, which is based on purely prudential and pastoral reasons.

But there is on record a comparatively recent decision, in the above sense, by the Sacred Congregation of the Council. The Bishop of Annecy, in 1887, wishing to secure uniformity in pastoral ministration throughout his diocese, made, among other laws, one according to which no child that had not attained its twelfth year was to be admitted to First Communion. A parish priest objected to this statute, and the matter was referred to Rome:

An Decreta Episcopi Anneciensis sint confirmanda vel infirmanda in casu?

Resp. *Affirmative* ad primam partem, juxta modum. Modus est ne Episcopus parochos prohibeat ab admittendis ad primam Communionem iis pueris, de quibus certo constat eos ad discretionis aetatem juxta Conciliorum Lateranensis IV et Tridentini Decreta pervenisse.

Sanctissimus vero, in audientia diei 23 Julii jussit declarari verba *ad primam Communionem* esse intelligenda ad exclusionem primae Communionis *in forma solemni.*

The decision was variously interpreted, until a further instruction of the Cardinal Prefect made it plain in the following exposition: " Parochus potest S. Communionem administrare juveni quem ipse reputat *instructum* et quem dicit habere discretionem intelligendi id quod agit, sed *privatim* absque ulla solemnitate et publicitate; at cum agitur de administranda S. Communione *in forma publica et solemni* juxta morem ecclesiarum Franciae, observari debet decretum episcopale " (Cf. Mocchegiani, *Jurisprudentia,* tom. I, cap. IV, ad 1068).

THE RIGHT TO ADMIT CHILDREN TO FIRST COMMUNION.

Qu. I have just read the August number of your esteemed REVIEW.

Will you kindly inform me whether in the present canonical legislation Sisters are considered as *Clerici?* There seems to be a great difference between priests and ordinary lay-sisters.

We have a couple of boarding schools here, governed by Sisters, and although we never have. difficulties, it is good to know one's rights. Thanking you beforehand, I am very respectfully

FR. REGINALD YZENDOORN,
Vicariate Apostolic of Hawaii.

Resp. The question whether the right of religious (*Regulares*) to admit children to First Communion, irrespective of the pastor's claims, is confined to communities of priests, such as the Regulars of the Scholae Piae, is to be answered in the negative. That right belongs to the children's parents or to whomsoever these choose to commit it; and in the next place to the confessor. Canon Law does not admit of pastoral rights in this matter. " Puerorum ad primam Communionem admissio, inter jura parochialia minime accensetur," writes Mocchegiani, quoting Bouix (*De Jure Reg.,* tom. II, p. 210); and he adds "contraria opinio vix confutatione digna videtur " (*Jurisprudentia ecclesiastica,* tom. I, cap. IV, n. 1068).

It is on this principle that the S. Congregation decides such doubts as the one of which we gave an instance in the case referred to by our correspondent. The question whether Sisters come under the term *clerici* is hardly pertinent therefore.

SOME SUGGESTIONS FOR OUR CATECHISMS.

To THE EDITOR, THE ECCLESIASTICAL REVIEW.

It may or may not help to jot down what occurred to one old teacher when reading Monsgr. Dunne's suggestive article on this subject.

There is no need of apology for making suggestions. The feeling that our catechisms need improvement is quite general.

· It would be an improvement to impart a knowledge of what religion is; but can that be done by a definition? How much does a child really learn by definitions? Think how difficult it is for a child to give a definition of something already perfectly well known to the child. Suppose we say to the child: " Shut your eyes and tell me what a chair is." The child knows as much about a chair as I know; but it is beyond the child's power to define it in words. Definition is not the natural way of imparting knowledge to a child.

The additional catechetical instruction suggested by Monsgr. Dunne is needed; the problem is how to impart it. Instead of 25 questions he would have to ask at least a hundred, and make them much more concrete, before the instruction could be assimilated by children.

The Trinitarian division of the Apostles' Creed is a long step in the way of improvement.

The "old-time and common-sense division" of the catechism might still serve if consistently carried out. I do not know; for what appears a nice order of sequence to us adults may not be the order best suited for instruction of children. But anyhow it was too inconsistent as it stood. The sacramental system involves a large number of the most vital articles of faith, and yet it was placed outside of "what we are to believe." The Sacraments are not co-ordinate with the Church. They are part of the Church, and yet they were treated as if apart from the Church, under different general headings. The Baltimore Catechism has the following:

Q. Which are the means instituted by our Lord to enable men at all times to share in the fruits of the Redemption?

A. The means . . . are the Church and the Sacraments.

A pedagogical objéction to this arrangement is that it places an obstacle in the way of the children getting any complete idea either of the Church or the Sacraments. It is the definition-method and too mechanical. Monsgr. Dunne's Trinitarian division of the Creed suggests a more vital method. Connect the Church and *her* Sacraments with the abiding Presence of the Holy Ghost as closely in the catechism as they are connected in the Creed, and the children will understand whence it is that the Sacraments have their divine efficacy. They will understand it, not by any definitions that may be given, but by a proper sequence of facts, images, and ideas.

TEACHER.

THE REFORM IN CHASUBLES.

To THE EDITOR, THE ECCLESIASTICAL REVIEW.

Fra Arminio's article on the Chasuble is delightful. We know that our modern vestments are ugly, we would like to have chasubles more conformable to the beautiful chasubles of old; but where can we get them? Will Fra Arminio tell us the name and address of someone who makes them?

If there were a firm somewhere in the world that would make nothing but what was beautiful and rubrical, we could write or go there with confidence for what we wanted.

A gentleman who was sick and tired of reading " about " how Mass should be sung, asked me to tell him where he could hear the Proper and Common of the Mass as it ought to be sung. I suggested a certain Seminary near his home. He went there. I asked him how he liked it. He said: " It gave me a pain."

Don't tell us what we ought to have. Let us hear it and see it, and we will gladly follow. Let us have the names of half a dozen churches in the United States where everything is rubrical and beautiful, where all the ceremonies are correctly and reverently carried out, and we will go to see them and learn. One church that has everything correct, will do more to reform the Rubrics than thousands of pages of writing.

J. F. SHEAHAN.

Church of St. Peter, Poughkeepsie, N. Y.

THE INTRODUCTION OF THE OLD ROMAN (GOTHIC) CHASUBLE.

A correspondent who favors the introduction of the older form of chasuble, as suggested in the December number, but who apprehends difficulties on the score of prejudice, habit, and mercantile convenience, directs our attention to a paper on this subject by Bishop William von Keppler in the *Archiv. Christ. Kunst.* The Bishop proposes that the graceful style of the old Roman—miscalled " Gothic "—chasuble be first adopted in the cathedrals, where the distinction would be not only natural as befitting the more solemn ceremonial but would likewise be more easily understood as a mark of episcopal bearing. He suggests the Borromean form (for city churches) on solemn festivals, which would familiarize the faithful with the fact that it is not a question of change, as though the old vestments were censurable, but rather of an increase of beauty in the form of paramentics befitting the solemnity of exceptional services. For weekdays Bishop Keppler would recommend the old form of chasuble, but in the ampler fashion actually in use in Rome.

We outlined in the last number the general shape of the older form as contrasted with the cut-away fashion of the present-day, factory-made chasuble. In the February issue we shall bring exact patterns as made according to definite principles of Christian art and liturgical law.

It may be added here that the learned Luxembourg writer

on paramentics, Father J. Braun, S.J., endorses the opinion of the Bishop of Rotenberg, and stands for a gradual or discriminating introduction which will allow a proper place for the three kinds of chasuble mentioned.

THE FACULTY "DISPENSANDI AB IMPEDIMENTIS MATRIMONIALIBUS, IMMINENTE MORTIS PERICULO".

In the November number of the REVIEW on page 617, in summarizing the decision *de facultate dispensandi ab impedimentis matrimonialibus* (page 586), it is stated that " the faculty . . . does not apply to those who live in concubinage, but to any other cause " etc. By a printer's error the word " merely " before " apply " has been omitted, as will be plain if the reader refers to the document which accompanies the summary. Accordingly the faculty is to be understood as applying not only in case of concubinage, but in other cases also when there is need of providing for the relief of conscience.

THE OBLIGATION OF THE "ORATIO IMPERATA".

Qu. What is the law governing the " Oratio imperata "? For what length of time can a bishop indict an " imperata "? Does it continue in force after his death until a new bishop is appointed? Can an administrator " sede vacante " order an " imperata "?

I have been unable to find anything definite on the question in the various hand-books of Canon Law. I think the answer would interest quite a number of clergymen.   A. C. Z.

THE ALTAR-BREADS.

To the Editor, The Ecclesiastical Review.

In discussing the period beyond which altar-breads are not to be used, the point should, I think, be taken into consideration that old hosts, especially in a dry climate, are more likely to crumble. They leave numerous and minute fragments on the corporal. On account of their small size it is more difficult to gather these up with the paten. In consuming the Host one is apt to touch it with the lower lip or the teeth which causes such particles to separate more readily from a host dry from several weeks' age, and the fragments naturally adhere to the organs and are transferred to the rim of the chalice. When distributing Holy Communion, little pieces frequently become detached from the Hosts, falling on the Communion cloth or on the floor directly, or they adhere to the priest's fingers. In purifying the ciborium there will sometimes be considerable difficulty in getting all the minute particles out with the wine and water. All these difficulties savoring of possible irreverence can be avoided only by the use of fresh altar-breads.   R.

Criticisms and Notes.

NEW SERIES OF HOMILIES FOR THE WHOLE YEAR. By the Right Rev. Jeremias Bonomelli, D. D. Translated by the Right Rev. Thomas Byrne, D. D. Four volumes. New York: Benziger Brothers. 1909.

CATECHISM IN EXAMPLES. By the Rev. D. Chisholm. Five volumes. New York: Benziger Brothers. 1909.

THE SERMON OF THE SEA and Other Studies. By the Rev. Robert Kane, S. J. New York and London: Longmans, Green & Co. 1909.

HUMANITY—ITS DESTINY AND THE MEANS TO ATTAIN IT. By the Rev. Henry Denifle, O. P. Translated by the Very Rev. Ferdinand Brossart, V. G. New York: Fr. Pustet & Co. 1909.

Some helps for "the pulpit" and—may it not be so augured?—for "the pew", since *correlativa sunt simul et re et ratione*, as say the philosophers. When a bishop, with the wisdom, enlightened zeal, and the just sense of "actuality" which his preceding works show to be so eminently exercised by the present occupant of the See of Cremona, undertakes to write and have published four volumes of homilies, one may be assured in advance that the work will be worth while; will be solid and usable. And when one observes that a busy American prelate has given his time and labor to translating these volumes, the assurance becomes doubly assured. If with this *a priori* anticipation one takes up the volumes themselves, one quickly finds it justified.

These are homilies that explain. They illuminate and bring out the literal meaning of God's Word. They are not subjective aerial speculations, nor are they catenae of passages from the Fathers. Their author has utilized the wisdom of the great commentators, but he has passed it through his own mind, made it his own and set it down in plain language understood surely of his own people. Fortunately, too, the translation does justice to the original. The English is English, not a mongrel of foreign idioms. The priest who will give an hour or even less to the reading of the pertinent Epistle or Gospel homily need never let his people go without a solidly instructive and practical understanding of the divine word which the Church has selected for their support and comfort. The discourses may not lend themselves to outbursts of passionate oratory, or to inflated self-preachments; but they will supply the pastor with abundant food with which to strengthen and edify his flock.

If, moreover, in preparing for his Sunday discourses the priest will draw for illustrative stories on the *Catechism in Examples*, compiled by Father Chisholm in the work placed second on the above list, he can add not a little to the interest of the Scriptural commentary. Reference has previously been made in the REVIEW to this collection of illustrations designed for catechetical instructions, but equally available for all pulpit purposes. Not every story set down in the five volumes will appeal to every one who uses the work, but there is such a rich abundance of matter that usually something will be found adapted to one's purpose. It is easily the best collection of illustrative material to be found in English.

Reverting again to the above-mentioned Homilies, it should be noted that, though the preface promises Homilies for every Sunday of the year, should the priest who uses the work depend upon it for the sixth Sunday after Epiphany, he would have to content himself on that day with the experience of Old Mother Hubbard, when she went to the cupboard. It was probably an oversight that the author passed by the beautiful parable of the mustard seed and the leaven hidden in the meal.

The third book on the list above does not strictly belong to pulpit literature. The *Sermon of the Sea*, which gives it its title, was not uttered by human lips. The sea itself here preaches its own sermon. Rather is it the deep voicing the divine praises, the *benedicite maria et flumina Domino*. Besides this song of the sea there are a score of other " studies "—none dry—on subjects supernatural as these reflect themselves in nature, studies which reveal the spiritual in the material, the ideal in the sensible, the divine in the human. It were useless to set down here the titles of these studies, as the headings could hardly even suggest to the reader the matter or the lines of the thought. A casual persual of the pages might indeed lead one to side with the author's " candid " friends who " have sometimes accused him of literary affectation "; for almost every sentence scintillates with some brilliant of the imagination; so that one's eye is almost bedazzled by the multiplied radiations. If one takes, however, the author's assurance that he wrote " under the absorbing inspiration of nature " and " sought to express what he felt of its impetuous power " and therefore " spoke rather than wrote "—if one, in a word, tries to enter into the author's spirit and reads the book with the ear rather than the eye, the luxuriant wealth of fancy will not so much arrest the intellect from the embodied thought. The book belongs to the literature of power rather than of technical knowledge. The priest will gather from it inspirations and suggestions to quicken his spirit and to utilize the ministry of nature in uplifting himself and his people—to find the sermons in stones, tongues in trees, books in the running brooks, and the good in everything.

The lectures delivered by the learned Dominican historian, the late Father Denifle, and translated by Father Brossart, Vicar General of the Diocese of Covington, are not really sermons, though they were originally delivered from the Cathedral pulpit in Gratz, Austria. They are, strictly speaking, "discourses", reasoned elaborations of principles—principles in the first place rational, natural, that express the fundamental relations of man, individual and social, to God; in the second place principles supernatural, that grow out of the Incarnation and express the relation of the Catholic Church to the perfection, moral, intellectual, spiritual, of humanity—or rather the other way about, of humanity to the Church as the teacher and organ of grace and truth. These principles are carefully formulated and solidly established as real. They are then unfolded with rigid consecutiveness and a wealth of learning—philosophical, theological, and historical. The book is not such that one may read it while running. One must sit down leisurely and think along steadily if one would profit. The profit will be increased, by imparting depth and breadth of vision, and suggestive thoughts that the preacher can use, once they have passed into his own spiritual life. The translator " out of profound respect for the author has adhered closely to his mode of expression ". One could wish that equal tenderness had been exercised toward the reader. The English is not as smooth as one would like it, and does not facilitate the process of mental assimilation. The meaning, however, will nowhere escape the *willing* reader, who, moreover, may be the better for the increased attention demanded of him.

PREDIGTEN UND ANSPRACHEN zunaechst fuer die Jugend gebildeter Staende. Von Mgr. Dr. Paul Baron de Mathies (Ansgar Albing). Erster Band. St. Louis, Mo.: B. Herder. 1909.

Those of the readers of THE ECCLESIASTICAL REVIEW who may be acquainted with the numerous and varied writings of Ansgar Albing—for such is the author's pseudonym—will heartily welcome this latest literary venture of the gifted and versatile writer. The author, it is true, has in the *Predigten und Ansprachen* entered upon a new line of literary endeavor. But, whilst it need scarcely be said that sermons differ essentially in content, style, and method of handling, from other forms of writing, sacred and profane, we have here the same distinctive qualities of style and manner which mark the purely literary productions of the author.

Monsignor Mathies is a literary artist of recognized ability. Everywhere in German-speaking countries his novels, poems, and short stories have won for him general recognition. The author's high connexions in his native city—he is the scion of an old patrician family of Hamburg—and his intimate relations with the Austrian and Italian nobility have enabled him to portray with color and precision the manners, the aspirations, and the foibles of modern society, as is evident from his society novels. The style is distinctive and fascinating.

Similarly the author's poetic productions present a round of lyrics full of inspiration and charm. They are the finely finished utterances of a poet commenting upon men and happenings as they presented themselves to a mind keenly sensitive to everything that is beautiful and elevating.

While the author's poems and works of fiction aim primarily, though not exclusively, at affording his readers healthful exhilaration and ennobling enjoyment, his apologetic and ascetical works —such as *Religion in Salon und Welt, Nim und Lies, Harmonien und Disharmonien der Seele, Epistulae Redivivae*—are chiefly addressed to Catholics whose social position and environment are, in no small measure, responsible for the manifold dangers to which their faith and morals are exposed. The same phases of the author's productive and versatile mind, reflected singly in his novels, poems, short stories, published letters, apologetic and ascetical works, are to be found combined in the *Predigten und Ansprachen* before us. There is throughout an originality of manner that lends charm and interest to the book, converting what might otherwise have possibly proved a collection of dry and dull talks into eloquent and impressive sermons. The practical lessons which they convey are enhanced by the literary grace with which they are set forth. For the rest, the style is clear and plain throughout, at times even severely plain in its classic stateliness. The author delivers his august message with all the accompaniment of learning, depth of thought, and the reverential attitude which best becomes it. He has manifestly spent much time in study and meditation upon the Holy Scriptures and the liturgical books of the Church before committing these " Sermons and Addresses " to paper.

And this fact is no doubt the chief cause of that charming aroma of simplicity and directness—such as we associate with the *Parochial and Plain Sermons* of Cardinal Newman—which pervades the entire volume. The perfection of art is hidden in the careful proportioning of parts. In matter of fact, a refined and ideal temperament looks out through every one of them,—a temperament quick to perceive and happy to linger on the inner beauties and harmonies of the Catholic religion.

But whatever may be said of the literary and esthetic character of these "Sermons and Addresses", it is more especially their apologetic and ascetical worth that merits a particular recommendation. Thanks to his first-hand knowledge of Protestantism in various shapes and forms and to years of personal contact with Protestants of many shades, the author is in a position to estimate, at its full value, the happiness of membership in the Church of Christ. This is a favorite topic of the author. Moreover, his personal experience of the spiritual life, in many phases, entitles him to assume the responsibility of a guide and adviser to such Catholics, in particular, as by reason of indifference and worldly-mindedness stand most sorely in need of spiritual direction and enlightenment. In a candid and withal sympathetic tone the author directs, cautions, or reproves, as the spirit moves him. At one time it is the uncompromising postulates of Catholic dogma, at another the enrapturing beauty of Catholic ideals and the ineffable delights springing from a life of Christian perfection that he unfolds to his reader in his luminous and inimitable fashion; at another, with his finger firmly set on the pulse of the times, he discloses the multiform and complex evils that gnaw, canker-like, at the very vitals of religion, morality, and social well-being. Then, too, he does not hesitate, on occasion, to sound notes of warning to Catholics whose faith is dormant and whose devotion to the interests and demands of their holy religion is being displaced by, if it has not already succumbed to, cold indifference to matters of religious practice and belief.

The "Sermons and Addresses" comprise two parts. The first consists of twenty-four sermons for the Sundays and chief festivals from the first Sunday of Advent to Low Sunday. The second part contains eleven occasional sermons. I should recommend the *Predigten und Ansprachen* to all priests and educated laymen acquainted with the German language. Here the reader will find not only a collection of solid, practical, and inspiring sermons, but instructive and readable chapters on the great truths of the spiritual life.

O. L. L.

THE MEANING OF TRUTH. A Sequel to "Pragmatism." By William James. Longmans, Green & Co.: New York. Pp. xx-298.

The sub-title of this work but recently from the press recalls the whole war of words waged with rather unnecessary seriousness around the somewhat mystic "Pragmatism" championed during the last few years by Professor James. The present work, how-ever, will be a decided disappointment to all who have taken any real interest in the matter; since, so far from being a "sequel" to "Pragmatism", it is its merely diluted reiteration; for nine out of the fifteen articles which it contains either preceded that work, or were practically contemporaneous with it; and all are reprints ex-cepting two; one of which is an unimportant "dialogue" of ten pages at the conclusion of the work. With a similarly unimportant preface, these two articles form the only new portions of the work, and they are new only in a chronological sense.

Since, moreover, Pragmatism completely denies every ordinary an-chorage of daily human thought, no time need be spent in tracing its misleading etymology. Historically, the name and the system (?) originated with C. S. Peirce in 1878, and led an extremely anaemic existence until, twenty years later, Professor James of Harvard, by a liberal infusion of his peculiarly striking adjectives and adverbs, galvanized the new ideas into agile and seemingly robust life; so much so that they became everywhere known, and found especially ardent advocates in Schiller in England, Le Roy in France, and Papini in Italy. Peirce was very soon forced to bewail this active and powerful patronage, for his principal ideas had become ut-terly unrecognizable under the Jamesonic and other metamorphoses; and, abandoning the misappropriated name, he retained, and still further evolved, his original thought under the new designation of "Pragmaticism", a word ugly enough, he says, to no longer tempt kidnappers. Since then, the fortunes of the system have been very varied. Trained philosophers readily pointed out the palpable con-tradictions and absurdities of the theory; but the ordinary, half-read philosophical dilettanti eagerly welcomed a system which seemed to open long-closed doors with surprising ease, and to place even the great problems hitherto deemed far too abstruse for popular treat-ment within their convenient reach and command. Needless to say, the new hope was more brilliant than real.

In our own very brief account of Pragmatism and of its peculiar theory of truth, we shall restrict ourselves mainly to Professor James; since he is sufficiently expository and typical, and is especi-ally representative of American Pragmatism. His principal utterances are to be found in three different works following in close succession upon one another: *Pragmatism, A Pluralistic Universe,* and the present work. Professor James is not without a great deal of originality, but it is rather of expression than of thought. He leans heavily upon others. In his *Pragmatism,* he is very evidently inspired to a great extent by Papini. In *A Pluralistic Universe,* Bergson is avowedly his prophet, and in the present work, Schiller and Dewey lend him much aid, wherever his anxious pen is not evidently seeking the path of least resistance through the tangled mass of adverse criticism which has accumulated around his own ill-considered utterances. At times he becomes penitent, and regrets his unguarded language, but he also as soon forgets his confession, and loads his critics with the most drastic abuse.

Our own task is not unlike that of the bewildered professor. We must attempt what no Pragmatist has ever accomplished; that is, we must seek to induce some order into a maze of philosophico-theological thought which touches every branch of higher human knowledge, yet in which confusion reigns supreme. The mind naturally awaits a definition of the new system, but Peirce, James, and Papini all warn us not to expect a definition of Pragmatism. We can, therefore, only take advantage of those respects in which the Pragmatists themselves are the least involved; and, by doing this, we may say at once that Pragmatism includes three principal things: a mental attitude, a theory of reality, and a theory of truth. As to the first, Pragmatism is in open revolt against usual, intellectual methods. Regarding both reality and truth, " creative " is the word to keep in mind; for Pragmatists claim a really creative efficiency with regard to both; their kind of objective existences, and truth itself, being said to spring into their only real existence at Pragmatism's magic touch. According to this principle, that alone is true which, being tested by the demands of practical, daily exigences, works out in a way that is advantageous to us, and " guides us prosperously " in our daily wishes and needs. Reality owes its existence to the same means; and it must be remembered here that the Pragmatist does not talk thus as of a *test* of truth or reality, but of their very *fieri*, of their very coming into existence. We need not say that in this summary we shall weigh pragmatic utterances according to their objective value, and not according to the assurances of Pragmatists as to what they really mean.

And pausing a moment for the brief criticism which alone is possible here, we may quote and adopt, with regard to Pragmatism's rejection of intellectualism (often called " rationalism " in pragmatic manuals) the words of a recent newspaper critic concerning

Pragmatism as set forth by James. " There is somet
hilarity of sport in dragging out the inconsistencies, i
cerities, of a philosopher who has tried to defend ratic
tem which is professedly an attack on rationalism. F(
and nothing more, is Pragmatism. It is easy to show
philosopher ought, so far as the correspondence of log
ity goes, to be a complete sceptic ". In his first wor
James makes very strenuous efforts to appear thorough]
that he is dealing with the deepest and most importa
appealing, even, to the sense of responsibility with whic
and necessary creation of truth and of reality shoul(
every act. But, after becoming first irritable and ther
under the continual cross-fire of his adversaries, he ;
second work, an account of his troubled mental times,
says:[1] " I had literally come to the end of my concept
trade, I was bankrupt intellectualistically, and had to
base." And:[2] " I hoped ever for an intellectualist wa
difficulty, and it was only after reading Bergson that I
continue the intellectualist method was itself the fault.
philosophy had been on a false scent ever since the days
and Plato, that an *intellectual* answer to the intellectual
ties will never come, and that the real way out of the
consisting in the discovery of such an answer, consis
closing one's ear to the question ". As a natural resu
" I have finally found myself compelled to give ul
fairly, squarely, and irrevocably." To finish the narra
we may add that the next stage in the professor's menta
consisted in his going through Bergson's " inner cata
placing himself, that is, " at a bound, or *d'emblée*,"· a!
says, " inside of the living, moving, active thickness
All of which only moves the same critic to further cor
what will you do if, before the ink is fairly dry on yc
Proteus of the lecture hall is before the world with a r
his errors and a frank retreat to just such logical
you denounced him for not confessing?" This instan
the " inside of the real " is a recent and favorite pi
Bergson. It is of an essentially mystic and mysterio
but is partially described as an " inner catastrophe ", a
as it were philosophically climacteric change, which ;
sist principally in the negative attitude of refusing ev

[1] *A Pluralistic Universe*, pp. 291-2.

ordinary men believe, with a further consequence of liberty to believe whatever one's self may wish to hold. Professor James claims
to have taken the leap, and he recommends it most highly to others.
But, in very truth, the total result of Pragmatism's revolt against
intellectualism plus the bound *d'emblée* of Bergson and James is to
deprive their adherents of any even probable belief.

Regarding its second quasi-definite doctrine, that, namely, concerning " reality ", Pragmatism is emphatically a philosophy of the
" flux ". " The stubborn fact remains ", says Professor James[4]
" that there *is* a sensible flux ", and he excludes all else by practically
making his own such utterances as the following,[5] " ' Behind the
bare phenomenal facts ', as my tough-minded old friend Chauncey
Wright, the great Harvard empiricist of my youth, used to say,
' there is *nothing.*' " For Professor James and the Pragmatists, this
flux of sensation is the only real world, and for them,[6] " the world
stands really malleable, waiting to receive its final touches at our
hands." The pragmatic idea is that we, adventitiously touched, as
it were, by this " flux ", seize upon it, and build reality out upon it,
and thus augment the actual extension of reality; and this, not by
any mere rearrangement of its parts, or by borrowing any part of
preëxistent reality, but, by a truly creative act, causing the whole of
something to exist where there was absolutely nothing before. One
is here mildly reminded of Kant, but Professor James explicitly
warns us that Pragmatism is by no means Kantism. When we remember, further, that the power within us which thus " creates " sensible, or sensational, and therefore material, reality, is, for James,
our thought, and for Papini, our imagination, it is readily seen that
the resulting " reality " can only be of the most illusory and fantastic
kind.

Pragmatism's third doctrine, that of truth, claims a very open
field; for we are told [7] that " at present we have no definite notion
of what the word may mean." The old idea that truth consisted
in a relatively static correspondence of the mind with the thing is
expressly rejected, the word " static " itself being an object of especial abhorrence; and in the substitute thesis of Pragmatism, truth
—meaning all conceivable truth—exists, like reality, only in a
fusible, malleable condition; for we are told again [8] that " we have
to live to-day by what truth we can get to-day, and be ready to-
morrow to call it falsehood "; a precept, we may note in passing, that
Mr. James very faithfully follows. He himself had made, as far

---

[4] *Pragmatism,* p. 255.   [5] *Pragmatism,* p. 263.
[6] *Pragmatism,* p. 257.   [7] *Pragmatism,* p. 192.
[8] *Pragmatism,* p. 223.

back as 1897, some initial essays in this matter of truth, the results
appearing finally in a rather heterogeneous volume, *The Will to
Believe*; a somewhat unfortunate title, since in the hands of the
critics it became *The Will to Deceive, The Will to Make-Believe,*
etc., compendiously expressing their judgments upon it. In his later
utterances on truth, he is reporting Schiller and explaining that author's "humanism", rather than attempting any further analysis of
his own. Combining, however, the utterances of all its exponents,
it is clear that Pragmatism seeks to show that in regard to truth, not
less than in regard to reality, man is a true creator, that we see
" truth in the making," that we ourselves build truth out upon
truth, just as we are said to build reality out upon reality, and both
from nothing. Absolute truth, we are told, nowhere exists. Even
our most basic principles of thought are, for Pragmatism, only unusually fortunate, workable guesses which no actual experience has
as yet, indeed, disproved; but which might, at any time, and by any
accident, be seen to be wholly erroneous. A list of ill-starred
" truths" of this kind *de facto* shattered in this wholly unpre-
meditated manner is given by Professor James in his characteristically confident and flippant manner; and it will be noted that his
gaiety increases with the gravity of the subjects he attacks.
" Ptolemaic astronomy ", he says,[9] " euclidean space, aristotelian
logic, scholastic metaphysics, were expedient for centuries, but
human experience has boiled over those limits, and we now call
these things only relatively true, or true within those borders of
experience. 'Absolutely' they are false; for we know that those
limits were casual, and might have been transcended by past
theorists just as they are by present thinkers ".

As to this account of truth, Professor James's own later avowals
of complete scepticism form an all-sufficient commentary; and, as
we have said, the present work gives no additional light in this matter.
We only note that throughout this part of the author's work, there
is a woful confusion and confounding of many simple tests for
truth with truth itself; and a total lack of the distinctions and
divisions absolutely necessary for the proper understanding of,
questions involving many essentially different grades of being and
of action. If, like God, we saw all things in one all-perfect glance,
it would be different. Imperfect, as we are, we must divide and
subdivide, in order to reach anything like accuracy.

Passing to a rapid general view, it will be seen that any careful analysis of the entire matter of Pragmatism will show that it
refuses all Logic, denies all intelligible reality, ignores Psychology,

---

[9] *Pragmatism*, p. 223.

smiles at Mathematics as mostly " man-made ", abhors Metaphysics both General and Special, and in Ethics finds that to be good which is profitable here and now, and without any reference to any outside authority or sanction. In Theology, Pragmatism is simply blasphemous. Though continually talking about religion, James never even so much as mentions Christ, while in his pages, wandering Indian " swamis," Neo-Hegelian " One-Knowers ", and Fechnerian " Earth-Souls " all receive respectful consideration; after which it is less astounding to notice that a straggling " poem " of Walt Whitman, the loathsome " cow-pen " poet, furnishes the text for James's lecture on Religion. As far as anything definite can be extracted from his utterances, James is a confused, psychical-research kind of pantheist. Concerning the real God Himself, James says,[10] " The truth of ' God ' has to run the gauntlet of all our other truths. It is on trial by them, and they are on trial by it. . . . Let us hope that they will find a *modus vivendi* ". Speaking of accepting the evils of this world in the ordinary Christian spirit of resignation, on the ground that God's ways are unknown to us, and that He has some good reason for permitting such trials, James further says,[11] "A God who can relish such superfluities of horror is no God for human beings to appeal to. *His animal spirits are too high.*" And these flippantly blasphemous utterances could be indefinitely multiplied. We shall only say that perhaps the most characteristic note in all Pragmatism is its colossal assurance, and that it is rather too much for men whose antecedents can be known only through the various " Who's Who's," to ask us to rely upon their unsupported personal authority, and, at their simple request, to dismiss all that the world has thus far deemed valuable in the realms of thought, and to substitute for the granitic truth of the centuries the incoherent vagaries which betray complete poverty of mind regarding consecutive thought and the fundamental rules of right reason.

D. DEVER.

THE BERLIN DISCUSSION OF THE PROBLEM OF EVOLUTION. Full Report of the Lectures given in February, 1907, and of the Evening Discussion. By Eric Wassmann. St. Louis, Mo.: B. Herder; London: Kegan Paul. 1909. Pp. xiv-266.

The cause and circumstances which gave rise to the " Berlin Discussion," authentically reported in the present book, will probably be already known to the reader, as they have been made known generally through the press. Father Wassmann, it will be remembered,

---

[10] *Pragmatism,* p. 109.   [11] *Pragmatism,* p. 143.

in his work on *Modern Biology* advocated a form of evolutionism of organic species within the sub-human kingdoms.   This book was animadverted on by Professor Haeckel in certain popular lectures which he had delivered in Berlin in April, 1905.   Father Wassmann felt called upon to answer his critic publicly, and when subsequently he was invited by a committee of representative German scientists to deliver a course of lectures on his theory of evolution he accepted the invitation.   The three lectures were given on the 13, 14, and 17 February, 1907.   On 18 February there was a public discussion of the subject dealt with in the lectures, eleven prominent men of science or letters appearing on the platform as opponents of Father Wassmann.   The volume at hand embodies a full report of the lectures and the discussion.

In the first lecture the author considers the doctrine of evolution as a *scientific* hypothesis and theory.   He argues that the transformation of sub-human species is perfectly compatible with the Christian theory of origins, and he furnishes some evidence for such transmutations from his own private special study, the ant family and their guests.   The second lecture deals with evolution *philosphically,* and proves that it is quite distinct and should be separated from atheistic or pantheistic monism as well as from the specifically Darwinian hypothesis.   Darwin's method of natural selection is inadequate—though it is subsidiary—and must be supplemented by the idea of *internal* adaptivity of organisms.   In the third technic it is shown that the soul of man, being a simple and spiritual substance, can certainly not be accounted for by any evolutionary process. Concerning the body, the author says that "the Church has not promulgated any definite decision as to the nature of the substance employed by God in the creation of man.   Theologians, however, following constant tradition and the opinions of the ordinary teaching authority in the Church, have constantly maintained that the human body was formed of inanimate matter.   Perhaps this is all that can be said on the theological side of the question. . . . . Zoology and its attendant sciences within their proper sphere are perfectly free to discuss the scientific side of man's origin.   The assured results of theology need serve them only as an external standard, for one truth cannot contradict another.   If science reveals some undoubted truth, theologians will accept it.   I can vouch for the accuracy of this statement" (p. 55).   It need hardly be said that the natural sciences have as yet discovered no evidence and no serious arguments for the bestial descent of man's body.

Whilst one who is familiar with the evolutionary discussion will discover no new arguments *pro* or *con* in Father Wassmann's lectures, he will find, first, some interesting illustrations drawn from the author's specialty—entomology—which seem to indicate "the formation of *new species, genera, and families*" (p. 13) ; secondly, he will probably find nowhere else within the same compass so clear, methodical, and all-around satisfactory a presentation of what is said by experts for and against the evolution of organic types.

About two-thirds of the volume is devoted to the report of the so-called Berlin Discussion. It must have been a dramatic spectacle, the Jesuit priest standing before a Berlinese audience of two thousand persons (mostly non- and anti-Catholics) and confronting eleven adversaries obviously determined, if not to confute, certainly to confound the defendant! It had been at first arranged that Father Wassmann should be allowed to speak at least twice: once after the first and again after the last speaker. By some unexpected change in the program which could hardly be called undesigned, Father Wassmann was given but one opportunity of rejoinder, and that was after his opponents had occupied three hours in objecting—from 8.30 to 11.30 P. M. One who has had no experience of the tactics of infidels would believe it, to say the least, improbable that distinguished men of science could fall into such illogical argumentation, much less could be guilty of such substitution of personal attack for reasoning as was manifested in this Berlin Discussion. The unbiased reader will find it very easy to agree with Father Wassmann's own modest summing-up of the event—that his eleven opponents did not collectively succeed in encountering and refuting him on the ground of science and philosophy; that some of them strayed from the subject and turned a scientific discussion into an attack on the Church, doing this in the name of free science ; that they thus furnished the best proof that the opinions which Father Wassmann presented both as a Christian and a scientist do not clash with the principles of free research (p. 257).

We may note in conclusion that the translation is unusually well done into clear idomatic English. It would have been better had the translator adhered to a uniform method of giving the titles of German books. Sometimes they appear in German but usually in English. In the latter case the reader may be led to suppose that the book cited exists in English, whereas it seldom does. Thus Father Wassmann's other books which have not been translated are given in English title equally with those that have been translated. How shall the reader distinguish?

UNE ANGLAISE CONVERTIE. .Par le Pere H. d'Arras.   I. " Ma Conversion," recit autobiographique, par Madame d'Arras.   II. Notes,
souvenirs, correspondance.   Introduction par la Comtesse R. de Courson.
Paris: Gabriel Beauchesne & Cie.   1909.   Pp. xvi-212.

The story of Madame d'Arras' life was written at the solicitation
of Mgr. Guillibert, Bishop of Fréjus and Toulon. He had heard her
give some oral account of it, which so pleased him that he asked her
for a written sketch of it with the understanding that he might
publish the same after the lady's death. A commonplace reviewer,
charmed at sight and sincerely thrilled by the spontaneous vivacity,
pathos, genuine persuasion of the *récit autobiographique,* also groans
in spirit over the conventional and stereotyped religiosity, undiluted
cant, or something much similar, in the supplementary portions.
And possible faults to the front, be it furthermore objected that a
great deal of the supplementary matter belonged strictly to an inner
family circle, and not, with propriety, to any outer public. At
least not in the form now given; for whilst the convert's personal
relation is of a throbbing reality that should move every susceptible
Christian ,heart, and must humanly touch even heretics and unbelievers, with any particle of sentiment in their constitution: one is
considerably doubtful whether the supplements will affect anybody
but the " rigid righteous ". Whereas, of course, the publican and
sinner stand in much deeper need of edification.

Madame d'Arras, whose maiden name was Louisa Augusta Lechmere, was born at Worcester, 9 February, 1829; of a distinguished
aristocratic lineage, resident in England from the time of the Norman conquest. Her immediate ancestors, however, were no longer
Catholic, but even stiffly " bigoted " Protestants, and utterly intolerant of everything " Popish ". Her mother withal, and a governess, later on the scene, were strongly Calvinistic. Indeed the objective background of the personal narrative brings out into full relief the *Protestant* sides of the Anglican Communion, generally regarded, until the Tractarian reaction. The singular contrast will
also suggest itself herein, that although the " Church of England "
has always looked askance at the " unchurched " Lutherans of
Continental Europe, the Lutheran " orthodox " practice retained
several features distinctly nearer to the Catholic usage (the cross,
candles, Communion wafer, etc.) than the ordinary practice of
Anglicans prior to Dr. Pusey and the Ritualists. Miss Lechmere's
very first glimpse of Catholic rites, when as a child of nine years
she visited Boulogne-sur-Mer, left a permanent impression on her
observant faculties; till then accustomed to the " chill " of a meagre

bareness of worship. There was a richness, fervor, heartiness in the Catholic devotions that even a child, with eyes and ears alert, soon seized with joy. But Miss Lechmere underwent several phases of Anglican education before finally reaching the Catholic centre. Her Anglican confirmation, strangely enough, since her parents were such radical Protestants in doctrine, occurred in the "advancing" Ritualistic parish of *St. Paul, Knightsbridge*, London; this being the family residence quarter in town. Perhaps this merely reflects the frequent Anglican "comprehension", or "Broad Church" platform. At any rate, when Miss Lechmere answered in the accepted catechism fashion, *two* sacraments generally necessary to salvation, the Rev. "Puseyite" Vicar corrected: "Yes . . . but there are five other sacraments." In like manner, her manual of instruction for Holy Communion detailed a broadly "comprehensive" diversity of Anglican teachings on the *one* supreme Eucharist; ranging from "Real Presence" (High) to spiritually memorial, or Calvinistic and *Low*. At Brighton, however, when happening to attend a true Catholic Mass, about a twelvemonth after her Anglican confirmation, our subsequent convert experienced an unaccountable emotion during the solemnity of *elevation*: "I adored even still in ignorance of the Mass, and in spite of myself." Meanwhile, as the Tractarian reaction spread, her father one day declared in anger, he would shut his doors on any child of his that should ever presume to turn Catholic. Miss Lechmere became all the more eager to know the whole "secret" of Catholic doctrine; and so accidentally lighted on a controversial tract containing a convert's profession of faith. She forthwith attentively proceeded to *collate* the same, text for text from her "Protestant" Bible; with the result that she "admitted all the dogmas of Rome, without so much as having previously read a Catholic book or consulted a priest." Still she continued attending Anglican rites: wherein, to be sure, the Rev. *Puseyite* rector's sermons gave her "more and more the desire to embrace the Catholic religion." Notwithstanding the clause: "At that epoch, to become Catholic was deemed a great dishonor for the person and the family." Somewhat of the *social* caste therein implied, as by the "Four Hundred's dictum: 'You know, the *nice* people all belong to our (Episcopal) Church.'"

"At this juncture, we were sojourning in the country. There was a Catholic church in the neighborhood, but I knew not exactly where. In course of a walk one day, I stood face to face with this church. Imagine my feelings! I trembled with agitation at the thought of meeting a priest, and was already wondering: If he convinces me of the truth, what shall I do?" Whom she met, in fact, was a certain *Brother Cenairs* (a Redemptorist) : and through him, the Superior, Father Laus. On disclosing her desire of becoming a Catholic: " I remember being quite astonished that he did not immediately propose to baptize me. Ignorant as I then was, I understood that the Catholic priests did everything to gain converts, and received them irrespectively of conditions." Father Laus, instead, gave her good spiritual counsel, a prayer-book, crucifix, and catechism. She subsequently met an earnest Father Ludwig, of the same Order, who guided her in the successive steps toward Catholic profession. But some vehement family " storms " had also to be painfully, not far from " desperately " weathered, when her parents got wind of the situation. There was even downright blows on occasion (*mais des coups de poing*: not simply, gusts of the aforesaid " wind "). Even *materfamilias*, " usually so gentle, so kind, so tender, was greatly enraged. She tore from the wall a rosary once brought me from Ireland, for a *curio*, then, and overwhelmed me with reproaches . . . " Also imprecated *paterfamilias* the fires of hell, were this Catholic resolve to take effect in a child of his. When exiled to her room for a month, to be nourished with volumes violently opposing the Catholic faith, Miss Lechmere, contrary to the expected purpose of a book denouncing *Virgin Worship*, culled from it some beautiful praises to the Blessed Virgin, and shaped them into a small " office ", all her own. " Since then, *Salve Regina* has ever been one of my favorite prayers." Next she was sent on a visit to an Anglican uncle, resident at Brampton Brian, Herefordshire. Here she enjoyed the happiness of kindred affections, but it was a vain move to check her Catholic resolve: the more because the Reverend uncle took even his Protestant religion chiefly in the way of a parson sportsman: " impassioned for the horses, the dogs, the sports; above all the chase to the fox." Whose *deacon* once bringing the message, an infirm parishioner desired to commune on the morrow: " Impossible for me to attend to this tomorrow. I leave at five in the morning, and the meet is scheduled at seven."

Her health becoming shattered by the emotional strains that she underwent, Miss Lechmere's parents (she was yet a minor) at last gave their conditional consent to her Catholic purpose; but she was first to receive thorough *Protestant* instruction: whose dispensing oracle should be none other than " Monsieur Bennett, clergyman of the Puseyite Church of St. Paul, Knightsbridge "; the same who had prepared her for Anglican confirmation. A sympathetic adviser, in many respects; yet insistent on his lines of opposition to the *Roman* Catholic Church. Miss Lechmere's one clinching answer: "If the Church can have erred in her doctrine, the promise of Jesus Christ is void: the gates of hell have prevailed, and our Lord was not thus the Son of God." Monsieur Bennett also *confessed* his "Romish" ward; but much to her surprise, the *forms* he did use were identical with those in a Catholic manual she had received from Redemptorist Father Ludwig: Monsieur Bennett having simply *pasted* the like in his Anglican volume! In conclusion of the confession, she was bidden to read the "protestation of St. Francis of Sales, borrowed from *Garden of the Soul.*" Whilst this Puseyite clergyman allowed her to believe, if she chose, in Purgatory and prayers for the dead, he still personally pronounced *en chaire*: "There is no such thing as Purgatory, however consoling the belief therein"! As touching the absolution, this, it appears, had to be deferred (in those days) to the Anglican Bishop of London. Her penance, absolution or none, was to fast through Lent until six in the evening; daily rising at five. His Anglican Successorship to the See of London, just then, was nothing of a Ritualist, and "seemed to have no very lofty idea of his power to absolve. I am not sure that I had much faith in it myself, indeed; but I should have done almost anything, at the moment, for a little repose and peace of soul."

Eventually, when twenty-one years old, she was permitted to consult a Catholic priest with a view to practical decision. "Dr. Wiseman, at that time Apostolic Vicar, afterward Cardinal Archbishop of Westminster," was "the only priest in whom they had any confidence"; and it was arranged for Miss Lechmere to meet him. Even here, some hitches occurred: Mrs. Lechmere would neither allow a Catholic person to darken her doors, by way of escort; nor lend her carriage, nor otherwise enable her daughter to visit Dr. Wiseman consistently with British decorum. A note to him resolved the dilemma: he would send a Catholic gentleman, in a carriage . . . "The course of true love never did run smooth!" When Miss Lechmere started to meet this conveyance, at a point agreed, the *rendez-vous* failed; and by sheer "Providence" of luck, in the mixed London throng thereafter, she "hailed" a carriage that possibly might be the one at issue; and so it proved. The subsequent steps were all successful: some temporal difficulties notwithstanding: the convert's "whole fortune", at a certain pass, amounting to three shillings and sixpence. Her first Communion occurred on a Saturday, 14 June, 1850. Several years later, she "espoused Monsieur d'Arras, a Catholic full of faith, devoted to the cause of Pope and King." Her family became reconciled, in a measure; though she was disinherited, barring a stinted indirect "settlement ".

Three of her four children were destined to Church vocations: Father Henry d'Arras, who first "wore the cassock in 1880"; a daughter Marguerite, in the Carmelite Order; another daughter, with "Little Sisters of the Poor."

Apart from the phrasing and exaggerated "religiosity", as to some it would appear in the added chapters, these, too, contain passages of salutary merit. One can roundly subscribe the following comment, referring to the delight of Madame d'Arras in the "major offices and liturgical prayers of the Church": "I have scant use for all those booklets of sentimental devotion, wherein you find nothing substantial; *spiritual pastry*, were I fain to style them. People go to Mass with these tracts; flit from one sentiment to another, instead of nourishing their souls with the magnificent prayers of Holy Mass, the prayers of the Church herself, so powerfully assisting our conjunction with the priest. And then the Psalms! I never hear *In exitu Israel* without profound emotion: methinks every word a right theme for meditation."

Madame d'Arras "died in the Lord", on 31 October, 1907. Monseigneur Guillibert applies to her Saint Paul's commendation: *Charissimam quae multum laboravit in Domino.*   W. P.

THE CHRISTIAN PHILOSOPHY OF LIFE. By Tilmann Pesch, S. J. Translated from the German by M. C. McLaren. London: Sands & Co.; St. Louis, Mo.: B. Herder. 1909. Pp. xiv–637.

A SPIRITUAL CANTICLE OF THE SOUL AND THE BRIDEGROOM CHRIST. By St. John of the Cross. Translated by David Lewis. Introduction by Benedict Zimmerman. New York, Cincinnati, Chicago: Benziger Bros. 1909. Pp. xxiv–317.

PSYCHOLOGIE DES MYSTIQUES CHRETIENS. Poeme de la Conscience: Dante et les Mystiques. Par Jules Pacheu. Paris: Perrin & Cie. 1909. Pp. 400.

If mysticism is, as some authorities define it, "the love of God", then are all reasonable Christians, in so far as they love God, mystics, and all saints who love God in an eminent degree the living masters and the examples of mysticism. Among the saints, however, some more than others possess the power and the providen-

love in the Book of the Exercises. The latter embodied his in three works entitled *The Ascent of Mount Carmel, The Dark Night of the Soul,* and *The Spiritual Canticle of the Soul.* The volume above, entitled *The Philosophy of Life,* is constructed on the basis laid down by St. Ignatius. Most of our readers will probably know of the late Tilmann Pesch through his voluminous scholastic writings — the *Cursus Lacensis* and the *Welträthsel.* All who are familiar with these writings are aware that their author was not simply a learned expositor of scholasticism. He was this, but he was more. The very exuberance of his style, both Latin and German, pointed him out as an overflowing, an outgoing character —a man in whom the love element, the mystical in the true sense of the term, dominated, controlled, directed the mind, the visual, the speculative faculty. It is well that he has left us in his *Philosophy of Life* the expression of this practical side of his personality. Calling it practical, we do not mean to ignore, much less to deny, its theoretical and expository character. Like the *sacra doctrina* of the Master, St. Thomas, whom he knew and loved so well, on whose writings he commented so wisely and so abundantly, his science is here *speculativa sed eminenter practica.* He has taken the book of his other and more immediate master, Ignatius, as his basis and starting-point, and upon it he has constructed a Philosophy of Life. The "Exercises", however, furnish only the ground plan and the broad ideas that pervade the superstructure. These ideas he has moulded and fashioned into manifold shapes, while within and around them he has built countless others drawn from many sources—Scripture, theology, philosophy, science, literature, personal experience. The book is a collection of "thoughts" following the soul's orbit—its journey from and back to God, pursuing "the Way", Christ, and terminating in union with God Himself through perfect love. There are more than a hundred and eighty chapters—enough to outline without attempting to exhaust a large variety of subjects and furnishing abundant food for meditation or reflective reading and oral instructions.

The translation is on the whole well done, clear, and readable. Here and there it might be made more faithful. For instance, at page 20 where what apparently is meant for some of Fichte's teachings the text says, " I postulate myself ", etc. *Posit* is what Fichte says, which is not the same as *postulate.* At page iv Bishop Kneipp is mentioned. The lowly apostle of the *Wasserkur* would have deprecated so lofty a title, even though in his latter days he did wear the purple of a *Hausprelat,* a monsignor.

The *Spiritual Canticle* embodies the culmination of the philosophy of life as conceived and wrought out by that master of mystical science, St. John of the Cross. His preceding works, *The Ascent* and *The Dark Night,* systematize the truths and laws that concern the soul's passage from sin by repentance and mortification (*via purgativa*) unto the life of solid virtue (*via illuminativa*). The present volume treats principally of the highest stage of the spiritual life on earth—that which is attained by generous and heroic souls—the life of conscious union with God. The Spiritual Canticle consists of forty stanzas which may be said to contain an abridgment of the Song of Songs, and therefore to picture under the Scriptural symbolism of espousals the blessedness of the soul that has attained to union with God. The stanzas were composed by St. John during his imprisonment at Toledo (December, 1577, to August, 1578). At the request of the Carmelite religious whom he directed he wrote a continuous commentary on the poem—interpreting each line and expression. This commentary is presented in the above volume, the translation being substantially that of Mr. Lewis's second edition, with a luminous introduction by Father Zimmerman. The work embodies the supreme " philosophy of life ", the highest wisdom. Few are chosen of the many called to this sublime life. The priest whose vocation it may be to guide the elected few can, it need hardly be said, do nothing more secure than follow the direction of so experienced a leader as St. John of the Cross.

M. Pacheu's *Psychologie des Mystiques* is a description of mystical experience in its broadest significance; as embracing, that is, the inner phenomena of the spiritual, the supernatural, life in all its stages — purgation, illumination, and union. The groundwork and the principal materials are taken from the *Divina Commedia* of Dante, and the Book of the Exercises of St. Ignatius. The facts gathered from these classics of the spiritual life are amplified and illustrated by matter drawn from the other great mystical writers, St. Francis of Assisi, St. Teresa, St. John of the Cross, and many others. The work, as we have just indicated, is for the most part descriptive. The author has another volume preparing in which he purposes giving a critical psychological analysis of the mystical experiences described in the volume at hand. The latter, however, is an independent work and may be recommended for its luminous treatment of the subject, and its reverent and thoroughly Catholic spirit.

THE SCIENCE OF ETHICS. By the Rev. Michael Cronin, M. A., D. D., Professor, Cloncliffe College, Dublin. Vol. I. Dublin: M. H. Gill & Son; New York, Cincinnati, Chicago: Benziger Bros. 1909.

LEHRBUCH DER NATIONALOEKONOMIE. Von Heinrich Pesch, S. J. B. I–II. Freiburg, St. Louis, Mo.: B. Herder. 1909.

The German work here introduced is probably the most comprehensive and thorough treatise on political economy in that language, and one may search the kindred literature in the other languages without coming upon its equal. Political economy, when rightly viewed, is a science "subaltern" to Ethics, that is, it is the development of ethical principles applied to the establishment and maintenance of public well-being. It is therefore rooted in and logically grows out of moral philosophy. The German language is fairly well supplied with works on the latter root-science. Not so with English. Heretofore, we have had no single work in which the science of ethics is adequately treated.

Happily in the English book above introduced we find the first of what promises to supply the long-felt need of a comprehensive treatment of ethical foundations solid enough to support an economic superstructure such as is embodied in the German work before us. The first four chapters of the volume cover the ground familiar to the student of scholastic philosophy—human acts, their final end, the specific distinction of good and evil. This portion is, of course, almost exclusively expository of fundamental concepts—the metaphysics and psychology of morals. With the next chapter—on the moral criteria—the student approaches the more controverted questions, and as the ensuing chapters unfold he finds himself in the midst of conflict, where his adversaries of to-day and yesterday press upon him from every side—foes with modern weapons, sharp-shooters with breach-loaders, at ready command. Freedom and morality, duty, hedonism, utilitarianism, evolutionism, the moral faculty, intuitionism—the mere mention of these chapteral headings suggests to the knowing reader what a field bristling with fierce battle is here outspread. The ensuing chapters on "synderesis", the consequences of morality, habits and virtues, cover ground more peaceful, troubled rather by skirmishing than by war; while the final chapters on law and rights close the work once more amidst the din of battle.

Throughout it all the student feels the security begotten of the consciousness that he has before him a leader who, while skilled in modern tactics and equipped with modern arms yet wears an armor wrought of mail that has been reforged according to the latest processes of science and linked in à way that leaves fullest play to hand and limb. Or, to change the figure, the reader feels that the foundations on which he stands are of granite set on a base of granite; granite chiseled and fitted together block for block with an eye to modern purposes and demands. No competent student will read the chapters dealing especially with evolutionism—biological (Spencer, Leslie, Stephens), psychological (Mill, Bain, Royce), transcendental (Hegel, Green), without being impressed first with the clarity and justice with which the opposing theories are presented; secondly, with the thoroughness of the criticism; thirdly, with the author's mastery of his own principles, and the keenness with which he distinguishes the error from the truth in his adversaries' opinions, utilizing the one while discarding the other.

The foundations are here laid deep, broad, and solid—proportionate to the weighty structure of special Ethics, with its important individual and social questions, and to the economic problems, such as are discussed in the German volumes introduced above.

The first volume of Father Pesch's work appeared some four years ago and was then described in the REVIEW. The second volume has but recently been published, it having been delayed by the author's illness. Father Pesch evolves his science, it need hardly be said, right out of its philosophical principles. He begins with the relations of man to his natural environment—man as " lord of the world " through labor; and in society; the ministry of nature. These relations involve the conceptions of wants, goods, value, exchange, etc.—economic ideas which are carefully analyzed at the opening of the first volume. Society and sociology take the next place in order—occasion here being given to compare the excessive evolutionistic theories of society with a saner philosophical construction. The roots and support of the social organism—the family, the state, and private property—are in turn examined in the light of old principles and new views. The foregoing topics occupy almost half of the first volume. The second half is devoted to a comprehensive study of economic activities and their organization—individualism, socialism, and " solidarity ", being the central ideas—and to the science of economics in its ideal structure, laws, and method.

The general aim of the first volume is therefore to lead up critically and constructively to the specific end of economic theory—the general well-being of a nation. The whole of the second volume is engaged with the study of the essence and the causes of that welfare. *In was besteht der Volkswohlstand und wie ensteht er?* The answer to this large double question is carried through five generous chapters: 1. The older economic theories (the Mercantile, Physiocratic, Industrial or Individualistic, and Collectivist; over against these Father Pesch establishes his own—" the social-labor system ", as he calls it—the system of coöperation or solidarity) ; 2. the public weal as effectively attained under the latter system; 3. the concrete determination of public welfare in the individual nation; 4. the land and national well-being—climate, soil, geographical territory; 5. the people and welfare—problems of population, Malthusianism, race and nationality, popular health, education, religion, morality, " the classes and the masses ". It will be noticed from the foregoing outline that the present portion of the work is confined to general politico-economic activity and theories. The special organization thereof on the lines of production and exchange and the sub-departments thereof will be treated of in a future volume; upon which will follow other volumes devoted to special industries, finance, statistics, etc.—volumes to be prepared by specialists in these studies. The breadth and comprehensiveness of the entire program are thus apparent. The imposing foundations thus far laid down assure the strength of the future edifice.

GRADUALBUCH. Auszug Haus der Editio Vaticana, mit Choralnoten, Violinschluessel, geeigneter Transposition, Uebersetzung der Texte und Rubriken. Herausgegeben von Dr. Karl Weinmann. Regensburg, Rome, New York, Cincinnati: Fr. Pustet. (Typographers of the Holy Apostolic See and of the S. Congregation of Rites.) 1909. Pp. 396–128–134.

tions exclusively in a tongue which they do not understand, and which the greater number of priests will not, and in many cases can not, interpret to them in their native speech, then we exhibit one of those saddening phenomena of institutional sectarianism which would substitute formalities for sincere and useful realities, and which confound lip-service of uniform sound with real unity of belief and worship. What we contend for in the use of ritual in the administration of the Sacraments, applies in some measure to the use of the Vatican Gradual, which is to further congregational chant as well as understanding of the liturgy, unity of sacred action and decorum in the public services of the Church. Our singers are not Roman or Italian seminarists, who make their living in the service of chantries and endowed vestries. They are young men who are engaged in some useful trade or profession, or they are schoolboys whose parents have to support them. They cannot give the time to learn Latin with any hope of understanding the liturgical text which they are to sing, even if their own vernacular were, like the Italian tongue, much closer related to the Latin than it is.

In view of this indifference in those who are to worship in the Latin rite, it must be considered a wholesome measure, likely to help toward carrying out the purpose of the Pontifical legislation, to have the vernacular accompany the Latin text in the authorized chant books, and to replace the archaic, square notation, by the five-line stave with notes which our young people can read like the music which they learn in the schools. This is what the Pustets have done for their German patrons. They have likewise recognized that it is altogether impracticable, not to say extravagant because of the needless expense, and an obstacle to the actual introduction of the Roman chant, to find it printed in a volume which the mere holding of requires much strength and courage on the part of the singer; it also takes money needlessly out of his pocket, for a big bulk of paper and print, a large proportion of which he does not, can not, use in his whole life-course as a chanter.

We therefore welcome Dr. Weinmann's *Gradualbuch* as remedying both the above-mentioned inconveniences, and we strongly recommend a like version for the use of English choirmasters and chanters. The *Gradualbuch* is an excerpt from the *Editio Vaticana*. Its practical features emphasized are: 1. It contains only such chants as suffice to answer the common liturgical needs and conditions of the Church. For extraordinary and local circumstances the complete edition can easily be substituted. 2. The chants are written in the familiar keys of modern music, and are therefore transposed to a middle pitch usually tending toward the lower manual, and with an eye to actual practice. Most organists in case of need, will find it easy to alter the transposition into a higher or lower key. 3. The common objection that such transposition interferes with the melodic line and the freedom of phrasing claimed for the Gregorian or choral chant, is met, at least to a great extent, by the retention of the old form of square notation, and by the absence of rhythmic and dynamic marks, which thus leaves the chanter at liberty to follow the traditional changes of phrasing and sustaining. 4. An interlinear translation of the Latin text gives the chanter an opportunity of understanding and appreciating what he sings; and this simple device has unquestionably a decided influence on the manner of his chanting the Latin. " Psallere cum corde " is impossible for those who have no idea of the meaning of the words they sing. 5. The responses of the Gradual, such as the *Tractus*, which are intended for soloists are given merely as text, since they may be recited on a single note; or, if variations are called for on special occasions, they are easily mastered by a soloist chanter. 6. And, last of all, this Gradual, which answers all the ordinary needs throughout the liturgical year, is much cheaper than the bulky editions now in hand, although we are not unmindful of Dr. F. X. Mathias's *Epitome ex Editione Vaticana* which adopts the modern notation.

CAEREMONIAE MISSARUM SOLEMNIUM ET PONTIFICALIUM aliarumque functionum ecclesiasticarum. Opera Georgii Schober, C. SS. R. Editio altera revisa et aucta. Ratisbonae, Romae, Neo Eboraci et Cincinnati: Sumptibus, chartis et typis Friderici Pustet. 1909. Pp. 427.

THE HOLY SACRIFICE AND ITS CEREMONIES. An explanation of its mystical and liturgical meaning. By M. C. Nieuwbarn, O. P., S. T. L. Translated by L. M. Bouman. London: Burns & Oates; New York, Cincinnati, Chicago: Benziger Bros. 1909. Pp. 111.

The occasion of the republication of the second book above
listed gives us an opportunity of commenting briefly upon a liturgical study of the Holy Sacrifice which, whilst not alone in its scope
or form, comes nevertheless as a timely addition to the English literature of the subject. The Dominican author briefly outlines the
Catholic teaching on the Holy Mass, describes the ceremonies, illustrates the rite in its solemn action, and explains the use, forms,
colors of the sacred vestments, the essential qualities of chalice, paten,
and other instruments of the sacrificial worship. Whilst the method
pursued in the exposition, as well as the ground covered, is largely
the same as that of Father Gavin's excellent little manual, *The
Sacrifice of the Mass*—an explanation of its doctrines, rubrics, and
prayers—or Archbishop Howley's *Explanation of the Holy Sacrifice
of the Mass*, there is the difference of style and detail, not to mention the critical something which recalls Father Charles Cowley
Clarke's *Liturgical Notes on the Mass*, or the more extensive survey
of this subject by the Sulpician Father Vigourel in his *Synthetical
Manual of Liturgy*, translated for us by Father John Nainfa of the
Baltimore community.

DIRITTO E PERSONALITA UMANA NELLA STORIA DEL PENSIERO.
Prof. Giorgio Del Vecchio. Pp. 32. Zamorani e Albertazza: Bologna.

L'ETICA EVOLUZIONISTA. Nota Critica. Prof. Giorgio Del Vecchio.
Pp. 12. Rivista Italiana di Sociologia. Roma.

The first of these two pamphlets was intended to outline the
course of the " Philosophy of Right " given by Prof. Del Vecchio
at the University of Ferrara, and might aptly be entitled " The
Historical Evolution of Ethical Ideas." In it the author furnishes
a remarkable instance of the fact that " in moralibus finis saepe in-
ficit opus "; for in it the author reveals the by no means commendable purpose of his otherwise laudable and conclusive vindication
of the existence and the liberty of the personal *Ego* that Spencer
so explicitly denies. This purpose is to supplant the evanescent
Ego of Spencer with one that shall not only be permanent, but shall
also be supreme as the only fount of cognition and the only source
of law. In the author's view, the modern development is such as
to demonstrate that " what is *a priori* in the order of cognition is
also *a priori* in that of ethical jurisprudence ", meaning that the individual, as such, is first and last in both. His *Ego*, therefore, is
so very independent and so very free that it becomes in its sole self
and in the most absolute manner the only and the ultimate founda-

tion and standard of all morality. The idea of a creating, and therefore justly ruling, God, or of any other extrinsic authoritative entity, is, in the mind of the author, only an illusory projection of this autonomous *Ego*; and, in the same view, this misleading figment of the imagination has in the past been a very heavy incubus on human progress, and still remains as a most troublesome heritage of ignorance and comparative imbecility, obscuring the true light of juridic science, and perpetuating, on the one hand, the most destructive traditions of servility, and on the other, that of usurped authority; and in both cases most lamentably impeding the proper onward progress of the race.

The author hails with delight what he considers to be the already accomplished intellectual vindication of this *Ego* by Kant and Fichte, but deeply deplores the lagging behind of practical science with regard to its more speculative congener, and also bewails the annoying persistence with which we retain the slavish, degrading idea that man may, after all, have a master, and that there may perhaps be some extrinsically adjudicated punishments and rewards concerning which it would be well to take timely thought.

The principal thesis of the book is hopelessly at variance with consciousness, reason, and fact; and it is accordingly labored and obscure. Yet the work as a whole is not altogether devoid of ingenuity or of erudition, the part devoted to the mutual relations of Philosophy and Jurisprudence and their respective historical developments giving especial evidence of studied elaboration.

The author finds that in the ancient civilizations Philosophy and Jurisprudence were amalgamated and blended into one somewhat confused whole, rather than distinctly outlined in themselves, or accurately co-ordinated with respect to each other. Amongst the Greeks, philosophical ideas predominated; while the more practical Romans accented jurisprudence at the expense of any more explicit cultivation of purely speculative science; both Greek and Roman thought, however, finally flowing, to a great extent, together through the deep influence of Stoic Philosophy upon Roman juridic forms; its impressive rigidity fitting it well to be the practical norm of that sternly imposing people; and the " Jus Gentium " forming finally the magnificent synthesis of all that was best and highest in either Greek or Roman juridic conceptions, and remaining as the principal and classic fount of all subsequent civil ordination. Throughout, however, the individual was merged with the state, to an extent that almost elided his personal standing; this lack of clear distinction and of proper co-ordination being, in the mind of the author, the especially weak point in the whole of ancient juridical thought and practice.

With the appearance of Christianity, the author finds the first distinct assertion and acknowledgment of individual right and of personal dignity; but with it also he deplores the ascribing of what he considers a false cause for this supremely desirable effect. For he says that in this case the elevation of the individual was not due, as it should have been, to a recognition of man himself as the supreme and sufficient norm of all things whether rational or ethical, but to the immission of a divine element, coming from an over-ruling God, and demanding respect as such; thus leaving the really absolute autonomy and inherent supremacy of human nature as completely unrecognized as before.

Yet even this vicarious title to consideration was not long allowed to exert its beneficent practical influence in the direction of individual liberty; for—always according to the author—there soon entered an element more deplorable still, the element of self-assumed human authority, a factitious " Church ", whose egotistic and ambitious prelates unwarrantably asserted their own necessity as guides for the practical development of this divine principle, and for the attainment of its connatural recompense in a future life, and thus riveted the ancient bonds of individual enslavement only more closely, more gallingly, and more hopelessly than before. Freedom could only come again when, not only these usurping human intermediaries, but also the very concept itself of any extrinsic norm or of any future sanction would have been ruthlessly cast aside. And after the long night of the dark and middle ages which inevitably followed upon such fundamentally erroneous principles, the author sees in the Renaissance and in the Reformation the first Samsonic struggles of the long-enchained *Ego* and the first flamings of a light that was to bring it at last to a finally effective vindication of long-deferred right. The Renaissance represents the struggles of the *Ego* toward the throne of supremacy in the cognitive order, struggles which became triumphs only with the explicit vindications of Kantism; the servitude of the ethical order being finally sundered and cast aside in the mighty upheaval of the Reformation; in which we are to see, therefore, the victorious *Ego's* final rupture and rejection of all his extrinsic moral fetters, and of all his heavenly, yet falsely, imposed moral bonds. The author naïvely admits that the revolution has not proved to be wholly complete either in the speculative or in the practical order; that systems of philosophy that should have excluded God still retain Him; and that the Reform forged a dogmatism not less absolute than that which it was supposed to destroy; but he as naïvely informs us that the present is not the time or the place to explain these facts which militate

Supposing, however, the *Ego* to have been freed to the extent and in the manner described, it is said to have made still further progress, by becoming the dictator, and not the follower, in regard to the state; which relation the author rather strangely designates as "morality"; so that, in this view, positive human law is to be modeled upon human nature as this is known and interpreted by individual reason; and the *locus* of the juridic struggle is no longer to be between the Church and the Empire, but between the individual and civil society, between personal liberty and the corporate laws of the state.

As we have already indicated, the author is obliged to confess that this elaborately interwoven theory of the *Ego* in its nature, struggles, and destiny has always had its difficulties; being persistently shackled with forms derived from the old Greek and Latin days, from the odious Church, and from unduly encroaching civil enactments. But in addition to this we are told that a new and supremely perilous crisis awaited it at the beginning of the eighteenth century. Heretofore, it had only been neglected and ignored; but at the period in question its very existence was threatened by the dissolving and decomposing tendencies of empiric psychology, which denied to personality any substantial existence, and reduced it to the sum of coincident psychical states. Naturally enough, this philosophical upheaval, though valiantly resisted, had its reflex in the practical order; and led to the consistent denial of this fugitive *Ego* as the ultimate base of all law, and to the provisional substitution of historico-theoretical ideals of a shifting and extremely doubtful character.

The present state, therefore, of philosophico-juridical science, as described by the author is one of dislocation. Instead of a solid study of the true foundation in the *Ego*, one is now forced, we are told, to deal principally with the radically erroneous ideas and enactments of modern civil society, with the not remote danger of specifically juridic science being wholly disintegrated and dissipated in the stern, unpitying attrition of the positive sciences, or of meeting the even more ignoble fate of living on without identity in the historico-dogmatic *mélange* called sociology. The regeneration and resurrection of juridical science must await that of speculative philosophy in general. Both must free themselves at all cost from the ever more exacting and more peremptory demands of positivistic tendencies.

has vast consequences, eliminating, as it does, all idea of a creation and of a Creator in the only comprehensible sense of these terms; and he also sees that in this line of negative distinction the positivistic attitude of some students of science is not less efficacious than his own. But while he looks calmly upon the supposedly final cancellation of God by the engines of positivism, he is dismayed at the prospect of his own *Ego* disappearing in the same general ruin, and would gladly stem the modern tide wherever it threatens to engulf his own cherished ideas, theories, and conceptions. We have already marked his emphatic protest against Spencer's empiric invasion of Ethics, and his motive in so doing is now plainly apparent, being nothing less than the substitution of his own *a priori Ego;* a purpose which the author himself admits to be as yet but very slightly effectuated. He terminates his analysis, nevertheless, with a rather faint act of faith in our human powers of resuscitation, and voices the hope that the human mind will yet recognize and assert its own primary position as the creator of knowledge and of right; and will, accordingly, regulate individual and social relations in a manner conformable to this fundamental conception; and he concludes this preliminary address with the assurance that he will bring to his teaching the sincere enthusiasm of his moral conscience, an assurance that would seem to indicate that the author had unconsciously fallen back into the old, time-honored ways of thinking and speaking, since it is by no means easy to see just what such an expression would mean in the professed terms of its author.

The tendencies revealed in this work are extremely important, since, in the professed domain of Ethics and of Law, they represent an obstinate refusal to recognize the only authority which can make either intelligible, the supreme authority of God Himself; and they likewise represent an equally determined denial of man's essentially dependent position, as well as that persistent desire and purpose to prove him supreme which has never been absent from human history, yet was never more widespread or more pronounced than now; linked, as they are, with the cognate creative powers claimed under Pragmatism and similar modern theories. Yet we feel that this simple exposition is all that is necessary or desirable here, since an adequate criticism covering, necessarily, the whole range of theoretical and practical science is manifestly impossible, while a few fundamental tenets of sane philosophy and a brief appeal to consciousness would form their all-sufficient refutation.

L'Etica Evoluzionista is nothing less than a critique of a critique of Spencer's psychologico-ethical system. It is a study of G. Salvadori's work of the same title, which, in turn, is devoted to an interpretation and vindication of Spencer's ethical ideas. In considering this example of Salvadori's exegetical methods and results, Professor Del Vecchio renders two distinctly valuable services. He utters a valid protest against that unwarranted species of commentary which commends an author by changing him, and he accurately indicates some of the more grave defects which render the biologico-evolutionistic theory of ethical relations wholly unfit to serve as a basis for any scientific concept of morality. Incidentally, he also shows that Spencer himself and many of his followers were not wholly unconscious of these fatal faults of the system.

It is not difficult to discern the wide significance of Spencer's own admission that the doctrine of evolution did not serve him as a guide to the extent that he would have desired; and for those who wish accurately to understand the question—certainly fundamental in Ethics—of human personality with all its far-reaching consequences, the author introduces the following quotation from Spencer's *Principles of Psychology* (I, p. 501 ff.). "When, after a certain composite mass of emotion and thought has arisen in him, a man performs an action, he commonly asserts that he determined to perform the action; and by speaking *as if there were a mental self* [the italics are ours] present to his consciousness, yet not included in this composite mass of emotion and thought, he is led into the *error* of supposing that it was not this composite mass of emotion and thought which determined the action. . . . To say that the performance of the action is, therefore, the result of his free will, is to say that he determines the cohesions of the psychical states which arouse the action; and as these psychical states constitute himself at that moment, this is to say that these psychical states determine their own cohesions, which is absurd. Their cohesions have been determined by experiences—the greater part of them, constituting what we call his natural character, by the experiences of antecedent organisms; and the rest by his own experiences. The changes which take place at each moment in his consciousness, and among others those that he is said to will, are produced by this infinitude of previous experiences registered in his nervous structure, coöperating with the immediate impressions on his senses: the effects of these combined factors being in every case qualified by the psychical state, general or local, of his organism." Del Vecchio very justly marvels, when, in open opposition to this explicit declaration, Salvadori, professing to interpret and explain his principal, says, "Without doubt there is in the Ego a new activity which evolves itself freely, and which cannot be considered as a merely passive product of past

generations and a simple result of physical and social environment."
And the marvel increases when Salvadori again declares that "the
doctrine of evolution does not tend to the negation, but in very
truth to the affirmation of moral liberty and of responsibility."

All must agree here with Del Vecchio that these utterances of
Spencer are hopelessly, because fundamentally, irreconcilable with
those of Salvadori; that the antecedently determined *Ego* of the
supposedly misunderstood Spencer is an essentially different concept from that of the freely acting agent of his interpreter; that
this independent *Ego* and the personal liberty implied by its existence would, therefore, introduce a new and fundamentally dif-
ferentiating element into Spencer's biologico-evolutionistic deter-
minism; and that, as a final conclusion, the system of Spencer, which
thus reduces the *Ego* to the mere sum of antecedently determined
coincident psychical states, could never give the reason why that
Ego, or any other, should ever be the subject of praise or blame, reward or punishment; or why, in fact, there should be any ethical
system at all.   D. DEVER.

THE SACRAMENT OF DUTY, AND OTHER ESSAYS. By Joseph Mc-
Sorley, Paulist. New York: The Columbus Press. 1909. Pp. 284.

"To be cheerful, humble, honest, brave, constant, reverent; to
wage ceaseless war against the myriad forms of selfishness which obstruct the path to the higher life; to care fervently for the Blessed
Christ, and seek an ever-closer communion with the indwelling
Divine Spirit; these are aims and endeavors which the soul indeed
recognizes as its finest opportunities, but which the flesh grows weary
of pursuing." Father McSorley writes, and writes well, from a desire to strengthen belief in these aims and ideals, to keep alive the
realization of spiritual values, to foster the ambition to grow in
reverence and hope and unselfishness, despite the discouragements
that beset the struggle through life on earth. And for such end the
essay, which clothes its purpose in manifold guise suited for gaining
the attention of the moody and divers-minded reader, is better
adapted than the moralist's treatise which appeals to men already
convinced and fails most often to attract those whom it is chiefly
intended to correct.

"Soul Blindness," the "Sacrament of Duty," "On Being Cheerful," "Open-Mindedness," "The Ideal Man," "The School of
Paul," "God in the Soul," "Modern Life," and the epilogue upon
"The Unconverted World," are themes which have close affinity,
like cause and effect or substance and accidents. Whichever way we

read them they lead us to the same end, namely, the increased endeavor to be cheerful, humble, honest, brave, and reverent. The language which Father McSorley speaks is pure, discriminating, natural, and that is saying much for the value of a book that speaks of things spiritual to the man of the world.

Literary Chat.

The *Outlook* (11 December) has a keenly appreciative sketch of Father Tabb's life, under the title *Poet and Priest*. " Like Brother Azarias, whom he resembled in the quietness of his spirit and the shyness of his nature, Father Tabb was all his life out of the rush of affairs." Yet "apart from the world, his heart was deeply engaged with the fortunes of his kind. He had a rare genius for condensing his emotion or thought without sacrificing clarity or beauty. . . . A casual glance at the lyrics brings out his deep religious feeling, his passion for nature, and the refinement and purity of his sentiment." The writer illustrates by some lines quoted from Father Tabb's collection of poems, the deep sense of intimacy between the world of nature and the God who made it, expressed with a refinement of style and a spontaneity of feeling characteristic of the best art.

Father Tabb was an intimate friend of Sidney Lanier for many years, and their kindred tastes gave to the friendship a rare union of purpose in literary work. "Professor Bright, of Johns Hopkins University, who knew him well, describes him as frank and jovial, and the soul of wit in his intercourse with his friends. He saw the beautiful side of everything. . . He was an extremely exacting craftsman, unwilling that his little verses should go forth until they had received the last touch from his trained hand. Men of Father Tabb's temper, of his quietness of spirit, his genius for meditation, and his unworldliness of aim, are rare in any country. In this busy, hard-worked America of the twentieth century his little songs have come like rivulets of pure and refreshing water from a hidden fountain." This is true praise.

Among the edifying output of Franciscan literature in the English tongue must be mentioned an attractively printed little volume on the *Life, Virtues, and Miracles of Fr. Magin Catala, O.F.M.*, one of the Spanish missionaries who went to Mexico in 1786 and was later on active in the work of evangelization and colonization in California, and who has left a tradition among the natives which has earned him the title of the *Holy Man of Santa Clara*. Father Zephyrin Engelhardt is already known to our readers, not only as an indefatigable missionary, but also as a student who has opened up for the Catholic historian much that lay hidden in the scattered archives of the old missions in the far West. He is author of a volume *The Franciscans in California*, and another entitled *The Franciscans in Arizona*. Besides this he has written much on the subject of missionary work in general.

young women of our country and age, as contained in the *Family Sitting-Room Series.* (Flynn & Co., Boston.)

Dr. Thomas O'Hagan issues a little volume entitled *Essays, Literary, Critical, and Historical* (Author's edition, Toronto), in which he brings together some studies and interpretations of literature and history which have appeared in American periodicals at odd times. They are original and in places contain sharp criticisms of local methods in education. *The Degradation of Scholarship* is an arraignment of the Public and High Schools of Ontario which would strike the unbiased reader as somewhat overdrawn, if the author did not challenge its contradiction by offering proof of the inefficiency of the Provincial teachers and by citing from the reports statements of educational officials that seem to bear out his criticism.

A volume of superior merit as a text-book of Rhetoric is P. Nikolaus Schleiniger's *The Principles of Eloquence*, translated from an enlarged and revised edition of the Jesuit Father Karl Racke, by Joseph Skellon, with a preface by F. King, S.J. (Kegan Paul, London). In the section dealing with the arrangement of compositions, and in another treating of the mastery of the emotions, the author is especially clear and instructive. The selections are thoroughly Catholic, that is to say, they cover illustrations from lay orators of classical worth, among them Edmund Burke, Pitt, Lord Chatham, Lord Erskine, Lord Brougham, Grattan, Sheridan, O'Connell, Lord Beaconsfield, and Gladstone. A separate section is devoted to American orators, such as Patrick Henry, Sargent Prentiss, Webster, Clay, Seward, Lincoln. The list of spiritual orators includes Wiseman, Thomas Burke, Newman, Manning, Purcell, Spalding, Kenrick. Everything about the book, its form and contents alike, commend it to the use of students in seminaries and for private culture. (B. Herder.)

Steadily, if slowly, our didactic literature of Catholic philosophy is developing. Text-books, manuals, there are in many varieties. What has hitherto been lacking is a short outline of the history of philosophy. The demand has recently been supplied by Father Coppens, S.J., the well-known author of several other useful compendia. Within the limits of less than one hundred and fifty pages Father Coppens has succeeded in synopsizing the story of philosophy—Eastern, Greek, Roman, Patristic, Medieval, and Modern. This may sound incredible, but it is true none the less. Of course, not a great deal can be told within so narrow a compass of any particular system or thinker. Nevertheless, there is enough for an intelligent survey, enough for a text-book in the hands of a competent teacher, enough for an outline to be filled in by a professor, enough to introduce an intelligent reader to a larger work, like Turner's *History of Philosophy*, or Finlay-Stöckl's kindred work.

Here and there a critic might detect an exaggerated statement; as where it is asserted that Darwin in his theory supposed "that whatever can be imagined to have happened has actually occurred" (p. 118). This, of course, is hyperbole. A few other such blemishes might be pointed out. Again, Alfred Wallace is said not to have "included man in the series of evolution" (ib.). Wallace, we believe, excluded from the evolutionary process the *higher faculties* of man, not the human organism with its purely organic powers.

Although the Catholic press in France pours forth an incessant stream of books—religious and philosophical—very many, indeed most of which, are instructive and attractive, some of the older books of a generation past have not lost their hold on the reading public. There is, for instance, Père Gratry. His works, while perhaps not quite classical, seem to have taken permanent rootage. Quite recently his *Morale et la Loi de l'Histoire* has passed into its fourth edition (2 Vols., Paris: Téqui). Seeing that the work originally appeared just as forty years ago, this may not be deemed a very remarkable perdurance. And yet its comparative longevity arrests attention and calls for an explanation. The latter may lie partly in the charm of style, though mainly it must be sought for in the principles and personal appeal which the work embodies and fulfills. Père Gratry was temperamentally drawn to those Catholic principles that answer immediately to the religious and the volitional elements of human nature. He saw as well as spontaneously felt those revealed truths that find their natural adjustment to man's will and feeling. While his appeal did not overlook the intellect it touched immediately the aspirations and ideal tendencies. It was human and personal. Hence its natural adaptation to the modern spirit, which in so far is not necessarily modernistic. The moral law and the law of history are in the work above mentioned shown to be co-extensive. The moral law of nature is seen to be the natural reflex of the law of the Gospel—do unto others as you would have them do unto you; and the latter is shown to be the law or principle on which the preservation and progress of human society depend. Without being explicitly so styled, the work is a Catholic philosophy of history—Catholic, that is, universal in compass; and Catholic in the sense that it builds upon the Catholic, that is, the natural, adjustment of human personality to God and the supernatural order, the *anima naturaliter Christiana.*

Under the title *Dieu, Lectures Théologiques,* Canon Berthé has arranged a catena of excerpts from the Fathers, Doctors, and eminent theologians of the Church, illustrating the Divine existence, nature, and attributes. The passages are arranged on the plan of the corresponding topics in St. Thomas's *Summa Theologica*—the work, also, from which the greater part has been adapted. As a store-house of illustrative material representing the best thoughts of the masters the volume will be found useful and suggestive. The book has been neatly made up by Bloud et Cie. (Paris), the well-known publishers of series styled the " Library of Science and Religion," a series containing so many little treasure-troves of things valuable. Amongst the latest noteworthy accessions to the series are *Morale Scientifique et Morale Évangelique devant la Sociologie,* a brief essay by the eminent physician and professor (Montpelier) Dr. Grasset, on the relative efficacy of naturalistic and Christian ethics for healing the present social disorders; *La Survivance de l'Ame chez les Peuples non-civilisés,* a study in comparative religions, by M. Bros, establishing the belief in immortality prevailing amongst savage nations. The booklet is valuable for its compact mass of evidence. *Les Arguments de l'Athéisme,* by M. de la Paquerie, a succinct criticism of the antitheistic objections urged by Kant, Spencer, Hebert, Dantec, Büchner. Then there is *Petau,* a learned and luminous sketch of the works of the great Jesuit theologian Petavius, by the Abbé Jules Martin. Each of these neat and valuable little books—and many hundreds more of their kind—can be bought in Paris for half a franc! Surely wisdom in these days goes almost a begging for acceptance!

tain the influence which it has communicated." Then, after developing this thought in relation to public speech, he goes on to show how "private instruction is more effective when it is practicable to give it," and he illustrates the fact by the experience of the "political campaigner," "the evangelist," the college "tutorial system," and "the confessional which gives untold strength to the Roman Catholic Church because in the confessional an individual gives counsel to an individual". Further on he continues: "Society —that kind of society in which men talk much and say nothing—is a great waste of time, the more pitiable because it is also a waste of opportunity. To converse ought to mean what the dictionaries tell us it does primarily mean—to live with another. Conversation ought to be a real interchange of life. What is the sense of this modern reserve which forbids us from talking about the matters which really interest us? Is it because we have so little life to impart? Do we keep the curtains of our soul down lest the world should see how empty the rooms are?" Then, after some illustrations of personal experience to the contrary, he adds: "When I get in literature a glimpse, to me a very enticing glimpse, of the French *salon* of the seventeenth and eighteenth centuries, I wonder whether the woman's clubs of the twentieth century are any improvement—are not rather the reverse. In the one was the play of an intellectual conversation, a real communication of life; in the other there are the silent audience and a learned or eloquent speaker— sometimes" (p. 48).

The Macmillans publish a new volume by Jacob A. Riis, author of *Children of the Tenements, The Battle with the Slums, How the Other Half Lives,* and other works which have done much to light up the dark recesses toward which scores of prophetic moralists and writers on Sociology have turned their melancholy microscopes to discover and discuss theories, but theories for which we needed actual data as well as the courage to face and trace the sad conditions to concrete causes. These data Mr. Riis furnished in his earlier books, and it has earned for him the approbation of the nation of his adoption, as well as the proud gratitude of the Danish sovereign and people to whose educational influence he largely owes the qualities of mind and heart that have been exercised in fostering among us republican ideals of a high standard. It has sometimes been said that Mr. Riis is a partisan; that he allows religious or anti-religious proselytism to mar his philanthropic work. His writings demonstrate the contrary. We say demonstrate, not merely assert. For there is in them that quality of strong personal presence which rarely deceives, least of all when the writer discusses not merely the objective results of study or professional experience, but the intimate motives of his action as they reveal themselves in his antecedents and in the circumstances of his ordinary life. We have the story of his life by himself, not told indeed in a spirit of self-adulation, but as a record of experience well calculated to help the young American toward the true realization of our national ideal of citizenship. The *Making of an American Citizen,* which is practically an autobiography of Mr. Riis, is to our mind one of the most healthful books that can be put into the hands of an American youth. And the new volume, *The Old Town,* might be called a supplement inasmuch as it furnishes the reader of the former volume with the background of the story of the Danish youth who, true to the instincts of a love for right, gave vent to his ambition to do, and to be helpful, amid the novel and trying circumstances which beset the immigrant. The volume is redolent of his love for home, his sympathy with the stranger, his eagerness to face new and difficult conditions, and a generous intolerance of shams and of the temporizing spirit that delays reform.

The Old Town is the story of Ribe, a town on the North Frisian coast of Jutland, where the author was born. It gives us a picture of a quaint and honest civilization that is fast passing away, memories of boyhood's simple joys, of places and persons in which local traditions and time-honored national virtues are represented. There are touches throughout the book of respectful allusions to ancient Catholic customs still surviving in the life of the town, grouped about the old Dom Kirche with its altar and its symbols of pre-Reformation days. It is a book that breathes reverence and unaffected loyalty for whatever is true and good and fair; and for that we commend its reading to those who, to their respect for the old things and tolerance for the right things, even when they are not labeled according to our own notions, join the appreciation of American freedom in its recognition of honest speech and square dealing.

Father Schuyler's *The Courage of Christ* is the first of a series of four small volumes that are to analyze and interpret the characteristic virtues of Our Lord's Sacred Humanity, with a view to engage our imitation of the Master who became Man that He might show us the Way that leads to eternal life. It is a timely as well as an attractive theme, for in the midst of the manifold secondary issues that are foisted on our attention as the essentials of happiness, everything that urges a return to the simple ideal of Christ's life and teaching is of much value. Courage in action, in mental suffering, in physical suffering, and the courage that can sustain the hope of eternal joys by perseverance in well-doing, is a fundamental quality—the gift sometimes of inheritance, to be guarded from turning into pride of life; sometimes as the fruit of prayer, to be daily renewed, lest the thorns choke its growth. The book is handsomely furnished. (Peter Reilly, Philadelphia.)

Books Received.

THEOLOGICAL.

DIEU. LECTURES THÉOLOGIQUES. Extraites de l'Écriture Sainte, des Pères de l'Église et des principaux Auteurs ecclésiastiques. Par L. Berthé. Paris: Bloud et Cie. 1910. Pp. xii-263. Pr. 5 frs.

LES CONFESSIONS DE SAINT AUGUSTIN. Traduction d'Arnauld d'Andilly. Introduction et Notes par Victor Giraud. Paris: Bloud et Cie. 1910. Pp. 223. Pr. 1 fr. 20.

THESAURUS CONFESSARII seu Brevis et accurata summa totius doctrinae moralis. Auctore R. P. Josephi Busquet. Editio quarta, digestior, locupletior et castigatior. Paris: Bloud et Cie. 1901. Pp. xvi-784. Pr. 5 frs.

EPITRES DE SAINT PAUL. Leçons d'exégèse. Par C. Tousaint. I. Lettres aux Thessaloniciens, aux Galates, aux Corinthiens. Paris: Gabriel Beauchesne et Cie. 1910. Pp. xxiv-506. Pr. 5 frs.

DE SCRIPTURA SACRA. J. V. Bainvel. Paris: Gabriel Beauchesne et Cie. 1910. Pp. 214. Pr. 3 fr. 25.

DE SACRIFICIO MISSAE, Tractatus asceticus continens praxim attente, devote, et reverenter celebrandi. Auctore Joanne Bona, Presb. Card. Ord. Cisterc. Cum Approbatione Rev. Ordinariatus Ratisbon. Ratisbonae, Romae, Neo Eboraci, et Cincinnati: Sumptibus et Typis Friderici Pustet. MDCCCCIX. Pp. xvi-208.

CAEREMONIAE MISSARUM SOLEMNIUM ET PONTIFICALIUM aliarumque Functionum Ecclesiasticarum. Opera Georgii Schober, Congregationis SS. Redemptoris Sacerdotis. Editio altera revisa et aucta. Ratisbonae, Romae, Neo Eboraci et Cincinnati: Sumptibus, Chartis et Typis Friderici Pustet. MDCCCCIX. Pp. xii-427. Preis: broch. M. 3; gebdn. M. 4.

LE PAIN DES PETITS. Explication dialoguée du Catéchisme par l'Abbé E. Duplessy. Tome I: Le Symbole des Apôtres. Tome II: Les Commandements. Paris: P. Téqui. 1909. Pp.: Tome I, xiv-255; Tome II, 255. Prix, 2 fr. le vol.

NON MOECHABERIS. Disquisitiones medicae in usum Confessariorum. Fr. A. Gemelli, O.F.M., Doctor Medicinae et Chirurgiae, Prof. ad. honorarius hystologiae, Lector Medicinae Pastoralis. Rome, New York, Cincinnati: Fr. Pustet. 1910. Pp. 248. Price, $1.50.

A COMPENDIUM OF CATECHETICAL INSTRUCTION. By the Very Rev. Angelo Raineri. Edited by the Rev. John Hagan, D.D., Vice Rector, Irish College, Rome. In two Volumes. New York, Cincinnati, Chicago: Benziger Bros. 1909. Pp. 573. Price, $4.25 net.

COURAGE OF CHRIST. By Henry C. Schuyler, S.T.L. Philadelphia: Peter Reilly; London: Kegan Paul, Trench, Trübner, & Co. 1909. Pp. 127. Price, $0.50 net, postage 6c extra.

LEARNING THE OFFICE. An Introduction to the Roman Breviary. By John T. Hedwick, S.J., Georgetown University. Ratisbon, Rome, New York, Cincinnati: Fr. Pustet & Co. 1910. Pp. 93. Price, $0.35.

OFFICIUM ET MISSA PRO DEFUNCTIS, cum Absolutione necnon Exsequiarum Ordine, cantu restituto jussu SS. D. N. Pii Papae X. Editio Ratisbonensis juxta Vaticanam. Ratisbonae, Romae, Neo Eboraci et Cincinnati: Fridericus Pustet. 1910. Pp. 95.

PHILOSOPHICAL.

THE APPROACH TO THE SOCIAL QUESTION. An Introduction to the Study of Social Ethics. By Francis Greenwood Peabody, Plummer Professor of Christian Morals in Harvard University. New York: The Macmillan Co. 1909. Pp. vii-210. Price, $1.25 net.

THE ELEMENTS OF SOCIAL SCIENCE AND POLITICAL ECONOMY. Especially for use in Colleges, Schools, Clubs, Guilds, etc. By the Venerable Archpriest Lorenzo Dardano. Translated from the Italian by the Rev. William McLoughlin, Mount Melleray Abbey. Dublin: M. H. Gill & Son, Ltd. 1910. Pp. xxvii-180. Price 3/6.

LE SENS COMMUN, LA PHILOSOPHIE DE L'ETRE ET LES FORMULES DOGMATIQUES. Suivi d'une étude sur la Valeur de la Critique moderniste des preuves Thomistes de l'existence de Dieu. Paris: Beauchesne et Cie. 1910. Pp. xxx-312. Pr. 3 frs. 75.

MORALE SCIENTIFIQUE ET MORALE ÉVANGÉLIQUE DEVANT LA SOCIOLOGIE. Par le Docteur Grasset. Bloud et Cie. 1910. Pp. 64. Pr. 60 centimes.

LES ARGUMENTS DE L'ATHÉISME. Par J. L. de la Paquerie. Bloud et Cie. 1910. Pp. 64. Pr. 60 centimes.

LA VALEUR SOCIALE ET L'ÉVANGILE. Par L. Garriguet. Paris: Bloud et Cie. 1910. Pp. 315. Pr. 3 frs. 50.

PRAGMATISME, MODERNISME, PROTESTANTISME. Par Albert Leclère. Bloud et Cie. 1910. Pp. 296. Pr. 3 frs. 50.

DOCTRINES RELIGIEUSES DES PHILOSOPHES GRECS. Par M. Louis, Professeur au Grand Séminaire de Meaux. (Bibliothèque d'Histoire des Religions.) Paris: P. Lethielleux. 1909. Pp. vii-374. Prix, 4 fr.

LA MORALE ET LA LOI DE L'HISTOIRE. Par A Gratry, Professeur à la Sorbonne. Membre de l'Académie Française. Quatrième édition. Paris: P. Téqui. 1909. Pp.: Tome I, xii-329; Tome II, 379. Prix, 7 fr. 50.

LE MODERNISME SOCIOLOGIQUE. Décadence ou Régéneration? Par l'Abbé J. Fontaine. Deuxième édition. Paris: P. Lethielleux. 1909. Pp. lix-515. Prix, 6 fr.

GREAT ISSUES. By Robert F. Horton, Author of "Inspiration and the Bible", "Revelation and the Bible", and "Verbum Dei". New York, Toronto, London, Melbourne: The Macmillan Co. 1909. Pp. vi-384. Price, $1.50 net.

DEVOIR ET CONSCIENCE. Par P. Gillet, Dominicain. Paris, Bruges, Rome: Desclée, De Brouwer & Cie. 1910. Pp. 323. Prix, 3 fr. 50.

HISTORICAL.

ERASME ET LUTHER. Leur Polémique sur le Libre Arbitre. Par H. Humbertclaude. Paris: Bloud et Cie. Pp. xxiii-297. Pr. 4 frs.

L'ÉGLISE ET LA MONDE BARBARE. Histoire Générale de l'Église par Fernand Mourret. Paris: Bloud et Cie. 1910. Pp. 496. Pr. 6 frs.

L'ART, LA RELIGION ET LA RENAISSANCE. Essai sur le Dogme et la Piété dans l'Art religieux de la Renaissance italienne. Par J.-C. Broussolle. (Leçons données à l'Institut Catholique de Paris.) Ouvrage accompagné de 139 gravures. Paris: P. Téqui. 1910. Pp. xiii-491. Prix, 5 frs.

SAINTE BATHILDE, REINE DES FRANCS. Histoire Politique et Religieuse. Par Dom. M.-J. Couturier, O.S.B. Paris: P. Téqui. 1909. Pp. x-367. Prix, 3 fr. 50.

BISHOP DE MAZENOD. His Inner Life and Virtues. By the Very Rev. Eugene Baffie, O.M.I. With Portraits. New York, Cincinnati, Chicago: Benziger Bros. 1909. Pp. xxvi-457. Price, $1.80 net.

CATHOLIC EDUCATIONAL ASSOCIATION BULLETIN, Vol. VI, No. 1, November, 1909. Report of the Proceedings and Addresses of the Sixth Annual Meeting at Boston, Mass., July 12, 13, 14, and 15, 1909. Catholic Educational Association, Columbus, Ohio. Pp. vii-477.

EIN ÖSTERREICHISCHER REFORMATOR. Lebensbild des heiligen P. Klemens Maria Hofbauer, des vorzüglichsten Verbreiters der Redemptoristenkongregation. Von P. Adolf Innerkofler, C.SS.R. Mit oberhirtlicher Druckgenehmigung und Erlaubnis der Ordensobern. Regensburg, Rom, New York und Cincinnati: Druck und Verlag von Friedrich Pustet. 1910. Pp. xxii-914. Preis: broch. M. 5; gebdn. M. 6.20.

LIFE OF MARY WARD, Foundress of the Institute of the B.V.M. Compiled from Various Sources. With an Introduction by the Right Rev. Abbot Gasquet, O.S.B. New York, Cincinnati, Chicago: Benziger Bros.; London: Burns & Oates. 1909. Pp. xxv-140. Price, $0.85 net.

A HISTORY OF CHRISTIANITY IN JAPAN. Vol. I. Roman Catholic and Greek Orthodox Missions. Vol. II. Protestant Missions. By Otis Cary, D.D. New York, Chicago, Toronto, London: Fleming H. Revell Co. 1909. Pp. 431 and 367. Price, $2.50 each volume.

REPORT OF THE COMMISSIONER OF EDUCATION FOR THE YEAR ENDING JUNE 30, 1909. Volume I. (Whole Number 411.) Washington: Government Printing Office. Pp. xii-598.

LE BRAHMANISME. Notions sur les Religions de l'Inde. Par Louis de la Vallée Poussin. Paris: Bloud et Cie. 1910. Pp. 127. Pr. 1 fr. 20.

LA SURVIVANCE LE L'AME CHEZ LES PEUPLES NON-CIVILISÉS. Par A. Bros. Paris: Bloud et Cie. 1910. Pp. 64. Pr. 60 centimes.

PÉTAU—1583—1652. Par l'abbe Jules Martin. Paris: Bloud et Cie. 1910. Pp. 72. Pr. 60 centimes.

DENYS D'ALEXANDRIE: Sa Vie, Son Temps, Ses Œuvres. Par Joseph Burel. Paris: Bloud et Cie. 1910. Pp. 125. Pr. 2 frs.

L'AVENIR DU CHRISTIANISME. Première Partie: Le Passé chrétien: Vie et Pensée. Tome IV—*Histoire de l'Église—du IIIe au XIe siècle.* Par Albert Dufourcq. Paris: Bloud et Cie. 1910. Pp. 356. Pr. 3 frs. 50.

PETITE HISTOIRE DE L'ÉGLISE CATHOLIQUE AU XIXE SIÈCLE. Par Pierre Porette. Paris: Bloud et Cie. 1910. Pp. 128. Pr. 1 fr. 20.

THE LIFE AND TIMES OF BISHOP CHALLONER (1691-1781). By Edwin H. Burton, D.D., Vice-President of St. Edmund's College, Old Hall; Fellow of the Royal Historical Society. In two volumes. New York, London: Longmans, Green, & Co. 1909. Pp. Vol. I, xxxv-403; Vol. II, viii-367. Price, $7.00, *net.*

MISCELLANEOUS.

THE UNBIDDEN GUEST. By Francis Cooke. New York, Cincinnati, Chicago: Benziger Brothers. 1910. Pp. 255. Pr. $1.25.

SERMON DELIVERY. A Method for Students. By the Rev. George S. Hitchcock, B.A. New York: Benziger Brothers. 1910. Pp. 82. Price, $0.75 *net.*

LA REPRÈSENTATION DE LA MADONE á travers des âges. Art et Littérature. (Avec Figures.) Par Joseph-H.-M. Clément. Paris: Bloud et Cie. 1910. Pp. 71. Pr. 60 centimes.

THE ROMANCE OF THE SILVER SHOON. A Story of the Sixteenth Century. By the Rev. David Bearne, S.J. New York, Cincinnati, Chicago: Benziger Bros. 1909. Pp. 195. Price, $0.85.

ROUND THE WORLD. A Series of Interesting Illustrated Articles on a Variety of Subjects. Vol. VII: Trees, Historic, Wonderful, and Ordinary. Furs and Fur Hunters. German Folk Lore. Floating Mines. Santa Catalina Island. Gold Mining in Mexico. Mountain Climbing in America. Old Style Writing. Canoes and Canoeing. Hunting Rubber in the American Tropics. Outdoor Bird-Taming. The Landmarks of Old Virginia. With 100 Illustrations. New York, Cincinnati, Chicago: Benziger Bros. 1909. Pp. 223. Price, $1.00.

PHILEAS FOX, ATTORNEY. By Anna T. Sadlier. Notre Dame, Indiana: The Ave Maria. 1910. Pp. 349. Price, $1.50.

THE WOMAN WHE NEVER DID WRONG and other Stories. By Katherine E. Conway, author of "Lalor's Maples", "The Family Sitting-Room Series", etc. Boston: Thos. J. Flynn & Co. Pp. 140. Price, $0.50.

Plate I.

1. Artistic and harmonious colors.

2. Spectral «liturgical» colors.

THE

ECCLESIASTICAL REVIEW

FIFTH SERIES.—VOL. II.—(XLII).—FEBRUARY, 1910.—NO. 2.

WHAT IS AN ADEQUATE COURSE OF SCRIPTURE STUDY?

IN the December number of the REVIEW the Rev. Father
Campbell pleaded for a course of Positive Theology in our
Seminaries, and all who read his words must have concurred
with him that some such course is a necessity. We are not at
present concerned with that question but with another which
is of even greater importance. Fr. Campbell says: " The
school of Scripture will aim at giving its students a first-hand
knowledge of the content of the Sacred Scriptures, and incidentally a knowledge of the disputes about them." He adds:
" This is, of course, the complete antithesis of our present use;
but it remains for those who cry out on all change as a rupture with the past to inform themselves whether our present
use be not a lapse rather than a continuation."

Of late years there has been an awakening regarding Biblical studies; we are flooded with Biblical periodicals, with
Reviews, with " Studies ", with Commentaries, etc., and anyone who takes up by chance any Review in our public
libraries must feel a sense of something akin to dismay when
he sees how vast is the field of Biblical knowledge now ex-
ploited. And many an earnest Rector of a Seminary feels
also a sense of shame at the inadequacy of our Seminary-
teaching on these points. And yet what can we do? Our
courses are already too crowded; our curriculum is as full as

up for students who have at the most five or possibly six years in the Seminary and who have very little time for study and who have an already crowded curriculum; who are, too, as we know to our cost, only too often neurotic and hardly in a fit physical state for study.

At the outset we must beware of being too idealistic. A certain Biblical Professor in a Seminary persuaded his Rector that the Scripture course was hopelessly inadequate, and he at length prevailed upon him to write to a non-Catholic friend of his and obtain for him the prospectus of a neighboring Protestant training-college. The results were disastrous! "Why!" ejaculated the Rector after he had looked it through, "it is nothing but Greek Testament! None of that stuff for me! Give them plenty of Dr. Hay and good old Dens. They were good enough for me and my fellow-students. Why can't they be enough for you? If your young men produce as many Bishops as my class did, they will do uncommonly well!"

And so, too, now. If we turn over the prospectus of the *École Biblique* at Jerusalem or that of Rome, we feel carried away with enthusiasm and yearn to try and do likewise. Yet it is clearly impracticable. We have no time for courses in Aramaic, in Assyrian, in Cuneiform, in Epigraphy, in Semitic Religions, etc., etc., nor, be it added, are such things in the least necessary for our Seminaries. No sane Rector would of course ever dream of taking over such a system wholesale but some might be tempted to adapt it to their own Seminaries. Is such a thing possible? We venture to answer most emphatically in the negative. Such prospectus cannot be adapted; they must be taken in the lump or not at all. They are meant solely for the future professor and are in no sense intended for the man who is destined for the active ministry. Yet no one wants to keep these latter in the background; they are the backbone of our Seminaries, and it is for them we must primarily provide, while at the same time we are bound to keep before our eyes the fact that some of them must become professors in their turn and must not be able to retort that their Seminary training has in no sense equipped them for their work.

But is it possible to give such a Biblical course in our Seminaries as shall serve equally well for the priest on the mission and for the future professor? We maintain that it is and that moreover such training is the best. For, after all, what is necessary for the priest on the mission? Is it necessary for him to know all the latest vagaries of the " Higher Criticism "? Need he be well informed regarding the latest archeological " find "? Is it requisite that he should be able to give a critique upon the textual theories of Westcott and Hort? Need he be a " Papyrologist "? No! He needs none of these things. *But he does need a good sound knowledge of the text of the Bible itself,* and that is what is wanting in so many, not merely in priests engaged in mission-work, but even in some who call themselves " critics " and are actually Professors! And this, we maintain, every Seminary course should aim at imparting before all things, for it is surely the foundation of all Biblical study whether for preaching or for lecturing. In old days it used to be the custom to commit a great deal of the New Testament to memory, and a preacher has no greater asset, while such knowledge would often save the " critics " from serious blunders; the lecturer, for instance, who endeavored to persuade his hearers that since, in Genesis 37 : 25 and 28, the men who bought Joseph are called " Ishmaelites " and " Midianites ", the whole story must be regarded as the combined work of two distinct authors, would hardly have fallen into such an error if he had read, or at least remembered, the eighth chapter of Judges.

The days are gone by—let us hope, for ever—when the Scriptural course in the Seminary was the same for all the students alike, when the man just admitted and the deacon expecting to be ordained in a few months' time were all alike expected to attend the lectures on whatever book of the Bible was being given that year. Knowing nothing whatever of the contents of the Bible, the tyro was expected to derive profit from lectures which were at the best hopelessly uninteresting and which were almost certainly beyond his capacity! Is it a marvel that such men after five or six years of such drudgery never opened the Bible after quitting the Seminary?

But even now are we really much better off? What is the course generally in vogue? In many Seminaries a year may be devoted to " Introduction ", and then immediately upon that follows a course of two lectures a week on one of the Gospels, generally that of St. Matthew, which is too long to really finish in any satisfactory manner; and then in the subsequent years the student may see another Gospel or an Epistle of St. Paul, with perhaps a desultory commentary on the Acts of the Apostles. During one year a Book of the Old Testament may possibly be done. And a student who gets a course even such as this may think himself fortunate, for in many cases nothing half so comprehensive is attempted. But if we turn to some Seminaries which are better equipped, what do we find? Sometimes a year devoted to what is known as " General Introduction ", another year given to " Special Introduction ", and then three years of exegesis. Truly fortunate are students who get a course so well arranged as this and none but he who has tried to give it single-handed can know what hard work it is. But even then the apparent want of results is most discouraging. Do we really find that men go out on to the mission with a real love of the Bible? Do we find that they habitually read it or that their preaching depends much upon the actual text of the Bible? It must be confessed that such results are not often apparent. Or, again, do we find that men so trained are well equipped for the professorial chair? They will be the first to tell you that when they began to teach they found themselves very ill-equipped indeed!

It is not easy to assign an adequate cause to this apparent failure, but perhaps an analysis of the best of the courses depicted above will serve to explain its want of results.

In the first place a year, the first year, was given to General Introduction, and such questions as Inspiration, the Versions, the History of the Canon, etc., were touched upon. In the next year came Special Introduction, and the student was taken hastily through some of the principal books of the two Testaments. Perhaps, too, in those first two years he picked up a smattering of Hebrew; more probably he began it but dropped it in disgust! After this introductory course, which certainly sounds well, the student attended the course of exegesis, and if he was fortunate enough to fall under a good professor he may have seen in a fairly satisfactory fashion a Gospel, an Epistle, and possibly an Old Testament book. But ask such a man after his course whether he knows much about the Bible. No one expects him to say he does, nor would we believe him if he did say so; but what we do want him to be able to say is that he is immensely interested in Biblical questions, and that he finds he can use his Bible profitably in the pulpit and for his own spiritual life. If he cannot give this answer there must have been something wrong with his Biblical course—supposing always that he has done his duty at the Seminary. But now test him a little and try to find out what he has learnt; ask him some simple question, about the Psalter for example. It is the part of the Bible he knows, or ought to know, best; but what does he really know? We do not expect him to be able to give a reasoned explanation of the " Exurgat Deus "; we should not even be surprised if, like the young priest in *My New Curate,* he translated " Herodii domus dux est eorum " by " The palace of Herod is their leader." But ask him some simpler question; ask him which are the Messianic Psalms; which are the " Passion " Psalms; or, passing to the New Testament, on which he has to preach every Sunday, ask him where the Parable of the Prodigal Son is to be found; ask him whether there is any passage which is to be found in all of the four Gospels; again ask him which of the Evangelists narrates the story of the Divine Infancy, which of them has an account of the Ascension. These questions may seem puerile, but we confess to thinking them test-questions in the case in point, for our object is to discover what our newly-ordained priest knows about the Bible itself. It is of small importance whether he can tell us what Harnack or Driver think of a certain book, for such knowledge is worse than useless unless accompanied by a deep knowledge of the Bible itself; and that—we repeat once more—is the real aim, or rather should be the real aim of all Seminary Biblical teaching. Yet can we say that it is the result generally attained? We fancy not. Is it not rather the case that our priests know better what is said about the Bible than what the Bible says about itself? Canon Sheehan's Curate knew something about the Codex Vaticanus—or thought he did; but he got into trouble over the " heron "!

What, then, is the fault with the curriculum sketched out above? We venture to think it is this: when a divine comes to the Seminary we presume that he already knows his Bible, whereas just the opposite is the case. And that we do so presume—at least tacitly—is evident from this that we put the General Introduction first, instead of after the Special Introduction. We know that the curriculum-framers will raise a protest and say that this is the only logical order. But is abstract logic always necessary? Is it the best guide in teaching? We must reckon with facts, and the fact which faces us is that our students do not know the text when they come to their first lectures. A young divine, fresh from college and with a brand-new Bible in his hands, listens to a professor who lectures him upon Inspiration and the history of the Canon. The Inspiration of what? The Canon of what? He has only the vaguest idea. Not long since a Professor of Philosophy of great standing combated some views propounded by the present writer anent Inspiration; when he was confronted with certain facts from the Book of Judith which— so the writer maintained—could not be explained on his theory, he retorted, " I do not know the Book of Judith, but I am sure your theory is wrong! "

In those words we have the root of the difficulty; what he should have said was, " I do not know my Bible well enough to dogmatize about the theory of Inspiration ". And yet what else are we doing when we put before a raw " freshman " theories of Inspiration before he has even a vague notion of the subject-matter of Inspiration? We pass over the fact that any solid theory of Inspiration must be essentially philosophical, and our tyro has presumably done no Philosophy! But we shall at once be told that it is just as absurd to put the Special Introduction first as to put the " General Introduction " first, and we can already hear cavilers saying : " What ' freshman ' is capable of understanding such questions as ' the Mosaic authorship' of the Pentateuch, or the ' Documentary Theory ', or the Messianic character of certain Psalms, or the Synoptic Problem, etc., etc. ?" We cordially agree, no " freshman " can be expected to tackle these questions; they are the controverted questions of the age; they are the arena of all the most recent conflicts in the world of Biblical science. But we shall be told that they are *fundamental* questions and therefore must be treated first! Once more it is the old fetish of abstract Logic! Are we heretical in saying this? Perhaps we are, but at any rate we fancy we are practical and this is a practical if not a logical age. Let us look facts in the face. These great questions are the vexed problems of to-day; they are the ones which torture matured minds; they are the ones which will be brought before a young priest the moment he comes out into his parish and meets interested unbelievers. For example, he sits in a drawing-room and hears some remark about a new archeological discovery which—so it is maintained—has once more shown the absurdity of supposing that poor old Moses wrote the Pentateuch! Now if he is a wise man he will hold his tongue until he is asked for an opinion. But supposing he is asked what he thinks on the question, what will he say? He has been ordained a year; he has had three or four years of theology; that horrible question of the Mosaic authorship was forced down his throat when he was in his second year of Philosophy; he hardly knew at the time what the Pentateuch was; he had certainly not read it then and since then he has not had the time for anything except his Gury, etc. But people are waiting for an answer! He is a lucky man if he escapes without an uneasy sense that he has made an exhibition of himself!

But we can hear a critic saying, It is easy to pick holes. But what remedy do you propose? You say you would not have the General Introduction first, because it supposes a knowledge of the text which, according to you, students do not possess; and you will not put Special Introduction first, because the questions treated of in that course are the vexed questions of the day and demand a trained mind. What will you do?

Before answering we must call to mind the precise object we have in view. The goal we aim at is to produce students who shall have a good practical knowledge of the text of the Bible, who shall be sufficiently *au courant* with modern difficulties to avoid making wild and foolish statements, and who, when they leave the Seminary, shall have solid foundations for further Biblical study. We maintain, and we feel that all who have examined the question will bear us out in what we

books remains upon their shelves covered with dust. Our first object, then, must be to interest them in it. In other words we must teach them how to read the Bible. How many devout souls there are who for years have read their daily chapter and yet have no real knowledge of the Bible! This is because they have never been taught to read it intelligently. A student, then, needs in his first year to be shown the principal divisions of the Bible; he must be shown how it is divided into definite groups, i. e. the Law, the Historical Books, the Sapiential Books, the Prophets Major and Minor, and finally the Historical Appendix in Maccabees. Concurrently with this he must learn the ordinary system of chronology and should be taught to arrange the various Books according to the dates to which they approximately belong. He must at the same time be shown how the Prophets fit into the historical framework and thus throw light upon the history as given us in Kings and Chronicles. Nor must the Geography be forgotten, for it, more perhaps than anything else, serves to fix points in the memory and adds a most fascinating interest to the dry details of the history. And the books themselves must be divided up according to their subject-matter. To take a concrete example; we divide Genesis into the history of the Patriarchs, i-xi; of Abraham, xii-xxv; of Isaac, xxvi-xxviii: and of Jacob and Joseph, xxix-l. There is of course some overlapping, but the division may stand for practical purposes. We now take each of these periods singly and enter into details. The governing principle in this first section is that of *elimination,* and we analyze it, pointing out as we proceed the various Toledoth which serve to indicate the divisions of the whole book. As we advance from period to period the history is dwelt upon and the geographical details, with the assistance of the black-board, are pointed out; we see Abraham journeying from Ur and passing through Haran until he finally settles in Canaan; we point out the various visions vouchsafed to him and his children, the covenants God made with them, and the providential care He ever exercised in their regard. The genealogies are worked out, and it is shown how they served as the framework for the history. At the same time we shirk no difficulties; the sins of the chosen stock are not glossed over, for we are not teaching children;

the so-called doublets are pointed out in the Creation story and in the stories of Abraham and Isaac at Gerara and in Egypt. Parallel passages in the Bible are also indicated, e. g. St. Stephen's speech in Acts vii, and the discrepancies which have been singled out by critics are not glossed over, though we do not attempt any explanation, for that would take us outside our sphere. The Messianic prophecies in Chapters 3 and 49 are indicated and their importance insisted on, but no detailed commentary is made. Above all, constant reference is made to archeological finds, especially when treating of Ch. 14, for it is certain that nothing better serves to stimulate interest than the wonderful story of the " Resurrection " of Palestine and the Far-East as worked out by the spade.

Some will, however, object that at this rate we should never finish the Bible in the year. But we only treat Genesis in this way. This book is fundamental in more senses than one, and if students do not at the outset grasp its mode of construction and arrangement, and if they do not seize upon its position as the key to the whole of Sacred Scripture, they will fail to understand many things in the rest of the Bible. But we shall be asked whether we treat of the question of the Hexæmeron and of the precise character of the first eleven chapters. If we have made our position understood above, it will be evident that we cannot afford to treat of these questions in any systematic way, for such questions are beyond the freshman; we point out the difficulties when it appears necessary to do so; we lay stress on the witness of the cuneiform accounts of the Creation and the Deluge, but we do not enter into details of theological interpretation, for the reasons assigned above. Again, it will perhaps be objected that it is absurd to point out a difficulty and at the same time furnish no answer; but three courses are open to us: we can either pass over the difficulty and its solution or we can dwell upon the difficulty and the answer. But if we elect the former course some student is almost certain to single out that difficulty and it will be made evident that we have passed it over. Moreover we may not at the moment have an adequate answer ready if we have not intended to touch the question, and the result will not tend to increase the confidence which students must have in their professor. If, on the other hand, we elect the latter course we find ourselves involved in. difficulties, for the students are not prepared to assimilate an answer which can be considered really satisfactory; moreover we have not the time for such treatment of the question. It seems, then, best to strike a mean and not to shirk the difficulty but point it out frankly, with the conviction that such a course is far more likely to prove a safeguard to the student than either of the above alternatives.

The rest of the Pentateuch can be treated much more briefly, provided the framework is duly worked out and the salient points of each book dwelt upon. When we enter upon the study of the Historical Books we shall need an introduction on the methods of the Hebrews in writing history, though this may be as slight as possible. But the historical framework *must* be mastered and the names and dates of the kings and of the principal events must be committed to memory. Here again archeology plays an important part in interesting the student. By Easter we ought to have finished the Historical Books, and there will remain the Sapiential Books and the Prophets. This sounds like a great deal of work to cover before the summer examinations, but the professor will probably find that by this time the students will have become accustomed to his methods and will have learnt to read the Bible for themselves in an intelligent fashion; and this of course will make his work much easier. Moreover it will not be necessary to read every book; it will suffice if a good knowledge of the main divisions is obtained. But it will be important to see that the interconnexion of the Prophets and the history is clearly grasped.

We now pass to the second year of study. If the first has been well done, two results will have been obtained; the students will have a real interest in the Bible, and they will have a very fair knowledge of its contents and of the arrangement of the various Books. They are now prepared for an examination of the question: How did we get our Bible? They know what the Bible is; they can now enter upon the study of questions which must of course have been touched upon already, viz. the Versions, the MSS., the formation of the Canon, and finally the burning question of Inspiration. For this last question it must be confessed they are even now hardly ripe, but at any rate they are capable of appreciating the data furnished by the Bible, even if they are not capable of fully grasping the philosophical aspects of the problem. The second year over, students may now begin the exegesis of some New Testament Book. They are fairly well equipped for the work as they have a practical knowledge of the contents of the whole Bible and are quite capable of appreciating the differences between the New and the Old Testament. But what kind of lectures on the Gospel are they to attend? Supposing that that of St. Mark is chosen, are the students to be dragged through a wearisome exposé of the Gospel, word for word? We must bear in mind the goal we are to have in view. These students are to go out shortly on the mission; they are to be prepared then for practical work. Is it any good to burden them, or rather their note-books, with a heap of minute comments on each verse? What student ever looked at his note-books after leaving the Seminary unless some controversy forced him to do so? And if he did then look them up he probably found that he had no notes on that particular point! Similarly it is no good furnishing him with a quantity of notes on the "Higher Criticism". No, what students want, whether they are to be simply on the mission or professors later on, is, we repeat, a good working knowledge of the text. For the text is the best commentary, as St. Bernard said long ago. If a student goes out knowing well the divisions and arrangement of the Gospels, if he knows where to look for the various parables and miracles, where to turn for controverted points; if he has formed for himself by diligent reading a fair idea of our Lord's life and ministry; if he has grasped the different features of that life as depicted by each Evangelist; if he has taken the pains to compare for himself only two or three parallel passages as set forth by the different writers—then he will have a fair, and above all, a practically useful knowledge of the Gospels.

But, once more, how are we to teach the Gospel we have chosen? It is customary to begin by an introduction, which may be either longer or shorter as the professor chooses. But if what we ventured to say above about the impracticability of giving the General Introduction before the Special was justified, it would seem only logical to argue that here also the introduction should not precede but follow an ac-

quaintance with the text to be studied. Let us suppose that
we are going to give the Gospel of St. John. The introductory matter is enormous and notoriously difficult; it is essentially a question of details. Are students capable of appreciating it? We fancy not. But if it is insisted that each
student must first read the whole Gospel for himself and that
not chapter by chapter but as much as he can at a stretch—
no one who has not so read a Gospel or an Epistle can imagine
how differently it reads and how different an impression it
makes on us when so read; and if he has been shown how to
read it intelligently, i. e. with due regard to its main divisions, then he is in a better position to appreciate an introduction. Yet even then it seems to us that the introduction can
be much more profitably given, and with a great saving of
time, if it be postponed to the end when students are thoroughly acquainted with the subject-matter and when, too,
in the course of the commentary many passages have already
been pointed out to them which have an important bearing
on the introductory questions.

Yet here again we have certain reservations to make; they
may sound revolutionary, and we only suggest them for what
they are worth.

It will have been noticed that we have said nothing so far
about Special Introduction to the New Testament. We did
this for several reasons. In the first place, the time is short;
in the second place, the New Testament is so much more
familiar to students than the Old that there is not the same
need for insisting on their becoming acquainted with its contents before beginning their studies. But our main reason
for the omission was that if we give the Introduction to the
New Testament at the outset it is apt to be forgotten by the
time students come to the study of the actual books. Now if

duction to the Gospels as a whole. And this introduction should take the form of an examination of the contents of the Synoptic Gospels with a comparison of the contents of St. John's Gospel. A few parallel passages from the Synoptics might be compared and thus the student would be introduced in a practical way to the Synoptic Problem, which must be treated in the concrete if at all. He should also be taught to draw up for himself lists of the parables and miracles occurring in each Gospel, and if he can learn these by heart so much the better. If the first half of the year were devoted to this, a very practical commentary could be given on any one Gospel—St. Mark's for choice—in the latter half of the year, and we are certain that good results would accrue.

If in the second year the student received a similar introduction to the Epistles of St. Paul and a brief but thorough commentary on any one of them—not that to the Romans!— he would have a better knowledge of the New Testament than most who have waded through our Seminary course. His third, and presumably last year, might profitably be devoted to some Old Testament book treated in the same way; this would enable the professor to return to certain Old Testament problems which he was unable to treat as fully as he could have wished at an earlier period in the student's career.

Anyone who has had the patience to read the foregoing pages will probably feel that there are two main difficulties which call for solution: first, where shall we find professors capable of such thorough work? and secondly, in the schemes roughly sketched out above, what preparation is made for the formation of Biblical professors?

Perhaps one answer will satisfy both queries. We said at the outset that our aim was to put forth a scheme which, while keeping in view primarily the needs of those who are destined for the mission life, should yet serve as a preparation for the formation of professors. Now in the scheme thus sketched it is evident that there is no provision made for the special training of professors, but we fancy that the ground has been well prepared for their after equipment. Students who have been so prepared are capable now of taking up a systematic

namely a thorough practical knowledge of the text. We presume of course that such men have been warned that they are destined for the work of teaching afterwards and that they have at least a smattering of Hebrew and that their knowledge of Greek is at least passable. Now how are we to secure their full equipment? They need special training and for that they must have thoroughly trained masters; no dilettanti will do; students must be able to go to each lecture with the assured feeling that the lecturer is fully up to his work and is master of the subject. The answer then is patent: such candidates for posts as Biblical Professors must go to one of the Écoles Bibliques which now exist. It is expensive work, it must be admitted, but it is an expense which will be well repaid. If such a student goes to Rome, he will have the advantages of a trained staff of professors and of a good library. If he goes to Jerusalem he will have in addition the inestimable advantage of living amid Biblical scenes and thus steeping himself in Biblical lore in the unchanging East where everything he sees will remind him of the Old and New Testament, and where he will learn to interpret the Bible through the best of all mediums, namely association with the very scenes in which so many Biblical events were enacted. Moreover at Jerusalem he will have the further advantage of thoroughly trained men who have devoted their lives to the study of the Bible and whose names as professors and as writers are already household words.

HUGH POPE, O.P.

Doctor in S. Scripture and Professor of Biblical Exegesis, Collegio Angelico, Rome.

THE REFORM IN CHURCH VESTMENTS.

I. THE COLOR OF PARAMENTICS.

LAST year, whilst the sessions of the Catholic Congress in Germany took place in the beautiful city of Düsseldorf, a somewhat unusual spectacle was presented to the vast assem-

Catholicity in Bohemia, where the free action of the Church was being hampered by the agitations of a powerful Socialist faction. There had been the usual brief discussion following the address, and the signal of the chairman had announced the time limit for comment, when the president of the assembly stepped to the front of the platform to introduce a lady— Madam Helene Stummel [1] who was to make a plea in behalf of a much-needed reform of church vestments. She spoke with such admirable grace, and showed so complete a mastery of her subject in every detail and motive, that she quickly won the attention and sympathy of the audience. The result was a unanimous resolution adopted by the Congress to further by all legitimate means the efforts of the speaker to restore the delicate craft of correct and dignified paramentics to its former place of honor among the ecclesiastical arts.

It was on this occasion that the writer of the present article received the first impulse toward taking up the study and aiding in the reform which tended toward securing the proper shape, color, material, and use of ecclesiastical *paramenta,* since these features had, through a gradual process of deterioration, been lost sight of, and were constantly being replaced by modern models not at all in accord with the symbolism of the ancient forms and colors which play so important a part in ecclesiastical art. Madam Stummel kindly placed her writings [2] at my disposal, permitted me to discuss the subject with her in detail, and assisted me most disinterestedly in every possible way for the purpose of bringing the matter before the readers of the ECCLESIASTICAL REVIEW. In sub-

---

[1] Frau Helene Ludovica Erica Stummel is well known in German art circles, not only by her writings on the subject of paramentics, but also as the organizer and director of a practical School of Design for the production of sacred vestments. She is the wife of Friederich Franz Maria Stummel, whose historic paintings in Berlin, Cologne, Luxemburg and other important centres, have placed him in the foremost rank of the Düsseldorf School· to which Overbeck, Deger, Karl Müller, Ittenbach, and other artistic interpreters of Christian ideals belong. Herder's *Konversations Lexikon,* which speaks of his works, also mention the merits of Helene Stummel as an exponent of paramentic art. These merits have been recognized not only throughout Germany and Austria, but likewise in England, Belgium, and Italy. The Sovereign Pontiff, Pius X, recently evinced his appreciation of her labors by decorating her with the medal *Pro Ecclesia et Pontifice.*

[2] *Die Paramentik vom Standpunkte des Geschmackes und Kunstsimels;* Kevelaer: Jos. Thum. *Die Paramentik.* A series of Essays in " Stimmen ausden Missionen." Pfaffendorf. Also essays in " Pastor Bonus," Trier, and " Die christliche Frau," Freiburg. ·

mitting the results of my inquiries to the American and English-speaking clergy I entertain the hope that the suggestions here offered, imperfect as they are, may stimulate others more gifted in this direction to devote their talents to the cause of restoring the proper kind and use of paramentics in the glorious service of our churches and to the honor of religion.

Whilst it must be conceded that, during the last fifty or sixty years, thanks to the efforts of men like Montalembert in France, of Pugin, Morris, and in a measure also of Ruskin, in England, of August Reichensperger and others in Germany, much progress has been made toward purifying the aims of Christian art in its various departments, the one branch of paramentics, which is intimately bound up with the divine service and which is so important a factor in all public worship, has been seriously neglected. Christian artists have hardly given it a thought, and as a result it has completely fallen a prey to that enemy of all true art—*commercialism.* The introduction of machine methods with their mechanical reproductions has supplanted the delicate ingenuity of the Christian mind, and prevented the employment of that fine artistic sensitiveness of the human hand which is capable of giving to a work the simple esthetic yet rare character so much admired in medieval embroidery. Furthermore, commercial speculation, by employing every mechanical device of modern machinery, has debased the quality of materials for church goods and lowered them to the level of ordinary and cheap articles of fashion or domestic wear.

Commercialism in the production of art, and mercenary speculation by which the material used in the manufacture of church goods has gradually deteriorated, were however not the only causes which lowered the standard formerly maintained for the making of vestments. There was a third element which contributed to the degrading process, and which caused a setting aside of the true liturgical colors, and brought about a substitution of an entirely false composition in symbolical arrangement and meaning, and in artistic taste. This deterioration arose, strangely enough, from the excessive application of scientific research to the sphere of art, and created a chronic disease of bad taste in color.[3] This somewhat ab-

[3] Cf. *Die Paramentik*, by H. Stummel, p. 18.

normal perversion of taste proceeded from an attempt to establish a harmony of colors based upon the phenomenon of the so-called spectral analysis; that is, the decomposition of the white light of the sun when seen through a prism. Scientific analysis, which takes no account of the actual productions of the old masters in art, necessarily drew false conclusions regarding the value of colors apart from their appearance through the solar spectrum. The colors of the spectrum are presented to us as something so absolutely pure that no existing pigment or dye can possibly attain to their sharpness, distinctness, and purity of tint. The fact is, there are no pure colors in nature. The white, red, blue, or yellowish colors of light as they pass through the ether are neutralized or dulled, so as to soften and blend the colors of individual objects, thereby also bringing them nearer to each other. This is what the Germans, in speaking of art, call *Stimmung,* that is to say, a harmonizing or attuning of the various tints into one concordant whole. Thus we speak of the blueish moonlight and the golden noon-day sun. Steeped in this neutral tone each color loses in sharp definition what it gains in harmony and affinity with other colors. And just as the pure, undiluted colors of the solar spectrum cannot be found in nature, so are they all wanting in classical art. If we examine the rare Persian and Gothic tapestries preserved in the South Kensington Museum, or the paintings of the old-master schools represented by Van Eyck and Rubens, or the superb mosaics of Venice, Ravenna, and Aix la Chapelle, we shall find this blending of analytically separable and scientifically distinct colors. The same principle is applied to the colors employed in the making of vestments. One of the most notable examples of perfect color combination is to be found in the collection of *paramenta* in the Musée Cluny of Paris. Here red is made use of to produce the greatest color effect, and it inclines most often to the terra cotta, the yellowish red. Naples yellow and ochre yellow produce good light effects. Green and purple appear only as mixed colors, mild and soft; green in the brighter hues, inclining to the yellowish; whilst in the darker hues it is almost a blunt blue. Purple often appears as a plum brown, or reddish gray, with sometimes a warmer, sometimes a colder-toning. Blue resembles indigo, the color of the sky at night, and always appears as a soft, blended tone, with which brown and black naturally harmonize. Whether the one or the other of these colors predominate as the fundamental tone of the accord, the result is always perfect harmony, so as to produce an impression of tranquillity and peace in the beholder.

In the accompanying illustration (Plate I, Number 1) we have a reproduction of the color scale to which I have reference. There is nothing glaring, blazing, obtrusive about these colors and tones. Yet they present a richness, fulness, and clearness despite the subduing glow which pervades the whole. In No. 2 (Plate I) we have on the other hand a sharp, loud and obtrusive color scheme, creating a sense of irritation in the beholder. Yet these latter colors, both inartistic and untrue to nature and symbolic truth, are the ones which we find most frequently reproduced in the vestments of the day. They are the colors of the spectrum produced by means of chemical dyes.

Great changes in the art of dyeing have been caused by the discovery of what are known as the aniline dyes. The author of *Arts and Crafts Essays* states that their discovery, while conferring a great boon on the science of chemistry, and while doing great service to capitalists in their hunt after profits, has greatly injured the art of dyeing, and caused an absolute divorce between the *commercial process* and the *art* of dyeing. Any one desirous of producing dyed textiles with artistic quality in them must entirely forego the modern and commerical methods, and adopt those which are at least as old as Pliny, who speaks of them as being old in his time. In another essay [4] Mr. Morris speaks in the following terms of the process of dyeing with aniline: " A hundred years ago the processes for printing on cloth differed little from those used by the Indians and Persians; and even up to within forty years ago they produced colors that in themselves were good enough, however inartistically they might be used. Then came one of the most wonderful and most useless of the inventions of modern chemistry, that of the dyes made from coal-tar, producing a series of hideous colors, crude, livid—and cheap—which every person of taste loathes, but which never-

[4] "Textiles" in *Arts and Crafts Essays*, p. 33.

theless we can by no means get rid of until we are able to struggle successfully against the doom of cheap and nasty which has overtaken us." [5]

One word more about the old dyes and their artistic and economic value. "They all make in their simplest forms beautiful colors; they need no muddling into artistic usefulness when you need your colors bright, and they can be modified and toned without dirtying, as the foul blotches of the capitalist dyer cannot be. Like all dyes, they are not eternal; the sun in lighting them and beautifying them consumes them; yet gradually, and for the most part kindly. These colors in fading still remain beautiful, and never, even after long wear, pass into nothingness, through that stage of livid ugliness which distinguishes the commercial dyes as nuisances, even more than their short and by no means merry life." [6] Of the greatest importance for paramentics is the fact noted by Mr. Morris, that no textiles dyed blue or green, otherwise than by indigo, keep an agreeable color by candlelight; many quite bright greens turning into sheer drab. Under this head is to be classed a certain commercial green known as "gas-green" which has found its way into our liturgical colors and is much in vogue.

About the middle of the last century it began to be generally recognized by churchmen that the later "baroque" textiles, with their fantastic, often quite Japanese patterns or unsightly flower-bouquets, were in no wise suited to the sincerity of the divine service or the grave and earnest spirit of the Church. Apart from the unnaturalness of color and form, it was true that the liturgical rules relating to the color and shape of vestments and especially to their symbolism had been arbitrarily set at naught.

To remedy these abuses the Sacred Congregation of Rites issued a decree which directed attention to a more careful observance of the Rubrics of the Roman Missal in regard to the color of the vestments,[7] and forbade such combinations of

[5] In Persia the importation of aniline colors is strictly prohibited. Cf. H. Stummel, "Freude an schönen Stoffen" in *Jahrbuch für Aesthetische Kultur.* Trier, 1908.

[6] Morris: *Of Dyeing as an Art.*

[7] "Servetur strictim rubrica quoad colorem paramentorum." (S. R. C. 12 Nov., 1831.)

colors as made it difficult* or impossible to distinguish a primary and ground color.[8] By an arbitrary and thus mistaken reform movement which adopted the latest conquests of science—the colors of the spectrum and the aniline dyes to reproduce them—a new but mischievous standard of uniformity came into vogue. In place of the typical liturgical colors formerly in use, the reformers took their standard from the color-scale of the spectrum, and in conformity with this scale they began to manufacture the materials for church vestments and their ornamentation. Samples of the material were sent to all parts of the Catholic world as representing "church goods in liturgical colors", and thus arose the catchword "liturgical colors", which has been misleading the representatives of the paramental art throughout Europe.[9]

If any one is disposed to doubt that the color of the vast majority of our vestments is inharmonious, let him place a modern vestment beside a medieval one, no matter of what century; one glance will convince him. Indeed if we wished to apply a practical test, let us ask any woman of taste to wear a dress made in what are called liturgical colors; she would at once reject the fabric as being unnatural in color. Among what are called or rather miscalled "liturgical" colors in our church goods' catalogues, the greens and purples are especially offensive to any one who has true artistic perception. This we come to realize more keenly when we read the beautiful explanations of the symbolism of the liturgical colors to be found in the writings of such authors as St. Bernard, St. Bonaventure,[10] Cornelius à Lapide,[11] Gihr[12] and others. Of green Gihr says: " Green holds a middle place between the strong and weak colors; hence it is the most refreshing and gratifying to the eyes. When Spring awakens, woods and meadows, hills and valleys germinate and sprout and blossom and diffuse their odorous breath far and wide; all nature unfolds new life and growth, clothes herself in fresh, lovely green, and holds out the hope of a rich harvest. Green is the

[8] S. R. C., 23 Sept., 1837. Cf. Gihr, *The Holy Sacrifice of the Mass.* 6th. Ger. ed., p. 270.

[9] H. Stummel, *Die Paramentik,* p. 25.

[10] S. Bonav, *Vitis Mystica,* c. 17-22.

[11] In Apoc. 7, 9.

[12] L. c., pp. 272-284.

symbol of hope. Green is in harmony with the very nature of the Church—she is a mighty tree, which lifts its top majestically toward heaven, spreads its shady branches and leaves in benediction over the earth, resplendent with the richest blossoms, bringing forth choice fruits of grace and virtue [13] in abundance. She is the watered garden of the Lord; Christ, the good shepherd, leads his sheep to ever green pastures. The Church clothes herself in green vestments to express her joyous, lively hope of the ever lovely and eternally verdant meadows of the heavenly paradise,[14] of the incorruptible inheritance and the unfading crown of glory in Heaven (I Pat., 1, 4, 5)." Now it is impossible to recognize in the rich verdure thus described by the liturgical writers anything like the green of the stuff commonly exhibited by our dealers in church goods, as its flashy and stark obtrusiveness can neither be called refreshing nor gratifying, nor does it remind us of the "ever lovely and eternally verdant meadows". Take a handful of grass or a fresh green bough, or a bit of moss or fern growth, and place it beside a newly ordered green vestment; it will give you a palpable proof of the vast difference between our present "liturgical" green and the pleasingly soft and mild green of the plant world from which the liturgy borrows its color beauty. If on the other hand you compare these products of nature with some well-preserved green vestment of the old times or—which is more to our present purpose—with the reproduction (Plate II, Green) of one of Mrs. Stummel's chasubles, you will find the resemblance striking and pleasing, like the sight of sunlit meadow and shady woodland, all of which indicates the sense of hope and peace or of tranquil gladness.

Regarding the use of purple color in church vestments Gihr says: "Purple, inasmuch as it approaches the sober gray of ashes, suggests the earnest spirit of penance; on the other hand, it also resembles the darker shades of the violet flower (*violaceus* from *viola*), suggestive of that modest retirement which avoids the gaze of men, and hides in the deep valleys and forest recesses, where it blossoms and exhales its fra-

[13] Hence the Church aptly sings in her office "Mentis perustae vulnera munda *virore gratiae*."

[14] Constituat te Christus Filius Dei vivi intra *paradisi sui semper amoena virentia* (Ordo commend. animae.)

grance as if satisfied to do so alone for its Creator. Purple is symbolic of unassuming humility, holy retirement, gentle sorrow of heart, burning longing as if consumed by the silent homesickness and desire for Heaven. Purple, thus in the first instance, expresses sorrow; but not complete and universal sorrow. It is a sorrow and affliction tempered and subdued by hope and confidence like rays of joy entering the shades of this valley of tears." The purple silks and satins, as we find them dyed with aniline according to the custom of manufacturers of vestments during the last fifty or sixty years, will hardly answer to this explanation. There is nothing about them to dispose us to " Gentle sorrow of heart, holy retirement, and unassuming humility ". They are too loud, too self-assertive and aggressive. Surely those who produce such materials and those who tolerate them or even find them appropriate can hardly have studied the purple hues which nature presents to us in such manifold forms. " Before the sun rises, night being already past, the earth reposes under a wonderful veil of purple gray mist, which envelopes every object in awe-inspiring mysteriousness. Then, when day gradually begins to break, the sun throws out its refulgence as it advances in the heavens, and its warm rosy tints reflect, and its rays warm and brighten the purple-gray mist, which slowly retires before the coming light. Thus even this *Morgenstimmung* furnishes us with two shades of purple, the one inclining to the ' dark gray of ashes ', the other to a reddish violet glow like the aurora. Bright daylight reveals the violet, the manifold hues of the pansy, the delicate brown of the mellow plum, the rich light of the clustering grape. Masses of storm-clouds hanging over a slate-quarry form a canopy under which the grandest colors resembling purple satins are displayed, on which the golden darts of lightning swiftly sketch wondrous designs." [15] The author of this new reform, sanctioned and encouraged by the Holy See, has, as is evident from her writings, an eye and a heart for the beautiful colors of nature. Nature has been her school, her text-book, and by following its indications she has been able to produce work that acts as a mirror of God's creation. Compare the purple vestment in Plate III with any of the same

[15] H. Stummel, in *Stimmen aus den Missionen.* No. 13.

color now in use, and you have an object-lesson in what the pretended "liturgical" purple is and what it should be.[16]

But there is another liturgical reason for eliminating aniline green and purple from the color scale of ecclesiastical vestments. According to all approved authorities on liturgy a distinction is to be observed between strong and weak colors used in the sacred worship, to indicate the spirit of the ecclesiastical year. There are in the life of the Church days and seasons of joy and triumph, of hope, fear, affliction, and of deepest mourning. *White* is "the color of light and the symbol of brightness and glory, of heavenly joy, blessedness and transfiguration." White is as such the most important and most prominent color in the liturgical series, and represents the extreme limit of all color in the direction of light. *Red* is the strongest, most lively and most gorgeous of the prismatic colors. It is "the color of fire and blood, and symbolizes the flaming, devouring heat of love which is enkindled in the heart by the Holy Ghost; the victorious love which sacrifices the greatest and dearest earthly possession—life—in martyrdom, and which triumphs in dying."[17] Of green and purple and their symbolism we have already spoken. *Black* marks the extreme boundary line of all colors in the direction of darkness. "It is the color which represents the extinguished light of life and joy, of death and the grave—the symbol, consequently, of the deepest sorrow, and of mourning called forth by death."

It is a commonly received although erroneous idea that the color of the vestments must be loud and blazing in order to be effective. "It depends on what we understand by *effective.* The song of the nightingale is effective; yet it is soft, mild, agreeable whilst still heard at a great distance. The crowing of the 'shrilly' cock is no doubt more obtrusive, yet in the

---

[16] The silk for this chasuble was dyed according to the directions of Madame Stummel, who also had the design made, and supervised the completion of the whole work, which is here accurately copied in plates made in Germany under the lady's personal supervision. It is of course only one of several shades of the true liturgical purple, which whilst it may vary in lightness or depth, is entirely distinct from the "bright" colors of bluish or reddish hue affected by the negro races and by children who are fond of the gaudy. Thus we may have a vestment the purple of which almost approaches the rose color and the liturgical and symbolical significance is truly reflected thereby.

[17] Gihr, l. c.

sense of being agreeable it can hardly be called more effective." [18]

When we have obtained good fabrics in proper colors, the
important question then is the coördinating or grouping of
the different combinations of color employed in the making
of vestments. To assemble different hues of color into a beautiful complex requires judicious and artistic arrangement of
the parts. Now the chief source from which we may draw
a correct standard of judgment in this matter is the book of
Nature. It was in the field, the meadow and the wood that
the ancient Hebrews sought inspiration for designing and
ornamenting the gorgeous vestments of their high-priests.
" As the sun when it shineth, so did Simon, the high priest,
the son of Onias, shine in the temple of God. And as the
rainbow giving light in the bright clouds, and as the flowers
of roses in the days of the spring, and as the lilies that are
on the brink of the waters, as an olive-tree budding forth, and
a cypress-tree itself on high, when he put on the robe of glory,
when he went up to the holy altar." (Ecclus. 50: 6-12.)

And here we may learn something of the order to be observed from the *spectrum* or picture formed by the decomposition of sunlight. In the color-scale of the spectrum each
color has its contrasting color: red has green; blue, orange;
violet, yellow. These pairs of colors are, so to speak, hostile
to each other, and if combined into one produce a shabby
black. In paramentics the color-contrasts of the spectrum are
sure guides, but the colors themselves must be subdued,
blended, i. e. obtained by using artistic vegetable and insect
dyes, not the crude, livid aniline ones; and it must always
be remembered (a fact insisted on at the outset of this
essay [19]) that the absolutely pure and sharp-toned colors of
the spectrum are not found in nature. The effect of these
contrast-colors is far more satisfying if three artistic qualities
are brought to bear on them and the tones to be combined
display the weaker contrasts of *light* and *dark, colored* and
colorless, warm and *cold.*[20] Blue and all grades of blue are
cold. Yellow and all grades of yellow are warm. Red and

[18] H. Stummel: *Die Paramentik*, p. 31.
[19] See Plate I.

Plate III.

green may be warm or cold according to the ground tone. Even without the added charm of embroidery any grouping of colors founded on these contrasts will be beautiful and effective. Of course the size of the surface must be taken into consideration. The medieval chasuble—the only one answering to the Latin name, *planeta*—with its narrow forked-cross, needs no other ornamentation. It is a different matter with the kind of chasuble much used at present, which is made in the shape of a violin-case. To render this sort of vestment at all presentable—no easy matter when we consider its absolutely inartistic shape—it is advisable to keep to one color throughout; a red chasuble, for instance, would then have a red cross well outlined with appropriate borders, and, if possible, tastefully embroidered, and so on.

What has been said thus far must suffice here as an indication of the requirements in color for church vestments. There is something to be said about the character of the ornamentation or embroidering, as also of the shape of the vestments used at the Holy Sacrifice. Of this I expect to treat in a subsequent article.

GEORGE METLAKE.

Cologne, Germany.

THE STORY OF ST. CLARE.

THE story of St. Clare is so intimately entwined with that of St. Francis in popular sentiment and imagination that it seems difficult to think of the one Saint apart from the other. And it is certain that the gentle influence of the Assisian Abbess played no small part in fashioning the life and forwarding the work of the Umbrian *Poverello*. Not only was St. Clare " the chief rival of the Blessed Francis in the ob-

yet so strong, so human and yet so other-worldly—and in that spirit she threw around poverty an ineffable charm such as women alone can impart to religious or civic heroism.   After St. Francis was gone, Clare proved herself the faithful heiress of his ideals, the fearless exponent of his teaching; and when those ideals were in danger of demolition, because some of the disciples of the *Poverello* would fain have tempered his teachings by the dictates of worldly wisdom, it was Clare who struggled to uphold them beyond all the rest.   That struggle lasted more than a quarter of a century: it ended only with her life.   But the victory lay with Clare,[2] whose steadfast striving after an ideal through good report and evil report, no less than her engaging example of "the praying spirit that worked as it prayed", did much to guide the women of her day toward higher aims.

St. Clare called herself the "little flower of St. Francis," [3] and St. Bonaventure tells us that she diffused around her the fragrance of springtide.[4]   Something of that fragrance clings to the story of her life after all these centuries and lends it a special charm.   It is truly one of those lives that can teach perfection without sacrificing poetry.   And, in so far as it may be allowable to associate romance with such a subject, the friendship of St. Francis and St. Clare forms one of the most romantic chapters in the Lives of the Saints.   For more than one reason, then, the story of St. Clare opens up a page of medieval biography full of import and pathetic interest even for those who are not especially students of the Franciscan Legend.

It cannot, however, be concealed that the personality of St. Clare is in some sort as elusive as it is winsome.   Easy as it is to grasp the main and deeper lines of her life-story, a detailed study of it is beset with no small difficulty.   This difficulty seems to arise largely, if not chiefly, from the fact that there are very few documents extant bearing on the subject that can be relied upon.   Indeed, it may be said that the

---

[2] Only the day before her death did St. Clare succeed in obtaining the Papal Bull in which the Poverty Francis had sought and taught was sanctioned in all its pristine purity.

[3] See her Rule—" Regula Sororum Pauperum " in *Seraphicae Legislationis Textus Originales* (Quaracchi, 1897) p. 52.

[4] See *Legenda Major S. Francisci* (Ed. Quaracchi, 1898) p. 37.

sources of our knowledge as to St. Clare are scanty in proportion as they are abundant in the case of St. Francis. And if so little, comparatively speaking, has been written of late years about St. Clare and the beginnings of her Order, notwithstanding the widespread interest in the early Franciscan movement which has been such a marked feature of recent literature, it is due mainly to the dearth of information we possess in her regard.

This lack of material, be it ever so regrettable, is not altogether surprising. It is not so much that the life of St. Clare was overshadowed by that of St. Francis, as a recent writer has contended,[5] as that it was in great measure a hidden one. There is no good reason to believe that she ever once stepped beyond the threshold of San Damiano from the time of her instalment there in or about 1212 up to her death some forty-one years afterwards.[6] With St. Francis it was far otherwise. He lived almost continually, so to say, in the public eye closely followed in all his journeyings by observant chroniclers. It is not, therefore, to be wondered at if contemporary writers have left us such a complete record of the doings and sayings of the *Poverello,* and such a meagre account of St. Clare. So far as concerns outward events there was probably little to relate.

Premising this, it may be worth our while to mention the documents from which our knowledge of St. Clare is chiefly drawn. These sources, as they are called, of the Life of St. Clare are few and easily classified. They comprise (1) some fragments of the Saint's correspondence;[7] (2) a Testament attributed to her;[8] (3) some early bulls bearing on her life,[9]

[5] See "The Personality of Clare of Assisi," by the late Sir Home Gordon, Bart in the *Oxford and Cambridge Review* (London, Constable), No. 5, 1908, Michaelmas Term.

[6] It can no longer be concealed that the pretty story told in the *Fioretti* as to how St. Clare and St. Francis ate together at the Porziuncola, is —like many others of that ilk—wholly devoid of historic foundation. It is surely a pity to have to confess this, but the demands of truth are imperative.

[7] Four charming letters to Blessed Agnes, Princess of Bohemia, who founded a monastery of the Clares at Prague, are all that remain to us. They are given by the Bollandists, *Acta SS.,* Martii I, pp. 505-507.

[8] It may be found in the *Seraphicae Legislationis Textus Originales,* pp. 273-280.

[9] These Papal documents, which include the famous *Privilegium Paupertatis,* the definitive approbation of the Rule of St. Clare, and the Bull of Clare's canonization, are printed in the *Bullarium Franciscanum* of Sbaralea, tt. I and II, passim.

and (4) a contemporary biography.[10]   If we except such occasional references to St. Clare as occur in the early lives of
St. Francis,[11] these are the only sources, properly so called,
of the history of St. Clare now at the disposal of students.
This is no place in which to discuss the critical questions connected with these sources.   Succinctly stated, one finds nothing or next to nothing in St. Clare's letters to the Princess
Agnes which throws any light upon her life.   On the other
hand allusions to her vocation and the beginnings of her
Order are not wanting in the Testament which has come down
to us under her name.   It is only fair to state that the authenticity of this latter document has been called into question.
But it seems safe, on the whole, to say that it may well be
the handiwork of the Saint.   It is no easy task to thread one's
way through the early bulls touching the life of St. Clare
that are scattered through the first two weighty tomes of the
Franciscan Bullary, and it requires a patient spirit of research
to disentangle the complicated early history of her Rule which
these documents unfold.   Concerning the contemporary biography of St. Clare it is enough to say that its author withheld
his name and that at an early stage of its existence this life
passed into the *mare magnum,* as it has been called, of Franciscan anonymity.   By and by St. Bonaventure came to be accredited with its paternity, but it is now quite clear that the
work never emanated from the gifted and prolific pen of the
Seraphic Doctor, and most modern critics are agreed in
ascribing this contemporary biography to Thomas of Celano,
the famous first biographer of St. Francis and the reputed
author of the *Dies irae.*   Be this as it may, it was evidently
written on the very morrow of St. Clare's death, and, in so far
as it represents the collected impressions of the Saint's companions, it is more surely her *vera effigies* than any later work
can ever be.   Moreover, it gains an additional interest as being
the earliest attempt to give a presentment of the Saint in
writing.   It is to this biography, then, taken in conjunction
with St. Clare's own writings and the early bulls touching her
life, that all subsequent works on the subject bear back.   From

---

[10] Edited by the Bollandists, *Acta SS.,* Aug. 11, (12 Aug.), pp. 754-768.

[11] See for example *I Cel.,* 18, 19, 116, 118; *II Cel.,* 204-206; *Tres Socii,*
CXIV, No. 60; Bonav. *Leg. Maj.,* IV, n. 6, p. 37.

these three sources the ground-work of our knowledge of St. Clare is derived.

It is well known, however, that not all the early documents bearing upon the Saint's life have come down to us. For example, only a fragment of the rule of life which St. Francis gave to Clare at the beginning of her religious life is known to exist, and of the "many writings" which the *Poverello* addressed to the Clares [12] not more than a few lines have survived.[13] The Canticles he composed for the Sisters of St. Clare and the last blessing he sent them in writing [14] and other manuscripts of equal importance for the life of St. Clare have likewise perished or at least disappeared.

But how, it may be asked, did the Poor Clares ever suffer documents such as these to pass out of their hands? This question calls for a brief digression. It is enough for us to recall that the Chapter General of the Friars Minor, assembled at Paris in 1266, ordered that the "Ancient Legend" [15] should no longer be read and should to the utmost of the power of all the Friars be destroyed.[16] There have been some differences of opinion as to the precise aim of this ordination.[17] There can unfortunately be no doubt as to its effects: it resulted in a desperate war being waged upon all the early Franciscan documents, especially those which were known to relate to St. Francis's will as to the observance of Poverty.

---

[12] "Scripsit nobis formam vivendi . . . et plura scripta nobis tradidit." Testamentum B. Clarae, l. c., p. 276.

[13] These lines owe their preservation to the fact that St. Clare inserted them in the definite Rule of her Order, confirmed the day before she died.

[14] See *Spec. Perfectionis* (Ed. Sabatier), p. 180 and p. 215.

[15] Under this title the authorities of the Order appear to have comprised a collection of the primitive biographies of St. Francis, as opposed to the "New Legend" composed by St. Bonaventure in 1263. See *Speculum Perfectionis* (Ed. Sabatier), p. CLXII.

[16] The text of this decree is as follows: "Praecipit Generale Capitulum per obedientiam quod omnes legendae de beato Francisco olim factae deleantur et, ubi inveniri poterunt extra ordinem, ipsas fratres studeant amovere" etc. See Ehrle *Die ältesten Redactionen der Generalconstitutionen des Franziskanerordens* in *Archiv.* (1892), p. 39; also Little, *Decrees of the Chapters General of the Friars Minor 1260-1282* in *Eng. Hist. Rev.*, t. XIII (1898) pp. 704-8.

[17] Its aim was no doubt the controversy then ravaging the Order as to the observance of the Rule, but see Van Ortroy, S.J., in *Anal. Boll.*, t. XVIII, p. 174; Lemmens, *Doc. Ant. Franciscana*, pars II, p. 11; Ed. d'Alençon in *Études Franciscaines*, t. I, p. 656; Faloci in *Misc. Franc.*, t. VII, p. 159; Little in *Eng. Hist. Rev.*, Oct., 1902, p. 651.

It was doubtless about this time that Brother Leo, as we learn from Ubertino da Casale, confided his famous *rotuli* and *ceduli* for safe keeping to the care of the nuns in the Monastery of S. Chiara at Assisi and in order to save them to posterity.[18] Ubertino tells us, however, that "to his great grief" these manuscripts of Leo had been "partly scattered" and "perhaps lost, at least many of them".[19] And this fact seems to furnish a valuable clue to the disappearance of some, at least, of the Clares' documents also. For, relating as these documents did in part to the question of Poverty, they would have been no less exposed than Leo's *scripta* to the attempts of the abbettors of laxity. Apart from this consideration, if we take into account the vicissitudes through which the Monastery of S. Chiara at Assisi—not to mention other less fortunate foundations—has passed during the six and a half centuries of its existence, the wonder is rather that the nuns there have succeeded in saving any of their early documents at all. Only those who have been privileged to read a touching MS. chronicle of *Memorie* preserved in the archive and written at different periods by religious who had witnessed what they record, can form any idea of what the community at S. Chiara had to suffer in consequence of oft-recurring wars and revolutions. More than once within the last hundred years the religious have been brutally expelled without being allowed to take anything, whilst their monastery was pillaged and turned over to the soldiers as a barracks or the cells were let out as lodgings. Who can tell how many a precious volume and manuscript may have perished in this way? In any event, it may be affirmed that the Clares at Assisi are in no wise accountable for the loss of their early documents bearing on the life of St. Clare and the history of their Order. Throughout the history of the monastery of S. Chiara its archive has been guarded with jealous care,[20] and when no other means of saving the treasures remained, the nuns hid them not less wisely than well. Witness the pious ruse by

---

[18] Ubertino's testimony on this point may be found in his remarkable book, *Arbor Vitae Crucifixae Jesu*, which he composed on Mount La Verna in 1305. See the edition printed at Venice, 1485, lib. V, c. 5, fol. E III r. a.

[19] *Arbor Vitae* l. c.

[20] The same is true, as a whole, of the other early monasteries of the Clares I have visited at Spello, Foligno, Perugia, and elsewhere.

which the original Bull of Innocent IV confirming the Rule of St. Clare was preserved. This precious document, which for centuries was thought to have been lost, was found by the abbess in the spring of 1893 at the Monastery of S. Chiara wrapped inside an old habit of the Saint!

The belated recovery of this important Bull awakened considerable interest not only for its own sake but also because it led to the hope that some other missing documents of the early times might also be hidden at S. Chiara, awaiting, as it were, to be discovered. That such is not the case may now be positively affirmed. In January of 1908 the present writer, having obtained the necessary leave to enter within the *clausura* at S. Chiara, made a minute and protracted examination of the archive there and of every other nook and corner on the premises likely to conceal aught of interest, sounding the very walls lest perchance—as not infrequently happens—some hidden treasure might be secreted behind them. The Breviary of St. Francis which his companions Leo and Angelo committed to the nuns at S. Chiara for safe keeping, besides many other interesting relics, are there, but in vain I looked for any trace of the MSS. which Leo confided to their care or for any of the much-desired early documents bearing upon the history of St. Clare. Of a truth, I was hardly so sanguine as to expect to find them. Indeed it was not so much by the hope of finding the documents in question that I was led to make the search at S. Chiara as by the desire of setting at rest once for all the mooted question as to the probability of some at least of the missing documents being hidden in that monastery. My quest of documents there also served to disclose the existence of many interesting early bulls and other "pergamena", some of these yet unpublished.[21] It may be added that, thanks to the courtesy of Mgr. Tini, Vicar General of Assisi, I was able to make sure that no early MSS. touching the history of St. Clare lie lurking in the archives of the Cathedral of S. Rufino either. In the hope that some clue to certain of these documents might perhaps be found in the episcopal archives of Spoleto, I also visited that ancient city, but upon being informed by the Vicar General,

---

[21] I have since published a list of them: See the "Inventarium omnium documentorum quae in archivo Proto-Monasterii S. Clarae Assisiensis nunc asservantur," in the *Arch. Fran. Hist.*, an I (1908), fasc. II—III, pp. 413-432.

Mgr. Faloci-Pulignani—who is also editor of the *Miscellanea Francescana*—that there were no documents there of any kind earlier than the Council of Trent (1546) I reluctantly abandoned the search. Although the ceaseless search for Franciscan documents which has been pursued so eagerly for several years past has not tended to throw any new light upon the life of St. Clare, I yet cherish the humble hope that it may lead to the discovery of some fresh materials bearing on the subject. In the meantime the materials at our disposal, albeit incomplete, are sufficient to enable us to form a clear outline of St. Clare's life and character.

She was reared in an atmosphere of religion and her childhood was one of precocious yet engaging piety. The first event of public interest in her life took place during the Lent of 1212. St. Francis was then preaching at the Church of San Giorgio in Assisi. Deeply moved by his " words of spirit and life " Clare felt that the " Master had come and was calling to her ". She gave her heart to Francis and he in turn consecrated it to God. There are few more dramatic pages in any biography than Clare's midnight flight from her father's house toward an unknown future. Having forced her way through a walled-up door [22] she hurried out of the slumbering town and across the intervening fields even down to the tiny chapel of the Porziuncola in the plain below; as she drew to it the *Poverello* and his companions advanced to meet her bearing flickering torches, and Francis, having cut off her hair, clothed her with the coarse, beast-colored tunic and knotted cord worn by Francis and his Friars. Then and there the grand old Order of the Poor Clares, in whose bosom there now repose so many generations of Saints, was founded, however unconsciously, through this brave, venturesome, even reckless, act of one frail young girl. Clare was not yet eighteen when she underwent this great spiritual crisis called her " conversion ".

The first of the " weaker sex " to embrace the new mode of life marked out by the *Poverello,* Clare was destined to become the " valiant woman " of the early Franciscan movement. In some respects, perhaps, Clare was even more virile than Francis

[22] In old Assisi the door of a house through which a dead body had been carried out used, it appears, to be walled-up and was known as a " porta di mortuccio." Many vestiges of this usage still remain.

himself. Witness, for example, her interview with Gregory IX at San Damiano. The venerable Pontiff, who regarded absolute poverty as impossible for cloistered women, visited Clare and urged her to accept some possessions for her community. "If it is your vow that hinders you from doing so," he added, "we absolve you from it." "Holy Father," replied the gentle abbess, "absolve me from my sins if you will, but I desire not to be absolved from following Jesus Christ." [23] Clare's conduct on that occasion was hardly less heroic than when single-handed she routed the band of Saracen mercenaries who had scaled the walls of San Damiano. Nor was that the first time she had faced men without flinching and vanquished them.

But with all her strength of will Clare had a woman's tenderness and she showed it in a woman's way. Thus we read that when the nights were cold Clare was wont to go through the dormitory at San Damiano's and to put warmer covering over such sisters as seemed to be ill-protected against the rigors of winter. This tenderer side of the Saint's character is portrayed by her contemporary biographer no less charmingly than the empire she exercised over the hearts of her spiritual children. Brave and cheerful to the last, Clare, in spite of her protracted and painful infirmities, caused herself to be propped up in bed so that she might continue to spin altar-linen for the poor churches among the Umbrian hills. And when during an access of suffering Cardinal Rainaldo exhorted her to patience, Clare replied, "Believe me, dear brother, that ever since the day I received the grace of vocation from our Lord through His servant St. Francis, no suffering has ever troubled me, no penance has been too hard, no infirmity too great." Nothing truly is more touching in the Saint's later life than this her unfaltering devotion to the memory of Francis. Then, as in the heyday of her girlish enthusiasm when his preaching first touched her young heart, Francis was, after God, the master light of all her seeing. [24]

[23] Pope Gregory yielded and so far gave away to Clare's views as to grant her the celebrated "Privilegium Paupertatis," by virtue of which she might never be constrained to receive any possessions whatsoever. The original of this precious document is preserved at the monastery of St. Chiara in Assisi, and I have been courteously permitted by the abbess to photograph it.

[24] "Erat columna nostra," she says in her will, "unica consolatio post Deum et firmamentum." See Testament. B. Clarae, in *Seraph. Legis. Text. Orig.*, p. 276.

And it was fitting that the early companions of Francis should be with her as she lay dying at San Damiano to read aloud the Passion of our Lord according to St. John, even as they had done twenty-seven years before when Francis was led away from earth by " Sister Death ".

Such, in briefest outline, are some of the salient traits of Clare's life and character as portrayed in the early documents, and so taking are they that one is eager to learn more about her. To meet this demand later biographers of the Saint have felt justified in drawing upon other sources and even, it is to be feared, on their imagination.[25] This method of hagiology, however desirable for the purpose of edification, can never, in the long run, do aught but harm, since it tends to change and deform the figure of Clare. I would be the last to disparage any of the " Lives " of the Saint written by Italians, Spaniards, or Frenchmen of note, which have enjoyed indeed a certain vogue on the Continent.[26] Doubtless these works have all served a useful purpose in their day. But the atmosphere which pervades them is scarcely that of history, and they are all sadly spoilt by insufficient knowledge of the original sources. In spite of the marked improvement in this respect noticeable in the monograph of Father Leopold de Chérancé,[27] and the larger work since edited by the French Colettines,[28] there is up to the present no life of St. Clare in circulation which seeks to portray the Saint as she appeared to her contemporaries. That seems to be what is most needed. May the forthcoming celebration of the seventh centenary of the foundation of the Poor Clares start such a work on its way !

Fr. Paschal Robinson, O.F.M.

Franciscan Convent, Washington, D. C.

[25] Witness, for example, the elaborate yet wholly fabulous pedigree with which they have burdened St. Clare and which one is surprised to find resuscitated by Jorgensen.

[26] Perhaps the best known of these lives are these of Giuseppe da Madrid (Rome, 1832), Locatelli (Assisi, 1854), Demore (Paris, 1856; new German translation by Schmid, Ratisbon, 1906), Richard (Paris, 1895), etc.

[27] *Sainte Claire d'Assise;* Paris, Poussielgue, 1902, pp. xiv-253.

[28] *Histoire de l'Ordre de Sainte Claire,* Lyons, 1908.

THE TRIBUNALS OF THE ROMAN CURIA.

II. The Sacred Roman Rota.

FROM early times the Roman Pontiff was accustomed to appoint chaplains whom he commissioned to examine certain causes. At first these chaplains were wont by *hearing* evidence to take informations and then to make a report to the Sovereign Pontiff, who would himself give the decision. For this reason they were called *Auditores,* not being yet empowered to decide cases. When afterwards they received additional authority to enable them to give judgment, the former name or title (*Auditores*) was retained.

Why the term *Rota* was employed to designate this Tribunal has been the subject of controversy. The most probable opinion appears to be that a revolving stand (*Rota*) was used, on which were kept legal documents frequently consulted by the *Auditores.* Another opinion is that this Tribunal was so called because the judges were accustomed to sit at a *round* table; some, too, thought that the name was given because the judges delivered their opinion in *rotation.*

These judges constituted a college and were called *Auditores causarum sacri palatii apostolici.* Nicholas IV (1288-1292) appointed some judges to take charge of civil suits for the Papal dominions; Clement V (1305-1314) instituted an independent court for ecclesiastical cases. These two courts were afterwards merged into one. John XXII in his Constitution, *Ratio juris* (1331), issued certain ordinances, regulating the rights of Auditors of the Rota and prescribing the form of oath to be taken by them. At one time there were as many as twenty Auditors of the Rota, but the number was fixed at twelve by Sixtus IV in 1472. The head of the Rotal College was called the Dean, whose duty it was to preside at general meetings and to exercise supervision over the other officials of the institution.

FORMER COMPETENCE OF THE ROTA.

This Tribunal at first took cognizance of only those cases which by special commission of the Sovereign Pontiff were assigned to it. Afterwards two classes of cases became the customary matter of its jurisdiction, viz. litigious cases of a spiritual character, such as benefices, and civil cases arising within the Pontifical Territory. At no time was it usual for this Tribunal to be occupied with criminal proceedings. After the institution of the Roman Congregations, the labors of the Sacred Rota, which had reached their climax in the fifteenth century, began to diminish notably. The chief reason for this diminution of its functions was that the Roman Congregations acquired authority to decide questions upon matters which had previously belonged to the competence of the Rota. Then, since 1870, when the Roman Pontiff was robbed of all his temporal possessions, there were no longer any purely civil cases to be tried by this tribunal. Hence in recent times the *Auditores* of the Rota, since they no longer had their former work to perform, were assigned to other employment; in particular, they have assisted the S. Congregation of Rites, being made judges of validity in the apostolic processes of canonization and beatification.

PRESENT POSITION OF THE ROTA.

We shall best understand the changes effected in the Sacred Roman Rota by a study of the words of the New Constitution, *Sapienti consilio,* indicating those changes. " As the Tribunal of the Sacred Roman Rota, which in former times was an object of universal praise, has in these times through various causes almost ceased to judge, the result has been that the Sacred Congregations have been burdened excessively with forensic cases. To meet this evil, following the lines laid down by our predecessors, Sixtus V, Innocent XII, and Pius VI, we not only ordain ' that for the future contentious cases, civil as well as criminal, requiring judicial procedure with trial and proofs, shall not be received or taken cognizance of by the Sacred Congregations ';[1] but we moreover decree that all contentious cases, not major ones, which are treated in the Roman Curia, shall for the future devolve to the Tribunal of the Sacred Rota, which we do by these Letters again call into exercise according to the *Special Law* which we place in the appendix of the present Constitution, without prejudice, however, to the rights of the Sacred Congregations as above set forth."

[1] Letter of the Secretariate of State, 17 April, 1728.

In the foregoing words the Sovereign Pontiff alludes to the cause of the new legislation regarding the Roman Rota. The Sacred Congregations, as distinct from the other departments of the Roman Curia, were overcrowded with business, owing to their treating many cases in forensic manner. Various Pontiffs endeavored to remedy this inconvenience: especially, Sixtus V (1585-1590), Innocent XII (1691-1700), and Pius VI (1775-1779). Now the present Sovereign Pontiff, Pius X, makes two definite enactments, the one prohibitive, the other affirmative. The Roman Congregations are no longer permited to try any cases according to judicial process, whether civil or criminal. The affirmative enactment is that all contentious cases which are not *major* and which are to be treated according to judicial process in the Roman Curia, belong exclusively to the tribunal of the Sacred Roman Rota. Besides, the Roman Pontiff lays down that this tribunal of the Rota is to be regulated by certain statutes which are termed *Lex Propria,* Special Law, published as an appendix to the Constitution, *Sapienti consilio.*

LEX PROPRIA.

The *Lex Propria,* to which allusion is here made, consists, so far as relates to the Rota, of three chapters, treating respectively of the constitution, competence, and mode of procedure. We shall give here a brief summary of the enactments contained in these chapters, leaving the reader to study for himself the text as published in the *Acta Apostolicae Sedis* (20-29).

The Constitution of the New Rota.

to the priesthood sits in the first place after the Dean. When the Deanship of the Rota becomes vacant, that Auditor succeeds to the office of Dean who has held the first place after the Dean. Each Auditor appoints an assistant for himself with the approval of the Rotal College and the consent of the Sovereign Pontiff: each assistant retains his office at the will of his Auditor. The Sacred Rota must also have a Promoter of Justice and likewise a Defender of the sacred bond of marriage, of religious profession and of sacred ordination. These officials must be priests, Doctors of Theology and of Canon Law, appointed by the Pope on the recommendation of the Rotal College. Notaries are to be appointed after concursus by the Rotal College, and the appointment is to be confirmed by the Roman Pontiff. As many Notaries as will be required are to be thus appointed: two of them at least must be priests, who alone are to perform the duties of Notaries in criminal cases of clerics and religious. Each Auditor after nomination, before assuming his office, must take an oath in presence of the whole College and of one of the Notaries to fulfil his duties with fidelity. Each assistant will take a similar oath as will also the other officials of the Tribunal, in presence of the Dean and of one of the Notaries. The Auditors, assistants, and other officials are bound to secrecy in the performance of their respective duties: if they violate this obligation or cause grave detriment to litigants through negligence or fraud, they are bound to pay damages. The Rota gives its decisions in one of two forms, either through a commission of three Auditors, or through the full College, unless the Sovereign Pontiff otherwise ordain for a particular case.

Competence of the Holy Roman Rota.

The competence of this Tribunal is set forth in four canons (14-17) of the *Lex Propria*. It decides in the first instance those cases committed to it by the Roman Pontiff, acting either *motu proprio,* or at the petition of the contesting parties; it also decides such cases as have been tried judicially by Ordinaries in the first or second instance and are legitimately appealed. Besides, it settles in the last instance cases already decided in the first or second instance by Ordinaries or by any other tribunal, when the causes have not passed into *res judicatae* and are legitimately appealed to the Holy See.

Limitation of Jurisdiction.

What are termed *Causae majores,* on account of their object or of the persons concerned in them, are excluded from the authority of this Tribunal. It is not here proposed to mention in detail all the causes which are to be held as *majores,* and over which, therefore, the S. R. Rota has no jurisdiction. Let it suffice to say that they refer to questions of more than ordinary moment, such as matters of doctrine, the general discipline of the Church, beatification and canonization of saints, approbation of Religious Orders, creation of episcopal sees, the union or dismemberment of dioceses, the appointment, transfer, or deposition of bishops. There is another class of causes in which this tribunal of the Rota possesses no authority, viz. when Ordinaries give decisions without observance of judicial procedure, there can be no appeal to the Roman Rota; such questions are to be brought before one of the Roman Congregations according to the character of the matter in dispute. If this Tribunal were to examine even incidentally into questions of either class and pronounce sentence, the sentence would be *ipso jure* null.

Method of Judicial Procedure.

This portion of the subject is minutely set forth in canons 18-34 of the *Lex Propria,* so that the reader may safely see for himself what is permitted and required on the part of litigants, plaintiff, and defendant; what the Judges may allow or must prohibit. Each contestant may plead his own cause or he may engage the services of a procurator or advocate. There must be a statement of the case in writing. No oral informations are allowed: nor is there any oratorical effort permitted to either party in the suit. Sometimes, however, leave is given for special reason to speak to the Bench of Auditors. Limitations are placed regarding the time allowed for answering the statement of each litigant, as also regarding the length of such answers, while the Judges are vested with authority to deviate for just reason from those limitations. The Auditors meet on an appointed day for a secret discussion of the case. Each one brings his vote in a written opinion, which contains not only the conclusions he has arrived at, but also the proofs, whether of law or of fact. In this discussion an Auditor may recede from his conclusion, if he think it just and necessary. The sentence of the Court is that of an absolute majority of the Auditors present, so that in the ordinary bench of three Auditors, two votes are sufficient and necessary for a valid sentence. The reader may here be left to study the statutes on the Procedure of the Rota. He cannot fail to be convinced that these statutes are marked with great consideration for the common good and that nothing has been left undone to procure full justice for the contending parties.

M. MARTIN, S.J.

St. Louis University.

[TO BE CONTINUED.]

FATHER ERIC WASMANN, S. J.—MODERN BIOLOGIST.

DARWINISM never enjoyed the vogue in Germany that it obtained in England. Indeed it may be well to recall that it was only in English-speaking countries that natural selection as an explanation of evolution—Darwinism in the true sense—made its way successfully. Among other nations, however, it attracted wide attention, but received only scattered acceptance, and that as a rule not from the greatest among the scientists of the period. France was quite antipathetic; but above all Germany furnished the typical example of refusal on the part of the great discoverers in the biological sciences to accept Darwinism at anything like English values. Almost as a unit the distingusihed German biologists of the past two generations were not Darwinians. They rejected the new theory entirely or accepted it only with many modifications and limitations. This is so different from what is usually supposed to have been the case—for ordinarily it has been assumed that Darwinism met with practically universal acceptance from teachers of biology all over the world—that some details of the real situation deserve to be mentioned.

Of the great biological workers in Germany who were contemporaries of Darwin practically no one accepted the teaching of natural selection as an important process in biology. Some slight influence they admitted that it had, but it was of no weight for the essential problems of evolution. A leader among the men who took this stand with regard to Darwinism was Virchow, one of the greatest of the German biologists of the nineteenth century, the father of modern Pathology, and in his time one of the greatest of living anthropologists. He had been deeply interested in every phase of the application of the cell doctrine to man and to disease and to the problems relating to man as the highest of the animals. If there was anyone who by his training and lifelong mental occupation was eminently fitted to judge of the significance of the Darwinian theory as regards the higher animals and man at least, surely it was the great German pathologist. From the very beginning, however, he refused to go with the tide that set in toward Darwinism, and to the end of his life he remained a consistent opponent of the theory. He sometimes went so far as to say that a half-century of biology had been wasted in Europe trying to bolster up the Darwinian theory instead of making observations simply for what they were worth to science.

Virchow's great colleagues in Germany were practically unanimous in their agreement with him in this matter. Embryology is often supposed, because of the succession of stages which it presents in the embryo, to afford definite support to the evolutionary hypothesis and to encourage the acceptance of Darwinism. Each animal or human being passes through a series of stages which strikingly recalls the evolution of the race, and this was supposed to make the acceptance of the Darwinian theory comparatively easy. Von Baer, the greatest of the German embryologists during the nineteenth century, a man who received world-wide recognition for his contributions to his favorite science, absolutely refused to accept Darwinism, however, and though he lived on until many of the lesser minds around him in Germany had yielded to the facile, plausible explanation of many as yet insoluble problems afforded by Darwinism, he continued until the end of his life absolutely to refuse his acceptance to the Darwinian theory. In this he was imitated by Naegeli, probably the greatest of German comparative anatomists, and by Von Kölliker, one of the most successful investigators in human anatomy.

What was true among the great scientific workers in the biological sciences relating to man and the higher animals, was also true in other biological departments. It was on botany that the Darwinian theory rested with most assurance as furnishing evidence for the transmutation of species as the result of natural selection. Darwin's studies in botany represent his greatest work in science. Indeed it was the thoroughness of his methods of investigation in this and the exquisite patience of his researches that deserve for him a place among the great scientists of the nineteenth century. The reputation acquired among scientists because of his botanical studies was transferred by his disciples to his theory and made to bear great weight for it. The most distinguished of German botanists in the nineteenth century, Wigand, whose work stamped him as one of the world's most accomplished botanists, did not accept the Darwinian theory, however; but, like the great German biologists of other departments, he absolutely refused to concede that Darwinism contained any important contributions to biological science.

What was thus true in Germany of the greatest investigating scientists and biologists of the latter half of the nineteenth century was true to a much greater degree than is commonly supposed for the same class of men in English-speaking countries. Agassiz, for instance, probably our greatest teacher of paleontology and geology in America, could not understand how scientists brought themselves to accept Darwinism. In one of his letters he speaks of it as a mania. He wrote to Sir Philip De Gray Egerton in 1867:[1]

My recent studies have made me more adverse than ever to the new scientific doctrines which are flourishing now in England. This sensational zeal reminds me of what I experienced as a young man in Germany, when the physio-philosophy of Oken had invaded every centre of scientific activity; and yet, what is there left of it? I trust to outlive this mania also.

Cope, another of our great American paleontologists and zoologists, who is usually considered to have been one of the greatest of our investigators in biological sciences during the last generation, was not a Darwinian but a neo-Lamarckian. Many other names might be mentioned in the same connexion.

Sir J. William Dawson, the distinguished Canadian paleontologist, whose reputation can best be appreciated from the fact that he occupied the honorable position of President of the British Association for the Advancement of Science, remained until the end of his life, about ten years ago, a strenuous anti-Darwinian. He had no sympathy at all with the theories of evolution that are supposed to have revolutionized science. He did not hesitate to declare that the popularity of these theories was mainly due to their superficial character. Anyone who knew enough of science really to test their value did not hold them. In his article on Evolution for the *Universal Encyclopedia* he said:

The vague and indefinite application of the term evolution to all these modes of development and to their innumerable and complicated causes and determinations has perhaps more than anything else tended to disgust men of common sense with this protean and intangible philosophy, and to divorce it more and more from the alliance of rigid science. On the other hand its vague and shadowy character, and the pretension to explain all things by one dominant idea have great charms for the unwary and enthusiastic crowd, and it gives a cheap and easy way of appearing learned and philosophical, which has a peculiar attraction for an age characterized by a superficial and confused expansion of thought and discussion, and by an intense craving for the exciting and sensational. These elements of the thought of the age must for some time longer give currency to the abundant coinage of a mint which so easily converts the base metal of speculation into the semblance of scientific conclusions.

the fittest. The younger German school of biologists emphasized very much this aspect of the question.

One of the workers in biology in Germany whose influence
has been felt very materially in this reaction against the shallow evolutionary theories of the nineteenth century has been
Eric Wasmann, a Jesuit priest well-known for his contributions to the science of entomology and for his discussions of
the broader problems of evolution. When, two years ago,
there was a debate in Berlin on the subject of evolution, while
Haeckel represented the radical side, Father Wasmann represented the conservative; and it was generally conceded that
Haeckel, far from making new adherents for his special interpretation of Darwinism, had lost ground among his German
compatriots as the result of the controversy. Indeed the beginning of the serious discrediting of Haeckel dates from that
time, and Haeckel has constantly lost in popular sympathy and
has had to confess that he modified many of his designs for his
books in order to make them fit in with his theories, though
they were supposed by his readers to be pictures direct from
nature. If Wasmann has been nothing else but a factor in this
newer view of Haeckelism, which has existed for long among
scientists, but is gradually spreading even among the people,
his career would be interesting; but he counts for much more
than this, and his scientific work merits for him a place among
the great biological observers of the present generation.

His work has been done almost exclusively on ants and their
parasites and guests. This would seem a curious and rather
anomalous occupation for a Catholic priest, and above all perhaps a Jesuit; but science is a sacred subject and even the
smallest things in nature have an interest that connects them
with the Creator and the universe, so that nothing is really
small. Long ago Tennyson said to the flower in the crannied
wall " If I could know thee root and branch and all, I would
know what God and man is," and the Universe is so connected
together that a man " cannot stir a flower without disturbing
a star "; and so nothing in the world of nature is really unimportant.

Father Wasmann's interest in ants was not accidental, for
very early in life his attention was drawn to them; but during
his younger years as a Jesuit his health was despaired of be-

cause of consumption and as a consequence he was required to pass practically all of his time out of doors. He utilized the enforced leisure of his convalesence in studying the ants in the College garden, and in time came to be looked upon as one of the greatest of living entomologists. Evidently his story should be of far more than passing interest for American Catholics.

Eric Wasmann was born at Meran in South Tyrol some forty miles south and slightly west of Innsbruck, in what is an intensely Catholic country. His parents, however, were converts who came from Hamburg and who had found the faith in the midst of this Catholic people. His father, Friederich Wasmann, was a distinguished pupil of the great German religious painter Overbeck, and was looked on as one of the important German artists of the nineteenth century. His son Eric's studies were made in the Gymnasia at Meran and Hall and in the Jesuit boarding-school under the title of Stella Matutina at Feldkirch. Even in his student days young Wasmann occupied himself, as we have said, a good deal with entomology. At the completion of his Gymnasium studies in spite of his interest in science young Wasmann entered the Jesuit novitiate. This was in 1875, when he was about sixteen years of age and at a time when the May laws were in full force, so that he had to go for his years of novitiate to Holland. He applied himself very seriously to his vocation, and in 1879 began to exhibit marked signs of pulmonary consumption.

This forced on him the necessity to live the outdoor life and pursue his favorite study of the ants. In spite of his delicate health he was able to complete his studies for the priesthood and was ordained in 1890. By this time his health had im-

certain explanations of them. These articles in the *Stimmen* are really the biographical data for his development as a scientist, and they furnished ample evidence to his superiors of the advisability of giving him further opportunities for scientific study which resulted in his graduate work in zoology at Prague.

After his studies at Prague Father Wasmann devoted himself entirely to writing scientific articles with regard to insects and certain scientific problems connected with them until he is now looked upon as one of the world authorities on these subjects. The foundation of his reputation was laid in a series of observations of very great value. The scientific reader will perhaps best appreciate this when told that during the something more than twenty years from 1886 to the present time Father Wasmann has written nearly 200 articles with regard to the guests and parasites of ants and termites. The relations of these to their hosts was very little known when Father Wasmann took up the subject, and this chapter in entomology is largely his. Anyone acquainted even superficially with this series of observations will not be surprised that Father Wasmann should be considered an authority in entomology. His observations required infinite patience, great ingenuity and care in the drawing of conclusions. How well the work was accomplished the general reception of his papers by the critics furnishes the best evidence.

It was after this work had been largely accomplished that the true scope of Father Wasmann's scientific abilities made itself felt. The study of ants and their guests and parasites does not seem important for the great problems of biology to the ordinary man, but his deep study of insect conditions soon led him to very important conclusions. Ordinarily it is assumed that there is a gradation in the intelligence of animals and that the more nearly they resemble man in their anatomy the more similar are they to him also in manifestations that have some analogy to reasoning power. The ants, however, and indeed all of the insects—for the bee and the wasp must be included in this category—represent a distinct contradiction of this idea. While not at all resembling man and far distant from him in the zoological scale, their mani-

called psychological order. All of these insects and especially the ants have social qualities, that is they live in communities and help one another and have many manifestations of that mutual aid which characterizes man as he rises in the social scale.

It is evident, then, from the study of the insects that there is no relation between the development of the nervous system and the capacity for doing ingenious and helpful things. Animals that much more nearly approach man in their anatomy are not at all equal to the insects in their ability to do many things that would seem to require reasoning power, if we were to translate animal actions into human ways. His studies of insects, then, naturally led Father Wasmann into the field of animal psychology, as it is called. His contributions to this field, which began with his studies on *The Combined Nests or Colonies of Ants,*[2] and which went into its second edition later, was followed up by his studies on *Instinct and Intelligence in the Animal Kingdom,*[3] which is now in its third edition in German, and finally in his *The Psychic Life of Ants as Compared with the Higher Animals,* originally issued in 1897, but now in its third edition, and his *The Psychic Faculties of Ants,* originally published in 1899.

These studies in comparative psychology brought him out of the narrow field of entomology into the wide field of general biology. It was his contribution to this under the title of *Modern Biology and the Theory of Evolution*[4] which attracted worldwide attention. This eventually brought him into controversy with Haeckel, and it represents one of the important contributions of German biology to the theory of evolution. Of course it met with decided opposition. It showed mercilessly how little evidence there is for evolution, and above all showed the utter lack of foundation for the common belief that there is abundant evidence that Darwinism and natural selection represent an important factor in biology. The work was resented however, rather than criticized. A generation of

[2] *Die Zusammengesetzten Nester und gemischten Kolonien der Ameisen,* Muenster, 1891.

[3] "Instinct and Intelligence in The Animal Kingdom," Authorized translation of the second and enlarged edition. Herder: St. Louis, 1903.

[4] *Die Moderne Biologie und die Entwicklungstheorie.* St. Louis, Herder. 1904.

teachers had been occupied with the thought of spreading Darwinism as an assured fact. In spite of Virchow's prophecy made in 1887 at the meeting of the German physicians and naturalists in Munich, when he criticized Haeckel so severely and said that those who wanted to teach Darwinism popularly would regret it, because their teaching would have to be taken back and the consequence would be a serious set-back for science in popular estimation, they had gone on teaching it. Now there was assembled convincing evidence that Darwinism was plausible but not scientific, and that it would have to be given up and the field left open for further investigation before any theory of evolution could be advanced.

These three steps, first of observation with regard to the insects, then of analysis and synthesis of his previous knowledge to show its bearing on comparative psychology, and finally his employment of all his previously collected materials to bring out the present position of evolution in biology, represent the successive phases of Father Wasmann's career. It is because his writing on evolution at the present time is founded on important contributions to both the deductive and inductive side of biology that his opinion with regard to the evolutionary theory carries so much weight. It has seemed worth while, then, to take up each of these phases of his career and to present to American readers some idea of just what he accomplished in order that his place as a scientist among scientists may be properly appreciated.

Father Wasmann's observations have mainly, as we have said, been made with regard to the guests of ants and termites, the Myrmekophiles and the Termitophiles as they are called in scientific language. In the Netherlands *Tijdschrift V. Entomologie* for September, 1890, he published "Comparative Studies of Ant and Termite Guests." In the German *Zeitschrift für Entomologie,* of 1890, he published "Observations on a New Ant Guest from Brazil." In 1891 he published in the Netherlands journal above mentioned "The Ants and Their Guests in Holland, and Limberg." In the biological *Centralblatt* for 1891 came "Remarks on the International Relations of Ant Guests," while the Proceedings of the Vienna Society for Zoology and Botany for this same year contained a paper on "Some New Guests of the Termites." During the next year there were other articles on newly-discovered guests of the ants and the termites, and each year thereafter saw further studies along this same line. In 1894 he published a book on this subject containing some 231 pages with annotations regarding the mode of life, also descriptions and plates, of the new forms. In 1895 he studied some further specimens from Brazil. He continued for many years to add to European scientific knowledge on this subject.

He was greatly aided in this matter by his brother Jesuits throughout the world who sent him specimens of all kinds. This constituted the principal reason why he was able to describe so many new species, though the development of his powers of observation enabled him to differentiate many species hitherto unrecognized in Europe. He succeeded with the help not only of brother Jesuits but of the missionaries of other Orders who in distant countries had become interested in his work in making a magnificent collection. The number of specimens in that collection, as furnished me by a student of his some two years ago, is astounding to the non-scientific mind accustomed to think of ants as just ants and to consider that there may of course be a couple of dozen or more of species but that even these are more due to the scientific overprecision of collectors than to real differences of nature. In Father Wasmann's collection there are no less than 2,000 species of ants and termites. There are about 1,200 species of the guests of ants and termites of various kinds all over the world. Father Wasmann's interest in another branch of entomology will be appreciated from the fact that this collection contains about 1,500 species of European beetles.

With regard to instinct there is probably no one who in recent years has made such important contributions to the scientific side of this subject as Father Wasmann. His many years of familiarity with insect life in which instinct plays such a large rôle, has eminently fitted him to discuss this subject with thorough knowledge of all the results of recent observation. His first controversy with scientific men was along this line, and his Jesuit training in scholastic philosophy and in the nice distinctions that the old-time philosophers made so well, enabled him to throw clear light on many dubious questions. Above all it enabled him to point out fallacies and

indicate where distinctions should be made so as to avoid ob-
scuration of sense. His illustrations drawn from his favorite
study of entomology are eminently illuminating and at the
same time add so much of interest to his philosophical treatment of the question that his books have been widely read and
have gone through several editions in different languages.
His definition of instinct and the discussion of it in the third
chapter, " What is Intelligence and What is Instinct? " in his
book *Instinct and Intelligence in the Animal Kingdom,* illustrate this very well:

Consequently instinct signifies both from an etymological and historical point of view, *a sensitive impulse* which induces a being to
perform certain actions *the suitableness of which is beyond the perception of the agent that performs them.*[5]
    It is instinct that induces the male larvæ of the stag beetle before
its transformation into a pupa, to produce a cocoon, the size of which
is far greater than that of the pupa, and thus to provide in advance
for the length of the future antlers of the imago which is to come
forth from the larva.   It has never even seen a developed stag beetle,
and no amount of reflection on its part could hit upon the clever idea
of its eventual destiny to become a male stag beetle with mighty
antlers on its head.   It is instinct that impels the female of the
leaf roller (*Rhynchites betulae*) to make an incision into a birch leaf
after an extremely ingenious mathematico-technical problem, that
was—by the way—not introduced into human science before 1673,
and then to roll up that leaf in the shape of a funnel as a depository
for its eggs.   Neither by experience nor by reflection could the little
weevil gain an idea of that problem, nor could it even know that it
would lay eggs at all, from which young leaf rollers would eventually
develop.   It is instinct that makes the young bird which is unacquainted with any nest of its own species, collect after pairing little
stalks and blades of grass and similar material for a warm nest, in
which its fledgings are to be hatched; for neither by experience nor
by thought or reflection could it know before its first season of breeding, that it would even lay eggs, and that these eggs would have to
be hatched, in order to produce a new generation of its own kind.
It is due to instinct, when a dog that suffers from tapeworm eats
artemisia absinthium, although it never otherwise touches this plant;
for a study of medicine would be requisite to hit upon such a suitable
treatment by its own experience.   It is instinct, finally, that causes

[5] Italics ours.

the new-born babe to express its feeling of hunger by crying and seeking its mother's breast; for it could not possibly have previously recognized by experience or its own thinking the suitableness of its cries and its attempts to suck.

What is it then that *essentially characterizes* these different instinctive actions? It is the circumstance that *their suitableness lies beyond the perception of the respective agent.* The *unconscious suitableness* (adaptiveness) is, consequently, the essential criterion of instinctive, in contradistinction to intelligent, actions.

Not without purpose was it pointed out in each of the previous examples that the respective agent not only lacked *experimental knowledge* of the suitableness of its acts, but that it likewise was unable to attain that knowledge by means of its *own deliberate reflections.* Animal psychology (ordinarily so-called) considers in a one-sided manner only the former point of view, and neglects the latter.

This was a fine philosophic note to inject into the discussion of instinct then so rife, and which had been carried on mainly with the idea of obliterating the old distinction between instinct and intelligence, for this would break down the barrier between man and the animal and make it comparatively easy to argue for the development of man in the course of evolution from the animals. Father Wasmann's work in this line began a reaction which brought the whole subject of instinct to the bar of scientific criticism once more, with the result that many accepted popular notions were emphatically condemned.

How much such a criticism of the subject of instinct and intelligence in animals is needed is plain to anyone who knows the exaggerations of many presumed students of nature on this subject. Ex-President Roosevelt, himself a naturalist of recognized ability, protested vigorously not long since against the abuses of many authors of stories of animal life in this matter and stamped them indelibly with the name of " nature faker ". John Burroughs, one of the most charming of American writers on nature subjects, has not hesitated to characterize many of the tales of animals written by the new school of nature story-writers as mere fiction. He has insisted that the placing of their books in the hands of children with the inevitable assumption that they represent truths of nature is sure to do harm. It is all right to write fiction, but it should be stamped as fiction and not masqueraded as truth; above all not as truth learned from close study of nature. What is true for popular writers on this subject, however, is more or less true also for even scientific students on the subject who allow themselves to be carried away by their enthusiasm, to the extent of translating the actions of animals as if done according to thought processes of their own, and then dilating on so-called animal intelligence.

One of the most difficult problems in the differentiation of instinct and intelligence is that which concerns the various sounds produced by animals, by which they communicate their affections and their wants and even certain sensitive perceptions to other sentient beings. It has often been argued that these modes of communication, either by noises of various kinds or by signals, represent exactly the same thing as human speech, though in an undeveloped form. Father Wasmann has argued for the essential distinction between these modes of communication in animals and in mankind. His knowledge of entomology (for among insects particularly such modes of communication are very strikingly illustrated) enables him to treat this subject authoritatively. His method of treating it furnishes an excellent example of the way in which he discusses all of the difficult problems relating to instinct and intelligence and their differentiation. Although the quotation is rather long, it well deserves a place because of the importance of the subject, the frequency with which it comes under discussion in recent years, and the light that it throws on Father Wasmann's application of his scientific knowledge to philosophic problems.

There exists a perfect parallelism, that is demanded by nature, between the cognitive and appetitive powers and their manifestation through signs which can be perceived by the senses. This parallelism is as remarkable in man as it is in the brute. In the stage of infancy, and before all use of reason, the babe manifests its psychic impressions and feelings by inarticulate sounds of pain, joy, desire and pleasure. Even adults act in a similar way, and in the first outburst of passion generally give inarticulate utterance to those vehement affections in which the activity of the sensitive appetite prevails. But when sober reflection is restored, when reason gains its sway and the superior appetite predominates, the same adults manifest their psychic life by phonetic or graphic symbols which are properly arranged in thought and expression. They speak or write a rational language according to rational and grammatical rules. This parallelism clearly shows that the animal possesses only a sensitive and not a spiritual perception and appetite, and explains why its perceptions and affections are never expressed by arbitrary symbols, but only by those immediate and natural signs which follow the instinctive laws of sensitive association of . representations. Moreover many animals are forced by the circumstances in which they live to communicate their sensitive perceptions and affections to other sentient beings. A dog will scratch at a closed door and bark and whine until it is opened. Such methods of communicating sensitive affections belong to the same class of natural signs as the mating sounds of animals, the chirping of crickets, the knocking of certain beetles (anobium), or the different melodies of birds. The alarm cries of certain animals against enemies, and the cries by which our animals of the same species are warned of impending danger belong to the same category. Even the so-called feeler language of ants which is not immediately connected with the propagation of species or with individual needs of self-preservation, but subserves manifold wants of social co-operation, to an extent not met with in any species of higher animals, even this means of communication which bears the most resemblance to human speech, does not ascend above the level of immediate natural, spontaneous and sensile signs, it is not determined by individual deliberation.

It cannot be denied that all these different forms of "animal language" exhibit an *analogon* of human speech. Still they are essentially different. Pseudo-psychology may ignore this difference: scientific psychology must acknowledge it. Animal language is never the result of an intelligent reflection on the part of the brute to use arbitrary, fixed sensitive signs which may have been conventionally agreed upon as the fit expression of psychic experiences with the view of being understood by other animals. It is simply the outcome of the laws of sensitive instinct which imply with physical necessity the use of a certain sound or a certain tap of the feelers to express and communicate a certain sensitive affection. The language of ants published in our "Vergleichende Studien", offers further proofs of this conclusion. These remarks will, I trust, suffice to clear up the true relation between speech and intelligence.

Father Wasmann did not hesitate to declare that he owed many of his conclusions on the subject of instinct and intelligence to the principles laid down by the scholastic philosophers. His tribute to St. Thomas in this matter was probably a surprise to the modern scientists, so occupied with recent scientific observations that they could scarcely believe that an old medieval philosopher had by deduction, after a small number of observations, reached conclusions worth while considering by a modern scientist with many observations in his possession, in the midst of our era of natural science. Father Wasmann said:

It will interest modern men of science to learn that Thomas of Aquin attributed to animals the powers of sensitive perception and appetite in the very same terms as we have done, and that he divided the interior sense powers in a similar manner. This fact alone is weighty evidence for the truth, that the cherished and unceasingly repeated reproach of modern scientists against scholastic philosophy of making a machine of the animal, in letting it be exclusively guided by a "blind instinct", is due to a total ignorance of the teachings of that philosophy which it has become fashionable to disparage and discredit.

And so the scholastics are to come into their own once more through the reverent devotion of students who know both science and scholasticism and do not merely criticize what they ignore.

Father Wasmann's most important work, however, has undoubtedly been his contribution to the current discussion of evolution by his book on *Modern Biology and the Theory of Evolution.*[6] This went through three editions in about as many years. It was originally published as a series of articles in the Jesuit periodical *Stimmen aus Maria Laach,* during the years 1901, 1902, and 1903. While it met with very vigorous criticism, many of its bitterest critics could not help but acknowledge the scientific value of the work done by its author or the right his scientific achievements gave him to be heard on so important a subject. The amount of space their criticisms took up in important scientific journals shows how significant this latest contribution to the theory of evolution was considered to be. Lotsy, the professor of Biology at the University of Leyden, and the author of a text-book on *The*

[6] *Die Moderne Biologie und Die Entwicklungstheorie,* Von Erich Wasmann, S.J., Herder: St. Louis, Mo., 1906.

Theory of Descent, said: "Wasmann is a Jesuit but at the same time he is one of the best zoologists of our time, and his observations on the life of ants for example demand our highest admiration."

Perhaps no recent set of incidents serves better to bring out the fact that science has not set the world free—though that is the boast of many a scientist—than the reception accorded to Fr. Wasmann's book in certain scientific quarters. Many scientific critics have not hesitated to be quite intolerant of his opinions. They have emphatically declared that, while his science is all right, they cannot bear the presumption of a Jesuit in daring to inject himself into a scientific discussion. They have insisted that when he discusses science his opinions are all right, but just because the monistic theory of evolution would eliminate the spiritual world and therefore creation, that Wasmann's defence of an opposite system of thought which on scientific principles shows the necessity for a creator, cannot be listened to for a moment. It is this attitude of intolerance when the days of intolerance are supposed to be over, that is most amusing. Men are evidently men, and whether they are defending scientific or theological opinions they are likely to cling to their own views because they are their own views, and to consider that other men cannot be quite candid if they disagree with them. Even in science, then, orthodoxy is our " doxy " and heterodoxy is other peoples' " doxy ". Any one who disagrees with us must not be quite straightforward or must be at least a little disingenuous. It is the world-old position men have taken with regard to one another repeating itself even in these days of the supposed absolute freedom consequent upon the scientific development of recent times.

Father Wasmann in discussing the evolution theory first reviews the history of the idea of evolution in the world, showing that it existed among the Greeks and has never been entirely ignored whenever men have thought deeply upon biological problems. He shows above all, in a very interesting ten pages of his first chapter, that biology is not the modern science that it is often supposed to be, but that its development can be traced from Aristotle and through the great medieval thinkers Albert the Great and Roger Bacon. He shows that there was considerable discussion of evolution during the eighteenth century, and that, though at the beginning of the second quarter of the nineteenth century the idea of the constancy of species had triumphed in scientific circles, the case for the transmutation of species had been presented very fully and very strikingly by a number of biologists and above all by Lamarck, who well deserves the name of the Father of Evolution. He sets forth a complete theory of evolution in his book published in the very first year of the nineteenth century.

Then he takes up the question of the place of Darwinism, and shows the position that it holds among the various theories of evolution. He insists particularly on the correction of the false notion, which is so popular, that Darwinism and the theory of evolution are equivalent conceptions. Evolution was in the world long before Darwin, who presented merely a new theory of explanation for evolution. He endeavored to explain the origin of species by means of natural selection on the principle that the breeding of new species depends on the survival of the fittest and the struggle for existence. The accurate meaning of the word Darwinism, then, is natural selection as the explanation for things as we see them. Just as soon as Darwinism is thus limited, as it should be, it is easy to follow Father Wasmann's emphatic conclusion that it is scientifically inadequate, since it does not account for the origin of attributes fitted to the purposes for which they are attuned, for these must be referred back to the interior original causes of evolution. In a word, it is the question of adaptation that shows the serious failure of Darwinism to explain the qualities of living things as we know them. This has been pointed out very emphatically in this country by Professor Thomas Hunt Morgan in his book on *Evolution and Adaptation.*[7]

A typical example of Father Wasmann's treatment of the question of evolution as applied to man will perhaps illustrate his scientific objective mode of thought and argument from facts, since the whole subject cannot be reviewed in a brief article. One of the phases of the argument for the evolution even of man's body from that of the animal he meets very successfully, is that founded on the presence of what are called rudimentary organs. There are in man's body a number of

[7] Macmillan, N. Y., 1903.

organs the use of which we do not know and many of them have been declared to be the now useless remains of organic structures that were of use in previous stages of evolution, when the human body was gradually being perfected out of the animal body. It would be surprising were it to be generally known how many people consider this one of the most telling arguments for the evolution of man. This hypothesis of man's development from the animal they declare explains perfectly the presence of these rudimentary or vestigial structures, as they are called, because they are supposed to be vestiges of previous stages of existence, while no other theory makes it at all possible for us to understand how they can possibly have come into existence in the human body, because they have no purpose and are most of them, apparently at least, in gradual process of disappearance, so that we can foretell their fate from what the evolutionary theory tells us of their past history.

Father Wasmann points out that the most significant feature of our recent advance in knowledge with regard to the rudimentary organs is that, while we have been accustomed to think of them as useless because we did not know enough about them, increase of knowledge has shown us very clearly that many of them are extremely useful in ways that we did not at all suspect. The thymus and the thyroid glands, for instance, formerly considered to be useless, are now known to be extremely important ductless glands pouring a secretion into the blood which is of great significance for health and strength. The so-called hypophysis cerebri, which used to be considered a rudimentary remnant of a cyclopic eye that existed in certain animal bodies, presumedly the ancestors of man, has now proved to be a very significant secretory organ the secretion of which has something to do with the regulation of growth and probably also with the regulation of the circulation at the base of the brain. Father Wasmann admits that certain organs, as for instance the rudimentary muscle of the ear, may be really vestiges of a previous condition of man, though not necessarily pointing to an animal ancestry of man. The same thing may be true he admits for the appendix.[8]

[8] As far as the appendix is concerned, there are very few physicians now who continue to believe that this is a useless organ. Recent investigations

Wasmann's treatment of the question as to the attitude that Catholics should assume toward the theory of evolution is especially interesting and, while thoroughly conservative, is eminently scientific. He has summed it up at the beginning of the article on evolution in the fifth volume of the *Catholic Encyclopedia.* With scholastic exactness he insists on the necessity for distinctions, so that the different meanings of the word special evolution may be understood before an answer is made. He says:

We must distinguish, (1) between the theory of evolution as a scientific hypothesis and as a philosophical speculation; (2) between the theory of evolution as based on theistic principles and as based on a materialistic and atheistic foundation; (3) between the theory of evolution and Darwinism; (4) between the theory of evolution as applied to the vegetable and animal kingdoms and as applied to man.

He takes up each one of these headings and makes his answer very direct and positive. The theory of evolution is as yet only a scientific hypothesis. The formation of species has been observed in so few cases as to constitute no absolute truth. Fossil forms of the horse, of ammonites, and of many insects, furnish an indirect proof for the generic relation of many systematic species. There is no evidence whatever for the common genetic descent of all plants and animals from a single primitive organism. The greater number of biologists consider that whatever evolution there is must be polyphyletic, that is from many different primitive organisms. This theory does not in any way contradict the Christian conception of the universe. Scripture does not tell us in what form the

of large numbers of patients from whom the appendix had been removed apparently go to prove that the secretions of the appendix have much to do with the regulation of fermentative conditions in the lower bowel. It must not be forgotten that we constantly carry around with us in this portion of our anatomy a very offensive mass of excrementitious material. In spite of this we are as a rule neither inconvenienced ourselves nor do we inconvenience others because of this condition. There are many factors that play a rôle in this protective mechanism. Various glands of the intestines, especially those which secrete white blood-cells, are engaged in it. The appendix is largely a mass of lymphoid tissue giving off such protective cells. In this it closely resembles the tonsils which guard the entrance to the digestive tract, while the appendix stands guard at the lowest portion of the digestive tract. Persons from whom the appendix has been removed nearly always have some trouble with the proper function of their lower bowel, and their history after its removal shows this very clearly.

present species of plants and animals are originally created. by God. As early as 1877 Knabenbauer stated that " there is no objection, so far as faith is concerned, to the doctrine of descent of all plant and animal species from a few types." [9] Neither is there any essential opposition between the Christian interpretation of nature and the principle of evolution as a philosophic speculation which makes the history of the animal and the vegetable kingdoms upon our planet, as it were, a versicle in a volume of a million of pages in which the natural development of the cosmos is described, and upon whose title page is written: " In the beginning God created Heaven and earth."

As for the beginning of evolution, natural science not only does not accept spontaneous generation, but has proved that, so far as we know, it does not occur. We cannot assume then in any theory of evolution that living things begin without some adequate cause for them. Evolution without God, then, as the Creator is unthinkable. The first organisms must be produced by a creative act. In any theory of evolution that accepts Christianity a creative act is also demanded for the origin of the human soul, since the soul cannot originate in matter. The atheistic theory of evolution contradicts the position of science with regard to spontaneous generation and fails to explain the origin of the human soul and must be frankly materialistic.

believe that man's body, having been prepared in the process of evolution for the reception of the human soul, had this soul directly infused into it, but this is merely a hypothesis, and recent science has rather tended away from the idea of direct bodily descent from the animals rather than toward the accumulation of proofs in this direction.

Wasmann's exposition of this conservative side of evolution in the controversy in Berlin not only attracted attention but made many thinking people realize that our generation had been hurried into conclusions not justified by scientific knowledge. The controversy created a storm in the German press with at first a tendency to resent the fact that a Catholic clergyman scientist should set himself up in opposition to German University professors of science. Before the end, however, there were many signs of revulsion of feeling in favor of the doughty champion of conservatism who so bravely and, it could not be denied, so successfully faced antagonists who might be expected to swamp him at once. A good idea of this change of feeling may be gathered from a sentence in the German *Hochland,* a non-Catholic journal: " The disgraceful fact remains that Wasmann, an insignificant priest, in consequence of his training and not of his intellectual abilities, speaking as a philosopher, routed our collective scientists, and in the course of the discussion displayed the greatest intellectual self-possession in combating that scientific arrogance which deals with truths that are limited to an existence of twenty-five years."

Father Wasmann's life shows very well just what the attitude of the Church toward the study of physical science even by clergymen is. Two of the most distinguished contributors to modern biology in the last fifty years, Abbott Mendel and Father Wasmann, have been priests. Far from their devotion to physical science proving any detriment to their careers as clergymen they have been held high in honor as a result of their successful scientific studies. Both of them belonged to religious orders; one of them to the Augustinians from which Luther withdrew 400 years ago, but the Order still continues to flourish and its members are still, as they were in Luther's time, among the most distinguished scholars in their periods; the other belongs to the Jesuits, whose members are directly under the control of the Pope and who would not devote themselves to physical science but for the fact that not only is there toleration, but the most direct encouragement, of this form of intellectual effort on the part of the Papacy.

Biology is usually supposed to be the most unorthodox of sciences in its tendency. It is usually assumed that a man cannot know modern biology deeply and retain his ardent faith in religious principles. The lives of these two distinguished clerical scientists are a direct contradiction of such assumptions, and show that it is not biology itself but certain unscientific developments of it quite unjustified by the science itself that have been leading men astray. Father Wasmann particularly has called attention to this. He has very aptly compared our time to that transitional period of human thought which succeeded the publication of the Copernican theory when men were suddenly led to realize that the earth instead of being the centre of the universe was a small planet, in a small solar system, one of many in an immense universe. Men at that time were inclined to think that such an entire change of view with regard to human importance meant the end of old religious ideas. In the modern time the theory of evolution has worked something of the same revolution in many men's minds. Just as men learned however that the Copernican theory was quite compatible with Christianity, so they are now learning that the evolutionary theory is quite compatible with religious beliefs and Christian traditions. Father Wasmann sees the reaction in scientific minds against materialism, and hails the awakening of a new spirit more favorable to Christianity among the younger scientists all over the world.

JAMES J. WALSH.

Fordham University, New York.

ECCLESIASTICAL HERALDRY.

II.

4. ECCLESIASTICAL HERALDRY IN GENERAL.

IF, before taking up the question *de jure,* we investigate the question *de facto* of ecclesiastical heraldry, we find in the ancient monuments, and particularly episcopal seals, that church coats of arms came into use very little later than civil ones; for, even in those early times, many bishops were feudal lords and crusaders. The usage of ecclesiastical blazoning may safely be said, then, to have originated at the beginning of the fourteenth century, and that from this time forward, when the Cardinals of the Holy Roman Church took the initiative, its practice very soon became universal.

There is but a single instance of an earlier use of papal arms surmounted by the tiara, namely those to be seen on the tomb of Pope Lucius III, who died at Verona A. D. 1185 and lies buried in the cathedral of that city. In the next known instance, the tomb of Pope Honorius IV ($+$ 1287) bears in front the coat of arms of the Savelli, withont any tiara. A last instance, which is sometimes mentioned, is that of Innocent IV ($+$ 1254); but it should be borne in mind that his monumental tomb was built only about fifty years after his death: there, indeed, we see his family coat of arms (that of the Fieschi), crowned with an ogival tiara, behind which are passed the two traditional keys *per saltire* (crossed in form of a cross of St. Andrew). However, all the masters of heraldic art agree that in the fourteenth century the usage of armorial bearings was a fixed one, and that the Sovereign Pontiffs were then in the habit of surmounting their coat of arms with the tiara and keys.

We mentioned above that the Cardinals were the originators of the regular usage of the ecclesiastical escutcheon. The circumstances of the time were dramatic: Emperor Frederick II within and the Turks without were waging war on the Church of Christ. To remedy these evils, Pope Innocent IV, who is proclaimed by the historians, "nobilis genere sed vita nobilior," called the First Council of Lyons (1245) and there solemnly excommunicated Frederick and had subsidies voted for a crusade. Now, it was on this same momentous occasion that the Pope granted to the Cardinals the use of the red hat. Naturally enough, this distinctive emblem was soon reproduced on their armorial bearings, and from that time the red hat took the place of the mitre above their coat of arms; then came the tassels (strings which served to fasten the hat under the chin) the representation of which was also gradually and variously introduced.

As to episcopal coats of arms, it is impossible to trace any of them further back than the middle of the thirteenth century. Before that time, the episcopal seals usually represent a bishop, with crozier and mitre, seated on his throne or standing; later on, there appears the coat of arms itself on the verso of the seal; next, the crozier above it, then the mitre, and lastly both the crozier and mitre. Still later, there is visible the influence of Italy and the Cardinals, who, instead of crozier and mitre, had only a cross, with one or two crosslets according as they were bishops or archbishops. And to that same influence must be referred the later superposition of hat and tassels. Such is the evolution of the episcopal coat of arms.

A word about prelatic heraldics follows next. Armorial bearings are one of their privileges, and the various colleges of prelacy are distinguished by the number and color of the tassels, as also by the color of the hat: the present usage in this matter has been once more defined by a recent *Motu proprio* of Pope Pius X (1905). There are two great classes of prelates, secular and regular, the latter comprising more particularly the abbots of the Benedictine Order of Canons Regular, etc.

But what of the question *de jure,* or in other words, by what right are our bishops entitled to coats of arms? It would be childish to claim for it the authority of Holy Scripture, as some medieval writers, " gentlemen of leisure ", have done. For instance, there are actually under my eyes the coats of arms of the twelve tribes of Israel! The various emblems are taken from the last words of Jacob to his sons and of Moses to the twelve tribes (Gen. 49 and Deut. 33). And there is there the " Benjamin lupus rapax ", of whom St. Augustine devises so beautifully in the second nocturn for the Conversion of St. Paul; and thus we have the authen-

tic (?) coat of arms of the great Apostle, " a wolf passant ",
etc. But, not to take too much space, I must refer the curious
reader to the erudite Cornelius à Lapide [1] who, in the line of
symbolism, has literally a mine of information about the
twelve precious stones in Aaron's breastplate, which he then
compares with the twelve pearls set in the foundations and
gates of the new Jerusalem.

Leaving aside, then, this *argumentum accomodatitium* from
Holy Writ, let us remember what we have already stated,
that " arms or coats of arms are emblems of nobility or dignity, legitimately given or allowed by the sovereign power,
and which serve to distinguish persons, families, societies, and
corporations." Now, all history proclaims that in the ages
of faith, and hence at the very cradle of heraldry, there was
no visible power, spiritual or temporal, more universally recognized as supreme than the Sovereign Pontiff of all Christendom, whose *triregno* or triple crown was the emblem of
highest dignity. Hence in the degrees of nobility his place
was ever the very first: " Pope, Emperor, King, Cardinal,
Marshall, Duke and Prince, Marquis, Count or Earl, Vis-
count, Baron, Knight." The cardinals are the princes of his
court, the bishops and prelates his noblemen. And the sad
fact of the Holy Father being for the present despoiled of
part of his temporal power and independence, does not in any
wise weaken his secular and imprescriptible right.

In this connexion and in conclusion, it is a subject of legitimate pride for us Americans to hear the highest tribunal of
this nation solemnly proclaim, in the face of so many apostate
governments, that the suggestion made in the Philippine case,
as in the Porto Rico case, that the Catholic Church was not a
legal person entitled to maintain its property rights in the
courts, did not require serious consideration when " made with
reference to an institution which antedates by almost a thousand years any other personality in Europe." And our Supreme Court reminds all courts that " the Holy See still
occupies a recognized position in international law, of which
the courts must take judicial notice. The proposition (or
objection) that the Church has no corporate or jural personality, seems to be completely answered by an examination of

[1] Comment. in Exod. 28, and in Apoc. 21.

the law and history of the Roman Empire, of Spain, and of Porto Rico down to the time of the cession, and by the recognition accorded to it as an ecclesiastical body by the Treaty of Paris and by the law of nations." This is the remarkable opinion handed down by Chief Justice Fuller himself.

Such then is our answer to the question propounded, " By what right are our bishops entitled to armorial bearings? " It is a privilege granted to them by the recognized most ancient and most venerable sovereign power on earth.

5. ESSENTIALS OF ECCLESIASTICAL HERALDRY.

After this short sketch of the history of heraldry in general and the origins of ecclesiastical heraldry in particular, we now proceed to the more practical subject of the essentials of ecclesiastical heraldry. But, before taking up this second part of our task, we wish to make our own a timely remark of Mr. de Chaignon La Rose (who, by the way, deprecates being an Anglican), in the article from the *Magazine of Christian Art* quoted above, as it gives us perhaps the principal key to the glaring blunders we cannot help noticing in not a few of our prelates' coats of arms. " It is but fair," says our writer, " to state that European ecclesiastical heraldry has always been somewhat more capricious than has lay heraldry, and has proportionally more often contravened the broad underlying principles of armory. The reason is that it has been less subject to official supervision." In England, as far back as 1240, there was formed a first Roll of Arms, and a second one in 1413; besides, a Herald's College was established in 1483, and at repeated intervals there were Herald's Visitations, all in order to avoid confusion and abuses. England still has its Kings of Arms, an office which was left vacant in France in the year 1830. " But," continues Mr. de Chaignon, " since a bishop or spiritual lord did not derive his rank from a temporal prince, his arms and the arms of his spiritual fief or see were, by general courtesy, exempt from official regulation, although he might, and often did, invite this regulation. In England, however, by the practice of centuries, and on the Continent also, this exemption has been generally conceded." This statement explains then, and to some extent excuses, if it does not justify, the deplorable condition of some of our ecclesiastical heraldry. Now, a ready remedy seems to be at hand, and, if the present writer be allowed a suggestion, something like a Herald's College could easily be established in our great St. Mary's Seminary, Baltimore, whence was lately issued that much-needed and up-to-date volume on the *Costume of Prelates,* which also contains an elaborate chapter on heraldry.[2]

Be that as it may, the first point to settle in our essentials is what sort of arms may be used by our prelates. The heraldists have classified them, in respect of the right to bear the same, under the following heads: (1) arms of sovereignty, as for popes, emperors and kings, and our sovereign States; (2) of pretension, when a right to some territory is claimed, as the King of England from Edward III up to 1801, *rex Franciae;* (3) of concession, granting part of royal arms, which explains the prevalence of the lion in England, the fleur-de-lys in France, and the eagle in Germany: instance, Charles VII ennobling the Blessed Joan of Arc; (4) of community, as bishops' sees, chapters of canons, abbeys, universities, towns (mural arms), societies and corporations; (5) of family, paternal or hereditary; (6) of choice, after ennoblement, often *parlantes;* (7) of patronage; (8) of alliance; (9) of succession, and (10) of adoption.

Now, the practical rules according to sound heraldry are the following:

A prelate should keep the coat of arms of his family, if he is of noble descent. We have at least one instance of this in the United States, the present Archbishop of Boston, who has divided his coat of arms between his adopted one (the Holy Cross recalling his Cathedral and Bishop de Cheverus) and the one of the O'Connells. His predecessor, the said Bishop de Cheverus, and likewise Bishop de la Hailandière of Vincennes, for what motive is not known, never used their family arms in America; whilst the late Bishop de Goesbriand of Burlington showed the ones of his family with ducal coronet, viz. " azure, a fess or " (on a blue field, a gold fascia).

A bishop belonging to a religious Order generally *impales* or divides half and half his own arms with those of his Order, or places these *in chief* on the upper tier of the shield: in-

[2] The Rev. John A. Nainfa, S.S.; publishers, John Murphy Co.

stance, Archbishop Falconio, who thus shows the Franciscan coat of arms.

The arms are personal to the bishop, and in this country, where the dioceses are not feudal corporations, they do not belong to his see, as is wrongly believed sometimes: for instance, the coat of arms which is generally given in public print as our Cardinal's, is the same as the one formerly used by Archbishop Maréçhal, and perhaps Archbishop Carroll, representing the Assumption, whilst the Cardinal's personal coat of arms is entirely different.

Hence, *a bishop should never use the coat of arms of his predecessor.* Of this mistake we have unfortunately several examples: the late Bishop Horstmann used the one of Bishop Rappe; the late Bishop MacCloskey of Louisville the one of Bishop Lavialle; and a few of the living bishops could make their *mea culpa* on this score.

And if, out of friendship or in token of reverence, a bishop wished to *assume part of another's coat of arms,* this should not be done without previously *altering* it, so that the two be not alike. Our Holy Father himself furnishes an instance, for, as we stated, part of his arms are taken from those of his friend the late Bishop of Treviso; the late Archbishop Bourgade of Santa Fe also took the modified half of Archbishop Lamy's coat of arms.

The reason of these rules is found in the foremost requirement of heraldry, embodied in the trite sentence: "Arma sunt *distinguendi causa."* For, by the very fact that they make known the personages whose dignities they denote, they serve a very useful and practical purpose. To quote an eminent authority, Mgr. Barbier de Montault: "Ecclesiastical coats of arms are placed at the head of all official documents, manuscript as well as printed, so as to show from whom they emanate. They are usually engraved on the seal, appear over the main entrance of churches and convents, on sacred vessels, church vestments, and decorations of the sanctuary, on the chasuble, cope, dalmatics, and ends of the canons of the mitre, etc." Let us add from other writers that these arms should also be found, in church, on the canopy of the episcopal throne, and on the front part of a prelate's priedieu; in his own house, the prelate marks with his coat of arms whatever belongs to him personally, as his plate, tapestries, cushions, etc.; it should also be painted over the entrance door of the bishop's house, and on both doors of his carriage; besides, on festive occasions, on programmes, engrossed addresses, menu cards, etc.[a] Lastly, what more appropriate decoration could there be of a bishop's reception parlor, than the gallery of his venerable predecessors, showing their portraits and coats of arms?

Let us now study the coat of arms itself and its component parts, which are, first of all the escutcheon or *shield,* then the exterior ornaments called also the *crest,* and finally the *motto.* In a coat of arms (Latin, *insignia seu stemmata*) the principal part is the escutcheon or shield (Latin, *scutum,* French, *écusson*), because, even all alone by itself, by the figure it contains it designates its possessor. There are in the shield three things to consider: (1) the *field* or surface of the shield, (2) its *tinctures* or colors, and (3) the *charges* or figures it bears.

(1) *The Field.*—As to the field, which is nothing but the escutcheon itself as the background for the tinctures and the

1. VARIOUS SHAPES OF ESCUTCHEON OR SHIELD.

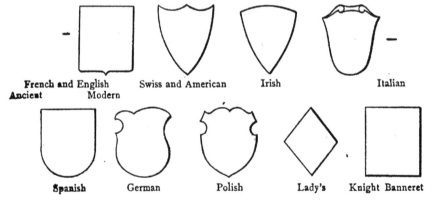

French and English   Swiss and American   Irish   Italian
Ancient   Modern

Spanish   German   Polish   Lady's   Knight Banneret

charges, we will state, at the outset, that *the shape of the shield is an indifferent matter* and that it may be chosen at will. But to satisfy the very natural sentiment which attaches us to the *natale solum,* " our own, our native land," we shall

[a] Nainfa, *Costume of Prelates.*

here reproduce the various shapes and forms of the shield according to divers nationalities. The most convenient one for all styles of blazonry seems to be the modern French-English form. (See illustration 1.)

The heraldists have assigned special names to the *nine points* or places which are found on the field, designations of primary importance for correct blazoning (describing and representing of armorial devices). The upper portion of the shield or chief has its *dexter* (right) and *sinister* (left) points, where are located the corresponding dexter and sinister cantons of the chief; in the middle portion or *fess* is found the center or heart point, above which is located the honor or collar point; in the lower part or base we have again a dexter and sinister point with their respective cantons of the base. (Illustration 2.) It will be noticed that dexter

2. POINTS OF THE SHIELD.

2	1	3
Dexter	CHIEF middle	Sinister
	4 honor collar	
	5	
Dexter Flank	FESS center, heart	Sinister Flank
	6	
	nombril	
8 Dexter	7 BASE	9 Sinister

1. The middle *chief* point.

2. The dexter chief, dexter canton of the chief.

3. The sinister chief, sinister canton of the chief.

4. The honor point, or collar point.

5. The *fess* point, or center, heart point.

6. The nombril or navel point.

7. The middle *base* point.

8. The dexter base, dexter canton of the base.

9. The sinister base, sinister canton of the base.

judgment " (*sic*), the honor point is his *collar* (compare the collars of army and navy) ; the *heart* is in the center, flanked by right and left arms, and lastly the *legs* are figured in the dexter and sinister base points. One thing, however, is certain of heraldic practice, it is that the chief is the place for the sky, and the base likewise for the ground.

A third and last item of information pertaining to the field are the divisions of the same. (See illustration 3.) And in

3. DIVISIONS OF THE SHIELD (PARTED OR PARTY).

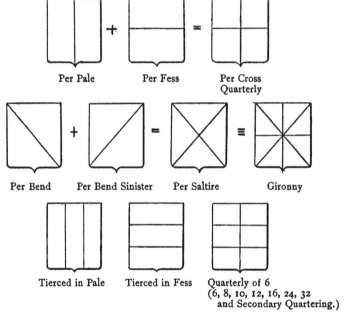

Per Pale	Per Fess	Per Cross Quarterly

Per Bend	Per Bend Sinister	Per Saltire	Gironny

Tierced in Pale	Tierced in Fess	Quarterly of 6 (6, 8, 10, 12, 16, 24, 32 and Secondary Quartering.)

addition to simple right lines and curves, dividing and border lines assume various forms; they are then said engrailed, indented, wavy, embattled, dovetail, etc. But all these divisions

Analecta.

ACTA PII PP. X.

AD V. E. JOSEPHUM GALASANCTIUM CARD. VIVES, PRAE-
FECTUM S. CONGREGATIONIS DE RELIGIOSIS, CIRCA TITULUM
FRATRUM MINORUM.

Eminentissimo Signor Cardinale,

Nelle nostre Lettere Apostoliche sulle tre Famiglie francescane, abbiamo stabilito, che quella dei Frati Minori uniti
da Leone X e Leone XIII di s. m. sia chiamata col glorioso
cognome e nota storica e distintiva di *Unione Leoniana,* prin-
cipalmente quando fosse opportuno per evitare ambiguità e
confusione negli atti pubblici. Ora, volendo che nelle sacre
Congregazioni della Romana Curia sia in perpetuo osservata
una norma uniforme nella pratica di queste Nostre disposizioni, ordiniamo che il titolo di *Ordine dei Frati Minori dell'*-

(*c*) nelle controversie e dispareri, che potessero nascere fra le tre Famiglia francescane.

In tutti gli altri casi poi, purchè a norma delle ultime nostre Lettere Apostoliche si sottintenda sempre la nota storica e caratteristica di Frati Minori dell'Unione Leoniana, che li differenzia dalle altre due Famiglie, concediamo che le SS. Congregazioni possano usare del semplice titolo di *Frati Minori, Ordine dei Frati Minori, Ministro generale dei Frati Minori.*

Incarichiamo Lei, Signor Cardinale, di communicare queste nostre disposizioni a tutte le SS. Congregazioni Romane per la piena osservanza, e Ci confermiamo a Lei affmo.

PIUS PP. X.

Dal Vaticano, li 15 Dicembre 1909.

S. CONGREGATIO CONSISTORIALIS.

I.

DE COMPETENTIA SACRAE CONGREGATIONIS CONCILII SUPER CONFRATERNITATES ET PIAS UNIONES POST CONSTIT. "SAPIENTI CONSILIO".

Proposito dubio, " utrum competentia super confraternitates a Constitutione *Sapienti consilio* tributa sacrae Congregationi Concilii se extendat quoque ad confraternitates et pias uniones quae dependent ab Ordinibus et congregationibus religiosis, vel erectae sunt in eorum ecclesiis seu domibus; an potius haec reservata sit sacrae Congregationi de Religiosis ".

Emi Patres S. Congregationis Consistorialis, praehabito Consultoris voto, in generalibus comitiis diei 9 Decembris 1909 respondendum censuerunt: *Affirmative ad primam partem, negative ad secundam.*

Facta vero, die insequenti, de his relatione SSmo, Sanctitas sua resolutionem Emorum Patrum ratam habuit et confirmavit.

C. Card. DE LAI, *Secretarius.*

L. * S.

SCIPIO TECCHI, *Adsessor.*

II.

DE COMPETENTIA SACRAE CONGREGATIONIS DE PROPAGANDA FIDE SUPER NONNULLAS SOCIETATES MISSIONUM.

resolvendum sequens dubium: " utrum S. Congregatio de Propaganda Fide etiam post Constit. *Sapienti consilio* suam jurisdictionem exercere debeat super societates, sive Lugdunensem pro missionibus ad Afros, sive Parisiensem pro missionibus ad exteras gentes, nec non super seminarium Mediolanense S. Caloceri seu Institutum Mediolanense pro exteris missionibus, denique super pontificium seminarium SS. Apostolorum Petri et Pauli de Urbe ad exteras missiones, praesertim quoad ea quae respiciunt eorum regulas, administrationem, atque opportunas concessiones ad sacram alumnorum ordinationem requisitas ".

Et Emi Patres S. Congregationis Consistorialis, votis duorum Consultorum aliisque perpensis, responderunt: *Affirmative in omnibus.*

Die vero 10 Decembris 1909, facta de his relatione SSmo, Sanctitas sua resolutionem Emorum Patrum ratam habuit et confirmavit.

C. Card. DE LAI, *Secretarius.*

L. * S.

SCIPIO TECCHI, *Adsessor.*

S. CONGREGATIO RITUUM.

DIOECESUM GALLIAE ET BELGII ATQUE UTRIUSQUE DITIONIS COLONIARUM

CONCEDITUR CLERO DITIONUM GALLIAE ET BELGII ET UTRIUSQUE COLONIARUM OFFICIUM CUM MISSA DE S. COLETA VIRGINE.

IN PROPRIO DIOECESANO

DIE 6 MARTII

IN FESTO S. COLETAE VIRGINIS

Duplex.

Omnia de communi Virginum, praeter sequentia:

.

In I Nocturno

In Quadragesima: De Virginibus praeceptum.   *Extra Quadragesimam, de Scriptura occurrente.*

In II Nocturno

Lectio IV.

Picardiae civitatis Corbeja, dioecesis Ambianensis, sanctae Coletae natalibus ex matre sterili et sexagenaria, illustris effecta est.   Haec ab ineunte aetate coepit ardentius colere officia caritatis: ita ut quidquid habere poterat, hilariter pauperibus largiretur.   Orationi assidue vacans, solitaria loca quaerebat, tenerum ibi corpusculum affligens, ieiuniis carnem spiritui subiiciens, catena ferrea cilicioque numquam aut raro depositis, humi cubans, cum eam necessarius somnus occupabat.   Quartumdecimum aetatis annum agens, orationibus impetravit a Domino, ut corpus suum, quod exiguum remanebat, subito ad iustam magnitudinem excreverit: ac vultus venustas, ne forte alicui occasionem praeberet delinquendi, in terreum colorem mutaretur.   A daemonibus frequenter lacessita, diversisque apparitionibus exagitata, vulneribusque toto corpore lacerata, ab oratione tamen numquam recedebat: in qua saepe in ecstasim rapta Angelorum visione et colloquio potiebatur.

Lectio V.

Facultatibus pauperibus distributis, tertii Ordinis sancti Francisci regulam professa, novas praecedentibus austeritates superaddens, in reclusorium successit; ubi per triennium morata, vitam plane coelestem aggressa est, nudis semper pedibus, etiam hiemis tempore incedens, et continuis ieiuniis corpus suum pene conficiens.   Tum se ad reformandum seraphici Francisci pene collapsum Ordinem, a Deo varie admonita, destinare cognovit: cui humiliter diu reluctans, linguae oculorumque usu deperdito, tandem voluntati divinae sese subiicere coacta est. Utroque autem sensu mox in integrum restituto, divino Spiritu afflata, Apostolicae Sedis adire praesentiam decrevit, ut a Summo Pontifice praedictum opus exsecutioni mandandi facultatem exposceret.   A quo benedictione accepta, susceptoque praedictae reformationis mandato, in patriam rediens,

Lectio VI.

Cum autem summo studio, tam antiquis monasteriis re-
formandis, quam novis exstruendis incumberet, ingruentes
difficultates admirabili constantia superavit. Paupertatis semper studiosissima fuit, unica tunica, eâque districta contenta,
angustissimam cellam in angulo habens, nulla supellectili in-
structam, praeter stramineum saccum, qui ei pro lectulo erat.
Caritate, patientia, humilitate, mansuetudine ceterisque virtutibus decorata, dono etiam prophetiae illustris, abdita fidei
mysteria divinitus edocta, ita penetravit, ut de his altissime
dissereret. Multis tandem, et maximis patratis miraculis,
morte sua ante biennium praecognita, omnibus Sacramentis
munita, hortatisque sororibus ad regularem disciplinam, obdormivit in Domino, pridie Nonas Martii, anno millesimo
quadringentesimo quadragesimo septimo, Gandavi in Flandria,
in monasterio a se aedificato; in quo sacrae eius reliquiae as-
sidua veneratione primum excultae, postremo a monialibus,
e coenobio depulsis, anno Domini millesimo septingentesimo
octogesimo tertio, Poliniacum, tunc Bisuntinae dioecesis in
Gallia, in Clarissarum monasterium translatae fuerunt, ubi
usque nunc piissime asservantur. Eam denique Pius septimus
Pontifex Maximus, nono Kalendas Iunii, anno octingentesimo
septimo supra millesimum, novis riteque probatis prodigiis
coruscantem, solemni pompa Sanctorum albo recensuit.

In III Nocturno

Homilia in Evangelium Simile est regnum coelorum decem
virginibus, *de eodem Communi.*

In Quadragesima, IX Lectio de Homilia feriae.

IN APPENDICE MISSALIS

Missa Dilexisti, *de Communi Virginum, praeter sequentia:*

ORATIO

Domine Iesu Christe, qui beatam Coletam virginem tuam
coelestibus donis cumulasti: tribue quaesumus; ut eius virtutes
aemulantes in terris, gaudiis cum ipsa perfruamur aeternis:
Qui vivis et regnas.

tibi offerendo, mentes nostras refove: quibus, in eo suscipiendo, beatam Coletam ad mores populi tui instaurandos replere voluisti. Per Dominum.

POSTCOMMUNIO

Fac, Domine Iesu Christe, ut beata virgo Coleta, sponsa tibi fidelis, divinae caritatis flammiam excitet in cordibus nostris; quam ad perennem Ecclesiae tuae gloriam, innumeris virginibus inseruit: Qui vivis et regnas.

DECRETUM

Sanctam Coletam, quae coelitus missa, non modo ad regularem disciplinam pluribus in locis collapsam, in utraque Francisci Assisiensis et Clarae familia instaurandam, verum ad ipsam Ecclesiam Dei reparandam superna ope delecta fuit, magno pietatis studio christifideles, praesertim in Galliae, Germaniae et Belgii regionibus merito prosequuntur. Siquidem inclyta haec Virgo, divino aestuans amore, atque in proximos caritate flagrans, tum rigidiores poenitentes summa austeritate assidue aemulata, tum egenos ac maxime aegrotos benignissime complexa, distributis antea in pauperes suis facultatibus, tertii Ordinis sancti Francisci regulam professa, consiliis evangelicis arctissime inhaerens, omnium virtutum culmen attingere visa est. Mundo mori omnimode cupiens, in *reclusorium,* uti aiunt, secessit, ibique triennium morata est. Divinitus dein admonita, moderatoribus annuentibus, ex illo egressa fuit. Haud multo post, Spiritu divino afflante, ad reformandam vitam regularem Clarissarum, quibus a Romano Pontifice cooptata fuerat, indubiis accedentibus signis, sapienti consilio impigre adlaboravit. Incredibile dictu est, quantocius reformatio a Coleta feliciter peracta fuerit, quamplura exstructa monasteria, adaucto in dies monialium numero, instaurata ubique arctioris disciplinae Clarissarum ratio, adhuc late virescens: quam plurima sanctitatis specimina Ecclesiae Christi contulisse compertum est. Nec satis: zelo succensa Coleta virorum quoque religiosorum familiam primi Ordinis excitavit, qui Coletani idcirco appellati, uberrimos fructos retulerunt, et sacculo decimosexto ab Apostolica Sede Fratrum Minorum Ordini, lubentibus animis, fuerunt inserti.

nullis iniuriis, aut calumniis, nedum conviciis infracta, mulier fortissima mirifice perfecit; perditis nimirum populorum moribus emendandis intendit, et grassanti schismati in Occidente delendo; missa propterea ad Concilium Constantiense sapientissima epistola. Coletae virtutum et miraculorum fama, Italiam, Galliam, Germaniam aliasque pervagata regiones, undique ad ipsam confluebant gentes, opem a Deo Coletae precibus consecuturae: quinimmo viri praestantes virtute ac doctrina eam conveniebant, tamquam sanctitatis et perfectionis christianae magistram et exemplar: quos inter Vincentius Ferreri, Ioannes a Capistrano et Ioanna Arcensis virgo, uti fertur; quae, ad Galiam sospitandam tunc temporis excitata, beatorum coelitum honores, orbe plaudente, nuperrime assecuta est. Quibus omnibus permoti, Rmus Dnus Fulbertus Petit, Archiepiscopus Bisuntinus, in qua dioecesi primum sanctae Coletae coenobium exstat, ac Rmus P. Dionysius Schüler, Minister generalis totius Ordinis Fratrum Minorum, nacti occasionem primi labentis saeculi ab ipsius inclytae Virginis canonizatione, sanctissimo Domino nostro Pio Papae X supplicia vota porrexerunt, ut festum sanctae Coletae ad cunctas Galliae et Belgii regiones, atque ad earumdem gentium Colonias extendere dignaretur: quorum vota libentissime obsecundarunt fere omnes sacrorum Antistites Gallicae et Belgicae ditionis, praeeunte Emo et Rmo Dno Cardinali Petro Coullié, Archiepiscopo Lugdunensi, et Galliarum Primate: iis enim in locis, sive tantae Virginis nativitate, sive rebus mirifice gestis, sive pretiosa eius morte, vel ipsius reliquiarum custodia, Coletae nomen in benedictione est ac pari veneratione. Quare Rmus P. Franciscus Xaverius Hertzog, Societatis S. Sulpitii Procurator generalis, et Rmus P. Franciscus Paolini, Postulator generalis Ordinis Fratrum Minorum, huiusce causae respectivi Postulatores, Officii proprii ac Missae de sancta Coleta exhibitum schema supremae sanctioni eiusdem sanctissimi Domini nostri humillime subiecerunt. Sanctitas porro Sua, eiusmodi precibus peramanter deferens, una cum litteris hac de re postulatoriis sacrorum Galliae et Belgii Antistitum, ab infrascripto Cardinali Sebastiano Martinelli sacrae Rituum Congregationi Praefecto relatis, festum sanctae Coletae virginis, sub ritu duplici minori, in universis Galliae, Belgii et utriusque Coloniarum regionibus, die sexta Martii (vel, hac impedita, prima subsequenti die libera iuxta Rubricas) quotannis recolendum decrevit, cum suprascriptis Officio et Missa: servatis Rubricis. Contrariis non obstantibus quibuscumque.   Die 25 Augusti 1909.

Fr. S. Card. MARTINELLI, *Praefectus.*

L. * S.

PHILIPPUS CAN. DI FAVA, *Substitutus.*

ROMAN CURIA.

Official announcement is made of the following honors and appointments:

29 October, 1909: The Rev. Maurice M. Hassett, D.D., Rector of the Cathedral of Harrisburg, made Domestic Prelate.

The Very Rev. Thomas Joseph Shahan, D.D., Rector of the Catholic University of America, Washington, made Domestic Prelate.

Sign. Narciso Hamel, General President of the Society of St. Vincent de Paul, Quebec, Canada, made Commander of the Order of St. Gregory the Great (civil class).

6 November, 1909: His Eminence Cardinal Francesco di Paolo Cassetta, appointed Protector of the Order of Minims.

17 November, 1909: Giuseppe Rosales y Gutierrez de Bustillo, of the Philippine Islands, made Knight of the Order of S. Sylvester.

22 November, 1909: The Rev. D. Edoardo Ferreira, Secretary of the Bishop of Cordoba (Argentina), made Domestic Prelate.

29 November, 1909: Mons. Francesco Cherubini appointed Sub-Secretary of the S. Congregation of Religious.

18 December, 1909: The Very Rev. P. Francis Fallon, Provincial of the Oblates of Mary Immaculate in North America, promoted to the Bishopric of London, Canada.

The Rev. James O'Reilly, Rector of the Church of St. Anthony, Minneapolis, of the Diocese of St. Paul, Minnesota, promoted to the Bishopric of Fargo, United States of America.

Studies and Conferences.

OUR ANALECTA.

Roman documents for the month are:

1. The Holy Father, in an official letter to Cardinal Vives, Prefect of the S. Congregation of Religious, declares that the members of the Franciscan Order commonly known as Friars Minor, are to be distinguished as *Friars Minor of the Leonine Union* in all official documents in which the three branches of the great Franciscan family are mentioned or in which special privileges of the Friars Minor are set forth. The object of this declaration is to avoid confusion, since both the Conventuals and the Capuchins are known by the name of Friars Minor as a general term applicable to all the institutes of the original Franciscan foundation.

S. Congregation of Consistory: 1. Decides that the competence of the S. Congregation of the Council extends to the confraternities and pious unions which depend on religious Orders or Congregations, although the latter themselves are subject to the S. Congregation for Religious.

2. Decides that missionary societies, such as that of Lyons for the African missions, of Paris and Milan for the foreign missions, are subject to the jurisdiction of the Propaganda.

S. Congregation of Rites publishes a new office and mass in honor of St. Coleta, Virgin, obligatory for France, Belgium, and their respective colonies.

Roman Curia announces a number of appointments and honors.

A REMEDY FOR MIXED MARRIAGES.

·Church. The Denver *Catholic Register* also quotes the article extensively. And, by the way, here is the text of the mandatory conclusion of a Pastoral of Bishop Matz of Denver, dated 2 February, 1907: " Therefore we demand that any Protestant wishing to marry a Catholic submit to a course of instructions, to prepare himself for the discharge of his duties in helping to raise a Catholic family. *We shall grant no dispensation, unless this request is complied with*—and we warn Catholics to take up this matter in time with their non-Catholic suitors. The raising of a Catholic family in a mixed marriage, where the father is a Protestant, is a most difficult task; but if the mother happens to be Protestant, then it becomes almost impossible. Therefore *we positively shall refuse to grant a dispensation in a mixed marriage where the woman is a non-Catholic,* and we warn all Catholic young men against forming such acquaintances with a view to contracting marriage." It may not be inopportune to mention in this connexion a little brochure of which we have spoken with warm commendation in these pages before; we mean Father J. T. Durward's *A Short Course in Catholic Doctrine,* especially written for the above purpose. This non-controversial and comprehensive little work contains twelve chapters, and ends with the conclusion " Finis sit initium ", which it has been and will certainly be for many a soul who is of good will.

CATECHETICAL INSTRUCTION AT THE EARLY MASSES.

Since the Holy Father in 1905, through his Encyclical on Christian Doctrine, urged the necessity of instructing the faithful carefully and continually in the rudiments of religion, there has been a great revival of the old practice of catechetical instruction at the low Masses on Sundays, and at Vespers. The Sovereign Pontiff himself suggested a method by which the contents of the Catechism could be conveniently covered in a course of five years, devoting one year to each of the following divisions: Creed—Sacraments—Decalogue—Prayer—Precepts of the Church.

This plan has been followed, as an eminent missionary assures us, in many places. In not a few dioceses the bishops have prescribed the course definitely according to a published program which all pastors are obliged to follow. Thus a New York paper informed its readers recently that with the beginning of the New Year the clergy of Brooklyn have entered upon a new method of Sunday services. We quote:

The first day of the season of Advent yesterday was marked by an innovation in the Brooklyn Catholic Diocese.

Bishop McDonnell ordered the clergy to dispense with sermons at all Masses hereafter, except the last Mass on Sundays. The priests, instead of preaching sermons at the half-past 6, 8, 9 and 10 o'clock services, are to give instructions based on the Catechism of the Church. According to Mgr. Joseph McNamee, Rector of St. Teresa's Church, Brooklyn, the plan is in vogue in Ireland. Bishop McDonnell contemplated introducing it in his diocese a year ago, but deferred action until he heard from Mgr. McNamee, who when abroad made special inquiries into the matter. The monsignor's report of his observations caused Bishop McDonnell to act.

Every priest in the diocese received at the direction of Bishop McDonnell a book containing the formula of the new method of instruction. Mgr. John I. Barrett, diocesan secretary, explains the object as follows:

"The idea is one which will help grown people through these plain instructions to get a deep and fine conception of all that the Church has to offer. The priests will take up and unfold in the most careful, plain way, the teachings of the Sacraments, the Commandments, the Apostles' Creed, the Hail Mary, the Lord's Prayer, and the acts of contrition, of faith, of hope, and of charity. It is quite probable that an entire year will be spent in instructions in the Apostles' Creed alone, and by the time the last leaf in the book of instructions has been turned ten years will have elapsed."

THE "CORRECTED" FORMS OF THE HYMNS IN THE VATICAN GRADUALE.

It is credibly stated that the long delay in the appearance of the Vatican Graduale is, at least partly, due to a difference of opinion as to the inclusion of the "corrected" or of the "original" forms of the older hymns. The Graduale has made manifest to the world the fact that the Commission on Chant felt not merely the desirability, but the necessity, of a return to the older texts. Some hymnologists, Catholics as well as Protestants, have expressed their dislike of the changes in text made by the Correctores of Urban VIII—changes which replaced the older and less polished diction, and the unquantitative rhythms, by classical diction and metres. Perhaps on this score alone a return to the original forms was desirable. But in at least one obvious case, such a return was a necessity, if the original chant melody was to be restored. Our present *Coelestis urbs Jerusalem* was originally the rugged but fine old hymn *Urbs beata Hierusalem*. The Correctores were apparently offended by the rugged diction and the unclassical rhythm of the old hymn, but unfortunately, in the revising process, changed wholly its metre (from trochaic into iambic), so that the chant melody could not, without much mutilation, be used for the revised hymn. The attempt to do this, as seen in the Ratisbon Vesperal, was an awkward one. The mutilated chant melody was scarcely singable by those whose ears had been attuned so often to the melody of the *Pange lingua gloriosi Corporis mysterium*. In the body of the Vatican Graduale, only the older and unrevised texts of hymns are given (e. g. the *Pange lingua . . . proelium,* and the *Vexilla Regis prodeunt*). It is now said that the S. Congregation of Rites differs with the Vatican Commission on the Chant in respect of the return to the original hymn-texts. It does not desire to have the older, unrevised forms, and, *pendente lite,* the Antiphonary cannot, of course, appear. It would seem that the S. R. C. had begun much earlier its protest against the unrevised hymns; for the appendix to the Graduale gives both the unrevised forms (with notation) and the revised forms (without notation). One of these hymns thus given in both forms, is the *Veni Creator Spiritus,* which offers one little illustration of the difficulty found more obviously in the *Coelestis urbs Jerusalem*. The older form of one line is: *Dextrae Dei tu digitus,* and the corrected form is: *Digitus paternae dexterae*. The melody offers only one note for the syllable *Dex;* so that the singer is forced to crowd, somehow or other, the two syllables: *Digi* into the melodic space of one syllable. Accordingly, the Graduale italicizes the second syllable: Dig*i* in order to indicate the fact that both syllables must be sung to but one note of the melody. The difference of opinion between the S. R. C. and the Vatican Commission is a fundamental one. Something must be sacrificed—either the original form of the melody (in certain hymns) or the revisions made by the Correctores. One obvious way out of the difficulty would of course be, to retain the original melodies, but to give an additional revision to the hymns, which would restore the proper rhythms for singing, while eliminating the prosodial defects of the old hymns. This would reduce the difficulty to a matter of taste, although it would sacrifice that pleasant flavor of antiquity which is one of the precious heirlooms of the whole liturgy—ceremonial and vestments as well as music and hymnody.

FATHER BOARMAN'S ANSWER TO THE CRITIC OF HIS CATECHISM.

To the Editor, THE ECCLESIASTICAL REVIEW.

After receiving from all sides so many strong endorsements of my little catechism, I am well pleased to see the impression it has made upon "Scrutator", an unbiased writer who, having examined it critically, declares that it has "many admirable qualities as a catechism for children". He has, however, found a few things to which he takes exception. The comments of "Scrutator", as published in the November number of the REVIEW, I look upon as another endorsement of the manual; and I shall be happy to incorporate into the booklet whatever seems commendable. No catechism is perfect, and the best catechisms are always the result of the combined wisdom and experience of many minds. Regarding the several items to which attention was called, I beg to submit the following reasons for my views:

1. Man was defined as a creature composed of a body and a "*spiritual*" soul. The word "*spiritual*" was used designedly to offset the dangers of materialism which teaches so many blighting errors concerning the nature of the soul of man.

2. The question and answer on the formation of the body of Eve make it plain that God breathed a living soul into the body of Eve.

3. I do not think that the date of the birth of Christ can be better stated than by saying that, "Christ was born about nineteen hundred years ago".

salvation is generally attributed to those acts of Christ more manifestly meritorious, namely, His sufferings and death.

6. In naming the chief works of Christ, the Catechism mentioned only the great "abiding" works of His mission. Hence miracles were omitted; though, in the preceding answer, miracles were
enumerated amongst the chief means by which Christ proved Himself the Messiah.

7. In defining "Tradition", I gave the "*objective*" definition;
because this definition seemed to me most conducive to the instruction
of children.

8. My argument for the Catholic Church from the unbroken line
of Popes is this: The continuity of the Catholic Church with the
Church of the days of Peter proves that the Catholic Church is the
true Church founded by Christ upon Peter: But the unbroken line
of Popes from Peter to our day proves this continuity. Therefore,
etc.   .

9. Amongst the several necessary conditions of salvation for those
who are out of the body of the Church, I gave this one: "They cannot know the true Church." I used the word "*cannot*", in prefer-
ence to "*do not*", because "cannot" seems to express more clearly
the idea that there must be no moral guilt in their ignorance.

10. The Catechism uses the word "pledge" in the ordinary ac-
ceptation of the term as a firm resolution to abstain from intoxicating drink, etc. As I understand it, a resolution indicates the
present determination of the will, but a resolution can change without contracting sin. But promises and vows go further and bind
under pain of sin to future fulfilment.

11. Though it be true that most working people in our country
cannot keep the Holidays of obligation as they should keep the
Sundays, yet a Catechism could scarcely be excused if it neglected
to lay down the general law of the Church.

12. The Six Sins against the Holy Ghost are usually cited in
catechisms. They are called sins against the Holy Ghost because
they put into the heart unusual obstacles to the workings of the Holy
Spirit.

13. The definition of "hell" leaves out the word "state", because it seems to me that the word "state" adds little to the definition; and also because the Scriptures invariably speak of hell
as a place of torments; and the Catechism of Trent calls it a "teter-
rimus et obscurissimus carcer".

14. It seemed to me good to state the reasons why Christ insti-

15. To try to make it clear that not any kind of desire for baptism will supply the baptism of water, I stated the theological truth, that this desire for baptism must go with, or be accompanied by, the perfect love of God which is charity.

16. The answer to the question regarding the meaning of the olive oil and balm used in Confirmation was adopted verbatim from the Pope's Catechism. The answer seems to me both beautiful and instructive.

I beg to extend my sincere gratitude to " Scrutator " for his good suggestions and earnestly solicit recommendations for the improvement of the little manual which is now spreading rapidly.

MARSHALL I. BOARMAN, S.J.

Cincinnati, Ohio.

THE COLORS OF VESTMENTS AS ILLUSTRATED IN THIS NUMBER.

In order to show the difference there is between the truly liturgical colors for vestments and the aniline-colored stuffs of which our vestments are now commonly made, we have had the colored plates illustrating the contrast reproduced by a German firm after models selected and approved by Herr Fritz Stummel. Accordingly Plate I shows the harmonious and artistic colors in all their shades from light to dark. They are the result of a careful examination of the best-preserved medieval embroidery. In contrast with these we place on the same plate (Fig. 2) the colors *erroneously* styled liturgical or church colors, as far, indeed, as it was possible to reproduce in print the aniline-colors used for dyeing the silk, which affords a peculiar surface that permits these colors to come out in a sharp and garish vividness hardly attainable on paper.

Plate II shows a green vestment; the figuring is of a cooler shade; the ground a warm moss-green relieved by a lighter yellowish tint in the cross. The ornamentation of the latter is effectively enhanced by the delicate contrast of salmon-colored material with a border worked with thread-of-gold.

Plate III represents the color of a vestment in the reddish-brown purple which was deemed exceedingly rare and precious, because it reproduced a shade of purple attained only by a combination of perfect tones in red and blue according to the ancient dyers' art. There is a decided contrast between it and the modern violet so frequently affected for purple vestments. The bright lines of the cross are formed by little beads gleaming with the varied hues of mother-of-pearl. The ornamental work within the bars forming the cross is composed of delicate aglets in gold, according to an old pattern of embroidery much employed in medieval vestments.

THE AGE AND AUTHORSHIP OF THE MOSAIC PENTATEUCH.

Qu. Some time ago the Biblical Commission issued a decision to the effect that Moses is to be considered the author of the Pentateuch. How is this decision to be reconciled with the fact of the discovery of the monumental *stele* of the Code of the Babylonian King Hammurabi, which dates back to the time before Abraham, and which contains the identical laws found in the Pentateuch. In other words, the Mosaic laws were known nearly a thousand years before Moses is supposed to have written the Pentateuch. Is the Biblical Commission infallible?

Resp. The Biblical Commission is not and does not pretend to be infallible. Nevertheless it is perfectly correct in its decision.

That decision does not declare that Moses is the author of the Pentateuch. It simply declares that the arguments thus far advanced by the so-called higher criticism, resting chiefly on internal evidence, are not convincing enough to dislodge an ancient, authentic, and consistent tradition, which has heretofore been unanimously accepted by the legitimate and natural Jewish and Christian guardians of the Bible, and which has always attributed the substantial composition and authorship of the Pentateuch to the Jewish prophet and liberator Moses.

The teachers in the Catholic Church are therefore instructed to maintain this ancient tradition, and not to raise doubts which are unwarranted by any conclusive evidence to the contrary.

At the same time the Biblical Commission makes clear what it understands by the expression " Mosaic authorship ". That expression does not necessarily mean that Moses originated and wrote or even dictated the contents of the Pentateuch, in

simply means that the contents of the Pentateuch were originally collected and promulgated by the Jewish lawgiver,
Moses; that they were accepted as a code of laws under his
personal authority established by divine sanction; and that,
as we have them at present in the Pentateuch, they are substantially the expression of that divine sanction, without any
addition, diminution, or alteration that might vitiate the design of Moses as the divinely-inspired lawgiver.

Such a conception of " Mosaic authorship " does not exclude the idea that Moses availed himself of previously-existing legislation, traditions, and personal experiences. But all
these had a special divine sanction which caused him to embody them in his code. If in times of subsequent reforms it
became the duty of other legislators, such as Joshua, the
Judges, Prophets, and Priests, inspired by a similar divine impulse, to recast the original code and adapt it to new conditions, it still remained substantially the old Mosaic law, and
its authorship was so far and explicitly recognized by tradition that the scribes at times incorporated the original form of
expression adopted by Moses, side by side with its later modification made by other inspired legislators and reformers.
Thus we have duplicates of the very fundamental laws, the
ten Commandments, actually in two distinct and slightly different forms of words—Exod. 20: 2-18, and Deut. 5: 6-22.
A papyrus (Nash-Burkitt) of the Apostolic age, discovered
during 1902 in Egypt, shows a still different Hebrew text of
the same Decalogue as it was in use among the Jews of the
Maccabean period.

The Mosaic authorship of the Pentateuch does not then exclude the notion of a previously-existing code of legislation,
either such as had explicit divine sanction or such as was a
remnant of that legislation preserved in the light of the
natural law. Of the former we have an example in the address of God to Noah (Genesis 9) in which some of the positive elements of the Mosaic legislation are first indicated [cf.
Lev. 17] and from which Hebrew tradition evolved the so-
called Heptalogue of the proselytes. These were incorporated
in part in the Mosaic Decalogue, and sanctioned in the first
Apostolic Council for the converts from paganism.

It need not surprise us therefore to find similar expressions not only of the natural law but of the positive law, as we find it in the Mosaic Pentateuch, among the nations which, as descendants of Noah and his sons, received the traditions of Noah and the commands of right living revealed to him by God.

The Church nowhere teaches or maintains that the Mosaic law is the first expression of a divine revelation, either written or orally transmitted. What she teaches is that the Law of Moses as incorporated in the Pentateuch, is there written by a direct impulse from God, and is, so far as we have any records, the most perfect and complete code of moral, dogmatic, and disciplinary legislation known to man. The *Code of Hammurabi* contains many laws and ordinances which sound like the laws of Moses; but it is very far from true to say " that it contains the identical laws found in the Pentateuch ".

To any one who wishes to compare the two codes, and to get a good notion of what the *stele,* discovered by De Morgan in the ruins of the old Elamite capital, Susa, contains, will find Dr. Davies's little manual, *The Codes of Hammurabi and Moses,* excellent for the purpose. It gives the history, text with parallels and comment, authorities, and indexes to a complete understanding of the Hammurabi Code.

Father Scheil was the first to make a good (paraphrasing) translation of the 247 laws preserved in the monument. There is a fracture or erasure on one side of the stone, which has destroyed the reading of some thirty-five of the 282 numbered laws. Prof. Davies, of the Ohio Wesleyan University, has taken note of all the principal versions, so that the reader gets a clear and all-sided view of the document as far as is possible. The book can be obtained from Jennings and Graham (Cincinnati) or Eaton and Mains (New York).

FUNERAL RITE OF CHILDREN.

Qu. There is a custom with some foreigners of having the Mass of the Angels said at the funeral of an infant.

Will you kindly refer me to where I may read of how the Votive Mass of the Angels ranks on an occasion of this kind?

M. F. McG.

Resp. The said custom has the sanction of the S. Congregation of Rites. (Cf. *Decreta Authentica,* nn. 3481 Paris. et 3510 Aurelian.)

The Mass *De Angelis* is the one found at the end of the Missal among the votive Masses, beginning " Benedicite Dominum omnes Angeli ejus." It can be said only on days when ordinary votive Masses are permitted, as on semi-doubles; that is to say, it is *not* permitted on double feasts, on Sundays, within the octaves of Christmas, Epiphany, Easter, Pentecost,. and Corpus Christi; on the vigils of Christmas, Epiphany, and Pentecost; Ash Wednesday, and the ferial days of Holy Week; All Souls' Day, 2 November; in parish churches where but one Mass is said with procession on Rogation days. On these days the Mass of the feast or day is said in thanksgiving for the child's translation to heaven since it died in the state of innocence.

The Votive Mass *De Angelis* is said in white, *with Gloria,* with two orations added from the office (Mass) of the day, *without Credo,* the Preface common, unless the day be within an Octave or season that has its proper Preface. *Ite missa est* at the end.

After the Mass, which is offered in thanksgiving and not *per modum suffragii,* the rites prescribed in the Ritual *pro obsequiis parvulorum* are performed. The bells ring a joyous air and the music is in accord with the spirit of gratitude for the happiness of a holy innocent. (Cf. ECCLESIASTICAL REVIEW, Vol. XXII, p. 634; Vol. XXIII, p. 187.)

QUESTIONS PROPOSED TO THE EDITOR OF " THE ECCLESIASTICAL REVIEW. "

Under the caption of *Studies and Conferences* the REVIEW publishes each month communications from correspondents, mainly in the form of questions which the Editor answers, or on which he comments when occasion calls for it. This-

also as censor, book-agent, translator, writer of inscriptions, designer, almoner, advocate "in causis criminalibus clericorum ". We have repeatedly stated in these pages that we cannot, as Editor of the REVIEW, undertake any such obligation, and that the appearance of the Conference Department in our pages is not to be interpreted as a pledge that we shall reply either by private letter or in print to questions addressed to us by readers of the REVIEW.

The reasons for this limitation must be obvious when it is remembered that the REVIEW addresses itself to some twenty-thousand English-speaking priests, many of whom find it convenient at one time or another to have their theological or pastoral doubts disposed of by addressing them to the Editor or to the publisher. We say " to the publisher ", because a large number of priests pay their subscription bills in some such form as this:

Dear Editor—Enclosed $3.50 to renew my subscription to the REVIEW. Would you please answer in your next, or by return mail with the receipt, the following questions which came up in a discussion among a number of priests last evening, etc.

The number of such questions to which replies are expected " in the next number " or " by private letter " often amounts to several hundred. It is impossible to publish all the answers in the REVIEW; first, because our space is limited; secondly, because many of the questions are not answerable or have been answered in previous numbers, often within the same volume; thirdly, because some of the answers may easily be found in any manual of theology, liturgy, ecclesiastical history, or encyclopedia, or they are so local and personal as not to permit publication of them without the risk of creating false impressions and animosities.

Nor can we always answer by private letter. There is a very great difference between the readers of an ordinary popular magazine or newspaper and the readers of a professional ecclesiastical periodical. The latter are nearly all in a position which prompts discussion, inquiry, and readiness to write for information. No other class of professional men are in the way of meeting so many urgent and intricate doubts and difficulties, to which superior judgment, precedent, or definite legislative authority needs to be applied. It is not surprising therefore that the number and character of the questions which come to us are disproportionately large and serious. Accordingly the information and advice sought from the Editor often demand more than a perfunctory reference to decrees, statistics, sources, or precedent cases. Nor can the solution be referred, as in a newspaper or ordinary intelligence office, to a secretary or reference clerk whose memory serves as an index of general information.

Whilst the Editor endeavors to answer by private letter, in most cases, the important queries proposed to him, it is hardly fair to assume that, besides preparing a magazine which furnishes definite information of a professional and practical nature not easily accessible in any other form to our clergy, he should at the same time act as an attorney general in ecclesiastical and pastoral affairs for the large and critical body of readers of THE ECCLESIASTICAL REVIEW. There are official tribunals in every diocese, with opportunities of appeal to metropolitan courts, to the Apostolic Delegation, and to the Roman Congregations. These are open to every priest, and they are professedly instituted to decide questions of practical importance for ecclesiastics. The Editor of the REVIEW seeks to supply useful material for its readers, and a full measure of it. Beyond this he neither desires nor has he the ability to assume the duties of auditor in affairs which properly belong to ecclesiastical authority, or to supply information "on call" regarding matters which are easily to be found in theological text-books, and in manuals of liturgy or apologetics.

Let us say it once more. The *Conferences* which appear in our monthly issues are published for the purpose of furnishing opportune information to priests who prefer to read their pastoral theology in that form. They are not intended to serve

withdraw their subscription. We on our part regard the terms of our mutual contract with our readers to require no more from us than to furnish them the REVIEW.

A very estimable priest wrote to us some time ago complaining that we did not acknowledge or answer his queries. He stated that he would have been quite willing to make extra compensation for the extra services, as is done in the case of lawyers and consulting physicians, if we would only fix our terms. Our answer to this is that we have no terms; that we devote all our services to the REVIEW, apart from our obligations to our diocesan in the position assigned to us as professor in the Seminary. At the same time we wish also to say that, if we had the strength or energy and time, we would gladly respond to the wishes of all sincere inquirers, no matter how far out of our ordinary line or compact their demands might be. And in such case we would be simply acting out the privilege of our priestly calling to serve our brother-priests without any compensation in money or temporal commodity.

CELEBRATIO MISSAE PER SACERDOTEM NON JEJUNUM.

Qu. Can the permission which the Holy See has granted to those permanently sick—to receive Holy Communion after taking some liquid nourishment—be extended to priests who are in the same condition and desire to say Mass? In other words, may such priests say Mass after taking some liquid food?

Resp. The Decree (7 December, 1906) of the S. Congregation of the Council permitting persons who have been sick for a month, without any sure prospect of recovering soon (*absque certa spe ut cito convalescant*), to receive Holy Communion, once or twice a week (if they live in a community or house where the Blessed Sacrament is reserved), after having taken some liquid by way of drink, extends to priests as well as laymen. Since, according to an official interpretation by the same Congregation (6 March, 1907), it is not required that the person who is ill, should be confined to bed, the inference that a priest may take Holy Communion by saying Mass, seems legitimate, so long as in the judgment of the physician the patient cannot sustain the fast, and on the other hand the confessor deems it advisable that his penitent should receive the Blessed Sacrament.

STIPEND FOR THE SECOND MASS.

Qu. There appeared in a Roman journal not long ago a communication from the Congregation of the Council, dated 7 August, 1909, in which a decision is rendered in answer to a request of the Bishop of Breda in Holland, granting to the clergy of that diocese the privilege of accepting a stipend for a second Mass whenever they are obliged to duplicate. In the course of the discussion of this decision it is stated that "Our Most Holy Lord, the Pope, has been graciously pleased to decree that faculty be given, as it is given by these presents, to the Ordinaries of missionary countries to permit for just and serious reasons that priests subject to them may and can receive a stipend for the second Mass also."

Since the diocese of Breda has, in virtue of the Constitution *Sapienti consilio,* ceased to be subject to the jurisdiction of the Propaganda, its status is identical with that of our dioceses of the United States, which have likewise ceased to be under the jurisdiction of Propaganda as missionary dioceses. Are we therefore to understand the above words of the Holy Father to imply that priests in the United States (missionary in the same sense as those of the diocese of Breda, although, like it, our dioceses are no longer under Propaganda) enjoy the right of accepting a stipend for the second Mass in cases of legitimate bination? It would seem so; although I have not seen in the REVIEW any mention of this privilege, which would be a very important one for us.

Resp. The decision referred to appeared in the *Acta Apostolicae Sedis,* 15 October, 1909, and is of a merely local character, as its introductory argument indicates. It simply extends a faculty, granted to the clergy of some missionary countries, and formerly also to the diocese of Breda. In virtue of this extension the clergy of Breda, although now no longer under the jurisdiction of the Propaganda as a strictly mission-

of some charity (*in causas pias*), especially the maintenance of poor priests. From this charitable fund in behalf of poor priests, those are not excluded who have themselves contributed to the fund by their offer (of the stipend for the second Mass), provided they are in need of such help.

The decision has therefore no application to priests outside the diocese of Breda, unless they have a special indult to that effect.

RESERVATION OF THE BLESSED SACRAMENT IN PRIVATE CHAPELS.

Qu. In a manual of liturgy I read: " Asservatio SS. Sacramenti in capellis seu oratoriis non permittitur, nisi in praedictis oratoriis missa *quotidie* celebretur uti patet ex pluribus Decretis S. Rituum Congregationis, praesertim ex uno Bajonen, diei 14 Maji 1889 ad II." Does this obligation extend to the United States in such manner as to prohibit the reservation of the Blessed Sacrament in chapels where Mass is not said daily?

Resp. The disciplinary conditions for reserving the Blessed Sacrament in private chapels are based upon the principle of securing due reverence to the Real Presence. This principle of reverence requires that a priest should be the guardian of the tabernacle, by having the custody of the key, the duty of renewing the Sacred Species at fixed intervals, the dispensing of It to those who desire to communicate out of devotion or by way of viaticum, and of presenting It to the worship of the faithful at Benediction.

To secure the maintenance of this guardianship with its requirements of renewal, distribution, and adoration, the Church prescribes that Mass must be said periodically in chapels where the Blessed Sacrament is reserved. The period or interval between the Masses is not fixed by a uniform law, prescribing daily Mass, because it is not essential for the security and reverence of the Blessed Sacrament that Mass should be said every day. In some places it is both possible and desirable that the Mass should be said daily. This is the case in Catholic countries, since this mode of guarding the Real Presence is calculated to attract worshippers. There the privilege of reserving the Blessed Sacrament would be granted only on condition that Mass is celebrated " daily ", which term is to be interpreted however in a general sense, as when speaking of something done usually once every day, although accidentally it may be omitted now and then.

In missionary countries, or in places where there are only few to attend Mass, the rule is less stringent, and the faculty of reserving the Blessed Sacrament in private chapels is given to bishops to use at their discretion, always with the understanding that the chief principle of reverence, as explained above, be maintained. Our bishops frequently obtain the faculty of permitting the Blessed Sacrament to be kept in chapels where Mass is said three times or, at least once, a week. The indult granted in individual cases for reserving the Blessed Sacrament in private chapels, as in convents, etc., usually contains the phrase " servatis servandis ", which means that a light is to be kept constantly burning before the tabernacle, and that Mass is to be said at the altar, if possible daily, or at least once a week—" dummodo quotidie, si fieri potest, aut saltem semel in hebdomada Missa celebratur " (cf. Van der Stappen, Vol. IV, qu. 150 ad II.).

THE OLD ROMAN (GOTHIC) CHASUBLE AND THE ARTISTIC SENSE OF THE AMERICAN CLERGY.

him to serve her. An attempt was made to organize a society on similar lines in this country, but, on account of our great apathy and indifference to Christian art, it never gained a solid foothold. I wonder how long the clergy here are going to accept everything that the commercial supply houses see fit to furnish them? We will never have a decent art until these supply houses become educated to look beyond the pocket-book into the eyes of true art, or until individual artists are picked up and encouraged to do their best far away from the blighting influence of mere commercialism.

I know a few men who could start such an independent source of art supply. But who will give them orders sufficient to keep them alive? Until the bishops and the clergy realize our present stultifying position in regard to art and take some active steps to bring about healthier conditions, Christian art will remain a dead fish.

JOHN T. COMES.

Pittsburg, Pa.

BEAUTIFUL VESTMENTS AND RELIGIOUS COMMUNITIES.

We might add to the suggestions given in the foregoing letter that we feel sure many of our religious communities would be prepared to take up the work of ecclesiastical art-needle work and the paramentic industry, both from a sense of love of what is really beautiful and as a means of occupying young girls in the wholesome and elevating tasks of church ornamentation.

This work has three distinct advantages for convents. It promotes the external beauty and decorum of sacred worship there. It is an educational factor for our young people, who would thereby learn to discriminate and appreciate what is truly beautiful in form and in its symbolic meaning—two elements entirely absent from the average liturgical uses of to-day. Thirdly, it would enable many of our communities to add to the means of increasing their modest income by an ennobling industry, at once devotional and educational in its trend.

Sisters of the Holy Child, whose English training and Irish love of the old faith have led them to the use of Gothic vestments on great festive occasions in their motherhouse at Sharon Hill. We are convinced that these nuns would lend their help to the introduction of graceful paramentics, perhaps by the establishment of classes in their academies where the rules of the art could be taught. Doubtless there would also be other communities glad to take up the work, so that the difficulty proposed by a correspondent in our January number is not so great as might be assumed.

Our chief appeal must of course be made to the clergy. If we would but get rid of the pestilential notion of getting ugly things for God's house merely because they are the cheaper things, we should give more glory to God, raise the tone of our worship, sustain incidentally in many cases a charity by giving the money for church vestments to struggling religious who make them properly rather than to secular manufacturers who consult their private interests, however charitable they may otherwise be.

Regarding the manufacturers, however, it is to be said that they are mostly willing to furnish what is expected of them, and that they would no doubt make for us becoming chasubles if we showed the disposition to require them at a reasonable cost.

Ecclesiastical Library Table.

RECENT BIBLE STUDY.

I. **Prof. Bacon's Views.** I. THE SYNOPTIC PROBLEM. *a. The Problem Stated.* The Synoptic Problem or the question of the literary dependence of the first three Gospels was formerly solved in three different ways, by the theory of mutual inter-dependence, the theory of written sources, and the theory of oral tradition. In recent years the second Gospel plays the most important part in the explanation of the difficulty. It may be said that the whole problem is even stated in terms, as it were, of the second Gospel. For the synoptic material is divided into three great parts: first, the whole of the second Gospel (661 verses) is said to be incorporated by the first Gospel and the third, excepting only fifty verses; secondly, there is certain material common to the first Gospel and the third, amounting to at least 185 verses, not found in the second Gospel; thirdly, a third kind of material is peculiar to either the first Gospel or the third, without being found in either of the other two synoptic Gospels. How shall we explain these phenomena?

b. Recent Literature. The higher criticism has endeavored to make the problem almost wholly its own; such men as Wernle, Schmiedel, Weiss, Wellhausen, Harnack, Loisy, Sir John Hawkins, Burton, and Burkitt, have eagerly pursued the documentary analysis of the sources. The philological side of the question has been accurately studied by Gould and Swete, not to mention a number of German scholars, and Menzies has supplied the historical sidelights. A general statement of the present problem has been given in an article entitled "A Turning Point in Synoptic Criticism" in the *Harvard Theological Review,* for 1 January, 1908. The technical detail for the critical solution of the problem will be found in such scientific publications as *The American Journal*

in Yale University.[1] The writer professes to express his answer with absolute frankness, without mental reservation, in terms intelligible even to the student unfamiliar with Greek, and ignorant of the course of technical discussion. He introduces indeed the necessary historico-critical discussions into the heart of the commentary itself, but is careful to exclude the mechanism of processes and technicalities.

c. Assumptions. From the very start the writer is careful to make clear his critical principles. He is going to do for the Gospels what the Graf-Kuenen school has done for the Pentateuch. As the historical books of the Old Testament are judged in the light of the conditions as reflected in the prophetic writings, so must the Gospels be explained in the light of the great Epistles of St. Paul. Prof. Bacon distinguishes three periods in the earliest history of Christianity: the first embraces the actual events that took place in the life of Jesus Christ; the second contains the Christian belief, institutions, and practices in the Greek-speaking churches, a cross-section or a photographic view of which is given us in the great Epistles of St. Paul written a full score of years before the earliest Gospel was written; the third is expressed in the history of Christ as we find it in the Gospels or the summaries of the anecdotes which formed the evangelic tradition, told and retold for the sole purpose of explaining or defending beliefs and practices of the contemporary Church. Hence, according to the Professor, the Gospels are not strictly historical records of the life and the doctrine of Jesus Christ; they are etiological narratives. The reader can not be satisfied to be told, that such and such is the sacred writer's meaning. He demands an opinion on the question, was it so, or was it not so? What was the common starting-point from which the varying forms of the tradition diverge?

· *c. Endorsements.* Prof. Bacon assures us that the Abbé Loisy's criticism on St. Mark came into his hands after he had written the last line of his present work, and he is gratified at the coincidence of results independently attained by himself and the French Abbé in his recent *Évangiles synoptiques* (1908), especially the chapter of the Introduction entitled *Le second évangile.* This appears to be a reply to the apologists

[1] Yale University Press, New Haven, Conn.; Henry Frowde, London,. Toronto, and Melbourne: 1909.

of tradition who commonly urge the fact that no two critics are of one mind in their analysis. The writer might have appealed to Nicolardot's little volume entitled *Les procédés de rédaction des trois premiers évangelistes;*[2] for this writer too agrees with Loisy in the opinion that the Evangelists highly idealized, changed, and even invented parts of their narratives. He too investigates the question how much is due to the individual final redactors of the Gospels in the progressive development of the subject, and he solves the synoptic problem by an appeal to the theory of two sources.[3] Prof. Bacon would no doubt have mentioned J. Weiss as another kindred critic, if it had not been his principle, not to distinguish in his volume between his strictly original contributions and the opinions previously advanced by other critics, on the plea that the scholar will know what had already been said, and the general reader will not care.

d. Prof. Bacon's Solution of the Problem. Thus far we have dealt with Prof. Bacon's preliminary principle of historic development in the inspired writings of the New Testament, an assumption without which his critical analysis of the Gospels would be quite impossible. We shall now briefly indicate an outline of his solution of the synoptic problem. He considers the fundamental proposition that Mark is the literary groundwork of Matthew and Luke as now generally admitted, after an earnest debate lasting for seventy years. He believes that the second principle is accepted with almost equal unanimity; Matthew and Luke are independent compilers of Mark with another evangelic writing denoted by the symbol *Q,* and containing the teaching of Jesus. He admits that this principle is proved only by a disproof of the interdependence of Matthew and Luke in the coincident material not found in Mark. The writer considers these two principles as the demonstrated features of the so-called synoptic or Two-Document Theory; nor does he attempt to set forth its other portions as far as the first and third Gospels are concerned. But the second Gospel is studied more carefully.

2. PROF. BACON'S STUDY OF ST. MARK. *a. Assumptions.* The following suppositions concerning the second Gospel are simply assumed by Prof. Bacon: (1) The author of the Gospel in its present form is not John Mark, traditionally reported to

---

[2] Paris, 1909: Fischbacher.   [3] Cf. *Revue du clergé français,* LVII, 169-172.

have been its writer, but he is designated by the symbol *R*, indicating the Redactor or ultimate employer of the material used in the composition of the Gospel. Hence all legendary anecdotes about John Mark are severely excluded. (2) The Evangelist's story once went on to relate the substance of the early narrative of Acts, and may have even ended with the planting of the Gospel in Rome, as the Book of Acts does. This, the Professor tells his reader, is as certain as anything in the field of critical conjecture can be. How then was this original ending of the second Gospel lost? To appeal to accident is to surrender the problem rather than to suggest a reasonable theory. Mr. Bacon finds it quite enough to account for the disappearance of the original ending, that it contradicted Luke and was too little honorific to Peter and the Apostles; the third Gospel and Acts formed a more extended and a less radically Pauline publication. Mark was thus reduced to "the interpreter of Peter" who was supposed as confining himself to "the things either said or done by Christ."

b. Relation of Evangelist to Apostles. The ancient tradition preserved by Papias knows that Mark does not agree with Matthew in order, but claims that he "made no mistake while he thus wrote down some things as he remembered them; for he made it his one care not to omit anything that he had heard, or to set down any false statement therein." The Gospel appears therefore to be represented as the Memorabilia of St. Peter; St. Justin Martyr uses this name explicitly. Dr. Bacon critically investigates this relationship of the Gospel to Peter, and finds that part of its contents shows no intrinsic evidence of proceeding from St. Peter; in other portions he discovers duplicates of matter already told. He denies to the Evangelist that insight into the real factors of the history which we should justly expect from one who had even a modicum of personal acquaintance with one of the Twelve. The author of the Gospel is dominated by theoretical considerations, often manifestly derived from the Pauline Epistles, especially the Epistle to the Romans.

c. Sources of Second Gospel. But the second Gospel draws not merely on the material of the Pauline Epistles, but also on the source independently employed by Matthew and Luke, which is designated by the symbol *Q*. Dr. Bacon is convinced that in this use the Evangelist, *R*, uniformly pragmatizes, materializes, exaggerates in the interest of his demonstration of the divine sonship of Jesus on the basis of miracles. In fact, R must have used Q to embellish and supplement an earlier and simpler narrative which may be designated as P, or Petrine. Moreover, R does not add the two documents mechanically, but he appears to quote Q from memory only. Again, the Q document as employed by R must have been embellished already with the narrative of the Baptist's preaching, the baptism, and temptation of Jesus. It seems that R derived certain portions from Q as it fell into the hands of the third Evangelist, i. e. from Q^{LK}; similarly, other portions must have been derived by R from Q as employed by the first Evangelist, i. e. Q^{MT}. Instead of either Q^{LK} or Q^{MT} Dr. Bacon often uses the symbol X, so as to denote an unknown source.

d. Relation of Redactor: 1. To the Jews. Regarding P and Q as the principal sources of the second Gospel, it may be asked what character must be attributed to the work of the compiler, to R. Dr. Bacon is convinced that he is emphatically anti-Judaistic. He shows himself not merely independent of Jewish legalism, but denounces the ceremonial system as " doctrines and precepts of men." The Jews are the people that " honor God with their lips while their heart is far from Him ". This anti-Judaistic redaction is not confined to a few passages, but enters into the substance of the Gospel.

2. To the Apostles. In the next place, Dr. Bacon considers $R's$ attitude toward the kindred of Jesus, and toward SS. Peter, James, and John. He finds that the kindred of Jesus appear but twice in the Gospel: first to lay hands on Jesus, and again in the words of the Master, " a prophet is not without honor save in his own country, and among his kin, and in his own house ". As to St. Peter, the Gospel makes known all the instances in which he appeared in an unfavorable light. SS. James and John too appear only twice in the Gospel: first when they are rebuked for their intolerant spirit, and next when they ambition the first seats in the kingdom. In the three instances in which SS. Peter, James, and John play a separate rôle, at the raising of Jairus's daughter, in the Transfiguration, and in Gethsemane, Dr. Bacon sees a special preparation for their future martyrdom.

3. To St. Paul. What has been said represents a merely negative characteristic of R; he is emphatically anti-Judaistic.

Dr. Bacon believes that *R's* positive character is his Paulinism. How does the writer prove it? He appeals to the manner in which the Evangelist conceives his task, to the conception of what constitutes the apostolic message. *R* is charged with leaving his readers completely without information on the law of Jesus. Like the fourth Evangelist, *R* writes solely that his readers may believe that Jesus is the Christ, the Son of the living God. The doctrine of the Cross forms the only exception. It is simply the Pauline principle of the mind that was in Jesus, the continual repetition of the doctrine—" he that would save his life shall lose it ", " he that followeth Me, let him take up his cross and come after Me." This is *R's* Sermon on the Mount.

II. Review of Prof. Bacon's Views. *1. Summary.* It has been seen that Prof. Bacon starts with two assumptions: the principle of historical evolution in Christian doctrine, and the fact that the synoptic Gospels represent a more advanced stage of development than the Pauline Epistles. Then he adopts the Two-Source theory as the proper solution of the synoptic problem, rejects John Mark as author of the second Gospel, and advances the critical conjecture as to the original extent of the Gospel. Coming to the question of sources, the Professor finds that the second Gospel was written under the influence of the Pauline Epistles, though a Petrine document, *P,* and a collection of Christ's teachings, *Q,* together with two more or less known documents, Q^{LK}, Q^{MT}, *X*, constitute the immediate literary parentage of Mark. *R,* the redactor or compiler of the Gospel in its present form, did not join these documents mechanically nor even scrupulously; he writes from memory with an anti-Judaistic, anti-Apostolic, and Paulinian tendency. What is the reader to think of Prof. Bacon's results?

2. Doctrinal Development. The Catholic reader knows that

represent a later doctrinal stage than the Pauline Epistles, P. P. Flournoy in an article entitled "The Real Date of the Gospels"[4] shows that the Gospels must have been written soon after the events which they relate. He urges that the theological development found in the Book of Acts, the Epistles, and the Apocalypse, is further advanced than in the Gospels; hence the period of the Gospels must be earlier than that of the Epistles, the Book of Acts, and the Apocalypse. The danger of a change in the oral tradition, and the custom of writing memoirs as implied in Luke 1: 1-4, must have given occasion to an early composition of the Gospels. Another motive for the same would be found in the early spread of the Christian doctrine into various countries. Flournoy is of opinion that the Gospels are mutually independent productions.

4. The Two-Source Theory. Dr. Bacon may be correct in saying that the Two-Source theory of the literary genesis of the synoptic Gospels has been adopted by most scholars. It cannot be supposed however that it has been universally regarded as the best solution of the problem to be solved. Gieseler, Westcott, Wright (second edition) are a few among many who have not seen fit to abandon other solutions of the difficulty. There are phenomena which Hawkins pronounces inexplicable on any mainly documentary theory. An appeal to a lax method of reproduction, or to a want of the sense of inspiration, or to the Evangelists' endeavor to emphasize their own peculiar views of Christian history and doctrine, will not satisfy scholars of all classes. Besides, it is hard to explain such a phenomenon as the so-called dualism of Mark on the Two-Source theory.

5. John Mark. In the next place, Dr. Bacon eliminates John Mark from the authorship of the second Gospel. James Moffat in a review of Bacon's book, which appeared in the *Hibbert Journal* (Oct., 1909), takes exception to this elimination. First, the process appears to be due to a personal prejudice against John Mark; as long as he is the writer of the Gospel, it can hardly be regarded as advocating Prof. Bacon's Paulinism. Besides, the wary reader will pull himself up at

6. Original Ending of Mark. The critical conjecture that the second Gospel in its original ending covered certain parts, or perhaps the whole, of the period of Acts is not upheld by any argument worth discussing. If Dr. Bacon expects his reader to tolerate it as the theory of a scholar, he must extend the same tolerance to his reader's want of accepting it as a scientific result.

7. Mark's Sources. Mr. Moffatt [5] expresses his disagreement with Dr. Bacon's view that the writer of Mark's Gospel used the Logia or *P*-source; the reviewer is not alone in his opinion. To cite only two other recent authorities, we may appeal to M. A. Camerlynck, Professor of Scripture in the Seminary of Bruges, and M. H. Coppieters, Professor in the University of Louvain.[6] These writers are advocates of the Two-Source theory in their solution of the synoptic problem, but they are more reasonable in their estimate of St. Mark. According to them the first Gospel depends on Mark, the Logia, and an unknown source; the third Gospel has for its sources Mark, the Logia, and a Palestinian source; but in the second Gospel they find neither internal nor external evidence for any literary sources.

8. Mark's Character. Finally we arrive at the section of Bacon's work which deals with the character of *R,* the compiler of the second Gospel. What the author describes as anti-Judaistic tendency in the second Gospel, is easily accounted for, on the one hand, by the mutual attitude of Christ and the Jewish leaders, and, on the other, by the pretension of the Judaizers in the early Christian communities. The position held by St. Peter in the Gospel has been used by other scholars as a proof for the Petrine origin; as St. Matthew is the only Evangelist who relates that he had been a publican, so St. Peter would naturally relate his own shortcomings in his relation of Christ's life and teaching. The Paulinism ascribed to the second Gospel is perhaps the weakest point in Prof. Bacon's work. Mr. Moffatt writes about this feature:[7] " The elimina-

is valid, in spite of all that adherents of this theory, from Volkmar to Pfleiderer and Loisy, have urged. The ' Paulinism ' with which they operate is too arbitrary a factor in many cases; it is defined with over-precision and applied with too much looseness. The primitive church was much richer and simpler than the outcome of a mere antagonism between Jewish-Christian and Pauline parties; and while there are ample traces of the early apostolic age in the conceptions of Mark's Gospel, they scarcely amount to a proof that the editor was a partisan of Paul. Schweitzer, Zimmerman, and B. Weiss are surely on a truer historical line in their protest against the tendency to read Pauline tenets into the second Gospel. . . . Furthermore, if ' Mark' is Pauline, how are the resurrection traditions so different? and why does Mark emphasize the proof from miracles, which Paul seems to have passed by? "

Historicity of the Second Gospel. After reading Prof. Bacon's views on the second Gospel, the student will naturally be anxious to learn how the writer can save the historical character of Mark. In this regard, the author appears to occupy the standpoint of our so-called Modernists. This question has been ably discussed by E. Roupain,[8] A. Durand,[9] J. Bricout,[10] S. Protin.[11] Roupain urges that the Modernist method proceeds a priori, and neglects historical data which prove the trustworthiness of the synoptic Gospels. Bricout treats the subject in a popular way, in the form of a sermon; Protin first surveys the different hypotheses advanced for the solution of the synoptic problem. He then points out the deficiencies of modern Biblical Criticism, showing that it starts with several false assumptions. Among the latter we may notice the denial of the supernatural, the supposed enthusiasm of the inspired writers, and the late origin of the Gospels together with the early authorship of the Pauline Epistles. The writer urges the fact that the critical elimination of the Easter and Pentecostal miracles destroys the main argument for the supposed enthusiasm of the Evangelists.

[8] Les synoptiques et l'exégèse moderniste; *La Revue des sciences ecclésiastiques et la science catholique,* 1908, August.

[9] Les Évangiles synoptiques de M. Loisy; *Revue pratique d'apologétique,* 1901, September.

[10] La valeur historique des Synoptiques; *Revue du clergé Français,* LVI, 423-430.

[11] La valeur historique des Synoptiques; *Revue Augustinienne,* XIV, 63-71.

Criticisms and Notes.

THE GREEK FATHERS. By Adrian Fortesque. London: Catholic
Truth Society. 1908. Pp. xvi–248.

"This little book contains outlines of the lives of the great Greek
Fathers, from Athanasius to John Damascene, with a list of. their
chief works and a few bibliographical notes. No one will expect to
find anything new in what does not profess to be more than a series
of popular sketches. The only object of the book is to give in a
small space, and in English, a general account of what is commonly
known about these Fathers. I have described their lives and adventures rather than their systems of theology . . . This little book
is meant for laymen." The Fathers treated are Saints Athanasius,
Basil, Gregory Nazianzen, John Chrysostom, Cyril of Jerusalem,
Cyril of Alexandria, John of Damascus. One may add that while
the treatment is popular, it is yet distinctly learned, in its bearings.
The topical mechanism in fact is quite formally professional, and
will rather shelve the book among laboratory manuals of information than with volumes of detached entertainment.

One feature of the sketches that will appeal especially to Catholics, is the voluntary tribute shown to have been accorded by those
"first magnitude" lights of the East to the See of Rome and the
Power of the Keys, in matters affecting the integrity of Christian
doctrine, and involving its ultimate supreme exponent. Here if
Athanasius, the "greatest bishop in the East, the mighty patriarch
who held the second see of Christendom, the leader of the Catholics
against Arians, and the greatest of Eastern Fathers, appealed
solemnly to Rome, it was no case of patriarchal jurisdiction: Egypt
had nothing to do with the Roman patriarchate. The only claim
the Pope could have to interfere in a quarrel at Alexandria was his
claim to universal jurisdiction over the whole Church of Christ."
And all this was expressly confirmed, as well, by the Eastern Synod
of Sardica, A. D. 343.

Church of Rome, the Churches of Italy, Spain and all the West;" and that with him there signed the two Roman priests, Vitus and Vincent.   Among his eminent contemporaries in Egypt, by the way, we find Athanasius personally acquainted with St. Antony and Pachomius; whilst his *Life of St. Antony,* "one of the great standard books on the spiritual life," is reckoned as a primary cause in the conversion of St. Augustine.   The best edition of his collective works is said to be even still the Benedictine (St. Maur) edition, as published in Paris, 1698.

On their merely human side, there is more to attract us in two of the distinguished Cappadocian Saints, Basil and Gregory Nazianzen. The author himself is disposed to rate St. Basil as "personally, perhaps the most attractive of the Greek Fathers."   There is a picturesque setting withal about his early life in Pontus, and almost a modern student's tone in the period of his culture studies at Athens, in boon companionship with Gregory Nazianzen.   St. Basil's election to the metropolitan see of Cæsarea in Cappadocia, came directly in recognition of his generous and efficient conduct in relieving a dire famine in that country, wherein he both sold the remnant of his possessions that he might feed the starving, and also "persuaded merchants, who wanted to sell what corn they had kept in their barns, at an enormous profit," to sacrifice the iniquitous advantage.   When St. Basil, as Metropolitan of Cæsarea, was threatened by the Pretorian Prefect Modestus with "confiscation, exile, torture and death unless he would accept the Cæsar's religion" (the Arian heresy), he withstood so firmly that Modestus exclaimed: "No one has ever yet spoken to me so freely."   "Perhaps," answered Basil, "you have not yet had much conversation with a Catholic bishop." Valens, the Arian Emperor in question, came afterward in person to see and hear so resolute a subject, and even engaged him in theological discussion.   It would appear that on one such occasion, the imperial cook "chimed in," on the Arian side, but was discomfited by Basil's irony over the culinary grammar therein betrayed.   At all events, Valens learned to respect Basil's invincible worthiness, and ceased to molest him.

St. Basil freely corresponded with prelates in the West, and was on very cordial terms with St. Ambrose of Milan.   Like Athanasius (with whom he also corresponded), Basil appealed to the supreme jurisdiction of Rome, as in requesting Pope Damasus to use his authority to restore peace in the Arian troubles: "The only remedy for which evils is a visitation from your mercy."   Besides his renown as a saint, an organizer of monasticism in the East, and a chief liturgist of the "Orthodox" Church, Basil ranks as one of the best Greek writers of the fourth century; being "immeasurably" superior in point of style of St. Athanasius, though less ornamental and flowing than St. John Chrysostom. There appears to be no specific mention, in the author's list of St. Basil's works, of a certain delightful treatise introduced in America some years ago for a text-book in later Greek, on the use of pagan culture for Christian students; though the treatise cannot fail, both wholesomely and indelibly, to influence all who know it. We are told that St. Basil's dogmatic work on the Holy Ghost (*De Spiritu Sancto*), in defence of the equality and consubstantial nature of the Third Person of the Blessed Trinity, "has always been the standard work on the subject." His 365 extant *letters* are said to be peculiarly diversified, and vividly characteristic. His collective works were first published (in Greek) at Basil, 1532; whereas the best edition, as in the case of St. Athanasius, is still credited to the Benedictines of St. Maur (Paris, 1721-1730; reprinted in 1839). The sketch of St. Basil also contains a brief account of his younger brother, St. Gregory of Nyssa.

If St. Basil impresses one as being "personally, perhaps the most attractive of the Greek Fathers," then surely the very crotchets of St. Gregory Nazianzen render him personally the most palpably human. His very adjunct, Nazianzen, expresses his radical and never surmounted repugnance as to being even so much as nominally associated with his titular see of *Sasima*: "most odious place in the world, barren, solitary, ugly and generally detestable. He had never been there. Indeed, it is more than doubtful if he ever went to his diocese at all." So posterity has yielded to his own intense antipathy in the matter, by designating him only after his Cappadocian birthplace; or native *locus*, rather, since he was born at Arianzos, *near* Nazianzos. He had evinced similar disaffection, though less in degree, when ordained to the priesthood; though here his opposition proceeded from the rational motive that he desired to be a monk, and live apart from the world. There are very pleasing glimpses, on his genial side, of his intimate friendship with St. Basil, and of their studies at Athens; where they dwelt, moreover, as "lambs in the midst of wolves," as touching their Christian ideals in the presence of heathen culture (still flourishing, in those times, at Athens) and unedifying morals. Even that ancient, and sometimes barbarous, custom of "hazing" did there prevail; and one is amused with the local rivalries between Cappadocians and Armenians:

Those Christians, doubtless, who pivot their constructions of the Church on the article of adult baptism (by immersion, too) can find practical support for their argument in the fact that both St. Basil and St. Gregory Nazianzen deferred baptism till they were twenty-seven years old. But the like delay was gaining greater and greater disfavor in the Church; and afterward, "St. Basil and both the Gregories (Nazianzen and Nyssa) wrote strongly against it." One of the most momentous periods in the career of St. Gregory Nazianzen is that wherein he presides over the See of Constantinople (379-381), during a troubled season of heresies (Arian and *Pneumatomachian*); and also pending that "second General Council," which defined the attributes of the Holy Ghost. It is chiefly in the Eastern Church that St. Gregory Nazianzen is exalted as " Gregory the *Theologian* ": maybe thus, if one may so conjecture, not because the Catholic Church at all undervalues his theology proper, but simply for the fact that still greater theologians afterward "abounded" in the Church of the West. There is a certain latent humor in the author's familiar ascription: " He is the patron saint of people who do not want to be bishops "; this both allowing for the fabled category, "sour grapes," while yet paradoxically consoling, it may chance, here and there some vexed or overburdened bishop, who might gladly forego the episcopal office, were the charge of it one of desire alone.

St. John Chrysostom is defined so inseparably by his eloquent surname, the " Golden-mouthed," that the Catholic liturgy admits the distinction by official sanction. " The only other case of a surname in the text of the Roman Missal is that of St. Peter Chrysologus (Golden-speeched), Archbishop of Ravenna (+ 450), the Western counterpart of St. John Chrysostom." His early background is Antioch in Syria; and among his masters in culture there we find the philosopher Libanius, friend of the Emperor Julian (and one of the most graceful portraitures in the vast "shades" of Gibbon). It was during his priesthood at Antioch (386-398) that John won his oratorical fame, which rated him not only the first preacher of Antioch, but one soon to become the most renowned in the world. It is the practice of Greek preachers down to this day to "model themselves on Chrysostom," let alone their occasional artifice of memorizing some sublime passage from his sermons to relieve, by the dramatic effect of the same at an opportune point, their less rhetorical endowments. His most celebrated particular sermon still is the " Homily on the Return of Flavian," preached on an Easter morning, in fervent joy for the Emperor's pardon in the scandal of the "profaned" imperial statues; wherein Flavian, the aged Patriarch of Antioch, had proved a victorious intercessor with

Theodosius. " Teach this story to your children, and let them tell it to future generations, that all may know for all time how great is the mercy of God to this city."

There is much charity of eloquence in his appeal to the rich and comfortable to provide at least in their *stables* " a place where Christ may lodge in the form of the poor. You shudder at such an idea? It is still worse not to receive Him at all." The distinctive theological note, or dominating content, in the writings of St. John Chrysostom, is, " by universal consent," his absorption in the Holy Eucharist, the most frequently recurrent theme through his works at large. He likewise very plainly recognizes the *Primacy* and *ecumenical jurisdiction* of the Pope of Rome.

St. Cyril of Jerusalem achieved celebrity first of all on the ground of his peculiar excellence in the sphere of catechetics; and his twenty-three catechetical *homilies* " form practically all " of his extant works. He also stands out in the contemporary prophecy, so to speak, as a grave Christian eye-witness of Julian's pantheistic attempt to restore the Temple in Jerusalem. Whereof the author sagaciously observes, in a note by the way : " If only poor Julian had taken up any less hopeless cause than that of the gods he would have been the greatest Emperor since Constantine." For Julian's design, to be sure, with reference to the Temple, was merely to equalize the " God of Israel " with all the " gods of the nations ": and curiously *to date*, by the way, we have now the report of a *Freemasonry* plan to rebuild the Temple, perhaps in expectation of some new Messiah? In summary of St. Cyril's permanent distinction, the author quotes this passage from the Roman Martyrology : "At Jerusalem St. Cyril, Bishop, who, having suffered many injuries from the Arians for the faith, and having been many times driven from his see, at last rested in peace, illustrious with the glory of holiness; of whose untarnished faith the second ecumenical synod, writing to Damasus, gave a splendid witness "; and likewise the Collect for his Mass: " Grant us, Almighty God, that by the prayers of blessed Cyril, the Bishop, we may so know thee, the only true God, and Jesus Christ whom Thou didst send, that we may always be counted among the sheep that hear His voice." His *catechisms*, in fine, are furthermore valuable for incidental information about rites and ceremonial at Jerusalem in the fourth century.

St. Cyril of Alexandria, though second only to St. Athanasius in the line of Patriarchs of Alexandria, " has incurred an undeserved unpopularity because during his reign a Christian mob murdered Hypatia." From that accident of sarcasm in murder by a " Christian mob " (and a most horrible fatality it was, in truth) St. Cyril is every whit acquitted, in the light of impartial findings; although, at best, there was a certain "despotic" force of character in the present St. Cyril which rather compels than invites admiration. But this does not lesson his intrinsic importance in the annals of theology, nor his princely bearing as one of the typical "Christian Pharaohs." His theological fame, "Seal of the Fathers," rests on his cardinal defence of the Catholic faith against Nestorianism; which was formally condemned by the Council of Ephesus (431). The sketch, at this point, includes a very interesting digression, both antiquarian and freshly modern, on Ephesus and its Turkish survivals. What is to be remarked, again, as of singular Catholic moment, is that St. Cyril attended this Council as direct "legate" of Pope Celestin of Rome: "As legate he presided, and the Latins had received instructions from the Pope to acknowledge him as such and in all things to be on his side." And at the second session of the same Council, the Roman delegate Philip, a priest, uttered these historic words on the Primacy: "There is no doubt, indeed it is known to all ages, that the holy and most blessed Peter, Prince and Chief of the Apostles, column of the faith and foundation of the Catholic Church, received the keys of the kingdom, and that the power of forgiving and retaining sins was given to him, and that he till the present time, and always, lives and judges in his successors" . . . Pope Leo XIII declared St. Cyril of Alexandria a Doctor of the Church; and even apart from his championship of the faith against Nestorianism he excelled in the province of systematic theology: closely rivaling, in this respect, for the Eastern Church, St. John Damascene; which signifies, in turn, somewhat of a parallel Eastern attainment to that of St. Thomas Aquinas in the West. We learn that the only complete edition of his works was the one published by J. Aubert, a canon of Paris, in six folio volumes (Greek), in 1638.

St. John of Damascus (+ c. 754) is reckoned chronologically the "last of the Fathers, unless we count St. Bernard, in the West: in any case, the last Greek Father." Strangely enough, he spent all his life under the government, and sometimes under the *protection* (against a Christian Emperor) of a Mohammedan caliph. This protection was needed on account of the Iconoclast prosecution: "At that time Leo the Isaurian ruled the Roman Empire, who raged like a furious lion against the venerable eikons and against the orthodox congregation of the Church." The biographic details on John of Damascus being relatively meagre, the author complements the still graphic sketch of him by rich background views of Damascus and an austere, but romantic and "high relief" projection of Mar Saba, the chief monastery (St. Sabas) in Palestine; whither John withdrew in temporary retreat from the world, but was recalled by the Patriarch of Jerusalem, to be ordained as an active priest. However, he soon again returned to St. Sabas: "this eagle flying away sought his old nest." His hymns are very widely known, and have become, to some extent, the common property of "all who profess and call themselves Christians." "Pope Leo XIII declared St. John Damascene a Doctor of the Church, and appointed 22 March as his feast."'   W. P.

ELEMENTI DI ASTRONOMIA. Adolfo Muller, S.J. Vol. II. Astrofisica-Astroconaca. Pp. viii–600. Desclee, Lefebvre & Oo. Rome.

In this second volume of his work, Fr. Müller deals with Physical, rather than with Descriptive Astronomy; and enters with no little detail upon the general problem of cosmic evolution. The volume does ample credit to the successor of the late Fr. Secchi. It evinces a thorough and practical knowledge of the many questions of General Astronomy; and in the concise suggestiveness of its formulations, as well as its continual cross-references, it facilitates intelligent and really valuable acquaintance with the subject of which it treats. Whilst most of the recent advances in astronomical science are noted, we miss some that might have been included, such as, for example, Lebedew's researches and results concerning the Pressure of Light, and Nichols's and Hull's determinations of its energy. Similarly we should look for a wider discussion of the factors in the conservation of heat in our central luminary and in the other suns of the universe. The more recent studies concerning light are very interesting; they are considered by Poincaré and other noted physicists, and they mark at least some advance toward a solution of the long-standing enigmas constituted by the corona, the zodiacal light, and other similar and more extended cosmic phenomena.

from preëxisting developments can never be postulated without an
open defiance both of the basic principle of proportionate causality,
and of the mute, yet eloquent testimony of adequately considered
paleontological fact.   In this mediate position, the author justly
holds, there is nothing intrinsically repugnant to Catholic theology
or Catholic thought; and he adduces in proof of this assertion the
absolutely unfettered freedom of the divine energy both as to objects and modes, the constant record of ecclesiastical traditions, traditions sufficiently summarized in St. Augustine's "*rationes semi-
nales*", and the hesitancy, as old as the Church, which Catholic
writers have always felt in assigning any finally definite interpretation to the Mosaic Hexæmeron.

Since, however, the author very properly refrains here from any
ex-professo treatment of evolution, we too shall treat it but slightly
now ; only observing that in these disputed matters we too often lose
sight of our position of possession, which here, as elsewhere, is often
nine-tenths of the law.   If there is anything certain concerning the
whole question of evolution, it is that all its specific conclusions are
uncertain.   Probability added to probability will never make certi-
tude, and it is a troublesome and wholly uncalled-for tactical mistake to give to even one of the merely tentative theories of evolution
the altogether superior character of demonstrated fact.   We most
sincerely approve of all sane geological and other cognate studies.
We applaud all the very curious and very interesting results which
they have already attained.   But with an omnipotent Creator as the
real, unquestioned agent in regard to both mountain and mollusk,
and with His ways explicitly and confessedly inscrutable to our gaze,
we can certainly await something more than an inchoate science's
assurance, before we feel obliged to accept even the millions and millions of years and the vast elemental upheavals which may—or may
not—have preceded man's fitful appearance in God's endless eternity.
The authors of every new system must, by the very nature of the
case, prove every step of their way.

Fr. Müller presents the earth to our view in its supposed primary
state of highly heated gas roughly spherical in form, with its gradual
cooling, its at first elastic crust, its primeval floods of rain, its suddenly formed, and as suddenly toppling, mountains, its sedimented
seas, its emerging continents, its final granitic firmness, its flashing
volcanic violence, its soil-clad hills and plains, its beauty and its life.
All this is set forth by the author with a wealth of detail, a consistency of sequence, and a fertility of imagination, which make very
pleasant reading, even if it is continually accompanied with a good-
natured kind of scepticism concerning the objective reality of those
wondrous days of a world's preparation.   Whatever else may be

said, a real tribute is due to the patient minds that have so carefully elaborated and so poetically portrayed the entrancing story of creation's " might have been."

But many minds go deeper, and amongst them many that have no means of investigating these unrecorded days for themselves. And these are harassed with doubt, as to what they should, and should not, believe concerning them. The atmosphere is full of a new kind of learning. Reason, we are told, has outstripped faith, and has turned squarely upon it, forbidding and barring its further progress. Star-eyed science has, we are assured, fully penetrated all the factitious webs that silly astrologers and crafty churchmen had spread between honest ignorance and dawning truth, and has hurled them aside forever. Theology is condescendingly, yet firmly, told that it must now at last and definitely yield up and disavow all its old-time beliefs. The "Argument from Design" and all similar demonstrations have been hopelessly undermined, we are told, and utterly ruined by the advances of Darwinism. The "childish" acceptance of the Mosaic six thousand years as the age of our world can excite nothing more now, we are patronizingly informed, than an amused kind of pity. Old forms, it seems, are in general passing away forever; and regarding the future we can be certain of nothing, except that it will in nowise resemble the past. And concerning all this, we can only say here that Catholic apologists cannot be too careful in treating of these ultimate realities, and that no weak, unworthy concession should be allowed to sap the very foundations of the Church's philosophical defence.

DANIEL DEVER.

A GRAMMAR OF THE OLD TESTAMENT IN GREEK ACCORDING TO THE SEPTUAGINT. By Henry St. John Thackeray, M. A., Sometime Scholar of King's College, Cambridge. Vol. I: Introduction, Orthography and Accidence. Cambridge: University Press. 1909. Pp. xx-325.

declension and comparison of adjectives; numerals; pronouns; and verbs. Throughout the Accidence division, there is a continual collation with classic forms and usage, besides a detailed attention to the Septuagint forms as such. The body of the work is also reinforced by a list of Principal Authorities (German, French, English) ; and there is a catalogue of Noteworthy Verbs (pp. 258-290), with philologic and literary data to each. Undoubtedly the most inviting feature of the work for those mere amateurs of Old Testament lore who have never obtained a knowledge of Hebrew, will be the section entitled Semitic Elements of LXX Greek.

A great deal of the philological research, the grammatical "dry bones" of statistical data, in this patient volume, is designed to subserve the twofold aim of illustrating the general subject of Hellenistic Greek; whereof the French scholar Psichari justly remarks, "La Septante est le grand monument de la κοινή "; and of contributing carefully collated results toward some ultimately approximate reconstruction of a "primitive" text of the Septuagint, for as the author says: "we are still far from the period when we shall have a text, analogous to the New Testament of Westcott and Hort, of which we can confidently state that it represents, approximately at least, the original work of the translators."

In reducing the supposed Hebraisms of the Septuagint diction to their lowest resultant terms, the author duly considers that curious correlation of verb and cognate participle, noun or adverb, which represents, it would appear, the Hebrew construction known as "infinitive absolute." But he then shows that though this usage is typically Hebraic, it is also passably and coincidently Hellenic, and must therefore be excluded from the category of wholly unalloyed Hebraisms. He follows the like argument in other such cases of "reduction," showing that where the Hebrew had any parallel in Greek at all, the translators merely made the best of that accidental sanction, sometimes giving general currency, through the diffusion of the Septuagint text, to what had else remained a sporadic, or more or less isolated, usage in Greek or Hellenistic. That cognate reduplication is also locally adopted in the New Testament, notably by St. Luke. (One might likewise recall the Vulgate analogy, as in *congregans congregabo*).

As the residue Hebrew element in the Septugint is exceptionally prominent in the case of names of persons and places, one is both grateful for the space allowed to Proper Names under Accidence, and yet prompted to repeat the wish expressed above, that the author, when dealing with Hebrew terms, had given still ampler attention to radical definition; resolution of significant constituents, too, in compound forms. Primarily, of course, this latter task belongs rather to the whole sphere of Biblical interpretation than to the province of the Septuagint; but even for a secondary detail, full treatment herein were quite plausibly in season.

The author's Index labor is quite generous: an index of subjects, index of Greek words and forms, index of Biblical quotations. We beg to wish him Godspeed with his projected second volume; and withal we can devoutly wonder a little that our Catholic scholarship, though by no means neglectful of Septuagint study and research in the past, has not rather magnified than "averaged" the subject: if only on the side of its genuine *relic* value, in the life of the Church. Even more directly, in fine, than the Hebrew Scriptures, the very words of the Septuagint text were used by our Lord and the Apostles; by the Evangelists, Prophets, and Martyrs of the early Church: Peter and Paul, St. James, John and Jude, quote not from the Hebrew rolls, but from the familiar Septuagint Greek. And undoubtedly that older Septuagint editor, Dr. Leander Van Ess, was not unconscious of this hallowed association when he appended the pious "vow" to his preface (*Dabam Darmstadii, ultimis anni 1823* diebus) : " Ceterum nil magis in votis est, quam ut hisce sacris graecis litteris Studiosorum aliorumque Virorum commodis consulam et utilitati, salutique æternæ; quod sincere et pure voluisse mihi sat est, cui et Deus benedicens gratiam addat et effectum, incrementumque."

W. P.

THE SUPREME PROBLEM. By J. Godfrey Raupert. Buffalo: Peter Paul and Son. 1910. Pp. xx–339.

gives to those with which saints and other Christian writers have
filled the centuries. Nevertheless, new forms of the true solution—
for of course there is essentially but one solution—are needed to
meet the ever-shifting phases of error and sophistry and doubt with
which the human spirit of pride and fleshly tendency, subtly moved
and directed by the spirits of darkness in the guise of angels of
light, are continually beclouding the truth. A true solution in a
form that is in many respects new—new especially in the fresh
light which it sheds upon certain phases of the problem—is presented in the book at hand.

The sub-title indicates the scope of the work. It is "An Examination of Historical Christianity from the standpoint of human
life and experience and in the light of psychical phenomena."
Historical Christianity rests on the two dogmas, the fall of man,
and his restoration and redemption through Jesus Christ. Mr.
Raupert addresses himself first to the former of these fundamental
truths. With a wealth of psychological analysis and illustration
drawn from universal experience and the constant testimony of
conscience he proves that, while the traditional doctrine of the
Fall is one of the essential revealed constituents of the Christian
religion, it alone affords a rational and adequate explanation of the
darkness and weakness of the human intellect and the disorderly tendencies of the human will—wounds in man's specific faculties at-
tested by constant experience, individual and racial. The line of
argument thus suggested may not seem to be new and certainly it
is not if tested by the *nil novi sub sole.* Nevertheless Mr. Raupert
gives it a fresh setting, draws out its implications and, presenting
it in its relations to adverse theories, gives it renewed life and
strength. The effect of the Fall to which he devotes special attention is the devil's dominion over man. The teaching of the
Bible and the Church on this subject is familiar. That the un-
palatable and "unscientific" doctrine is assailed and denied at the
present day, especially by the "New Theologians", is almost
equally well known; but, as Mr. Raupert well observes, "an age
which dissolves the Personal God into a mere abstraction, and which
denies the supremacy of human conscience, can scarcely be expected
to believe in the existence and personality of the evil one" (p. 81).
But here again as always "God fulfils Himself in many ways",
nor is one even evil custom permitted to "corrupt the world".
It is significant, as it is hopeful, that an increasing number of
eminent scientists devoted to "psychical research" are coming more
and more to admit that certain portions of what are classed as
spiritistic phenomena are explicable only on the theory of extraneous

intelligence acting on and through human media. That these discarnate agents are diabolical, they are slow to confess. None the less the evil nature and disastrous effects of the phenomena in question are such as to point unerringly to positive malign intelligence in their cause. This, we think, Mr. Raupert has satisfactorily established in his work on *Modern Spiritism*. While he covers substantially the same ground in the corresponding chapter of the book before us, he here adduces fresh personal experiences of individuals who by lending themselves to spiritistic practices have fallen victims to unmistakable diabolical obsession and possession. If the book consisted simply of this one chapter it would have justified its writing and publishing.

The second half of the volume is devoted to the other fundamental doctrine of historic Christianity—the restoration and redemption of man. Mr. Raupert here proves that, first, this truth alone, while explaining man's moral disorder, leads to true self-knowledge and sheds light on the mystery of evil (p. 273) ; secondly, it furnishes a remedy for moral disorder, a means of forgiveness of sin, and a way to moral liberty (p. 277) ; thirdly, it explains the mystery of pain, affords the helps to bear it and thereby attain moral perfection (p. 302) ; fourthly, it offers the means of restoration to the supernatural order. The final conclusion is summed up by the author in the words of Newman: " Either the Catholic Religion is verily the coming of the unseen world into this, or there is nothing positive, nothing dogmatic, nothing real in any of our notions as to whence we come and whither we go " (p. 327). These truths, for the rest familiar enough to everybody, are, like the truth discussed above, that of the Fall, given fresh strength and a living personal meaning by the light of experience in which Mr. Raupert sets them, the literary allusions with which he has illustrated them, and the illuminating contrast with contrary doctrines with which he has compared them. A critic bent on finding flaws might of course succeed in his search. There are not a few typographical errors, which however touch nothing vital, and are accounted for by the publishers' note. Here and there connected quotations from different authors are not clearly delimited (e. g. at pp. 249-251), and an occasional statement might be modified in the interest of accuracy. These are of secondary moment, however, and do not affect the substance of a work of such sterling value—a work that forms a welcome addition to our apologetic literature, one that is a strong weapon of defence and attack, one that is made of the iron of ancient truth, wrought by the newest processes into the unbreakable yet flexible steel that is needed in modern tactics—a work

which, while employing the method of experience in confirmation
of the truths of faith, escapes the excess of that irrational pragmatism which would make the truth itself consist in its sole response
to experiential needs; a book which, written by a layman from the
"standpoint of a layman", will appeal to the layman, though not
to him only, but to every thoughtful and reflecting mind.

THE NECROMANCERS. By Robert Hugh Benson. St. Louis, Mo.: B.
Herder. 1909. Pp. 374.

Given a reprobate theme, one cannot look for a decidedly pleasing consequence in either treatment or the reflex reaction upon
healthy mortals. At the very best, this volume is unevenly written.
There are passages, incidents, felicitous interludes, discovering excellent fine art of style, and quite a perfection of exact depiction
in the keen miniature vogue of a Meissonier; there are touches of
intaglio realism in effects of sympathetic nature, as in the minor
interlude on cats, forsooth; as in the southwestern rain-storm, to
bespeak romance on momentary levels of the sterling truest. On
the contrary, there is platitude of conventional padding; whereas, by
stringent requirements, a volume under four hundred pages in bulk
ought not to afford any waste at all, of inferior lapses. One questions, again, the fairly moral value of attempting to reproduce, as
the book seems to attempt in its proper climax, sheer morbid lunacies.
Is anybody helped, *except* by his redemption of consummate style,
through De Quincey's *Confessions?* They probably neither help nor
hinder, where an opium habit once rules in fatuous entire possession
of its unanswerable victim; and one suspects, by analogy, that their
infatuated seizure is equally averse to moral suasion, the warning of
bitter example, the whole sway of reason, in victims of cocaine,
hypnotism, and the stilted subtleties of theosophy, spiritualism, old
Gnostic vagaries but freshly revived and modernly conditioned.

The *Necromancers*, in outline, is very simple. A candid, im-
pulsive, rather moody young Englishman, Catholic convert withal,
has fallen in love with a pretty face, an artless maid of Non-
conformist Philistia. She suddenly dies; and in his agitation of
grief still passionately edged, as it were, he drifts into the toils of
mediums; whose ultimate uncanny tricks appear to land him in
melancholic insanity. We say purposely "appear" to land him
thus; because the aforseaid climax proper is hardly worked out with
a sure master-hand, such as a hospital specialist might be expected to
wield in describing some parallel case of lunatic distemper: in
short, the really professional side of the theme, in that closing por-

tion (which, furthermore, is left in implicit suspense) is blurred, and even clumsy. Neither does the sane Catholic foil to this foolish young man, his adoptive sister, Maggie Deronnais, fully hold her own in the scene which else could have become a real "scene" for dramatic tension. Between the sustaining Catholic doctrine of Communion of the Saints, guardian angels, instant and effectual dominion of the powers of light over the demons of darkness, there is a great gulf set; and Maggie's consistent sanity of equilibrium became too incoherently shaken when the trial came between faith supreme and moonstruck demonism.

Father Mahon, the robust, but phlegmatic, stolid, narrowly routine Catholic priest in the story, is disposed to regard all spiritualistic heresy with blunt contempt, sanguine unconcern as touching any vital danger to the Catholic faith from such passing phenomena; and the Church, of course, does eternally weather ephemeral aberrations of one sort and all sorts. Nevertheless, the very skyward self-confidence of spiritualistic professors lures many dependent and shallow disciples from the firm anchorage of the one only revealed Catholic truth and faith; so that even the most sanguine pastors have cause to note the ever-lurking wolf, be his disguises never so silly, never so specious and flimsy. For while the Church at large infallibly wins the final day against every error, still the loss is positive and baneful to those individual "sheep" who become seduced.

Some of the personal descriptions are admirable. We give a sample. Enters Mrs. Stapleton, "a New Thought kind of person".

"So I understand," said the old lady, with a touch of peevishness. "A vegetarian last year. And I believe she was a sort of Buddhist five or six years ago. And then she nearly became a Christian Scientist a little while ago."

Maggie smiled.

"I wonder what she'll talk about," she said.

"I hope she won't be very advanced," went on the old lady. "And you think I'd better not tell her about Laurie?"

"I'm sure it's best not, or she'll tell him about Deep Breathing, or saying Om, or something. No; I should let Laurie alone . . ."

.   .   .   .

"It's too charming of you, dear Mrs. Baxter," Maggie heard as she came into the drawing-room a minute or two later, "to let me come over like this. I've heard so much about this house. Lady Laura was telling me how very psychical it all was . . . how suggestive and full of meaning!"

all was very suggestive and significant and symbolical of something else to which Mrs. Stapleton and a few friends had the key."

Indeed, the overweening sophistries, intellectual inflation, occasionally impudent patronage of conceited Gnosticism, as the "New Thought" resolves itself to be in the last resort, are sketched with a free and adept hand; while still the composite volume comes very far short of the full grasp of treatment in *Frankenstein*, to cite an effort of distinctive success in the "transcendent" line; to say naught of De Quincy's rhetorically *sustained* flights, in a morbid vein; and let alone the full-bodied compass of a *work* by Dickens: *Bleak House* the ghostly.

ORGELBUOH ZU J. MOHRS "OAEOILLIA" ZUR 32. Auflage neu herausgegeben von Johann Singenberger und revidiert von F. X. Engelhart. Erstes Heft: Messgesaenge. Pustet, 1910. (Quarto, three-quarter leather,) 102 pages.

Contains no less than six Masses from the Vatican Kyriale, transposed into suitable keys, in modern notation, and provided with organ accompaniment; as also five sets of hymns arranged for appropriate singing at Low Masses, with text in German. The volume thus forms the first part of the organ accompaniment to the "Caecilia" of J. Mohr, which has already appeared (Pustet, 1909) in its newest form. The many editions of this compact and comprehensive little volume testify to its great usefulness; but the most recent edition necessitated the quarto volume of accompaniments to the Vatican Chant selections. The five sets of hymns—constituting equivalently five "Masses"—should prove of the greatest service for Low Mass, as they provide texts appropriate for the several portions of the Mass, arranged in proper sequence for both singers and organist, while the fact that five such "Low Masses" are provided ensures interesting variety and avoids the bane of monotony.

Literary Chat.

Sedgwick Mather, Professor of Neurology at the American College of Neuropathy, Philadelphia. The book has barely 150 pages, but it covers the subject comprehensively enough for most practical purposes and in a style intelligible to the average educated reader. The physiology of the brain and nerves is the dominant subject. Anatomy is subordinate. The illustrations are very good and sufficient as far as the nerves are concerned. A few more on the brain would have enhanced the value of the book, which is very neatly made up by McVey (Philadelphia).

We have coupled above general readers of culture with students of psychology, for in these days when knowledge covers the earth, like the sea, the lines of demarcation between special student and general reader seem to have become faded, if not quite erased. However this may be, another work that appeals proportionately to both classes in question is *Stundenbilder der Philosophischen Propädeutik* by the Rev. Peter Vogt, S.J.—that is, omitting the untranslatable figure, *Stundenbilder*, a brief introduction to philosophy. The gateway to philosophy is, of course, logic; but as psychology, though independent, is closely connected with logic, the author introduces his readers to philosophy in the present volume through psychology and reserves the logical ingress for a future volume. It is not meant to be a technical treatise on psychology but rather to furnish supplementary matter with which the teacher can expand his commentary on his text-book and with which the educated reader may orient himself on the pertinent questions. The author's standpoint is dominantly empirical and covers the general phenomena of consciousness—knowing, feeling, tending. The strictly " rational " or metaphysical subjects concerning the soul as such are introduced in connexion with the special psychical phenomena. The reader who will take the title literally and study " the hour-pictures " one a day will find that by the time he has surveyed the sixty *Stundenbilder* into which the matter is divided he will have acquired very considerable information on a subject which it concerns him most to know, himself; information which is accurate and based upon extensive research, as the bibliographical references attest; and yet information which the author's happy style has made comparatively easy of assimilation. The book is published by Herder (Freiburg; St. Louis, Mo.).

From the psychology of life to the psychology of death is an easy, because a natural, transition. *Trauer und Trost* is the title of a recent book, written by an Austrian priest, Anselm Freiherr von Gumppenberg, and published by Pustet & Co. (New York). It treats broadly and spiritually of death. " Sorrow and Comfort at the graves of dear dead " is the full title of the book and suggests the scope and character of the contents.

Sermons with us are not usually delivered at the grave, but in the church. The place and the occasion lend them perhaps at times elements of strength which the candid panegyrist knows they do not inherently possess. The effective funeral sermon requires, of course, proportionately at least as much care in preparation as does any other sacred discourse. With the best endeavors, nevertheless, a priest may find his own fund of ideas pertinent to a subject upon which he is obliged so often to preach, inadequate to the demand. To him, if he read German, a book like *Trauer und Trost* will prove a rich treasury of suggestive ideas and sentiments, beautifully and feelingly expressed—suggestive only, of course, for a book of the kind can be no more.

moral life, and shows that, while all genuine love is rational, all rational operations have union with God, as the supreme good in itself, for their end. He
does not war with the Schoolmen, but he presents their teachings in a more
life-giving form to our age; and while he is no innovator in thought, he will,
we think, impress a new movement on the mind of the age that will be as
salutary as powerful " (*Works*, Vol. I, p. 381). This is high praise coming
from so discriminating a critic as was Dr. Brownson, especially when one
remembers the very severe handling to which he subjected Père Gratry's *Logic*.
The reviewer's prophecy remained unfulfilled. M. Gratry impressed no
" new movement on the mind of the age." Nevertheless, however, the affective rather than intellective temper of thought which he pursued and advocated is attuned to one of the tendencies of the modern mind and in so far
as that tendency is just and reasonable Père Gratry's writings can but serve
to keep it normal. Therefore we have from time to time welcomed in these
pages the republished issues of his books. The latest of these reprints is his
Commentaire sur l'Évangile selon S. Matthieu (Paris, Téqui), in two small
volumes. The commentary is in no wise literal or methodically exegetical.
The chapters of the Gospel are given, in French, and divided into sections.
Then follow detached reflections on a salient thought selected from the individual sections. The reflections are discursive and affective. Those who
meditate on the Gospels can hardly fail to have their spiritual sense quickened
and their affections nurtured by following these thoughts of Père Gratry.

Those who read Spanish will find a little book entitled *La Iglesia y el
Obrero*, by P. Ernesto Giutart, S.J., interesting and useful, especially in preparing discourses for workingmen. In a very clear straightforward style the
author pictures the conditions of the workingmen in pre-Christian times, the
influence of Christianity on labor, especially by abolishing slavery, promoting
guilds, opposing unjust usury, establishing institutions of charity, influencing
civil legislation favorable to labor. The concluding chapter summarizes the
teaching of Leo XIII on the conditions and rights of workingmen.

Another practical little book for the Spanish reader is *La Cruzada de la
Buena Prensa*, by the Bishop of Jaca, D. Antolin López Pelaéz. The illustrious prelate makes many wise and timely suggestions concerning the utiliza-
tion of the press in the cause of truth, and the special duty of the clergy
in the matter.

A neat little brochure of less than a hundred short pages, all filled with
true wisdom, is *Pensamientos escogidos de Santa Teresa*. The editor, P.
Pons, S.J., has extracted thoughts from the writings of St. Teresa pertinent
to the meditations of St. Ignatius and arranged them according to the order of the Book of Exercises.

A recent Spanish work of more scholarly and professional, though none the
less of profoundly spiritual significance, is *San Juan: estudio critico-exegetico
sobre el Quarto Evangelio*, by the learned Jesuit professor, P. Murillo. The
work embodies, with notable additions and elaborations, the lectures delivered
by the author in the Seminary of Madrid before the students of Exegesis
preparing for the licentiate in the Faculty of S. Scripture. The work is a
testimonial no less to the ability of the auditors who, it may be assumed, assimilated its contents, than to the erudition and spiritual insight of the lecturer. The volume contains a critical introduction to the Gospel, in which

et Congregaciones Ecclesiasticas segun la disciplina vigente—a short treatise on the canon law of the subject with special notes on the secular Tertiaries; and *Los Esponsales y el Matrimonio segun la novissima disciplina*, a canonico-moral commentary on the *Ne temere*. The latter two volumes are from the pen of the well-known Jesuit professor, P. Juan Ferreres.

———

"Catholicism and Happiness" is a well-written and remarkably rational paper by a Protestant clergyman, the Rev. R. L. Gales, Vicar of Gedney, in which the author dissipates the rather popular notion that the wealth and prosperity of Protestant countries stands for desirable conditions of living; indeed, the "benighted Popish countries," assumed to be unprogressive, are actually the best conditioned so far as the great mass of the people are concerned. His conclusion, after considering the facts, is that the sum of human happiness was not increased by the substitution of Puritanism for Catholicism in the religious changes of the sixteenth century. (*Hibbert Journal.*)

———

In the same issue of the *Hibbert Journal* (January) appear two articles on the late Father Tyrrell. Baron Friederich von Hügel recounts from letters which passed between himself and his friend during the last twelve years of the latter's life, the facts and sentiments which portray the unfortunate priest as he manifested himself in his most intimate relations. The picture thus drawn, whilst thoroughly sympathetic, does not ignore certain shortcomings of Father Tyrrell. "Nobly disinterested, fearless to a fault, warmly affectionate, truly humble, and full, in his depths, of the specifically religious passion and instinct, yet he was indeed much of a hero, but not a saint, if by sanctity we mean faultlessness; for he had his very obvious faults—a vehement temper and a considerable capacity for bitterness when writing." Such is the writer's estimate of the priest whom he believes to have been wronged as well as misunderstood by the Roman authorities who nevertheless could not rob him of his Catholic faith. One might be inclined to accept all that Baron von Hügel says about Father Tyrrell's nobility of character and power of intellect, or even what he says about the narrowness of the human element in religion which can manipulate the issues of legitimate authority to wrong purpose. Yet no argument or reasoning can alter the fact that Father Tyrrell, in an evil hour, not merely criticized authority by setting up his own standard of interpretation of truth against tradition— right or wrong; but that he defied the authority which he himself recognized as indeed the legitimate and only medium of sacramental communication from God to men. To toy with error, as he did with Old Catholicism, fully convinced that it did not stand for the Church of God, was criminal in a sense which no true authority could condone. Rome had no alternative in formulating its verdict concerning Father Tyrrell. If the means which brought about this verdict were bound up with low motives in his accusers, it would indeed be deplorable, as would be any injury done to a mistaken apologist of truth; but that would not lessen the justice of the sentence, which stands independent of all charges of personal malice or imbecility in the opponents of the accused.

•

most glaring inconsistencies as a thinker, not to speak of the ugly sallies of temper which mark its references to Pius X and Cardinal Mercier.

The *Centenary of Catholicity in Kentucky* by the Hon. Ben. J. Webb, published twenty-six years ago by Charles A. Rogers, comes to us as a reminder that the story of the last quarter of a century is needed to complete the interesting record of that pioneer period of faith and missionary zeal. Among the prelates who have guarded and shaped the destinies of Catholicity in Kentucky during this time is Bishop Maes, himself the first historian of the district as described in that intensely engaging biography, the life of Father Nerinckx. The Bishop has lived through this unwritten history and made a large part of it. It would be interesting and instructive to have in writing his recollections of this period so as to bring Judge Webb's work up to date.

Father De Zulueta is a zealous advocate of Eucharistic devotion, especially of frequent Communion, as his writings on the subject testify. The last book from his pen is *The Eucharistic Triduum*—an aid to priests in preaching frequent and daily Communion. It is in fact a translation from the French work of Père Jules Lintelo, S.J., and is a practical manual of instruction on Holy Communion. We note the list of books quoted and recommended, from the French, English, and Spanish. Among the list of English works we should like to see included Bishop Hedley's admirable volume on the Blessed Eucharist, as well as Father Dalgairns's on Holy Communion.

A practical manual, of use to seminarists and priests, who find it necessary to pay some attention to the culture of voice and speech, and to deportment and gesture in preaching, is a booklet of eighty pages by the Rev. George S. Hitchcock, B.A., published under the title *Sermon Delivery*, a method for students. (Benziger Bros.)

Books Received.

BIBLICAL.

EL NUEVO TESTAMENTO en Griego y Español. Texto Griego conforme à la tercera edicion critica de Federico Brandscheid. Version Española por el Padre Juan José de la Torre, S.J. Con licencia ecclesiastica. Friburgo, Brisg., St. Louis, Mo.: B. Herder. 1910. Pp. 752. Price, $2.60.

A LIFE OF CHRIST told in Words of the Gospels. Arranged by Mary Lape Fogg. Boston: Angel Guardian Press. 1909. Pp. 195.

ARETAS IV, König der Nabatäer. Histor. Exegetische Studie zu II Par. 11:32. Von Dr. Alphons Steinmann, Prof. Lyceum Braunsberg. Freiburg, Brisg., St. Louis, Mo.: B. Herder. 1909. Pp. 44. Price $0.27.

THEOLOGICAL AND DEVOTIONAL.

DICTIONNAIRE APOLOGÉTIQUE DE LA FOI CATHOLIQUE contenant les Preuves de la Vérité de la Religion, les Réponses aux Objections tirées des Sciences humaines. Quatrième édition entièrement refondue sous la Direction de A. D. Alès, professeur a l'Institut Catholique de Paris. Avec la collaboration d'un grand nombre de Savants Catholiques. Fascicule III: Concordats—Dieu. Paris: Gabriel Beauchesne et Cie. 1910. Cols. 641-960. Prix 5 francs.

THE PENITENT INSTRUCTED. A Course of Eight Practical Instructions on How to Make a Good Confession. By the Rev. E. A. Selley, O.E.S.A. New and Revised Edition. London: R. and T. Washbourne, Ltd.; New York, Cincinnati, Chicago: Benziger Brothers. 1909. Pp. xxii-169. Price, $0.35.

THE CAUSES AND CURE OF UNBELIEF. By N. J. Laforet, Rector of the Catholic University of Louvain. Revised, Enlarged, and Edited by Cardinal Gibbons. With a Chapter by the Most Rev. P. J. Ryan, D. D., LL.D. Philadelphia: H. L. Kilner & Co. Pp. 278.

CATHOLIC BELIEF; or, A Short and Simple Exposition of Catholic Doctrine. By the Very Rev. Joseph Faâ de Bruno, D.D., Rector-General of the Pious Society of Missions. Author's American Edition edited by the Rev. Louis A. Lambert, author of *Notes on Ingersoll*, etc. Two Hundred and Ninetieth Thousand. New York, Cincinnati, Chicago: Benziger Bros. Pp. 387.

THE CONVERTS' CATECHISM OF CATHOLIC DOCTRINE. By the Rev. Peter Geiermann, C.SS.R. St. Louis and Freiburg: B. Herder. 1910. Pp. 110. Price $0.10.

SS. DOM. N. PII X EPISTOLAE ENCYCLICAE (Series Prima) Latin, with German translation on opposite pages. Containing the Encyclicals, 4 Oct., 1903 to 8 Sept., 1907. Freiburg, Brisg., St. Louis, Mo.: B. Herder. Pp. 121.

SS. DOM. N. PII X EPISTOLA ENCYCLICA de S. Anselmo, archiepiscopo Cantuariensi. With German translation. Freiburg, Brisg., St. Louis, Mo.: B. Herder. Pp. 75. Price $0.27.

SS. DOM. N. PII X EXHORTATIO AD CLERUM CATHOLICUM. With German translation. Freiburg, Brisg., St. Louis, Mo.: B. Herder. Pp. 54. Price $0.22.

THE EUCHARISTIC TRIDUUM. An Aid to Priests in preaching Frequent and Daily Communion, according to the Decrees of the H. H. Pius X. Translated from the French (second edition) of Père Jules Lintelo, S.J., by F. M. de Zulueta, S.J. London: R. and T. Washbourne, Ltd.; New York, Cincinnati, Chicago: Benziger Brothers. 1909. Pp. xxv-225. Price $0.75 *net*.

MEDITATIONES Ven. P. Ludovici de Ponta, S.J., de Praecipuis Fidei Nostrae Mysteriis, De Hispanico in Latinum Translatae a Melchiore Trevinnio, S.J. Edit. August. Lehmkuhl, S.J. Pars IV complectens meditationes de Mysteriis Passionis D. N. J. C. &c. Friburgi, Brisg., St. Louis, Mo.: B. Herder. 1909. Pp. 468. Price $1.45.

LITURGICAL.

NOVUM CAEREMONIALE PRO MISSA PRIVATA ex " Ephemeridibus Liturgicis " excerptum. Opella juxta novissimas S. R. C. declarationes exarata. Petrus M. de Amicis. Romae ex typographia I. Artero ad Montem Citatorium. 1910. Pp. 96.

PHILOSOPHICAL.

THE SUPREME PROBLEM. An Examination of Historical Christianity from the Standpoint of Human Life and Experience and in the Light of Psychical Phenomena. By J. Godfrey Raupert. Buffalo, N. Y.: Peter Paul & Son. 1910. Pp. xx-339.

FAITH AND REASON. Showing how they Agree. By the Rev. Peter Saurusaitis. New York: Christian Press Assn. Pub. Co. Pp. 149. Price $0.20.

THE WONDERS OF THE UNIVERSE. What Science says of God. The Scientific Discoveries of our Day in the Language of the People. By the Rev. James J. Meagher, D.D. N. Y. Christian Press Association.

HISTORICAL.

HISTORY OF MEDIEVAL PHILOSOPHY. By Maurice De Wulf, Professor at the University of Louvain, Doctor of Philosophy and Letters, Doctor of Laws, Member of the Royal Academy of Belgium. Third Edition. Translated by P. Coffey, Ph.D., Professor of Philosophy, Maynooth, Ireland. New York, London: Longmans, Green, & Co. 1909. Pp. xii-519. Price, $3.00, *net*.

VIE DE SAINTE MARTHE, Modèle des Filles chrétiennes. Par Comtesse Saint-Bris. Leur Rôle dans l'Église et dans la Société. Deuxième Édition. Paris: P. Téqui. 1909. Pp. xviii-240. Prix, 2 fr.

THE CATHOLIC WHO'S WHO AND YEAR BOOK, 1910. Edited by Sir F. C. Burnand. London: Burns and Oates, Ltd.; New York, Cincinnati, Chicago: Benziger Brothers. 1910. Pp. xlii-387.

ST. VINCENT DE PAUL AND THE VINCENTIANS IN IRELAND, SCOTLAND AND ENGLAND, A. D. 1638-1909. By the Rev. Patrick Boyle, C.M. London: R. and T. Washbourne, Ltd.; New York, Cincinnati, Chicago: Benziger Brothers. 1909. Pp. 318. Price, $1.25.

THE PAPACY AND THE FIRST COUNCILS OF THE CHURCH. By Rev. Thomas S. Dolan. St. Louis, Mo.: B. Herder; London and Edinburgh: Sands & Co. Pp. 189. Price $0.75.

MISCELLANEOUS.

DESIDERATA. Nach fünf Jahren. Zwei Mädchengeschichten, Von Auguste v. Lama. Regensburg, Rom, New York and Cincinnati: Fried. Pustet & Co. Pp. 382. Price $0.75.

PAPERS AND ADDRESSES: Theological, Philosophical, Biographical, Archeological. By the Most Rev. John Healy, D.D., LL.D., M.R.I.A. St. Louis, Mo.: B. Herder. 1909. Pp. 559. Price $2.25.

ORGELBUCH zu J. Mohr's Caecilia. Zur 32 Auflage neu herausgegeben von Johann Singenberger, und revidirt von F. X. Engelhart. Heft. I. Messgesänge. Regensburg, Rom, New York and Cincinnati: Fried. Pustet & Co. 1910. Pp. 102. Gr. folio.

COAT OF ARMS OF POPE PIUS X

THE
ECCLESIASTICAL REVIEW

FIFTH SERIES.—VOL. II.—(XLII).—MARCH, 1910.—No. 3.

LIBERALISM AND USURY.

THE liberal creed, not very long ago the standard of religious, political, and social orthodoxy in Europe and America, is now held in its entirety by few. During the greater part of the nineteenth century it held undisputed sway. Learned professors taught its dogmas in the universities; critics took them for granted in their estimate of new productions in all the departments of learning; politicians assumed their truth as the basis of the laws which they enacted and the political measures which they adopted. Then sometime after 1870 a change began to set in. The appearance of socialism like a black cloud on the horizon, the open discarding of almost all moral restraint by large and increasing numbers, the frank avowal of hedonism as the only end of human existence, the squalor, the physical and moral hideousness of our large centers of population, all these causes began to produce their effect on thinking minds. Could this be the right road of progress after all? Were the doctrines and ideals which had led to these things founded on truth and in reality? Were the dogmas of liberalism so certain and self-evident after all? To put such questions was to shake the glittering but unstable edifice of liberalism to its foundations. It soon became clear that the imposing structure was for the most part built up of no more solid materials than lath and plaster platitudes, and its occupants began to abandon it in streams. Even those stalwarts who refused to abandon the rickety dogmas of liberalism altogether, found themselves under the necessity of re-interpreting them and accommodating them to the changed conditions of the times.

The present seems a suitable opportunity for studying this remarkable movement in human history. To trace in outline, at least, some of its features will be interesting and not without instruction. I propose in this paper to take the subject of usury.

From time immemorial usury and usurer have been ill-sounding terms. The old civilizations of Babylonia as well as those of Greece and Rome had found it necessary to make usury laws. Philosophers, quietly studying the matter in the dry light of reason, had come to the conclusion that usury was a practice most contrary to nature. The Old and the New Testament condemned it. The Christian Church declared whoever denied that usury is a sin to be a heretic. The civil legislation of all Christian nations agreed in prohibiting and punishing it. But this consensus of opinion among the wisest and the best men who had ever lived was quite sufficient to grate on the liberal mind. The very fact that the doctrine was old, traditional, and universally accepted, made it repugnant to the liberal creed. In his celebrated letters on Usury, Bentham lays down the proposition "that no man of ripe years and of sound mind, acting freely and with his eyes open, ought to be hindered, with a view to his advantage, from making such bargain in the way of obtaining money as he thinks fit: nor (what is a necessary consequence) anybody hindered from supplying him, upon any terms he thinks proper to accede to" (p. 2). In so many chapters of his book Bentham discusses all the reasons that the wit of man ever devised for restraining men's liberty from agreeing to pay what interest they liked for a money loan. He triumphantly refutes them all. Neither the prevention of the crime of usury, which indeed is only a bad name given to a quite laudable transaction, nor the prevention of prodigality, nor the protection of indigence, nor the protection of simplicity, affords rational grounds for usury laws. According to Bentham such laws are not only ineffectual: they are positively mischievous, inasmuch as they raise the rate of interest and thus increase the difficulties of the borrower. The historical prejudice against usury is readily explained as the fruit of envy and malice, for the spendthrift has ever been the favorite of mankind, if not of fortune, while one who saves and looks after his property has ever been unpopular. The celebrated passage in which Aristotle showed that money is barren is treated by Bentham with light banter and pleasantry. Bentham's *Defence of Usury* was published in 1787 and began slowly to produce its effect. By the middle of the next century it had so changed the opinions of lawyers, legislators, and business men, that in the year 1854 the usury laws were abolished in England. Most of the Continental nations quickly followed suit, and the view which educated men generally took of the question was expressed with fitting conciseness and cocksureness by Lecky in his *History of European Morals.* He there writes: "When theologians pronounced loans at interest contrary to the law of nature and plainly extortionate, this error obviously arose from a false notion of the uses of money. They believed it to be a sterile thing, and that he who has restored what he had borrowed, has cancelled all the benefit he received from the transaction. At the time when the first Christian moralists treated the subject special circumstances had rendered the rate of interest extremely high, and consequently extremely oppressive to the poor, and this fact, no doubt, strengthened the prejudice; but the root of the condemnation of usury was simply an error in political economy. When men came to understand that money is a productive thing, and that the sum lent enables the borrower to create sources of wealth that will continue when the loan has been returned, they perceived that there was no natural injustice in exacting payment for this advantage, and usury either ceased to be assailed, or was assailed only upon the ground of positive commands." [1]

It may be remarked in passing that if the sterility of money is an error, it was an error which was not shared by theologians alone. Philosophers, statesmen, lawyers, and the great bulk of mankind in general, were all on the same side. Lecky had no right to single out the theologians for his condemnation. But the reference to political economy is of most interest to us at present. "The root of the condemnation of usury," says Lecky, without a shadow of doubt on the matter, "was simply an error in political economy." Like a good liberal, Lecky invokes the dogmas of political economy;

[1] *History of European Morals,* i, p. 94.

anything which is contrary to them cannot be sound.   However, since Lecky wrote, this particular dogma of the political economy which was then in vogue has been exposed to many a rude shock from several different quarters.   The historical school of political economists, represented in England by such men as Professor Ashley and Dr. Cunningham, has pointed out that, although the modern conditions of industry and trade may make it perfectly reasonable to charge and receive interest on a loan of money, it does not follow that it would be reasonable under all conditions.   On this point it will be of interest to quote the words of the present Lecturer in Economic History in the University of Oxford:

With our modern knowledge and experience [writes Mr. L. L. Price], we think it foolish and mischievous to prescribe a legal maximum rate of interest, beyond which no one may legally lend or borrow.   We argue that the effect of such a law is not to prevent the needy man from borrowing at a higher rate, but to make him pay still more, to compensate the lender for the risk which he runs of being detected by the law, and losing both interest and principal. We point to the means by which such laws could be evaded, and we contend that it is better to leave matters to the ordinary market influences, making stringent provisions, and devoting our efforts to the enforcement of these provisions against violence and fraud.   And so we pass an unqualified condemnation upon the usury laws.

But if with such an historical economist as Dr. Cunningham in his *Growth of English Industry and Commerce,* or Professor Ashley, in his *Economic History,* we shift our standpoint, and go back in imagination to the state of medieval society, and supply the circumstances of historical fact amid which these laws were enacted, we begin to qualify our condemnation.   We see that there was no such opportunity for the investment of capital as there is now, and that the possessor of a large sum of money could scarcely apply it to any productive enterprise or use it himself in such a way as to realize a profit.   If then he lent it, and the security were good, and the money repaid, he rendered a service to another man, but himself sustained no loss.   Nor was it the prosperous who would borrow,

look of the Oxford Professor is wider, and consequently his judgment is more tolerant. But an attentive consideration of the facts will show us how well founded this tolerant judgment is, and enable us to be still more tolerant. Although, of course, money existed in the Middle Ages, it was comparatively scarce and formed but a small portion of the national wealth. Landed property was by far the most important form of wealth; personalty, which now far exceeds realty in value, was then almost a negligible quantity. Municipal law regulated the succession to landed estate and imposed on it the chief part of the public burdens of the state. Personalty was too insignificant to attract the attention of the revenue officers of the crown, and of the civil lawyer, and accordingly it fell under the jurisdiction of the Church. This seems to be the explanation of the remarkable dichotomy which is observable still between the English law of realty and of personalty. But money was not only scarce in the Middle Ages; its functions were restricted to providing a measure of value and a ready means of exchange. As yet it scarcely existed as capital, capital being taken to mean a stock of money which can be readily applied to different productive enterprises which offer an opportunity for gain. Especially in the country parts a natural economy still prevailed in England in the thirteenth century.[3] The population was fixed to the soil and obtained a livelihood from the produce of the small holdings which it held of the lord, or from rations distributed by him in consideration of services rendered. The great households lived on the produce of their estates, and when the produce of one estate was exhausted they moved to another. Even in the towns trade was fettered by all sorts of laws, customs, and regulations. It was organized in gilds subject to strict prescriptions as to the conduct of business and as to the number of journeymen and apprentices who might be employed. The

which brought about the industrial revolution a century ago, was still in the womb of the future. As Dr. Cunningham writes: " In dealing with the Christendom of earlier ages we have found it unnecessary to take account of capital, for, as we understand the term in modern times, it hardly existed at all. In the fourteenth and fifteenth centuries we may notice it emerging from obscurity, and beginning to occupy one point of vantage after another, until it came to be a great political power in the State." [4]

But if the functions of money in the Middle Ages were almost confined to furnishing a measure of value and a medium of exchange, if it hardly at all, or only by way of exception, existed as capital, the only valid reason for exacting interest on a loan of money was necessarily something extrinsic to the loan itself. If risk was incurred by lending the money, or if there were loss to the lender because he was obliged to withdraw money from a profitable enterprise in order to make the loan, the lender of money was of course justified in exacting interest for his loan. He was not bound to benefit his neighbor with loss to himself, except when an alms was due out of charity; it was only right, and acknowledged as such by everybody, that the borrower should recoup the lender for any loss that the latter incurred by making the loan. But if the lender incurred no such loss, if the money would lie idle and useless in its owner's coffers unless it were lent, and if it was as safe or safer in the hands of the borrower and sure to be restored at the time agreed upon, then there was no ground for demanding interest on a loan. The money would be borrowed to discharge a debt, to pay a contribution levied by the overlord, to pay a fine, or perhaps to purchase wine or some other article of luxury; the borrower made nothing by it: the only functions of money as yet were its uses as a measure of value and a medium of exchange. It passed out of the hands of the borrower in fulfilling these functions; he derived no profit from its use; it was what canonists called it, a fungible, a good consumed as far as its then owner was concerned in the very first use of it. There is no ground for charging interest here. The price of a good which is consumed in the first use of it is the price of that use. Professor

[4] *Western Civilization*, ii, p. 162 (1900).

Cassel writes: "All economic goods may be divided into two categories, those which satisfy our wants in being consumed at once, and those which afford a series of useful services before they are worn out. Food is an instance of the former category, houses of the second. This line of subdivision is one of the most fundamental in economic science. The price paid for an article of immediate consumption is of course the same as the price paid for the use of this article. This is not so in the case of an article belonging to the second category. The price paid for the single useful service it affords is one thing; the price paid for the article itself is quite another thing." [5]

Inasmuch then as money in the Middle Ages was not yet a form of capital (an instrument for the production of wealth); inasmuch as its only functions, speaking generally, were to serve as a measure of value and a medium of exchange, and no profit was as a rule made on a money loan by the borrower, the Church was quite right in teaching that in these circumstances there was no justification for taking interest on a loan of money; that to do so was to commit the sin of usury.

But, it may be said, the Church's action in this matter put a restriction on trade and hindered the development of commerce. In reply to this common objection it may be said that it was not the Church which imposed the restriction, but natural justice and fair dealing. Justice and fair dealing are sometimes a restriction on trade nowadays, but nobody thinks of blaming the magistrate for requiring the rules of justice and fair dealing to be observed by traders.

Beyond this it may be doubted whether the laws against usury were in fact any great restraint on trade. Trade was then in the hands of special gilds, or companies, largely confined to towns and occasional fairs, and hemmed in on all sides by laws, customs, and jealously-guarded privileges. Ordinary people had no loose capital to employ in trade, and if they had had it, gentlemen would never have demeaned them-

cantile enterprise, or employing an agent to trade for him, or embarking in trade on his own account. The Church made no difficulty about profit being gained in trade if only the trade were honest. It may then be safely asserted that the usury laws imposed no undue restrictions on trade.

One of the chief differences between the Middle Ages and modern times is that money has become capital in the interval. Some would say that this is the fundamental difference between the Middle Ages and our own times, and the cause of all other differences. No precise date can be assigned for the beginning of the capitalistic age. As Dr. Cunningham says: "It would be still more hopeless to try to treat the intervention of capital as an event which happened at a particular epoch, or a stride which was taken within a given period. It is a tendency which has been spreading with more or less rapidity for centuries, first in one trade and then in another, in progressive countries. We cannot date such a transformation even in one land; for though we find traces of capitalism so soon as natural economy was ceasing to be dominant in any department of English life, its influence in reorganizing the staple industry of this country was still being strenuously opposed at the beginning of the present [nineteenth] century." [6]

Whenever the change took place, money is certainly capital now, and one of its principal forms. Anyone who has saved a sum of money finds no difficulty nowadays in employing it productively; innumerable investments of all sorts compete for the money of the capitalist, and little or nothing can be done without its aid. The whole world lies helpless in the toils of Moneybags, as the socialist bitterly complains.

Will the fact that in the conditions of modern life money has become capital serve to explain and justify the taking of interest on a loan of money? The socialists angrily deny it. They maintain that Aristotle and the Christian Church were perfectly right when they condemned interest and usury as contrary to nature. Money, they say, is always and essentially barren. All wealth is produced by labor, as Adam Smith, Ricardo, and the classical school of economists, taught. The classical school of economists, however, wrote in favor of

[6] *Western Civilization*, p. 163.

the moneyed classes, and they carefully abstained from drawing the obvious conclusion from this fundamental principle of modern socialism. If labor produces all wealth, then all wealth is the fruit of labor and belongs to the laborer by natural justice. The laborer indeed needs capital, and to get it he is obliged to have recourse to the capitalist, who takes the opportunity to rob him of a portion of the fruit of his toil. The capitalist as such does not work; the money which he lends produces nothing; all the produce is due to labor. The capitalist would obtain all that is due to him if his loan without interest were paid back to him at the time agreed upon. The laborer produces more than is absolutely necessary for his support by working long hours and exhausting his strength; he thus produces surplus value; but instead of enjoying all the fruit of his labor himself, as in justice he should do, he is compelled to hand over the surplus value to the capitalist to pay interest on his loan. The capitalist then is nothing better than a robber of the worst type; he lives on the plunder of the poor.

Anti-socialists have no difficulty in showing that this reasoning is utterly fallacious. The fundamental principle that labor is the only source of wealth is false. Labor is indeed one of the sources of wealth; but it is not the only nor the chief source. Those commodities which can be produced in any quantity at will by common labor do indeed tend to gravitate in value toward the cost of the labor which produced them; but beyond this it is impossible to go with the labor principle. Land, mines of all sorts, forests, diamonds and precious stones, works of art, scarce objects of value, patent goods, have a value altogether out of proportion to any labor that may have been spent on them and independent of it. Even in those

ing the fruits of his toil twentyfold or a hundredfold. The work done by a steam-engine on the railway is not merely the reproduction of the labor bestowed on its manufacture plus the labor of the engine-driver and the stoker: the steam-engine is an instrument by means of which the energy stored up in coal and steam is captured and made to work in the service of man. As Mr. Mallock says, it is not merely crystallized labor; it is crystallized mechanics, crystallized science, and crystallized inventive genius, working with the forces of nature.

Although the socialist reasoning is unsound and fails utterly on its constructive side, it has served to discredit the classical political economy from which source it derived its fundamental principle. Furthermore it has compelled anti-socialists to examine more deeply into the grounds of interest with a view to its explanation and justification. It has been found that it is by no means an easy task to explain how capital produces interest, and to justify that interest. Böhm-Bawerk, the celebrated Austrian economist, after many years of study, wrote two books on the problem—*Capital and Interest* and *The Positive Theory of Capital.* The first is an exhaustive history and criticism of the numerous and varied theories that have been advanced in explanation of the matter, and the second contains a lengthy exposition of his own view. After an interesting historical account of the canonist doctrine on usury, Böhm-Bawerk discusses the modern theories, grouped under four heads: the Productivity, Use, Abstention, and Labor or Exploitation theories. We have already seen something on the last head; a word must now be said on the others.

The production of wealth, or of economic goods, or of those material conveniences which meet our wants and have an exchange value, is commonly said to be the result of the action of three factors—land, capital, and labor. The produce is due to the activity of these three factors, and so it is only equitable that a share in the distribution of the product should fall to each. Rent thus goes to land; wages to labor; and interest

tility of land aided by labor certainly produces economic goods; a share of the produce therefore is in justice due to the owner of the land and to the laborer. But what does money used as capital produce? Even if it aids in the production of goods, it does not follow from this that it produces values, much less surplus value, and the emergence of surplus value is the phenomenon to be explained. Whatever value the product has is due, says the Productivity theory, to the factors of production. Two parts are due respectively to land and to labor; the third is due to capital. But all the value that there is in this third portion of the product was already in the capital when it was applied to production. The productivity of capital then cannot explain the emergence of surplus value in the shape of interest on capital.

The Use theory is a modification of the Productivity theory, and it asserts that interest is due to the use of capital. This theory fails to recognize the great economic fact, insisted on by the Schoolmen, and the foundation of the canonist doctrine on usury. Capital has no use beyond its consumption. When the borrower has paid for its consumption or use, he has paid for the capital; and when he has paid for the capital, or stock of money, he has paid also for its use. Böhm-Bawerk is fully conscious that the prejudices of most modern economists are against him in this matter. "It is indeed", he says, "essentially the same question as was in dispute centuries ago between the canonists and the defenders of loan interest. The canonists maintained that property in a thing includes all the uses that can be made of it; there can, therefore, be no separate use which stands outside the article and can be transferred in the loan along with it. The defenders of loan interest maintained that there was such an independent use. And Salmasius and his followers managed to support their views with such effectual arguments that the public opinion of the scientific world soon fell in with theirs, and that to-day we have but a smile for the 'short-sighted pedantry' of these old canonists. Now fully conscious that I am laying myself open to the charge of eccentricity, I maintain that the much-decried doctrine of the canonists was, all the same, right to this extent—that the independent use of capital, which was the object in dispute, had no existence in reality. And I trust to succeed in proving that the judgment of the former courts in this literary process, however unanimously given, was in fact wrong." [7]   Böhm-Bawerk goes to the roots of the question and shows conclusively the truth of his contention that the scholastics on this point were certainly in the right.

The Abstention theory, worked out by Senior and others, looks upon interest as the reward of abstaining from the immediate consumption of one's wealth.   Capital is the fruit of saving; to save I must abstain from immediate enjoyment; this abstention deserves compensation, which it receives in the form of interest on the capital devoted to production.   Lassalle and the socialists poured ridicule on the idea of the abstinence of the capitalist.   The idea of a Rothschild or a Carnegie, who cannot consume their wealth with the best intention in the world to do so, and who yet deserve reward for their abstinence, was too ridiculous in socialists' eyes.   Böhm-Bawerk, however, prefers this theory to any of the others, and indeed it is closely allied to his own.   That in brief consists in this.   The problem of interest is a problem of value, and value depends upon facts of psychology, upon the wants and estimates of men who desire the satisfaction of those wants; but it is part of man's nature to esteem future goods less than present goods of the same sort and quality; so that $100. possessed at present is equal in value to $105. a year hence. Therefore in charging five per cent interest on the loan of $100. for one year the lender is merely demanding an equivalent in value for his loan.   Böhm-Bawerk's criticism has had a great effect on modern economic thought; but his own view has not met with anything like general acceptance.   Objections to it have been raised on the ground that it is by no means new as Böhm-Bawerk seems to suppose, and that it explains nothing.   Granted that in common estimation $100. of cash in hand is worth $105. to be paid a year hence, what reason can be assigned for this common estimation?   It does not seem to be an ultimate fact of human nature. · A bird in the hand is ordinarily indeed worth two in the bush; but this is because of the uncertainty whether the two in the bush will ever be in the hand.   If the birds were securely fixed in the

birds in the bush would be worth two in the hand, perhaps even more under certain circumstances. Similarly it is the element of uncertainty, or present need, or a good opportunity for immediate and profitable investment, which makes $100. in possession worth $105. a year hence. If these elements are excluded it is quite conceivable that in certain circumstances common estimation would consider $99. to be paid a year hence a fair equivalent for $100. of present money. The possibility of the rate of interest sinking below zero, and the depositor having to pay the banker for keeping his money safely for him, is recognized by economists of standing.

Böhm-Bawerk, with other economists of the Austrian school, adopted the theory of marginal utility to settle the value of commodities. In substance the theory amounts to this. Prices of commodities depend on subjective valuations of buyers and sellers from first to last. A cobbler, for example, has made a number of pairs of shoes, of which some are for sale. What will be the price per pair? He wants some for his own use and for the use of his family; the subjective value of the pairs of shoes necessary to supply these wants will be very high. A change of shoes is desirable; but still a second pair will not have such subjective value as the first pair has. Then in descending scale of subjective value a third pair may be desirable to supply the place of one nearly worn out, and so on to the last pair, the pair that the cobbler could most easily do without. The utility of this last pair of shoes is the mar-

society of men, and that it is the social estimate of society which is the cause and the measure of exchange value. This is precisely the doctrine of the common estimation, the standard of prices according to the Scholastics, rediscovered by modern economists.

The whole situation is one of great interest for the theologian. He sees that not only England, but Austria, Germany, and other Continental nations have reverted to usury laws in less than fifty years after they had discarded them; some main elements in what we may call the political economy of the Catholic Church are being brought back with honor from the ignominious exile into which they had been thrust by the liberal school. The dogmas of that school are decried and reprobated not only by socialists, but by the most accredited economists. Will the canonist doctrine on usury come to be generally recognized again as true? We have no hesitation in saying that there is every prospect of it, that in fact this is largely the case already, but that ignorance of what the real canonist doctrine was prevents the general recognition of the fact. The substance of the canonist doctrine on usury consisted in the assertion that *per se* it is against justice to demand a price for a money loan over and above the restitution of the loan itself. In the matter of money it is not possible to distinguish the price of the substance of a loan and the price of its use, as it is possible to distinguish the price of a house and the price of a lease of the same house. While insisting on this the canonists readily admitted that there were certain extrinsic titles for exacting interest on a loan of money. In other words, they taught that circumstances may justify interest on a loan which in other circumstances would be unjust. This is quite a common opinion among recent economists, and it has been adopted and developed by such an authority as the American economist F. A. Walker. Modern capitalism seems to be such a circumstance. Nowadays a man may readily borrow $5000. without anything passing between lender and borrower besides a piece of paper. With this loan the borrower can easily purchase land, machinery, shares in commercial or industrial companies, or other agents of production where the distinction between the value of the substance of the good and the value of its use and product is quite valid and legitimate. Money thus used is capital, and it represents, and is in modern times readily exchangeable for, all sorts of productive goods. Money then used as capital is virtually productive, and for all practical purposes it may be looked upon as a productive good itself. As Professor Cassel says: " The most important achievement hitherto obtained by the discussion, which has been going on for so many centuries, is that the question, For what is interest paid? may now be regarded as definitely settled. It is stated, once for all, that interest is the price paid for an independent and elementary factor of production which may be called either wäiting or use of capital, according to the point of view from which it is looked at." [8] If this be conceded, and I think that in the circumstances of the modern capitalistic world we need have no difficulty in conceding it, the question of usury is settled for the theologian.

T. SLATER, S.J.

St. Beuno's College, St. Asaph.

CIRCA LICEITATEM CUJUSDAM OPERATIONIS CHIRURGICAE PROPONUNTUR DUBIA NONNULLA.

est; et secundo, ut ii, qui arte medica sanabiles existunt, a morbis curentur, qui, deinde, recuperata valetudine, domum redire permittuntur.

Attamen finis ille duplex non est unicus censendus. Illis namque a commercio hominum segregatis, qui aliis periculo vitae vel sanitatis esse possunt, boni tam physici quam moralis ipsius societatis humanae ratio ita habetur. Quod quidem bonum tunc efficaciter obtineri potest quando de insanabiliter aegrotis sermo est. Si vero de illis qui ad tempus, curationis gratia, in nosocomiis supradictis vitam degunt, de iis, prae- sertim, qui vitio venereo laborant, quaestio agitatur, alio modo res se habent. Illi enim vix a pessima vivendi ratione revo- cari possunt; quo fit, ut a nosocomio liberati et ad vomitum reversi, contractoque matrimonio, vel etiam nullo contracto, liberos procreare incipiunt, qui typum gestant illorum de quibus supra diximus.

Ad incommoda et damna ista sat gravia praeveniendo prae- cavenda, recursum, his ultimis temporibus, habuerunt medici ad operationem quandam " vasectomy " dictam, qua viri et etiam mulieres ad prolem generandam inepti efficiuntur.

Operatio ista vasectomiae eo modo in viris peragitur, ut facta incisione per scrotum seu cutem et membranas quae testes cooperiunt, vas deferens prius forcipibus prehensum per totum dividatur;[2] quo facto statimque retracto cultro, vulnus ipsum contractione musculi[3] clauditur quin ulteriore opera chirurgica opus sit.

Simplicissima et etiam brevissima est haec operatio, tes- tantibus ipsis medicis; nec ullo medicamento somnifero indiget patiens. Similis quaedam, quamvis longe difficilior operatio, divisione scilicet oviducti, in mulieribus peragi potest quae eumdem effectum sterilitatis producit. De viris autem est adhuc notandum quod post vasectomiam peractam eodem modo ad copulam conjugalem peragendam illi sunt apti ac fuerunt antea.

Praeter effectum sterilitatis, de quo hucusque diximus, alios etiam effectus, quos psychicos vocant, ex tali operatione sequi,

---

[2] Si ea, quae heic dicta sunt, minus cum dicendi ratione apud chirurgos usitata quadrare videntur, hujus rei ea erit duplex ratio; tum quia simplicitati consulendum esse duximus; tum etiam quia minutiae hac in re vix aliquid utili- tatis ad quaestiones morales inferius instituendas conferri possunt.

in confesso est apud plures medicos; id, quod locum habet in iis, praesertim, qui vitiis contra sextum dediti sunt. Isti miseri, facta vasectomia, novam quasi vitam agere incipiunt; ab habitibus pravis, utcumque inveteratis, abstinent;[4] et ad tentationes superandas fortiores et promptiores redduntur. Cujus rei sufficiens, ni fallor, reddi potest ratio, si prae oculis habentur ea quae de secretione testium egregie statuit Brown-Séquard; quem, qui majorem hac de re scientiam habere cupit, consulat; at hic locus non est quo plura de hac questione ponamus.

His igitur de modo· quo operatio vasectomiae peragitur deque hujus operationis effectibus qui generandi potentiam spectant, sic breviter indicatis, ulterius ad moralistam spectat liceitatem vasectomiae juxta principia theologiae moralis determinare, eo praesertim casu, quo haec inscio omnino et ita forsan invito patiente perficitur. Qua de re duplex, ut videtur, oriri potest quaestio.

Primo, an quis licite tali operationi se submittere possit? Secundo, potestne medicus talem operationem facere casu quo patiens hujus effectum ignorat?

· Primo quaesito distinguendo respondendum est; vel enim agitur de eo qui hanc operationem in se fieri permittit eo animo ut sterilis effectus voluptate matrimonii gaudeat quin onera ex liberorum sustentatione et educatione prevenientia sentiat; vel quis intendit praecavere mala quae, docente experientia, ex procreatione filiorum evenire possunt; ut puta, si mulier nequit parere quin vita ejus periclitetur, aut foetus edit mortuos sive ita morbo vel deformitate aliqua affectos, ut vitam agere diu nequeant. Duplex hic casus, uti perspicuum est, matrimonium jam contractum respicit. De viro, autem, in-

intenditur. Quam si quis directe quaerat, procul dubio mortalis peccati erit reus. Secundus casus, vero, non est tam facilis solutu. Sed, ut videtur, ponitur in hac secunda hypothesi actio ex qua duplex sequitur effectus. Praecaventur enim mala supra indicata, et iste est effectus bonus. Deinde, frustratur finis primarius matrimonii, et habetur effectus malus. Id unum est, ergo, quaerendum; an, nimirum, effectus ille bonus mediante effectu malo sequatur. Res sane ita esse videtur. Etenim bonus ille effectus eo praecise obtinetur quia, facta vasectomia, vir filios amplius procreare nequit. Propterea, etiam in hoc secundo casu contra. liceitatem dictae operationis statuendum esse videtur.

Secundi quaesiti adhuc difficilius est responsum. Agitur praecipue de casu quo operatio vasectomiae in eos fit qui defectivi (*defectives*) vel degenerati (*degenerates*) appellantur, ad impediendum, videlicet, quominus, quum nosocomio valedixerint, progeniem, quam ex Capellmann jam descriptam habes, possint amplius propagare. Estne, igitur, licitum tales homines indiscriminatim sterilizare, uti loquuntur medici, etiamsi operationis effectum ignorent? Hoc opus, hic labor. Sed si quam opinationem hac in re mihi liceat habere, pro liceitate talis agendi modi standum esse puto. Summopere, enim, ut jam dictum est, societati humanae interest ut, qui matrimonii juribus fruuntur, progeniei sanae gignendae sint capaces. Praeterea, jus, quo unusquisque lege naturali gaudet ad matrimonium ineundum filiosque habendos, est ita alienabile ut cessare possit; tum quando directe a quopiam renuntiatur, ut fit ab iis qui sacris ordinibus innitiantur vel vota solemnia nuncupant; tum etiam quando cum jure validiore pugnat: jus enim validius praevaleat necesse est.

Et revera, si bono societatis, utpote communi, cedere debet bonum privatum individui, id etiam sequetur quod, quando hoc cum illo incompatibile est, auctoritas civilis individuum privare potest juribus quibus aliunde jure poli gauderet, si prius bonum secus obtineri nequit. Porro, si auctoritas civilis libertatem et vitam ipsam hominibus pravis privare potest ut, poenis istis perterriti, alii a criminibus patrandis abstineant, quare defectivi jure prolem habendi privare nequeunt: quod certe jus et bonum libertate et vita est minus valde? Et est notandum nos agere non solum de iis defectivis qui uxorem sunt ducturi; verum etiam de illis multis qui, nullo contracto matrimonio, filios nihilominus procreant, qui, deinde, usque fortasse ad majorenitatem adeptam expensis civitatis ali ac sustineri debent; et etiam postea, quum ingenium ac indolem paternum secuti, ob crimina patrata in carceribus conjiciuntur.

Et quis forsan nunc videbit totam rem de liceitate vasectomiae plus minusve theoretice agitatam hucusque fuisse. Ad praxim quod attinet, negari nequit quin abusibus quam plurimis locus daretur, si declarata semel liceitate hujus operationis penes medicum ipsum esset in singulis casibus discernere utrum sit facienda annon. Satis enim notum est, ut de aliis rebus taceam, non paucos dari medicos quorum conscientia progressum continuum et quasi geometricum facere videtur versus limitem quem significant mathematici symbolo O. Res sane lugenda.

Practice igitur interventus auctoritatis civilis requiri videtur, quae statuat in quosnam et quibusnam in casibus haec operatio sit facienda. Nec hoc dictum est, ac si potestas civilis arbitrarie omnino et nullo habito respectu juris naturalis agere posset. Jus enim naturale ex una parte sartum tectum maneat oportet; dum ex altera statum civilem spectat ut mediis aptioribus et efficacioribus ad civium salutem temporalem procurandam eorumque bonum tum physicum tum morale promovendum rite utatur.

Sed ne quid nimis. Presenti quaestionem utcumque agitasse sufficiat. At ne formidemus nos sacerdotes quaestiones hujusmodi discutere ac in illas enucleandas aciem ingenii interdum dirigere. Hoc enim saepe postulat vel ipsa salus animarum nobis concreditarum. Urget quoque alia ratio, ut nempe quum medici nos adeunt consilii capiendi caussa quomodo diversis in rerum adjunctis licite agant, eos tute ac rite edocere simus parati.

STEPHEN M. DONOVAN, O.F.M.

Washington, D. C.

THE FUNCTIONS OF CHURCH BELLS IN OLD ENGLAND.

BELLS "CHRISTENED".

REFERENCE has already been made in a former article [1] to the designations borne by some of the bells in England; as " Great Tom " at Oxford, " Big Ben " at London, and " Old Kate " at St. Mark's, Lincoln. These are, however, merely pet names or nicknames. But it must be borne in mind that in pre-Reformation England nearly every bell was christened, and christened with a religious name. Those of Crowland Abbey were named Pega, Bega, Tatwin, Turketyl, Betelin, Bartholomew, and Guthlac. This peal was destroyed by fire in 1091. The bells of the Priory of Little Dunmow, Essex, were in 1501, according to an old chartulary, recast and baptized:

> Prima in honore Sancti Michaelis Archangeli;
> Secunda in honore Sancti Johannis Evangelisti;
> Tertia in honore S. Johannis Baptisti;
> Quarta in honore Assumptionis beatae Mariae;
> Quinta in honore Sanctae Trinitatis et omnium sanctorum.

And the tenor-bell at Welford, Berkshire, bears the inscription: " Missi de celis habeo nomen Gabrielis, 1596."

The bells were, of course, not actually baptized with that baptism which is administered for the remission of sins; but they are said to be christened because the same ceremonies which are observed in christening children are also observed in consecrating bells,—such as the washing, the anointing, and the imposing a name: all which, however, may more strictly be said to represent the signs and symbols of baptism than they may be called baptism itself.

Bells are not baptized for the remission of sins, because the original sin of a bell would be a flaw in the metal, or a defect in its tone; neither of which the priest undertakes to remove. There was, however, a previous ceremony of Blessing the Furnace when the bells were cast within the precincts of a monastery, as they most frequently were in former times; and this may have been intended for the prevention of such defects.

The brethren stood round the furnace, ranged in processional order, and chanted the Psalm containing the verses:

Praise Him in the sound of the trumpet: praise Him upon the lute and harp.
Praise Him in the cymbals and dances: praise Him upon the strings and pipe.
Praise Him upon the well-tuned cymbals: praise Him upon the loud cymbals.
Let everything that hath breath praise the Lord.

Then followed certain prayers, after which the molten metal was blessed, and God was asked to infuse into it His grace and overshadow it with His power, for the honor of the saint to whom the bell was to be dedicaed, and whose name it was to bear.

FUNCTIONS OF BELLS.

I. THE RELIGIOUS USE OF BELLS.

How perfectly the parish church and its priest kept in touch with the pulse of the people is in nothing better proved, probably, than in the plurality of parts played by church bells in the political, parochial, and personal experiences of the people.

Summoning to divine services, emphasizing a particular season in the Church's year, announcing the consecration of the Sacred Elements, the time of the Angelus, the passing of a soul, etc.; this is their primary and most frequent use.

1. *Tolling for Church.* This is said to be a relic of the Ave Bell which, before the Reformation, was tolled before the service to invite worshipers to a preparatory prayer to the Blessed Virgin.

According to a Lincoln Minster time-table (circa 1400), in summer:

5 A. M.—Matins at daybreak (after 5 peals of bells). Three Masses *in aurora.* Lauds.

12 Noon.—(Second Ave bell). Choir boys at school.

1.30 P. M.—First peal, followed by four others.

3 P. M. — Evensong. *Placebo* and *Dirigo* (Collation in Lent).
  Compline. Boys at play.

6 P. M.—(Third Ave bell). Boys' supper. *Salve Regina.* **Pray**-
  ers in Dormitory. (The Ave bells later than 1400.)

7 P. M. (or Sundown)—Curfew. Scrutiny in the closed church.
  Searchers' supper. Watchman plays the flute to mark the
  hours. (Choir recites Psalter all through the night, changing relays at midnight, if there is a Canon lying dead.)

2. The *Curfew* has, for an extended period, been a most
important time-teller. It has often been asserted that William the Conqueror introduced the curfew custom into England, but it is highly probable that he only enforced a law
which was already in existence in the kingdom, and which was
a custom prevalent throughout Europe in the eleventh century. It was not an original idea of William's. The curfew
was early to be found all over France, Italy, and Spain; and
it is said that its ringing at Carfax, in Oxford, was instituted
by Alfred the Great. There were several wise reasons for
its enforcement by William of Normandy: (1) As a safeguard
against fires, at a period when a large portion of the houses
were built of wood; (2) as a precaution against surprises by
attack from an enemy, as the lights would afford an indication
as to the location of the foe; (3) as a check on the Saxon
beer-clubs, where William had every reason to anticipate the
hatching of treason.

In 1103, Henry I modified the curfew custom by making it
no longer compulsory. According to the " Liber Albus "
(which gives a curious picture of London life under the later
Angevin kings, beginning with Edward I), it was an offence
for any person who was armed to wander about the city after
curfew had rung. At Tamworth a bye-law was passed in
1390 which provided that " no man, woman, or servant should
go out after the ringing of the curfew from one place to an-

complains that soon the curfew will ring, and that if she is found in the streets the " watch " will take her to prison.

The curfew, which was more or less enforced as a domestic regulation for many centuries, gradually died out of use; but in old market towns and remote villages, where the shadows of antiquity still linger on the threshold of home, it is still observed. And it is really surprising to find in how many places it still exists. A touching case is that of many American towns, especially in the New England States, which have retained it as a legacy from the Pilgrim Fathers, who were so unwilling to abandon any of the customs of their old homeland. At Charleston, in 1851, for instance, two bells rang nightly (at eight and ten in summer, and at seven and nine during winter). The first bell was the signal for the young children to say good-night; at the second bell the " watch " for the night was set, and after that no servant might step outside his master's house without a special permit.

3. *Advent Bells.* In many an English parish the Advent bell was rung each evening during the month of December. In others it was rung on the last three Mondays in Advent. In most cases the ringing is in the evenings, as during the day the ringers are engaged in their respective occupations. In some parishes, especially in Northamptonshire and Oxfordshire, the ringing takes place at five in the morning.

4. *Christmas Bells.* No one who has read Charles Dickens is ignorant of the Christmas chimes. Indeed, all of us are more or less fondly familiar with the merry peal which heralds in the happy Christmas morn:

> Merrily the bells are pealing:
> On the past will memories dwell;
> Thoughts of absent friends come stealing;
> In our hearts we wish them well.

But there is one bell still rung at midnight on Christmas Eve, in some places, which is worthy of mention here. It is known as the " Old Lad's Passing-bell " or " Devil's Knell ". After the last stroke of twelve o'clock (midnight) the age of the year is tolled, as on the death of a person. The origin of this quaint custom was the belief that the devil died when Christ was born.

Mr. Baring-Gould tells an experience he had the first

Christmas Eve he spent at Horbury, near Wakefield, where this custom is still perpetuated.   He knew nothing of this singular knell, when he retired to bed, on that Christmas Eve, to be awakened at midnight by the tolling of the bell.   He says: "My window looked out into the churchyard, and was, in fact, opposite the tower door.   I was greatly shocked and distressed, for I had not heard that anyone was ill in the parish, and I feared that the deceased must have passed away without the ministrations of religion.   I threw up my window and leaned out, awaiting the sexton.   Then I counted the strokes —three, three, three: Then I counted the ensuing strokes up to one hundred.   Still more astonished I waited impatiently the appearance of the sexton.   When he issued from the tower, I called to him: ' Joe, who is dead?'   The man sniggered and answered, ' T'Owd Un, they say.'   ' But who *is* dead?' I repeated.   ' T'owd chap '! came the reply.   ' What old man?   He must be very old indeed!'   'Ay!   He be owd; but for sure he'll give trouble yet!'   It was not till next day that the matter was explained to me."

5. *Holy Innocents.*   Quaint as is the reason for the " Devil's Knell " at Christmas Eve, so beautiful is the idea of that pretty custom, observed in some parts of England, of ringing a muffled peal on Holy Innocents' Day, in memory of that ruthless massacre of those earliest Christian martyrs.   At Norton (near Evesham) after the muffled peal has been rung in commemoration of the martyrdom of the Babes of Bethlehem, the bells are unmuffled, and a joyous peal is rung for the deliverance of the Infant Jesus.

6. *Baptisms.*   Peals at Baptisms, though rare, are not unknown.   There are still parishes where it has been usual (from time unknown) to ring the " Christening peal ".

7. *When Carrying the Viaticum.*   Handbooks were common in the thirteenth and fourteenth centuries, advising, instructing, and exhorting the clergy as to their duties and the

an instruction on the administration of Extreme Unction, with
a kind of Office for the Visitation of the Sick:

> When thou shalt to sick gone,
> A clean surplice cast thee on;
> Take thy stole with thee right,
> And pull thy hood over thy sight.
> Bear thy host anont [upon] thy breast
> In a box that is honest.
> Make thy clerk before thee gynge [go]
> To bear light and bell ring.

8. *The Passing Bell.* This was the hallowed bell which,
in pre-Reformation times, used to be rung when a person was
in extremis. It had a double purpose: (1) to scare away the
evil spirits which were supposed to lurk around the dying,
ready to pounce on his soul; (2) to announce to the parish
that a soul was passing from time into eternity, in order that
the neighbors might of their charity pray for the soul which
was so soon to be beyond human help, that it might have a safe
passage into Paradise.

Instead of ringing the Passing Bell, the Athenians used to
beat on brazen kettles, at the moment of a decease, in order
to scare away the Furies.

The *Advertisements* of 1564 has: " Item, That when any
Christian body is in ' passing ', that the bell be tolled . . .
and after the time of his ' passing ', to ring no more but one
short peal, and one before the burial, and another short peal
after the burial." Canon LXVII, 1604, directs: "And
when any is ' passing ' out of this life, a bell shall be tolled

advice of his Chancellor, instructed his clergy in 1880 that "The short peal prescribed by the Canon to be rung before and after the burial is essentially a part of the Burial-ritual of the Church."

9. *The Soul-bell.* This was rung after the spirit had returned to Him who gave it, that the living might pray for the dead. This is the "ringing-out" knell referred to in the above passages. Besides being rung a few hours after death, the soul bell was sounded again at stated intervals—at the month's end, the three months' end, and so on. Surtees, the antiquary, alludes to this custom in the ballad of "Sir John le Spring":

> Pray for the soul of Sir John le Spring,
> When the black monks sing and the chantry bells ring.
> Pray for the sprite of the murdered knight,
> Pray for the rest of Sir John le Spring, etc.

10. *Hand-bell at Funerals.* A hand-bell was always rung before the funeral procession, and still is (or was, to within recent times) at University funerals in Oxford. Even so late as (about) 1735, in the diocese of St. Asaph—and doubtless in other dioceses too—psalms were chanted during a funeral procession, and a bell was rung before the corpse, as far as the churchyard.

One, a certain Thomas Nash, made a curious bequest in 1813. He bequeathed £50 a year to the ringers of the Abbey Church, Bath, "on condition of their ringing on the whole peal of bells, with clappers muffled, various solemn and doleful changes on the 14th of May in every year, being the anniversary of my wedding-day; and also on the anniversary of my decease, to ring a grand bob-major and merry peals unmuffled, in joyful commemoration of my happy release from domestic tyranny and wretchedness."

A singular, but beautiful custom still exists in the village of Horningsham, Wiltshire, where at the burial of a young maiden a wedding-peal is rung out, instead of the doleful tolling of the muffled knell.

11. *The Banns-Peal.* This is still heard in some places. It is a peal rung after the publication of the banns of marriage. It is usually chimed after morning service on the first Sunday that the banns are "put up"; but this is by no means the uni-

versal practice, as in some parishes it is rung on the first and third Sundays; and in others on the third Sunday only. In a few parishes the banns-peal is rung on all three Sundays.

12. *The Agnus-Bell.* Formerly the English churches seem to have possessed a small bell, named the Agnus-bell, which was (judging by its name) rung at the "Agnus Dei". The parish-church of Hemswell possessed one. In many churches, bells and other articles were returned in 1566 as lost or missing, without any satisfactory reason being given for their absence. In many cases they were, no doubt, secretly abstracted in order to prevent their destruction; in others they may have been hidden. It is probable that in a large number of instances they were taken to the houses of the people who saved them, and that in after years they were lost or destroyed.

It was no uncommon practice to convert the small hand-bells into mortars. Indeed, this was done in 1566, in the parish of Hemswell, already quoted: "ij. hande belles sold to Robert Aestroppe one of the sayd churchwardens to make a mortar off".

13. *The Sacring-Bell.* Before the Reformation, a sacring-bell was to be found in every church in England. A small sacring-bell was discovered in Bottesford Church (Lincolnshire) during its restoration in 1870. When the plaster was removed from the west end of the south aisle, it was seen that one of the stones in the wall was merely loosely placed in position, and not built firmly in like the rest of the masonry. It was removed, and behind it, in a hole (evidently made to hold it) was found the bell. This bell is now in the custody of the Society of Antiquaries, London. There seems to be some difficulty in always distinguishing between the sacring-bell and the Sanctus-bell. In some cases they appear to be the same; in others they seem quite distinct.

14. *The Sanctus-bell.* The introduction of the Sanctus (or Sancte) bell is attributed to William of Paris, in 1097; or to Cardinal Guido, in 1200. This bell hung in a cot, built for itself, within the church. The position of the Sanctus-bell cot was on the east end of the roof of the nave.

Some of these pre-Reformation " cots " still remain *in situ* in some of the Old-English churches. The writer has seen one in a village outside Warminster, Wilts., and at Tewkesbury Abbey. There is one at the parish-church of Mells, near Frome. The church belongs to the Perpendicular period, and dates back to about 1450. The cot for the Sancte-bell is formed above the chancel-arch. A lever is attached to the stock of the bell, to which was linked a connecting-rod, which went through the chancel-roof, ending in a loop or ring at such a height from the floor that it could be reached by a hook provided for that purpose. The bell was hung in such a manner that the down-pull and return would cause the clapper to strike the bell three times, so that three pulls would ring the Angelus.

Thus : 1—2—3
1—2—3
1—2—3.

II. THE SECULAR USE OF CHURCH BELLS.

So far our attention has been confined to the religious use of the Old-English church bells. But no article on this subject would be complete without some reference also to the secular purposes they frequently fulfilled.

1. *To allay Storms*, etc. Bells were believed to allay storms, disperse lightning and thunder, stay a pestilence, extinguish a fire, and scare away demons. That the English of the sixteenth century held this belief is proved by an entry in the Churchwardens' Accounts of Spalding, Lincolnshire: " 1519, It'm; pd. for ryngny when the Tempest was, iij d."

According to Dr. Brewer,[4] it is still by no means unusual, in France, to ring church bells to ward off the effects of light-

an hour to "lay a gale of wind." But the most recent instance with which the writer is acquainted, happened in England in 1899. The curious survival of this quaint superstition was at Dawlish, that pretty, quiet, little seaside resort
in Devon. The bells rang furiously when the storm was at
its height. And it appears that the bell-ringer holds a special
appointment for the purpose.

2. *To guide Wayfarers.* There are, in England, a number
of ancient bequests for ringing bells and lighting beacons to
guide travelers at night. As church bells were very useful
in directing the people home on dark winter evenings, in the
days when lands were unenclosed and forests and wild moors
abounded, charitable folk often left money to pay the sexton
for his labor in ringing at suitable times, when the sound of
the church bells might be of service to some belated traveler.

At Hessle, near Hull, a lady who had lost her way on a
dark night, and was guided safely home by the bells, showed
her gratitude in a practical way by leaving a bequest to the
parish clerk on condition that the church bell should be rung
every evening. And at Workingham, Berks., a Richard
Palmer left in 1664 a bequest to the sexton for ringing the
bell every night at eight, and every morning at four o'clock
—one reason for ringing this being " that strangers and others
who should happen, on winter nights, within hearing of the
ringing of the said bell, to lose their way in the country,
might be informed of the time of the night, and receive some
guidance into the right way ". Nor was it land travelers
alone for whom such provision was made. The bell-rock,
with its lighthouse, was so called from the bell which the
monks used to toll, in order that mariners might be warned
of their danger.

3. *To summon the Easter Vestry.* In some places the
church bells are rung to call together the Easter Vestry meet-

4. *To announce that an Apprentice was out of his Indentures.* A few parishes still cling to an old custom of ringing the church bells to publish the fact that an apprentice in the parish is "out of his time". This is done at Waddington by one or two strokes on the tenor bell.

5. *The Market-bell and the Fair-bell.* It was a very general custom in bygone days to ring the church bells on the day of the local market-day, whether weekly, fortnightly, or monthly; also at the period of the annual fair, to ring the bells at the commencement and close, that the people might know when the fair had begun and ended, as special local laws were in force during this period.

6. *To announce the Arrival of the London Coach.* This was the practice at Derby. When the coach drove through the town, in the olden times, it was usual to announce its arrival by ringing the church bells, that all such as had fish coming might hasten to the coach and secure the fish whilst fairly fresh.

7. *At Wife-Sales.* The latter half of the eighteenth century has gained an unenviable reputation in England by the frequent wife-sales that occurred at that period. These sales were duly reported in the newspapers, without any special comment, as ordinary items of news. The then popular belief was that a husband might thus put away his wife, provided the sale was transacted in a public place, and the woman was handed over to her purchaser with a halter about her neck. In some instances the church bells announced the sale; and in a few places tolls were collected similar to those charged for animals brought to the public market on market-days. This infamous practice of selling wives lasted into the middle of the last century; but there have been isolated cases of it still later.

Whilst still an Anglican, and the married rector of Lavington, Dr. Manning regularly performed the humble office of tolling the church bell. It was part of the discipline he imposed on himself. And on a bitter winter's morning he was to be found ringing away at the village tocsin calling the "yokels" from their beds to spend a few moments in prayer, ere they went to their long and arduous day's labor in the

who rang the bell which called them would be there, stately and immaculately spruce, for all his lusty ringing.

A song for the times, when the sweet church-chimes,
　Called rich and poor to pray,
As they opened their eyes, by the bright sunrise
　And when evening died away.

The squire came out from his rich old hall,
　And the peasants by two and by three;
The woodman let his hatchet fall,
　And the shepherd left his tree.

Through the churchyard dew, by the churchyard yew,
　They went both old and young;
With one consent in prayer they bent,
　And with one consent they sung.

JOHN R. FRYAR.

THE TRIBUNALS OF THE ROMAN CURIA

III. THE APOSTOLIC SEGNATURA.

IN treating of the Tribunal of the Apostolic Segnatura, the Apostolic Constitution, *Sapienti consilio,* has only the following words: " We have also deemed it well to restore the supreme Tribunal of the Apostolic Segnatura and by these present letters we do restore it, or rather we institute it in the manner determined in the above-mentioned law, suppressing the ancient organization of the Papal Segnatura of Grace and Justice." According to the legislation here set forth a Supreme Tribunal of the Apostolic Segnatura is now instituted, to be regulated by statutes which are given in the *Lex Propria*; and the Papal Segnatura heretofore existing is suppressed.

The term, Segnatura, or Signatura, took its origin from the fact that, when petitions of various kinds were presented to the Sovereign Pontiff, the answer to each petition was accompanied with the signature of the Pope. Some petitions were sent in order to obtain favors; there were others whose

them.   For a considerable period a distinction was made between those Referees who were concerned with questions of favor and those who were to give their opinion upon the rights of contestants.   Pius IV in the Constitution *Cum nuper* (1 July, 1562) refers to these two species of Referees as recognized by ecclesiastical usage.   However, for a long time the same body of Clerics gave their opinion on both kinds of petitions.   Sixtus V in the Constitution *Quemadmodum* (22 September, 1586) reduced the number of Referees and defined more exactly the qualifications needed for the office.   Subsequently the Referees of Justice were divided by Alexander VII in the Constitution *Inter cetera* (13 June, 1656) into those who possessed the power of voting and those who were devoid of this power. By the same Constitution he established a College of voting Referees, twelve in number.   In recent times the Segnatura of Justice had only few functions to perform, such as to decide controversies regarding the nullity of certain judicial acts, while all the duties formerly devolving upon the Segnatura of Favor have been performed by the Sacred Congregations.   By the legislation of the Constitution *Sapienti consilio*, both the Segnatura of Justice and that of Grace are now abolished.

THE APOSTOLIC SEGNATURA UNDER THE NEW LEGISLATION.

This Tribunal, which has been instituted by the present Sovereign Pontiff, will be best understood from the Statutes which are set down in the *Lex Propria* and which may be found in the *Acta Apostolicae Sedis* (pages 29-31).   So far as the *Lex Propria* refers to the Apostolic Segnatura, it is contained in canons 35 to 43 inclusive, wherein two subjects are treated, viz. the constitution and competence of this tribunal, and its method of judicial procedure.

Constitution and Competence of the Apostolic Segnatura.

This tribunal consists of six Cardinals chosen by the Sovereign Pontiff, who also designates one of them as Prefect. There is also an Assistant or Secretary, who under the direction of the Prefect is to do all that may be required for the preparation and expedition of cases.   There is likewise appointed at least one Notary, whose duty it is to assist the Secretary, and one custodian of the office chamber of the Segnatura. The former official should be a priest; the latter should be a layman. Besides, Consultors are appointed by the Sovereign Pontiff in order that they may examine and give their opinion on whatever questions may be presented to them by the tribunal. Whatever regulations have been made for the officials of the Rota in regard to their nomination and discipline are to apply *cum proportione* to the officers of this Tribunal.

Its province is confined to questions relating to Auditors of the Rota and to the sentences pronounced by them. Thus if objection be made against an Auditor, or if he have inflicted injury upon any one, it belongs to the Apostolic Segnatura to investigate the case and to give judgment thereon. Similarly, if a charge of nullity be brought against a sentence of the Rota, or if a demand be made for entire compensation against a Rotal sentence which has already passed into a *res judicata,* it appertains to the Apostolic Segnatura to take cognizance and give judgment.

Mode of Judicial Procedure.

In the first of the six canons (n. 38) upon the subject contained in the *Lex Propria*, it is laid down that a petition for compensation, as also a petition for the introduction of a case of nullity against a sentence of the Rota, may be admitted within a period of three months after the finding of a document, or the ascertaining of a cause justifying recourse to these remedies. But it is declared in the following canon (n. 39) that this petition for compensation does not suspend the execution of judgment. This tribunal is nevertheless empowered to issue an order to restrain execution, or to oblige the victorious party to give security for making full compensation.

In order that a case may be brought before this tribunal, a statement must be presented to the Secretary of the Segnatura. This official along with the Cardinal Prefect must examine the statement and declare whether it has sufficient foundation or not. In the former supposition it is admitted; in the latter it is rejected. When a criminal case is brought against one or more of the Auditors of the Rota on the ground of violation of secrecy, or on the ground of damages inflicted through null or unjust acts in their judicial capacity, strict canonical procedure prescribed by Canon Law is to be observed. In the trials against Auditors on other grounds, the Apostolic Segnatura is not bound by all the canonical observances, looking solely, as it should, to the attainment of truth, citing however interested parties and fixing some term for the presentation of claims. Other particular regulations to be observed by the Apostolic Segnatura in its judicial procedure are found in canons 41, 42, and 43 of the *Lex Propria* and need not here be given in detail. In the last mentioned canon (43) there is a general regulation set down, viz. that for the proper expedition of judicial business, whenever the special rules given for the Apostolic Segnatura are insufficient, this tribunal is to be guided by the laws laid down for the S. Rota and by the enactments of common law.

M. MARTIN, S.J.

St. Louis University, Mo.

[TO BE CONTINUED.]

A NEW TRANSLATION OF I COR. 9: 3–6

My defence to them that examine me is this:
Have we not a right to eat and to drink?
Have we not a right to have a sister-woman go about, as well as the rest of the Apostles, and the brethren of the Lord, and Cephas? [1]
Or—I alone and Barnabas—have we no right, without working?

ST. PAUL is defending himself: " My defence . . . is this." He is asserting and proving a right which his enemies denied. " Have we not a right?" In order to understand his defence, we must know what the accusations were that were brought against him. And we must examine his arguments to see what right he is claiming and proving. Then we will be ready to examine and understand the text.

ACCUSATIONS AGAINST ST. PAUL.

St. Paul founded the Church at Corinth. He stayed for a

---

[1] The Catholic translation of these words reads:
" Have we not power to lead about a sister, a woman?"
The common Catholic interpretation makes these women ministering matrons, who supplied the wants of the Apostles, as they did those of Jesus when He was alive. (Mt. 27:55; Lk. 8:1).
The Protestant translation (R. V.) reads:
" Have we no right to lead about a wife that is a believer?"
The Protestant translation and interpretation make these women the wives of the Apostles.
The translation and interpretation given in this paper differ from both.

time with Aquila and his wife Priscilla (or Prisca). Afterward he hired lodgings from Titus Justus, whose house adjoined the synagogue (Acts 18).

During the year and a half that St. Paul remained at Corinth he accepted nothing for himself or Barnabas or for the women who helped him. He supported himself and his helpers by working at his trade of tent-making and by the contributions of friends received from other places.

One reason why St. Paul accepted nothing was to encourage the Corinthians by his own generosity, to be more generous to their needy brethren in Judea. St. Paul often had to beg for money; even in this letter (16: 1) to them he has to ask for a collection. Another reason may have been to shame his lazy brethren who did nothing, and who wished to live on the Church. Concerning this class he uses very strong language in his Epistle to the Thessalonians :

Ye need not that I write to you . . . to work with your own hands, as I commanded you. (I Thess. 4 : 9-11.)

If anyone will not work, neither let him eat. (II Thess. 3 : 10-12.)

You yourselves know how ye ought to imitate us . . . neither did we eat bread for naught at any man's hand. (II Thess. 3 : 7-8.)

St. Paul's generosity in refusing for himself and his helpers what the other preachers accepted, money from the Church, was used by his enemies as an argument against him. If he had a right to support from the Church, they said, he certainly would have taken it. His not taking it was an acknowledgment that he had no right to it, and also an acknowledgment of his inferiority to the other Apostles. Some were mean enough to assert that his apparent generosity was only a cloak to hide his covetousness, to throw people off their guard, in order to enable him to steal more from the collections for the needy brethren.

Let us now take St. Paul's arguments. From them we will see clearly the one question at issue—whether or not he had a right to be supported by the Corinthians when he was laboring for them. He never used this right; he never will; but he had it. From his non-use of it his enemies tried to prove its non-existence. In his arguments St. Paul completely silenced his opponents; his arguments were unanswerable.

St. Paul's Arguments proving his Right to support from the Corinthians.

1. What soldier ever serveth at his own charges?
Who planteth a vineyard and eateth not the fruit thereof?
Or, who feedeth a flock and eateth not the milk of the flock? (9 : 7).

Every one has a right to be supported by the work to which he gives his time and labor. It is a simple matter of justice. The whole world admits it. St. Paul was a Christian soldier fighting for the Church; the Church therefore should support him. His Corinthian converts were the vineyard that he had planted; they were the sheep that he had fed with the Gospel, therefore he had a right to be supported by them.

2. St. Paul's next argument (the same argument in another form) is taken from the law of Moses:

Saith not the law also the same?
For it is written in the law of Moses, Thou shalt not muzzle the ox when he treadeth out the corn. Is it for the oxen that God careth? Or saith he it, as he doubtless doth, for our sake?
Yea, for our sake it was written: because he that ploweth ought to plow in hope, and he that thresheth in hope of partaking. (8-10.)

The right of every one to be supported by his labor was impressed on the Israelites by a remarkable law: they were not allowed to prevent the animals from eating the food that they were treading out. St. Paul's enemies treated him worse than they did their oxen. The Corinthians were the land that St.

Even if the Corinthians had given him carnal things (food and drink) they would still be his debtors, for there is no comparison between the spiritual things that they had received from him, and meat and drink (carnal things).

4. An argument *a fortiori*:

If others partake of this right over you, do not we yet more? Nevertheless we did not use this right.   (12.)

The labors of St. Paul for the Corinthians were greater than those of all who succeeded him; therefore he had a greater right to support from the Corinthians than they.

5. Know ye not that they that minister about sacred things, eat of the things of the temple, and they that wait upon the altar have their portion with the altar?   (13.)

This is another argument from the Mosaic law.

6. Even so did the Lord ordain that they who proclaim the gospel, should live of the gospel.

But I have used none of these things: and I write not these things, that it may be so done in my case.   (14-15.)

St. Paul's six arguments are one and the same argument in different forms: "The laborer is worthy of his hire" (Lk. 10: 7).   It is self-evident.   The whole human race asserts it.   The law of Moses enforced it.   Jesus proclaimed it.   When He sent His disciples to preach, He would not allow them to take money with them: He wished those to whom they preached to support them.   He said: "The laborer is worthy of his food" (Mt. 10: 10).   St. Paul and his helpers, both men and women, labored for the Corinthians during his stay of a year and a half at Corinth; therefore they had a right to support from the Corinthians.

never took anything, and never would; but. he asserts and proves, and more than proves, his right by unanswerable arguments, in order to confound his malicious enemies who had undermined his authority at Corinth.

We have finished our introductory remarks, and are now ready for our text. We will first take the words of the text one by one, and then take the sentence as a whole.

THE WORDS OF THE TEXT.

μὴ οὐκ ἔχομεν ἐξουσίαν. *Have we not a right?* There are two negatives in this sentence, *me ouk.* If the two are equivalent to one, the sentence may be translated: Have we *not* a right? or, Have we *no* right? If the two negatives neutralize each other, the sentence should read: Have we *a* right? The reader may take whichever he prefers.

To eat and to drink, i. e. without working at our trade; in other words, at the expense of the Church, like the rest of the Apostles. " Have we not a right to eat and to drink?" taken alone, does not make sense. No one denied St. Paul's right to eat at his own expense, or when his friends paid for it. What they denied was his right to eat at the expense of the Church.

Have we not a right? The repetition of these words makes the sentence more emphatic.

ἀδελφὴν γυναῖκα περιάγειν. *(To have) a sister-woman go about,* i. e. at the expense of the Church. No one denied St. Paul's right to the help of women at his own or at their own expense.

A sister-woman. R. V. is right in putting these words in apposition; the older versions were wrong in separating them.

Brother and sister were the names that the first Christians used in addressing and in speaking of each other. A sister-woman may mean a Christian woman, a woman " who is a believer " (R.Vm) ; or it may be a technical term for those women who devoted their time to religious work, instructing and preparing women for baptism. Sister to-day is the technical name for members of religious communities of women.

Go about, περιάγειν, in classical Greek is both intransitive (to go about) and transitive (to lead about). In the New Testament it is found six times [2] and always means to go about.

---

[2] "And Jesus *periagen* (went about) in all Galilee teaching." (Mt. 4: 23.)

These six texts are the only ones in the New Testament in which *periagein* is found. In half of them it expresses the going about of Jesus on His missionary journeys; in one, the going about of the Pharisees on their missionary journeys; in another, the going about of Elymas after he had been struck blind; and in the remaining text shall we not translate as it is translated in all the other texts? If we do, it tells us of the going about of the sister-women on their missionary journeys into the houses of the women, whither the apostles could not go, to instruct them and prepare them for baptism.

As well as the rest of the Apostles, and the brethren of the Lord, and Cephas. Who these men were does not matter, at present; they worked and were supported by the Church; St. Paul worked and therefore had the same right to be supported as they. These words make what goes before intelligible.

Have we not a right to eat and drink, *as well as the rest,* i. e. at the expense of the Church? Have we not a right to have a sister-woman go about, *as well as the rest,* i. e. at the expense of the Church? The sister-women who helped the other missionaries were supported by the Church; those that helped St. Paul supported themselves, or were supported by him. They had a right to support from the Church because they worked for it; St. Paul had a right to demand support for them, for they were an absolute necessity in the beginning; without their aid the blessings of Christianity would have been restricted almost exclusively to men.

Or—I alone and Barnabas. All the other missionaries at Corinth except himself and Barnabas got their living from the Church.

οὐκ ἔχομεν ἐξουσίαν; *Have we no right?* i. e. to meat and drink, and the aid of the sister-women.

Without working, i. e. working at our trade of tent-making. μὴ ἐργάζεσθαι, lit. not to work; or without working; to forbear

---

"And Jesus *periagen* (went about) all the cities and towns teaching." (Mt. 9:35.)

"And He *periagen* (went about) the villages preaching." (Mk. 6:6.)

" Woe to you Scribes and Pharisees, hypocrites: for *periagete* (ye go about) sea and land to make one proselyte." (Mt. 23:15.)

Elymas the sorcerer "*periagon* (going about) sought some one to lead him by the hand." (Acts 13:11.)

"Have we not a right to have a sister-woman *periagein* (go about)?" (I Cor. 9:5.)

working. A.R.V. To stop working. These or any other equivalent phrases are correct translations.

We will now take the sentence as a whole, and then we will be ready to answer objections:

The Sentence.

It is a compound sentence: its two members are connected by the disjunctive conjunction *or.* I will put it diagrammatically to make it clearer, and I will put in italics the words that are understood.

I.
Have we a right
(bis)

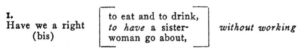

without working

as well as the rest of the Apostles, and the brethren of the Lord and Cephas?

2. Or—I alone and Barnabas—

have we no right

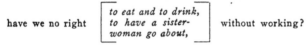

without working?

In both members of the sentence we have: the same subject *we*; the same verb, *have*; the same object, *right.* There are two coördinate clauses in the first member of the sentence: "Have we a right," is repeated: (1) Have we a right to eat and to drink? (2) Have we a right to have a sister-woman go about? It might have been repeated oftener, e. g.: (1) Have we a right to eat? (2) Have we a right to drink? (3) Have we a right to have a sister-woman go about?

St. Paul's enumeration is not complete; he had also a right to clothing, shelter, and other things; but he mentions only two—*food*, without which no one can live, and the *help of sister-women*, without whom there could have been but few women converts.

The complete object of the sentence is: "A right to eat and to drink and to have a sister-woman go about, without working " (i. e. at your expense).

To eat, etc. is expressed in the first member, and understood in the second. *Without working* is expressed in the second member, and understood in the first. It is easily un-

In the first member we have a double negative, *me ouk*; here we have treated it as an affirmative, since two negatives sometimes neutralize each other. The reader may substitute "Have we not" instead, if he wishes.

There is but a single negative, *ouk,* before "have" in the second member of the sentence, so this clause must be negative: "Have we *no* right?" If we insist on the meaning of the disjunctive conjunction *or,* which binds the two members together, since *or* makes two members mutually exclusive, it will determine the meaning of the two negatives in the first member. When one member having *or* for a connective is negative the other member must be affirmative, and so the sentence must be, as we have written it: "Have we *a* right . . . or, have we *no* right, to eat," etc.

QUESTIONS AND OBJECTIONS.

1. Who were the sister-women who aided St. Paul and Barnabas at Corinth? Phoebe probably was the chief one. St. Paul speaks of her as "Phoebe our sister, who is a servant of the Church that is at Cenchreae." [3] (Rom. 16: 1.) Priscilla (or Prisca), the wife of Aquila, was another invaluable assistant of St. Paul. She with the aid of her husband converted the great Jewish Scripture scholar Apollo (or Apollos). [4] St. Paul speaks of her and her husband as "my fellow workers in Christ Jesus." (Rom. 16: 3.) He mentions her first; she is also mentioned first in the Acts,—an evidence that she was more prominent in evangelical work than her husband. Of

were needed.   St. Paul alone could preach to all those who came to his house, but he needed several sister-women to visit the Jewish and Gentile women in their homes.

2. The fact that no other New Testament writer uses *peri-agein* in a transitive sense (to lead about) is no proof that St. Paul may not have done so.   Therefore, it may be argued, the meaning of his words may be: " Have we not a right *to lead about* a sister-woman?"

No, this cannot be his meaning; for whilst he was at Corinth for a year and a half he led no one about.   He stayed at the house of Titus Justus, working at his trade most of the time, and preaching to those who came there on the Sabbath day and at other times.   He led no women; he sent them, to go about to those women who wished to be instructed in the Christian religion.

3. But may St. Paul not be speaking of something that he did not do, but which the other Apostles did?   He says: " Have I not a right . . as the rest of the Apostles?"

The only thing the others did which St. Paul did not do, was to take pay for services performed.   This is the only question of which St. Paul is talking.   He is talking of the things that both he and others did; he preached and they preached; he had women to help him and so had they; all his work was given gratis, whereas for theirs they received pay.   This is the only point in which they differed.   The whole question is about work, and the right of everyone to be paid for his work.   The forgetfulness of the one and only question at issue is the cause of all the confusion that had arisen about the meaning of I Cor. 9: 3-6.

APPENDIX.

THE PROTESTANT TRANSLATION OF GYNE IN I COR. 9: 5.

Gyne is the Greek word translated in the Catholic versions *woman*, and in the Protestant versions *wife*, in this text.   The nominative case is *gyne*, and the accusative case *gynaika*.

In the first edition of the Authorized Prot. Version the text was translated: "Have we not power to lead about a sister a *wife*", with *woman* in the margin. . In later editions the alternative reading

I will give the reasons *pro* and *con*, for this rendering, in conversational form, a Catholic and Protestant being the speakers.

Protestant: Is not the Greek word *gyne* a more honorable term than its English equivalent *woman*?

Catholic: Yes, it is. *Gyne* is the word that the Evangelist puts in the mouth of Jesus when He is speaking to His Mother from the cross (Jn. 19: 26).

P. Did not the Greeks use the word *gyne* more commonly than the specific words for wife, in speaking of their wives?

C. They did; even some English-speaking men say " my woman " oftener than " my wife ".

P. When we meet the word *gyne,* how can we tell whether the woman spoken of is a wife or not?

C. Sometimes we cannot tell; but usually it is evident from the context. The means of determining its meaning are the same in Greek as in English, e. g. if a man says, my woman, your woman, his woman, their women, we know that the women spoken of are wives.

P. That is one means of determining the meaning of *gyne*; but the verb *periagein* determines its meaning just as well. If a respectable man leads about (*periagein*) a woman, the woman led about must be his wife.

C. I have shown that *periagein* in the New Testament is always intransitive; it means *to go about*, not *to lead about*.

P. But I do not accept your translation or explanation. I take it transitively, to lead about. The woman that a respectable man leads about is his wife.

C. If you are talking of a man who is leading about animals, of a guide leading about tourists, of a professor leading about his scholars, whether they are men or women, *periagein* is the proper word. But even in English a man is not speaking respectfully of his wife, if he says he leads her about. In Greek *periagein gynaika* could not be tolerated; this phrase is not found anywhere in the whole of Greek literature, where there is any question of husband and wife.

C. We are foreigners to Greek, and yet we can see the difference between *periagein* and *periagesthai;* we cannot suppose any such ignorance on the part of St. Paul. Greek was the language that he spoke and wrote, and wrote correctly too. James Hope Moulton, who has revised his father's edition of Winer's Grammar says: "'The N. T. writers were perfectly capable of preserving the distinction between the active and the middle'. Such is the authoritative summary of Blass (p. 186), which makes it superfluous for us to labor any proof." [6]

P. But Winer says that "perhaps" the active is used for the middle even in Xenophon's Cyr., 2, 2, 28 (Winer, p. 322).

C. Xenophon is speaking of a boy led about (*periagein*) for immoral purposes. In that case it does not matter which voice is used, whether he was led about (active) or led about with oneself (in one's company) (middle).

We can see no reason for supposing that Xenophon intended to use the more honorable term (*periagesthai*), and by mistake or oversight used the less honorable term (*periagein*). Was Xenophon a "foreigner who had not a native's instinctive insight" into the Greek language?

It is a waste of time to try to make the sister-women spoken of in I Cor. 9: 5, wives by the aid of *periagein*. Some of these women were wives, some widows, some maidens: all were workers in the Lord. It is only as workers that St. Paul considers them; as such they deserved support from the Church for which they were laboring.

J. F. SHEAHAN.

Poughkeepsie, N. Y.

THE ORGANIZATION AND PRESENT CONDITION OF THE GREEK CHURCH.

I.

THERE is no doubt that one of the most deplorable and tragic events in the history of the Church is that which was formally commenced under Photius in the ninth century and consummated under Michael Cerularius in the eleventh; and it may be safely said that there is no question of a like

this significant question are simply amazing. True, one's sense of proportion is always liable to be affected by the perspective of time and space. We are attracted by the comparatively trivial matters that happen during or near our own time and at our own doors more than by the momentous facts of the far distant East, centuries agone. To use a parallel simile with one of our great English writers, a manslaughter in Boston attracts more attention than a Buddhist rebellion in China.

To keep our sense of proportion correct we must remember that there was a far greater and more lamentable schism in the Catholic Church in the ninth century, than that witnessed in the Reformation during the so-called golden age of unity of the sixteenth century. It is sad enough to think of the twenty-one millions of Anglicans and sixty millions of Evangelical Germans, but sadder still to think of the ninety-five millions of Orthodox Easterns, children of the great apostolic churches of Alexandria, Antioch, Jerusalem,—names whose glory is second only to the See of Peter.

The great Eastern Schism was that which separated Constantinople from Rome in the ninth and again in the eleventh century. I am not now speaking of the Nestorians, who left the Church after the Council of Ephesus, and whom the Emperor Zeno drove out of his empire into Persia. Nor do I refer to the four great bodies that fell away after the Council of Chalcedon, — the Egyptians, Abyssinians, Syrians, and Armenians. All these great bodies had existed for centuries before the greatest of all schisms cut away Eastern Christendom from Rome.

This great Eastern Schism has been attributed to Photius and Michael Cerularius. Without wishing to defend or extenuate the evil wrought by these disobedient and ambitious men, I may say that they were the occasion rather than the cause, just as the discussions on the *Filioque* or the *Epiklesis* were the pretexts and not the real reasons for the separation. The true cause of the separation is to be found in political reasons and the growing ambition of the bishops of Constantinople. The Greek Patriarch, making use of the racial rivalry, the want of mutual sympathy, the jealousies and narrow nationalism by which the East and West were divided, had a fatal effect in bringing about the Schism. Originally there had been but three patriarchal sees, Rome, Alexandria and Antioch. Rome ever, as now, held the first place and exercised her jurisdiction over the whole Catholic Church. Their rank was already an ancient custom before Constantinople was ever heard of, yea even the bishop of Constantinople or Byzantium, as it was called, had no claim to any rank. He was under the Metropolitan of Heraclea. In the year 323, the emperor Constantine moved to Byzantium and made it the capital of the empire. The New Rome was to be the equal of the Old, and so its bishops did not see why they could not have a share in the honors. The emperors, who kept shamefully interfering in ecclesiastical affairs, did everything to favor their rise, for the more the minds of their subjects were turned to Constantinople the better for their centralizing policy. Alexandria, Antioch, and Jerusalem went down in importance, being tainted with Monophysism; and we find John the Faster of Constantinople, in the sixth century, assuming the title of Ecumenical Patriarch,—a title sternly opposed by Gregory the Great. Even Pope St. Leo as early as the fifth century had to protest against the usurpation of the Byzantine prelates: " The presence of the Emperor," he says, " may constitute a royal residence, but it does not create an apostolic see, divine affairs not being regulated after the manner of human matters." We do not wonder, then, that centuries before the final disaster the Patriarchs of Constantinople and their followers hated Rome. They wished to be in the religious sphere what the emperors were in the political—the spiritual chiefs of the East. The emperors were always publishing civil decrees to regulate church matters, so that in the ninth century we find Eastern " Orthodox " Christendom mostly the same as the Byzantine Empire. They strove to withdraw themselves as far as possible from the See of Rome. Many bishops, it is true, such as St. Chrysostom and St. Flavian, had recourse to the Holy See; the canons of Sardica had sanctioned appeal to the Roman Pontiff, and both bishops and priests had used the right. Even the emperors themselves had more than once recognized the Primacy of the See of Rome. Nevertheless out of the fifty-eight patriarchs who succeeded each other in the See of Constantinople from Metrophanes in 315, to Photius in 857, twenty-one were heretics or suspected of heresy. Altogether, if we add up all the periods, we find during the 464 years between the founding of Constantinople and the seventh General Council, no less than 203 years during which the Byzantine Church had been out of communion with Rome and the West. But these interruptions were only passing. To all these causes which prepared men's minds for schism, add the state of servitude to which the emperors had striven to reduce the clergy and the efforts of the imperial policy to withdraw itself from the influence of the Holy See, and one has the principal causes of the great break of the ninth century.

At the death of Theophilus in 841 the Byzantine throne was occupied by Theodora, who acted as regent for her son Michael III, known in history as Michael the Drunkard, on account of his depraved and drunken habits. During the fourteen years of her reign she restored the images to the churches and ejected the Iconoclast John from the patriarchate. Her benign influence brought prosperity and order to the empire until the year 865, when the intrigues of her brother, the incestuous Bardus, deprived her of her power and commenced the trouble that culminated in the fatal schism. Cæsar Bardus was the tutor and uncle of Michael the Drunkard. Having forced Theodora to retire, he influenced the

tius to violate the canons in the case of Theodora's monastic investiture, Bardus encompassed the downfall of Ignatius. He made out the Patriarch to be a seditious man, who was in league with Theodora in a conspiracy. Bardus succeeded, and Michael, who took his uncle's part throughout, had the Patriarch deposed and dragged with his adherents to the island of Terebenth, and Photius a layman appointed to the patriarchal throne. This layman was gifted with all the qualities that make the head of a sect—unbridled ambition, talents, indomitable courage, and hypocrisy. Nevertheless his enterprise would have failed if the state of the émpire had not favored him. In six days, in defiance of Canon Law, the new patriarch received Holy Orders from the hands of an excommunicated bishop. To legitimize this sacrilegious usurpation there was a pretence of election, and to silence the many voices raised in opposition, Photius and Bardus felt that they must have the Pope on their side. They wrote letters to Rome claiming that Ignatius had resigned voluntarily and was living retired and honored in a monastery. The emperor on his side affirmed the same things and sent an ambassador and four Greek bishops, with the most magnificent presents, to beg the Pontiff to send thither legates who would pacify men's minds, troubled by the revival of the Iconoclastic party. But neither hypocrisy, nor lies, nor presents succeeded with the Sovereign Pontiff — the indomitable and glorious Nicholas I. He refused to ratify the irregular ordination of Photius, but consented to send two legates to Constantinople to examine the facts in the case. The legates, Rodoald and Zacharias, were bribed by the emperor and took part in the deposition of Ignatius in a Council of three hundred and eighteen bishops, whom Photius and Bardus had seduced.

On their return to Rome they tried to deceive the Pope, but when he had read the acts of the Synod, he saw at once that the legates had been unfaithful and protested against all they had done. The Pope later on declared that Photius had fallen from the priesthood. Ignatius was reinstated, and the perfidious legates were excommunicated. The emperor at the instigation of Photius wrote letters refusing to recognize the spiritual supremacy of Rome. Seeing that he was supported by the emperor and having surrounded himself with numerous creatures among the clergy and people, Photius considered himself strong enough to try a schism. He assumed the title of Ecumenical Patriarch, which several of his predecessors had appropriated to themselves against the will of the Pope, and wrote an encyclical to the Oriental bishops to convene them in Council at Constantinople. In this encyclical he accuses the Latins of five crimes: they fasted on Saturdays; they eat butter, eggs, and cheese in Quinquagesima week; they imposed the yoke of celibacy on the priests; they denied the priests the rights of administering Confirmation; and they changed and corrupted the Creed by the addition of the *Filioque.* All his points are local customs which no one has ever tried to impose on them, yet his document becomes the charter of the Schismatical Church.

For ten years Photius had triumphed when suddenly a dramatic change took place. Bardus and Michael in a drunken debauch met their death. Philip of Macedonia, who was suspected of being the perpetrator of the crime, became emperor and sought peace. He expelled Photius and re-established Ignatius. The latter and the emperor turned their eyes toward Rome—the mother and mistress of all churches. An embassy was sent thither. The false acts of the Council convened by Photius were condemned and burned, and Adrian II, who had succeeded Nicholas, once more renewed the condemnation of his predecessor. The embassy returned to Constantinople accompanied by three legates from the Pope, who were charged to preside at the Eighth Ecumenical Council, held at Constantinople, in which Ignatius was re-instated in his see. Union with Rome was thus re-established, but the germs of disunion remained. Nevertheless the union subsisted until the death of Ignatius in 877.

In the meantime, Photius gained the favor of Basil by working up a mythical pedigree for him. His party, already a strong one, wanted their hero back and as the see was now

As soon as he was thus recognized, Photius wanted a coun- · cil to meet at Constantinople, his primary motive being to counteract the effect of the one that excommunicated him. Pope John sent legates who behaved nearly as bad as those sent by Nicholas I. Photius was master of the Council. He violently abused the Synod of 869, and renewed his charges against the Latins, especially the *Filioque* clause, and claimed Bulgaria as a part of the Patriarchate of Constantinople. This schism lasted until the death of Basil, when Photius once more had to go into exile. Leo the Philosopher, the son and successor of Basil, had personal reasons for hating Photius; he expelled him from his see and confined him in a monastery where five years later he died. Such was the end of the man whom the Schismatical Greeks venerate as a saint on the sixth day of February, and whom we rightly regard as the Luther of the Greek Schism, and the greatest enemy Christian unity ever had.

For nearly a century and a half after the second deposition of Photius, the union of the Greeks with the See of Peter remained unbroken. Under seventeen successive Patriarchs they continued to recognize the supremacy of Rome, until the reign of Michael Cerularius in the year 1053. With less education and less ability than Photius, Michael had in common with him ambition and the art of falsifying Pontifical documents; still nine years elapsed before he thought himself secure in setting aside completely the yoke of Pontifical authority. In the midst of " perfect peace ", he issued complaints against the Latins, and to the charges of Photius he added new ones,—such as the custom of shaving; of eating the flesh of strangled animals; of bishops wearing rings; and of conferring baptism by only one immersion. Above all he sharply upbraided the Latins with consecrating in unleavened bread,—a usage, we may remark, which even the virulent Photius had not thought of condemning. It was by this question of leavened or azyme bread that Michael Cerularius drew to his party the Greek patriarch of Antioch. But he did not confine himself to recriminations; he closed the churches of the Latins throughout all his jurisdiction, desecrated the Blessed Sacrament, rebaptized those who had received baptism according to the Latin rite, and excommunicated those who had recourse to Rome. The Pope sent three legates to recall the patriarch to a sense of his duty. They were received by the emperor, but the patriarch refused to see them. The legates, finding their efforts useless, proceeded to spiritual penalties. It was the sixteenth day of July, 1056, and Santa Sophia was full of people and priests. The Holy Liturgy had just begun when the three legates walked up the aisle of the great church and placed their bull of excommunication on the main altar. As they turned their backs, they said, " Let God see and judge." Michael made the people believe that the legates were imposters and had not been sent by the Pope. He worked unceasingly to strengthen the schism, drawing with him the bishops of Bulgaria, and the partiarch of Antioch, and probably those of Alexandria and Jerusalem, now negligible quantities under Moslem jurisdiction. After the schism Michael became by far the strongest man in Constantinople until his death just as he had been condemned for treason.

Here ends the greatest and most disastrous quarrel that ever rent the Church of Christ. Here is the worst story of arrogance and insolence on the part of the enemies of Rome; and, despite the attempts at general reunion and partial reunion, the great schism still continues. Nor did the capture of Constantinople by the Crusaders in 1204 help to bring back union; on the contrary, it increased the hatred of the Greeks against the Latins and broadened the separation still more, and with good reason.

tinople has a primacy of honor but not of jurisdiction. At first there were but four patriarchs, but since the schism eleven others have been added. As each state liberated itself and formed into an independent political entity, so its church became an ecclesiastically independent church, though the patriarch of Constantinople strongly resented this. So there are at present, exclusive of the four patriarchates and the autocephalous church of Cyprus, the following national churches, really independent and self-governing: Russia, Servia, Greece, Montenegro, Roumania, Bulgaria, Carlovitz Bosnia, Herzegovina, Hermannstadt, and the monastery of Mount Sinai. Although they are independent of one another, they all recognize each other as sister churches in Jesus Christ. They are entirely separate from Constantinople, and maintain with it only a communion of belief and of liturgical rites. The Russian branch, which contains four-fifths of the Eastern schismatic Christians, is under the power of the Czar; with him lies the choice of the members of the Synod and their dismissal.

The great turning-point in history for the Greek Church was the Turkish conquest in 1453, when Constantine XII died so honorable a death. The Christians were allowed to keep their religion and customs, and the patriarch, while degraded through having been invested by the Sultan, and compelled to pay a heavy bribe for his appointment, yet became the civil head of his people. But I believe this latter privilege has disappeared since 1856. He is named for life and cannot be deposed except for the crime of high treason. The Synod, however, can demand his deposition either for violation of the " Orthodox " faith or maladministration of the patriarchate. This last point has often been the cause of intrigue and consequently of unjust depositions, so much so that scarcely any patriarch now reigns more that three successive years. At present there are three or four ex-patriarchs waiting until the wheel turns that they may be again re-elected.

To assist him in his spiritual and temporal functions, the patriarch has a Council called the Holy Synod, composed of twelve bishops of metropolitan rank, and a mixed Council, of four members from the Synod and eight laymen, elected by the orthodox population of Constantinople. Appeals from the decisions of bishops are tried by the Synod, whose judgments are final.   To it alone belongs the right of judging the patriarch, and pronouncing on his guilt or innocence, except in the case of high treason, which is reserved to the Council of State.   It regulates the ecclesiastical revenues and makes their distribution, and its meetings are generally held on Sundays or feastdays after divine service.

When the patriarchal see is vacant, the Synod as well as the archbishops and bishops present in Constantinople, in the presence of the Government commissary, vote on the choice of three candidates of metropolitan dignity.   The choice is handed over to the community or nation, who mark one of the three candidates, whom they accept by the ancient exclamation of "Axios".   The Synod then transmits the result to the Porte to be confirmed by the Sultan, who has even then the right to reject him.   The newly-elected after the payment of a large sum, which is often an inducement to the Sultan to unjustly change patriarchs, receives the *Berat* in which his powers and privileges are determined and detailed as follows:

The patriarch has the direction of the Orthodox Greek churches and monasteries, and the superintendence of their financial administration.   He may at his pleasure nominate and depose the archbishops and bishops.   It is on his proposition that the Porte grants the Berats necessary to newly-nominated bishops.   The patriarchs of Alexandria, Antioch, and Jerusalem cannot come to the capital without the permission of the patriarch and his Synod.

The patriarch and his vicar have the entire duties on marriages and wills.

The patriarch has the right of inflicting penalties on members of the clergy conformably to the canons of the Church.   All the faithful are rigorously bound to obedience to the patriarch, who can strike them with excommunication and refuse them ecclesiastical burial.

position. It is made in large vessels and consecrated on Maundy Thursday. Both priests and people fear the excommunication of the patriarch, for it deprives them of all defense before Mussulmans and of ecclesiastical sepulture, if they die unabsolved. His revenues are considerable. The Court pays him five hundred thousand piastres a year; the dues from metropolitans and bishops amount to three hundred thousand piastres; the faithful contribute one hundred and twenty thousand; while Austria contributes fifty-eight thousand for Herzegovina and Bosnia. So he has an annual income of $47,500. Add to this all the property of bishops, priests and monks who die without legal heirs. In return, however, he has to pay the Porte twenty thousand piastres as an annual royalty, and ten thousand a year for the Sultan's body guard, besides his large bribe for his *Berat*.

The deplorable condition of the Greek churches in Alexandria, Antioch, and Jerusalem, reduced to a few thousand, cut a small figure; still they preserve their ancient prerogatives. While independent of the patriarch of Constantinople, like him they have their synods and spiritual privileges, yet it is only through his mediation they receive the *Berat*, maintain relations with the Ottoman Government, and exercise civil authority.

The archbishops and bishops are named by the patriarch and his Synod, and they receive through him their *Berat* from the Porte. They must be celibates, thirty years old, and as such are practically always taken from the monasteries. In every parish a collection is taken up annually for them by a commission of laymen who gather offerings from house to house. Besides these, there are the ordination dues, the taxes for dispensation, dues for marriages, burials, the blessing of water on Epiphany Day and the honoraria for Masses; like the patriarchs, they have their synods and helpers, more or less numerous according to the importance of their diocese.

The parochial clergy consist of a curé, whose work is to baptize, marry, and perform the funeral services; of a *pneumatics* or confessor, who must be forty years old and approved by the bishops; and of an *ephemerios* who celebrates Mass and recites the canonical hours. The revenues of the clergy are very meagre. A marriage costs from five to ten piastres; a funeral three to five; a baptism one to three; and a requiem from two to five. The priests are generally married. While the Sacrament of Orders is a diriment impediment to marriage, yet if they are married before ordination they can keep their wives. Once they are raised to the priesthood, however, they can never afterwards contract marriage, even if they become widowers, nor will one be raised to the priesthood if he marries a dishonored girl.

Through want of discipline and system, the parochial clergy are sunk in crass ignorance and deplorable indifference, as the writer knows to his sad experience. Through being cut off from Rome, which is the source of all the sciences, of order, and discipline, the focus from which intellectual and moral illumination radiates, they sink deeper and deeper in spiritual and moral degradation. They are taught to read and write in a monastery and they know the ceremonies of the Church. They wear a cassock, cloak, and kalemankion; are not tonsured, but wear long hair and beard. It is only when they are suspended and degraded that they are shaven and deprived of their hair.

Monasticism is a very important feature of the Greek Church, and the monks belong either to the Order of St. Anthony or of St. Basil, the latter being more numerous. The large monasteries are called Lauras, wherein each of the monks have a separate dwelling, but assemble in the common refectory and for devotions. Most of them are not priests and they never have the care of souls outside their monastery. Many writers tell us they are the most perfect relic of the fourth century left in the world. The abbot of the larger monasteries is called an *archimandrite*, and the abbot of the lesser an *hegumenous*. A woman who should lodge in a monastery of men would be excommunicated, and the same would be the case with a man in a convent of women.

The greatest monastery in the world or rather monastic republic is that of Mount Athos. Five years ago when the writer visited this famous mountain there were in that colony over 7,500 monks, and the priests therein spent over eight hours each day in the recitation of the Holy Office.

The present rule of faith in the Greek Church agrees in great measure with that of the Latins. They use the same

Bible, including the Deutero-canonical books. They accept
only the first seven Ecumenical Councils. They hold in common the seven Sacraments, the Sacrifice of the Mass; the veneration of the B. V. M., the saints, images, and relics; also the
hierarchical degrees of ecclesiastical orders and monasticism.
They reject the universal supremacy of the Pope, which they
loudly proclaimed before the schism, and acknowledge the infallibility of an Ecumenical Council, though they have never
held one since their separation from the See of Peter. At
Constantinople they baptize by a triple immersion, while the
Russian Church considers baptism by immersion a matter of
rite not of dogma. Directly after baptism, which is an elaborate ceremony, the priest administers Confirmation and gives
to the child Communion under both kinds. They strongly object to the fire of Purgatory, as if the Latins had defined this
teaching, yet pray and offer sacrifices for the dead that God
may have mercy on them on the day of general judgment.
They claim that the Holy Ghost proceeds from the Father
alone and are indignant at the addition of the *Filioque*. As regards Transubstantiation there is no real difference between
them and the Romans, but they believe that the change does
not take place until the *Epiklesis,* that is the invocation of the
Holy Ghost that follows the words of institution in their
Liturgy. They use paintings and engravings, but admit of
no images in relief or embossed work. They deny the Immaculate Conception inasmuch as it was defined by Rome.
They insist that confession of the laity ought to be free and
voluntary; for which reason they are not compelled to confess
annually, nor are they excommunicated for neglect. They
have no confessionals and absolve with a deprecatory form.
For the Sacrament of Extreme Unction or, as they call it,
Euchelaion, seven priests are required, though in case of
necessity one suffices. The matter is olive oil with which they
mix a little wine, and it is blessed by the priest just before it is
used. At present the priests bless the rivers and streams on
the Epiphany, and as soon as the blessing is over, men and
women plunge into the water and immerse themselves three
times. Marriage is surrounded with curious ceremonies,
among others that of crowning the bride and groom with
little brass crowns which make them look indescribably ridi-

culous. Marriage is forbidden within the seventh degree, and fourth marriages are never allowed. The tie is indissoluble, though they pretend it can be dissolved by adultery, and no person, under any provocation, can marry again while the other spouse is living.

In spite of great inconveniences the Orthodox countries still use the Julian Calendar, for it is a point of honor with them, as it was with the English till 1740, not to accept the corrections of a Pope. Their year begins 1 September, and contains four great fasts: the fast of Lent; the fast of the Mother of God, from 1-15 August; the fast of Christmas, from 15 November-24 December; and the fast of SS. Peter and Paul, from the first Sunday after Pentecost to 28 June.

The Liturgy of St. Chrysostom is the one they ordinarily follow, though on certain feasts they use the Liturgy of St. James and St. Basil. A Greek priest celebrates Mass only on Sundays and greater feast days. The first thing that attracts the attention of a stranger on entering a Greek church, is the great *Ikonastasis* or picture screen that hides the altar and sanctuary. It has three doors: the middle or sacred door which when open reveals the altar, the deacon's door, and the door for the servers. Behind this screen in the middle of the sanctuary stands the altar,—a solid square stone covered with a linen cloth over which is a silk embroidered cover extending down to the ground on all sides. Only one Mass each day can be said on this altar. Of course a Greek priest (except the Armenians and Maronites) celebrates with leavened bread. He uses a sponge instead of a purificator, and a holy lance or long knife for cutting up the bread. This bread is a round loaf marked with divisions; the parts to be consecrated have a cross marked upon them. The priest cuts this piece away with the holy lance, singing at the same time, " The Lamb of God is sacrificed." The other pieces are put aside, in honor of the Blessed Virgin and other saints. The

During Mass the Greeks observe several distinct postures which are considered actually essential. On reaching their respective places, they uncover their heads and make the sign of the cross by joining the first three fingers of the right-hand, by which it is implied there are three persons in the Sacred Godhead; but they finish the form of the cross from the right to the left shoulder.

In the Greek as well as in the Latin Church the faithful must sanctify the Sunday by assisting at Mass and abstaining from servile work. Their funeral services are elaborate, commencing at the home, continuing in the church, and concluding at the grave. The dead are generally carried in an open bier, their boots on, the face uncovered, and in many places a coin is placed in the hand. Nor do they forget their dead notwithstanding their idea of Purgatory; they continually offer the sacrifice of the Mass and perform other penances in honor of their departed dead.

And now the question may be asked, Is there any hope of reunion? Unhappily there is no immediate prospect. For Catholics and Schismatics it would be an untold blessing. Secular prejudices still rankle. The Sovereign Pontiffs on their side have neglected nothing to make union easy and lasting. They have always allowed the preservation of Eastern rites, nay they have forbidden in most precise terms the abandonment or modification of them in anything whatever, excepting the abuses that had crept in and the reforming of what was contrary to faith. Of late years attempts have been made by the Anglicans and the Old Catholics of Germany to join these Eastern Schismatics, but the latter have just resented the proposal. Pius IX made advances for reunion in 1847, and again gave a general invitation to the Greeks to attend the Council of the Vatican, but all in vain. Again the gracious, kind, and forgiving letter issued by Leo XIII in 1894 was answered by the late patriarch, Anthimos VII, in rude and undignified terms. Poor Anthimos! Even before his answer was published, he was deposed by his own Synod. Such is the fate of an Erastian church; sooner or later they will die out in indifference or in still more modern errors. The detached branch can have only one history,—it lives for a while by its own sap, then it languishes, dries up, and perishes.

It takes all the obstinacy of heresy and all the ignorance of the masses to keep the eyes closed to the truth. May the good God hasten the day when His children from the East and from the West will be reunited in one fold and under one shepherd in the bonds of peace.

WILLIAM LEEN.

Walker, Iowa.

THE REFORM IN CHURCH VESTMENTS.

II. ORNAMENT AND SHAPE.

THUS far the question of proper liturgical colors, a subject that deserves much more extended treatment than can be given it here, has been chiefly discussed in these pages. We now come to the question of proper ornamentation by means of embroidery. Here too a lamentable deterioration from the ancient practice of ecclesiastical embroidery and good taste appears in the prevailing fashion. There exists a singular but almost universal misconception on the part of vestment makers of to-day, to the effect that every vestment *must* be embroidered, no matter *how*. And yet, as Walter Crane justly remarks, plain materials and surfaces are infinitely preferable to inorganic and inappropriate ornament. The chief aim of embroidery should be not merely the exhibition of precious material tastefully employed but, at least in paramentics, the further development of liturgical symbolism. " It is not worth doing," says Morris,[1] " unless it is either very copious and rich, or very delicate—or both. For such an art

"liturgical colors". A third firm puts them together. It would be nothing short of marvelous if the result were anything but inharmonious, if our sacristies were not over and over again replenished with the same tasteless stoles, chasubles, dalmatics, antependiums. Formerly these things were done under the guidance of some artist of refined instinct, and a knowledge of the needs and meaning of what was demanded for the divine service. Now it is a matter of commercial routine. The members of an altar society or the Sisters of a convent wish to embroider a stole or a centre-piece for a chasuble. If they lack the proper training in the art of designing for church embroidery they promptly apply to a religious goods manufacturer, who is ready to put his patterns at their disposal. Since it is much less expensive to get this machine-made embroidery, the arrangement suits all parties. But it is a sad departure from the purpose and viewpoint of the Church which would have us exercise exceeding great care in the choice of material and pattern, and in the making of these garments for the sanctuary of God's tabernacle. We forget that design in this case "should embody living thought, artfully expressed"; devotion which offers all that is best in material and form and the skill which combines them into a fair offering to God.

In embroidery as in every form of art the question of design is of paramount importance; for on the arrangement of lines and masses and their relations to one another the harmonious unity of the whole depends. Before making a design, the conditions under which the finished work is to be seen must be carefully considered; the material and the grouping of colors and the details of combination must be ever borne in mind. And here a vast field opens to women possessed of talent, taste for art and zeal for the House of God! Hundreds of women spend years of study and large sums of money to become painters, musicians, singers, lawyers, doctors, and what not. Many hundreds and thousands more are looking about for some suitable calling or occupation during their surplus time. How many devote themselves to the study of paramentics—a woman's art *par excellence*, an ennobling, a refining art—to the designing and making of artistic ornaments for the divine service? How many of those who actually embroider for church use have studied the history of the art? How many know the traditions of the art, the methods and principles which experience has found to be true and useful? Without this preparatory training not only artistic designing, but even the proper interpretation of an artistic design, is out of the question.

In connexion with the subject of ornamentation it is necessary to say a word on the use of lace in the making of vestments. " Shall I buy a lace alb, or a plain alb, or one with embroidered edges?" Every priest, I suppose, has been confronted with this question at some time or other. Usually it is answered by selecting a " lace-alb " for the greater feastdays, it being assumed that lace adds to the beauty of the simple white garment always worn beneath the chasuble. An embroidered alb for Sundays and second-class feastdays, and a plain alb for ordinary days, are the customary classifications.

The alb, as its various names (*alba vestis, linea, sc. tunica, talaris tunica, camisia*) indicate, is supposed to be a white linen garment falling in graceful folds down to the feet of the priest. I say " is supposed to be ", because in reality the alb is but too often an ungainly, bag-shaped tunic, made to fit everybody in general and nobody especially. The cincture serves thus to gather and hold up yards of superfluous material so as to give at least some shape to an otherwise hideous costume. This was not always the case. During the Middle Ages the alb, as well as the amice and the cincture, was frequently ornamented with gold and silver. As early as the ninth century we find samples of albs in which strips of costly embroidery, of purple or gold cloth, were sewed on the borders of the alb. These ornaments could be removed to facilitate washing. From the eleventh to the seventeenth century the so-called *parura* or *paratura* were much in vogue. These were rectangular-shaped colored pieces of ornament, attached to the front and the rear of the alb, to both sleeves, and to the amice. They were usually finished in red, and symbolized the

style of ornamentation, and its symbolism gives emphasis to the *manipulum fletus et doloris* which the priest at Mass fastens upon the left sleeve of the alb.

The sixteenth century marks the advent of lace into paramentics. It appears to have been a Venetian and Flemish fashion in secular dress and thus crept into the making of the sacred vestments. If the makers of vestments had confined themselves to the carved-ivory-like scrolls of Venetian raised points, or the dignified, solid Brabant laces at first in use, we should not quarrel with them; but these beautiful productions of medieval handicraft have given place to machine-made counterfeits, possessing neither artistic value nor any quality of preciousness whatever. What was said above regarding the selection of embroidery is true of lace also; that is to say, unless you can get the real article, do without it altogether. "Without finish of handicraft," says Alan S. Cole,[3] "producing beautiful ornament suited to the material in which it is expressed, lace worthy the name cannot be made." Why, then, insist on trimming an alb with yards of cheap, unseemly cotton point-net? Lace trimmings, especially when they are not in right proportion to the body of the alb, detract from the dignified character of the garment. Priests are men, and it is easy to make them appear ludicrous when wrapt up in lace— trimmings affected by women only. Artists have not objected to painting kings, ministers, and marshals with *jabots* and ruffles, but we look in vain for examples of flowing robes trimmed with a foot and a half (or worse still, with six inches) of filmy tissue. No artistic mind would care to see the Sixtine Madonna or the popes and doctors of the *Disputa* robed in lace trimming of this sort. If lace is used at all to embellish an alb or a surplice, it would perhaps be advisable to confine its use to tastefully designed, hand-made insertions, avoiding lace edges altogether. Insertions being narrow will not be so expensive, and, if made of good, stout material, will stand a great deal of wear and tear.

I cannot conclude these remarks on paramentics without at least touching on the vexed question of the *shape* of the chasuble.

The chasuble originated in the picturesque light loose cloak

[3] *On Lace.*

of the better class of Romans. It was called *planeta,* on account of its many folds, and *casula,* because it enveloped and protected the body like a casement.[4] A great preacher of the thirteenth century compares the chasuble to a bell and to the vault of the sky, and says it symbolizes the all-embracing love of God for men. About the middle of the fourteenth century the chasuble was subjected to a process of mutilation, which ended in the beginning of the seventeenth century by leaving nothing of the original vestment except the name and the opening for the head. In proportion as it decreased in size it increased in stiffness, until in front it resembled, as Pugin says, the body of a wasp, and in the rear a board. Needless to say, nearly every vestige of its former beauty and mystical significance is gone, and many of the rubrics of the Missal and Pontifical can be explained only by supposing that our present chasuble is something quite different from what it really is.

" But," it will be asked, "isn't the present shape by far more economical and convenient than the ancient one? It may be so; but the economical and the convenient cannot surely be regarded as the chief standard in the making of church vestments—not even in the making of garments for everyday wear. But I am not concerned with the standards governing secular wearing apparel; in paramentics liturgical symbolism and artistic beauty should surely be maintained. No attempt has been made to introduce the bell-shaped chasubles of the tenth and eleventh centuries still worn in the Eastern Church; but the instinct of correct ecclesiastical taste has asserted itself more definitely by the adoption of the Gothic vestment in use from the end of the thirteenth to the beginning of the sixteenth century, and often called Bernardine[5] and Borromean chasubles. Although not so full of folds and so dignified in appearance as the Greek chasubles, anciently in use throughout Europe, which we still admire in painted windows, frescoes, and statues, and which may still be seen in some of our museums and sacristies, these Gothic chasubles are suggestive of dignity and grace. They symbol-

---

[4] " Casula per diminutionem a casa dicitur, quod totum hominem tegat, quasi minor casa."—*Catalanus apud S. Isidorum.*

[5] Erroneously so styled by Canon Bock in his *Geschichte der liturgischen Gewänder des Mittelalters.*

ize what the chasuble was meant to suggest, namely the ample charity which embraces men in godlike fashion, the contrary of which is apparently symbolized by the violin-shaped and pieced garment with open sides, worn at the holy Sacrifice in these days.

Besides its manifest esthetic superiority, the Gothic chasuble has a practical advantage of no little importance—it never disfigures the wearer, no matter how small of stature he may be. Being a garment, and not a uniform or a coat-of-mail, it is not rigid and hard, but soft and pliable as the silk of which it is made. It need not be tied to the body in order to provide against the possible unpleasant consequences of a genuflection.

About the middle of the last century, Canon Bock of Aix-la-Chapelle, in Germany, and Pugin in England, inaugurated a movement in favor of the long-repudiated Gothic chasuble. A lively controversy followed, and the matter was referred to Rome. At first it looked as if the introduction of the old style would be absolutely forbidden; for Rome is slow to admit even a return to ancient and approved forms, when there is no question of sin or principle involved, and when the suddenness of a reform is apt to bear all the appearance of an uncalled-for innovation likely to scandalize the uninformed. But the decree of the Congregation of Rites (21 August, 1863) did not receive the Pope's approbation.[6] At present chasubles of the later medieval style may be used without hesitation.[7] In most of the churches of the Archdiocese of Cologne hardly any other kind is used at present on feastdays. Although the Gothic chasuble is still a rare thing in Italy, where tradition holds out (except in the German national church of the *Amina*), Pius X, with his broadminded outlook into the world, approves of it. When Mgr. de Waal some time ago openly criticised the present shape of the chasuble,[8] His Holiness agreed with him and said: "Ha perfettamente ragione, e il piu brutto possibile, questa forma." [9]

[6] See Pruner, *Pastoraltheologie*, vol. I, p. 56; and Braun, *Die priesterlichen Gewänder des Mittelalters*, 174.

[7] *Caerem. Episc.*, t. 2, c. 8, nr. 19, (edit. 1886, 150).

[8] In August, 1906, when vestments and sacred vessels were presented to the Holy Father for the stricken districts of Calabria.

[9] *Pastor Bonus* (Trier), September, 1906, p. 569.

Some twenty years ago, the present Bishop of Rottenburg, the learned and art-loving Wilhelm von Keppler, treated the question of the chasuble from the esthetic and practical points of view. He suggested that to preserve some distinction, the larger, so-called Bernardine style of the thirteenth and fourteenth centuries, be adopted in all cathedrals and the richer city churches for solemn feasts, while the less majestic and somewhat narrower Borromean style of the fifteenth century might be used in all churches on Sundays and feast-days. For ordinary days he recommended the retaining of the Roman form to which the people are accustomed in many places, provided it be given a respectable width.[10] These propositions, which are based on sound sense, might aptly receive the careful consideration of our liturgists and of all who, having the beauty of divine worship at heart, find it possible to influence the adoption of the reform in paramentics.

Indeed, the question: What can be done to remedy the present low standard in material and form in the manufacture of church vestments, or how can we restore the beautiful in color, shape, and technique, which were once characteristic of the garments of the sanctuary?—has an obvious answer. Let those who are responsible for the existing poor taste become the pioneers in the revival of good taste. This effects in the first place the dealers in church goods, then the clergy, the communities of nuns, altar societies; in fact, all who make, sell, buy or use vestments. The dealers in church goods are bound to conform to the canons of ecclesiastical symbolism and taste. Their standard of excellence should not be, as is only too often the case, the immediate market value, or possibility of profit, but rather both becoming beauty and serviceableness. On the other hand, the " buying public " must also be equipped with a full appreciation for true art; since the demand usually regulates the supply both as regards quantity and quality. Instead of tempting or even forcing the maker of vestments to cater to the false taste of the buyer, the buyer should continually stimulate the maker to higher, more perfect efforts. He must have a high standard of excellence in wares and not accept imitations for the real thing. It may be well in this matter to follow the advice given by William

[10] *Archiv für christliche Kunst,* 1888, n. 4.

Morris in his *Hints on Pattern-Designing*: " Have as little as possible to do with middlemen," he says, "but bring together the makers and the buyers of goods as closely as possible. Eschew all bargains, real or imaginary (they are mostly the latter), and pay what a piece of goods is really worth. Get to understand the value of intelligent work, the work of men's hands guided by their brains, and to take that, though it be rough, rather than the unintelligent work of machines or slaves, thought it be delicate; refuse altogether to use machine-made work unless where the nature of the thing made compels it, or where the machine does what mere human suffering would otherwise have to do."

These are some few suggestions in aid of the movement toward a revival of paramentics along true artistic lines. If it be true, as has often been remarked, that a movement which has any vitality at all must expect to encounter opposition as well as sympathy and support, then it is a consolation to think that the movement in favor of which I have entered this imperfect plea has had its share of both. But as the cause is good and noble, opposition will give way to sympathy, and sympathy lead to appreciation, and appreciation to unselfish effort, sure to be blessed with success, in His own good time, by Him who " greatly desires the beauty " of His Spouse and the splendor of the " house where His glory dwelleth." [11]

GEORGE METLAKE.

Cologne, Germany.

[11] Ps. 44, 12; 20, 8.

Analecta.

ACTA PII PP. X

<small>Ad rmum. Antistitem Generalem Societatis Sulpicianae.</small>

Dilecte fili, salutem et apostolicam benedictionem.—Redditae sunt Nobis tuae nuper litterae: in quibus quidem gratum fuit, quod tuam et Societatis, cui praesides, omnem in Nos observantiam declarabas; sed illud etiam gratius, quod addebas de vestra voluntate Nobis fidelissime obtemperandi, praesertim quod ad institutionem Cleri adolescentis attinet. Hanc enim

Nobis ac libet, cumulate vestris partibus satisfacturos, divina adiuvante gratia. Huius Nos auspicem, et benevolentiae Nostrae testem, tibi, dilecte fili, et omnibus vel magistris vel discipulis Societatis Sulpicianae apostolicam benedictionem grato cum animo impertimus.

Datum Romae apud S. Petrum, die XII Decembris MCMIX, Pontificatus Nostri anno septimo.

PIUS PP. X.

___

S. CONGREGATIO DE RELIGIOSIS.

I.

DECLARATIO CIRCA STUDIA A RELIGIOSIS PERAGENDA.

Nonnulli Superiores Generales Ordinum et Institutorum huic Sacrae Congregationi Negotiis Sodalium Religiosorum praepositae humillime exposuerunt difficultates, quas parit immediata executio recentiorum Declarationum circa studia d. d. 7 septembris 1909; sive quia alumni in propriis illorum Collegiis degentes, qui ad Novitiatum ingrediendum iam existimabantur sufficienter apti, in Collegiis ipsis, ad statum curriculum studiorum perficiendum adhuc permanere debent; sive quia ipsae novitiorum domus per aliquod tempus claudendae erunt, quum haud facile sit reperire alumnos ad tramitem Declarationum undequaque instructos.

Ideoque supplices preces dederunt, ut, quousque iuxta placita huius Sacrae Congregationis res apprime ordinentur, praefatas Declarationes benigniori quadam ratione interpretari fas esset.

Sanctissimus autem Dominus Noster Pius Papa X, cui haec omnia infrascriptus Cardinalis Praefectus retulit in Audientia diei 21 decembris 1909, rem mature perpendere dignatus est aequa lance cum expositis difficultatibus bona librando, quae ex immediata executione dictarum Declarationum Ordinibus et Institutis provenient, quae quidem bona non potest esse, quin cedant in utilitatem ipsius Ecclesiae Universae. Et sane, hisce praesertim difficillimis temporibus, aequali ac Sacerdotes saeculares debent scientia pollere Sacerdotes Regulares, quorum consilia Fideles non minori sane fiducia expetere constat;

litatem; quod si nonnullos abuti contingat scientia, Ordinis vel Congregationis sumptibus acquisita, et ante ingressum in Novitiatum discedere, melius est illos abire, quos ex hoc ipso patet non habuisse propositi constantiam, imo nec amplectendae vitae religiosae animum vere sincerum; longe minor est Ordinibus et Institutis timenda iactura, si minus frequentati, vel prorsus vacuae per aliquod tempus novitiorum domus existant, quam si plenae Sodalibus non adaequate institutis; praestat selectus numerus alumnorum stabilium, quam magnus praetereuntium, integre summopere curandum, ut id quod numero erit inferius, spe reddatur uberius.

His igitur aliisque permotus argumentis, idem Sanctissimus Dominus Noster minoris faciens difficultates expositas, supplicibus precibus haud annuendum, idque omnibus Superioribus Generalibus Ordinum et Institutorum in normam et regulam significandum duxit.

Contrariis quibuscumque minime obstantibus, etiam speciali mentione dignis. Romae, die 71 decembris 1909.

Fr. I. C. Card. VIVES, *Praefectus.*

L. * S.

D. L. JANSSENS O. S. B., *Secretarius.*

II.

DUBIA CIRCA PROFESSIONEM RELIGIOSORUM.

Ab hac Sacra Congregatione, Negotiis Religiosorum Sodalium praeposita, sequentium dubiorum solutio expostulata fuit, nimirum:

I. Quidam Religiosus, dimissus, ab una Domo Ordinis, de consensu Superioris Generalis, in alia Domo eiusdem Ordinis

Et Sacra eadem Congregatio respondendum censuit, prouti respondet:

Ad I. *Negative* ad primam partem; *Affirmative* ad secundam.

Ad II. *Affirmative* ad primam partem; *Negative* ad secundam.

Atque ita rescripsit, die 4 ianuarii 1910.

Fr. I. C. Card. VIVES, *Praefectus.*

D. L. JANSSENS O. S. B., *Secretarius.*

S. CONGREGATIO CONSISTORIALIS.

DE RELATIONIBUS DIOECESANIS ET VISITATIONE SS. LIMINUM.

I.

DECRETUM

SERVANDUM AB OMNIBUS LOCORUM ORDINARIIS

QUI S. CONGR. DE PROPAGANDA FIDE SUBIECTI NON SUNT.

A remotissima Ecclesiae aetate repetenda lex et consuetudo est, qua singuli Episcopi, statis temporibus, Urbem petant, ut sanctorum apostolorum Petri et Pauli limina venerentur, suaeque statum dioecesis exponant Apostolicae Sedi: cuius rei illustria monumenta veteres Ecclesiae annales suppeditant.

Eiusmodi autem facti ratio in ipsa Ecclesiae natura et constitutione nititur, atque a sacro Petri primatu necessario fluit, cui christiani gregis universi commissa custodia est, per divina illa praecipientis Domini verba: *pasce agnos, pasce oves.* In utroque autem munere, quum visitationis sacrorum Liminum, tum relationis de statu dioecesis, debitae Petro eiusque successori submissionis et reverentiae continetur officium.

Verum, quamvis unum et alterum huius legis caput tot antea saeculis viguerit, serius tamen hac de re certior invecta est disciplina. Est enim Xysto V tribuendum, quod is, Constitutione edita die 20 mensis decembris 1585, cui initium *Romanus Pontifex,* congrua ratione determinaverit, quibus temporibus et qua lege visitanda sacra Limina essent et reddenda ratio Summo Pontifici de pastoralis officii implemento a Patriarchis, Primatibus, Archiepiscopis et Episcopis: quibus etiam prospexerunt encyclicae litterae sacrae Congregationis Concilii, datae die 16 mensis novembris 1673. Abbatibus autem *nullius dioecesis* cautum est per Constitutionem Benedicti XIV, datam die 23 mensis novembris 1740, quae incipit *Quod sancta.*

Haec obtinuit ad nostros usque dies disciplina. Verum, effectis hodie multo facilioribus ac tutioribus dioeceses inter et Sanctam Sedem commerciis, iam praesentis aevi conditionibus haud respondere visa sunt ea, quae in memoratis Constitutionibus decreta fuerunt circa visitationes ad sacra Limina ac dioecesum relationes ad Apostolicam Sedem.

Re mature agitata in coetu Emorum Virorum Pontificio Iuri in unum corpus redigendo praepositorum, conclusa ab iisdem, SSmi D. N. Pii Papae X iussu, ad hanc S. Congregationem Consistorialem delata sunt, eidemque commissum iudicium, utrum et quomodo eius coetus consilia publici iuris fieri atque in usum deduci possent, etiam ante promulgandum ipsum Codicem.

Nunc vero, omnibus diligenter perpensis, iisque inhaerens quae a memorato coetu PP. Cardinalium deliberata sunt, S. Congregatio Consistorialis, de mandato SSmi Domini nostri, Eoque adprobante, decernit quae sequuntur:

Can. I.

Abrogata lege temporum, quibus hactenus visitanda fuerunt sacra Limina 'et relatio Sanctae Sedi exhibenda de statu dioecesis, omnes locorum Ordinarii, quibus dioecesani regiminis onus incumbit, obligatione tenentur referendi singulis quinquenniis ad Summum Pontificem de statu sibi commissae dioecesis ad normam canonum infra positorum et novi *Ordinis* praesenti decreta adiecti.

Can. II.

§ 1. Quinquennia sunt fixa et communia, incipientque a die 1 mensis ianuarii anno 1911.

§ 2. In primo quinquennii anno relationem exhibebunt Ordinarii Italiae, et insularum Corsicae, Sardiniae, Siciliae, Melitae, aliarumque minorum adiacentium.

§ 3. In altero, Ordinarii Hispaniae, Lusitaniae, Galliae, Belgii, Hollandiae, Angliae, Scotiae et Hiberniae, cum insulis adiacentibus.

§ 4. In tertio, Ordinarii imperii Austro-Ungarici, Ger-

§ 7. Et ita per vices continuas singulis, quae sequentur, quinquenniis.

Can. III.

§ 1. In prima cuiusque Ordinarii relatione ad singula quaesita, quae in adiecto *Ordine* continentur, distincte responderi debet.

§ 2. In relationibus quae sequentur sufficit ut Ordinarii ad quaesita in singulis articulis contenta dicant, utrum novi aliquid habeatur, necne.

Adiicient vero quomodo et quo fructu ad effectum perduxerint monita et mandata, quae S. Congregatio in sua responsione ad relationem significaverit.

§ 3. Relatio latina lingua est conficienda.

§ 4. Subsignanda autem erit, praeter quam ab Ordinario, ab uno vel altero ex *convisitatoribus*, qui de statu dioecesis magis conscii sunt et de ea testificari possunt.

Ipsi vero circa ea quae ex relatione noverint, si publici iuris non sunt, gravi secreti lege adstringuntur.

Can. IV.

§ 1. Omnibus et singulis pariter praecipitur ut, quo anno debent relationem exhibere, beatorum apostolorum Petri et Pauli sepulcra veneraturi ad Urbem accedant, et Romano Pontifici se sistant.

§ 2. Sed Ordinariis, qui extra Europam sunt, permittitur ut alternis quinquenniis, idest singulis decenniis, Urbem petant.

§ 3. Huic obligationi Ordinarius, vel ipse per se, vel per Coadiutorem aut Auxiliarem Episcopum, si quem habeat, satisfaciet; vel, iustis de causis a S. Sede probandis, per ideoneum sacerdotem qui in eadem dioecesi stabilem commorationem teneat.

Can. V.

Si annus exhibendae relationi adsignatus, ex toto vel ex parte, inciderit in primum biennium ab inito dioecesis regimine, fas erit Ordinario ab exhibenda relatione, et a visitatione sacrorum Liminum peragenda pro ea vice, abstinere.

Can. VI.

§ 2. Annis autem 1911 et 1912 a relatione et visitatione abstinere licebit Ordinariis, de quibus in §§ *2 et 3 can. II*, qui
anno 1909 iuxta veterem temporum periodum legi satis-
fecerunt.

Qui vero de statu suae dioecesis referent, hi ad normam
novi *Ordinis* a S. Sede statuti huic muneri satisfaciant.

CAN. VII.

Denique cum sacrorum Liminum visitatio et relatio dioecesana ad Apostolicam Sedem non sint confundendae cum
lege de visitatione pastorali dioecesis, idcirco vigere pergunt
praescripta a Concilio Tridentino, sess. XXIV, cap. III *de
reform.*, his verbis expressa: *Propriam dioecesim* (Episcopi)
*per se ipsos, aut, si legitime impediti fuerint, per suum ge-
neralem Vicarium aut Visitatorem, si quotannis totam propter
eius latitudinem visitare non poterunt, saltem maiorem eius
partem, ita tamen ut tota biennio per se vel Visitatores suos
compleatur, visitare non praetermittant.*

SSmus autem D. N. Pius Papa X, his canonibus et adiecti
Ordinis normis mature perpensis, iussit haec omnia promulgari et evulgari, mandavitque ut ab omnibus ad quos spectat
integre serventur, contrariis quibuslibet minime obstantibus.

Datum Romae, die 31 mensis decembris anno 1909.

    C. Card. DE LAI, *S. C. Consistorialis Secretarius.*

L. * S.

        S. TECCHI, *Adsessor.*

Ordo Servandus

IN RELATIONE DE STATU ECCLESIARUM.

NORMAE COMMUNES.

Prooemium Relationis.

Cap. I.

Generalia de statu materiali.

3. Indicetur paucis et perspicuis verbis,

(*a*) origo dioecesis, eius titulus seu gradus hierarchicus cum privilegiis potioribus: sitne archiepiscopalis, quot et quas habeat suffraganeas sedes; si sit episcopalis, cui archiepiscopali suffragetur: si immediate subiecta, cui metropolitano debeat adhaerere pro synodo;

(*b*) extensio dioecesis, ditio civilis, caeli temperatio, lingua;

(*c*) locus residentiae Ordinarii cum indicationibus necessariis ut epistolae tuto mittantur;

(*d*) summa incolarum et praecipua oppida: quot inter incolas sint catholici; et si varii adsint ritus, quot catholici in singulis; et si adsint acatholici, in quot et quales sectas dividantur;

(*e*) numerus sacerdotum saecularium, clericorum et alumnorum Seminarii;

(*f*) utrum et quot *capitula* canonicorum, aliique sacerdotum coetus ad instar capitulorum sint in dioecesi;

(*g*) quot sint paroeciae vel quasi paroeciae, cum numero fidelium in iis quae maximae vel minimae sunt; in quot vicariatus foraneos aliasve circumscriptiones paroeciae dividantur; quot aliae ecclesiae vel oratoria publica adsint; sitne sacer aliquis locus celeberrimus, et qualis;

(*h*) utrum et quaenam instituta religiosa virorum habeantur, cum numero domorum et religiosorum sive sacerdotum sive laicorum;

(*i*) utrum et quaenam instituta religiosa mulierum, cum numero domorum et religiosarum.

Cap. II.

De fide et de cultu divino.

4. Utrum divinus cultus libere in dioecesi exerceatur: sin minus, unde obstacula proveniant, a civilibus ne legibus, an ab hostilitate perversorum hominum, vel acatholicorum (si ad-

6. Utrum generatim ecclesiae et sacella publica satis instructa sint iis quae ad fabricam ac supellectilem pertinent; et quaenam generatim cura habeatur ut eadem munda sint et decenter ornata.

7. Utrum in singulis ecclesiis inventarium omnium bonorum et supellectilium habeatur, et quomodo custodiatur, ne morte rectoris aut alio quolibet eventu contingat ut aliquid subtrahatur aut disperdatur.

8. Utrum sint ecclesiae in quibus res vel supellectiles habeantur materia, arte, antiquitate pretiosae, praesertim codices vel libri, picturae, sculpturae, opera musiva arte vel antiquitate insignia; quomodo custodiantur; sintne haec recensita in inventariis, et an de iis speciale inventarium penes Curiam servetur.

Cautumne sit ne quid etiam tenue, sed ratione materiae, artis vel antiquitatis pretiosum, sine licentia S. Sedis et iudicio peritorum venumdetur.

9. Utrum singulis diebus, mane et vespere horis opportunioribus, ecclesiae pateant fidelibus.

Utrum debita vigilantia custodiantur ne sacrilegiis, profanationibus aliisve damnis obnoxiae sint.

10. Utrum, dum sacra peraguntur, ita omnibus fidelibus pateant, ut quilibet vel pauperrimus absque gravamine vel rubore libere ingredi, ibique adstare valeat.

11. Utrum aliquando ecclesiae vel sacella adhibeantur ad aliquem profanum usum, ad academicos coetus, musicos concentus, aliaque id genus.

12. Utrum in omnibus ecclesiis et sacellis in quibus SSma Eucharistia asservari debet vel potest, conditiones a iure requisitae ad conservationem SSmi Sacramenti accurate serventur: et an cura sit ut altare SSmi Sacramenti cultu, munditie et ornatu emineat.

13. Utrum poenitentiae tribunalia collocata sint in patenti ecclesiae loco, et cratibus instructa iuxta canonicas leges.

tratione sacramentorum aliisque sacris functionibus liturgicae leges serventur.

Irrepserintne singulares consuetudines, et quaenam: num hae S. Sedis auctoritate aut vetustissimo usu rite approbatae dici queant, aut saltem toleratae: et si tales non sint, quid fiat ut prudenter deleantur.

Speciatim vero utrum lingua et cantus liturgicus iuxta S. Sedis decreta adhibeantur.

16. Utrum graves errores contra fidem serpant inter dioecesis fideles. Adsintne e clero qui eisdem infecti sint. Quaenam huius mali fuerit vel adhuc sit causa. Quid fiat ut eidem malo occurratur.

17. Utrum consilium *vigilantiae* et officium *censorum* ad haec praecavenda institutum sit: quibus personis constet: et an diligenter munera sua ipsae adimpleant, et quo fructu.

Cap. III.

De iis quae ad Ordinarium pertinent.

18. Quibus bonis et reditibus mensa Ordinarii polleat. An et quali aere alieno gravetur.

Quomodo administratio geratur: utrum independenter ab auctoritate civili, necne; an seorsim a ceteris dioecesis vel piorum operum bonis et proventibus, vel cumulate; qua methodo et per quas personas.

19. Utrum adsit domus Ordinario dioecesis propria, vel privatam ipse conducere cogatur. In utroque casu num aedes ita instructae sint, ut Ordinarii dignitati congruant, et luxum non redoleant.

20. Cum quibusnam personis Ordinarius habitet, et quaenam sit earum vitae ratio.

21. An, a quibus S. Sedis officiis, et quibusnam specialibus facultatibus et privilegiis ipse qua Ordinarius instructus sit.

22. Quomodo residentiae legi satisfaciat.

23. Quoties consuescat in cathedrali templo vel alibi sacris functionibus interesse aut pontificalia peragere.

24. Qua frequentia sacris concionibus et pastoralibus litteris clerum ac populum instruat. Et quatenus sit impeditus a praedicando, an per alios opportune suppleat.

25. Quot et quales adsint in dioecesi casus reservati: et quibus Ordinarius committat facultatem ab eisdem absolvendi.

26. Qua frequentia sacramentum confirmationis administret; et utrum pro dioecesis conditione petitionibus fidelium satisfacere ipse per se valeat: et, si ipse non valeat, quomodo et per quos suppleat.

Utrum in huius sacramenti collatione canonicae regulae de aetate confirmandorum ac de patrinis serventur.

27. Utrum ipse per se vel per alium Episcopum sacras ordinationes contulerit.

Et in hoc peragendo, dum studuit dioecesim locupletare idoneorum sacerdotum copia, utrum sartum tectum servaverit Tridentini Concilii praescriptum non promovendi qui non essent necessarii vel utiles ecclesiae pro qua assumuntur.

28. Utrum ipse per se, vel per Vicarium generalem aut per alios viros a se deputatos totam dioecesim ita visitaverit ut singulis annis vel saltem bienniis de statu singularum paroeciarum certam notitiam habere potuerit.

An visitando paroecias, praeter ea quae pertinent ad divinum cultum, populi mores, religiosam puerorum et adolescentium institutionem, legatorum satisfactionem, aliaque; visitationem quam vocant personalem cleri peregerit, singulos audiendo, ut cognoscat quae sit eorum vitae ratio, qui spiritus precum, quod studium procurandae proximorum salutis, aliaque.

29. Utrum curaverit ut Conciliorum et S. Sedis leges et praeceptiones in dioecesi nota fierent et ab omnibus servarentur.

30. Utrum dioecesanam synodum congregaverit; et si nullam coegerit, an, quomodo et quanam potestate suppleverit.

31. Si sit metropolitanus, an provinciale concilium, aut saltem collationes seu *conferentias* episcopales habuerit, et quoties.

Exemplar eorum quae in *conferentiis* communi consilio conclusa sunt ad S. Sedem (si adhuc factum non fuerit) transmittat.

Cap. IV.

De Curia dioecesana.

33. Utrum habeatur Vicarius generalis qui tum virtutis ac doctrinae opinione tum gradus doctoralis auctoritate polleat: et quot aliis ministris constet dioecesana Curia.

34. Utrum et quot adsint examinatores et iudices synodales aut pro-synodales.

35. Utrum adsit tribunal ecclesiasticum cum suis administris rite constitutum; aut saltem possit constitui, si necesse sit.

36. Utrum Curia dioecesana aedes proprias convenienter instructas habeat cum tabulario, in quo pars secreta documentorum tuto ac seorsim ab aliis documentis custodiatur. An archivum ipsum sit bene ordinatum.

37. Quaenam taxa in usu sit pro actis Curiae rependendis; an et quando approbata; et an conformis ceteris quae in provincia ecclesiastica aut regione vigent.

38. Utrum Ordinarius cognoscat querelas adesse ob Curiae taxas; et an in re praesertim matrimoniali concubinatus, aut alia mala accidisse sciat ob earum gravitatem seu ob rigorem exactionis earumdem. Quomodo taxarum proventus erogetur.

39. Utrum ex multis, aut ex aliis titulis speciales alii proventus Curiae sint: et quomodo erogentur.

[TO BE CONTINUED.]

PONTIFICAL APPOINTMENTS.

By decree of the S. Congregation of Consistory:

8 January, 1910.—The Rev. Joseph John Rice, parish priest of St. Peter's, Northbridge, in the Diocese of Springfield, Mass., has been elected to the Episcopal See of Burlington, Vt., U. S. A.

19 January, 1910.—The Right Rev. Neil MacNeil, Bishop of St. George, Newfoundland, has been elected to the Archiepiscopal See of Vancouver, Canada.

8 January, 1910.—The Holy Father has appointed the Benedictine Father Pietro Bastien, editor-in-chief of the *Acta Apostolicae Sedis.*

Studies and Conferences.

OUR ANALECTA.

The Roman documents for the month are:

LETTER OF THE SOVEREIGN PONTIFF to the Very Rev. Henry Garriguet, Superior General of the Sulpician Society, commending its devotion to the training and educating of seminarists.

S. CONGREGATION OF RELIGIOUS: 1. Announces that the recent (7 September, 1909) declarations regarding the course of studies to be followed by Religious Orders and Institutes, must be carried out. The Holy Father has carefully considered the difficulties urged as being in the way of the immediate execution of the new regulations, but does not deem them serious enough to justify a modification of the above-mentioned declarations.

2. Solves two doubts in regard to the recent Decree (7 September, 1909) about the profession of Religious previously dismissed or dispensed from vows.

CONSISTORIAL CONGREGATION publishes a Decree concerning the diocesan reports and visitation *ad limina*. (A full commentary on this Decree and the *Normae* to be observed by the bishops will appear in connexion with the complete text of the document.)

ROMAN CURIA issues list of new Pontifical appointments.

ECCLESIASTICAL HERALDRY.

Two colored plates giving the coat of arms of His Holiness Pope Pius X, and that of His Excellency the Apostolic Delegate, will be found in this number of the REVIEW. Herewith we give their heraldic explanation and description.

He was born at Riese, Diocese of Treviso, province of Venice, 2 June, 1835; a student at the seminary of Padua, 1850; ordained *priest*, 18 September, 1858; parish priest and chaplain at Tornbolo (Diocese of Treviso) 1859; archpriest at Talzano (same Diocese), 1868; Canon, Chancellor, and Vicar-General of Bishop Callegari at Treviso, 1875; preconized *Bishop* of Mantua (province of Milan), 10 November, 1884; created *Cardinal*-Priest of the title of St. Bernard ai Termi, 12 June, 1893; and promoted *Patriarch* of Venice, 15 June, same year; elected *Pope* 4 August, and crowned 9 August, 1903.

COAT OF ARMS OF THE HOLY FATHER: "Azure, a mullet of six points or, and in base an anchor of three branches proper, bendwise, and emerging from tossed waves vert; on a chief argent, the lion of Venice proper, holding a sword of the second."

Translation: A blue shield holding a six-pointed star of gold, and in its lower part an agitated sea with a three-forked anchor bent to right; the upper part, or chief, shows the arms of Venice, viz. the Lion of St. Mark with a book and golden sword, all on silver field.

Explanation: When made Bishop of Mantua, Pius X adopted from the coat of arms of his Bishop, Mgr. Callegari (whom he created a Cardinal, soon after his exaltation) the field, star and sea, and added the anchor, discarding also Bishop Callegari's motto " Spes nostra "; it means, then, that " His hope is in the Star of the Sea." Later, when promoted Patriarch of Venice, as is customary, he added in chief the arms of Venice, changing, however (to conform with heraldry), the blue field to silver, the golden lion to natural, and the star from silver to gold, thus giving us " Ignis ardens."

II.

HIS EXCELLENCY THE APOSTOLIC DELEGATE, Archbishop Diomedes Falconio, O. F. M.; born in Italy, 1842; Bishop of Lacedonia (Italy), 1892; Archbishop of Acerenza and Matera

COAT OF ARMS OF HIS EXCELLENCY THE APOSTOLIC DELEGATE
THE MOST REV. DIOMEDES FALCONIO, O. F. M.

azure, a mullet of the second; fourth sable, a falcon couped or, armed gules; on a chief argent, the *conformities of St. Francis.*"

Explanation: The four quarters are the coat of arms of the Falconi (armes parlantes, falcon). The chief shows the coat of arms of the Order of St. Francis (the Stigmata), its field, however (to conform with heraldry), having been changed from blue to silver.

His Excellency received the pallium when residential Archbishop of Acerenza and Matera. The cross of a Knight of Malta is here left out, as having been a personal, not transferable, distinction of a member of the Falconi family. The motto, attributed to St. Francis of Assisi, is " Deus meus et Omnia—My God and my All."

ALOYSIUS BRUCKER, S.J.

VERNACULAR HYMNS AT DIVINE SERVICE.

Qu. A question arose lately among some priests and it was resolved to send it to you for solution. A pastor who had been using *Prayers at Mass for School Children* was told by another that it was not allowed to sing the Gloria, Sanctus, etc. in the vernacular during a low Mass, and as proof he brought forward a decree of 31 March, 1909, which reads: " Utrum preces et hymni liturgici, v. g. Introitus, Communio, hymnus Lauda Sion, a choro musicorum in lingua vernacula cantari possint infra Missam privatam; an vero ejusmodi cantica tantum prohibita sint coram Sanctissimo exposito, ad normam decreti S. C. R. n. 3537 Leavenworthien., 27 Feb., 1882 ad 3?. Respondit: —Negative ad primam partem, juxta decretum relatum n. 3537 Leaven. 27 Feb., 1882 ad 3; ad secundum jam in primo provisum." The decree 3537 to which reference is made reads: " Num liceat

be covered very well by the judicious remarks at pages 239-241 of last August's REVIEW. As, however, the singing of some particular hymns is in debate, we ask you to be so kind as to give a decision. It may be added that while the Sanctus in the compilation of prayers alluded to is translated literally, the Gloria is given neither literally nor wholly, so that the decree, however interpreted, may not concern it. Enclosed is a copy of the prayers referred to.

EDWARD P. GRAHAM.

Resp. We repeat here what was said on this subject in the August number of 1909, namely that the singing of hymns in devotional exercises during low Mass or Exposition and Benediction of the Blessed Sacrament, is not contrary to the liturgical prescriptions, unless these hymns are used in such a way as to supplant the liturgical chant which is prescribed in these functions and which must be in Latin.

The low Mass at which our school children attend does not exact any kind of liturgical chant. The faithful who assist at such Mass can pray, sing, or meditate, if this helps them to attend more devoutly and intelligently to the private offering at the altar. The public service of a High or Solemn Mass in which the people take part alternately with the celebrant, and in which they are represented by the liturgical choir, is a very different thing; and at such service it would be unbecoming to respond in the vernacular to the celebrant who chants the intonations and sacred addresses in Latin. The unity of the service and the harmony of the solemn sacred act demand that it be conducted in the one language, the Latin of the ancient Roman Church, which the priest chants aloud.

Does the decree cited above for the Diocese of Leavenworth, even if we admit its universal application, controvert this view? We think not. The Bishop asks for certain information in the following terms:

Devotionem erga SSmum Cor Jesu, quoad *externum cultum, uniformem ac liturgicis legibus apprime consonam* reddere cupiens, a S. Rit. Congregatione sequentium dubiorum declarationem humillime expetivit:

1. Num liceat Sacerdoti celebranti, ante vel post expletum Missae Sacrificium, publice *recitare preces vel hymnos in lingua vernacula,* v. gr. Novemdiales B. Maria Virginis vel alicujus Sancti, *coram SS. Sacramento publice exposito? — Resp. Affirmative, quoad preces tantum.*

2. Num liceat Sacerdoti coram SSo. Sacramento solemniter expasito ob devotionem SS. Cordis Jesu in Ecclesia publice celebranti, recitare actus vel alias preces in honorem ejusdem SS. Cordis in lingua vernacula ad auditum populi fidelis adstantis, ita ut ad istas preces vel actus ipse respondere valeat?—*Resp. Affirmative;* seu provisum in proecedenti.

3. Num liceat generaliter, ut chorus musicorum (i. e. cantores) coram SSo. Sacramento solemniter exposito decantet hymnos in lingua vernacula?—*Resp. Posse:* dummodo non agatur de hymnis Te Deum et aliis quibuscumque liturgicis precibus, quae nonnisi latina lingua decantari debent.

In analyzing the terms of this decision we must remember that the S. Congregation is proverbially careful in taking simply the literal sense of any doubts proposed to it. In the first of the above three questions the Bishop asked, whether the *celebrant* during Exposition of the Blessed Sacrament might recite prayers or (chant) hymns. The answer is: Yes, he may recite prayers, but he may not chant hymns, in the vernacular. Nevertheless the people, i. e. the congregation or even the choir, may chant hymns in the vernacular, as is very clear from the answer to number three, so long as the liturgical hymns prescribed for Benediction are not in question.

That the celebrant at Benediction should not *chant* or even intone hymns in the vernacular seems quite proper and reasonable, since such a practice would soon interfere with liturgical consistency. The same distinction would apply to the second question, in the instance of the chanting of prayers and responses, alternating between the celebrant and the congregation, such as the invocations to the Sacred Heart. The third

debent " is not that Catholics may not sing translations of
Latin hymns at their devotions in common, but rather that
those Latin hymns that are an *integral* part of the liturgical
service may not be chanted in the vernacular (when that implies their omission in the Latin as prescribed).

In using the expression " *externum cultum, uniformem ac
liturgicis legibus apprime consonam (devotionem) reddere
cupiens,*" the interrogator plainly indicates that he has in mind
the liturgical features of the service only, which does not include such devotions as those of the children at low Mass, except under the particular circumstances which give to this
Mass the character of a public or solemn parochial function.
The latter case would seem to exclude the regular chanting
by a choir (sanctuary choir) of the solemn parts of the Mass
in the vernacular, for the obvious reason that it would supplant
the solemn service prescribed for a liturgical function like
Mass (quasi-solemn), which is to be Latin.

But in the weekday Mass of the school children there is no
such perversion. They sing only snatches or parts of the
translated hymns as a matter of devotion; and even on Sundays, when their Mass may be regarded as a parochial liturgical act, they do not chant the Mass as such, i. e. in its entirety, in the vernacular. To sing the Gloria or part of it, and
the Sanctus, as given in the excellent booklet of *Prayers at
Mass for School Children*, is not singing the Mass, as the
liturgy interprets the term: it is singing God's praises. And
if we could not do that by using words which have the approval of ages of devotion, we should have to keep silent altogether; for to sing simply " Glory be to God on high " might
be construed by a narrow interpreter as violating the letter
of the law which seemingly prohibits the translation and use
at Mass or Benediction of the Gloria, etc.

To show that we are not forcing an unwarranted interpretation of the decision of the S. Congregation, we may refer
to the contexts of the decrees which forbid in general the use
of the vernacular in the liturgy mainly because the custom of
introducing " concentus indecoros et a ritu ecclesiastico
alienos, non sine divinae Majestatis offensa et Christifidelium
scandalo " into the sacred functions, has from time to time
tended to supplant and render of secondary importance the

liturgical prayers and chants. Hence Gardellini, referring to such legislation as the Constitution of Alexander VII *Piae sollicitudinis*, distinguishes between exercises of devotion which he calls *praeter-liturgicae* and those called *liturgicae* to be performed during Exposition of the Blessed Sacrament. Thus he removes the one-sided and over-rigorous interpretation of an old decree (S. R. C., 24 March, 1657) which reads:

Minime tolerandum abusum hujusmodi (utendi cantiones in lingua vernacula), sed, vel adsit SS. Sacramentum, vel non, omnino Episcopus idem prohibeat in ecclesiis cantiones, vel quorumvis verborum cantum materno idiomate.

Strictly interpreted this would mean that no Catholic would be free to sing ever a word of his mother tongue aloud in the church, which is an absurd supposition.

Furthermore, there are many decisions making it plain that the use of vernacular hymns in the sense above explained is altogether proper and lawful.

Utrum consuetudo canendi Hispano idiomate carmina aliosque similes modos musicos coram exposito SS. Sacramento aut in ejus processionibus, etc. tolerari possit?—Resp. Attenta consuetudine tolerari posse. (27 September, 1864. S. R. C.)

Custom, therefore, and the bishop's approval are all that is required in cases of doubt whether a function is exclusively liturgical or devotional.

Commenting on this and similar decrees, the late Bishop of Alton, in a Pastoral Letter (23 February, 1880), wrote to his clergy: " Since, then, bishops may permit the people to sing in their mother-tongue at Benediction, we wish such to be done, knowing well from experience that this will conduce much to devotion and will bring many to adore at the feet of Jesus in this exposition who would otherwise remain away." What is said of Benediction applies to other liturgical functions, and *a fortiori* to the low Mass for children.

names under the heading of Roman Curial Appointments and Honors. The latter class includes as a rule some Americans, who are made knights, marquises, monsignori, and the like, with decorations appropriate to their rank as classified Roman aristocrats. Now I can understand how these things are done in Europe, with its hereditary divisions of society. But I think that in America they are entirely out of place and even contrary to the spirit of our people, if not also to the letter of the Constitution. At all events the way Americans look on these titles is one of amusement, if not of disdain or irritation, though there are no doubt many people who like decorations and millinery display. The incongruity is furthermore evident in that such " honors " as have no particular religious meaning, but are solely rewards or favors, should come from the Church. They do not seem to fit in with the motto and well-known disposition of the present Pope—" Instaurare omnia in Christo ", unless indeed, as we may assume to be the case, he really does not sympathize with all this show, but merely yields to pressure from the outside by according such honors at the request of influential persons whom he does not want to offend.

My immediate reason for writing to the REVIEW on this occasion is, however, not to complain but rather to have some light, whether these honors belong to the temporal power or to the spiritual, particularly since the REVIEW is known to have a sane way of dealing with such questions. In the present case it seems to me to be the wrong thing to publish such " honors ", for it encourages the undemocratic spirit which destroys the popular ideals of our national government. The same might be said about the discussion of Ecclesiastical Heraldry. Priests and bishops who have the cross for their weapon and the faith for their shield can afford, it seems to me, to do without escutcheons, and be the better for the absence of them in our democratic land.

CANDIDUS AMERICANUS.

Resp. In publishing the appointments of the Roman Curia, we simply follow the official course of the *Acta Apostolicae Sedis*, since they have a documentary value as records of fact, distinct from their purpose or from the standpoint from which the American reader regards them.

As to the series of papers on Ecclesiastical Heraldry, our object is to interest ecclesiastical readers in the significance and symbolism of an institution which, whilst it often subserves the purpose of marking purely social distinctions that are contrary to the spirit of our democratic Republic, has nevertheless the purpose of classifying practical and worthy aims of moral manhood and religious principle. For, whatever may have been the origin of the adoption of symbols by which churchmen, who often were secular princes, meant to indicate their official and personal rank, it has with us at the present day quite another meaning. The ecclesiastical heraldic devices of our bishops are not designed to indicate their past lineage and family distinction, but to express some conscious principle or sentiment on the part of their possessors as underlying and governing their conduct as occupants of the sacred position to which they have been called. They are, then, to use a common phrase, a trademark as it were and pledge of official integrity, as well as of personal aspirations; and in this sense they have their value among those who understand and accept their meaning.

That our bishops should have adopted this particular method of signifying their official aims arises from their necessary association with the Church authorities of Europe, and from their obedience to an older discipline which unites the brotherhood of the Catholic episcopate with its religious head, the Sovereign Pontiff at Rome. To the student of history the process of evolution which created a system of heraldic distinction closely interwoven in many cases with family valor and the secular domain, must be plain enough; and the traditions thus created have exercised their influence upon churchmen in missionary countries newly opened to Catholic Christianity, such as America. The spirit of democracy which has become a real factor in the United States, asserted itself only after the Church had been organically established here, and the task of reconciling or modifying old ecclesiastical institutions (even though they are of a purely external and accidental nature) by the assertion of republican principles is not one that can be performed by civil legislation alone.

Furthermore, it must be kept in mind that these external forms of dignity with their traditional attachments serve chiefly the purpose of maintaining authority in the moral order by elevating it in popular estimation through religious symbols. Ornament and ceremonial further the legitimate aims of authority when they inspire reverence, and hence were always accessory to the proper service of religion in the Old

Testament worship and in the Christian Church. In the same way they become part of the secular public life and create the system of distinctions, titles, and honors conferred in the army and civil service.

On the other hand, it would be mere quibbling to deny that such honors and decorations as have the character of a reward for past services or of a favor, when bestowed on an American citizen by any foreign government, are contrary to the sense and law of the American commonwealth. The only plea on which such distinctions and titles can be accepted by American citizens who claim to carry out the democratic principles of our Republic, is that they are conferred as tokens of actual responsibility or authority in the ecclesiastical, that is the missionary, sphere of religious work. And as a matter of fact these honors have no other meaning to Catholics. Roman counts and marquises and monsignori are not, we believe, recognized as such by the American public in official life. They do not even rank at receptions or public assemblies as do princes and ambassadors of foreign courts, to whom our Government accords their respective honors of precedence by courtesy. Indeed the American could not claim such recognition without forfeiting his American citizenship. Such decorations as go with these titles are of much the same character as the secret-society emblems and titles used in our numerous American fraternities. They are purely private distinctions of class affiliation and as such calculated to inspire respect among the members of these associations.

ECCLESIASTICAL TRAFFIC.

There is no lack of legislation intended to prevent the constantly recurring attempts on the part of individuals to convert the interests of the Church into sources of private gain. The vendors of articles of devotion, the devotees who constitute themselves commissioners of charitable enterprises from which they derive a regular income, the pious nuns who needlessly contract for palatial buildings with a view of creating a debt which strengthens their appeal to charity, the priest who erects a presbytery and church on a scale which betrays the expectation that the place will grow quickly to be a cathedral parish with proportionate accommodations—these and kindred seemingly respectable vagrancies are familiar in city and town. They all make the claim that Catholics in general are bound to give them the patronage of their purses. To prevent irregularities arising from this sort of unauthorized canvassing it is necessary that there should be constant and active supervision.

In this connexion a recent pastoral of Archbishop Glennon may serve as a model. The Archbishop writes:

I desire to call the attention of the clergy and laity of the diocese, especially in the city, to certain regulations that obtain, and which if faithfully observed would tend to minimize if not entirely eliminate certain abuses.

1. It is a rule, for instance, that no one shall *collect moneys for charitable or religious purposes* indiscriminately through the city unless such a person has the permission of the Archbishop, and the same in writing. This rule applies to the priests and Sisters and religious in general, and is especially true of those who come here from the outside. Not unfrequently does it happen that they who travel under religious garb are unworthy of the confidence or patronage of charitable people and sometimes turn out to be fraudulent. Of course, exception may be made in the case of the " Little Sisters of the Poor " or representatives of established charities that are personally known to the charitable public.

2. From time to time the Catholic public are imposed on by unscrupulous agents who would *sell them worthless pictures, cheap literature or tawdry articles of devotion,* demanding for them a price that is exorbitant, and relying on the religious sentiments of their victims to promote a sale.

AN IMPORTANT CASE FOR THE MORAL THEOLOGIAN.

We direct the attention of professors of Moral Theology and of confessors generally to the *Casus Conscientiae* discussed by the Rev. Stephen M. Donovan, Professor in the Franciscan College attached to the Catholic University. The *Dubium Circa Liceitatem Operationis Chirurgicae quae dicitur Vasectomia* is practical for two serious reasons. The operation is in the way of being widely adopted by surgeons as the most expeditious and safe way of preventing physical and moral degeneration. Secondly, it recommends itself to the State boards of charity and education as a means of lessening crime, thus minimizing the responsibility and expenditures for the maintenance of public order and the housing of criminals. Hence measures have been enacted, as will be seen from the statements made below, by which the operation obtains legislative protection, and the question thus becomes one of ethical importance to the lawyer as well as to the physician and confessor. Fr. Donovan also furnishes us the following details regarding the practical aspect of the matter.

In the section on Preventive Medicine and Public Health, at the sixtieth annual session of the American Medical Association, held at Atlantic City, in June of last year, a very interesting and able paper on the subject of vasectomy was read by Dr. C. H. Sharpe of Indianapolis, Indiana, who was, perhaps, the first of the medical profession to advocate the operation as a preventive of crime.

It is the opinion of Dr. Sharpe, and perhaps of physicians generally, that innate criminal propensities, besides being hereditary, are likewise due to definite pathological conditions of the nervous system,—neuronal defects, as he calls them—thus making habitual crime more a matter of physical ailment than a moral evil for which the individual can be held accountable. Allowing the truth of this theory, it can easily be seen what a difficult matter it is for the confessor to draw the line between an objectively sinful act that is deliberate

without much difficulty. But it is somewhat different with the dypsomaniac. How far shall we hold him responsible in the sight of God for the periodical excesses that not seldom bring him to the brink of the grave? The principles laid down by theologians regarding the nature of a sin committed as the result of an acquired habit are true enough in themselves; but their application to particular cases is beset with so many difficulties that a decided feeling of relief comes over us when we hear of the physician's giving new force and meaning to a truth which we all have learned in psychology, namely, that the will, though free, is not supreme.

Whether, however, vasectomy will, in all cases, be productive of the psychical effects claimed for it by Dr. Sharpe and others, remains to be seen. As Dr. F. C. Valentine of New York remarked in the course of the discussion which followed the reading of Dr. Sharpe's paper: "That vasectomy can impart stamina of moral strength, the ability to resist immoral impulses and temptation, as suggested by the author, is, I must confess, an entirely new idea."

In March, 1907, a law was enacted in the State of Indiana making it compulsory for every institution in the State, entrusted with the care of confirmed criminals, idiots, rapists, and imbeciles, to appoint upon its staff, in addition to the regular institutional physician, two skilled surgeons of recognized ability, whose duty it shall be, in conjunction with the chief physician of the institution, to examine the mental and physical condition of such inmates as are recommended by the institutional physician and board of managers. If, in the judgment of this committee of experts and the board of managers, procreation is inadvisable, and there is no probability of improvement of the mental and physical condition of the inmate, it shall be lawful for the surgeons to perform such operation for the prevention of procreation as shall be decided safest and most effective.

and Utah.   And it is expected that before long all the States of the Union will have legislated for the sterilization of habitual criminals, idiots, and other " defectives ".

Criminologists are coming to recognize the fact that criminal habits and tendencies are largely hereditary; and that the most effective and rational method of dealing with crime is that of prevention by sterilization.   Such is the burden of an article on the subject by Judge W. W. Foster of New York, in *Pearson's Magazine* for November, 1909.   In the opinion of the editor " it is the most important contribution that has been made on one of the great social questions of the day ".   Perhaps this savors of exaggeration.   Still, the article is valuable as tending to show the present attitude of jurists, criminologists, and members of the medical profession in regard to this important question.

CELEBRATION OF MASS BY A PRIEST NOT FASTING.

To the Editor, THE ECCLESIASTICAL REVIEW.

In the February number of the REVIEW there is asked a question whether the permission granted to the permanently sick in reference to receiving Holy Communion when not fasting can be extended to infirm priests so that they may celebrate after having broken their fast.

Contrary to the opinion expressed in the response, I do not think that it is allowed.   At least in one case last spring to my own knowledge the permission was refused.   Moreover Father Noldin in his *De Sacramentis* (edition 1908, p. 176) says that this " concessio extendenda videtur ad omnes infirmos (non tamen ad sacerdotes, ut celebrare possint)."

ANDREW BYRNE.

St. Bernard's Seminary, Rochester, N. Y.

Resp.   When we stated that the permission granted to the permanently sick, of receiving Holy Communion without fasting, extended to infirm priests, *under the same conditions*, we reasoned from the logic of the case, saying that the inference seemed legitimate, so long as there was no positive prohibition to the contrary.   It may well be that, for reasons of prudence, and because there is special danger of abuse, the Holy See would forbid this interpretation.   If so we are glad to be corrected; but we should like to be positive and avoid equi-

ANENT THE REFORM IN CHURCH VESTMENTS.

To the Editor, The Ecclesiastical Review.

My hearty congratulations upon the movement you have started for the very desirable reform in our church vestments. Enclosed is a typical letter showing that you have many well-wishers with you in this matter:

> I read in the paper of the conversion of your whole Community (also of the Sisters). Let me sincerely congratulate you. After reading *The Lamp* which you have sent me for some time, I felt that before long you would have to take this step in order to be consistent. May the example of your Society make an impression upon other communities of ritualistic Episcopalians. But please do not be like the Rev. A—— B—— who was once an Anglican and is now a Catholic priest; in his fervor and abjuring of his former faith he looked upon everything he had before used as horrible and sacrilegious; his Gothic chasubles and beautifully shaped stoles, he had quite determined to burn up. I begged him to give them to me, which he did. I blessed them and have used them now for many years. For this missionary locality we are able to readopt the venerable old style of chasuble and stole and ignore the horribly shaped modern French, Spanish, and Italian styles. In Germany, especially in the Archdiocese of Cologne, the ancient pattern is used extensively. How priestly and becoming are also the all-linen albs and surplices.
>
> Sacerdos.

The Lamp, February, 1910.

Your correspondent, although what he refers to has happened

many years ago, will never forget the impression he received when present one day at a High Mass celebrated by Dom Guéranger, Abbot of Solesmes, assisted by two of his monks, who were, like himself, arrayed in Gothic vestments. It was indeed priestly and decorous beyond expression. And Dom Guéranger has good claims to be considered a good judge in all liturgical matters.

Herewith I send you also a beautiful cut of St. Ambrose, in Gothic chasuble and with the ancient low mitre, the model no doubt which inspired St. Charles, whose chasuble you illustrated in your first article. Note that this design is by L. Seitz, the painter so much beloved by the artistic Leo XIII. *Prosit!*   A. B.

THE DOMINICANS AND GOTHIC VESTMENTS.

To the Editor, THE ECCLESIASTICAL REVIEW.

It may perhaps please the readers of THE ECCLESIASTICAL REVIEW who are interested in the reform of church vestments, to know that the Dominican Fathers in Lewiston, Maine, and in Fall River, Massachusetts, have been using Gothic vestments for a good many years, and that they find no trouble in having them made by the ladies of the parish. These same vestments are also used by the Dominicans in Canada.

I have always found these vestments, when well made, to be as convenient as any " violin-case " chasuble. I say *when well made,* because some ladies like to have them nice and *stiff,* and for this purpose put some kind of strong canvas under the lining. In this case the vestment is so inconvenient that it can hardly be used. If the priest will give himself the trouble to oversee the work and explain matters, this can be easily avoided.

FR. THOMAS MARIA GILL, O.P.

THE MAKING OF VESTMENTS.

In reply to questions for directions regarding the proper material, form, measurements, and ornamentation of chasubles, we give below some illustrations indicating the liturgical requirements. The drawing shows the cut of the three kinds of chasubles, showing a section of each in their relative proportions. The middle figure (2) gives a part of the ordinary chasuble which, for reasons of present convenience and economy, would be continued in use at the daily Mass in most

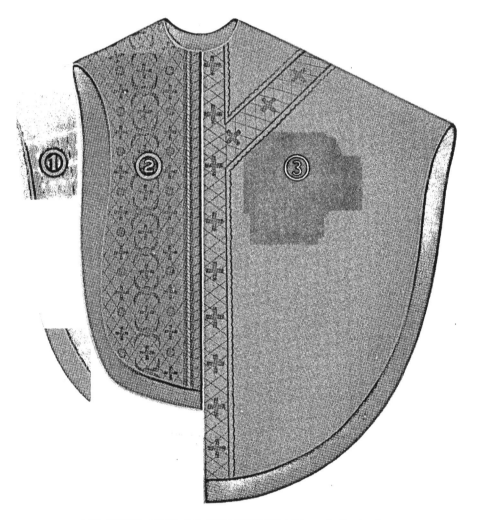

RELATIVE SIZE OF CHASUBLES (*Shown in Sections*)

1   For Use on Festivals in Parish Churches
2   For Daily Use   3   For Cathedrals

rubbing and partial wear of the latter in front and at the sides; and it is infinitely more graceful, draping the figure of the priest more reverently and suggesting the sacrificial and pontifical character of the sacred presbyter. This form of vestment is easily made by any person familiar with the normal art of needle-work. No. 3 shows the more stately form of Gothic vestment suitable for use in Cathedral and monastic churches. This is the style of vestment which the *Caeremoniale Episcoporum* assumes that bishops wear at solemn functions.[1]

The measurements of the three sizes as contained in the following tables are approximately those given in the work by Father Joseph Braun, S.J., on the method of making and ornamenting ecclesiastical vestments.[2]

	PRESENT FORM.	FESTAL FORM.	CATHEDRAL FORM.
	Fig. 2.	Fig. 1.	Fig. 3.
Length from the neck down (back)....	3 ft. 10 in.	4 ft. 1 in.	4 ft. 5⅛ in.
Length from the neck down (front)....	3 ft. 4 in.	3 ft. 8 in.	3 ft. 11¼ in.
Width across shoulders and arms	2 ft. 6 in.	3 ft. 11 in.	4 ft. 11 in.
Width from neck over each shoulder and arm	1 ft.	1 ft. 9⅓ in.	2 ft. 3½ in.

These measurements are simply suggestive and may be slightly modified to suit the size of the person as well as the weight of material used. The form (No. 1), which we have called *festal* or Borromean, permits of some variation. St. Charles is represented as having worn different kinds of chasubles, one of which is preserved in St. Mary Major in Rome, and which he used while he was archpriest of that Basilica. It is more in the shape of our modern chasubles. Shortly before this time, however, Pope Paul IV had attempted to stop the tendency of cutting down the old (Gothic) form of vestments, but his reform appears not to have suc-

---

[1] " Induitur planetâ quae hinc inde super brachia aptatur et revolvitur."— *Caerem. Episcop.* Lib. II, c. 8, n. 19, edit. typica.

[2] *Winke für die Anfertigung und Verzierung der Paramente.* 1904. B. Herder.

ceeded.[8]   St. Charles, applying the method common to the
pastoral prudence of Saints, gradually restored the old custom in Milan without departing greatly from the usage at
Rome.   A chasuble which belonged to the Saint, and which
is preserved in the Cathedral of Milan, has slightly greater
dimensions in width across the shoulders and arms over the one
shown in St. Mary Major at Rome.   It closely approaches the
measurement which we have given here as *festal*.   It is, therefore, only in this sense that it can be called Borromean.   Regarding the demands of material, color, and ornamentation, we
refer the reader to the article on the subject in this and the
preceding number.   For the rest, good judgment and a sense
of propriety must be consulted.

A PROPER DIVISION OF PASTORAL LABOR.

According to St. Paul, a priestly vocation does not imply
the possession of all the gifts which mark the efficient dis-
penser of divine graces in the sacred ministry.   " Quosdam
quidem posuit Deus in Ecclesia, primum apostolos, secundo
prophetas, tertio doctores—exinde gratias curationum, guber-
nationes, interpretationes sermonum . . . Aemulamini charismata meliora.   Et adhuc excellentiorem viam vobis de-
monstro." [1]

Now we have everywhere excellent preachers among our
clergy, also excellent catechists, priests who have the special
grace to attract and make themselves understood by children,
or by the simple-minded faithful.   Of some pastors our people
say that, to have a visit, in sickness, from Father N. is like
having the pain of disease lifted away, and the hope of
better times installed in one's heart.   Other priests again
have a talent for administration: they can raise money without being hard in demanding it and have ways of not accepting it from those who can ill afford to give, yet whose generosity is awakened to aid the priest' effort in other ways.

But half of the effect of these different abilities in different

[8] At least not permanently.   Oldvinus, in the third volume of his *Vitae
Romanorum Pontificum*, speaking of Paul IV, writes: " Pontificum indumenta,
quae a majestate formaque desciverant, suo splendori ac figurae· restituit."
Roma. 1677. 832 cit. apud Braun.

[1] Cf. I Cor. 12 and 14.

priests is neutralized by the good Fathers not being properly harnessed. Father Lingua Sapiens, a good preacher in a large parish, draws the people on Sundays to hear him, though he is known to be a poor hand at building a church, and has too much earnestness to attract the children or the sick by the genial manner which inspires personal sympathy. The following Sunday Father Felix, the second assistant, preaches a lonely sermon, without end, until all grace of patience has dried up in the pews. Father Raucus is singing the High Mass and adds to the tortures by his lack of ear, though people know him to be an admirable organizer and disciplinarian in school. The three priests bear each other no grudge, for they can exchange the compliment of poor preaching, or wretched chanting, or shy ways of meeting people.

In the presbytery parlor an analogous process of contrasts goes on all through the week. Father Prudens knows his theology and can tell what sort of questions to ask when there appears some matrimonial tangle, though he makes a mess of everything he undertakes in a business way, and has all the tramps, book-agents, and promoters after him. All the while Father Practicus sits upstairs wondering when he is going to get a parish, so that he may show the world what he can do in the way of saving money for the Church and doing things according to system and with promptness.

In short, here are three or four men, all bright, willing to work, and respected for their special abilities, hindering and interfering with each other quite unconsciously, the one building up a corner, the other tearing it down to get room for his own addition. This is ecclesiastical, but it is lamentable, and it would not be tolerated by leaders in any great business enterprise in which men combine to attain practical results for the common good.

Obviously it were wiser to distribute their powers in such a way as to permit each to attain a complete success by the use of his special gifts, without exposing him to the risk of failures in other lines, wherein he also lessens the efficiency of his brethren by the gaps he creates in their work. If a priest of ability is selected to fill certain positions and functions for which his gifts fit him, he is likely to be successful and contented. The creditable results which he achieves will enhance the value of the Catholic cause and name. Thus we might have a supply of priests who learn to use their natural powers all the better for being placed in the position where something definite is expected of them, and where credit is given in proportion to their application to their particular duties. The service which demands the use of voice in preaching, or culture in the chant, or practice in administration, church building, hospital work, etc. can be indefinitely developed. The assignment of special tasks can be adjusted as in any other condition of life where men are active for a common service. The project is feasible, at least in some places, and would be apt to elicit imitation wherever it is possible.

The notion that this would militate against the apostolic spirit can be sustained only if we carry such specialization to excess. There is no reason why, under the present system of promotion, a parish priest should be selected simply for administrative ability, excepting in places where such is particularly needed. He can supply what the congregation needs through his assistants. The rector of the Seminary would be a good judge and the bishop a good arbiter (if he were to consult the former) as to where to place young priests, after a test period under a prudent rector; and duties could be easily adjusted. By such methods our people would get a better ministry than they do in most cases, over and above the grace of the sacraments, to which they are to be attracted rather than driven.

A NEW PASCHAL CANDLE.

Qu. Would you be kind enough to give some information on the law requiring a new Paschal Candle annually? If there is such a law, it seems to me to be a good means of swelling the manufacturers' profits.   J. E. M.

Resp. Whilst there is some disagreement among the liturgists as to the obligation of renewing the Paschal Candle for the annual blessing on Holy Saturday,[1] the character of the ceremonial seems to indicate the propriety of having each year a new and unblessed candle for the Paschal celebration.

---

[1] See ECCLESIASTICAL REVIEW, Vol. XVIII, p. 212; also Vol. II, p. 286, and Vol. IV, p. 284.

Coppin, in his *S. Liturgiae Compendium*, seems to have no doubt of the obligation: " Cereus paschalis debet esse (1) novus seu non benedictus, vel saltem totaliter refectus; (2) totus ex cera, et non ex ligno depicto; (3) ex cera albi coloris; (4) ornari potest depicta Crucis effigie ad loca clavorum, deinde effigie Christi resurgentis aliisque insignibus." [2]

A writer who signed his communication " J. F. S.," commenting on this subject in the REVIEW, some years ago, made the following pertinent suggestion: The Paschal Candle is lighted on five Sundays of the Paschal time, and from the beginning of Mass until the end of the Gospel on Ascension Day. It burns for about two hours during the solemn Mass, and for about an hour during Vespers; that is to say, altogether *sixteen hours.* Let the candle manufacturers put " sixteen hour " wicks in their candles, and we will have a new candle each year . . . If the pastor will explain to the people the meaning of the Paschal Candle,[3] he will easily find someone in his parish who will be anxious to have the honor of donating it each year.

OFFICIAL CATHOLIC CHURCH STATISTICS.

The *Official Catholic Directory* for 1910, published by the M. H. Wiltzius Company of Milwaukee and New York, reports a Catholic population of nearly fourteen and a half million (14,347,027) in the United States. There are over eight million inhabitants (8,240,052, according to reports) in the Philippines, Porto Rico, and Hawaii, who profess the Catholic religion. This, with a Catholic population of two and a half million (2,538,374) in Canada, gives us over twenty-five million Catholics for the American continent. The Catholic population under the British flag is estimated at 12,053,418. Deducting from this number the French Canadians and other Latin elements of the population, we have an English-speaking Catholic body of upward of thirty million. And these people are for the most part better conditioned politically, economically, and morally, and, if not more gifted naturally, apparently more intelligent in the practical interpretation of the Catholic faith, than the people of

---

[2] N. 423 (edit. Stimart).
[3] See ECCLESIASTICAL REVIEW, Vol. IV, p. 280 ff.

South America, or of Italy, Spain, and France, where the Catholic Church is being persecuted by the progeny of its Catholic founders, and the faithful Catholic population finds itself in a helpless and irreligious minority amid Catholic institutions and traditions.

As an offset to this statistical estimate of our Catholic population we have the report of the Department of Commerce and Labor in the United States Government Census (released for use after 29 August, 1909), which is in fact an abstract of the first report of the statistics for the year 1906. It summarizes the progress of the Catholic Church in the United States as follows: " In 1890 the Protestant bodies reported 68 per cent of the total (religious) membership; the Roman Catholic Church, 30.3 per cent, and ' all other ' bodies together, 1.7 per cent. The rate of increase shown for the Roman Catholic. Church was 93.5 per cent, more than twice that for all Protestant bodies taken together, 44.8 per cent." Again the report says: " The Roman Catholic Church reported the highest number of members per organization, 969." For the Protestant bodies as a whole, the average number of members per organization was only 104.

As to the virility of religious life among Catholics, when compared to that of the combined Protestant churches representing 185 denominations (in 1906), the Government Census shows that, while the membership in the Catholic Church is nearly equally divided between men and women (49.3 male and 50.7 female), the Protestant bodies as a whole have only 39.3 per cent of male against 60.7 per cent of women communants. Nor is this difference due to the predominant. male element among immigrants who profess the Catholic religion, as is the case with the Russian Schismatic (Greek Orthodox) Church, in which 93.9 per cent of the members are men.

A third contribution to the statistical element of religious bodies in the United States comes from Dr. Carroll's annual

Regarding the balance of the two sexes in the membership
: writes: " In the Roman Catholic Church the sexes are
:arly evenly balanced, 50.7 per cent to 49.3 per cent. In
rotestant bodies the proportion of women is nearly 61, to 39
:r cent men. The increase of the Roman Catholic property,
cording to Dr. Carroll, is over 147 per cent.

In view of the not inconsiderable difference in the statistics
rnished *officially*, it may be asked whether the report of the
'iltzius *Directory* is not swelled beyond the actual figures by
ι optimistic mode of reckoning which accepts as Catholic
erybody who comes within reach of traditional Catholic in-
ience. " He ought to be a Catholic," is a phrase that is fre-
iently applied to a class of men who have no faith, although
ey were baptized in the Catholic Church; and the pastoral
nsus-taker might easily be induced to count such men as
longing to the fold if they become for one reason or another
ancial contributors to our institutional church or allied chari-
s and philanthropies. But, if there be such padding, it is
iily overbalanced by the number of professed Catholics who
ve no permanent domicile and who do not come under the
rsonal observation of a pastor, at least as churchgoers and
quenters of the Sacraments. They are laborers and artisans
o move about from town to town or shift from parish to
:ish, hear Mass and confess where they find a church open,
1 call for the nearest priest when they are about to die;
. no church register contains their names as pewholders or
'ishioners.

f there be reason to glory in a spontaneous increase of num-
s in the Catholic population of our country, because it
:rs hopes of confirming free activity in the exercise of a
e and honest citizenship through the profession and prac-
of the high moral principles inculcated by the Catholic
gion, we must also recognize the unquestionable fact of
1ense losses to the faith among the people who should
m that faith as a birthright. We may assume that th

them false. The defections summarized in his volume entitled *The Decay of the Church of Rome,* are, so to speak, chronic in the Catholic body; they are not formal apostasies, but constant fallings-off through want of caretakers and husbandmen to gather the harvest and prepare the ground for seedtime.   Bishop England's report, seventy years ago, that we had lost nearly three million of the descendants of Catholics, has been corroborated again and again; and we believe that, according to a quotation of Mr. McCabe's from the *N. Y. Freeman's Journal,* there are no less than twenty million people of Catholic extraction in the United States who to-day support the cause of Protestantism in one form or another. That this loss is going on, either from lack of priests or from lack of methods and zeal where we have sufficient priests, need not be doubted in view of the enormous number of people in all walks of life who profess no religion, while they bear the marks of unmistakable Catholic parentage in name or fatherland.

The remedy for this is Catholic organization, Catholic unity, Catholic schools, and, as a result, Catholic life apart from the mere profession of faith.

THE WILTZIUS DIREOTORY AND ITS PREDEOESSORS.

. In commenting on the reports of the Wiltzius *Directory,* referred to in the preceding note on Catholic Church Statistics, we wish to endorse the very efficient work of the Editor, Mr. J. H. Meier, to whom the firm has entrusted the care of the *Directory.* It is accurate as far as it can be made so, and shows evidence of an unusual expenditure of care and labor. This does not mean that faults may not be discovered in it. But the extraordinary usefulness of the volume is not in any measurable degree diminished thereby.   Without such a manual the clergy would be deprived of a valuable means of orientation, almost an essential reference book in some cases. The current issue of the book is a sort of jubilee number, being the twenty-fifth of the series undertaken in 1886 by the Milwaukee firm of Hoffmann Brothers represented to-day by the M. H. Wiltzius Company.

The history of official Catholic Clergy lists and directories for the United States is not one of unbroken success, as might be supposed by those who are unfamiliar with such publication enterprises.

The first attempt at printing an official Directory of the Catholic Church in the States was made nearly a century ago. In 1817 Mr. William Creagh, a New York bookseller, published a list of the missionaries, churches, religious houses and institutions, together with an ecclesiastical calendar and such general information on Catholic topics as might be found in current books of Christian instruction. Five years later, in 1822, Mr. Creagh printed a second issue under the title of *The Laity's Directory to the Church Service.* The volume was revised and corrected by the Rev. John Power of old St. Peter's Church, New York. The demand for the little book must have been limited, for the next publication of a Church Directory was eleven years later, when James Myres, from his " shop " near the Cathedral in Baltimore, Maryland, issued the *Metropolitan Catholic Almanac and Laity's Directory* which kept on appearing every year until 1848.

In 1849 F. Lucas, Jr., took up the publication which had sold in a small 16mo form for twenty-five cents, and of which " the seventeenth number is now offered to the public ", as the preface of that year's issue informs us. In the following year Mr. Lucas enlarged the volume, which appeared regularly each year without alteration, except for the change of firm name to " Lucas Brothers " in 1855.

For the year 1858 we find the publication office of the Directory again in New York, under the title of *Dunigan's American Catholic Almanac and List of the Clergy for 1858.* Messrs. Edward Dunigan and Brother, the publishers, inform us that the task of publishing the Directory was imposed upon them by ecclesiastical authority and that " every copy costs more for printing and paper than it sells for; the advertisements alone enable the publisher to suffer such a moderate loss as he can be reasonably expected to bear." It appears that this volume was ordered to be printed at a late date (in February), after it was found that Lucas had failed to publish the reports. In the issue for the following year (1859), the new publishers, Messrs. John Murphy and Company, of Baltimore, make the statement that Messrs. Lucas Brothers " had declined the farther publication of the Directory ", and that " the late Council of Baltimore by a special resolution requested us to continue the work. We felt it our duty to comply with a request from this high source."

The difficulties which beset the work may be gleaned from the unhesitating avowal of Mr. John Murphy in his issue of the volume for 1861 in which he writes: "A year ago we spoke of the very imperfect method adopted by many of the prelates to indicate the location of the clergy." This does not seem to have roused the prelates to any much greater energy, and as a result the official Directory failed to appear during the two following years, 1862 and 1863. Mr. Peter F. Cunningham, however, was equal to the emergencies as a publisher and issued in the meantime a small *Catholic Register* which had the approbation of the Bishop of Philadelphia, and which bridged over the series until 1864, when the firm of D. & J. Sadlier & Company took up the publication.

Sadlier's Directory was to be a decided improvement on the preceding issues, and so it proved. The publishers announced that they intended to make it permanent, and asked the Catholic Hierarchy to sustain their efforts. Although they had stated in the preface that " It is a matter of little pecuniary benefit to a publisher," the price they fixed upon for the volume aroused criticism, and in 1886, after more than twenty years' possession of the field, a rival Directory was issued by the Hoffmann Brothers of Milwaukee. They not only considerably lowered the price of their volume, but furnished a quarterly Clergy List by way of supplement. If their enterprise resulted in a financial loss which made them resign the publication to its present management, they at least gave the impulse and laid the foundation for an excellence that it would be difficult if not impossible to surpass under present circumstances.

Ecclesiastical Library Table.

The Science of Religion may be treated in a double way: one may investigate the facts, and one may scrutinize their origin, their connexion, and their development. The former part is a mere history of religion, tabulating religious customs, beliefs, and rites according to their documentary evidence. But it is hard for the human mind to know a number of parallel series of facts without comparing them; hence the so-called comparative religion naturally follows the history of religion.

1. **Historical Religion.** *a. Meaning of Historical.* The Rev. F. R. Tennant, D. D., contributed to the *Hibbert Journal*[1] an article entitled " Historical Fact in Relation to Philosophy of Religion " in which he considers the historicity of religious facts. The author first gives the three meanings of the word " historical ", i. e., actual, significant, and belonging to history. He employs the word in the first sense in the course of his present investigation. But then comes the question, how do we know the historical facts of religion? That " historical " must be taken in the sense of " actual " is confirmed by the rationalistic systems of Spinoza, and Hegel, and by science itself. Spinoza and Hegel as well as the scientist must learn their facts from experience or history; their deductions or generalizations are as empty as Kant supposed his categories to be. Dr. Tennant urges the actuality of the past not against any surviving shreds of extreme rationalism, but against a modern tendency to have faith based on what are called " the inwardly verifiable facts of the soul's experience ",

but its knowability is at times questioned in theological circles. Dr. Tennant believes that the method, or the methods, by which the establishment of facts in human history is sought, may be compared with those which are credited with solid results in the concrete sciences of nature. *a.* Large classes of facts are only inferred from their observable effects. The past is involved in the present in the case of human history as much as in that of geological evolution. The impression produced by a great personality on his age presents sufficient ground for arguing back to the historic life that wrought it. *β.* The second general method of establishing historical facts is by means of testimony. Those who discard the value of testimony in the sphere of history are bound in consistency to reject it also in the sphere of physical science. *γ.* The third kind of proof used by historians is again paralleled by a scien-. tific method. A hypothesis is formed to explain or interpret a collection of undisputed facts; if the consequences deducible from this hypothesis are found actually to follow, the hypothesis is said to be verified. The hypothesis in the sphere of history may be that a certain event occurred as testimony asserts it to have done.

c. Value of Historical Knowledge. Is it not strange that after this defence of an actual past, the writer expresses his conviction that historical testimony remains unworthy of absolute confidence? He accords the character of unquestionable necessity only to two kinds of knowledge: first, to the formal knowledge met with in the laws of logic or in the numerical and spatial relations of pure mathematics; secondly, to the knowledge of sense-particulars exclusive of any information whatever as to their relations. Historical truth, he insists, is at best highly probable truth. An historical religion, just because it is historical, can never be wholly a rational religion. Nevertheless, its adoption may be far more reasonable than its rejection. No more, and no less, would I claim for Christianity. The author is more reasonable, when he defends the value of our historical knowledge as far as practical life is concerned. He rejects the " short-cuts " to absolute religious truth through value-judgments, or through immediate individual experience; probability is the guide of life.

istorical Religion may be Scientific. Dr. Tennant does
why a hard line of distinction should be drawn between
religion and historical or revealed religion. The dismay have its uses, but it is not plain why historical
s of one kind should be appropriate data for philo-
ɔ manipulate, and historical elements of another kind
be excluded from the sphere of its operation. For it
ɪe denied that, after all, both historical and natural rest on one kind or another of historical data. The ex-
that Christianity is a " revealed " religion, and that
s which form its basis are too insignificant to form
ces of universally valid truth cannot be urged against
tific character. We can hardly endorse Dr. Tennant's
that Christian revelation would be natural, if philon-
nlarged or revised the common conception of " Na-
As long as philosophy gives a true definition of Na-
ɪristian revelation will always remain supernatural.
ɔther hand, the writer is fairly correct when he points
: the rationalistic habit of mind which demands un-
ɪ truth of reason and despises sense, lies at the root
ontention that the historical facts of Christianity are
ɪnificant to be the sources of universal truth.
nt Literature. We have developed Dr. Tennant's
at great length, because they give the reader a fair
the distinction between the so-called natural and his-
ɪligion, and they introduce him too into part, at least,
cience of Religion. The importance of this subject
inferred from a brief summary of its literature pub-
thin the last few years. E. C. Richardson has given
Alphabetical Subject Index and Index Encyclopœdia
lical Articles on Religion, 1890-1899." [2] Those who
work too bulky or too expensive, may read a care-
pared bibliography of the subject with critical ap-
ɪ of the various publications in the *Revue des Sciences
ɪiques et théologiques.*[3] A work of a different type

be complete in ten volumes of about 900 pages each.[4] The reader will judge concerning the contents of the work from such articles as " The Apostolic Age " by McGiffert, " The Ancient Arabs " by Nöldeke, " Mithracism " by Cumont, and " Buddhism " by de la Vallée-Poussin. The " Transactions of the Third International Congress for the History of Religions "[5] furnish another source of general information on the Science of Religion.

Special questions of the same Science have been treated by a number of writers among whom the following will be found to be of uncommon interest: Fr. Lagrange has studied the Messianism among the Jews of about B. C. 150—A. D. 200.[6] Two lectures on progress in religion delivered by F. Delitzsch and translated by F. L. Pogson[7] dwell upon the question "Whose Son is Christ?" J. Böhmer endeavors to construct an historico-religious framework for the kingdom of God.[8] G. D. Castor considers the kingdom of God in the light of Jewish literature.[9] R. Brook writes on " The Bible and Religion,"[10] explaining religion as experience, and the Bible as a means to resuscitate religious experience. P. Heinisch has studied the Greeks and the Jews in the last century before Christ.[11] The author first gives a picture of Greek culture and Jewish religion, the two elements out of which the Christian religion is said to have developed; but the author opposes to this system of syncretism the many entirely new ideas in Christianity, which imply a new divine impulse in the historic development of religion.

To these works may be added Galloway's " Principles of Religious Development,"[12] Miller's " Cosmic View of God and Man,"[13] Eucken's " Christianity and the New Ideal-

[4] Edinburgh, T. and T. Clark.

[5] Oxford, 1908: Clarendon.

[6] Études bibliques, Paris, 1909: Lecoffre.

[7] London, 1908: Green.

[8] Der religionsgeschichtliche Rahmen des Reiches Gottes; Leipzig, 1909: Dieterich.

[9] Bibliotheca Sacra, LXVI. 344-361.

[10] Interpreter, V. 296-305; 408-418.

[11] Griechentum und Judentum im letzten Jahrhundert vor Christus; Biblische Zeitfragen, I. 12:45. Münster, 1908: Aschendorff.

[12] Macmillan, 1909; p. 363.

ism," [14] Lewis's " Fundamental Principles Involved in Dr. E. Caird's Philosophy of Religion," [15] Warschauer's " Problems of Immanence," [16] Ridsdale's " Essay in Modern Metaphysical Philosophy in its Attitude towards Christianity," [17] Leuba's " Psychological Origin and Nature of Religion," [18] Coe's " Religion and the Subconscious," [19] and Hayes's " What have Facts to do with Faith?".[20]

3. Comparative Religion. *a. Method.* Christianity does not need to fear any true fact or any truly scientific method of research. But the Science of Religion, as it is carried on to-day, is certainly antagonistic to our Christian faith and practice. A. W. Hunzinger clearly shows the consequences of this study; he uses the positions of Troeltsch as representing the views of modern religious scientists. Their principles of immanence, development, and relativity are calculated to destroy not only the supernatural character of Christianity, but to undermine all religion. It is owing to a want of logical consistency on their part that they retain a religion called Christianity, though bereft of every supernatural element. We need hardly add that the adherents of this method subscribe to all the tenets of modern dogma as well as to the ethical monotheism which they ascribe to Jesus Christ. Hunzinger rejects energetically this Christianity built on the principle of immanence, and thus aids indirectly at least the true study of the Bible.

b. M. Reinach's "Orpheus". To illustrate the destructive effect of the modern method followed in the study of the history of religion, we shall briefly indicate the process followed by Solomon Reinach in his *Orpheus*.[21] The book deserves our attention; it has passed through a number of editions in French, and translations are being prepared in English, Ger-

[14] Translated by L. J. Gibson and W. R. Gibson; Library of Living Thought, Harper, 1909; p. 175.

[15] Quelle und Meyer, 1909, p. 62.

[16] Clarke, 1909, p. 242.

man, Russian, Spanish, and Italian.   The device of the work is, *Veniet felicior ætas*, and this happier time will see the destruction of all religions, leaving only the religion of social duty.   In the mean time, man is man indeed, but still obedient to the unreasonable instincts of the animal.   The golden age would have come much sooner, if man had followed the Greek rationalism instead of being swallowed up by the floods of the Eastern cults.   Rationalism began its work again at the time of the renaissance, in the eighteenth century, and in recent days.   It is not surprising to learn that these happy times will free the human mind from all bondage, but it is astonishing that M. Reinach is less intent upon setting free the savages from their horrid superstitions, and the Protestants from the few shreds of religious belief still left to them, than the Catholics.   As one goes on reading the work, one becomes more and more impressed that it is intended as an engine of war against the Catholic Church.

As to the make-up of M. Reinach's work, it opens with an introduction about the origin of religion, then contains six chapters concerning the religion of pagan nations, and finally closes with six chapters on the Jewish and the Christian religions.   Fr. de Grandmaison [22] and Fr. Lagrange [23] take exception to the lack of proportion shown in the *Orpheus*.   Religions professed by millions of believers in India, China, and Japan are dismissed in a few pages, though some of them interest our present time in a special way.   The dualism of the Chaldean and the Egyptian civilizations, the Sumerian question, and the problems of prehistoric Egypt, raised by the publications of MM. de Morgan and Flinders Petrie, have been wholly ignored.

Religion is defined by M. Reinach as the summary of scruples which impede the free exercise of man's faculties.   It is a rather suspicious character of this definition that it eliminates from the fundamental concept of religion what is generally regarded as the object of all religious sentiment; still, the author actually boasts of this discrepancy between

have given a definition of religion. But if he has not defined religion, he has at least destroyed it. An obstacle to
the free exercise of our faculties which springs from scruples,
impedes us only as long as our ignorance lasts. All the duties
and rights of religion have their source in ignorance; here is
M. Reinach's explanation of religion; our only real duty is to
free ourselves from all religious bonds, as it is our duty to
throw off the limitations of our ignorance which restrict the
exercise of our liberty.

As if the author's words were not clear enough, he qualifies
these religious scruples as so many taboos. Though he does
not define the word taboo, he makes it clear that it signifies
nothing but an irrational instinctive prohibition, an heirloom
which man derives from the animal, a categorical imperative
of human nature evolving from pure animality. Even the
Decalogue is nothing but an improved edition of an ancient
code of taboos. Here is the first root of religion; the second
is equally inherited from the animal, for it is animism. It is
true that the animal does not share its psychological confi-
dences with man; but the child and the savage are animists;
they project outside of themselves the will they exercise within themselves, and they people the world with a life and sentiments like their own. Animism, therefore, on the one side,
and the taboo on the other are the two main springs of religion. It is nothing but imagination on the one side and the
other, without reality and deceit, without revelation and im-
posture.

Historically considered, religion needs two more sources,
though they are less primitive than the two already indicated. The taboo appears to be connected with Totemism
or "a kind of worship paid to the animals and vegetables
considered as allied and related to our clan"; while animism
endeavors to subdue and utilize the dreaded and unknown
forces of nature, thus being connected with what M. Reinach
calls magic.

With this explanation of the origin of religion before us,
we may succeed in emancipating ourselves from the "scruples"
which limit the rightful use of our faculties. The taboo dissolves itself into the commands and prohibitions of the common law; animism vanishes into poetry; Totemism and magic

yield to the light of science. Thus man is emancipated from all the shackles of religion. The victory of M. Reinach might be complete, if his definition were correct, if he really explained the origin of a reality instead of describing a figment of his imagination. M. Reinach's religion is not that of the full-grown man, but at best of the savage and the child. But even here it is defective. The taboo only indicates the object whose touch and use is interdicted, without supplying any motive; on the part of the savage, it is fear, however superstitious, of the consequences of his transgression, that makes him respect the taboo. The animal is prevented from eating its young by a mere blind instinct, a real animal taboo; but the savage is prevented by fear and precaution from transgressing the taboo, which implies the belief in certain spiritual beings. Again, the taboo is purely restrictive in its character, while religion implies also the sentiment of admiration and affection for its God.

Fr. Lagrange [24] enumerates a list of inaccuracies of which M. Reinach is guilty in his parallels between the pagan and the Christian religion, and in his statements concerning the pagan beliefs. The reader will probably be more interested in the author's treatment of the Christian religion. He sees in Christian beliefs and practices nothing but purified survivals of the ancient rites of Totemism. The Resurrection, e. g., is explained by the alleged fact that a sacrificed divine animal never dies completely, but always finds a successor after a few days of mourning. M. Reinach is always ready with a number of sinister motives for the actions of the representatives of religion. Jesus offends the temple merchants in Jerusalem, St. Paul offends the venders of pious articles in Ephesus, Zola offends those who have a material interest in the devotions at Lourdes. When he comes to explain the origin of Christianity, and the Gospels in particular, the influence of M. Loisy is felt throughout. The citations of Scripture found in the Apostolic Fathers who lived before A. D. 150 must all be referred to the Old Testament. It was Marcion who about that time formed the first collection of books which anyway resembled our present idea of a Canon. No gospel was

[24] L. c., pp. 134 ff.

written by an eyewitness; the texts which appear to imply the contrary, are explained away with the help of one or another of Loisy's principles. Moreover, what is represented as a possible or plausible hypothesis by Loisy, is put forth as gospel truth by M. Reinach.

Nor can it be said that M. Reinach did not see whither his work tended; he assures us that he weighed his responsibility before he took it on him. Moreover, he professes to have written in such a way that his book can be read by the young as well as the old. Let us hope that a kind Providence will prevent the realization of his promise to publish in the future another work fit to be read only by " mothers ".

Criticisms and Notes.

HISTORY OF MEDIEVAL PHILOSOPHY. By Maurice De Wulf, Professor at the University of Louvain. Third edition. Translated by P. Coffey, D. Ph., Professor of Philosophy, Maynooth College, Ireland. New York, London: Longmans, Green, & Co. 1909. Pp. xii–519.

DIE GESCHICHTE DER SCHOLASTISCHEN METHODE nach den gedruckten und ungedruckten Quellen dargestellt von Dr. Martin Grabmann, Professor der Dogmatik am bischofl. Lyceum zu Eichstätt. Erster Band. Freiburg im B., St. Louis, Mo.: B. Herder. 1909. Pp. xiii–354.

The two books here introduced are mutually supplementary. The former is distinctively a history of the various systems of philosophy prevailing in the Middle Ages, while the latter is a history of the scholastic method, as such, which rose, developed, and reached its highest perfection during the same period. Professor De Wulf in his present work, as he has done in its predecessor, *Scholasticism Old and New* (English translation, 1907), keeps the distinction well defined between medieval philosophy and medieval theology. The former includes besides scholastic various other medieval systems of philosophy, alien and opposed to but synchronous with scholasticism. Medieval philosophy, especially its main current, the scholastic, drew its materials from many tributaries—chiefly, of course, from those that flowed through Greece, from Socrates, Plato, and Aristotle; also from the Neo-Platonists; likewise from the Fathers, notably St. Augustine. This multiplicity of origin makes it necessary for Professor De Wulf to begin his work with an outline of the Greek and Patristic philosophies (pp. 1-89). The narrative then proceeds through the first, the formative, period of scholasticism from the ninth to the close of the twelfth century (pp. 125-239) onwards to the highest development of medieval speculation attained in the works of St. Thomas (pp. 240-410). Then comes the period of decline during the fourteenth and the first half of the fifteenth century (pp. 411-459), followed finally by the transitional stage in which the new philosophies grew up, partly out of the old trunks, with many a fresh, if not always a vigorous, much less a fruitful, engrafting of their own. Over these fields of speculation Professor De Wulf conducts his readers, the while pointing out like an experienced guide the peculiarities of the landscape and the leading types of flora and fauna; but, much more like a trained student of nature, dwelling mostly on the geology of the ground he is traversing and pointing out the agencies that have diversified the surface, uplifted the hills, carved out the valleys and made the soil; indicating also how the various strata have been deposited and arranged; how their living types are interrelated; how their primal materials were formed and ordered out of the original chaos. But while thus playing the rôle of the expert naturalist, the author bids his observers note the sources whence he has drawn his knowledge and to which they may go for fuller information. The bibliographical apparatus of the volume, if not quite exhaustive, is ample in original and derivative material. The whole work is one which the earnest Catholic student will welcome as furnishing him with the fullest reliable exposition of the origin and medieval development of his philosophy to be found in the English language. He has already had at command a compendium of the same subject in Dr. Turner's general *History of Philosophy.* He has here its expansion and abundant documentation. The translator has done his work well, the rendering being clear and readable. The publishers, too, have added their share to making the book attractive. To non-Catholic readers likewise the work cannot fail of being instructive. They may by it be disabused or defended from the very general prejudice that no philosophy deserving serious attention existed during the thousand years of the Middle Ages; while it may serve to correct the erroneous and garbled accounts of medieval thought given with hardly an exception by the non-Catholic text-books on the history of philosophy hitherto written in English.

original and derivative sources. He has laid the great European libraries under contribution for manuscript materials and he has enjoyed the co-operation in his research of the late eminent archivist, Heinrich Denifle. The result, so far as the present volume embodies it, is a thorough presentation of the method and, by consequence, of the main contents of early scholasticism. The term scholasticism, however, must be here divorced not only from those unworthy associations with which prejudice has linked it, but also from those partial and imperfect conceptions under which it sometimes lives even in Catholic minds. After separating its true meaning from these false and one-sided interpretations, Professor Grabmann sums up his own definition substantially thus: The scholastic method is an endeavor by the application of reason, philosophy, and revelation, to obtain an insight into the contents of faith, in order thus to assimilate supernatural truths to the reflective understanding and so to facilitate a systematic synthesis of their totality, and also to enable the mind to meet the objections raised by natural reason against those truths. In its gradual evolution the scholastic method developed a technical external form in which it expressed and embodied itself (p. 37). It would be interesting to dwell upon the significance of this carefully formulated definition; but space forbids. Obviously the definition draws a clearly marked line between the inwardness and the outwardness of the thing; between the scholastic method as an ideal on the one hand, and its technical apparatus on the other hand. Moreover, the definition gives scholasticism its true place in the history of attempts at constructing world-views, complete syntheses of the totality of truth—an overly ambitious attempt, it may be thought, but none the less an actual, a historical attempt, an attempt which the mind is forced to make, if not in virtue of its natural constitution, at least by the fact that it is the receptacle of two orders of truths, natural and supernatural, truths which, lying side by side, in the same spiritual faculty clamor to their possessor for co-ordination into a complete harmonious synthesis. The most satisfactory answer to this demand has been reached by the scholastic method and is set forth in scholasticism as the resulting system. For the proof of this assertion we must refer the reader to the work at hand. The present volume covers only the Patristic beginnings and after-development down to the twelfth century. A second volume, now in perparation, is to carry the subject as far as the thirteenth century; whilst a third, the concluding volume, will tell of the scientific *Arbeitsweise* of St. Thomas and his great contemporaries—that is, of the highest perfection of medieval scholasticism.

GRUNDRISS DER BIOLOGIE oder die Lehre von den Lebenserscheinungen und ihren Ursachen. Von Hermann Muckermann, S.J. Erster Teil: Allgemeine Biologie. Freiburg i. Br., St. Louis, Mo.; B. Herder. 1909. Pp. xiv–173.

ELEMENTA PHILOSOPHIAE ARISTOTELICO–THOMISTICAE. Auctore P. Jos. Gredt, O.S.B. Vol. I. Ed. altera. Friburgi, St. Louis, Mo.: B. Herder. 1909. Pp. xxv–496.

Two books that at parts overlap. About one third of the latter volume is devoted to philosophical biology—that is to the fundamental principles of living organisms—while the former volume approaches the same truths from a more empirical gateway. Father Gredt after long experience in the field of philosophy adopts the plan of the older masters of placing natural philosophy at the very basis of the science. Accordingly, having explained Dialectics, he at once takes up *ens mobile,* descends into its nature, and, discussing the various hypotheses devised to explain it, comes forth satisfied with the hylemorphic theory alone. He then follows the properties of the *ens mobile,* as they flow from its essence, i. e. motion, time, space, quantity, and the rest. Next comes the *ens mobile animatum,* carrying the student into the domain of life where he observes and reflects on the phenomena and nature of organized life, in plant and animal, until finally he rises to the consideration of human life—the essence, properties, and faculties of the soul which is distinctive of man. The volume therefore deals with formal logic and philosophical physics including herein philosophical biology as it terminates in human psychology. A second volume, embracing Ontology (which as Metaphysics will include Epistemology and Theodicy) and Ethics, is in course of preparation. For the rest, as we have already recommended the work on the occasion of its first edition,[1] it may suffice here to re-emphasize what was then said in its praise, and to add that in its present form it is brought to a still higher degree of excellence both as regards the development and the disposition of its subject-matter. Its discussion of the nature of bodies and of life, while following the lines of the *philosophia perennis,* takes account of the modern physico-scientific theories.

The student who desires fuller information on the latter subjects can hardly·do better than to familiarize himself with Father Muckermann's *Grundriss der Biologie.* The present section of this work deals exclusively with General Biology. After an introduction on the biological sciences generally, their history and present

---

[1] ECCL. REVIEW, Vol. XX, p. 553.

concentration on the cell, the author gives an outline of the chemical constitution of organisms. The immediately sequent chapters deal with the structure, "the irritability", nutrition, development, propagation of cells. The closing chapters discuss the problems of heredity and the origin of cells, i. e. of organisms and hence of organic life. While distinct and in a manner independent in itself as an outline of General Biology, the present volume is only the first section of an extended work designed to be an exposition of Philosophical Biology approached from an empirico-scientific method. The other volumes of the series at present preparing are to treat: (1) of the organic world and the problem of evolution; (2) the biology of multicellar plants; (3) of multicellar animals; (4) the human nervous system and the senses. The program here outlined, it will be noticed, meets precisely that side of our philosophy which calls for development. Some excellent work indeed has already been accomplished on these lines, both by our more recent works in Latin, including the one introduced above, but more especially by those in the modern languages: by Maher in English, Gutberlet and Wasmann in German, Mercier in French, and by others. Much more, however, still remains to be done. The present contribution by Father Muckermann carries us considerably forward. It is an up-to-date exposition of the principal phenomena of organic life. While leaving out nothing of importance, it does not lose the reader in a wilderness of detail so as to obscure his vision of general principles. He is allowed to see the trees without missing the woods. The method is scientific but the technicalities are made plain by the author's clear writing and the addition of many illustrations. The figures and tables are for the most part excellent, distinct, and intelligible. Though not so minute as Wilson's well-known book on the cell—the general lines of which it follows—the volume is comprehensive enough in relation to its purpose as laying the empirical groundwork of a philosophy of organic life.

LES SEIZE CARMELITES DE COMPIEGNE: Leur Martyre et leur Beatification –17 Juillet, 1794 et 27 Mai, 1906. Par le R. P. Dom Louis David, O. S. B. Fort volume in 12, avec belle gravure. Pp. 162.

THE MARTYRS OF COMPIEGNE. Compiled by Eleanor Mary Willson. With Preface by D. Gilbert Dolan, O. S. B. Art and Book Company, Cathedral Precincts, Westminster. 1907. Pp. xiv–131.

The solemn Beatification in May, 1906, of that Virgin band of martyrs known as the sixteen Carmelites of Compiègne, who were beheaded on 17 July, 1794, at Paris, as the victims of the brutal fanaticism evoked by the Revolution, has directed attention to some examples of heroic holiness, almost forgotten, who died in the prisons of the French Republic—priests, monks, and nuns. Among the latter we have in this very account of the Carmelite martyrs the beautifully interwoven story of some English Benedictines who were imprisoned under the same roofs, and who incidentally became important witnesses and promoters in the process of Beatification of the Carmelite martyrs.

We have placed the French volume first, not because it has served as the original from which the English version might appear to be an abstract, but because the author has been in touch with and has used original documents in the possession of the Carmelite monastery of Compiègne, just as the compiler of the English volume has been able to avail herself of original sources furnished her by the English nuns of Stanbrook Abbey. These religious have been the keepers of the documents, traditions, and relics, which closely associated their religious sisters of a century ago with the beautiful choir of virgin martyrs whom their successors are privileged to honor as saints to-day. Apart from these features which distinguish the two volumes, the story is one that deeply moves and edifies, well told in either language. Both writers have, of course, drawn largely from the " Depositions " of witnesses who were examined during the process of Beatification ; also from a history written by one of the nuns, a contemporary of the Carmelite martyrs, who lived in the same monastery, and who by a mere accident, which she bitterly regretted all the rest of her life, was absent when the community was imprisoned and martyred. She lived for forty years after the martyrdom, and at the instance of her superior, Mgr. Villecourt, Bishop of Rochelle, and afterward Cardinal, she wrote the account of her sisters amid great physical sufferings. The MS. was published after her death, in 1836.

Besides these sources, which include references to several memoirs of the Carmelites at Compiègne by Canon Auger and the Abbé d'Auribeau, Madam Willson has had at her service a number of original documents preserved by the Benedictine nuns of Stanbrook Abbey, Worcestershire. As we have already mentioned, some English nuns were in the same prison with the Carmelites. Their cells were opposite each other. They had been there for several months and were to remain until after four of their number had died of ill-treatment, starvation, and cold. Dame Anne Teresa Partington was one of the survivors, and in a touching narrative she tells as an eyewitness how the French nuns departed taking affectionate leave also from their Benedictine Sisters whom they were not allowed to approach, by the motion of their hands. She relates in the words of Monsieur Donai, reliable eyewitness, how the Carmelites went to the scaffold, how beautifully they said the Litany of the Blessed Virgin, and how by an unlooked-for providence they suffered on the very feast of their patroness, Our Lady of Mt. Carmel. She bears incidental witness also to the testimony of Sister Mary of the Incarnation, whose story has been referred to above as a chief source of information regarding the character and personality of the sixteen virgin-martyrs of Compiègne. " One of this holy community," she writes, " happened to be absent when the rest were taken to Paris. She concealed herself in different places till the death of the tyrant, Robespierre, which happened on 28 July, 1794. When this monster was removed, she returned to her friends in Compiègne, and frequently visited us in prison. She gave us the names and ages of her sisters who were put to death." It appears that the mayor of Compiègne had called at the prison some days after the execution of the Carmelites with the purpose of bidding the Benedictines to prepare for a like end. They were in want of shoes and other garments; and when they informed the official of this fact, one of the jailers answered: " You will not want shoes long." But the mayor went into the opposite cells where the Carmelites had been but a few days before, and finding there some garments he brought them over to them. He did not realize how greatly valuable these clothes were to the Benedictine nuns, for they were precious relics of their martyred sisters. At Stanbrook are also documents which throw further light on the relations of the two communities to each other. Among the latter is a letter from the Abbess of the Benedictines at Woolton. It is addressed to Mother Mary Bernard, stating that the Abbess was sending her some relics of the Carmelite martyrs with whom she had been imprisoned at Compiègne. The signature, beautifully characteristic, is: " From your obliged humble servant MARY BLYDE, *Abbess Unworthy*."

But we have indicated sufficient of the contents of this biography to awaken the interest of those who love to read history in its best types of heroic devotion to religious ideals exemplified by those who in many respects bear the tokens of our common human weakness. One learns from these examples that to become saints we need not so much be gifted with virtue as to strive after it and to value sacrifice for its attainment.

THESAURUS CONFESSARII seu brevis et accurata summa totius Doctrinae Moralis. Auctore R. P. Josepho Busquet e Congregatione Filiorum Imm. Cordis B. M. V., Utriusque Juris Doctore atque Theol. Moral. Professore. Editio quinta, digestior, locupletior, castigatior. Bloud & Cie: Paris. Pp. 784.

To students of theology this portable and well-printed volume will prove a useful compendium both for a general review of moral theological questions and a reference book in doubts. Its arrangement is thoroughly scientific and therefore in the field of morals thoroughly practical. It gives the reader in the first place clearly expressed and well-limited definitions. In the next place, it states the principles upon which the use of doctrine and law in moral theology is to be based in each case, so as to permit legitimate application to human action. In the presentation of his subject the author follows the topical divisions and groupings of the older moralists, chiefly St. Alphonsus Liguori: *Actus humani—Conscientia —Leges—Peccata—Sacramenta—Poenae et Indulgentiae.* These questions are treated quite exhaustively, yet without needless verbiage; rather, like closely knit framework they fit and dovetail in such manner as to illustrate one the other in logical sequence. Everywhere account is taken of recent legislation, in the matter especially of the *nova forma Sponsalium et Matrimoniorum*; regarding stipends for Masses, daily Communion, reform of the Roman Curia, etc. To have these subjects treated succinctly and clearly is of great value to the average busy priest on our missions no less than to the theological student.

It is to be noted, however, that the author wrote his *Thesaurus* chiefly for the Spanish clergy; and this has led him to overlook certain important modifications of ecclesiastical law applicable to English-speaking countries. Thus the explanation of the *lex abstinentiae et jejunii* fails to refer to the indult for the families of workingmen, granted 15 March, 1895, and renewed 8 February, 1905, by which the use of flesh meat is allowed once a day on fastdays, with four exceptions.

Literary Chat.

morbid sensationalism. M. Nicolay's *Histoire des Croyances*, it need hardly be said, is a study in the fundamental supernatural beliefs of the various races and nations of men—a contribution to the history of religions not unlike the Abbé de Broglie's *Problèmes et Conclusions de l'Histoire des Religions;* though it approaches its subject from the standpoint of law and conduct—the decalogue being taken as the nucleus—while M. de Broglie is more concerned with speculative truths and doctrines. In his latest book M. Nicolay has given, if not so comprehensive a study of the field as he had surveyed in the preceding work, certainly a proportionately interesting summary of the practices of many peoples in regard to mortal crimes and penalties. Students who may be looking for information pertinent to capital punishment, homicide, war, human sacrifices, cannibalism, will probably find what they are looking for in this uneuphoniously entitled bloody story.

Until rather recently some of us were lamenting a dearth of solid and reliable works, by Catholic authors, on the history and science of religions. *Some* were complaining, but others seemed to be content that there were no such books, since the things of the sanctuary were thus being kept out of the laboratory. However, farther-seeing minds discerned that if the history and the science of religions—there is, of course, only one true religion, but there are many false religions more or less divergent from and contrary to the true—were to be saved from naturalism and materialistic evolutionism, if they were to be made allies not enemies of revealed truth, then must they be cultivated by Catholic minds, by minds having a view of the whole, the domain of faith as well as of history and science. And so it is gratifying to note our growing literature in this department. In English, it is true, we have not as yet many works of this kind. Still there are the excellent little booklets published by the Catholic Truth Society, with the promise of more such. Even in French there has been until lately little up-to-date literature available, outside of the two works above-mentioned by de Broglie and Nicolay. For the past year or two, however, the number of books of the class in question has multiplied rapidly. In the first place there are three distinct series in course of publication: The *Études sur l'Histoire des Religions* publishing by Beauchesne, and the *Bibliothèque d'Histoire des Religions* by Lethielleux, and the *Histoire des Religions* by Bloud et Cie. The former series was initiated by Bishop le Roy's *La Religion des Primitifs,* which is one of the very best studies in savage cults thus far produced. The book was previously reviewed in these pages. Of the second series just mentioned *La Religion des peuples non civilisés* par A. Bros, has also been previously recommended in the REVIEW. The latest accession to the same series is *Doctrines religieuses des Philosophes Grecs* par M. Louis (Lethielleux). It is a strong, an illuminating, and in many respects an original study of the religious attitude of the Greek thinkers from the earliest records to the time of Justinian. With sure philosophic penetration the author discerns the dominantly religious tendency pervading Hellenism and its consequently providential relation as a pedagogue to Christianity. At the same time and indeed because of this relationship, he shows how the return to Hellenism advocated by some recent writers would mean not simply turning back the hands on the dial but a reversal of the wheels of true human progress, moral and intellectual as well as material.

Still another series of works, one devoted, that is, to the Oriental religions, is initiated by M. Roussel's *La Religion Védique* (Paris, Téqui). The author is professor of Sanscrit at the Fribourg University (Switzerland) and writes with authority on the religion of the Vedas. He treats of the Vedic beliefs —the various deities—as well as the forms and ideals of worship; and at the same time proves that Vedism is not the primitive religion as some would have it. So far from its being the naive expression of early man's spontaneous reverence for nature, M. Roussel shows that the most authentic documents reveal it to be the outcome of a long traditional process of beliefs and practices that indicate religious and moral decadence instead of progress.

We have on a former occasion called attention to the brief essay on *Védisme* by M. de la Vallée Poussin. The same writer has recently produced a similar monograph on Brahmanism (*Le Brahmanisme*). It is published in the well-known series of *Histoire des Religions* by Bloud et Cie (Paris). Besides the succinct but illuminating account of the origin and growth of the dominating caste in Hindu life, religious, political, and social, the booklet contains a summary of the Vedanta, the essential philosophy of the Upanishads. The epitome is adapted from Deussen's well-known work in German, and, besides its historical value as an account of probably the profoundest product of the Indian mind, it is suggestive of the similarity to it and retrogressiveness of the modern systems of monism. Here again is there seen to be nothing new, in philosophical constructions, under the sun.

M. de la Vallée Poussin has also recently contributed a volume to the series above-mentioned (*Études sur l'Histoire des Religions*) entitled *Bouddisme, Opinions sur l'Histoire de la Dogmatique* (Paris, Beauchesne et Cie). The subtitle indicates both the spirit and the scope of the study. The author, unlike many of the camp-followers in the army of Buddhistic scholars, recognizes the obscurity that still enshrouds the subject—the documents, sources, and contents of the system that claims Cakyamuni for its founder. He presents, therefore, the best results of his research as opinions, reserving for himself the liberty of modifying them should the interests of newly-discovered truth so demand. Moreover, he limits his work to the doctrinal history, his effort being to present simply the genuine teachings, religious and philosophical, of Buddha and his disciples. The work is therefore purely historical and not apologetical or theological. At the same time the author does not conceal his opinion regarding the modern craze after Buddhism that has affected many minds especially in this country as well as in England and Germany. The system of Gautama has come to be looked upon as singularly privileged in the religious history—as having a purely rationalistic philosophy, an ideal compatible with modern science, an ethics without God or soul, and much more that does it *beaucoup trop d'honneur* (p. 2). "Some savants and many that are not so, tell us," says M. Poussin, "that Europe ought to go to school to Cakyamuni. On this point one might find somewhat summary the opinion of Barthélemy Saint-Hilaire. 'The only, but the immense service that Buddhism can render us is by its sad contrast to make us better appreciate the inestimable value of our own beliefs.' At bottom, however, the pupil of the great Orientalist Burnouf is right; it would be folly 'to exchange the bread of Western thought for the narcotics of the bhiksus' (the yellow-robed mendicant monks). 'Even after Buddhism has been stript of its immense baggage of trifles and silliness, and with proper pressure reduced to a sort of mystic positivism,' says M. Barth, 'nothing short of an incredible capacity for illusion is needed to pretend to extract from it anything that can be of service to us.' As to what is called Neo-Buddhism, 'it is enshrouded with a thick fog of credulity and charlatanry.'" This verdict of M. Barth is severe, but M. Poussin considers it just and he further adds that "one would waste one's time in trying to prove that Cakyamuni can teach us either philosophy or morality" (p. 4). This pronouncement of so eminent an authority as is M. Poussin is worth noting. It is, however, incidental to his work, which, as was said above, is purely expository, and is therefore the kind of book the student wants in order to get as near as possible to the real beliefs and speculations of a system that claims the allegiance, at the lowest estimate, of one-twelfth of the human race.

its form to-day may not hold good of its stage to-morrow. However, the writer has had this necessity of adjustment in view, and has happily seized the salient characteristics of the movement and formulated such general judgments as seem most likely to have longest endurance. These centre on the Moslem doctrine of the future life, fatalism, almsgiving, belief in Christ and His Mother, pilgrimages, warfare, the position of women, children and education, mysticism. Upon all these points the author says many things that are instructive, important and interesting. Especially is this the case with the closing chapter on the future of Islam. Such a contingency, as some have prognosticated, of a pan-Islamite invasion of the West he shows to be practically impossible. The political consistency of the Moslem peoples is far from adequate to such an effect. Nor is their religious coherence sufficient to balance the political divergencies. Besides, throughout Moslemdom there is an ever-growing upper stratum that is steadily evolving Western ideas and forms of material progress. The Young Turks are now fairly ubiquitous in Islam, and all are striving to assimilate European progress, many of them willing to sacrifice all but their essential religious beliefs, ready to go to school to Western teaching, and willing even to accept European domination for the sake of European civilization. The author sees in this approach of the Islamic East toward the West a hopeful sign which Europe should welcome and foster in the interests at least of human brotherhood if not of religious unity—indications of the latter being as yet below the horizon.

When the priest is asked, as he often is by young laymen, for advice as to what to read on Socialism, he need feel himself at no loss for an answer. What with books like those of Cathrein, Goldstein, Ming, Kress, Devas, and the lectures, tracts, etc. of which there are many, he can easily guide the inquirer. When, however, he is asked for some good solid and readable work (in English) on Sociology or Social Science or the Philosophy of the State, he finds himself at a loss what to say or where to look; for indeed there is not, we believe, any such work to be found, outside the few text-books of Ethics which devote some pages to Sociology. The field is one which Catholic scholars have yet to till.

It was this lack and this corresponding need that induced Father McLoughlin (Mt. Melleray, Ireland) to translate from the Italian a book which in English bears the title *The Elements of Social Science and Political Economy* (Dublin, Gill & Co., 1909). He has designed it "especially for use in colleges, schools, clubs, gilds, etc.," and doubtless it should meet this purpose, as such organizations have teachers and directors who ought to be able to utilize the work as a text-book. There is a great deal of important truth compressed into the ninety-odd pages devoted to Social Science, and to the somewhat smaller number of pages given to the topics that are grouped under Political Economy. To fix these giants upon what seems so Procrustean a couch has called for considerable skill and demands no less competent a demonstrator of the structure and significance of the members and tissues thus compressed. We fear the translator has been too considerate for his author and not quite enough so for his readers. The version will be clear enough to the attentive eye, but is not to be read by the running. Perhaps, however, it is best so. He that has to stop to look that he may see, will see most and longest. Anyhow the work is solid, thoughtful, comprehensive enough, and suggestive.

———

Passing from these outlines of Social Science to Professor Peabody's recent volume, *The Approach to the Social Question* (New York, The Macmillan Co.), one gets a sense of roomy liberty. The former book is mainly a summary of primary social and economic principles and their more immediate inferences, the latter a discursive consideration of the ways of adjusting the individual to society. How to maintain the two factors of experience—the individual and the social whole—"each without sacrificing the other, how to be a person and at the same time an efficient member of the social body; how to realize personality in terms of the common good—this in its many forms of statement is the Social Question," as Professor Peabody rightly conceives it to be (p. 19). The question "may be asked in terms of the family, where a man or a woman, conscious of individual rights, is at the same time a member of a group whose stability depends on sacrifice and service. It may be asked in terms of philanthropy; it may be asked in terms of the industrial order, where employer and employed have their distinct functions to perform, while the total movement of economic life holds them in its service." Usually, of course, it is asked and solutions are offered in the latter, the economic, sense. Professor Peabody views it, however, in its larger meaning of individual and social coördination. His main purpose is to analyze and illustrate this conception. He approaches it from the points of view of philosophy, social science, economics, ethics, and religion. That in working out so complex a program, in which science, philosophy, and religion are inextricably intertwined, the author makes some statements from which a Catholic must differ need hardly be emphasized—especially when it is remembered that the author is a Unitarian and no believer in our Lord's personal divinity. On the other hand, apart from such statements (and they are not so many as one might expect), the present volume, like its predecessor *Jesus Christ and the Social Question*, contains many wholesome truths, happily expressed, which one rejoices to meet with and to endorse. The educated Catholic student, especially the priest, will do well to read both books.

We have called Professor Peabody's work a "discursive consideration". It is reflective and theoretical, with practical applications close at hand. Students who wish to approach the same problem from a more detailed, analytico-scientific standpoint should read *Psychological Interpretations of Society*, by Michael M. Davis, Ph.D. It is one of the recent "Studies in History, Economics, and Public Law" emanating from Columbia University, and is published by the Longmans. Those who see no use in a sociology that does much more than prove that society is natural, not the result of mere compact, and has as an end the public weal—truths indeed which one may never cease insisting on but which call for a fuller and more concrete setting than they receive in our class-books—readers, in a word, who are content with social generalities should leave this book alone. They would only be distracted by the *cui bono?* query. Earnest inquirers, however, into the concrete interpretation of that abstract "property" of human nature called sociality; students especially who are endeavoring to keep abreast with the trend of present-day research into the psychological springs and laws of social life, will probably be helped by reading Mr. Davis's book, even should they find themselves unable to agree with all its facts and inferences.

Several communications have come to us from members of Religious Orders and others endorsing our plea for better and more tasteful ecclesiastical

and "De Ritibus Servandis in Cantu Missae," but it is likewise a fine piece
of liturgical bookmaking, offered at so reasonable a price that there is no excuse for its absence from any priest's library.

The Department of State, Washington, has sent out a note under the heading *The so-called "Spanish Swindle"*, in which Americans are warned against
an organization having its centre at Barcelona, with confederates not only in
the United States but in most other countries. Their work has been going on
for nearly twenty years, and in the main consists of an appeal from a political
prisoner of wealth in behalf of his daughter whose hidden fortune can be
restored through the advance of a small sum of money by distant friends.
These good people are to receive eventually a large share of the estate, but
their coöperation must be kept secret. What elicits our interest in the matter
is the fact that one of the central figures in this scheme represents himself
as a Spanish priest who ostensibly acts as the confidential agent in the case.
The story is one of knavery both as a scheme of obtaining money under false
pretences and as discrediting the "good priest" who is represented as both
fool and villain, though he is doubtless only a fiction.

We propose soon to give an extended review of Dr. Otis Cary's two volumes of *A History of Christianity in Japan* (Fleming H. Revell Co.). It is
a creditable piece of work from a non-Catholic witness. Incidentally we want
to note here that Prof. Harlan P. Beach of the Divinity School of Yale, who
has treated the subject in a very different and bigoted way, somewhat weakens
his own former testimony in referring to this work by praising Dr. Cary
(though, we believe, justly) as "one of the most scholarly among the entire
Japanese missionary force," and by declaring that Dr. Cary's book is "not
only remarkably accurate and symmetrically complete, but," etc.

The *Dublin Review* has been regaining its prestige of earlier days since
Wilfrid Ward became its editor. The subscriber gets a substantial return of
well-presented information on topics of interest to the present-day educated
Catholic; at the same time there is nothing ephemeral about the contents of
the magazine. The article which particularly attracts our attention in the
January number is that by Hilaire Belloc. Under the title *The International*
the author lays bare the true details of the Ferrer trial, and asks the very
pertinent question why these facts have been withheld from the general reading public throughout Europe and America. The evidence points to the existence of a highly organized, powerful, international association, whose operations in this and other similar political instances seem to coincide with the
outbreaks of simultaneous and equally organized attacks upon the Catholic
Church, and which suggest kindred origin and opposition. Mr. Belloc promises to answer the riddles thus raised in a second article.

Books Received.

THEOLOGICAL AND DEVOTIONAL.

A Treatise on the True Devotion to the Blessed Virgin. By the
Blessed Louis-Marie, Grignon de Montfort. Translated from the original
French by Frederick William Faber, D.D., Priest of the Oratory. With a
Preface by Cardinal Vaughan, Archbishop of Westminster. New York,
Philadelphia: P. J. Kenedy & Sons. 1909. Pp. xix-198.

Jésus. Quelques traits de la Physionomie morale de Jésus. L'enseignement ascétique de Notre-Seigneur; la pédagogie de Notre-Seigneur; Jésus dans ses relations avec les hommes; Prédication de Notre-Seigneur au point de vue didactique et oratoire. Par le R. P. Maurice Meschler, S.J. Ouvrage approuvé par Sa Grandeur Mgr. l'Archevêque de Fribourg en Brisgau. Traduit de l'allemand par l'abbé Christian Lamy de la Chapelle. Paris: Beauchesne & Cie. 1910. Pp. 169. Prix, 1 fr. 60, *franco.*

Graduale S. Romanae Ecclesiae: De Tempore et de Sanctis. SSi D. N. Pii X P. M. jussu restitutum et editum. Cui addita sunt festa novissima. Romae: Typis Vaticanis. MDCCCCVIII. Pp. xvi-335 and xxiii-559 (208 and 156). Price for two volumes bound, $2.75.

Theologie und Glaube. Zeitschrift für den Kath. Klerus, herausgegeben von den Professoren der Bischöfl. philosoph. theolog. Fakultät zu Paderborn: Drs. A. Kleffner, N. Peters, H. Poggel, B. Bartmann, H. Müller, B. Funke, J. Schulte, F. Tenckhoff. Jahrg. I, 1909, complete, pp. 864 with Index. Agent: B. Herder, St. Louis, Mo. Subscription price, free by mail, $3.00.

Lenten Sermons. Two Series: I. Sin and its Remedies. II. The Seven Deadly Sins. By the Rev. Francis X. McGowan, O.S.A. Second Edition. Ratisbon, Rome, New York, Cincinnati: Fr. Pustet & Co. Pp. 224.

PHILOSOPHICAL.

Grundriss der Biologie oder der Lehre von den Lebenserscheinungen und ihren Ursachen. Von Hermann Muckermann, S.J. Erster Theil: Allegemeine Biologie. Mit Illustrationen. Freiburg, Brisg. und St. Louis, Mo.: B. Herder. 1909. Pp. xiv-174. Price, $1.30.

Each for All and All for Each. The Individual in his Relation to the Social System. By John Parsons. New York: Sturgis & Walton Co. 1909. Pp. xiii-390. Price, $1.75, *net.*

Modernism. Some Notes. By the Rev. W. D. Strappini, S.J. London, Edinburgh: Sands & Co.; St. Louis, Mo.: B. Herder. 1909. Pp. 16. Price, $0.05.

Historia Philosophiae. Auctore Dr. Josepho Kachnik, C. R. Theol. Facult. Olomucensis Professore P. O. Editio altera emendata et aucta. Olomucii: sumptibus R. Promberger, bibliopolae. 1909. Pp. 132. St. Louis, Mo.: B. Herder. Price, $1.10.

Ethica Socialis seu Sociologia. Praelectiones Academiae. Auctore Dr. Josepho Kachnik, C. R. Theol. Facult. Olomucensis Professore P. O. Olomucii; Sumptibus R. Promberger, bibliopolae. 1909. Pp. 287. St. Louis, Mo.: B. Herder. Price, $2.25.

Die Freiheit der Wissenschaft. Ein Gang durch das moderne Geistesleben. Von Dr. Josef Donat, S.J., Professor Univers. Innsbruck. Innsbruck: Fel. Rauch; New York, Cincinnati; Fr. Pustet & Co. 1910. Pp. 494. Price, $1.50.

HISTORICAL.

Une Conversion de Protestants par la Sainte Eucharistie. Autobiographies. Par le R. P. Emmanuel Abt, S.J. (*Apologétique Vivante*—4.) Paris: Gabriel Beauchesne & Cie. 1910. Pp. 106. Prix, 0 fr. 90, *franco.*

LA RELIGION ASSYRO-BABYLONIENNE. Conférences donées a l'Institut catholique de Paris. Par le R. P. Paul Dhorme, O.P. (Études palestiniennes .et orientales.) Paris: J. Gabalda & Cie. 1910. Pp. xi-319. Prix, 3 fr. 50.

HISTORY OF THE SOCIETY OF JESUS IN NORTH AMERICA, COLONIAL AND FEDERAL. By Thomas Hughes of the Same Society. Documents. Vol. I, Part II, Nos. 141-224 (1605-1838). London, New York: Longmans, Green, & Co. 1910. Pp. xi and 601 to 1222. Price, 21 shillings *net.*

HISTOIRE DE S. FRANÇOIS DE BORGIA, Troisième Général de la Compagnie de Jésus (1510-1572). Par Pierre Suau, S.J. Paris: Gabriel Beauchesne & Cie. 1910. Pp. 591. Prix, 8 fr., *franco.*

THE CATHOLIC CHURCH IN CHINA FROM 1860 TO 1907. By the Rev. Bertram Wolferstan, S.J. London, Edinburgh: Sands & Co.; St. Louis, Mo.: B. Herder. 1909. Pp. 470. Price, $3.00.

DIE KIRCHLICHEN BENEDIKTIONEN IM MITTELÄLTER. Von Adolph Franz. Two volumes. Freiburg, Brisg.; St. Louis, Mo.: B. Herder. 1909. Pp. xlvi-646 and vii-764. Price, both volumes, $9.40.

HISTORY OF THE CATHOLIC CHURCH IN THE NINETEENTH CENTURY 1789-1908. By the Rev. James MacCaffrey, Prof. Hist. Eccl., Maynooth. Two Volumes. Dublin, Waterford: M. H. Gill & Son; St. Louis, Mo.: B. Herder. 1909. Pp. xxiii-487 and xv-574. Price, $4.00.

THE LIFE OF BLESSED JULIE BILLIART, Foundress of the Institute of Sisters of Notre Dame. By a member of the same Society. Edited by the late Father James Clare, S.J. Edinburgh, London: Sands & Co.; St. Louis, Mo.: B. Herder. 1909. Pp. 559. Price, $2.50.

DER EHRW. PATER LIBERMANN UND DIE NEGERMISSION. Von einem Priester der Kongregation vom Hl. Geiste. Verlag: Missionhaus, Knechsteden (Dormagen), Rheinland. 1910. Pp. 62.

THE NATIONAL CIVIC FEDERATION. Tenth Annual Meeting, New York, 22 and 23 November, 1909. President Seth Low's Report. Workmen's Insurance in Foreign Countries. Employers' Liability in the United States. Compensation for Injured Wage-Earners, etc. Old Age Pensions. Annual Reports of Woman's Department. New York: The National Civic Federation, Metropolitan Building, 1 Madison Ave. 1910. Pp. 347.

MISCELLANEOUS.

LIFE'S LITTLE DAY. A Book of Seriousness from Catholic Sources. Selected and arranged by D. J. Scannell O'Neill, author of *Converts to Rome in America, Our Country and Citizenship, Watchwords from Doctor Brownson.* Techny, Illinois: Society of the Divine Word. Pp. 78. Price: in paper cover, $0.15; cloth bound, $0.25.

ATONED. Adapted from the German by the Rev. L. A. Reudter; and THE TWO CHRISTMAS EVES. By J. C. K. Heine. Techny, Illinois: Society of the Divine Word. Pp. 238. Price, $0.50, postpaid.

THE ESCAPADES OF CONDY CORRIGAN. An Amusing Series of Irish Fireside Stories by Cahir Healy. Illustrated by H. Horina. Techny, Illinois: Society of the Divine Word. 1910. Pp. 172. Price, $0.50, postpaid.

THE FIRST DAY—GOOD FRIDAY.
The Burial of Jesus.

THE

ECCLESIASTICAL REVIEW

Fifth Series.—Vol. II.—(XLII).—April, 1910.—No. 4.

THE "THREE DAYS"

From Holy Thursday Evening to Easter Sunday Evening.

The illustrations for this article are from drawings made by Messrs. Arnold and Locke, Architects, Brooklyn, N. Y., from designs suggested by the author.

DAY. ITS MEANING.

DAY, when it means the time of light, can have but one meaning, sunrise to sunset; but when it means the seventh of a week, and includes both light and darkness, its starting-point is arbitrary.

We may measure the day of 24 hours, from midnight to midnight, or from sunset to sunset, or we may take any other starting-point we choose.

Our day is measured from midnight to midnight; the Jewish day in our Saviour's time began and ended six hours earlier, at sunset.

Before midnight, Jesus said to Peter: "The cock shall not crow *this day,* till thou thrice deniest, that thou knowest me" (Lk. 22:34; Mk. 14:30).

After midnight, came Peter's denials, and the cock crowing.

The first of these three days the Jews called Parasceve; the second Sabbath; the third we now call the Pasch. Good Friday, Holy Saturday, and Easter Sunday, are more familiar names, but these days of ours begin at midnight; the days of which we are about to speak began at sunset. They do not exactly coincide. The Church frequently uses the Scriptural day in her Liturgy; the Divine Office, for instance, does not begin at midnight, but with Vespers (evening song).

The First Day.—Parasceve or Good Friday.

Late Thursday afternoon, when the western sky was on fire from the setting sun, Jesus and His disciples were entering the Supper chamber. Soon the light died out in the western sky, and the Pascal moon rose full and bright over Jerusalem.

Now it is Thursday evening, we would say; but the disciples would say, "No; Thursday is over, and another day, Parasceve, has begun." For they began their day at sunset.

At the beginning of this day, Jesus eat the Paschal meal with His disciples; He washed their feet; He told them of Judas's treason; He instituted the Holy Eucharist; He foretold Peter's denials. Leaving Jerusalem He went to Gethsemane; there He suffered His agony; He was seized by the mob, was brought before the Sanhedrim, was condemned by Pilate, was led to Calvary, and nailed to the cross.

Toward the close of this day He died; at its close He was buried. In the Missal we say that Jesus instituted the Holy Eucharist, *pridie quam pateretur,* the day before He died. When midnight is made the dividing line, this is true; but according to the Scriptural division (that which Jesus Himself used), He offered the unbloody Sacrifice at the beginning, and the bloody Sacrifice at the end, of the same day.

Jesus died about three o'clock; then Joseph of Arimathea went to Pilate and asked for His Body. After securing permission, he brought fine linen, while Nicodemus went for ointment. When they returned to Calvary, they took the Body down from the cross, anointed it, wrapped a napkin about the Face and twined linen about the Body; then they carried it to Joseph's sepulchre near-by, rolled a great stone to the entrance, and departed to their homes. Their work was necessarily hurried, for they had to finish it before the

THE BURIAL OF JESUS.

Sectional View, showing Interior of Sepulchre.

THE SECOND DAY—THE SABBATH.

Jesus in the Sepulchre.

Sabbath, on which it was not lawful to work. Fig. 1 shows the procession to the Sepulchre, just before sunset. Fig. 2 is the same scene, but a sectional view, showing the interior of the Sepulchre.

THE SECOND DAY.—THE SABBATH: HOLY SATURDAY.

When those who buried Jesus hurried to their homes, the sun was sinking, and with it Friday ended. The first day was over, and the second had begun. From sunset on Friday to sunset on Saturday was the second day, the Sabbath; Holy Saturday we call it now. It was Limbo day. During the whole of it, the Soul of Jesus was with the blessed souls detained there; some of them for centuries had been awaiting His coming.

His Precious Blood dyed the ground about Calvary; His Sacred Body was in the tomb; His Soul was with them. Since the burial, Calvary and the Sepulchre were silent and deserted; no one was seen there; no sound was heard, unless that of the wind, of some stray animal, or of passing birds; but myriads of invisible angels were gathered there, about the Sacred Body and the Precious Blood, in loving adoration. The great city of Jerusalem was almost as still as the Sepulchre, just outside its walls; for this was the Sabbath and a " great Sabbath day ". But Sabbath though it was, the chief priests and Pharisees went to Pilate and said:

Sir, we have remembered that that seducer said, while he was yet alive: After three days I will rise again.

Command therefore the sepulchre to be guarded until the third day; lest perhaps his disciples come, and steal him away and say to the people, he is risen from the dead; and the last error shall be worse than the first.

Pilate said to them: You have a guard, go, guard it as you know.— (Mt. 27: 63-65.)

Whether this was on Saturday morning or later, we do not know. St. Matthew merely says: "On the morrow, which is after the Parasceve, the chief priests and the Pharisees came together to Pilate " (Mt. 27: 62).

If it was later than six o'clock on Saturday morning, more

than half of the second day was past. What was the meaning of their request, to have the sepulchre guarded *until* the third day? · For the next few hours until sunset? · Certainly not: the Jews did not care whether the Body of Jesus disappeared or not during the second day; if it did, it would have falsified His prophesy, for He said: " On the third day, I will rise again."

During the second day, and until the beginning of the third (sunset on Saturday), there was no need of a guard. It was from Saturday evening until Sunday evening, *during* the third day, that a guard was wanted. During would be a better word than until, in this verse.

" They, departing, made the sepulchre sure, sealing the stone, and setting guards " (Mt. 27 : 66). Where the guard was, at what hour they reached the sepulchre, when the chief priests and Pharisees met them there—these and other details are wanting. The guard probably reached the Sepulchre as quietly as possible. It is not likely that they marched in a body through the streets of Jerusalem, on that great Sabbath day. If they did, the whole city would have known it. Everything in the Gospels points to the utmost secrecy. The women had not heard of the guard, as their question shows: " Who shall roll us back the stone? " The change in public sentiment must have made the priests and Pharisees cautious. In all probability each member of the guard was notified to reach the Sepulchre before sunset, and to go there each one alone, and by unfrequented roads, so that they would be unnoticed. With the same caution, the priests and the Pharisees who had ordered the guard, reached the appointed place.

THE THIRD DAY.—THE PASCH : EASTER SUNDAY.

A. BEFORE THE RESURRECTION.

While the western sky was all aglow, the priests and Pharisees, with the guard at the Sepulchre, were anxiously watching it. When the sun had vanished, the Sabbath day was over and the third day had begun.

The guard rolled back the great stone from the door of the Sepulchre, and the priests and Pharisees entered with lighted torches, to assure themselves that the Body of Jesus was still there. They carefully examined the walls, the floor, and the

THE THIRD DAY.

Priests and Pharisees examining the Sepulchre

THE THIRD DAY—JESUS RISING.

ceiling, to make sure that there was no secret passage through which the disciples might steal in. Having satisfied themselves that all was secure, the guards rolled back the great stone, against the entrance; the priests put several cords across the great stone, sealing their ends to the walls of the Sepulchre, so that if the stone were moved, the broken seals would give evidence of it. They ordered the guard to remain there for the next twenty-four hours, and then they returned to their homes. The guard lighted a fire, as they had done two nights before (Jn. 18: 18), for the March nights were cold; they pulled their cloaks about them, and began their watch.

The examination of the interior of the Sepulchre is not mentioned in the Gospels; but it is a natural precaution they would not be likely to omit. They thought that the disciples would attempt to steal the Body, and we cannot suppose that they failed to examine whether they had done so already.

Fig. 4 shows the priests examining the Sepulchre. Fig. 5 shows the guards watching it after their departure. How many guards there were, whether a dozen or a hundred, we have no means of knowing. Since the disciples of Jesus were numerous (Jn. 12: 19), a large guard may have been deemed necessary; the more numerous it was the less would be the chance of bribing them all.

B. THE RESURRECTION.

Whilst some of the guards were standing at the door of the Sepulchre, and others were warming themselves at the fire, the Soul of Jesus returned from Limbo; His Precious Blood was gathered up and put back into His arteries and veins; Body, Blood, and Soul are united again, never to be separated any more. (The Divine Nature had remained inseparably united to all three, His Body in the Sepulchre, His Blood about Calvary, and His Soul in Limbo.)

Jesus is not alone: millions of souls, all the ransomed dead from Limbo, and all the angels of heaven are with Him.

Jesus casts aside the napkin about His Head, and the grave clothes that were about His Body, and, like an X-ray, passing through the rocky roof or wall of the Sepulchre, is risen from the dead, and the guards, all unconscious of it, are guarding an empty tomb.

Fig. 5 shows the moment of the Resurrection, Jesus rising. Fig. 6 shows Jesus passing through the roof of the Sepulchre.

In what direction Jesus left the Sepulchre we cannot tell, whether through the rocky roof, the side walls, or through the great stone that filled the entrance. No good reason can be given for supposing that He came through the great stone rather than through the roof or walls. Nothing could impede His glorified Body; with the silence and rapidity of light He was gone.

C. AFTER THE RESURRECTION.

The coming of the angel.

There was a great earthquake. For an angel of the Lord descended from heaven; and coming, rolled back the stone and sat upon it. And his countenance was as lightning, and his raiment as snow.

And for fear of him, the guards were struck with terror and became as dead men.—(Mt. 28:2-4.)

After Jesus arose—how long after we do not know—an angel came to the Sepulchre. His presence being ushered in by an earthquake, he took the great stone like a play-toy, rolled it aside, and sat upon it. The terrified guards, looking into the Sepulchre, which was lighted up by the brightness of his countenance, saw it empty. The sight of the terrible angel so frightened them that they became for a time like dead men. When they recovered from their fright sufficiently to run away, some of them went to those who had placed them there, and told them all that they had seen.

Artists have imagined that the guards saw Jesus coming out of the tomb, and that He terrified them. This is contrary to the Gospel account. St. Matthew tells us very explicitly, that it was the sight of the angel and his lightning-like countenance that terrified them. They did not see Jesus at all. He had risen before the angel came. It was not necessary for Him to have the stone removed, or to remove it Himself: He passed through the closed Sepulchre, just as He entered the closed room where the Apostles were, on Easter night.

Our illustrations (Figs. 5 and 6) show the Resurrection. The pictures that the artists have given us should be styled " After the Resurrection ", or " The Coming of the Angel ".

JESUS PASSING THROUGH THE STONE TOMB

AFTER THE RESURRECTION .
Coming of the Angel and Terror of the Guard.

The angels and the souls from Limbo were the witnesses
of the Resurrection. There were no human witnesses, unless
Jesus allowed His Mother to see Him rising.[1]

J. F. SHEAHAN.

Poughkeepsie, N. Y.

THE BIBLICAL COMMISSION AND THE DEGREES IT CONFERS.

IN the February issue of this REVIEW we discussed the question of the Biblical courses in vogue in our seminaries.
We endeavored to set forth what, in our estimation, constituted an adequate course which should, while catering primarily for the priest who is to go out on the mission, also
prepare, at least remotely, the priest who is later to become a
Biblical professor. In the present paper we propose to put
before our readers some account of the recent legislation of
the Church as expressed in the foundation of the Biblical
Commission and in the institution of the Biblical Degrees
granted by it.

It was in 1893 that Leo XIII published his immortal Encyclical entitled *Providentissimus Deus* in which he laid down
such clear principles touching the need of Biblical study and
the methods which should be followed in seminaries and universities where such studies were carried out. " It is our wish
and fervent desire," said the late Pope, " to see an increase
in the number of the approved and persevering laborers in
the cause of Holy Scripture; and more especially that those
whom Divine Grace has called to Holy Orders, should, day
by day, as their state demands, display greater diligence and
industry in reading, meditating, and explaining it." After
dwelling at considerable length on the work done in past ages

---

[1] Mt. 28:2 does not mention the Resurrection of Jesus through the closed
tomb, but it is so clearly implied, that there is no controversy about it. All
admit that it is the Evangelist's meaning.

The angel opened the tomb, and terrified the guards; he said to the women:
I know that you seek Jesus; He is not here, He has arisen (Mt. 28:6).

Evidently Jesus had arisen before the angel came and opened the tomb.

"He could pass through a closed sepulchre (implied by Mt. 28:2), and
closed doors " (Jn. 20:26). Hastings, *Dict. of Bible*, iv, p. 234, a.

"The Resurrection itself is not described. Like all beginnings, whether in
nature or in history, it is hidden from view." (Plummer, Lk. p. 546.)

The angel rolled away the stone of the sepulchre of Christ. "Not that He
might rise out of it, for He had already risen while the sepulchre was
closed." (à Lapide, l. c., Eng. trans.)

by Catholic exegetes, the Pope went on to point out how we
were to study the Bible:

Let our first care, then, be to see that in seminaries and academical institutions the study of Holy Scripture be placed on such a
footing as its own importance and the circumstances of the time demand. With this view the first thing which requires attention is the
wise choice of professors. Teachers of Sacred Scripture are not to
be appointed at hap-hazard out of the crowd; but they must be men
whose character and fitness are proved by their love of, and their
long familiarity with, the Bible, and by suitable learning and study.

There then follow most wise remarks on the method of
teaching which should be followed. It is these remarks which
served for the basis of our paper in the February issue.

Nine years later the Pope spoke once more, and this time
it was to give concrete expression to the doctrine he had laid
down in the previous Encyclical regarding Biblical teaching.
In this second Encyclical, *Vigilantiae,* dated 30 October, 1902,
Leo XIII instituted the Biblical Commission and he laid
down certain broad principles which were to guide its members. First, they were to keep themselves *au courant* with all
that could in any way concern Biblical exegesis; whatever
new discovery was made they were at once to endeavor to ap-
praise it as its true value and publish it for the advantage of
Catholic Biblical scholars. They were especially to pay attention to philology and Oriental languages and also to the study
of the original texts. Secondly, they were to do all in their
power to discourage Catholics from building up their exegesis solely on the works of non-Catholic commentators, and
were to insist on the rights of the Church as the sole inter-

vealed truths are brought into discussion, the members of the Commission are to arrive at a decision, as far as they can, on some of the more important of these controverted questions and thus prepare the way for the Apostolic See to decide finally what Catholics are to hold.

But Leo XIII was nothing if not practical, and he saw that it would be impossible for the members of the Commission to do good work unless they had a thoroughly good library at their disposal: "We assign to them therefore now a certain part of our Vatican Library and we will provide that there shall be there collected manuscripts and books of all periods, and these are to be at the disposition of the members of the Commission."

Pope Leo died in the following year, 1903; but his successor Pius X has not been slow to carry out the intentions expressed by the late Pontiff. On 13 February, 1904, he published the Encyclical *Scripturae Sanctae* in which, after referring to the two foregoing Encyclicals, he says that with a view to providing a supply of good professors for Catholic colleges he has decided to institute the Degrees of Licentiate and Doctor in Sacred Scripture. These Degrees are to be conferred by the Biblical Commission which will hold examinations at stated periods for that purpose. The conditions for candidature may be briefly stated thus:

1. The candidate must be in priest's orders; he must further have obtained his doctorate in theology in some approved University; he may belong to either the Secular or the Regular Clergy.

2. The examination must be in writing as well as *viva voce*.

3. Candidates may present themselves for the Licentiate immediately after taking their degree as Doctor in Divinity, but they may not present themselves for the Biblical Doctorate until a year has elapsed from taking the Licentiate.

4. For the Doctorate a written thesis approved by the Commission must be presented.

the Licentiate have been held, and priests from all over the world have presented themselves. Thirty-eight have passed, with varying degrees of success; many have failed. We mention this latter point because it is often said that Roman examinations are not a guarantee of knowledge; no one can complain that the examinations of the Biblical Commission are not severe enough; many candidates have been astounded at the very serious character they assume. The ex-Rector of Louvain University, Monsignor Hebbelynck, assisted at the last examination for the Licentiate and also examined in Coptic for the Doctorate. He expressed himself delighted at the solid character of the examination. And this is as it should be. Four have passed the Doctorate, and of these America claims one and England another. It is noteworthy that the majority of the candidates belong to the secular clergy; one Benedictine and six Dominicans, of whom one has also taken the Doctorate, represented the old Religious Orders; the rest are members of the secular clergy and the Religious Congregations.

The examination is, then, a high-class one, and there can be no shadow of doubt that it will do an immense good in the Church, since it will form professors whose attainments are guaranteed and who consequently are thoroughly capable of taking up the Biblical teaching in any seminary. Two points in the legislation for the Degrees seem to us primarily responsible for the success of the step taken by the Holy See. First of all, a candidate must be already a Doctor in theology. This ensures a certain stability and maturity which in the investigation of Biblical matters is of the highest importance. And secondly, the Commission is composed of members of various Religious bodies as well as of the secular clergy. It is in no sense attached to any one body. It is cosmopolitan. No one would have been surprised had Pope Leo XIII thought fit to entrust it to the Benedictines, for example, or to the Jesuits, or to the Dominicans whose Biblical School at Jerusalem was then already well-known. But the Pope did noth-

we have shown, vast. But that is in itself a safeguard. The examination has to be taken as a whole or not at all. It is illegal to break it up. And all who have any inside acquaintance with modern methods of " cram " will feel grateful that this is so. A candidate must have solid knowledge if he would pass; he cannot undergo a two-years' course of drastic preparation.

We will now give the program in full. It is probably familiar to many of our readers, but it will be more convenient to repeat it here.

AD PROLYTATUM.

IN EXPERIMENTO QUOD SCRIPTO FIT.

(A) Exegesis (*i. e. expositio doctrinalis, critica et philologica*) quattuor Evangeliorum et Actuum Apostolorum. *Pericope ex his, a iudicibus eligenda, exponetur nullo praeter textus et concordantias adhibito libro; de qua verbis quoque periculum fiet.*

(B) Dissertatio de historia biblica *iuxta materiam infra sub n. III assignatam.*

(C) Dissertatio de Introductione generali aut speciali *iuxta materiam infra positam sub nn. IV et V.*

IN EXPERIMENTO VERBALI.

I. Graece quattuor Evangelia et Actus Apostolorum.

II. Hebraice quattuor libri Regum.

III. Historia Hebraeorum a Samuele usque ad captivitatem Babylonicam; itemque historia evangelica et apostolica usque ad captivitatem Sancti Pauli Romanam.

IV. Introductio specialis in singulos libros utriusque Testamenti (*i. e. authenticitas, integritas, compositionis circumstantiae, scopus, divisiones generales*).

V. Introductionis generalis quaestiones selectae, nimirum:

1. *De Bibliorum Sacrorum inspiratione.*

2. *De sensu litterali et de sensu typico.*

3. *De legibus Hermeneuticae.*

10. *Inscriptiones Palaestinenses antiquissimae.*
11. *De kalendario et praecipuis ritibus sacris Hebraeorum.*
12. *De ponderibus, mensuris et nummis in Sancta Scriptura memoratis.*

It will be at once evident that this program embraces an immense amount of matter. In fact the only question which is not explicitly mentioned is that of the Formation of the Canon of the Bible, and even this is not wholly omitted since the Special Introduction to each book (IV) necessarily includes the question of its canonicity. Similarly, though the question of the Mosaic authorship of the Pentateuch is not explicitly mentioned, it must be faced when treating of the introduction to any book of the Pentateuch.

For the comfort of the student it must however be remarked that no specialistic knowledge is required. The examination is meant to test a student's general and fundamental knowledge. Wide reading is not demanded, but careful reading. We may now take each item as it figures in the program, and see what is expected of the student.

But before doing so it will be convenient to point out that another program in French is published for the further information of students. From this we learn that certain subjects are of higher importance than others; thus the three written papers A, B, and C, are not of equal value as regards marks; the first-named, A, lasts for six consecutive hours, and is marked twice as high as the other two, which last only three hours each. We must not however conclude that mere length of time rules the relative value of these papers; the examiners wish to point out the immense importance of New Testament exegesis.

Again, in the oral examination, Hebrew and Greek count for twice as much as the Special and General Introductions and the Biblical History. Here again it is question of foundations; the Commission feels that a sound knowledge of the languages of the Bible lies at the root of all true Biblical

our business to criticize it. This exegetical paper is concerned only with the Gospels and the Acts; it must be written in Latin, and it must be a solid, doctrinal, philological, critical examination of the passage proposed for examination. As we read in the French program, what is called for is the literal exegesis of the text, the legitimate doctrinal conclusions, a comparison of any real parallel passages, an examination of apparent contradictions, and finally the discussion of the principal variants between the text and the versions. In short, a candidate must have a good knowledge of the text of the Gospels and the Acts; he must be able to write a practical commentary on any portion; he must know the main difficulties which he is likely to encounter; he must have a fair grasp of the Synoptic problem, that is to say he must not talk nonsense about it, though at the same time, be it noted, he is not required to know all the theories and views that have been put forth regarding this vexed question. Similarly, when it is said that a knowledge of the principal variants must be shown, it is clear that no candidate is supposed to carry in his head a whole list of all the variants in the New Testament! But he must know the chief ones; if, for example, he has to comment on Acts, Chap. 8, he would be expected to know that there was a difficulty about v. 37; but no one could expect him to know all the vagaries of Codex Bezae!

As a rule, at least in all the later examinations, the candidate has had a choice of three distinct passages for this first written paper. Thus one year we find that one of the three following passages was proposed for examination: the Call of the Apostles in the Synoptic Gospels, the Parable of the Good Samaritan, the Cure of the Man born Blind in S. John, 9. Again, another year, a choice was offered between: the narrative of our Lord's Temptation in the Desert; the Discourse with Nicodemus; and St. Peter's address to Cornelius in the tenth chapter of the Acts.

Assiduous reading of the Gospels and Acts in the Greek and Latin text will undoubtedly form the best preparation for this severe test; a simple commentary which gives us the variants, discusses the parallels, and does not flinch from difficulties, is to be preferred to any more recondite work which will probably only confuse the student. But here a difficulty at once arises, where are such commentaries to be found? Are there any Catholic commentaries of the kind required? Have we got anything which can compare, for example, with the Cambridge Greek Testament for Schools and Colleges? We would prefer to leave this question unanswered; we will remark only that there are very few such commentaries to be found and that the best, on one New Testament book only, is by a nun! We do not say this by way of disparagement—far from it—but it makes one think! If the candidate has been engaged in teaching Holy Scripture his task will be rendered much easier. He will have been in the habit of correcting examination-papers; he will have been forced to express himself clearly and exactly in his regular class-work, and he will necessarily have acquired a great familiarity with the matter. At the same time a professor labors under certain difficulties when he presents himself for such an examination as this, for he has his mind formed and he has been accustomed rather to examine others than to be himself examined. He is, too, more aware of the difficulties, especially the big ones, and he is apt to think when he sees a certain passage set for examination that the examiner had a certain difficulty in his mind, whereas probably the examiner never thought of it. Hence the professor is in danger of overlooking points which to him may seem trivial but which he has to show that he knows. And if the professor is a specialist in any one line, his difficulty is intensified for he has to forget his special line and adapt himself to an examination which deals with general principles only and with fundamental knowledge only. Lastly it should be noted that for this examination no books are allowed except the text and the concordances. This seems to be interpreted by the presiding examiners as meaning that the Latin text with the assistance of the originals and of any simple version must be used. It goes without saying that it would not be permissible to bring into the room a version with notes of any critical value. A concordance to the Vulgate and to the Greek Testament is indispensable. Candidates have to provide their own books, viz. concordances and Bibles; but paper, etc., are supplied.

The second written paper is concerned with the Biblical History referred to under No. III. This embraces two parts, the history of the Hebrews from the time of Samuel to the Babylonian Captivity, and the Gospels and Apostolic history from the commencement to St. Paul's Roman captivity. This history is of great importance, as it is of course the foundation of the Bible; it is its framework, so to speak, and it would not not be too much to say that modern vagaries in criticism are mostly concerned with the history, so much so that we constantly hear it insisted that we must now completely re-write our Biblical histories according to the ideas of the Evolutionist School of Old Testament exegesis. Now the history of the Hebrews is so intimately bound up with that of the surrounding nations that a knowledge of the history of these latter as told us on the monuments of Babylon, Assyria, and Egypt, is absolutely essential to any real knowledge of the history of the Old Testament. Hence particular stress is laid on the history in its relation with the monuments. One question has been repeatedly asked in these examinations, viz. the story of Sennacherib and Ezechias particularly as illustrated by the monuments. Consequently the student must make himself familiar with the history which has been of late rendered accessible to us by the discoveries of such men as Maspero, Sayce, Scheil, De Morgan, Petrie, Mariette, etc. It is evident that we cannot all be Assyriologists or Egyptologists, but we can keep ourselves *au courant* with what is going on and we can learn for ourselves the main facts which serve to illustrate the Bible. And here again we may repeat that the student who has the best knowledge of the text of the Bible will have the greatest advantage, and nothing but assiduous and intelligent reading of the text will win this for us. Such knowledge is of special assistance in the oral examinations, as we shall see later.

The third and last written examination, like the preceding one, lasts three hours. It is in some sense the most difficult of all, because the matter is so vast. There are seventy books in the Bible, and the unhappy student has to know the Special Introduction to every one of them! This demands a knowledge of the book itself, a knowledge of what is generally said about it, of its authenticity, its date, its divisions, its most important parts, the doctrine contained in it, its canonicity, its place in the Bible history, etc. This will demand evidently much precis-work; some good Special Introduction must be read and studied and synopses must be formed which can be committed to memory. But if this portion of the examination is trying, it is the portion which will most repay us in the end, for the work requisite for attaining the necessary knowledge will give us a familiarity with the Bible-text which we can hardly otherwise obtain. A great deal will undoubtedly depend upon the student's skill in writing an examination paper. This needs practice; three hours may seem a long time and we may be disposed to fancy we can allow a certain amount of time to biting our pen; but it is not so. A student who really knows his matter will find the time none too long; indeed, unless he have a very clear idea of what he is going to say, and of how he is going to say it, he will find the time all too short. Moral Theologians divide moral circumstances as answering the queries *Quis, Quid, Ubi, Quibus auxiliis, Cur, Quomodo, Quando.* These same mystic words may serve for the general heading of our paper on the Special Introduction to any book of the Bible. This sounds like a " tip ", but such things are not to be despised.

HUGH POPE, O.P.

Rome, Italy.

[TO BE CONTINUED.]

THE ORIGIN AND PRESENT CONDITION OF THE RUSSIAN ORTHODOX CHURCH.

IN a former article [1] we explained the origin of the Greek Church, its organization, and present condition. Of its ninety-five million adherents, nine-tenths are under the dominion of the Russian Empire and among the Slav races. Notwithstanding these teeming millions of Christians, it must be admitted, of all the nations of Europe the Russian Empire was the least known in this country, until its late war with Japan brought it under the light of universal publicity. In nothing was this more evident than in the ideas commonly entertained even by educated Catholics relative to its religious condition. It is a country permeated with religion, where old traditions and primitive habits and customs are

ined. Its strength mainly consists in having
t those principles which can alone secure the
ation, namely, its deep religious feeling, and
ithority; for its monarchical principle is recog-
ed with a religious character which makes it
an eyes. In many minds the Russian religion
with the Orthodox Greek, but it is not Ortho-
:igin, nor is it Greek in language, constitution,

The Greek Church is composed of the Chris-
onfined to the territories of the Ottoman Em-
spiritual jurisdiction of the Patriarch of Con-
embracing about ten million individuals. The
, whilst it maintains with the Greek church
f belief and of liturgical rites and recognizes
hurch " in Jesus Christ, yet is completely inde-
id under the power of the Czar. Being by far
rt of the Orthodox communion, the Russians
that the Holy Synod had better take over the
the whole Orthodox church, for they openly
' Orthodoxy " is and should be Russian. If
ind vigor count in the matter they are correct,
itly possess these characteristics. According
1905 the number of Russians of the " Ortho-
:eeds eighty-six million. There are 50,000
ich 37,500 are parish churches, while the re-
onastic and cathedral churches. There are
: Empire sixty-six dioceses, governed by three
urteen archbishops, and forty-nine bishops. In
eses, the bishops have auxiliary bishops, whom
to assist them. The white or secular clergy
250,000 priests, 25,000 of whom receive sal-
imperial treasury. There are also 15,000
000 precentors who discharge the duties of
:, sacristans, beadles and singers. There are
for men, having 8,500 monks besides 7,000
d 362 convents for women, having 11,000
32,000 lay sisters and novices. The church has
ion four ecclesiastical academies, at St. Peters-

dents. About twenty million children are being educated, which clearly shows that at the present day the prevalent ideas relative to the lack of education in the Russian church are not well founded. The churches and monasteries also maintain 264 hospitals and about 1,000 alms-houses, while 28,000 libraries are attached, revealing the fact that the Russian clergy are no longer insensible to their sacred responsibilities. Since the war with Japan a great change has come over Russia, which is no longer recognized as a " despotism tempered by assassination," but a country whose people are brave, patriotic, self-sacrificing, and democratic. They love their *mir,* their country and their Czar with a love that passeth knowledge; blindly faithful to one form of fatalism, that whatever their " Little Father " decrees is for the best. The eyes of the civilized world are focused on this singular nation, and people are anxious to learn of its constitution and religion. Its inhabitants are raising themselves from the slough of servitude; superstition is vanishing before the rays of enlightenment; liberty of conscience is in the air, and the curse of state entanglement, clinging about the church like the poisoned shirt of Hercules, has been loosened by the now historic ukase of 30 April, 1905.

It is generally known that the first efforts to convert the Russian people to Christianity were undertaken in the ninth century by the two brothers, Cyril and Methodius, to whom in a great measure they owe their liturgy. A full account of their apostolic labors has been portrayed by Leo XIII in his admirable encyclical of September, 1880, addressed to the archbishops and bishops of the whole world. Being Greeks the two brothers brought with them the Greek rites as their form of worship, but instead of writing the Slavonic language in Roman or Greek letters, they invented an alphabet which afforded the Slav tongue the signs and means of a written language, which is used to the present day under the name of the Cyrillic or Slavonic alphabet. They translated into the Slavonian tongue all the liturgical books, besides the gospels and epistles used in the Greek rite, and instituted Mass to be said in the same. Complaints were sent to Rome, but, after an investigation, Pope John VIII approved of the use of the Slavonic language forever in the Mass and in the whole liturgy and offices of the Church, as is evident from his still extant letter to Sfendolpulk, Count of Moravia. The language of those liturgies, like that of the Latin, was never changed, although the people for whom they were originally drawn up, and amongst whom they still continue to be celebrated, have entirely transformed their ancient language, and are perfectly incapable of understanding it at the present time in its original form. The Slavonic missal was revised by an order of Pope Urban VIII in 1631, and his brief and approbation are prefixed to this missal reprinted at Rome in 1745 at the expense of the Congregation of the Propaganda.

Although SS. Cyril and Methodius had evangelized the southern part of Russia, the bulk of the nation remained buried in paganism till nearly a century later. In 957 Olga, the wife of Prince Igor, whilst on a visit to Constantinople embraced Christianity and received baptism from the hands of the holy Patriarch Polycuct, together with several of her suite. Nestor, the father of Russian history, calls her the " Harbinger of Christianity ". Returning to Russia she vainly endeavored to convert her countrymen, but not until 988, under her grandson, the Grand Duke Vladmir, was it finally established. Rambaud in his *History of Russia* tells us that, " when Vladmir had resolved to become a Christian, he marched against the Empire at Constantinople. Since this religion was a desirable thing, there was of course only one way in which a Norman and a gentleman could acquire it—by conquest. So he seized the Chersonesos, and then sent a messenger to the Emperor, Basil II, saying that what he wanted was three things, namely, priests to baptize him and his people, relics of saints for the churches, and Basil's sister for wife. If these wishes were not promptly complied with he would come and destroy Constantinople. The emperor forthwith granted his requests." Vladmir issued a proclamation inviting all his people, rich and poor, lords and slaves, to receive baptism under the penalty of being declared enemies of the prince. He introduced Christianity into other parts of his empire, founded a city named after himself, built churches, established priests in them, and founded schools.

Thus we see that Russia did not receive the Faith from the schismatic Greek church of Constantinople. SS. Cyril and

Methodius received faculties from Rome, and their difficulties were referred to and settled by Rome, and when Princess Olga and her grandson embraced Christianity, Constantinople recognized the supremacy of Rome. True, they received their first bishops and priests from Constantinople and were regarded as belonging to the jurisdiction of that See; nevertheless the new Church of Russia took no part in the great schism, but as it continued to receive its bishops from the schismatical capital it gradually lost direct relations with the centre of Catholic unity. Twenty years after the schism of Michael Cerularius was consummated, we find Pope Gregory VII sending legates to Grand Duke Demetrius with a letter that is still extant. Even the Russian bishops accepted the canonization of St. Nicholas by Pope Urban II, a Saint who is rejected by the Greek Church but who to-day is the popular and indeed the national patron of all the Russian people.

As the metropolitan See of Kieff, the head church of Russia, had been made dependent on the patriarch of Constantinople, the custom of receiving the primates of the Russian Church from Constantinople could not but result in drawing her into schism. Thus at the beginning of the twelfth century, Nicephorus, who was sent from Constantinople as primate of the church at Kieff, avowed himself schismatic, as is proved from an encyclical written by him against the Latins. During his primacy the Tartar invasion of Russia began under Genghis Khan. In 1224, the year of his death, the Tartars had proceeded as far west as Kieff, and sixteen years later they took and pillaged it. All communication with Catholic Europe was then cut off, and while Christianity was still retained by the people, the clergy came to recognize their princes as supreme alike in church and state. The taking of Kieff by the Tartars drove the Russian Christians northward and westward toward the little town of Moscow. The latter grew in importance, overshadowed Kieff, and became the origin of the present

Kieff, which divided the Russian church into two great juris-
dictions, those of Moscow and Kieff. The latter remained for
some time more or less faithful to Rome. At the Council of
Florence, when there were as many Catholics in Russia as
schismatics, Isidore, its metropolitan, voted for union, but
under the jurisdiction of Peter Moglia—better known as the
great champion of Orthodoxy—Kieff returned to communion
with the northern schismatic Russian church.

After the fall of Constantinople, the Grand Dukes of
Russia, who now called themselves Czars, assumed authority
over the primates of Moscow and freed them from all foreign
dependence. This was accomplished in 1589, by the erection
of the Orthodox Patriarchate of Russia at Moscow. Jeremiah,
the Patriarch of Constantinople, had bought his appointment
from the Turkish government, and he visited Russia in quest
of the purchase money. The Czar Feodor took advantage of
the occasion and enticed Jeremiah to erect Moscow into a
patriarchate wholly independent of Constantinople, an agreement which the latter readily embraced by raising the then
metropolitan Job to the dignity of patriarch. It was not the
simoniacal Jeremiah who gave the investiture to the new patriarch but the Czar himself, in these words: " Most worthy
Patriarch, father of all fathers, first of all the bishops of
Russia, I give thee precedence over all the bishops; I give
thee the right to wear the patriarchal mantle, the cap of a
bishop, and the great mitre; and I order that you be recognized and honored as a patriarch and the brother of all the
patriarchs." The principle here implied has been ever recognized by the schismatics of Russia. The East was always
prone to recognize the right of the Emperor to interfere in
the things of the sanctuary, from Constantius in 355 to
Nicholas II, the present Czar. According to the " Code of
Laws of the Russian Empire ", the Emperor is the supreme
defender of the dominant creed and of all that concerns good
order in the Holy Church. Theophanes Procopovich, the
favorite of Peter the Great and Bishop of Pskow, declared
that the Czars received from on high the power to govern the
church, but not to officiate. Emperor Paul I declared in
formal terms that " the supreme authority granted by God
to the Autocrat extends also to the ecclesiastical state, and

that the clergy must render obedience to the Czar as their head chosen by God Himself in all matters religious and civil." From the moment when the Czar gave the investiture to the patriarch, the Russian church became purely national, and in accordance with the invariable fate of all national churches, the Czars grew omnipotent in imposing their own wills on the church.

As long as the patriarchate of Moscow lasted, the Czars encroached more and more on the spiritual power, until that which was established by one was abolished by another. On 21 January, 1721, Peter the Great assumed to himself the right and duty of reforming the church as he had reformed the state. Having completely changed the administration of the latter he set up his capital on the Neva and started the new city of St. Petersburg. He replaced the patriarchate, purposely left vacant after the death of Hadrian, by a permanent Synod chosen by himself and somewhat on the basis of the Lutheran consistories. This was the Czar who, without alleging any cause, espoused the lascivious Catherine, while his wife Eudoxia was still alive, a matter that recalls the conduct of Bardus in the Greek church and Henry VIII in the Anglican.

This Holy Synod that rules the Russian church is the shadow of the Czar. It is composed of the metropolitans of Kieff, Moscow, and Petersburg, besides six other bishops appointed at the pleasure of the Czar. The Czar's chaplain and the head chaplain of the forces are also members; these latter two, belonging to the secular clergy, are married; but the chief man in the Holy Synod is the Procurator, a layman, generally a soldier. He is the real intermediary between the Czar and the Synod, " the eye and advocate of state affairs ". He has the direction of the Exchequer of the Synod, and of the numerous attendants employed by it, as well as the direction of ecclesiastical schools. The authority exercised by him over these administrations naturally gives him great influence over the progress of affairs submitted to the Synod as also over diocesan authorities. Russians themselves realize how completely their church now lies under the heel of the autocracy.

The oath imposed on the members of the Synod, from

Peter the Great to the present time, contains a phrase worthy of quotation: " Moreover I profess with oath that the supreme Judge of this Ecclesiastical College is the monarch of all the Russians, our most gracious Sovereign." By the institution of the Holy Synod, Peter became the sole effective patriarch in his dominions, the real guide of consciences; and that power has been exercised ever since, whether by the murderous Catherine, the crazy Paul, or the cruel Nicholas. The Constitution of the Holy Synod remains unchanged in its formation, and under it to-day the Russian church is the most Erastian body among Christians in the world.

Nor was Peter satisfied with substituting a permanent Synod for the patriarchate; he also drew up for the reform of the Russian church a canon which is to this day, with little modification, the basis of its organization. It is divided into three parts, the first treating of the Synod and the necessity of its creation; the second of matters relating to the church, clergy and laity; while the third refers to the members of the Synod and their functions. Then follows a complete Ecclesiastical Code, which imposes rules on the secular clergy, monks, and nuns, and abolishes provincial synods. The " Holy Directing Synod ", as Peter called it, is named in the liturgy instead of the patriarch. It decides all ecclesiastical questions, regulates religious instructions, governs the censorship of books and questions of ritual, and selects professors for the seminaries. It is the last court of appeal in religious matters, and all the clergy of every rank, monasteries and convents are under its jurisdiction. It decides matrimonial cases and cases of conscience, settles disputes between bishops and priests, and watches over the use of ecclesiastical property. By the Ecclesiastical Code attached to the canon it prescribes the right of confessors to break the seal of Confession when there is a question of a plot against the Czar, his government, or his family, where the penitent will not abandon his intention. The simple faithful must go to Confession and Communion at least once a year; otherwise they are to be denounced by their parish priest to the bishop, who informs the civil authorities, and the latter will prosecute them on the ground of being Raskolniks. It forbids monks the use of the pen except in case of extreme necessity, and prohibits nuns from taking their vows till they have reached the age of sixty. A later ukase, however, has fixed the age at forty. In a word, all the matters formerly pertaining to the jurisdiction of the patriarch are now in the province of the Synod. After this it is difficult to dispute the emperor's authority over the church.

On the establishment of the Synod, the bishops found themselves all on a level before this assembly in which centered all authority. If to-day we find some bearing the title of archbishop or metropolitan, these distinctions are merely honorary and lucrative, and the title is attached rather to the person than to the see. The nomination and election of bishops are no longer regulated by the canon of the Greek church. The Czar names the bishops on the presentation by the Synod of two names, but nothing is easier than to have included the one intended beforehand. As celibacy is requisite in a bishop, it follows that all the bishops belong to the monastic state, and this gives to the black clergy, as the monks are called, a great advantage over the secular or white clergy. Their salaries vary. While the metropolitan of St. Petersburg receives 5,500 rubles, or $4,125 a year, others receive less than one thousand. Besides this stipend they receive allowances to defray the expenses of their cathedral and household. To this we may add the proceeds of ordinations, burials, offerings made to miraculous pictures, church consecrations; and as the bishops are monks, they generally in a way remain archimandrite of their monastery, and thus enjoy the revenues still belonging to them, which consist of lands, mills, and fisheries of some value. The household is composed of two archpriests, a confessor, a steward, three deacons, and attendants who vary in number. These are maintained at the bishop's expense.

To help the bishop in the administration of his diocese, a consistory of six or ten members is selected from the *hegoumeni* of the monasteries and from the secular clergy. A lay secretary chosen by the Synod on the nomination of the chief procurator attends to all affairs even those of the clergy, down to the most minute details, and often to their disadvantage. His opinions and decisions are generally regulated by the amount of money he receives from the interested parties. He

, a host of clerks as mercenary as their master and
›ved only by the chief procurator. He is more
ın the bishop in the administration of his diocese,
o condition is the latter to enter into dispute with
radict his decisions. A bishop must reside in his
may not leave it, even to visit a neighboring
out permission from the Synod. He cannot call
ɔgether. Even for solemn functions, the number
mble to assist is limited to three beyond the regu-
f the parish, while synods and retreats are strictly
Any violation of these ordinances renders the
le to a fine or banishment without a trial at the
the Minister of the Interior. They can be trans-
one diocese to another even against their will,
of promotion and now as a sign of disgrace. In
bishop named Smaragdus who had occupied in
even different dioceses. The displeasure of the
ficient reason to retire a bishop to his monastery.
an clergy are divided into two classes, the white
ıd the black or religious, the latter so-called from
their dress. The white clergy may wear a dress
except black, though actual white is seldom worn.
led white clergy or popes in contradistinction to
black clergy from whom they are divided by an
g gulf of jealousy. In Russia alone has the cus-
l of requiring the marriage of all who are to be
ɔng the white clergy. As in the Catholic and
h, Holy Orders are a diriment impediment to
ıce clerics in minor Orders are obliged to marry
resent themselves for ordination to the diaconate,
ıate not being reckoned as one of the major
ave they perfect freedom in choosing their wives.
leacons have daughters; these daughters must
fe, and so it is prohibited to clerics to marry out-
ı class. The bishop is generally an ecclesiastical
n his own diocese and often forbids his students

a ukase of Alexander I published in 1814, the sons of popes and deacons should be placed at the disposal of the department of ecclesiastical schools, to be brought up for the priesthood, while the sons of noblemen and peasants who have priestly vocations are expected to join the monastic state. This plague of Levitism is one of the cancers eating into the life of the established church in Russia. Every secular priest or pope has generally with him a deacon and two clerks discharging the duties of sacristan, beadle, singer, etc., who partake of his various pecuniary resources—the priest receiving half, the deacon a quarter, and the remaining quarter is divided between the clerks. Many of the priests receive a yearly stipend from the imperial treasury, and besides this their incomes include offerings of the faithful for baptisms, marriages, confessions, Communions, and burials, as well as other perquisites from landed property and perpetual foundations for the dead. The landed property is often considerable; even in small parishes the pope has the usufruct of no less than fifty acres of glebe land. He tills his fields and plants his gardens whilst his wife attends to the household affairs. He with his deacon and clerks chant the Mass and Sunday office with all the pomp of the Greek ritual. He administers the sacraments according to the same rite, baptizing the children two or three weeks after their birth. Immediately after baptism, he administers Confirmation, by touching the forehead, lips, breast, hands, and feet of the child with a feather moistened with chrism, saying at each application: "Receive the seal of the Holy Spirit." Two weeks later the child is carried to the altar, where the deacon gives it a few drops of the Precious Blood with a spoon, from the chalice, saying: "N, servant of God, receive this sacrament in the name of the Father and of the Son and of the Holy Spirit." So much reverence have the people of the Russian church for the office of the priesthood, that they look upon their popes with solicitude and affection, and overlook their many faults, but they openly manifest that their respect is for the office and not for the man.

The black clergy or monks are more respected than the popes. They fill the episcopal sees and control nearly all the positions of honor in the church, though of late years the white clergy obtain the positions of embassy and military chaplains. The emperor's confessor is also a secular priest, and a member of the Synod, as also the Chaplain-in-chief of the Army and Navy. Hence the white clergy are assured of two voices in that assembly which governs the Russian church, voices very influential before which the majority is often compelled to bow. These concessions they have obtained within the past century, and their ambitions still tend toward the ranks of the episcopate; but here their efforts will be apt to fail, for a married episcopate was never known within the Orthodox church. The monks lead a celibate life and hence are the only members available for the order of bishops. They follow the rule of St. Basil, and from them are taken the professors and directors of seminaries and academies, the preachers for large towns, confessors, and prelates. Yet not always are the monks selected as professors. Men of Protestant tendencies, yea even Protestants themselves, such as John Von Horn, Graefe, and the unfrocked Capuchin, Fessler, who embraced Protestantism, are given chairs in their academies, thereby inoculating the minds of the clergy with a spirit of Protestantism very remarkable at the present day. To-day every phase of agnosticism that passes over the German universities is reflected in the ecclesiastical seminaries of Russia. This same spirit pervades the monasteries; and while there are virtuous and holy men to be found therein, their rule of Christian piety falls far behind the standard of Catholic conventual life; community life as understood by us, being almost unknown in Russia. The youths receive no instruction in the religious life; there is no novitiate, no period of probation. Their principal occupation is the recital of the long prayers and offices of the Russian liturgy. Everywhere the bureaucracy names the superiors, and these offices are stepping-stones to a higher career, which puts the organization at complete variance with the duties of the religious life. The last Saint canonized by the Holy Synod was the monk Seraphim, who died in the odor of sanctity at the monastery of Sarov in 1833, the Czar ratifying his canonization in Janu-

privilege of being interred within convent walls, and pilgrims replenish the alms-boxes most generously. The revenues attached to monasteries and convents are not calculated to maintain the highest ideal of the religious life, but act as a bait to entice another avaricious Peter or rapacious Catherine to confiscate these hoarded treasures.

In no country of the world is there more devotion to the Blessed Virgin and the saints than in Russia. The picture of Mary is found on the gateways, the principal buildings, in every shop, in every café or restaurant, and no Russian passes it without making the sign of the cross and saying a little ejaculatory prayer. Every family has its special *icon* or picture of Mary or one of the saints. These icons are of peculiar shape. The face and hands shine from the canvass as originally painted, but the headdress and halo, the clothing and drapery, are made in raised relief of silver or gold or pearls, and present a somewhat grotesque appearance. No one can pay a Russian a higher compliment than by taking some deferential notice of his icon, upon entering or leaving his dwelling or place of business. Before it he offers up his morning and evening prayers, and he never fails to consult the saint whom it represents, on all occasions of a doubtful or hazardous nature. At the funeral the priest walks in front carrying the *icon* of the deceased and at the grave it is laid upon the coffin. The walls of their churches are covered with them, and young and old do reverence before them, by bowing, crossing, and kissing, and other pious gesticulations. Their churches are usually square in form with five domes; a large one in the middle and four small ones at each corner of the building, to typify Christ and the four evangelists; where there are three domes they typify the Holy Trinity and where there is only one dome it represents Christ the Saviour. These domes are painted in gaudy colors, and are surmounted by lofty double-armed crosses which from the distance attract the eye of the traveler and relieve the monotony of the vast plains.

Up to a few years ago, any member of the Russian church who joined another communion, would incur the penalty of death. It was a crime punishable with from six to ten years' imprisonment with hard labor, to utter any word in public against the state church. To write against it was punishable by exile to Siberia, and to convert any person from the state religion incurred the same punishment. The Russian who should venture to follow his conscience and leave the Orthodox church for another religion was banished from his native land. Such was the case with Prince Gallitzin and Madame Swetchine. The children of all mixed marriages must be brought up as members of the dominant church. Yet in spite of this severity of the laws there are millions of native Russian schismatics called Raskolniks.

The present population of Russia is about 130,000,000, and in spite of the intolerance of the government, 25,000,000, exclusive of Roman Catholics, Jews, and Moslems, live in schism from the established church. These are known by the name of *Starovertzi* or Old Believers. They are also designated by the more general name of Raskolniks, that is to say, dissenters. They separated from the Russian church in the seventeenth century, when Nikon, the patriarch of Moscow, reformed the Russian liturgical books. In the course of time, many errors due to the negligence of copyists had crept into them. To remedy this Nikon corrected them with the help of the ancient Greek and Slavonian manuscripts. Then arose violent discussions; some cursed and anathematized Nikon. They separated from his communion, and owing to their immovable tenacity to the old customs they are designated by the name of Raskolniks. They were hunted down, exiled, tortured, and burned by Peter the Great; and their history is one of the wierdest stories in all the religious movements of the world. Soon they split into two factions known as the " Priestly " and the " Priestless " Old Believers. Those sects that have preserved the priesthood are the less radical and differ only from the Orthodox in the matter of Nikon's changes. After much persecution they receive to-day more tolerance, and are anxiously sought after as converts to the established church. On the other hand, the " Priestless " Raskolniks hold the wildest beliefs, and are broken into numerous sects. Some of them to hasten the second coming of Christ preached suicide and then quarreled about the mode. Others known as Duchobors, who believe in the reincarnation of our Lord, fled to Canada and gave much trouble to the government in 1898, by going out to meet Christ on his second coming, to a place where they would have died of cold or hunger if their foolish project had not been prevented. Before the death of Father John of Kronstadt a new sect had sprung into existence called "Ioannity". Many of the peasants had formed such a high idea of his sanctity that they thought he was the Messiah and great excitement had been caused by this preaching, until the police and ecclesiastical authorities took measures to prevent the propaganda. Thus numberless sects have grown out of the Nikon movement, all designated by the opprobrious name of Raskolniks, many of whom are still persecuted, and as usual answer persecution by a tenfold fanaticism. The religious tolerance now proclaimed has brought them relief at last.

For the last few years the attention of the world has been specially fastened upon Russia. A change has taken place in the constitution of the Empire and freedom of conscience was granted by a ukase issued by the Czar 30 April, 1905. The war with Japan helped the religious movement. The present Czar is a fair-minded man and the rebuke administered to the Procurator of the Holy Synod, M. Pobedonostzeff, when the former ascended the throne, was a noteworthy indication of his religious toleration. This Procurator was the most arrogant and intolerant bigot that ever occupied the high position, and his civil counsels to Alexander III induced the policy of the persecution of Catholics which disgraced his reign. To find Nicholas II setting aside his counsels and furthermore granting to Mgr. Agliardi, the Pope's envoy to the coronation, the concession of precedence over all the other envoys was certainly an augury of better things, and better things have come, and a brighter day has dawned for liberty of conscience in autocratic Russia. The project of ecclesiastical reform since the ukase of April, 1905, has been going on in the Orthodox church, and the leading men in state affairs are deeply concerned in its interests. Formal petitions have been forwarded to the Czar asking for the freedom of the

trigue, are returning to unity with Rome. Four months after the ukase of April, 1905, a dispatch from Mohilev stated that 220,000 members of the Orthodox church embraced the Catholic religion in that bishopric alone. It is true that throughout the Russian church there always has been, and there still is, a party friendly to Catholics. Professor Harnack says: " People who understand Russia, know that there is a patriotic Russian party, in the heart of the country, in Moscow and among the most educated people, that hopes for an awakening in their church in the direction of the Western Church—that is, of the Roman, not Evangelical Communion —who work for this, and who see in it the only hope for Russia." It is from this party on the one hand and the Uniates on the other that one hopes for the beginning of an understanding. The historian Pogodin prophesied that, should the day of deliverance ever come, " one half of the peasants will join the sect of the Raskolniks and one half of the educated classes will become Catholics." Of late years the Greek and Russian churches are drifting apart in the matter of doctrine and discipline; while Russia, notwithstanding its taint of Protestantism yet tends toward Rome, its Greek sister tends toward skepticism, which it is steadily importing from Germany. The Russians in a certain way welcome a Catholic as being one of themselves, while a Protestant is looked upon with distrust and dislike. When Mr. Palmer of Magdalen College, Oxford, visited Russia, in the interest of uniting the Anglican and Russian churches, they said to him: " If we had any communication with your church, it would have to be through the Pope and the Church of Rome; we can not recognize you otherwise. Reconcile yourself with your own Patriarch first, and then come and talk to us, if you think you have anything to say to us."

While there are twelve million Catholics in Russia, it is a sad thing that they are mostly Poles, whom every Russian considers hostile to the emperor and the nation, and this is in reality one of the gravest difficulties in the way of union with the Holy See. Persecution for their religion has embittered the Poles against the Russians, and the rebellion of forty years ago has accentuated the hatred on both sides. Since Leo XIII in the evening of his long life showed a favorable disposition to come to terms with the Orthodox church, the question of reunion has been agitated by influential leaders in Russia, yet in some quarters the activity of the Orthodox church against Catholic teaching is very pronounced. This fact shows that a lively interest is being taken in the matter. Lately two cheap editions of the speech of Bishop John George Strossmayer at the Vatican Council in 1870 in opposition to the definition of the Infallibility of the Pope have been issued. Needless to say, Bishop Strossmayer receded from his extreme views expressed in that speech, and became the most zealous advocate and foremost defender of that dogma up to his death in 1905. The reason for publication is frankly given. Since the toleration of religious freedom in Russia Catholic activity in religious matters has begun; and may it continue!

Let us not despair of the future. The events of the last half dozen years have cleared the atmosphere and drawn Russia closer to her mother, Rome. If arrogance and tyranny and the powers of darkness, in the past, have kept this vast land— this Colossus òf the North—in their clutches, we know there is One who is stronger than they, who will bring about, in His own good time, the deliverance of His schismatic but not heretical people who have clung with more than human tenacity to devotion to the Mother of God and to the Saints of God's Church.

WILLIAM LEEN.

Walker, Iowa.

THE STORY OF A MODERN CAPUCHIN.

FRANCE is a land of strange contrasts. The changeable character of its people is reflected in the variety of vicissitudes which mark the course of its history. We are wont to

ness or thoroughness. They are intensely in earnest in the pursuit of good or evil. Severely and inexorably logical, they are eager to push principles to their ultimate deductions. They are not content, like other peoples, with the best possible or attainable, with half-way measures or methods—with Horace's golden mean. Directed into a right course, their finer qualities, their great natural gifts, their enthusiasm, thoroughness, earnestness, and resourcefulness lead to results which inspire high hopes for the future, when the evil influences that have warped and weakened their character, misdirected their energies, and retarded the development of their moral qualities, shall have spent their force. The good and evil, working in opposite directions and for opposite ends, the counter influences operating for the renovation or ruin of a country whose diminishing population is indicative of a decadent epoch, the lights and shadows, sharply defined, are graphically depicted in the life of a famous French Capuchin, Père Marie Antoine, a typical Frenchman and a typical missioner.

Born in 1825 and dying in 1907, this missioner's life overlaps two centuries. Though the greater portion of his work was done during the latter half of the nineteenth century, he had not ceased working until after this century had dawned, and may be said to have died, as he had lived, laboring for the salvation of the country and the race he loved with all the devotion of an apostle and the ardor of a patriot. Variously designated by his admiring biographer[1] as "the Saint of Toulouse", "the Apostle of Toulouse", "the Demosthenes of the people", "the new Peter the Hermit", and "the Apostle of St. Anthony", his life was spent among and for the people. He was a personality and a power in the France of his day. In the big book in which Père Ernest Marie of Beaulieu relates his busy and well-spent life with an amplitude of detail that leaves nothing to be desired, there is not a dry page in all the closely printed 680. It is largely autobiographical,[2] being mainly made up of minute and vivid de-

---

[1] *Le Saint de Toulouse.* Vie du P. Marie Antoine des F. F. M. M. Capucins. Par le P. Ernest Marie de Beaulieu. Préface de M. le Chanoine Valentin. Toulouse: L. Sistac, Éditeur-Libraire. 1908.

[2] He wrote his own Life in 1894 at the instance of his family, and dedicated it to his nephew, Joseph, Curé of Missècle, in the diocese of Albi.

scriptions of the multitudinous missions which he directed or in which he took part, and the various religious undertakings he promoted. Full of interest and animation, it sheds some very illuminative sidelights upon the social and religious condition of contemporary France.

The pretty little town of Lavaur, the antique Val d'Or or golden vale, in the centre of the valley of the Agout, which primitively grew up around a castle of the Counts of Toulouse, was his birthplace. The country round about it was evangelized in the beginning of the fifth century by its bishop, St. Alain, but early in the thirteenth century, having become the first stronghold of the Albigenses, the town was beseiged and captured by Simon de Montfort, who laid a heavy hand upon the heretical inhabitants. Leo Francis Augustine Clergue, for such was his name in the world, was the son of Frederick Clergue who combined the functions of a notary's clerk with those of court registrar. " God," said he in the autobiography he wrote in 1894, " gave me parents of admirable piety, of consummate virtue, and of a culture of mind above their social position. Their means had been formerly considerable, but in the troubled times of the Revolution, my grandfather having been hunted as an aristocrat, this furtune had been providentially destroyed. It was a grace. Is not poverty the root of all virtues, and the aroma that preserves them? Are not the work and thrift which come of it the wisdom and honor of life? " They were strong legitimists. " God and the King " was their motto. Madame Clergue showed the mettle she was made of. A group of men, knowing her sentiments, to vex her waved the revolutionary flag several times under her windows. She did not stand it long. Forgetting her feebleness, she suddenly made her appearance in their midst, and, snatching the flag, tore it into fragments and trod it under foot, putting her disturbers promptly to flight. Henceforward she was known as " la Vendéenne de la Carlesse " from the name of the street they lived in. Père Marie Antoine inherited from his mother the energy and force of character, the iron will, the indomitable firmness, and militant spirit which characterized his whole strenuous life, early formed to solid, manly piety in a home where family prayer was made in common, where his mother read a passage from the *Imitation* or the Lives of the Saints before each meal, and his father at dessert declaimed some of Racine's sonorous lines or a fable of La Fontaine. " When I was young," said Père Marie Antoine once to a pious lady, " I was an obstinate fellow, but I always wished to be a saint." The preacher was foreshadowed before the saint. He tells us how his child-companions called him " Pope Leo " (he was christened Leo through devotion to Leo XII), and gathered round him to listen to the little sermons he delivered when he was five or six years of age. He had been dedicated to the Blessed Virgin when he was an infant—his pious father taking him in his arms immediately after baptism and placing him on her altar, praying her to be a Mother to him and to adopt him as her child—and when he grew to manhood he dedicated himself to her. Eight times during his infancy he was near dying in his cradle, and eight times, at his father's prayers, Our Lady restored him to health. He was initiated into the service of the sanctuary by the venerable curé of Saint Alain, Père Noyer, an aged priest laden with the weight of ninety years and still more laden with merits, who had for curate his brother, another saintly priest beloved of the poor, who followed the brothers to the grave with the remark, " On n'en plantera plus de si bons *noyers; on n'en plantera plus!*" " Formed by such holy priests and such holy parents," said Père Marie Antoine, " from my tenderest years I had only one thought, one desire: to be a priest, to say Mass, and to preach. My pious parents hastened to second such a sublime vocation." Before he completed his eleventh year he was sent to the Petit Seminaire of Toulouse, where he was already called "the little Capuchin ". The venerable superior, M. Izac, predicted that he would one day become a son of St. Francis. One of his fellow students, Paul Goux, the superior's nephew, became afterward curé of Saint-Sernin and Bishop of Versailles, and another, Gabriel Monbet, the celebrated Abbot of La Trappe d'Aiguebelle. They were called " the three Louis Gonzagas of the Esquile," the name of the seminary.

The smallest incidents of his early life always remained fresh in his memory. Here is one which reveals a Franciscan trait as touching as it is characteristic in its simplicity. When,

two years before his death, the nuns of the Convent of Our
Lady of Charity of Refuge in the Rue Rémusat were cele-
brating his golden jubilee, he reminded them that it was in
their chapel he heard and served his first Mass in Toulouse;
how the then superioress used to give him a slice of bread and
jam for his breakfast, and how, instead of eating it himself,
he gave it to a poor man who waited for him at the corner of
an adjacent street. "We became great friends," he said,
"and it was a great joy to us to meet every morning. I sat
down while he ate the slice, and I remember his saying to me,
weeping, ' My little child, you'll be blessed by the good God! '
Not a day passed without this scene being renewed, and this
meeting with my old friend was a thing very sweet to my
childish heart, which suffered cruelly from being separated
from my father and mother, for whom I had the greatest affection. One day, after leaving my old friend the beggar, I
was passing along, sad and solitary, through the little street,
always thinking of my beloved parents, my heart painfully
oppressed with the feeling of being far away from them, when
I was suddenly stopped as it were by the sound of a voice.
This memory is so deeply engraven in my heart that I still
see the very place in the street where I heard that voice, and
could describe it. That voice said to me: ' My child, thy
father and mother, however much they love thee, cannot always be thinking of thee, but I always do. Will thou not
love Me? ' I knew that it was the voice of my God which
thus spoke to me, and, from that moment, I gave myself to
Him." To Our Lady he also turned for unfailing consolation in the absence of the loved ones. "She became," he
says, "my consoler and my guardian. I prayed to her every
day and placed upon her altar the prizes I had the good fortune to win twice a year." He specially besought her to obtain for him humility, confidence, and love. "Humility, confidence, and love," repeats his biographer, "there you have the
whole spiritual life of Père Marie Antoine to its close. Those
whom he directed and consoled in his long career will recognize the whole man in those three words, which sum up all
his exhortations, encouragements, sermons, and letters. Before teaching others, the man of God exercised himself in the

When he was twenty-two and a young prof
through that mysterious state called by mystics
of the soul. " God," he says, " prepared me foi
of His grace by an interior trial which ha
been the greatest in my life, strewn, however,
mercy with an infinity of sweetnesses." The
shed a ray of light upon the darkness that
during six months of mental anguish was utter
who found him in tears and said to him: " (
you pass through this state because He destines
some one who will suffer what you are suffe
this, he was not only resigned but asked for r
He attributed his deliverance from what he c
mense trial, this unfathomable desolation " to
intervention of the Blessed Virgin, who inspir
" an angelic pupil ", when making his first C
pray to our Lord at the moment he received Hir
on my professor." " He did so," relates Père N
" and at that very instant my martyrdom cease
began in my soul at the moment when the chi
the altar steps from the holy Table. I fell on
if pushed by an invisible hand; I shed a torren
arose in the peace and joy of an indescribable :
my soul has ever since preserved. All that the
have said of the dark night and martyrdom of
perienced and felt. I call this grace, the grace
then understood and learnt what Calvary and th
were. From that day the attraction toward the
came stronger; I could not approach the tabei
the presence of Jesus becoming, as it were, sen:
cibly taking possession of my heart. I seemed
saying to me: ' My son, thou seest Me here chi
Impossible for Me to go and convert that poor :
that poor invalid, that sad prisoner; go and
and do as I would do Myself '."

He was not slow in obeying the call. The

ing him to the poor, the lowly, the humble, the children, and the populations of the faubourgs, to him always the favorite portion of the flock. He drew some of his fellow students into this apostolate, creating several *œuvres,* such as that of the Blessed Sacrament, an association formed of his pious friends who daily sacrificed a quarter of an hour of the time allotted to recreation which was spent in adoration before the Tabernacle; and that of the hospitals and prisons, visited twice a week.

He was a pioneer in what has come to be called social action. That portion of the population who roam the streets of large cities to procure by painful, almost servile labor their daily bread, without fixed abodes, almost always wandering and thus removed from the pastoral purview, who, if they had had any religious principles instilled into them in childhood, soon lose them and stagnate in forgetfulness of every duty, a prey to ignorance more than misery and exposed to all the seductions of crime, moved his sympathies and stimulated him to action. To apply a remedy, he, along with some of his confrères, founded in the Seminary an association out of which sprang the work of the *petits Savoyards,* or, as we would say, city Arabs; and, so as not to lose sight of them when they grew up, that of the *petits métiers,* or small traders. Another work was to gather together, at the approach of Lent, the street porters, shoeblacks, and vagrants of all sorts to get them to fulfil the Easter duty. About twenty attended the first meeting in the Chapel of the Holy Thorn. Some of the street porters having plotted to spoil the work, it was deemed prudent not to go hunting them up but wait until they came. At first very few came of their own motion, and at the suggestion of those who did, a more convenient hour in the evening was fixed, as they had to be up before dawn to find work for the day and needed rest. When the time came, to their astonishment such a number of street-porters and poor toilers of all ages assembled—more than two hundred—that the chapel was quickly filled. The number increasing, it became evident that the zeal and familiar instructions of students, not yet invested with the priesthood, were insufficient for the object in view, and the co-operation of the Seminary professors was invited and secured. " How touching it was," relates Père Marie Antoine, "to see those men, after instruction, come up to the sanctuary and throng round us to ask us for medals of the Blessed Virgin which, kissing them, they put round their necks; and, better still, to ask us to lead them to the different confessors we had brought. ' I want one very much, Monsieur l'Abbé,' said some, ' and I'll want time, for it is ten, twenty, thirty, fifty, and even sixty years since I went to confession.' And the tears flowed from their eyes; the priests who so charitably heard them knew they were sincere. Others, blushing, whispered in our ears: ' Monsieur l'Abbé, I haven't made my first Communion.' And yet, sometimes the hair of the one who spoke was white. Others, still more confused, with sorrow and tears confessed that they had not sanctified their union by the sacrament of marriage." Confessions and instructions became more frequent, followed by an eight days' retreat, concluded with a general Communion in Easter week, when there were one hundred and forty communicants, nearly a dozen of whom made their first Communion then. The retreat produced miraculous effects. " The most obstinate sinners who had not yet responded to the call of grace," writes Père Marie Antoine, " fell on their knees at the confessor's feet bathed in tears, almost ill from sorrow, asking as a favor a penance equal to the greatness of their faults. ' See, it's thirty years,' said one of them, ' since I made my first Communion, and since that time, I don't think I entered a church once; but now I'm repairing this scandal.' In fact, seeing him overwhelmed with fatigue, coming to one of our exercises, ' Well, poor friend,' we said to him, ' you're ill?' ' No, Monsieur l'Abbé,' he replied, ' it's only a little weakness. See, since daybreak, I've been in my parish church on my knees at the foot of the altar, and I remained there until everybody saw me; I wanted to thus repair my scandal.' (It was Holy Thursday.) I turned aside to dry a tear and bless the Lord."

What he calls " a prodigy of mercy " is thus recorded: " Among the first-communicants there was one more interesting than the others. He was an old soldier nearly sixty years of age; his body, covered with wounds, and his scarred face were reminders of his intrepid courage. ' A confessor, if you please, Monsieur l'Abbé,' addressing the catechist, ' I've a terrible tale to tell him; I took to soldiering young and I haven't yet made my first Communion.' He threw himself at once at the confessor's feet, received a medal, and promised, on his word of honor, to come to the next service to continue his confession. But in vain we waited for him; he didn't reappear. Astonished at such forgetfulness on his part, we hastened to look him up in the square of the city where we had first found him: the place he usually occupied was vacant. His comrades approached to tell us that he had been seized with a terrible hemorrhage of blood and that they had taken him to the hospital. We hurried there and they led us to his bedside, where we found him unable to speak, so acute was his suffering. But, to express his gratitude to us, he pressed our hands, kissed them, and bathed them with his tears. He manifested a wish to continue his confession and make his first Communion. Our visits after that were frequent; his confessor saw him every day, and he had the happiness, assisted by the catechist, to bring him the Viaticum on the eve of his death, the first Communion which was also the last."

The catechist was the Abbé Clergue who, during his last years at the Seminary, devoted all his free time to this apostolate, seeking, with others, in the squares and crossways of the city the young Savoyards and children, giving them a sou after each instruction, and at the close of the year a pretty little wax taper and new clothes. "The character, gaiety, affability, and piety of the Abbé Clergue," says one of his coworkers, M. David, "fitted him very well for this ministry. He was more zealous, more the apostle, bolder than I in seeking them, finding them, and bringing them."

He was soon to enter on a higher ministry. At the approach of his ordination, after summing up in a few lines all that constitute the greatness of the priesthood, he wrote, *Diligis Me?* That is to say, "Lovest thou God alone in all and for all? If thou canst answer on the day of thy priesthood: *Deus meus et omnia!* then thou wilt be worthy to hear Jesus Christ say to thee, *Pasce agnos meos:* I confide to thee these souls, which are most precious to Me, and which ought to be to thee, as to Me, more precious than thy blood and thy life." His biographer discerns in these words a foreshadowing of his Franciscan and apostolic vocation.

[TO BE CONTINUED.]

R. F. O'CONNOR.

Cork, Ireland.

THE ROMAN CURIA.

The Offices.

IN the preamble of the Constitution, *Sapienti consilio,* the Sovereign Pontiff lays down that the Roman Curia is composed of Congregations, Tribunals, and Offices. Having treated at some length of the two former departments in previous articles of this REVIEW, it still remains for us to consider the third department, which comprises five Offices. These we shall now briefly discuss, following the order set down in the Constitution itself. The term Offices (*Officia*), it is hardly necessary to say, here designates certain secretariates established in Rome for the purpose of expediting ecclesiastical business.

THE APOSTOLIC CHANCERY—IN FORMER TIMES.

From the early ages of Christianity the Popes were accustomed to keep records of various pontifical acts, and officials were placed in charge of the archives containing these records. These officials were called *Scriniarii* and *Chartularii;* to these were added *Notarii.* The chief of these officials was termed *Protoscriniarius,* and his position became so exalted a dignity as to be conferred on bishops. It would seem that only in the eleventh century the word *Cancellarius* began to be applied to the holder of this dignity. It is not quite clear why he received this title. Some are of opinion that he was thus called because he was accustomed to *cancel* defective documents, while there are others who think that this name was given to him because he was wont to give audiences behind grating (*cancelli*). From the thirteenth century the chief official was no longer designated as Chancellor, but Vice-Chancellor, and the practice was continued even till the reorganization of the Roman Curia by the present Sovereign Pontiff. A reason for the use of the term Vice-Chancellor rather than Chancellor, has been found in the fact that formerly the prefectship of the Chancery was conferred upon a person of less exalted dignity than that of a Cardinal, so that when the practice was subsequently altered, a Cardinal in assuming the duties of the Chancellor was not lowered from his former dignity, since he did not receive the title of Chancellor, but performed his duties while retaining the more exalted dignity of Cardinal. In more recent times the prefect of this Office received another title, viz., *Summista* which was given to him by Alexander VIII in 1690. There was another official called *Regens Cancellariae,* who was also named *Subsummista,* because he acted as substitute for the Vice-Chancellor. Among the offices of the Chancery there were many others, such as *Notarius, Secretarius, Plumbator,* etc.; there was even a college of prelates appointed to assist in the functions of the Chancery which was called *Collegium Praelatorum de parco majori,* and which had a dean and secretary.

The scope of work for the Apostolic Chancery was for a long time very extensive, as may be shown from a letter of St. Bernard to Cardinal Haimerich, who was Vice-Chancellor at the time the letter was written. We shall here make a brief extract from the letter. " Siquidem cum nullum ferme fiat in orbe bonum, quod per manus quodammodo Romani Cancellarii transire non habet, ut vix bonum judicetur, quod ejus prius non fuerit examinatum judicio, moderatum consilio, studio roboratum et confirmatum adjutorio," etc. The Saint proceeds to say that the man holding this position should be regarded as the most fortunate, or the most miserable, since he either participates in all that is worthy, or else proves himself the enemy of all that is good; therefore rightly should he have all praise or censure corresponding to the results and the merits of his endeavors. Afterwards, when the Secretariate of Briefs and the Apostolic *Dataria* were separated from the Roman Chancery, and still more when the various Roman Congregations with their respective Secretariates were introduced, the Chancery became greatly diminished in the number of its functions. Still it continued to be competent to expedite all the acts of the Roman Pontiffs which by written law or the approved practice of the Curia should be published in *forma Bullae.*

THE APOSTOLIC CHANCERY UNDER THE NEW LEGISLATION.

by the legislation of the *Sapienti consilio.* For this end we naturally turn to the document itself and to any supplementary publications of the Holy See upon the subject. In the section of the constitution relating to the Apostolic Chancery allusion is made to three headings, the personnel, the functions, and the mode of procedure.

THE PERSONNEL.

As regards the first heading, it is simply stated that one of the Cardinals of the Holy Roman Church will preside over the Office and that he shall assume the title of Chancellor instead of Vice-Chancellor. Whoever holds the dignity of Chancellor holds likewise the Office of Notary in the Sacred Consistory. The reason for this latter enactment is quite obvious, since the official who performs the duties of Notary for the S. Consistory must be well acquainted with the great bulk of the business which has to be expedited by the Chancery. As to the reason for the title of Chancellor being given henceforth to the Cardinal appointed to preside over the Chancery, it may be assumed that the Sovereign Pontiff wishes to have it understood that the functions of the Prefect of the Chancery are sufficiently important to be performed by a member of the Sacred College, or in other words that the title of Chancellor is not beneath the Cardinalitial dignity. Along with the Prefect of the Chancery there is a Regent; also five Prothonotaries Apostolic; besides, there is an *Adjutor Studii* or Informator, whose duty it is to be well versed in the cause and, if this be a matter of considerable length, to give a synopsis of it.[1] In the Office of the Chancery there is a secretary who performs the duties of archivist, and there are likewise four writers. Each of these officials has his respective duties which may be found in the " Normae Peculiares," Chap. 6.

FUNCTIONS OF THE ROMAN CHANCERY.

tion of new dioceses and chapters, and the transaction of the other great affairs of the Church." In treating of the Consistorial Congregation we have seen that the chief part of its functions consist in the erection of new dioceses and the appointment of bishops in those places outside the jurisdiction of the S. Propaganda; and it belongs to the Apostolic Chancery to expedite these and other such grave affairs of the Church. It may be well to note that Papal Constitutions or Apostolic Letters are usually issued under the form of Bulls or of Briefs. There are indeed simple Apostolic Letters not issued under either of these forms, but as these do not present any special peculiarity, reference to them may be here omitted. Bulls are distinguished from Briefs inasmuch as the former relate to the more important business of the Church, and Briefs to the less important. The document called a Bull was formerly distinguished by being written in Gothic characters on strong brown parchment with a hanging seal of lead (*sub plumbo*) or gold. The seal (*Bulla*) bore on one side the images of SS. Peter and Paul, and on the obverse side the name of the Roman Pontiff. At the beginning of the reign of the late Pope, Leo XIII, a change was introduced on 29 December, 1878. Instead of the Gothic characters it was ordered that the ordinary Latin characters should be used, while only in the more solemn acts of the Holy See was the leaden seal to be attached. In the less solemn acts the seal itself was not to be attached, but only the impression of a red seal having the images of SS. Peter and Paul with the name of the reigning Pontiff inscribed around it.

The other kind of Papal Constitution, called a Brief, employed in less grave concerns of the Church, is written upon white thin parchment or vellum; sometimes ordinary paper is used, but always of excellent quality. Briefs are not expedited by the Apostolic Chancery, but by the Secretariate of State or by the Secretariate of Briefs to Princes, while it appertains to the Chancery to expedite Papal documents *sub plumbo* in the form of a Bull. On the subject of Bulls and Briefs the reader can find a very able and exhaustive article in the second volume of the new *Catholic Encyclopedia.*

MODE OF PROCEDURE.

Hitherto two modes of procedure have been employed by

the Apostolic Chancery. One was called the ordinary; the other was called the extraordinary method. The former was employed when the Rules of the Chancery were exactly observed, so that nothing was changed in the customary form or clauses, and when the expedition was effected through the ordinary officials. The extraordinary method was employed in three different ways, termed respectively *per viam secretam, de camera,* and *de curia.* The first of these, *per viam secretam,* signified that the Bulls were forwarded gratis and without strict observance of the rules of the Chancery; the second way, *de camera,* signified that, although a tax was imposed, the other rules of the Chancery were not rigidly observed; and the third, *de curia,* meant that the Bulls, after receiving the signatures of the Pro-Datary and of the Secretary of Briefs, were recorded at the Secretariate of Briefs and despatched *extra Cancellariam.* It should be here noted that these three modes of expedition have been suppressed by the new Constitution, and the ordinary method, *per viam Cancellariae,* alone remains in force. It is also deserving of notice that the College of Prelates, formerly known as *Abbreviatores majoris vel minoris residentiae,* is likewise suppressed by the Constitution and that their duties are to be performed by the Prothonotaries Apostolic.

THE APOSTOLIC DATARY.

ITS ORIGIN.

himself according to the well-known adage, " Papa non Datarius concedit gratias ".   In particular the Datary received
authority to grant dispensations in diriment impediments of
matrimony, in irregularities, in the alienation of ecclesiastical
property, and in conferring those benefices reserved to the
Pope which were not Consistorial.

FORMER PERSONNEL AND MODE OF PROCEDURE.

The *Datarius* or Prefect of the Datary was formerly a Prelate, but from the fifteenth century he has usually been a Cardinal; hence for the same reason as in the case of the Vice-
Chancellor, the incumbent of this office has been called
Pro-Datarius.   Under him there were three major officials,
viz., the Sub-Datary, the official *per obitum,* and the official
per concessionem.   It belonged to the first of these to assist
the *Datarius* in a special manner and to supply his place even
in the causes which were required to be brought before the
personal notice of the Roman Pontiff.   The official *per obitum*
had special charge of those matters which were brought before
the *Dataria* on account of vacancies occurring through death
(*per obitum*) ; the third official was put in charge of dispensations or concessions granted by the Datary (*per concessionem*).
The minor officials of the Datary were very numerous, and it
is not necessary to stop here in order to name them.   The
reader may consult the authors already cited for a list of the
minor offices.   For a long time it was customary to hold a
daily meeting of the Datary, at which the Cardinal Pro-
Datary and the three major officials were present.   The petitions were discussed at those meetings, and, if favorably received, were either granted by the Cardinal Pro-Datary, if it
came within his authority to grant them, or, if not, they were
proposed in audience to the Sovereign Pontiff.   Then, when
the appointments and dispensations and answers were made
or given, there were other officials to expedite them.   From
time to time various changes were effected in the procedure of
the Apostolic Datary.   Even within a few years prior to the
publication of the Constitution, *Sapienti consilio,* new regulations were made for this Office.   Thus petitions for dispensations were regulated by a Statute of 1897; and the procedure
for the grant of benefices was likewise regulated by an enact-

ITS PRESENT SCOPE.

The scope of the Datary has been greatly diminished by the Constitution, *Sapienti consilio.* It no longer possesses any authority to grant matrimonial dispensations; it cannot give any dispensation in irregularities, nor can it grant permission for the alienation of ecclesiastical property. According to the terms of the new legislation: " For the future the one special function of the Dataria is to be that of taking cognizance of the fitness of those who aspire to non-consistorial benefices reserved to the Apostolic See; to draw up and forward the Apostolic Letters conferring these benefices; to dispense from the requisite conditions for the conferring of these benefices; to look after the pensions and charges which the Supreme Pontiff shall have imposed for the conferring of them."

There are some ecclesiastical benefices which are conferred by the Consistorial Congregation, e. g., bishoprics not subject to the S. Propaganda. In countries subject to the latter the appointment to episcopal benefices appertains to the Propaganda itself with the confirmation of the Sovereign Pontiff. There are other ecclesiastical benefices which are not acquired through the Consistorial Congregation or through the Propaganda, and yet are reserved to the Holy See. It is this latter class of benefices which is entrusted to the supervision of the Datary. It belongs to this Office to determine the fitness of aspirants to these benefices, and to confer them through Apostolic Letters. The Datary has likewise authority in the conferring of those benefices to exempt from the conditions required by the ecclesiastical law. This authority is somewhat similar to what the Congregation of the Council possesses in regard to parochial benefices which may be conferred by Ordinaries. It is the duty of the Datary to take care of the pensions and charges imposed in conferring those non-consistorial benefices reserved to the Holy See.

REGULATIONS TO BE OBSERVED.

and by existing usage, in such manner, however, that the latter will not be in disagreement with the former. It is also laid down in the "Normae" that there should be a minute or written summary of the documents conferring the benefices, to be taken by an assistant; and this minute is to be preserved in the acts of the Datary. Besides it is mentioned in the "Normae" that no change is made in the method sometimes employed of conferring benefices by a decree of simple signature without the expedition of any Bull. When however benefices are conferred through Bulls, these are to be signed by the Cardinal Datary or, when this cannot be, by the Cardinal Secretary of State; in either case they should be countersigned with the signature of the official present who is first in the order of time after the *Datarius.*

THE PRESENT PERSONNEL OF THE DATARY.

It is expressly set forth in the Constitution that this Office is under the presidency of one of the Cardinals and that he will have the title of *Datarius,* not *Pro-Datarius,* as heretofore. A similar change, and for a similar reason is made, as has been seen, regarding the title of Chancellor in place of Vice-Chancellor.

What the other officials under the Cardinal President are, we are not told in the Constitution nor in the "Normae"; but in the *Acta Apostolicae Sedis* for January, 1909 (pp. 132 and 133), a list of the other officers is given. Among these may be named the *Subdatarius,* Prefect, Substitute, and four Consultors—in all fifteen without reckoning the Cardinal Datary. In former times it was necessary to have a much larger number owing to the more extensive duties which were to be performed by this Office.

THE APOSTOLIC CAMERA.
ORIGIN AND FORMER PERSONNEL.

This is another of the Offices of the Roman Curia and one whose origin can be traced back to the end of the eleventh century. The ecclesiastic who was placed over it received the title, *Domini Papae Camerarius.* From the middle of the twelfth century until the fifteenth, Cardinals were frequently appointed to this position, and since the latter date this dignity has been entirely confined to the Cardinalitial body.

Along with the *Camerarius* or Chamberlain there were three assistants, one of whom was called the Vice-Chamberlain, the second General Treasurer, and the third Auditor General. The first assistant or Vice-Chamberlain was always, after the seventeenth century, invested with the title of *Gubernator Urbis,* and sometimes even before that time. The General Treasurer had the guardianship of the Papal Treasury and also a supervision over certain officials termed *Collectores* and *Subcollectores.* The third assistant or Auditor General received considerable civil and criminal jurisdiction, and under his direction there was a tribunal of justice consisting of prelates and doctors of laws.

COMPETENCE OF THE APOSTOLIC CAMERA HITHERTO.

For many years the Apostolic Camera possessed authority for administering the rights and temporal possessions of the Holy See; it was, besides, a tribunal of fiscal causes, as also in some criminal and civil matters.[4] In modern times the functions of the Camera were limited to the temporal government of the papal dominions, so that when the Holy See was robbed of these dominions in 1870, there has scarcely been any proper function for this Office. However, during the vacancy of the Apostolic See it retained full authority in the Palace of the Pontiff. It belonged to the Cardinal Chamberlain to enter the Pope's chamber on the occasion of his death and to declare officially the fact of that death. The examination of the corpse was made in his presence, and he then entered upon the administration of the Apostolic Palace and made provision for the Conclave.

PRESENT STATUS OF THE APOSTOLIC CAMERA.

and administration of the rights and property of the Holy See, especially between the death of the Roman Pontiff and the election of his successor.

Now in regard to the functions appertaining to this Office and to the Cardinal Chamberlain, who is its President, during the interregnum, we are referred for information to the regulations contained in the Constitution of the present Pope entitled *Vacante Sede Apostolica.* It is to be noted that this important document contains the most recent legislation regarding the observance to be followed during a vacancy of the Holy See. Many of the requirements enacted by preceding Pontiffs are here confirmed, while a few of them are abrogated and new ones substituted. This Constitution, consisting of ninety-one sections, is divided into two main parts. The first part deals with the authority of the S. College of Cardinals during the vacancy; the meetings of the Cardinals, general and particular; the Sacred Congregations and the faculties they possess; and the obsequies of the Pontiff. The second part regards the election of the Roman Pontiff and contains seven chapters dealing with the Electors or Cardinals, Conclavists, i. e. those appointed to attend upon the Cardinals in Conclave, the entrance into Conclave, the *clausura* and secrecy to be observed by the Electors and Conclavists, the form of election, certain observances during election, the aceptance and proclamation of the election; finally the consecration and coronation of the new Pope. It is not proposed here to give an exposition of the contents of this Constitution, since for this purpose an entire article or more properly several articles would be needed; it is merely intended to ascertain from this document the duties devolving upon the Apostolic Camera and its President, the Cardinal Chamberlain, during the vacancy of the Holy See. In section 14 of this Constitution it is laid down that the Cardinal Chamberlain has charge of the temporal goods and rights of the Holy See and that he is assisted in the fulfilment of his duties by the senior Cardinal in each of the three Orders (Cardinal Bishops, Cardinal Priests, and Cardinal Deacons); he should also obtain the suffrages of the whole College of Cardinals upon questions of business. As soon as he has received information of the death of the Sovereign Pontiff from the Pre-

order to take possession and exercise control. He must also make a juridical investigation of the Pontiff's death and draw up an authentic certificate thereto; he should likewise after consulting the three Senior Cardinals just referred to, determine the most suitable mode of preserving the body of the dead Pontiff, unless the latter while still alive had made known his will upon the matter. The Cardinal Chamberlain is also required to affix seals to the private apartments of the deceased Pontiff, and to give information of the death to the Cardinal Vicar of the City. He must too in the name and with the consent of the College of Cardinals make whatever arrangements may be deemed expedient in the circumstances for defending the rights of the Holy See and for its proper administration. There are other duties to be discharged by the Cardinal Chamberlain, mentioned in the same Constitution, *Sede Vacante Apostolica,* such as to see that the oath of secrecy, obligatory under pain of excommunication specially reserved to the future Pontiff, be taken by the Conclavists at least one or two days before entrance into Conclave (Sect. 40). Then the keys of the Conclave are to be handed to the Chamberlain after it has been closed within and without; and the Chamberlain along with the three Cardinals already mentioned is to examine the hidden places and corners of the Conclave in order that no one forbidden should remain (Sect. 46). There are a few other details to be executed by the Cardinal Chamberlain, but being of less importance they are here omitted.

THE PERSONNEL OF THE NEW CAMERA.

THE MONK AS A WITNESS IN APOLOGETICS.

To forestall possible misapprehension as to the drift and purport of the following article, the author would beg the reader to bear in mind that what he has written here is but one of a series of connected studies. Some of these have already appeared in print (see *The Catholic World,* passim, 1907-1909), and others are shortly to follow, having for scope to describe Catholic and Roman Christianity as the fullest, most continuous and, withal, most vital expression in history of the primary claim once formulated by our Lord, that He is, indeed, the Way, the Truth, and the Life, and that His Church, as embodying His larger Self through the ages, must take on something of the same mysterious triad of characteristics. Whether one examines it in idea, or endeavors to follow its actual realizations in history, Monachism will be found to be but another of those arresting manifestations which make good the claim of Roman Christianity to be, not only a survival, but the only authentically uncompromising survival of our Lord's religion upon earth to-day. The timeliness of such a suggestion when Rome's instinctive attitude toward Monachism is taken into account will not have escaped the regard of those who have been struck by the extraordinary vitality of the coenobitical ideal, not merely among ourselves, but among latter-day Anglican and Lutheran bodies as well; and that, too, in an age somewhat too hastily assumed as unfavorable to its further development.—C. C.

IT was in the *Essay on Development,* published now nearly two-thirds of a century ago, and not yet fully mastered, it would seem, either by the general public to which it was obviously addressed, or by the theologians, Roman or Anglican, who have since taken the trouble to examine it, that the genius of Newman first ventured to sketch in outline the historic data for the argument that had led him, all unwittingly, to the threshold of St. Peter's See. Among the many remarkable positions in that elusive book, Monachism is briefly touched upon as one of those instances of " logical sequence " which prove, not only that Roman Christianity is not a corrupt Christianity, but that it turns out on investigation to be the only full and legitimate expression in actual history of our Lord's idea of a *growing* Kingdom of God upon earth. It was a large claim to make for an institution the evil of which has, in popu-

unwary of pitfalls that scarcely make for progress in Catholic thinking, and that certainly have not made for pleasantness in instances not a few that we could mention. Yet, in spite of all this, in spite, too, of its merely capitular and outline quality, the *Essay* remains, on the whole, one of the most stimulating pieces of constructive reasoning produced by the religious debates of the nineteenth century; and on that score alone, if on no other, it deserves the attentive study of all those who believe that the witness of history cannot be utterly without bearing upon the real mind of Christ and of the Church that His personality called into being.

And what we have said of the primary idea of the *Essay* itself will have to be applied, with certain conjectural restrictions, to its brief, but singularly illuminating, remarks on the rise and development of the monastic idea. The genealogical descent of that idea may be other than the argument avers. For the monk in the great Tractarian's view of him is described as a fourth-century product of the Catholic feeling for post-baptismal penance, and is, in no strict sense of the word, a New Testament creation at all. He has entered, however, so largely, so inevitably, and withal so congruously into the active life of the Church as to have become, *through the influence and growth of the obediential ideal,* part of the very fibre and substance of Catholicism itself. Such an account of the matter may satisfy Protestant prejudices, indeed; but will it escape the imputation of offense against those Catholic prepossessions in which the monastic life is currently viewed as a palpable and immediate derivative in logic, whatever it may prove to be in its actual history, of our Lord's hard teaching on the " counsels "? The answer is, of course, that Newman's concern is with the evidences that seem to make against Roman Christianity, and that in linking Monachism, as he does, to the ordinances which speedily revealed to Catholicism at large the Church's abiding conviction as to her power over post-baptismal sin, he has vindicated for the institution a dignity that length of time could not greatly enhance nor dearth of monuments ever enfeeble or destroy. Does he not tell us in so many words that " in the first ages, the doctrine of the punishments of sin, whether in this world or in the next, was little called for "? The monk, as we know him in history, had not appeared, because the time was too fervent to give occasion or significance to his coming. " The rigid discipline of the infant Church," we are reminded, " was the preventive of greater offenses, and its persecutions the penance of their commission; but when the Canons were relaxed and confessorship ceased, then some substitute was needed, and such was Monachism, being at once a sort of continuation of primeval innocence, and a school of self chastisement." [1] No historical scholar, we imagine, will be disposed to quarrel with that position; even if, as Newman himself was prepared to admit, " the sheepskin and desert of St. Antony did but revive the ' mantle ' and the mountain of the first Carmelite, and St. Basil's penitential exercises had already been practised by the Therapeutae."

It was the frank recognition, the instinctive sympathy it eventually met with at the hands of authority, and more especially on the part of St. Peter's See, that gave Monachism what we may call its biological opportunity and secured for it from the days of St. Benedict's reform its extraordinary and mysterious promise of life. How that recognition was, ultimately won, how it substituted definiteness, efficiency and life for the comparative formlessness which had hitherto characterized the same institution throughout the brooding East, how these qualities in turn reacted upon the corporate and hierarchial Church at large, knitting every portion of the mystical Body of Christ into *a discipline of obedience* that gave new significance to the old Apostolic plea for unity by emphasizing the essentially pragmatical note of our Lord's appeal to the general as well as to the individual soul,—how order, in a word, emerged from disorder, and heaven from what began as chaos, will be best understood by studying the careers of the four master spirits of the West through whom Monachism became supremely articulate, fruitful, and true. There are other names, no doubt, patriarchal names, too, which no student of its history can afford to ignore; but few if any of them stand out from the surrounding welter of religious effort as do the names of St. Benedict, St. Dominic, St. Francis of Assisi, and St. Ignatius of Loyola. Each of these, it is true, is a man of the Latin race and each of them appears

[1] C. ix, § 6; p. 395, edit. 1900..

at an acute crisis in the fortunes of Latin Catholicism; but
it is not less true that each of them is also more than Latin
in his outlook, and like the Church to which by an instinctive
loyalty he consecrates his gifts, the Latinism is transfigured
to a Catholic breadth which marks him as one in spirit and in
legitimate descent with Him who, though a Jew, is nevertheless for all men, the Way.

It is with the story of St. Benedict that the history of Monachism, as perhaps the most plastic and far-reaching of the non-
sacramental forces of Western Christianity, really begins.
Mabillon, basing his researches on the materials affectionately
put together by St. Gregory, has preserved for us all that
seems possible to be known of his unique and inspiring career.
It was a career, in many ways, rife with anomalies beyond the
measure usually found even in reformer Saints. He was born
in the last quarter of that moribund fifth century which, in spite
of the few commanding names that emphasize it, has left so
little impress on after-time. He was a patrician, who was
yet enamored of the simple life; a scion of the corrupt office-
holding class, who cared more for solitude than for curial
place. An insignificant Roman *municipium* in the Sabine
country, the *frigida Nursia*[2] of Vergil, was the home of his
boyhood. The best education of his time was open to him;
but he turned from it in dismay, preferring, in St. Gregory's
quaint phrase, to be " skilfully ignorant and wisely un-
learned "[3] rather than buy knowledge at the cost of innocence
which was the accepted price that youth only too commonly
paid for it in the Rome of that day. Reserved as a child
beyond his fellows, and revealing, even in boyhood, something
of that recluse spirit which ultimately attracted to him what
he appears most sincerely to have studied to avoid, the notice,
namely, of the religious world about him, he withdrew, while
yet a stripling, first to Afile and afterwards to Sublaqueum;[4]
in which latter place he lived in almost complete isolation for
a notable period of years. It was all but inevitable, taking
the religious temper of the time into account, and remember-
ing the credit he enjoyed with the monk Romanus who seems
to have acted in the capacity of patron toward him, that his

---

[2] *Æneid,* vii, 715.   [3] *Dial. S Greg. M.* ii, *Proleg.*
[4] Subiaco.

environment and mode of life should have brought him a name for sanctity. We are not surprised, therefore, to find his retreat broken in upon early in his career at the instance of a community of monks who were said to be in ill repute because of their laxity. Whatever judgment we are to pass upon the spiritual condition of these men, they could not, at the time, have been utterly past praying for; since they besought the youthful anchoret with much urgency to abandon his cave and take up his abode as abbot in their monastery. To this arrangement the Saint reluctantly consented; but as the event turned out, his going proved satisfactory to neither party. The firm discipline of the new superior only provoked the irritation of the tepid. The disaffection spread; and Benedict soon realized that his life was in danger. It was but one episode out of many like it, we must remember, in a morally chaotic age. The twentieth-century reader need not infer, of course, on that account that the ethical sense of the time was appreciably duller than our own. Even a monk, we imagine, may find performance a less obvious matter than theory; especially when precedent and opportunity alike combine to teach him how effectively conscience may be trained to enjoy its occasional holiday. If it be thought to afford a significant commentary on the monastic conditions of the world into which Benedict was thus apparently making so sad an entry, that a way of escape from his attempts at reform was sought for in a plot to poison him, we may possibly discover in the fine answer which St. Gregory describes him as making to his would-be murderers a forecast of the new spirit which his Rule was to infuse into the religious ideals of the West. " Did I not tell you before," he cried, " that my manner of life and yours would not agree? Go, seek a superior to your own liking; for me ye can no longer have with you." There was something prophetic in the brave words. The old monachism, good and bad alike, was doomed; *the new monachism with its fuller sense of obedience was about to be born.* It was in the more elaborate provision for religious domesticity, so to call it; in the detailed and child-like intimacies enjoined between abbot and monk; in the changed attitude toward work of every kind, and especially toward agriculture, which was taken up no longer as a pastime or a mere preventive of idleness, but as a set duty of the day, having the same spiritual value as prayer; it was in these things—none of which was unfamiliar, save in its juxtaposition and spiritual synthesis, perhaps—and, most of all in the profounder instinct inculcated for the Rule and the *septa monasterii,* as well as in the almost deliberate substitution of the Founder's ideal of *Pax* in lieu of the old Oriental notion of a recoil from secularism, which had actuated the discipline of the earlier coenobite, that much of this newness was eventually to be achieved. The victory was realized at last; by what strange processes, only the student who has mastered the story of Subiaco, of Monte-Cassino, and of the strange parallelisms of Luxeuil and Bobbio, can tell. The Benedictine reform or Rule thus became a kind of Aaron's rod. It swallowed up all others in the Latin Church, winning for itself a noble primacy which has endured now for nearly fourteen hundred years. Mediterranean, Celtic, Spanish, North African—one by one, they became mere memories; because they lacked, it would seem, that rooted and Catholic obedientialism, that pliability in the hands of authority, which the great St. Gregory, himself a Benedictine of the Benedictines, turned to such magnificent account in the missionary enterprise that brought the fair-haired English into the unity of St. Peter's faith. The secret of this enduring vitality lay undoubtedly in the Benedictine's conception of his vow. He made no explicit promise either of poverty or of chastity. To these obligations he was bound, indeed; because they were involved in the quasi-sacramentalism of his oath. They were parts of that all inclusive sacrifice by which his obedience was deliberately linked in charity to the self-abasement of the Cross. It would be idle to pretend, nevertheless, that the ideal so inspiringly conceived by the genius of St. Benedict never lost its hold upon the after-ages of the Church. Some of the most melancholy stories of monastic decline that the ecclesiastical historian has to record are to be found in Benedictine annals. The fact is quite true; but it has no more bearing on the essential witness of the Rule than many a corresponding decline in the general morals of Christendom could be said to have on the essential witness of Christianity itself. If there were periods of decline; there were also periods of renewal; and it is in this extraordinary power of recovery that the

worth of St. Benedict's reform reveals itself, quite as arrest-
ingly, one might urge, as in its original victory over those rival
institutes which perished, while it advanced by the Way.
Clugny, Grenoble, Citeaux are Benedict's achievements; as
are the mysterious re-awakenings in the hearts of clergy and
laity alike which were fostered by the disciplinary reforms of
the Synods and Popes of the eleventh and twelfth centuries.
It is only when the Friar movement begins at the dawn of the
later Middle Age that a crisis arises in the face of which Benedictinism seems for a moment to be resourceless.

It is not easy to name in a single breath the many recondite
influences, religious, scholastic, economic, or political, that con-
spired for so many hundred years to produce the parti-colored
thing that is spoken of—too often with a convenient sort of
Nominalistic glibness, we fear—as the mind of the Middle
Age. A mind, however, there certainly was; and it is early in
the thirteenth century that we observe it becoming both self-
conscious and articulate. However the preceding centuries
may be said to have grown and fabled and dreamed, the
maturer thirteenth enters into its inheritance with a certain
air of resolution. It was a time in which men were rejoicingly
alive to their opportunities and eager to reap the usufruct of
them, sometimes even by unwise ways. What part the emerging burgher class had in this awakening it might be rash to
affirm; but it is significant to have to note that there was an
influential burgher class at this stage of European development, and that its kinship with that vaguer general known
as the *people* was beginning now to be widely and profoundly
felt. The Benedictines had begun in the wilderness; but they
had never believed it to be essential to their vocation to restrict
themselves to the wilderness, even in their palmiest days of
monastic vigor and all-consuming zeal. They had drawn nigh
to the towns wherever the towns summoned them, fixing their
abodes well within the walls, or marking off a spot in the
quieter outskirts beyond, according to local, which sometimes
meant episcopal, need. Witness the foundations of St. Andrew's on the Cœlian Hill in Rome; of SS. Peter and Paul's,
afterwards known as St. Augustine's, in Canterbury; of St.
Martin-in-the-Fields in Paris; or that created by King Sig-
bert's gift at Westminster near London. Yet, in spite of this

attitude of Catholic reasonableness toward the town and the town's ideals, it seems true, on the whole, to maintain that the Benedictine spirit during the wonderful seven centuries of development that had intervened between its Founder's day and its present critical hour had never been directly in touch either with the burgher or with the villein class. It had recruited its ranks, for the most part, from the nobility; its great leaders, its reformers, its men of affairs had sprung from the governing orders; of citizen or churl, as such, it had hardly taken account; and then only by accident, as it were; yet these latter classes were gradually acquiring an importance that neither churchmen nor noble could afford any longer to ignore. When the elemental instincts which had been stirring fitfully in the heart of the earlier time, therefore, found expression at last in those vague forms of popular discontent which alarmed the promoters of the Lateran Synod in the opening years of the thirteenth century, it was to other men and to newer institutions that the vision and the opportunity came of preparing a way of escape from the peril.

Like nearly all of the wider spiritual movements that have sprung from the heart of Catholicism, the advent of the Friars was due partly to chance, and partly to a deliberate and inspired attempt to answer a great need. Dominic de Guzman was born in the year 1170, the third son of a distinguished and pious couple belonging to one of the ancient families of Castile. Francis of Assisi was born twelve years later. He was the son of Pietro Bernadone, a prosperous and ambitious cloth merchant of Umbria, married to a gentlewoman of southern France. Both were delicately nurtured, and both saw at close hand, and while they were still young, not a little of the stirring pageantry of life, as life was lived at the dawn of the thirteenth century in that most cultivated, most corrupt, because always half-pagan, corner of Latin Europe, known as the Kingdom of Provence. Few portions of the Mediterranean world have had so rich or so human a history; and fewer still, it is significant to note, have been so doggedly retentive of the very forces against which Catholicism instinctively prepares itself whenever it is speciously summoned out to war. It was here, by a singular fitness in the poetry of events, that the Friar movement took its rise; for it was here that Dominic was first brought face to face with the moral havoc created by that strange "Bulgarian error", the memory of which was to survive with such sinister persistence centuries after in the ugly word that still disfigures so many dialects of our Latin and Teutonic speech.   It was here, too, in the original country of the Troubadours, that Joy made for itself, in spite of the surrounding darkness, a religion and a cult which were destined in later years to suggest to Francis in his Umbrian home the quaint but holier conceit of the *Joculatores Domini* or Jongleurs of the Lord.   Dominic's great spiritual experience, in which the horror of the "Albigensian madness" first took possession of his heart, dates from the year 1203.   He had been invited to accompany an embassy along with his friend and patron, the saintly Diego de Azevedo, Bishop of Osma, in order to arrange the preliminaries of one of the royal marriages of the time.   The cavalcade crossed the Pyrenees and passed through Languedoc.   What the young Castilian saw in in that strange progress seems to have made so profound an impression on his character that he determined to devote his great gifts as a preacher to the work of building up religion in the land for the next ten years.   He bravely kept his resolution; but the years brought their supreme lesson before his immediate task was done.   It was the time of Pope Innocent's Albigensian crusade, a time, that is to say, of fire and sword and relentless expatriation; but tradition has described Dominic's actual share in that terrible series of events as one of pity and unremitting persuasion.

He saw that no man, however fertile in resource his zeal might prompt him to be, could cope with the witchery of spreading unbelief or bring an apathetic clergy back to a Catholic sense of responsibility by inquisitorial methods alone.   It was not soldiers and pursuivants that were needed; but the charity of a brotherhood and a campaign of ideas.   It all came about in the simplest way.   A rich citizen of Toulouse, one Pierre Cella by name, came forward with the gift of a house to be set apart

Rule under which his own character had been shaped for inspiration in the present juncture. The local bishop generously set apart certain tithes for the purchase of books and the support of the community. It was, in nearly every Scriptural sense of the word, a mustard-seed foundation; for in less than two years we hear of the Saint at Rome petitioning Pope Honorius for Papal approval of the *Fratres Praedicatores* or Preaching Brothers. The petition was not only granted, but the Saint himself was made " Master of the Sacred Palace ", an office that afterwards grew to be of commanding importance and that has been associated with the Order for the past seven centuries. Six years later the " little company of preachers " had grown to be a great brotherhood filling sixty convents and numbering eight distinct " provinces ". They also began to establish themselves not only in populous districts, but in the more important university towns. The intellectual forces which were to mean so much to the Friar movement had fairly started.

Meanwhile that other Saint, whose ties with the mysterious Provençal land were of so pleasant a sort that popular imagination derived his name from the ease with which he spoke its joyous speech, Francis,[5] the rich cloth merchant's son, was building up another " little society " in distant Umbria which was to be every bit as wonderful as Dominic's in its day; though it seemed to lack the initial stimulus and pomp of occasion that had lent so grave an interest to the Spaniard's task. The era was one of great conceptions and high ideals. In spite of the unrest of the South, and the spiritual apathy prevalent in many sections of the body ecclesiastical, poetry and Catholicism filled the very air that men breathed and made the general life of Europe exuberant and tonic. Not all the

unlike Dominic, he had been more than a beholder of the passing scene. What precise meaning we must attach to Thomas of Celano's words we cannot say; but even in their most mitigable sense they bear a sad weight of meaning.

There was [he writes] in the city of Assisi, which stands on the borders of the valley of Spoleto, a man named Francis, who from his earliest years was brought up by his parents frowardly, according to the vanity of the world; and by his long imitation of their wretched life and conduct he became himself still more vain and froward. . . . Almost until the twenty-fifth year of his age he miserably squandered and wasted his time. Nay, surpassing all his co-evals in his bad progress in vanity, he proved in more abundant measure an instigator of evil deeds and a zealot in folly. He was the admiration of all; and in pomp of vainglory he strove to surpass the rest in frolics, freaks, sallies of wit and idle talk, songs and soft and flowing attire; for he was very rich. He was not miserly, but prodigal; not a hoarder of money, but a squander of his substance. . . . And so, compassed about with the troops of the wicked, haughty and uplifted, he strutted along amid the open places of Babylon until the Lord looked down from heaven and for His Name's sake removed His fury far from him and curbed his tongue with His praise, that he might not perish utterly. Therefore, the hand of the Lord came upon him and the change wrought by the right-hand of the Highest, that through him assurance of restoration to grace might be given to sinners and that he might become to all a pattern of conversion to God.[6]

The Saint's conversion, in spite of popular impression to the contrary, was a gradual one, culminating at last in a supreme crisis that issued in a great resolve. After the fever that had struck him down at Spoleto and put an end to his dreams of military distinction, it was noticed that he had entirely changed his former manner of life. One of his friends taunted him one early morning with being in love and received the characteristic answer; " Oh, I shall some day marry a wife, fairer, richer, purer than any that your fancy can conjure up!" Did he even at that still halting date, have the " Lady Poverty " in mind, the poor and outcast flock of Christ,

---

[6] *The Lives of St. Francis of Assisi by Brother Thomas of Celano.* Translated by A. G. Ferrers Howell, L.L.M., Trinity College, Cambridge. New York, E. P. Dutton & Co. 1908.

whom he was to serve as no lover ever served his mistress
on this earth before or since! Or was it, as some of his interpreters solemnly assure us, Religion, whom he would pick up
from her fallen estate as King Cophetua did the beggar maid?
The genius of Dante divined better. It was no abstraction
that Francis loved. The strange break with his father and his
entrance upon the *Vita Nuova* he had conceived came in due
course. The way to Poetry and Happiness was, when all was
said and done, the old, half-forgotten Way of Renunciation,
the Way of Christ, in fine; but Renunciation was not the last
word; nor was it the most important word in this new Scholasticism of the heart. It was charity grown tender and universal and concrete: the poor were a kind of Eighth Sacrament. The genius of Giotto has happily familiarized us with
the broad features of the memorable interview in which this
Poor Man of Assisi came before Pope Innocent to secure the
Church's approval of his incorrigibly romantic Rule and Way
of Life. The story of the dream about the falling Lateran,
quite apart even from its rare spiritual significance, is valuable to the Catholic student as revealing the deeper conviction of Southern Europe on this particular phase of the Friar
movement; for it is scarcely going too far to assert that Fran-
ciscanism alone would have brought the masses back to orthodoxy and fervor, even if there had been no Dominic to inject
a stream of ordered knowledge into the over-run garden of
their faith. After many delays and disappointments, Honorius III confirmed the Rule in 1223. For a while it looked as
though Christendom had begotten but two types of really
serious men, the Black Friar and the Grey.

Of the subsequent fortunes of the Friar movement during
the next three centuries, of its prompt invasion of the universities, of its work in cathedral-town, in court, in hamlet, and
country-side; of its success, in brief, it is not our business to
speak in this essay. That success was instant and compelling;
and only not complete because human nature in the individual
conscience seems to be a blend of strangely incalculable elements that make wise men dumb. Its essential witness, however, which appears to have been the secret also of the anger
it eventually aroused, may be gathered from the cardinal facts
we have selected as illustrating our original contention that

Monachism, Roman Monachism, as opposed to the inchoate or barren forms that preceded Benedict's great revival, is to a most wonderful degree, whether we view it in idea or in actual history, a fresh argument for Catholicism as the Way. And that this is arguably true of the Friar movement in its main outline will appear, we think, if one will but consider the three qualities that mark it off from the Monachism which preceded it. It is its greater universality, its greater simplicity, that have made it so vital to souls at large during the past six centuries and more of its various existence; and more than this, it is in its closer and more avowed dependence on the great instrument of visible unity which the providence of Christ and the play of certain obvious forces in human history have established in St. Peter's See, that we shall find the secret of its deeper strength. Surely, it was a great thing to have achieved that. It was as though, in the easier confidence instinctively created by such a juncture of notes—felt everywhere throughout Christendom, rather than explicitly affirmed —the *Schola Christi* had been taken out of the cloister and set bravely down in the midst of the world. *In hoc mundo; sed non de hoc mundo!* The peoples of Europe were drawn more closely together in things Catholic than ever before; Christendom was more palpably and indefeasibly one. Its way of obedience, if narrower, was henceforth to be more definite; its lesson of loyalty easier to learn. Worldliness, ignorance, Scholasticism had tried it in the century before as by flood and fire; but Dominic and Francis had indicated a way of escape; the one by his propaganda of the true obedience of knowledge, the other by his propaganda of the holier obediences of love. Could the coenobitical principle go further than this?

The centuries that followed the great wave of the Friar movement have a history all their own. There are scandals and plenty to record; and the Friar, in more than one authentic instance, seems almost on the point of betraying the very principles he was apparently created to uphold; but, as in the case of Benedictinism, there was something in the Friar-

cence, it was doubtless owing to this very principle of coherence, imparted to the peoples of Europe by the Friars of the
earlier time, that saved the Church from worse disasters than
actually befell. If the Renascence itself, however, can be
said to mark a turn in the fortunes of Friarism that left it
unable to cope single-handed with the religious revolts of the
sixteenth century, the principle that the Friar himself stood
for received a fresh and most remarkable development at that
very juncture in the establishment of the Society of Jesus.
Here was an order, accepted by Church authority at a time
when orders could hardly be said to be in honor in an out-
raged Christendom, prepared to reinforce the coenobitical
idea without the aid of habit, enclosure, choir, or written
Rule. It was, as many thought at the time, and as everybody
must still allow who reflects upon the matter at all, one of
the greatest departures from precedent that Catholicism had
known. The high-hearted Hidalgo Saint whose genius conceived this extraordinary idea consented, it is true, to write
a Rule at last; but he insisted that in doing so he was yielding
to no pressure of the time, but rather to a permanent need in
unheroic human nature itself. However we are to explain the
anomaly, the fact remains that the Jesuit marks a sharper line
of cleavage in the continuity of history than any other exponent of the coenobitical ideal. In the eloquent tribute to the
great Society in which Newman sums up the evidence for his
particular reading of Monastic development we are told that
the secret of the Jesuit's power seems to lie chiefly in his insistence upon the law of obedience in a highly intellectual
age. That is true, as far as it goes; but as an explanation it is
both unphilosophic and vague. Has not obedience, after all,
made the substance of a monk's sacrifice from the beginning;
and who that has had living contact with the children, will
say that Benedict, or Francis, or Dominic has made light of so
primary a consideration in the establishment of a Holy Rule?
We once heard a wise novice-master of the Society, a man
of many varied accomplishments and university-bred, make
a remark on this very head which we think will bear pertinent
repetition here. " An old Jesuit had been asked by a shrewd
man of the world, one day, which were the qualities that made
most for success in the Society of Jesus. ' The very same

qualities that make for success in the world,' was the extraordinary reply." There was not the slightest hint, either of cynicism or irony, in the curious paradox of that story. It embodied, and embodied very candidly, a principle that St. Ignatius himself and every son of his deserving of the name, could be said to have followed since that memorable meeting on Montmartre which seemed at the moment to mean so little to the Church of God and the religious life over three centuries ago. The Jesuit is the true " spoiler of Egypt "; for the actuality of his faith has armed him with courage to steal one of the most practical of the world's secrets—the secret of that immediacy which so often proves too much for the " children of light" who are either " on a journey" when they ought to meet it, or " sleeping" or peradventure all but dead. It is in his cult of readiness, of efficiency that the real solution of the eternal mystery of the Jesuit will ultimately be found. It is this quality which gives character to his obedience itself; it is this same prepossession which accounts for that reasoned and scientific devotion to spiritual exercises which makes him, whether at home or abroad, as Newman rightly inferred, a man distinguished and apart. It is this same clear-sighted instinct for the measure that will work, for the idea that will do, that has made his much-discussed Order in other respects, and on the larger stage of ecclesiastical history, so rich in versatility as compared with other coenobitical families who have adhered to more leisurely and perhaps more lasting ideals. In the case of these earlier manifestations the instinct for obedience had expressed itself in a Rule; but in the case of the Jesuits it revealed itself in a method and form of prayer. Wonderful as the Institute or Code of the Society of Jesus is, considered as a mere piece of legislative wisdom, the *Book of the Spiritual Exercises* which that Institute was designed to interpret and complete, is far more wonderful still. What other manual of devotion, outside of Scripture itself, can compare with it in its clear and ascertained results? It infused new life into the heart of post-Tridentine Catholicism and gave a turn to the energies of the famous Counter-Reformation by which the Lutheran error was disfurnished of more than half its strength. If, as partisan scholars have often tried to show,[7]

---

[7] *Les Origines de la Campagnie de Jésus.* Hermann Müller. Paris, 1908.

its more central ideas were, indeed, borrowed from the *Exer-citatorio de la vida espiritual* of Dom Garcia de Cisneros, the Benedictine Abbot of Montserrat, it will nevertheless be found that the genius of St. Ignatius has shaped them to new and more compelling meanings and made of them an agency of almost ecumenical efficiency for the Church at large. He has endowed them with fresh and convincing significance; and it is through his recognition of them that they are so ex-traordinarily alive. What they did for his unique character they have wrought in measure, and according to the spiritual capacity of each, for all those generations of his sons, fervent, or common-place, or frankly lax, who have been submitted to their mysterious alembic since the Saint reluctantly sur-rendered his original plan of an " elect cohort of sixty " and went out into the highways and byways for material for his difficult crusade. It is on this *Book* that every Jesuit is formed long before he understands the canonical height or depth of his curiously elastic Rule. He may fail in a score of ways in after-life; but having felt the urgency of its most relentless, because most Spanish, logic, he can never again be quite as he was before. Readiness, efficiency, actuality—these must henceforth be the notes of his trained and pragmatical life. They must qualify his scholarship, which must inevitably lack the patient temper and perhaps, also, the depth of the Benedictine's, as they must give in turn a cast and touch of mystery to the pieties and to the very habit and feature of his outward man. Not in his obediences, therefore, but in his form of prayer, we should say, is the real soul of the Jesuit to be grasped and his amazing history understood.

Omnis spiritus laudet Deum! It is a sound Catholic instinct not to compare the Saints; and one equally sound not to wrangle over their works; for in this sense, too, is it pertinent to say: *their works do follow them.* If it is a far cry from Benedict to Ignatius, it is almost farther still from the latter's tumultuous day to the Church of our own time; Catholicism cannot but live. Yet what a way is opened up to the voyaging heart that listens to the central message of this story, what *industries of obedience* to the will that sincerely aspires to be " good "! *One alone is good,* it is written, even God; yet He that uttered that awful saying made that *Goodness* ineffably attainable to whoso will reach out after it. Peace, knowledge, tenderness, actuality—are not these some of the qualities by which men's eyes are opened to that " Goodness " and taught to reach out to it, when their hearts glow within them, as they walk disciplined in charity with Benedict, Dominic, Francis, or Ignatius *along the Way?*

CORNELIUS CLIFFORD.

Whippany, New Jersey.

IS SOCIAL REFORM WORK A DUTY OF THE PARISH CLERGY?

THERE is abroad a cry for social reform, and the Church cannot but be interested in the methods adopted to bring it about. Years ago Leo XIII pointed out the needed social reform in his Encyclicals, and offered a program for its safe execution by the combined action of Christian rulers, societies, and the clergy. In consequence there were earnest discussion and vigorous organization in Catholic circles. The present Pontiff, too, by warnings and directions has clearly shown what is his mind regarding effective social reform work.

In the secular order the makers and administrators of law are alarmed by the rapid change in the pulse of social bodies. The leaders of the people in America hardly find time to study the real causes of the general upheaval, and it would appear as if they disliked the philosophy of it. They undertake to cure the disease by attacking the symptoms from without. They are stirred by the appeal of the masses, and some form of social democracy is the remedy they propose. They fear revolution unless reform in this direction is assured.

There never was such close study of social conditions and never such helplessness to stem the tide. Naturally the question obtrudes itself: Can the Parish Clergy be of any assistance in social reform? Are they called upon to make any special effort to help in what appears to belong exclusively to the secular economic rulers? The first question is a dynamic one; the second is one of finality.

The possible influence of the Parish Clergy in the matter would not prove more than their duty to help, as citizens ought to, in a patriotic cause.

If their co-operation should however follow in virtue of their office to maintain and promote Christian morality and Christian faith, then they would be obliged as guardians of righteousness and Christian culture to do all in their power to work for social reform. This latter seems to be the case. The Parish Clergy are not an isolated body. They are the organic part of the Church. Their origin dates from the Founder of the Church. The development of their present form is not accidental. The grouping of parishes and dioceses under the leadership and guidance of the successor of the Key-holder and Chief Pastor, appointed by Christ, was not a chance evolution. Neither has the final purpose of the Church changed. That purpose still is to bring salvation to all, until Christ comes again to judge the living and the dead. The Gospel is to be preached; the faith is to be kept; morality to be nurtured; graces thereunto to be administered by the Church; " and blessed are they who are not scandalized ".

In that function the Parish Clergy are the organ of the Church, immediate to the laity. At so close a range, whatever touches the people in their temporality cannot fail to give new motives to the priest in his ministration of spirituality.

Human life is not divided. It is not one part natural, secular or temporal, and the other part supernatural, spiritual or eternal. The entire man must serve God. His ultimate happiness comes through faith and law made known by Revelation. They diffuse light and warmth into his mundane aspirations and keep him in justice and charity while he orders his material conditions. His world-view becomes fixed and defined by the revealed word of God. And to teach that word is the mission of the Church. History has proved that human action has no enduring motive of unity in its manifold uses on earth, unless the perfecting grace of God steady and illumine it. Now it is the mission of the Church to administer the grace of God.

Hence arises the question so much discussed: Is it not all that can be expected of the Parish Clergy if they properly preach the word of God and dispense His graces? Should they not let the body politic economize its own affairs? Political economists generally affirm it; though some allow the Church a considerable margin in the exercise of charity,

Equity and justice in civic matters, they hold, are solely within the competency of human law and custom. Social forms proceed from and are dissolved by forces entirely 'inherent in natural causes. Conditions are but sequences. Reform of policies comes through their very mistakes.

It is evident that such a view allows no room for punishment or reward of men's deeds in temporal matters coming from a higher authority than nature.

The sanction of law is nature, not God. If the citizen holds any religious views, they are apart from his duty to his fellows. His soul-life, prompted by convictions due to belief in a hereafter, is distinct from his commercial or industrial life. Such a view is certainly wrong. Man is entirely beholden to God, whether taken individually or socially. That is the fatal philosophy which divides man against himself. The Commandments of God oblige and direct conscience in all its operations. Man's relation to his fellowmen results from his relation to God—and that is religion.

Christ gave the human race not only religion, but the only true one, in which the graces of His atonement and redemption are to be administered by His Church. That Church shall not fail in its characteristics, and its service is infallibly sure to guide men in right living and to final happiness. Now is it not enough if the Parish Clergy of that Church teach the religion of Christ; should they enforce it, keep the sense of it alive by entering into the very midst of distracting, misformed economics? Should they not let business men attend to their business affairs, and hold aloof from politics?

If world-economics are quite independent of divine ordinance, if commercial enterprises are under the control of selfish or altruistic motives, and may pass unchallenged so long as they do not conflict with human law, or obstruct the course of government, then of course the members of human society need make no concessions to God's law, or to the law of the Church, or to divine faith, in purely business transactions, and the clergy have no duty outside the sacristy. They must indeed build churches and schools, teach catechism to children who are sent to school, and preach to such as are drawn by peculiar graces to hear them. They collect money and protect church property—for after all the clergy meet the requirements of certain constituents of the social body, and no human law can deny them that right. But they are not a part of modern business concerns. How different from the mind of our Lord! He came to regenerate. His life-giving doctrine, whilst it turned the thoughts of men to heaven, did reform their standard of living in their social intercourse. How strangely at variance with the ministry of the Christian dispensation as taught by the Apostles to the early Christians. Had the last two Popes in particular not urged bishops and clergy with such zeal to restore all things in Christ, to enter into the study of social conditions, and labor with all their might to make them better, one would be tempted to think their usefulness for temporal things had come to an end, and their continuance in office only due to tolerance of the powers of the world. Thus they would have ceased to be the salt of the earth and the light of the world. Evidently Leo XIII and Pius X would have us think differently.

The second point in this question, however, is stronger than the first. How can the Parish Clergy co-operate in social reform work? The theory is easy enough: but how make it practical? Indeed there are as many opinions in the matter as there are heads that trouble themselves about it. Let us begin with the first necessary supposition, that the Parish Clergy should do social reform work.

The work of the clergy is determined by the mission of the Church. Their ordinary duty is to make known truths of eternal salvation and administer the helps to secure it. The hierarchical order, the organization of the teaching Church describes the sphere of action of the clergy. Now is there in social reform work an additional, or extraordinary task for the Parish Clergy—one that naturally flows from their duty to make eternal things the unforgotten in temporal occupations?

forget, however, that man is to be governed in all cases by the standard of divine law. The ethics of human law are not independent of revealed precepts. Ignorance of Christ's doctrine may excuse, but does not annul the right and the duty of the clergy to teach it. Man's natural sense of equity, the reciprocal duties and rights of the human family are not the only nor the safest source of right living. Besides, selfish aims are so predominant, in spite of repeated assurances of optimism, that the love of neighbor is crushed out by them and the fear of God in consequence fails with it.

Who is appointed to perform the great service of keeping alive knowledge and fear of God, if not the Parish Clergy? They are the point of contact between Church and State in social economic matters. The Church is not a monitor only, a guide-post to point the way; but she infuses a life eminently conducive to temporal happiness. She does not preach hatred of the world nor escape from it, but it is her concomitant mission to assist in its uplift.

She opposes the flesh, the world, and the devil, because they are the enemies of the true and the good; because they rob God's creatures of their appointed bliss. They are foes of the natural as well as of the supernatural happiness of man. True, not all issues of a social economic character are equally moral. Whether it is expedient to build a railroad, or whether the size of the navy or army should be increased, cannot be decided by the Decalogue; nor can the Church arbitrate on the budget or on pensions.

But if the men who have to do these things are patriotic, and loyal, conscious that all power is from God, that they must do their duty for the good of the people in accordance with divine law, that they are responsible for their action to God, then it will appear how mighty the influence of the Church is to maintain a high degree of civilization and an

co-operation according to parish circumstances; for all parishes do not offer like opportunities. Again, the union of the
Parish Clergy in the work is of prime importance, lest they
lapse into local, isolated action and fail of encouragement.

Where should the Clergy secure that knowledge required
for preaching and how can they practise an effective ministry
in social reform work?

The study of social problems should begin in the seminary.
Whether that is best accomplished by a special course, or by
special attention given to social and economic problems in
ethics, or in moral and pastoral theology, need not be decided
here. What is here emphasized is the necessity of such study
by the future priest. A knowledge of ethical and moral principles, even casuistry dealing with cases of conscience in penance or canon law, are no longer sufficient for the cure of
souls. The priest will command a hearing on the ills and
cures of modern socialism, if he knows whereof he speaks.
When he is actually in charge of souls he must still learn and
observe. Indeed, then he experiences the vast difference between knowing and doing social reform work. There are
priests doing excellent work in this regard who never made a
special course in their seminary days. But that can be no
argument against the study of social questions by future ministers.

The strongest dislike for social reform work by the Parish
Clergy comes from a common opinion among them that their
ordinary ministrations are at all times entirely sufficient, and
that extraordinary knowledge and activity are for specialists.
It will be hard to dislodge that opinion. If it were not so
disastrous for the common good, it might be left undisturbed.
The corporate and individual initiative of the episcopate, in
imitation and obedience of the Holy Father, will however
hurry the great work, and before long the majority of the

reform work by the Parish Clergy is in the parish itself. Our parishes are such financial enterprises as leave the clergy no leisure for anything but liquidation and ministration. It is hard for them to act on St. Paul's advice to Timothy: " No man, being a soldier of God, entangleth himself with secular business ".[1] Temporalities in most cases so occupy them that the care for these unduly detracts their attention from the pressing social problems.

Perhaps, in time the congestion in parish finance work will yield to a more numerous clergy, who can divide their duties with more profit to social reform. In the meanwhile that work is likely, though it is much needed, to go by default. Organization and work should not all be left to the laity.

It needs no prophet to tell that when the scenes of social, industrial, commercial life shall be shifted, the Church and the clergy will be forced to the background, unless they prepare now to forestall this by active co-operation, " that the ministry be not blamed ".[1]

Perhaps the REVIEW will open its pages to a discussion of this very important question.

JOSEPH SELINGER.

Jefferson City, Missouri.

[1] II Tim. 2:4.
[2] II Cor. 6:3.

Analecta.

ACTA PII PP. X.

I.

Venerabili Fratri Gulielmo, Archiepiscopo Bostoniensi, ob Largitatem erga Pontificium Institutum Biblicum.

Venerabilis frater, salutem et apostolicam benedictionem.—
Pontificium institutum biblicum, quod vix exortum ab omnibus maxime probari accepimus, utpote divinarum rerum sci-
entiae provehendae perutile, tua modo auctum largitate, mai-
ora laetamur posse ecclesiae portendere. Pietate in Nos tua
nihil uberius: tuae vere pecuniae nulla prestantior usura
Cogitare etenim *de sapientia sensus est consummatus:* et *qui*
illam diligit, *diligit vitam.* Vitam porro dilexisti te praebendo
adiutorem operi quod, utpote Sacris Litteris explanandis de-

venerabilis frater, clero ac populo in quem pastorales tuae curae optime evigilant, peramanter impertimus.

Datum Romae apud S. Petrum die xxv Decembris MCMIX, Pontificatus Nostri anno septimo.

PIUS PP. X.

II.

SUMMUS PONTIFEX COMMENDAT PROPAGATIONEM SODALI-
TATIS SUB TITULO FOEDERIS A BONO PASTORE IN CIVITATE
WASHINGTON FUNDATAE ET INDULGENTIIS LOCUPLETATAE.

PIUS PP. X.

Ad perpetuam rei memoriam.—Exponendum curavit Nobis dilectus filius Parochus S. Patritii Civitatis vulgo: " Washington," Archidioeceseos Baltimorensis, se optata Patrum Concilii secundi Baltimorensis explentem in suo Curiali templo piam instituisse Sodalitatem quae sub titulo " Foederis a Bono Pastore " id potissimum precibus pietatisque operibus a Deo impetrare contenderet, ut integra inter Curiales fides servetur ac Sodalium necessarii et amici ad veram convertantur religionem. Cum autem huiusmodi Foedus ab Ordinario canonice erectum, ac recens ab hac Apostolica Sede indulgentiis locupletatum, uberes iam tulerit fructus, atque Antistitum suffragiis in alias Dioeceses non intermisse propagetur; enixae sunt Nobis ab eodem dilecto filio adhibitae preces, ut coelestes Ecclesiae thesauros, ipsi Foederi concessos, ceteris etiam in huius exemplum ortis Consociationibus largiri dignaremur.

Nos piis hisce votis obsecundantes, de Omnipotentis Dei misericordia ac B. B. Petri et Pauli App. Eius auctoritate confisi, cunctis Sodalitatibus in Statibus Foederatis Americae Septentrionalis de respectivi Ordinarii consensu iam erectis vel posthac erigendis, dummodo eiusdem sint ac praedicti Foederis nominis et instituti, omnes et singulas tum plenarias tum partiales concedimus indulgentias, quae ab hac S. Sede die septimo et vicesimo mensis Maii huius labentis anni pio, quod supra memoravimus, Foederi impertitae fuerunt. Universis

peris, item uno die a suae cuiusque Sodalitatis Moderatore singulis mensibus designanda, ab ortu usque ad occasum solis dierum huiusmodi; dummodo hi omnes vere poenitentes et confessi ac S. Communione refecti quamvis Ecclesiam vel publicum oratorium devote visitaverint et ibi pro Christianorum Principium concordia, haeresum extirpatione, peccatorum conversione ac S. Matris Ecclesiae exaltatione pias ad Deum preces effuderint, Plenariam quotannis lucrandam omnium peccatorum suorum indulgentiam et remissionem misericorditer in Domino concedimus. Iisdem praeterea Sodalibus qui corde saltem contrito piae in singulas hebdomades habendae exercitationi interfuerint, trecentos dies; denique iis, qui quae sequuntur preces: " O Jesu, Pastor bone, universas actiones hodie a me peragendas Tibi offero pro conversione patriae meae ac praesertim pro conversione N———," quocumque idiomate devote recitaverint, quoties id egerint, centum dies de iniunctis eis seu alias quomodolibet debitis poenitentiis, in forma Ecclesiae consueta, relaxamus. Quas omnes indulgentias, peccatorum remissiones ac poenitentiarum relaxationes etiam animabus fidelium in Purgatorio detentis per modum suffragii applicari posse indulgemus. Contrariis non obstantibus quibuscumque. Praesentibus perpetuo valituris.

Datum Romae apud S. Petrum sub Annulo Piscatoris die xxx Decembris, MCMIX. Pontificatus Nostri anno septimo.

R. Card. MERRY DEL VAL, *a Secretis Status.*

S. CONGREGATIO S. OFFICII.

INDULTUM PRO TERTIARIIS ET CONFRATRIBUS ORD. REDEMPTORUM B. M. V. DE MERCEDE.

Beatissime Pater,

Fr. Franciscus Gargallo, Vices-Procurator Generalis Ordinis Redemptorum B. M. V. de Mercede, ad S. V. pedes pro-

Die 9 Decembris 1909.

SSmus D. N. Pius Divina Providentia PP. X, in Audientia R. P. D. Adsessori S. Officii impertita, benigne annuit pro gratia iuxta preces, ceteris servatis de iure servandis. Contrariis non obstantibus quibuscumque.

Aloisius Can. Giambene, *Substitutus pro Indulgentiis.*
L. * S.

S. CONGREGATIO CONSISTORIALIS.

I.

Circa Competentiam Relate ad Matrimonia Mixta.

S. Congr. S. Officii litteris diei 27 Martii 1909 a S. Congregatione Consistoriali formalem declarationem petiit circa competentiam relate ad matrimonia mixta. Itaque proposito dubio in terminis ab Adsessore S. Officii statutis hoc est: "quale sia la competenza del S. Offizio in fatto di matrimonii misti, sia tra battezzati e non battezzati, sia tra cattolici ed acattolici, tanto dal lato pratico, ossia per la concessione delle dispense, quanto dal lato teorico, ossia per la risoluzione dei dubbi che possono sorgere su tale materia, anche nei riguardi del recente decreto *Ne temere*", Emi Patres, perpensis consultorum votis et re mature considerata, respondendum censuerunt: "Competentiam S. Officii se extendere ad omnia quae sive directe sive indirecte, in iure aut in facto se referunt ad Privilegium Paulinum et ad praefatas dispensationes. Et ad mentem, quae est: supplicandum SSmum ut statuat ac decernat ut quaelibet quaestio circa praefata matrimonia deferatur Sacrae Congregationi S. Officii, salva huic Sacrae Congregationi potestate, si ita censeat et casus ferat, quaestionem ipsam remittendi ad aliud S. Sedis officium".

SSmus, audita relatione infrascripti Cardinalis Secretarii, resolutionem ratam habuit et confirmavit, mandavitque ut in posterum quaelibet quaestio circa matrimonia mixta deferatur S. Congregatione S. Officii iuxta petita, sub lege tamen ut firma semper et in omnibus maneat dispositio decreti *Ne temere* in art. XI n. 2° et 3° statuta.

C. Card. De Lai, *S. C. Consistorialis Secretarius.*
L. * S.
Scipio Tecchi, *S. C. C. Adsessor.*

II

Circa Relationem S. Sedi exhibendam ab Alumnis Collegii Iosephini.

Proposito dubio, utrum veteres alumni Collegii Iosephini civitatis *Columbus* in America adhuc teneantur quolibet anno relationem S. Sedi exhibere, iuxta iuramentum ab iis emissum, SSmus Dnus Noster in audientia concessa Emo Cardinali Secretario die 21 Ianuarii currentis anni 1910, attenta nova rerum conditione inducta a Const. *Sapienti Consilio,* benigne dignatus est alumnos memorati Collegii dispensare et eximere ab annua relatione peragenda.

Carolus Perosi, *S. C. C. Substitutus.*

III.

De Relationibus Dioecesanis et Visitatione SS. Liminum. (*Continued.*)

ORDO SERVANDUS IN RELATIONE DE STATU ECCLESIARUM.

Cap. V.

De clero generatim.

40. Referatur generatim quinam sint cleri mores, qui cultus, ac doctrina, quod studium aeternae salutis proximorum, quae pietas: quaenam erga suum Ordinarium Summumque Pontificem obedientia et reverentia: quaenam inter sacerdotes concordia, coniunctio, caritas.

41. Utrum vestis talaris adhiberi possit et reapse adhibeatur a clero: et in quolibet casu an clerus habitu proprio et decenti induatur, nec sint hac in re scandala vel dicteria.

42. Utrum sacerdotes in missae celebratione praeparationem et gratiarum actionem debite peragant: an serotinae visitationi SSmi Sacramenti assueti sint: qua frequentia ad poenitentiae sacramentum accedere soleant.

quaestionibus moralibus, seu casibus conscientiae, itemque theologiae et liturgiae habeantur: qua frequentia, qua methodo, quo fructu.

45. Quae Ordinarii cura sit de iunioribus sacerdotibus, ut postquam sacerdotio initiati sunt studia non deserant, et pietate adhuc proficiant.

46. Pro emeritis sacerdotibus infirmis et pauperibus an domus aliqua habeatur in qua recipiantur et debita caritate sustententur: an saltem reditus speciales constituti sint quibus eisdem subveniatur.

47. Utrum adsint sacerdotes, qui quamvis viribus et iuvenili aetate polleant, otiosi tamen vivant, adeo ut inutiles vel etiam noxii dioecesi sint: quaenam huius rei sit causa, et an et quomodo huic malo occurri possit.

48. Utrum adsint de clero qui rebus politicis et factionibus civilibus immodice et indebite se immisceant, cum offensione aliorum et spiritualis ministerii detrimento: et quid factum sit, aut fieri possit ut intra iustos limites contineantur.

Et in dioecesibus ubi una vivunt catholici variorum rituum, aut diversae linguae, vel nationis, an idcirco adsint in clero contentiones et aemulationes: quid fiat ut exstinguantur, et spiritus Christi in omnibus inducatur.

49. Utrum, quod Deus avertat, aliquis habeatur sacerdos qui vitam minus honestam agat, aut agere publice videatur; vel cui imputetur aliquod aliud crimen post ultimam relationem dioecesanam patratum.

Nullane habeatur, quam Ordinarius sciat aut suspicetur in suo clero, violatio legis de observandis et vitandis in satisfactione missarum manualium.

Caveantne sacerdotes nedum a libris, sed etiam a diariis irreligiosis vel impiis legendis, nisi gravis et legitima causa intercedat.

50. Quid factum sit tum ad salutarem lapsorum correctionem, tum ad scandali (si adfuerit) reparationem.

Utrum et quoties suspensio *ex informata conscientia* in quinquennio irrogari debuerit; quo fructu; et quaenam sit regula quae in hoc adhibetur.

Cap. VI.

De capitulis.

52. Utrum adsit cathedrale canonicorum capitulum; quot canonicis et dignitatibus constet; et an adsint theologi et poenitentiarii officia.

53. Quomodo canonicorum, officiorum et dignitatum provisio locum habeat; utrum libere iuxta commune ius, an alia aliqua speciali ratione.

54. Utrum et quali praebenda singuli fruantur: et an haec distincte administretur; an potius vigeat regimen communis *massae.* In quolibet casu an specialis alia communis *massa* habeatur pro distributionibus quotidianis, pro missa conventuali, pro expensis fabricae et cultus.

55. Utrum, et a quo tempore capitulum suas habeat constitutiones legitime approbatas, et an eas servet.

56. Quale sit chorale servitium tam pro recitatione divini officii quam pro missae conventualis celebratione; quotidianum ne iuxta commune ius, an potius intermissum: et quo indulto.

57. Utrum, et quot adsint canonici honorarii: an excedant numerum a sacris canonibus statutum.

58. Deficiente cathedrali capitulo, an habeatur consultorum collegium; quot personis constet; quibus aliis ministeriis iidem vacent; et an ita proximi sint civitati episcopali ut facile congregari possint.

59. Quanam canonici vel consultores existimatione gaudeant in dioecesi. Utrum ipsi concordes inter se et cum Ordinario sint; an potius aliquid Ordinarius habeat, quod eorum de agendi ratione doleat.

60. An Ordinarius eos rite convocet, ut in negotiis maioris momenti consilium vel consensum iuxta sacros canones requirat.

CAP. VII.

De parochiis, earumque rectoribus.

63. Utrum omnes paroeciae de suo proprio pastore sint provisae: an potius adsint quae ab aliquo viciniore parocho vel ab aliquo canonico ad tempus regantur: quam ob causam: et an idcirco incommoda notabilia aut mala sequantur.

64. Utrum provisio paroeciarum fiat per concursum: et quomodo concursus ipse celebretur.

65. Utrum adsint paroeciarum seu animarum rectores ad nutum amovibiles.

66. Utrum, quibusnam sub conditionibus, et quo iure adsint paroeciae Ordinibus seu Congregationibus religiosis addictae.

67. Utrum habeantur paroeciae in quibus cura animarum habitualis penes capitula aliasve personas existat.

68. Utrum adsint paroeciae obnoxiae iuri patronatus ecclesiastico, vel laico, sive familiari, sive populari, sive regio: quaenam praxis vigeat in earum provisione: an et quaenam incommoda hac de re acciderint.

69. Utrum emolumenta, quae occasione administrationis sacramentorum, funerum, celebrationis missarum solemnium, attestationum, publicationum a parochis percipi solent, recognita sint ab Ordinario, vel diuturno usu probata.

Et an sive ob gravitatem parochialium taxarum, sive ob rigorem exactionis earumdem, inconvenentia aliqua et querelae, praesertim in re matrimoniali et in funeribus, deploranda sint.

70. Utrum et qua dote certa parochi eorumque ecclesiae generatim honestentur: an potius ex solis stolae incertis et fidelium oblationibus vivere debeant.

Si bonis immobilibus parochus eiusque ecclesia fruantur, quomodo administratio geratur, et quomodo caveatur pro conservatione patrimonii sacri alterutrius, vel utriusque.

In quolibet casu an parochi habeant quo honeste sustententur et quo expensis occurrant pro animarum cura et pro parochialibus functionibus necessariis.

71. Utrum parochi domum canonicam habeant; et an ibi cum parocho eius adiutores una vivant. Et si·ita non sit, an et quod studium habeantur ut hoc regimen inducatur.

72. Utrum, qua lege et qua observantia caveatur, ne quo-

libet sub praetextu, etiam ratione servitii, iuniores mulieres (etiam consanguineae, si cum parocho adiutores simul vivant) parochiales domus inhabitent aut frequentent: et an cura sit ne in parochialibus aedibus familiae consanguineorum parochi cum filiis et nepotibus degant.

73. Utrum libri parochiales adsint in singulis paroeciis, et ibi iuxta canonicas praescriptiones adnotentur quae pertinent ad baptismum, matrimonium ac mortem fidelium.

Speciatim circa matrimonium, an novissima lex servetur qua iubetur de peracto matrimonio inscriptionem fieri in baptizatorum libro ad singulorum nomen.

An habeantur quoque libri confirmatorum et status animarum, itemque tabellae seu libri missarum fundatarum et manualium, iique diligenter redigantur ac serventur.

74. Utrum in singulis paroeciis tabularium aliquod adsit, illudque in duas partes, publicam et secretam, divisum, et utrumque naviter custoditum.

75. Utrum parochi aliique animarum curatores debitam residentiam servent.

76. Utrum diebus festis missam pro populo applicent, sacrasque functiones ad diei festi sanctificationem proprias cum zelo et fructu celebrent: potissimum vero an evangelium explicent, et catechesim tam pueris quam adultis tradant, qua methodo, quo fructu.

An adsint hisce in rebus negligentes.

77. Utrum in audiendis confessionibus, sacra Eucharistia distribuenda, infirmorum adsistentia semper praesto sint, nihilque inconveniens, vel nulla querela hac de re habeatur.

78. Utrum, nisi gravis et legitima causa in aliquo speciali casu obstet, baptismum administrent et matrimonio adsistant in ecclesia, servatis solemnitatibus a Rituali Romano praescriptis.

79. Quomodo se gerant erga fideles qui, sectis secretis notorie addicti, vel alia quavis de causa extra Ecclesiae sinum

rii et parentum iudicio discretionis sunt capaces a sacra mensa non prohibeantur, nec diu arceantur.

81. Utrum parochi pro viribus curent fideles suos in fide roborare, ad sacramentorum frequentiam, praesertim ad S. Communionem etiam quotidianam excitare, et in christianae vitae more et puritate continere. Et ad hunc finem, praeter consueta sui officii munera.

(*a*) an aliquoties in anno, diebus praesertim solemnioribus vel tempore adventus, quadragesimae vel mariani mensis, praeconem et confessarium extraordinarium advocent;

(*b*) an identidem post aliquam annorum periodum sacras missiones in sua paroecia haberi curent;

(*c*) an pias devotiones ab Ecclesia probatas, ut expositionem SSmi Sacramenti, viam crucis, rosarium, mensem marianum, aliaque similia in sua ecclesia celebrent, et fidelibus commendent: et quaenam magis in usu sint in dioecesi;

(*d*) an studeant pueros, puellas et maioris aetatis fideles allicere ut ad pias uniones, patronatus, sodalitates vel consociationes catholicas se adscribant;

(*e*) an prudenter instituant vel saltem foveant opera socialia, quae Ecclesiae catholicae spiritu aluntur.

CAP. VIII.

Art. I.—De Seminario dioecesano.

82. Paucis dicatur quae sit Seminarii fabrica, novane an vetus, quot alumnis continendis capax, an disciplinaribus et hygienicis regulis respondens, an a servitutibus libera, hortis et atriis ad recreationem instructa.

Si vero dioecesanum Seminarium non unicum sit, sed in *maius* et *minus,* vel in plura alia aedificia divisum, exponatur

tur, indicetur quaenam sit haec congregatio, quando quibusnam conditionibus, et an ex S. Sedis venia curam pii instituti
susceperit, et an praefatis conditionibus satisfaciat.

85. Utrum habeatur magister pietatis, vulgo *director spiritualis,* in Seminario degens et nullo alio officio implicatus;
et an, praeter ipsum, sufficiens copia aliorum confessariorum
detur.

86. Utrum adsint deputati pro disciplina et pro oeconomia
a S. Concilio Tridentino praescripti: et an Ordinarius eorum
consilium iuxta iuris praescripta requirat.

87. Utrum magistri in Seminario convivant, necne: et an
quoad eorum idoneitatem, pietatem, agendi rationem (praesertim si Seminarium incolant) aliquid animadvertendum sit.

88. Quot sint actu Seminarii alumni: et an inter eos ad-
mittantur qui ad statum ecclesiasticum certe non aspirent.

An et quot externi alumni habeantur: qua de causa: et an
fieri possit ut et ipsi quam primum Seminarium ingrediantur:
interim quomodo vigilentur: an saltem cura sit ut ante sacram
ordinationem per aliquod notabile tempus in Seminario degant.

An et quot alumni extra dioecesim instituantur, ubi et qua
de causa.

Et vicissim an clerici alterius dioecesis in Seminarium dioecesanum recepti sint, quot, quarum dioecesum, et quibusnam
de causis.

89. Si unum sit Seminarium, et simul convivere debeant
aetate iuniores cum maioribus, an debitae cautelae adhibeantur,
ut seorsim hi ab illis et cum disciplina suae cuiusque aetatis
propria instituantur.

orum, quae quamvis in se innoxia, eos tamen a studiis suis distrahere possunt.

93. Utrum Ordinarius saepe Seminarium invisat et alumnos pro viribus ipsemet audiat, ut cognoscat quo spiritu educentur, quaenam sit eorum pietas, quinam in studiis profectus.

94. Quae regulae serventur in promotione alumnorum ad ordines: quale scrutinium habeatur et quale examen, ut constet quinam pietate, scientia, vitae integritate aliisque requisitis sacra ordinatione digni et idonei censeantur: an spirituales exercitationes praemittantur: an interstitia serventur: quo titulo ordinentur.

95. Utrum ab ultimo quinquennio extraordinarium aliquid in Seminario acciderit sive bonum sive malum.

96. Utrum adsit rusticationis domus, et ibi alumni feriarum tempore adunentur. Ea si desit, an et quae spes sit ut comparetur, et ibi alumni saltem maxima ex parte temporis agant ferias.

Interim dum ad suos revertuntur, an parochi naviter de iis curam habeant, et Ordinarium certiorem reddant de eorumdem agendi ratione: quaenam hac de re normae praescriptae sint in dioecesi.

97. Utrum cura sit ut maiores spei clerici, sive ante sive post susceptum sacrum presbyteratus ordinem, in aliqua pontificia studiorum universitate, sive Romae sive alibi, instituantur ut academicos gradus assequantur.

98. Si qui vero cum Ordinarii venia, vel eius mandato, publicas civiles studiorum universitates frequentant, an pro iis regulae a S. Sede statutae serventur, ut ipsi a perversione custodiantur, et a fide vel ab ecclesiasticae vitae institutis non deflectant.

99. Si clerici servitium militare obire cogantur, quae cautelae adhibeantur ut ii in stipendiis honestam vitam agant

Art. II.—De Seminario interdioecesano seu regionali.

101. Si in dioecesi habeatur Seminarium quo alumni plurium dioecesum vel totius alicuius regionis conveniant, et ipse loci Ordinarius huic Seminario praesideat, de eius statu fuse referat iuxta quaesita superius relata pro Seminario dioecesano.

Quod si huic Seminario ipse non praesit, indicet cuius immediatae directioni subsit, et exponat quid de eo fama ferat.

[TO BE CONTINUED.]

S. CONGREGATIO DE RELIGIOSIS.

DECLARATIO CIRCA DECRETUM D. D. 7 SEPT. 1909.

"DE QUIBUSDAM POSTULANTIBUS IN RELIGIOSAS FAMILIAS NON ADMITTENDIS."

Sanctissimus Dominus Noster Pius Papa X, in Audientia, die 4 Ianuarii 1910 infrascripto Cardinali Praefecto benigne concessa, decernere dignatus est, ut dispositiones Decreti Sacrae Congregationis de Religiosis, d. d. 7 Septembris 1909, *De quibusdam postulantibus in Religiosas Familias non admittendis,* ad mulierum quoque Religiosas Familias in posterum extendantur. Ideoque, absque speciali venia Sedis Apostolicae et sub poena nullitatis professionis, non excipiantur sive ad Novitiatum, sive ad emissionem votorum, postulantes:

1.° quae, propria culpa, e collegiis etiam laicis, gravi de causa, expulsae fuerint;

2.° quae a scholis domesticis, in quibus puellae speciali cura in spem amplectendae vitae religiosae educantur, quacumque ratione dimissae fuerint;

3.° quae, sive ut professae, sive ut novitiae, ab alio Ordine vel Congregatione religiosa dimissae fuerint; vel, si professae, dispensationem votorum obtinuerint;

4.° quae iam admissae, sive ut professae, sive ut novitiae in unam provinciam alicuius Ordinis vel Congregationis et ab ea dimissae, in eamdem vel in aliam eiusdem Ordinis vel Congregationis provinciam recipi nitantur.

Contrariis quibuscumque non obstantibus.

Romae, 4 Ianuarii 1910.

Fr. J. C. Card. VIVES, *Praefectus.*

L. * S.

D. L. JANSSENS, O. S. B., *Secretarius.*

S. CONGREGATIO RITUUM.

DE OFFERTORIO IN MISSIS CANTATIS.

Ab hodierno Rmo Dno Episcopo Curiensis Dioecesis proposito dubio: " An sustineri possit consuetudo quae in multis Ecclesiis minoribus Curiensis dioeceseos ab immemorabili tempore invaluit, ut nempe in Missis cantatis, exceptis quibusdam solemnioribus, celebrans Symbolum intonet, hocque recitato, immediate pergat ad Offertorium illudque conficiat, dum a Cantoribus Symbolum decantatur ? "

Sacra Rituum Congregatio, audito etiam Commissionis Liturgicae suffragio, respondendum censuit: *Negative* et serventur Rubricae et Decreta.

Atque ita rescripsit, die 11 Decembris 1909.

Fr. S. Card. MARTINELLI, *Praefectus.*

L. * S.   PH. CAN. DI FAVA, *Substitutus.*

PONTIFICAL APPOINTMENTS.

By decree of the S. Congregation of Consistory :

7 February, 1910.—The Rev. John Martin Janiz, of the Diocese of Cordova, Central America, elected to the Episcopal See of Santiago de Estèro, Argentina.

7 February, 1910.—The Rev. Abel Bazàn, of the Diocese of Cordova, Central America, elected to the Episcopal See of Paranà, Argentina.

7 February, 1910.—The Rev. John William Shaw, Rector of the Cathedral, Mobile, Alabama, elected to the Titular See of Castabala and Coadjutor of the Bishop of San Antonio, Texas.

7 February, 1910.—The Right Rev. Denis O'Donaghue, Titular Bishop of Pomario and Auxiliary Bishop of Indianapolis, elected to the Episcopal See of Louisville, Kentucky.

8 February, 1910.—The Rev. John Jeremiah Lawler, Rector of the Cathedral, St. Paul, Minnesota, elected to the Titular, See of Hermopolis and Coadjutor of the Archbishop of St. Paul, Minnesota.

The following were appointed Domestic Prelates :

7 January, 1910.—The Rev. John J. McCort, Rector of the Church of Our Mother of Sorrows, Philadelphia, Pa.;

The Rev. George Bornemann, Rector of St. Paul's Church,

Studies and Conferences.

OUR ANALECTA.

The Roman documents for the month are:

THE HOLY FATHER: 1. Thanks Mgr. William O'Connell, Archbishop of Boston, for the special interest he has shown in the work of the Pontifical Institute for Biblical Studies.

2. Commends the extension of the *League of the Good Shepherd,* established originally in St. Patrick's Church, Washington, and having for its chief aim the bringing of non-Catholics into the fold of Christ.

HOLY OFFICE grants an extension of opportunity for the gaining of the Plenary Indulgences attached to membership in the Confraternity of Our Lady of Mercy.

S. CONGREGATION OF CONSISTORY: 1. Declares that ecclesiastical decisions referring to mixed marriages, involving the *Privilegium Paulinum* and other dispensations, are to be invariably referred to the Holy Office, with the understanding that the said Holy Office may refer the same in special cases to some other competent tribunal.

2. Decides that the alumni of the Pontifical College of the *Josephinum* in the Diocese of Columbus, Ohio, are dispensed from making the annual *relatio* prescribed for the alumni of the Roman Pontifical Seminaries formerly under the authority of the Propaganda.

3. Continuation of the *Normae Communes* laid down for bishops in making their diocesan report and visitation *ad limina.*

S. CONGREGATION FOR RELIGIOUS prescribes that the regulations laid down by decree of 7 September, 1909, regarding the non-admission of certain classes of postulants into religious orders, are to be observed by religious communities of women as well as of men.

THE CASUS "DE LICEITATE VASECTOMIAE".

The last issue of the REVIEW (March, pp. 271-275) contained an article by Father Stephen Donovan, O.F.M., professor of Moral Theology in the Franciscan House of Studies attached to the Catholic University, Washington, in which he proposed for discussion the morality of a medical operation which has recently come into vogue among surgeons, and which in view of its effects as tending to counteract certain evils of inherited degeneracy, has been incorporated in the civil laws of several States of the Union, with the prospect of its being adopted by other States and territories of America.

In view of Father Donovan's hesitancy to offer an apodictic judgment regarding the case as stated, we referred it to Mgr. Canon De Becker, professor at the University of Louvain and a recognized authority in canon law throughout the Catholic world. We requested, moreover, that the case be submitted to the professors of allied theological branches at the University, inasmuch as it contained elements in which the judgment of specialists in pastoral medicine and ecclesiastical jurisprudence, no less than in moral theology, would be of importance.

The answer of the eminent professors of theology at the Louvain University is incorporated in the very clear and explicit judgment of Mgr. De Becker, as found below.

DUBIA.

I. An quis licite operationi quae vulgo dicitur *Vasectomia* submittere se possit, juxta modum a Rev. D. Prof. Donovan expositum?

II. Utrum medicus praedictam operationem facere possit casu quo patiens hujus effectum ignorat?

RESPONSA AD DUBIA PROPOSITA.

I. Dicendum non *probabiliter* tantum sed *certo,* juxta prin-

solo respectu conservationis proprii individui sed, insuper, sub respectu propagationis speciei, et consequenter, organorum ad hoc a Creatore destinatorum (unde gravitas peccatorum contra Sextum). Ex alia parte, gravis mutilatio in tantum permittitur in quantum est necessaria ad conservationem vitae.[1] Ideoque motivum allegatum plane insufficiens est ad excusandam dictam operationem.

II. Dicendum quod neque medicus neque auctoritas civilis ullum jus habent faciendi talem operationem homini sive volenti sive, a fortiori, ignoranti aut nolenti. De medici incompetentia res est nimis clara: quis enim dedit alteri (sive medico sive cuicumque privato homini) jus gravem perficiendi mutilationem proximo suo, dum ipse proximus, sub gravi, prohibetur ab ea admittenda? Ad auctoritatem civilem quod attinet, ea nullum jus habet relate ad vitam et libertatem *innocentium* et consequenter ea prorsus excluditur a jure mutilandi innocentem, etiam sub praetextu boni communis. Unde, sine ullo fundamento provocaretur ad principium in conflictu jurium. Quare plane subscribo sententiae R. P. Vermeersch, R. P. de Villers, R. P. Salsmans, *Professorum in Collegio Maximo Societatis Jesu, Lovanii,* dum dicunt:

"Doctrina quam sincera profecto mente et cum aliqua haesitatione proponit R. P. Donovan plane improbabilis et damnosa a nobis judicatur.

"1. In se mutilatio ista (nisi gravissima propriae valetudinis causa excusetur) non est *venialis* sed *mortalis.* Gravitas enim non tantum ex periculo vitae sed etiam ex functione qua privat judicanda est.

"2. Auctoritas publica *nihil* potest in vitam et libertatem innocentis, qualis est etiam homo aegrotus.

"Nec, cum agitur de Christianis, impedimenta matrimonii creare potest; multo minus potest imperare vel permittere mutilationem de qua in casu."

Scribebam Lovanii, 16 Feb. 1910.

JULES DE BECKER, J.U.D.

THE TEACHING OF SCRIPTURE IN OUR SCHOOLS.

To the Editor, THE ECCLESIASTICAL REVIEW.

In the February issue, Father Pope, O.P., points out that a certain number of priests leave the seminary with very little knowledge of the text of the Bible or of how to read it. He concludes that this is largely the result of a faulty seminary training in Sacred Scripture, and suggests some remedies. The present writer humbly doubts whether the remedies proposed are sufficient. Father Pope supposes that our young seminarians are quite ignorant of the Bible when they enter the seminary, and that it is this initial ignorance which paralyzes too often their Scripture course. This then is the fundamental trouble.

It is worth while asking ourselves what percentage of our seminarians (who are as a rule the graduates of our Catholic primary schools and colleges) have a fair acquaintance with their Bible before entering the seminary. Have they studied Bible History, and do they remember any of it? What did they learn about the Bible in the Catholic Colleges they attended? Was not at least one of the Gospels read through in Greek? It is not too much to expect that those who have studied Greek three or four years at a Catholic college should be able to read at sight any part of the Gospels. Some of our colleges however neglect the Greek New Testament altogether, and have no course of instruction in Sacred Scripture. If the courses in our colleges were better co-ordinated with the requirements of our seminaries we should no longer find the average young seminarian quite ignorant of the Gospel in Greek, and unfamiliar even with the New Testament in English. If, for example, the " Scripture Manuals for Catholic Schools " edited by Father Sidney, S.J., were in general use in our colleges, and the Gospel in Greek were studied as often as Greek be studied, our students would become familiar with the text and the meaning of the historical facts of the New Testament—the most useful part of the Bible for them to know. This, with a summary knowledge of Old Testament history and some general notions on the nature, inspiration, and inerrancy of Scripture, would be enough for an educated Catholic layman. It would moreover be an excellent preparation for a solid seminary course in Sacred Scripture such as Father Pope outlines.

JOHN J. O'GORMAN.

Canadian College, Rome.

"WHAT VESTMENTS SHALL WE WEAR?"

We have already referred to the unmixed note of approval that has reached us from different sources, clerical and lay, touching the proposed return to liturgical and tasteful vestments for divine service. This approval comes not from England only, where the revival of olden church discipline and good form in ecclesiastical decoration has been proceeding for a considerable time, and where it is moreover based on a very definite and respectable tradition; but it comes likewise from priests in America, where in many instances pastors have been obliged to devote their energies to provide housing for the Lord, irrespective of the requirements of a perfect liturgical service.

Let us emphasize the fact that, while the proposed modification is away from an almost universal custom (not to say abuse), it is not a merely useful change, whether viewed from the standpoint of taste, economy, or devotion, but it is also a perfectly legitimate one and one that does not require a dispensation from the Holy See. It is true there was published at one time under the name of the S. Congregation of Rites a decision which seemed to forbid the general adoption of the vestments commonly, though incorrectly, styled Gothic. This decision, however, has been omitted from the recent authentic collection of decrees, as we have already pointed out. The only form of chasuble the S. Congregation forbids to be used by the Latin clergy is the Oriental form adopted in the Greek services; but of this there is here no question, even though the ample chasuble recommended for cathedral use approaches it somewhat in form. The proposed modification is concerned only with the vestment that represents more truly the chasuble spoken of in the liturgy and prescribed by the established ecclesiastical laws which, like the statutes of St. Charles Borromeo in general, are for all priests models of correctness and in harmony with the spirit of the Council of Trent.

The Benedictines and Dominicans have maintained the ancient usage, and in many convents in the United States we find the so-called Gothic vestments actually used. Someone has said that the Jesuit Order is opposed to the reform. This we cannot credit; individual members of the Society may be, but hardly the Order. A recent editorial in *America,* a Catholic weekly conducted by the Jesuit Fathers, commented adversely on the efforts of the REVIEW to promote the dignity and holiness of the sanctuary service, especially in its influence upon the laity. The editorial writer's frequent and trivial criticisms on various serious subjects broached in the REVIEW, whether these happened to touch upon the utility of interpreting the liturgy for our people without interfering with the liturgical Latin of the service, or on the observance of the *Motu proprio* in the Church's chant, or on the liturgical form and the colors of the vestments, would fairly lead one to the conclusion that his comments have been and are inspired by mental limitations or bias. But we have never considered these criticisms as reflecting the sober Jesuit judgment. Elsewhere in these pages we have spoken of the noble work a-doing by *America,* and, as a co-laborer in the literary field and with like lofty aims, the REVIEW regrets that a lack of editorial honesty should hold even the slightest footing in the councils of *America.*

Withal, it is plain that unfair criticism in such matters will not in the least affect the judgment of our clergy and interested laity. Of this the REVIEW is assured by the letters we have received on the subject, letters which space and the general policy of the magazine alike preclude us from publishing here. If an exception is made in one case, it is because the letter comes from a priest who is respected alike for his zeal in behalf of liturgical observances and ecclesiastical art, and who is at the same time endowed with the practical good sense that takes account of the utility of Catholic teaching through the liturgy. We publish the parts of his letter which are directly pertinent to our subject, and if we take the liberty of withholding his name, we do so in order to forestall personal animosity:

To the Editor, THE ECCLESIASTICAL REVIEW.

I should like to call attention to the remarkable editorial in *America* for 19 February, 1910, entitled "What Vestments Shall We Wear?" First, let me protest against the flippant treatment of a very serious and important question; secondly, let me call attention to its manifest and positive unfairness as well as its self-contradiction. With regard to the latter, the writer says, "If the Holy See so ordains, priests will all exchange the present vestments for the modified ones; . . . we will do so with heavy hearts." Yet he seems to indicate that the Holy See would make the change only on account of the popular vote on the question, glibly quoting from Andrew Lang, and forgetting the obvious fact that in such matters the Holy See does not use the referendum. . . . If it be the policy of *America* to appeal to the popular sentiment in such matters as the observance of the rubrics, we may doubt whether the portion of the Catholic Church represented by the writer in *America* will " gladly," or even " obediently ", comply with any decree of the Holy See with regard to vestments.

The unfairness of the article is quite evident from the quip concerning the purchasing of vestments from Anglican Religious. In turning over the leaves of this same issue of *America,* I find that we are invited to go to [a non-Catholic company] for our church furnishings, which, I presume, include chalices, ciboria, ostensoria, etc., which are, in the judgment of many, quite as important in the service of the altar as are vestments; and when so high-class a journal as *America* tacitly requests its readers to go to non-Catholic sources for these furnishings, we scarcely see why they should cavil about going to people who have taste and experience, even though they are not Catholic. I happen to know that a number of very intelligent priests in the Middle West in despair of getting anything esthetic or artistic from the ordinary purveyors of church furnishings in their section of the country, have long been in the habit of procuring these from communities of religious women of the Protestant persuasion; and, as after all, it is a matter of business, there would not seem to be much more harm in it than in purchasing such furnishings from firms which, in many cases under Catholic names, are controlled by Jewish financiers.

THE QUESTION OF MANUFACTURING PROPER PARAMENTICS.

I.

To the Editor, THE ECCLESIASTICAL REVIEW.

I desire first of all to express my appreciation of Mr. Metlake's article in the February number; then, in reference to Mr. John T. Comes's letter in the same issue, to intimate that, until a suitable supply is forthcoming from U. S. A. (as suggested), vestments of the ancient forms and dimensions can be procured at somewhat modest figures from the Kulturkampf-exiled convent at Southam, near Warwick, whose card I enclose. I also send for your acceptance photos of three specimens of their output, two chasubles and a cope (with hood hung in front for photographing). I may say that details are complete down to pupils of eyes, eyelashes, and fingernails. The Erdington chasuble is 4 ft. 8 in. across at the widest part, and the Chester one 4 ft. 5 in. I would like to point out to those who propose to obtain some of these chasubles, that it is of no use getting them less than about 4 ft. 3 in. in greatest width (i. e. reaching, on the average man, down to the middle of the forearm), as then there would not be sufficient material to allow the graceful folds which are the soul of this type of vestment. In fact, 4 ft. 5 in. across is a good working size for priests of different heights. Of course, the chasuble will not be less than 4 ft. in length, behind.

There are only two Catholic providers in England of vestments of the highest class of embroidery, viz. Southam Convent and St. Katherine's Convent, Queen's Square, London, W. C., who have lately come over from Anglicanism, like your Society of the Atonement.

A. K. BRANDRETH.

Pembroke College, Oxford.

II.

To the Editor, THE ECCLESIASTICAL REVIEW.

Some interesting articles on Gothic vestments in this month's ECCLESIASTICAL REVIEW excite my sympathetic interest. Your correspondent, John T. Comes, gives an address of a Benedictine community at the Isle of Caldy as producing such work. . . . I should like to make known, however, the existence of the Benedictine Convent at Clyde, Missouri, where I have had vestments made in true Gothic shape, and excellent in texture and needle work. . . . The nuns are prepared to send drawings and specimens of the textiles when required.

E. FRANCIS RIGGS.

Washington, D. C.

THE QUESTION OF CHRISTIAN ART SUPPLY.

To the Editor, THE ECCLESIASTICAL REVIEW.

For several years we have followed with great interest the many instructive articles of the REVIEW, especially those pertaining to Christian art and art crafts, which indeed are of great value and help to a sincere priest when building, decorating, or furnishing his church. No doubt they were read by many priests, but, if I may apply the parable of the sower and the seed, much of the good seed has fallen by the wayside, has made no impression on the reader; and other some has fallen among the thorns of business cares and troubles, and these, together with false economy in purchasing the cheapest in the market, have choked it. And thus it happens that in this country so little progress is seen in the field of Christian art.

In Europe the principal attractions for tourists seem to be the various cathedrals and churches with their art treasures, where the esthetic sense is well pleased and gratified. In this country, however, we show to our visitors the federal and municipal buildings as evidences of the artistic taste of the inhabitants, and never think of bringing them to our churches, for we know and realize that these fall short in their artistic merits. It is a lame excuse, to say in order to justify the lack of taste in some of our churches, that this is a mission country where the churches are built and maintained by the contributions of the poor; for in our large cities we see costly church buildings, which could have been erected along the lines of truthful architecture and artistically decorated and furnished, and at less cost. Large sums of money have often been lavishly spent on the exterior of a church so as to render it an imposing structure, whereas the interior has been very stingily treated. The cheapest furnishings have been acquired; the cheapest artists have been engaged, and the result is naturally *cheap and inartistic workmanship*.

How is this evil to be remedied? Certainly not by critizing the bishops and clergy and placing all the blame at their door. A little self-knowledge and reason tell us that we all are fallible and liable to be mistaken in our views. Therefore it would be imprudent on our part to uphold our ideas and principles as the only true and correct standard to be accepted by all unconditionally. Such conceit is bound to bring about grave errors and to lay us open to censure. We should, however, at first make inquiry whether our views coincide with the spirit of the Church, mould our ideas accordingly, and then in all charity propose our views and principles to the logical minds of the bishops and priests.

The letter of Mr. John T. Comes[1] published in the February

---

[1] This letter referred the readers, among other sources, to a community of

number of THE ECCLESIASTICAL REVIEW, was of great interest to us in so far as it expresses his enthusiasm for Christian art and art crafts, and also discloses his sentiments and ideas. Enthusiasm is a valuable gift at the present time in a country where so much indifference is shown to true Christian art, and such enthusiasm is praiseworthy and the owner to be encouraged. But if the "Deutsche Gesellschaft für Christliche Kunst" seems to him to be the great exponent of true Christian art, we certainly differ with him. We do not deny the artistic merits of many of the members of that organization, nor question their good motives and intentions. But we leave it to the unbiased judgment of Catholic art critics to decide whether some of their work as reproduced in their periodical, comes up to the requirements of the Church as set forth in her councils and decrees. It may be that some of the members of that organization do not know of any laws and precepts of the Church in the realm of art. "The making or painting of pictures is not dependent on the unrestrained conception and inspiration of the artist, but on the lawful precepts and traditions of the Church. It is for the artist to put into beautiful and artistic form what the holy fathers, the builders of temples, have conceived." [2] The Christian artist who does not respect the laws of the Church concerning Christian art, cannot claim to foster true Christian art.

P. RAPHAEL, O.S.B.

Studio of Christian Art, St. Anselm's College, Manchester, N. H.

THE KEVELAER SCHOOL OF DESIGN FOR LITURGICAL VESTMENTS.

We have thus far refrained from referring in detail to the manufacture of vestments which is being carried on under the direction of Madame Stummel, the lady of whom George Metlake speaks in his able articles on "The Reform of Church Vestments",[1] lest the discussion of this important subject might take on the appearance of a commercial advocacy. But, having understood the importance of the matter, the question put by the Rev. J. F. Sheahan in his letter in the January number of the REVIEW (p. 85) becomes not only pertinent

---

Anglican Benedictines in Wales, no doubt because the matter of correct ecclesiastical vestments has been taken up by these communities as a specialty wherein they excel and in which their particular interest gives them a zeal as well as facilities not so common among Catholics.

[2] Conc. Nic. II, act. 7.

[1] ECCLESIASTICAL REVIEW, February and March, 1910, pp. 142 and 315.

but assumes a practical value for every priest interested in the reform. " We know that our modern vestments are ugly," writes Father Sheahan, " and we would like to have chasubles more conformable to the beautiful chasubles of old; but where can we get them? . . . If there were a firm somewhere in the world that would make nothing but what was beautiful and rubrical, we could write or go there with confidence for what we wanted."

Several houses where these vestments are made have already been mentioned, and we do not doubt that very soon others will be prepared to furnish what is wanted. Nevertheless, since the originator of this movement in its present phases, who, by her writings, lectures to the clergy and to Tabernacle Societies, and by practical illustration of the designs, colors, and artistic details of vestments, has won the commendation of the Sovereign Pontiff, is actually willing and prepared to furnish every assistance to priests wishing to procure correct vestments at a reasonable cost, it would seem to be the proper thing to apply to her directly for information.

To those who might be tempted to any misgivings on the score that the impulse of the movement comes from a woman, we would state by way of reassurance that Madame Stummel has abundant recognition of her qualifications to act as guide in this matter of paramentics. Indeed, the art belongs, so far as the production of vestments is concerned, much more to women than to the clergy. The divine ordinances of the Old Testament worship undoubtedly included the provision which assigned to matrons or virgins of the house of David the weaving of the temple robes and tabernacle veils; and a venerable tradition represents Our Lady at this task when the Angel approached her with the message of the " Ave Maria ". There is nothing unbecoming therefore in our receiving some lessons in this branch of ecclesiastical industry from a highly cultured and religious woman who has had better opportunities than are accorded to the average student of Christian art, to observe the needs of the sanctuary in different countries, and to discuss the subject with ecclesiastical dignitaries of every rank in Rome as well as in Germany. Very recently the Bishop of Luxemburg, whose diocese is, we are told, permeated with the traditions and taste of French ecclesiasticism, invited Madame Stummel to address a body of the clergy and students in his diocesan seminary, himself and the professors being present and fully approving the principles she explained regarding the shape and color of the vestments. The same report comes to us from other bishops and from ecclesiastical centres.

It may be of interest to priests and religious who expect to attend the Eucharistic Congress in Montreal this fall, to know that the President of the Congress, Mgr. Heylen, Bishop of Namur, has recommended Madame Stummel to the Committee as one of the speakers at the Congress. This will give an opportunity to many not only to hear her discuss the subject at the Eucharistic Congress, but also to obtain from her directly information on everything that pertains to this branch of ecclesiastical art.[2] Her last brochure, which has just been published, *Die Farbe der Paramentik,* and which appeared first in the *Archiv f. Christl. Kunst,*[3] goes into the details of the motives for a correct choice of liturgical colors. We understand that she is to bring with her to America specimens from a private collection of medieval and modern vestments to be exhibited at the Montreal Congress. As the lady speaks both English and French we trust that her presence in Canada will offer occasion for a visit to the chief centres of the United States where priests and religious will have the opportunity of hearing her and imbibing some enthusiasm in behalf of beautiful vestments for our sanctuaries. The initiative for this must, of course, come from the clergy or from the bishop of the diocese.

COMMUNION WITHOUT FASTING.

Qu. In reply to a question of a correspondent in your February number as to the right of an invalid priest to say Mass *without fasting,* the condition is presumed that, besides being out of bed, he is able, in a limited way, to attend to the duties of his calling. Could not the decree of the Congregation be likewise interpreted for the benefit of hundreds of laymen who are in poor health, not entirely

---

[2] Her present address is: Frau Helene Stummel, Kevelaer, Rheinprovinz,

disqualified for the exercise of their vocation in life, but unable, in the judgment of their medical advisers, to go abroad fasting?

S. C. B.

Resp. Assuming that the condition of the two patients is alike, there is no reason why the same principle should not apply to both layman and priest.

There is some difference between a priest's attending " in a limited way the duties of his calling " by the mere saying of Mass, and the going abroad of a layman for the exercise (even partial) of his vocation. The one involves simply the ceremonial of sacrificial reception of Holy Communion at his own hands; the other supposes an activity entirely distinct from the Communion and alien to it. To say Mass is the priest's ordinary way of communicating; and it implies hardly more exertion than that employed by a sick lay person who has to prepare for the reception of Communion at some inconvenience of movement and physical exertion.

AN AMERICAN LEAGUE FOR THE CONVERSION OF NON-CATHOLICS.

In another part of this issue we publish a Pontifical Brief in which the Holy Father recommends the extension of the *League of the Good Shepherd,* established originally at St. Patrick's Church, Washington, D. C. The League has for its motto " I know mine and mine know me, and other sheep I have that are not of this fold; them also I must bring, and they shall hear my voice, and there shall be one fold and one shepherd." These words of the Good Shepherd indicate the chief object of the League, which is the conversion of our

tiff's letter, which we here append in authorized translation, will show how much the Father of the faithful has at heart this work, in which all can unite by affiliation with the central sodality at Washington, where the statutes as well as a copy of the *Office* recited by the members may be obtained.

PIUS X. POPE.

Be it forever remembered:

Our beloved son, the pastor of St. Patrick's Church in Washington, Archdiocese of Baltimore, has made known to Us that in accordance with the expressed desire of the Fathers of the Second Plenary Council of Baltimore, he has established in his parish church the pious sodality of the League of the Good Shepherd which seeks as its special object, to obtain from God by prayer and good works the preservation of the faith among the parishioners and the conversion of their friends and relatives to the true religion. Since this League, canonically organized by the Ordinary of the Diocese and enriched with indulgences by the Holy See, has already borne abundant fruit and is rapidly spreading with the support of the Bishops into other dioceses, our beloved son as aforesaid, has earnestly besought Us to the effect that the heavenly treasures of the Church, which we have opened to this League, should likewise be made available for other associations which take the League as their pattern.

We therefore gladly favor this pious petition, and, relying on the mercy of Almighty God and the authority of the Blessed Apostles Peter and Paul, We grant to every association established or hereafter to be established in the United States of America with the consent of the respective Bishop and with the same name and scope as the said League, each and all of the indulgences, plenary and partial, which were granted to the League by the Holy See on the twenty-seventh day of May in the current year: To wit, a plenary indulgence to all the faithful of either sex who shall join one of the aforesaid associations, to be gained on the day of their admission; likewise, to the present and future members a plenary indulgence on the festivals of Easter, Christmas and Corpus Christi, including the first vespers of each festival; also the same indulgence, available from sunrise to sunset, on one day in each month to be selected by the director of each League; with the condition in all cases that the members truly repent of and confess their sins, receive Holy Communion, make a visit to any church or public oratory and there pray for peace among Christian Rulers, for the extirpation of heresy, the conversion of sinners, and the exaltation of holy mother Church. And We further grant, in the usual form, an indulgence of three hundred days to the members who, at least with contrite heart, shall attend the weekly devotions of the League; and one hundred days to be gained by each devout recitation, in any language, of the prayer: "O Jesus, Good Shepherd, I offer Thee all my actions of this day for the conversion of my country, and in particular for the conversion of N———." Finally, We permit all these indulgences, remissions of sins, and relaxations of penance to be applied by way of suffrage to the souls in Purgatory. Anything whatsoever to the contrary notwithstanding, the present concessions are to hold good in perpetuity.

Given at St. Peter's, Rome, under the Fisherman's Ring, the thirtieth day of December, nineteen hundred and nine, the seventh year of Our Pontificate.

R. Card. MERRY DEL VAL,
Secretary of State.

ADJUSTING MISUNDERSTANDINGS IN A PARISH.

To the Editor, THE ECCLESIASTICAL REVIEW.

May I intrude on your valuable space to make a suggestion? I am a priest of a diocese that is happily united and progressing rapidly since Rome sent us our first bishop; but occasionally little trials have to be borne by priest and people, and these could be easily adjusted if only we had an ecclesiastic capable of bringing about agreements when things go wrong. The thought occurred often to me that it would be a great relief to the bishop if we had in every diocese one or two experienced and tactful men who would know how to use the good offices of some zealous and conscientious layman to call upon both pastor and people in their difficulties and bring them together and put an end to their troubles in a broad-minded and common-sense manner. An example recently occurred in a neighboring diocese to which a friend of mine was called to act as intermediary in a bitter dispute that had lasted for several years. This good priest was asked if he could not do something to stop the quarrel and the scandal which had ostracized some and weakened the respect of others. Having a full knowledge of the case, he gladly accepted the task and went about it in the most informal way. He talked with the pastor and found him most willing to be reconciled and was authorized as peacemaker to tell the aggrieved parties that he would be glad to "let bygones be bygones" if they came back to the fold. In a few hours the bugbear of animosity which they held in their bosom against their pastor was dispelled and at his kindly invitation to go with him to the parochial residence they cheerfully assented. On entering the pastor's library they were met with a pleasant welcome, and the tactful intermediary opened up a conversation that had no connexion with the trouble. They talked of everything but the one thing that was uppermost in their minds, and after spending an hour very pleasantly together he said: "Now, gentlemen, I see you can get along very nicely on everything that does not pertain to your points of dispute. I want all of you to call off your dogs and henceforth live like friends." Not a word was spoken on the subject. The peacemaker had prepared both sides for the final issue; the cause was finished; and both have learned to avoid ever since their former errors.

Now, it might be asked, Why could not the bishop have done this himself? I answer, because the bishop should not be brought unnecessarily into disputes. He is the pastor of his diocese and, while there are many questions which he alone has the right to hear and settle, still there are circumstances in some cases that can be settled better without bringing his authority and official position into the arena. Besides, where there is some danger of his advice being refused, would it not be safer in such cases to make a trial of the method I have suggested in the first instance and, if this failed, let him enforce discipline at any cost?

It is sad to see how a few men laboring under the influence of wounded pride often cause breaches in the ranks of a whole parish and for want of timely correction and reconciliation often sow seeds of discord that take root and flourish for generations,—all of which might have been nipped in the bud by open-hearted, prudent, and kindly treatment. Men will fall out with one another in almost all kinds of business ventures and yet agree to live in peace; but once an antipathy to a priest is permitted to take root, it seems that no power short of a miracle or some great calamity can stop its growth and evil influences. I have heard from a priest on the mission of forty years' active service that some of the worst consequences to the faith arose from petty disputes followed by constant agitation which at last culminated in the most disastrous losses to the Church. And the remedy he offered was precisely what I have written. " Bring the parties together and let them make up, and whichever side refuses let the bishop force the recusant to obey at all hazards. Better to have unity and loyalty to authority among what you can count on than suffer a few to remain tormenting and disintegrating the whole body." These were his written words.

B. M. O.

ECCLESIASTICAL HERALDRY.

The explanation of the colored plate which is inserted at this page is as follows:

THE RIGHT REV. JOHN JAMES MONAGHAN, D.D., Bishop of Wilmington, Delaware; born in South Carolina, 1856; ordained priest at Charleston, S. C., 18 December, 1880; proclaimed Bishop of Wilmington, 26 January, 1897; and consecrated in Wilmington, 9 May, 1897.

COAT OF ARMS: " Or, a pine tree proper on a terrace vert; on a fess gules three mullets of the field."

Motto: " Deus incrementum dat." (1 Cor. 3: 6.)

Explanation: Steady progress of Christianity in the Diocese, which embraces parts of three States (Delaware, Maryland, and Virginia). The motto alludes to, " Paulus " (*first,*

COAT OF ARMS OF THE RIGHT REV. JOHN J. MONAGHAN, D. D
BISHOP OF·WILMINGTON, DEL.

Bishop Becker) " plantavit; Apollo " (*second,* Bishop Curtis) " rigavit; Deus incrementum dedit " (under the third or present Bishop).

TO A SEMINARIAN.

Although the scope of the REVIEW naturally excludes poetry, unless it serves as an illustration of some liturgical or pastoral theme treated in our pages, we make room for the following lines by the Rev. Michael Earls, S.J., of Woodstock College:

> Apart from restless marts, by God's high grace,
> You ply the looms of learning. Threaded thought
> Of Plato and the Stagirite well wrought
> With Aquin's warp and woof you deftly trace;
> And tints that science drew from stellar space,
> With what of earth the curvèd strata taught,
> And Faith's fair colors that Redemption brought—
> You weave into a garment for the race.
>> Work bravely in the lists for Truth arrayed
>> Unfearing what the present boasts, or lore
>> Hid in the womb of some far age's art.
>> Trust God for victory: as that Egypt maid,
>> Brave Catherine, won Grecian masters o'er
>> And changed to Christ the Athens in their heart.

THE PRECATORY FORM OF ABSOLUTION IN THE GREEK CHURCH.

·

This is not entirely precatory, inasmuch as it is partially declaratory, for the words "through me" are used.   But in the Russian Orthodox church the form of absolution is entirely declaratory, although commencing in the precatory form.   I quote from the *Trebnik* (Moscow, 1890), p. 38:

> May our Lord and God Jesus Christ by his grace and bounty towards mankind, forgive thee, my child,—all thy transgressions; and *I, his unworthy priest,* through his power given to me, *forgive and absolve thee* from all thy sins, in the name of the Father and the Son and the Holy Ghost, Amen.

In the Greek Catholic church the forms of absolution have always the declaratory form, almost in language like the Russian form just quoted.   For those who are desirous of comparing them, I would refer to the Greek Euchologion (Rome, 1873), pp. 195-208, and to the Ruthenian Greek Catholic *Trebnik* (Lemberg, 1873), pp. 102-117,—the forms of absolution being given in the Greek at page 208 of the Euchologion and in the Slavonic at page 117 of the *Trebnik*.

ANDREW J. SHIPMAN.

New York City.

II.

To the Editor, THE ECCLESIASTICAL REVIEW.

In reference to Mr. Shipman's comments on my article, "The Present Condition of the Greek Church," I beg to state that I fully agree with him as regards the form of absolution in the Russian Orthodox Church.   It is certainly declaratory.   But I was not discussing the Russian Church in that article.   That I treat in a separate paper in this number of the REVIEW.

As regards the sentence—"*They have no confessionals and absolve with a deprecatory form,*" Mr. Shipman says, "I do not think the latter part of this sentence is entirely correct."

Now it seems to me that the form of absolution taken from the Euchologion is entirely deprecatory.   The priest makes no declaration, but prays God *Himself* to forgive the penitent.   Even though he uses the words *through me a sinner,* he thereby indicates that he has not the power resting in him, but prays God to send it through him.   Father Adrian Fortescue in his original and scholarly work, *The Eastern Orthodox Church,* debating this very point, at pp. 422-423, taken from the same Euchologion (pp. 221-223), concludes: "From which it will be seen that the Byzantine Church

precatoriam obtinere certissime pariter constat ex eorum Euchologiis apud Goarium et Arcudium aliosque passim." Father Tanqueray in his *Theologicae Dogmaticae,* vol. iii, p. 506, discussing the *deprecative* form, says: " Negari nequit, quidquid in contrarium dicant nonnulli theologi, eam late in usu fuisse, *imo solam viguisse in Ecclesia Orientali* per multa saecula "; though he says further on, " Recentiori tamen aetate forma *indicativa* invenitur apud Graecos sive catholicos sive schismaticos ".

While I recognize Andrew J. Shipman as an authority on Russian ecclesiastical matters in this country, as his contributions to the *Catholic Encyclopedia* and other writings testify, and while I here acknowledge my indebtedness to him for some points of information relative to the Russian Church and especially the Russian Church in this country, I cannot agree with him in reference to the form of absolution in the Greek Church though fully appreciating his point of argument.

WILLIAM LEEN.

ALIENATION OF ARTICLES BLESSED BY THE CHURCH.

Qu. It is sometimes asserted that vestments, candles, beads, and similar articles liturgically blessed, if sold or given away, lose their blessing. The ECCLESIASTICAL REVIEW (Vol. XXVI, p. 724) quotes a decision of the S. C. Indulgences, 16 July, 1887, in which it is stated: " Indulgentiae amittuntur . . . si . . . venduntur (res benedictae)." Beringer in his work on Indulgences makes the same statement, citing several other decrees. He distinguishes, however, between articles simply blessed and such as are indugenced ;[1] whence I would conclude that blessed vestments, candles, etc. may be sold, so long as there are no indulgences attached to the blessing imparted. Is this correct?

Resp. An object that has been blessed remains blessed. Since the Church blesses all sorts of objects intended for the use of man, such as houses, lands, tools, food, etc., which are of a kind to be sold or given away, it stands to reason that

hibiting such alienation, apart from a sense of propriety and reverence.

It is different with objects distinctly *consecrated* for a specific sacred purpose. These may lose their consecration by being *desecrated*, that is to say by being rendered unfit for the purpose for which the consecration destined them. Such objects might be said to lose their blessing under certain conditions, since the consecration is taken away. They are by a general law, implied in their very consecration, not to be devoted to any other purpose than the one indicated by the consecration. Even these can be sold or given away, so long as they remain dedicated to the original purpose for which they were consecrated.

In like manner indulgences are attached by blessing to certain objects under the condition, regularly understood, that these objects may not be sold or alienated from their original purpose; and the indulgence is revoked or ceases to be applicable the moment this condition is violated. There is nothing in the fact of their being blessed that prevents their being sold or given away; only, the indulgence is then lost. They can be reindulgenced, however.

Criticisms and Notes.

DOM GUÉRANGER. Abbé de Solesmes. Par un Moine Bénédictin de la Congregation de France. Deux volumes. Paris: Plon-Nourrit & Cie. (G. Oudin & Cie.). 1910. Pp. 452 and 480.

Dom Guéranger is best known to the Catholic world at large by his great work entitled *L'année liturgique,* which, since its first appearance in 1841, has been issued in many editions and languages, as an authentic interpretation of Catholic worship and Roman ceremonial. In a sense, the "Liturgical Year" is a reflection of Dom Guéranger's life and character, set forth in his efforts to combat the separatist tendencies of Gallicanism by restoring appreciation for the Roman liturgy. But regarded by the historian of to-day in the light of an abiding influence which has contributed to the formation of Catholic thought and life in France, the eminent Benedictine presents a many-sided aspect of greatness. He was a reformer who interpreted Le Maistre to the statesmen who bore and distributed the honors of the Church; he knew how to discern the dangerous tendencies that grew out of the untutored zeal of a propaganda against the error fostered by De Lamennias and Gerbet; he could direct the powers of the literary genius with whom he came into contact, such as Madame Swetchine and Montalembert; he was capable of going to the foundations of religious life and building up a new Order which breathed the old spirit, so that the freshly-planted sprig became in truth the best representative of the ancient tree. In this he was like to his friend Lacordaire.

Ordained as a secular priest when barely past twenty-two years of age, the Abbé Prosper Louis Pascal Guéranger was made secretary of the Bishop of Mans who was in delicate health. Two episodes of this time, one at his ordination and the other almost immediately after the young priest's installation as chaplain, indicate the future trend of his mind and will. The ordaining prelate was the Archbishop of Tours. During the ceremonies the young candidate for sacred orders noticed that the Archbishop omitted the imposition of hands whilst reading the form and prayers from the Pontifical. Troubled at the possibility of an invalid ordination, the abbé said to the Archbishop: "Monseigneur, you are omitting the

was in their hands, when the latter said: " You are right, I beg your pardon; " and so saying he repeated the form with the imposition of hands. Some days later, while with the Bishop of Mans, the abbé related that he had said Mass in the chapel of the Ladies of the Sacred Heart, who followed the Roman Missal instead of the diocesan (Gallican) Proper commonly in use throughout France. For the sake of ascertaining the harmony which existed between Missal and Breviary, he afterwards read the corresponding Roman Office, and found it singularly attractive as compared with the local Breviary. He therefore asked his bishop to permit him to say the Roman Office regularly. The bishop consented, but reminded him that the diocesan Office was much shorter. The abbé saw no objection in this, but thought it might disconcert the bishop to have to assist at his chaplain's Mass said from a Roman Missal. " Why," replied Mgr. de la Myre, " is not the Roman Missal as good as ours?"

The foregoing incidents are not only characteristic of the man, but they give us the keynote to his subsequent activity. France was suffering from an hierarchical autonomy which alienated it from the centre of Catholic discipline and doctrine. To remedy the consequent separation between the episcopate of France which insisted upon Gallican prerogatives, and the authority of the Roman See, it was necessary to modify the system of episcopal elections in France. Guéranger saw this, and as a result published his reflections " Sur l'élection des évêques ". An admonition of this kind coming from a young priest of twenty-six years of age, was bound to prove ineffective, except in so far as it irritated the majority of the bishops and aroused sympathy in others who realized the danger of a civil church.

If the young abbé could not awaken the bishops to a spontaneous movement toward unity with the Head of the Church, he could make propaganda for a medium that would gradually produce a sympathetic feeling among the clergy at large in behalf of the Mother Church. This medium was the Roman Liturgy to be restored in France as a substitute for the Gallican Propria. But a theoretical or academical appeal would not be effective, he felt. The clergy might read his arguments, but he wanted them to act; and he would set them the practical example by organizing a re-

of tradition in behalf of the Roman Church as teacher and guide in matters of faith and morals.

But his critics, some of whom acted in a hostile and preventive spirit against him, despite the modest reserve with which he kept his personality out of view, objected that the champion of reform himself violated the first principle of order by establishing a Benedictine congregation which had no authority and was not affiliated with any recognized body of the monks of St. Benedict. This caused him to abandon his community for a time in order to enter and pass through the regular novitiate of the Benedictine Abbey of St. Paul in Rome. Having made his profession, he returned to Solesmes, where he was appointed Abbot and Prefect of all the Benedictine communities about to be established in France. Thus the foundation of Solesmes was to rank with similar institutions at Monte Cassino in Italy, and at Beuron in Germany. Soon he found opportunity of reviving the ancient spirit of Benedictine monasticism in other places. In 1886 he revived the order of Benedictine nuns by the establishment of the Abbey of St. Cecilia at Solesmes.

In the meantime he was incredibly diligent with his pen. He became one of the staunchest defenders of the doctrine of the Immaculate Conception, and the Infallibility of the Pope. In the latter sphere he practically silenced Père Gratry's oposition to the definition by his *Réponse aux dernières objections contre la définition de l'infallibilité.* In like manner he stood up stoutly for the prerogatives of the Roman Pontiff in the matter of temporal independence, by his *La Monarchie pontificale.* The tendency to oppose Gallican pretensions is apparent throughout all his writings, and they were in truth effective. Dom Guéranger had the blessing of a long life of nearly half a century spent in active service as a writer of apologetic literature. He died at the age of seventy during the first month of 1875. His great work *L'année liturgique,* though planned to completion, was never finished by him. Nine volumes came from his own hand, and the remaining three of the original French edition are by Dom Formage. What he did for the reform of Church Music is not only indicated by his well-known devotion to St. Cecilia, about whom he composed several volumes, but best of all by the zeal of his disciples who are faithfully laboring in his spirit, particularly the sons of St. Benedict of the Abbey of St. Pierre de Solesmes, at Ryde, Isle of Wight.

We understand that the work is being translated into English by the Benedictine Fathers themselves, and that we shall soon have an

THE SPIRIT OF AMERICA. By Henry Van Dyke, Professor of English at Princeton University. New York: The Macmillan Company. 1910. Pp. xv-276.

The author delivered a series of twenty-six conferences in the winter of 1908-1909, at the University of Paris, and the present volume contains the first seven of these conferences. The sixth conference, " Personal Development and Education," is a brief and sympathetic review of education in the United States. It could be wished, however, that his treatment of this supremely important subject had been more exhaustive and complete. His references to the elementary education of the country are concerned almost wholly with the public school system. There is mention, indeed, of the parish school system in the United States, but the extreme brevity of the reference to it cannot be reconciled with a broad and adequate survey of the vital forces in our educational life. The parish school system has certainly reached a stage that compels the attention of every serious educator, and calls for the thoughtful consideration of all who would give a really comprehensive view of the present state of education in America. An educational system which cares for more children in the elementary parish schools than the seven million people who constitute the population of Maine, New Hampshire, Vermont, Massachusetts, Rhode Island, Connecticut, Delaware, Montana, Wyoming, New Mexico, Nevada, and the District of Columbia, provide for in the public schools of these States, certainly deserved more than a sentence from one who presumed to interpret the Spirit of America, and who offered a multiplicity of credentials to show his fitness for the task.

Moreover, every student of educational development in America should recognize the deeply significant character and influence of the parish school system, which is as extensive as the country itself and which is keeping pace with every phase of the country's progress. The parish school system is and always has been a conspicuously prominent institution in the United States. It is the emphatic expression by the largest body of Christian people in the United States of a staunch loyalty to the fundamental and immovable principle that religion is an essential part of all true education. It is a protest against the widespread belief that religious teaching is the exclusive function of the home and the Sunday school. The sincerity of the loyalty of Catholics to these principles is demonstrated by the sacrifices which they are making in order to provide a right education for their children. Judged by their unselfish efforts in this respect, they are doing more for popular education than any other body of citizens. The proportions of their gratuitous assistance, often neither recognized nor appreciated, whereby they lessen the burden of taxation in the various communities may be seen by applying the average annual cost ($25) for the education of a child in the public school to the million and a quarter children in the parish schools. In addition to this indirect though actual offering to the treasury of their respective municipalities, Catholics contribute as much to the ·support of the public schools as their non-Catholic fellow-citizens.

Closely associated with this imposing material fact is a significant spiritual truth which has no parallel in the elementary schools of the public school system. There are in the elementary parish schools about 25,000 teachers; men and women who willingly and cheerfully have consecrated their lives to the service of their fellow-man with no thought of earthly reward, with no compensation other than that which provides the bare necessities of life, and with no intention of turning from their chosen calling save as age or infirmity may render them unfit to discharge the duties incumbent on them. These religious teachers offer to the world an object-lesson of simplicity of life and the highest social service. No competent educator can fail to see the difference in efficiency which must result from the efforts of those who dedicate their life to the work of education as compared with that which flows from the labors of those who, in the majority of cases, look upon the teaching profession as a merely transient occupation. With a full knowledge of all that the parish school system implies, Bishop Spalding spoke truly when he said that, in regard to education, " The greatest religious fact in the United States to-day is the Catholic school system, maintained without any aid except from the people who love it."

Doctor Van Dyke, in speaking, at p. 197, of the beginnings of education in the United States, refers to the " Dutch colonists of New Amsterdam who founded the first American public school in 1621 ", and to the " Puritan colonists of Massachusetts Bay who established the Boston Latin School in 1635 and Harvard College in 1636." In assigning 1621 as the date of the founding of the first American public school, our author is guilty of an historical blunder. Until recently the year 1633 was the generally accepted date for the founding of the first school, but a study of all the documentary evidence known to exist points to the conclusion that even this date must be set back four or five years. " In the light of all the present information," concludes an article on the " Date of the First School in New Amsterdam " (*Educational Review,* November, 1909), " we must fix the date for that school at some time after August 4, 1637, and, most probably, at about April 1, 1638." This is also the conclusion now arrived at by Dr. Burns, author of the *Catholic School*

System in the United States. In this connexion it is a matter of pride for Catholics to remember that "the earliest schools within the present limits of the United States were founded by the Franciscans in Florida and New Mexico." As early as the year 1629, nine years before the establishment of the oldest school in the thirteen colonies, "there were many elementary schools for the natives scattered through the pueblos of New Mexico." [1]

Doctor Van Dyke, after giving a summary of the public school attendance, the amount of money expended, the method of taxation by which the money is raised, the number of teachers employed, the average daily expenditure for each child, etc., says: "In addition to this number (16,600,000 pupils in the public schools) there are at least 1,500,000 children in privately endowed and supported schools, secular and religious. The Catholic Church has a system of parochial schools which is said to provide for about a million children" (p. 212). Doctor Van Dyke wisely consulted the Report of the United States Commissioner of Education in order to save himself from generalities in the statistics of the public school system. He should, we think, have taken the same precaution and turned to an authoritative source for the facts concerning the parish school system. There were, in the year 1909, actually enrolled in the parish schools of the United States well-nigh one million and a quarter pupils (1,237,251). The total number of children receiving a Catholic education under Catholic teachers in parish schools and various institutions was almost a million and a half (1,450,448). Between "about a million" and the above figures there is, to say the least, a material difference. In passing it might be noted that the flippant expression "is said" is wholly unworthy of being used in connexion with a system of education which is a concrete embodiment of the educational ideals of the Catholic people of America and which necessarily is and will be a vital factor in the life and development of the Republic.

For the rest, the book is extremely interesting and readable. But it is precisely for this reason and because of its importance that it has seemed well to dwell at some length on the author's serious fault of omission regarding the parish schools.

P. R. McDevitt.

---

[1] Dr. Burns, loc. cit., p. 39.

ETHIOA SOOIALIS. Auctore Dre. Josepho Kachnik. Olmucii, sumptibus R. Promberger; St. Louis, Mo.: B. Herder. 1909. Pp. 287.

HISTORIA PHILOSOPHIAE. Eodem auctore, et eodem bibliopola. Pp. 132.

One takes easily to the former of these two books. With its bright red and gold bands it quite binds you to itself; and as you open it out the great big letters smile at you from the clean pages. You are not used to such greetings from books of its class. Then, too, its name, its title, sounds alluring apart from its vowels, for sociology is in the air. Its offsprings are filling libraries and its legends make up books and magazines and countless catalogues that hypnotize the book-buyer. What you like also about the volume before you is that it is just the third part of Ethics, for you know the other two parts long ago; know them from your catechisms, you think, and your school-books. They give you the familiar principles, the roots of Ethics; this gives you the fruits; those you esteem: these you like. Moreover, the book comes to you from Moravia, a land of which your memories are few and dim, though they cling to your reading of the good king St. Wencislaus whose martyred remains rest in the old cathedral of the ancient Moravian town of Olmütz; where, too, is the venerable university, in the theological faculty in which the " praelectiones academicae " embodied in the book at hand were recently delivered. And so you read this new sociology. New as a book, and a work at least. But it is not sociology, of course, as you find it in Comte or Spencer, or Small and Vincent, or the others. These are historical and descriptive; psychological, likewise, in scope and method. Of such we have none as yet in Latin. What is before you is social philosophy, the philosophy of society—general, domestic, and civil. In so far the book is like almost any other scholastic treatment of social ethics, no more no less. What it has specially its own is that it deals mostly with the ethics of economics —with labor and wages largely, with Socialism also and property-right, and most largely with economic individualism—liberalism, as the author calls it—in its influence on agricultural, industrial, trades, and laboring conditions. These are all obviously important subjects, intensely alive in the popular consciousness. They all converge upon " the social question ", so that the book might be called a treatise on this problem—the righting, the equilibration, of economic opportunities. And since there are two extreme methods of solving the problem—the Socialistic and the individualistic, the " liberalistic ", the most of the discussion is devoted to these two erroneous solutions. The author's own solution, which, of course, follows the Catholic method of meeting the social iniquity, the existing unjust inequality, flows naturally from the rejection of the opposing extremes. On all the foregoing subjects the author writes learnedly and argues solidly and clearly. He has utilized much of the best European literature pertinent thereto and presents his matter first in its historic aspects, and then under its philosophical principles and in its practical bearings. The work is not beyond the average intelligent student, but the more one knows the more one will get from it.

The *Historia Philosophiae* by the same author is a brief outline of the history of philosophical speculation—ancient, medieval, and modern. One cannot, of course, expect much detail within the limits of so small a volume. There is barely enough for a text upon which a professor can enlarge, or which a student fairly familiar with the subject can utilize in review or for general orientation. For such purposes the book deserves commendation.

PSYCHOLOGY OF POLITICS AND HISTORY.   By the Rev. J. A. Dewe, M. A., Professor of History at the University of Ottawa. New York, London: Longmans, Green & Co. 1910. Pp. 269.

An interesting and an instructive book might be written on the philosophy of philosophy ; on the fundamental causes that have determined philosophical ideas and systems, and the growth and shaping of that unique world-philosophy which has found its home in Catholicism. Confining the suggestion to the latter subject, what a fertile field stretches out before one as one reflects on the development of that part of the philosophical organism which has to do with the science of knowledge as such. Almost a distinct organ it is in the body, evolved by conflict with alien and hostile types of thought. So, too, with scholastic psychology. Quite within our own day we have seen the abstract metaphysical truths on the soul and its faculties growing and shaping into a full concrete structure of tangible flesh and blood. Witness this in Father Maher's Stonyhurst *Psychology*. What, however, we have been looking forward to is a similar development of Social Ethics. The philosophical framework of this part of our system is, of course, firm and well knit. What it needs is more tissue roundness, more *embonpoint*. Would it were fatter ! We have no work in English that does for Catholic sociology what the work just mentioned has done for psychology— no work therefore that can be recommended as a guide to youth who are lead by choice or profession into the jungles of recent sociological literature outside the Church. In the meantime while we are awaiting for some such book to make its appearance let us welcome Father Dewe's *Psychology of Politics and History* as a very worthy herald or indeed in a large measure substitute.

As the title suggests, the book embodies the results of an effort to discover and formulate the psychological laws upon which the movements of nations toward perfection or decay depend. That there are such laws must be *a priori* certain, since they are at work in the individual members whereof nations are composed. The demonstration, verification, and concrete execution, however, of those laws are to be found in the history of nations, and it is from this source that Father Dewe draws inductively. The nation being the *homo major*, the laws that govern the *homo minor*, the individual, he shows by the light of history to be the grounds and norms of the progress and regress of collective peoples. Having pointed out the distinction between the substantial and the accidental in the life of a nation, he indicates the law of connexion between the psychological conditions and the aims of a nation. He distinguishes the social from the extra-social factors in national existence and shows how they are complementary to one another. The intellectual influence of statesmen and prominent thinkers on the popular mind, the true stimuli of national progress, the influence of the classic pagan religion on the State, the influence of Christianity on the State, the effects of international intercourse on individual national life—under these headings he has gathered a large amount of interesting facts—theory all illustrated by copious historical allusions. In a previous work he had shown to what extent the economic interpretation of history is justified. In the present volume he demonstrates much more thoroughly, convincingly, and interestingly that there are many more causes—efficient and final—at work in the moulding and guiding of national life than there are economical forces—causes intellectual, spiritual, religious. The present work therefore more than its predecessor furnishes the refutation of that materialistic theory which reduces all historical movements to economic agencies, which sees in human history only variations of the dominating ubiquitous struggle for food, clothes, shelter, and pleasure —the concrete struggle to solve " the stomach question ". Here and there a critic might find some slight inaccuracies of statement and the harmony-loving ear would be pleased with less alliteration in the diction. But these are *naevae*. On the whole the work deserves high praise; it supplies a need and it does it well. It is a book which the general reader as well as the student, and most of all the leader of men, will profit by.

MAN MIRRORING HIS MAKER.* The Priest of God's Church. Edited
from an unpublished MS. by F. O. P. London: Art & Book Co.
1908. Pp. 208.

The author of these reflections on the vocation, mission, and life
of the priest weaves together a series of meditations on the prerogatives of the sacerdotal state, in the fervid style of appeal common to the Latin ascetic writers. The topics—The Church Student,
the Public Life (of the Priest), the Mass, Calvary Priests, the
Blessed Sacrament, the Beloved Disciple, Renunciation, the Way
of the Cross, Perfection, Making Saints—are evidently the themes
originally of addresses conceived in the affective spirit of the fer-
verino made to missionary priests in community. One dislikes to
criticize a book which contains so much that is edifying and inspir-
iting, and which is evidently published with a high purpose of enriching the supply of spiritual reading for the clergy; yet we fear
that the volume will disappoint most readers of English, on account
of its style of appeal, since it is far removed from the sober habit of
reasoning and the simple statement of great truths and facts which
constitute in themselves the motive for priestly action.

It would be an error nevertheless to assume that the writer did not
have the practical side of the pastoral life in mind. He speaks of
the necessity of providing for the spiritual needs of society, of the
religious communities in the parish, of social gatherings, confraternities, guilds, etc.; but these topics are introduced in a more or less
spasmodic way, amidst ejaculations and prayers which evince the
strong feelings and desires of the speaker on the subject of pastoral
perfection; and amidst these sentiments the reader or the writer loses
sight of the chief theme indicated by the title of the chapter. If a
sense of reverence for the original form of these reflections inspired
the translator to give us a literal translation, he has done so, we fear,
at the expense of utility. The copy we have received is very badly
printed, from overtaxed linotype machines, and this too must detract from the appreciation of the volume, despite the beautiful
thoughts which it contains, and the elevated purpose which it serves.

CLERICUS DEVOTUS. Orationes, Meditationes, et Lectiones Sacrae, ad
usum Sacerdotum ac Clericorum. Accedit extractum ex Rituali
Romano. Cum approbatione Rev. Archiep. Friburgens. Friburgi
Brisg., sumptibus B. Herder: St. Louis, Mo. Pp. 488 and 15.

A convenient pocket prayerbook for ecclesiastics is a needed publication. *Clericus Devotus* fulfills all reasonable requirements of

parations and thanksgivings before and after Mass, morning and evening prayers, devotions suitable for visiting the Blessed Sacrament, the Office of the Sacred Heart, and Office of the Immaculate Conception; prayers before and after study, confession, etc. In addition to the various devotions practised by priests, we have meditations, some forty in number, arranged in brief points, which will be an aid not only to personal reflection, but to instruction for others. There are also, for the convenience of missionary priests, extracts from the Ritual giving the rites for Baptism, Communion, Extreme Unction, Funerals, and a number of ordinary benedictions. An appendix contains the exhortation of Pius X to the Clergy, and some prayers in English for the visitation of the sick. The little volume is neatly printed, and forms an excellent adjunct to the Breviary.

THE MYSTERY OF NAPLES. By the Rev. Edward P. Graham. Illustrated. St. Louis: B. Herder; London and Edinburgh: Sands & Co. 1909. Pp. 349.

Probably never before in all the Christian ages have the glimpses of the supernatural been so indifferently sought after, yet so universally discussed and so scientifically examined. Through all antiquity the interference of the unseen powers with the course of nature was accepted without difficulty by pagans and Christians alike. In modern times it is just the opposite. The common disposition is to assign natural causes for all that happens, and deny what cannot be accounted for; or, as the latter-day sceptic puts it, "Whatever happens is always natural, and what is not natural never happens."

In this connexion, the standing miracle, as it is called by Baronius, of the liquefaction of the Blood of St. Januarius has fascinated the interest of learned and holy men for five centuries and keenly attracted the scientific examination of ultra-critics for the past thirty years. A treatise on this miracle, *The Mystery of Naples,* by Father Graham, lies before me. A volume of 350 pages, which the author modestly calls a compilation, but which the reader will find to be a well-reasoned book that discusses the subject in a judicious and scholarly way. The "compilation" is so arranged that it is filled with arguments that evince painstaking research. He goes into the legends of the life, death, and translation of the Saint in a manner shrinking from no scientific aspect of the phenomena. Sound in historical research, yet not confusing, he shows the inadequacy of natural explanations, and from the cogency of his evidence he makes us believe in the genuineness of the miracle. Whilst it is true that legends may circle around the martyrdom of the Saint, the phenomenon of the liquefaction remains, and when ancient Parthenope became Christian Naples she chose for her patron and protector, the martyred Bishop of Benevento.

Born of noble parents, St. Januarius (St. Gennaro) became a Christian in early years and was made first Bishop of Benevento, A. D. 304. Under the reign of Galerius, while Aulus Timotheus was governor of Campania, Januarius and his companions, after many sufferings, were beheaded in the plain of Solfatara, 19 September, 305. The head and body of Januarius were buried in Marcion's farm between Puzzoli and the sea, and were afterwards transferred to Naples. From Naples the body was taken to Benevento in 817, but in January of 1497 it was brought back and deposited under the high altar of the Cathedral, and immediately the people experienced the protection of their Saint, for a plague that was then raging ceased forthwith. The date at which the head began to be preserved apart from the body is not known, but it is certain that it remained at Naples when the body was taken to Benevento. In 1305 Charles II of Anjou " caused a life-sized bust of silver covered with gold to be made, to contain with more respect and reverence the precious relic of the skull and in this it has ever since reposed." The pious custom of the Christians in the early ages of the Church was to preserve some of the blood of the martyrs in phials. Whether the blood of St. Januarius was buried with the body or not, we do not know; Father Graham tells us that " the question cannot be answered definitely ". He is of opinion that the blood was not with the head or body for six or seven centuries, because no trace of liquefaction has been recorded during that period. He places the time of the first liquefaction about 920. St. Peregrinus, during his visit about the beginning of the twelfth century, says it was then " a celebrated miracle ". Father Raphael Pica, who wrote a pamphlet on the miracle in January, 1909, published at Naples, gives an account of the first liquefaction in the first half of the fourth century, showing the spot where it occurred and the names of the prelates present. While this is possible, the account is thrown out of court by impartial critics for want of historical evidence. Professor Leon Cavène, a French Catholic layman, issued his *Le Célèbre Miracle de S. Janvier* in the beginning of 1909. It was enthusiastically received by dignitaries of the Church, and brought forth two articles from the able pen of Fr. Thurston, in the London

Tablet of May, 1909. Leon Cavène dates the first miracle of the liquefaction from the close of the fourteenth century. But this uncertainty of the first observation of the liquefaction need not specially trouble us; it is there, and how account for it? Since the year 1659 an exact record is kept of the circumstances under which each liquefaction took place, making a total of more than 5000 since the record began to be kept.

In the Office of St. Januarius (19 September) the liquefaction is described: " His blood is preserved in a vessel of glass in a concrete state, but when it is placed before the head of the same martyr it liquefies and boils in a wonderful manner, as if it were just recently shed; and this may be seen at the present day." The question is, how does it happen? How is the change from solid to liquid effected? Our author conclusively reasons that it is a miracle and cannot be accounted for in any other way. The weight of opinion is on his side, and two practical letters written for the London *Tablet* of last June by Fr. Graham, of Motherwell, Scotland, adds to the cumulative evidence collected by his namesake, our author.

It was my privilege in September of 1898 to be present in the Cathedral at Naples and witness this phenomenon at a special advantage. Glistening on the altar was the silver bust of St. Januarius containing the head. The glass cruet, half filled with congealed blood enclosed within the ostensory, beside which was a smaller cruet with a few traces of blood, was placed about five feet from the bust. The presiding official took the ostensory into his hands and recited certain prayers accompanied by the congregation. The prayers of the so-called " aunts of St. Januarius " in the forefront of the crowd could be heard above the voices of all, clamorously calling upon their patron. Within half an hour the hardened mass of blood diffused itself with a swift movement. A murmur spread through the crowd, " Il miraculo è fatto !" Then the relic was presented for the veneration of the worshipers who in turn came to the altar to kiss it. There is no concealing the miracle. Opportunity is given to all to view it plainly. On the second night of the octave as we went to the Cathedral to see it once more, the Archbishop was presenting the relic to the public to be kissed. One of the chaplains kindly invited the reviewer within the sanctuary where the Archbishop gave him ample opportunity to examine the liquefied blood. I cannot conceive how any individual who witnesses and examines the phenomenon can reject it without a secret skepticism in all miraculous intervention.

Eighteen times each year the blood is exposed. (1) On the eve of the first Sunday in May and on each of the eight days following, which our author says " may be in remembrance of the first removal of the martyr's body to the church without the walls." (2) On 19 September, the Saint's feast day, and on each day of the Octave. (3) On 16 December, as the festival of the Patronage of St. Januarius, a feast observed with great solemnity since the terrible eruption of 1631. While the blood rarely fails to liquefy in May and September, strange to say it repeatedly fails upon the December feast. During the nineteenth century, on the December feast, it failed to occur over sixty times out of one hundred. " On 6 May, 1527, the blood was found hard and it remained hard all during 1527 and 1528 and up to Saturday, 1 May, 1529: so for two years it did not liquefy. In 1628 two days passed before it occurred, and in May, 1835, there was no liquefaction at all. Likewise it had remained solid in 1551, 1558, and in 1569; whereas in 1556, 1557, 1560, 1599, and 1631, it was always found liquid."

The greatest scientists have failed to give any cause for these occurrences. It is not regulated by any definite or uniform laws, nor does it follow the sequence of cause and effect of physical rules. Sometimes it liquefies after a minute, sometimes after hours of prayer. The blood may remain liquefied for hours or it may solidify in a much briefer space. While the ampulla is half filled with blood when in solid form, the volume may increase to fill it, and when it solidifies again it by no means always returns to its former dimensions. Still more extraordinary, it increases in weight to the amount on one occasion of 27 grammes, as was proved when weighed by Abbé Sperindeo in September, 1902. Sometimes the liquefaction is partial, sometimes total. When solid it is the color of burnt coffee; when liquefied, of clear arterial blood. The color even changes from a blood red to a bluish, a black, or an ashy. Sometimes when brought near the head, the blood boils, bubbles, and froths (as Baronius says) " to seek to reanimate, as it were, before its time, the head from which it came and to which it shall one day be restored." In the diary kept in the " Treasure Chapel " of the Cathedral it is recorded that, on one occasion, the relic had perfectly liquefied and then suddenly hardened in the hands of a certain prince; while, no less strange, on another occasion it remained perfectly hard until certain persons were removed from the Church; then it suddenly liquefied.

That it is pure human blood cannot be doubted. On 26 September, 1902, two eminent Neapolitan professors of physics—Januario of the University and Sperindeo, with several other professors as witnesses, examined it by the aid of a spectroscope, with the following results: " There was seen to appear immediately the spectrum peculiar to human blood, a dark band after the line D, followed

by the other in the green region and a bright band between them. '
The examination proclaimed the contents of the phial to be human
blood.

At present and for some centuries the phials containing the blood
are hermetically sealed, but we know that at the end of the fifteenth
century, the phial containing the blood was open, for Charles VIII
when he visited Naples in 1495, before the miracle took place, was
given a silver rod with which to tap the surface of the dark solid
mass, and when it liquefied he could dip the same rod into the fluid
and lift it out dripping.

That a similar phenomenon of liquefaction is said to be observed
in a number of other relics such as St. Clare's, St. Stephen's, St.
John the Baptist's, St. Pantaleone's, St. Andrew Avellino's, St. Aloysius's, and St. Alphonsus Ligouri's, is no reason for discrediting that
of St. Januarius, but rather tells in favor of it, for if that of St.
Januarius stood alone in the world it would tend to excite our suspicion.

The chapter entitled " Januarius and the Flaming Mount " gives
an interesting account of the supposed relation between the Liquefaction and Vesuvius; while the chapter on " Explanations and Solutions " iconoclastically shatters the so-called solutions of those who
trust more to their own power of divination than to historic or scientific testimony.

Utter failure attended the attempt of Professor Albini of the
University of Naples to explain away the miraculous event, and
failure more disastrous and shameful befell Giaccio, Professor of
Chemistry, Podrecca of the infamous *Asino,* and Romualdi of the
discredited *Avanti,* when in 1907 before an anti-clerical audience in
Rome they produced a blasphemous parody on the miraculous blood.

Taking the mysterious relic as a whole, we are confronted with a
mass of evidence pointing unmistakably to supernatural intervention,
and since science can give no explanation of the liquefaction, we
must believe it to be miraculous. While the only miracles we are
bound to believe are the Bible ones, there are miracles outside the
Bible which are facts, and facts in general recommend themselves in
proportion to the amount and value of evidence in their favor. In
the case of the blood of St. Januarius no other solution up to the
present, save the intervention of Almighty God glorifying his martyred Saint, can satisfy our intellectual questionings.

The author is to be congratulated on his scholarly work, which
is here recommended to all who wish to be informed more deeply on
this supernatural relic. The author is sincere and earnest in his
statement of facts, and a perusal of the volume will help to keep
alive that sense of mystery and overruling power which is of the
very essence of the religious spirit.

W. LEEN.

Literary Chat.

Some time ago the want, in the English language, of a Life of St. Clare was discussed in these pages. We knew at the time that Father Paschal Robinson, O. F. M., had in his possession the MS. of such a Life, translated from the earliest authentic original ascribed to Fr. Thomas of Celano, of the Order of Friars Minor (A. D. 1255-1261), and that, if the erudite interpreter of St. Francis could but be prevailed upon to publish the same with such notes as his familiarity with the Seraphic group of Saints would enable him above all other Franciscan writers to add to the text, we should have a biography at once edifying and trustworthy. Now the Dolphin Press has succeeded in prevailing upon Fr. Robinson to publish this treasure, which comes to us in a handsome edition of the Life of "the little flower of St. Francis", decked in the sombre and chaste vesture of the Saint and "redolent with the fragrance of springtide", as St. Bonaventure has described her. It is charming reading, and whatever St. Clare's future biographers may attempt by way of illustrating the beautiful story of this virgin sister of St. Francis of Assisi in classical English, none can improve on the fascinating simplicity of the story as told by the Friar of Celano. We shall have more to say of this volume anon.

Franciscan literature grows apace, testifying to the universal interest in the Saint of Assisi and in everybody and everything associated with the great Umbrian reformer. We have already spoken of Father Paschal Robinson's first English rendering of the Life of St. Clare by Father Thomas of Celano. Almost simultaneously with it comes the announcement by the Messrs. R. & T. Washbourne, of London, that they have at press and will shortly issue a new Life of St. Clare. This second biography in English of the most zealous co-operator and imitator of the Seraphic Father, who trod closest in his footprints, and who was in her time the living embodiment of his Rule and its spirit, will be a translation, with additions, of the French Life by the Rev. Léopold de Chérancé, of Angers, already well and favorably known to the readers of English through his lives of St. Francis and St. Margaret of Cortona. The authorized translation is by Mr. R. F. O'Connor, from whose pen appears the first part of the history of a great Capuchin of our day, in the present issue of the REVIEW. Mr. O'Connor is favorably known as the English editor of the two biographies above mentioned. These have been highly praised by the reviewers. Father Léopold's " St. Francis of Assisi ", pronounced by the late Cardinal Vaughan to be " one of the most popular biographies of the Saint—graphic, attractive, tinged with spiritual ardor, and a most striking portrait of the man and of the day in which his life was set," was presented by Cardinal Logue to Pope Leo XIII, who commissioned the Irish Primate to send the translator his Holiness's special blessing. The book has run through seven editions in French and three editions in English, the third edition of the translation being made still more attractive by twelve half-tone plates.

This life of St. Clare is intended as the completion of a trilogy illustrative of three aspects of love, the law of life, pre-eminently of the higher life; St. Francis typifying seraphic love; St. Clare, virginal love; and St. Margaret of Cortona, "the Magdalen of the Franciscan Order", penitent love. Next to St. Francis, St. Clare was the most interesting and prominent personality in the great religious revival of the thirteenth century which, beginning at Assisi, spread all over Europe. The story of her life is interwoven with that of the Patriarch of the Friars Minor: the names of the son of Pietro Bernardone and the daughter of Favorina Scefi are forever inseparable.

The question of proselytism in Rome is one that has had its acute stages of late, and is sure to come up again and again in the course of time. In this connexion we want to keep before our readers an excellent plea recently made by a New York journalist who is not a Catholic, but who puts the argument for us in a nutshell in interpreting Mr. Fairbanks's failure to see the Pope. The article states that the Pope did not refuse to see our former Vice-President, who was in Rome as a private visitor, although he might well have done so. The Pope simply did not *invite* Mr. Fairbanks to a special audience. The editorial goes on to say:

"Mr. Fairbanks in Rome attended and addressed a religious Methodist organization, and he was present in Rome, to some extent, as a semi-official spokesman of this Methodist organization.

"This organization, acting doubtless within its legal rights, has made itself extremely offensive to the Vatican and to the Pope.

"It has gone to Rome to proselytize in a vigorous, aggressive and rather impolite fashion.

"Needless to say, it hasn't manufactured any genuine Italian Methodists, but it has succeeded, according to the statements of Archbishop Ireland, in insulting sincere Catholic believers, and deliberately and unnecessarily offending Catholic feeling in Rome.

"The Methodists, as stated, have a legal right to do this. Any man who stays inside the police regulations can do anything he likes in any city.

"But it is quite natural that the head of the Catholic Church should not care to receive with special honor the spokesman of a Methodist organization that is accused of making it a business to belittle the Catholic religion in Rome, and, by inference, to insult the head of the Catholic Church in Rome.

"Bishop William F. McDowell, of the Methodist Church, who supports the Methodists at Rome, says:

"'Our Methodist associations are in Rome for the purpose of doing Protestant work among a Catholic people, and the Catholic Paulist Fathers are doing a Catholic work among a Protestant people here. Charges that the efforts of Methodist missionaries have a "pernicious, proselyting effect" in Rome are no more true than the similar statement concerning the work of the Paulist Fathers in this country.'"

"Bishop McDowell is mistaken.

"America is a sort of 'free for all' religious country.

"It is preposterous to say that Catholics at work in America are at work 'in a Protestant country.' There is no recognized, official religion here. This country is not Protestant, or Catholic, or Mohammedan, or Christian Science, or Buddhist, or Confucian, or atheistic, or agnostic.

"*This is a republic which recognizes officially no religion, which is forbidden by its constitution to recognize officially any religion.* Here all religions and all religious teachers are on an equal footing.

"Catholics at work here are not proselying in a Protestant country. They are looking after their own people, after the millions of Catholics that have come here as Catholics from other countries, and after those that have voluntarily joined their Church.

"In Rome it is not so. Rome, historically, sentimentally, and *actually*, is the seat of the Catholic religion, the home of the Popes for ages.

"It is the Pope's liberality and generosity that keeps open the Vatican and St. Peter's, with their beautiful treasures, to the travelers of the world.

"The Pope is an old man, undergoing voluntary imprisonment because of his faith. The least that any decent foreigner can do in Rome is to respect his feelings, and the religion of which he is the head.

"And if Mr. Fairbanks did not know that, it is a good thing for the Pope to have impressed the fact on him.

"As regards Bishop McDowell's statement that the Methodist missionaries are in Rome to make Methodists of the Italians, we must say most respectfully that to anybody that knows Rome and Italians, that is a very interesting Methodist joke.

"Some Italians want Catholicism and some do not. Some want socialism and have it. Some want agnosticism. Some want no 'ism' at all.

"One thing is quite sure, the Italians do *not* want Methodism. And probably all of the real Italians that could be made real Methodists by a thousand missionaries in a thousand years could travel comfortably in one taxicab.

" The Italians are good-natured and will listen.

" They are also a practical race. They will accept spaghetti, chianti, macaroni, lire, or kind words from a Methodist missionary, or from any other kind of a missionary.

" But, if you take away from an Italian his Catholic religion, you do not make a Methodist of him—you make something quite different.

" In brief, respect for religion and religious teachers is one of the elements of common decency.

" Every man has a right to think what he chooses.

" No man has a right to insult the faith or the religious teacher of a great body of people.

" We believe that Mr. Fairbanks, or any other outsider sharing in demonstrations of disrespect for the Catholic religion or the head of the Catholic Church in Rome, needs to be taught a lesson. And we are glad that a lesson was administered."

Ansgar Albing (Baron de Mathies), the admirable grace of whose addresses was recently pointed out in these pages, has just published (Fr. Pustet & Co.) a charming little volume entitled *Harmonien und Disharmonien,* in which the author traces the varying moods of the soul, irenic and ironic. The aim of the volume is, of course, to spiritualize the tendencies of the will and to warn the young mind against the intoxicating influences of brilliant and passing acquisitions.

The Pustets have just published a new and extensive life of the Austrian reformer and Saint, Clemens Maria Hofbauer. The work is edited by P. Adolf Innerkofler, C.SS.R., and deserves further notice and interpretation in English.

One of the most attractive novels written of late and somewhat out of the common run of Catholic romance is the Marquise de Lanza's *The Dweller on the Borderland.* Its chief excellence lies in its analysis of the psychical elements at work in a rather delicate situation. A gifted young husband with a good-natured but commonplace wife is led to give up his position as a teacher in a country town in search after an ideal literary career in New York. After some disappointments he accepts a position as tutor to a bright boy who is under the guardianship of his aunt, a young widow, highly cultured and devoutly Catholic. A bond of mutual attraction arises between the tutor husband and the widow, and the well-poised manner in which the author brings about a struggle in which all the nobler faculties of mind and heart are called into play against the dangers of elective affinity, as Schiller would have said, constitutes the charm and climax of the story. The novel is, as we said, distinctly superior to the Catholic school novel meant for young girls' libraries, but rather of the order of Mrs. Ward's. John Joseph McVey, Philadelphia, publishes the book.

A new book by Mother Loyola is to be ready in May. The gifted author of numerous volumes for the instruction of children has not been heard of for some years. Her last volume *Home for Good* was published in 1907 by P. J. Kenedy & Sons. The present book, entitled *Heavenward,* and to be issued by the same house, is a treasury of spiritual direction for adult children. It is to have an introduction by Father Thurston, S.J.

The Charity Union (Charitas-verband für d. Kathol. Deutschland, Freiburg Br.) of Germany has just issued its report of the Conferences held in October last year at Erfurt. It deals chiefly with the methods for ameliorating the conditions of foreign emigration. A goodly portion of the *Auswanderer-problem* discusses the provisions made and to be recommended for immigrants to the United States.

Books Received.

THEOLOGICAL AND DEVOTIONAL.

MAN MIRRORING HIS MAKER. The Priest of God's Church. Edited from an unpublished MS. by F. C. P. New York, Cincinnati, Chicago: Benziger Bros.; London: Art & Book Co. 1908. Pp. xiv-208. Price, $0.75 *net*.

THE INWARD GOSPEL. Some Familiar Discourses addressed to Religious who follow the Rules of St. Ignatius. By W. D. Strappini, S.J. London, Burns & Oates; New York, Cincinnati, Chicago: Benziger Bros. 1909. Pp. 121.

LA LITURGIE ET LA VIE CHRÉTIENNE. Par A. Vigourel, du Séminaire Saint-Sulpice. Paris: P. Lethielleux. 1909. Pp. xx-504. Prix, 4 *fr.*

LA PRIÈRE DIVINE: LE "PATER". Par J.-M.-L. Monsabré, O.P. Cinquième édition. Paris: P. Lethielleux. 1909. Pp. 402. Prix, 3 *fr.* 50.

DIE SCHRIFTEN DES HEIL. FRANZISKUS VON ASSISI. Neue deutsche Ubersetzung nebst Einleitung und Anmerkungen. Von P. Maternus Rederstorff, O.F.M., Generallektor der Philosophie, Apost. Pönitenziar an der Lateranbasilika zu Rom. Regensburg, Rom, New York und Cincinnati: Druck und Verlag von Friedrich Pustet. 1910. Pp. 216. Price, $0.35.

DAS HIMMLISCHE VATERHAUS. Unterweisungen über die Freuden des Himmels. Zu Ehren des heiligsten Herzens Jesu, zum Troste und zur Erbauung des christgläubigen Erdenpilgers. Von P. Ludwig Lercher, S.J. Mit oberhirtlicher Druckgenehmigung und Erlaubnis der Ordensobern. (Aszetische Bibliothek—6.) 1910. Regensburg, Rom, New York und Cincinnati: Druck und Verlag von Friedrich Pustet. 1910. Pp. viii-192. Price, $0.70.

QUESTIONS OF THE SACRAMENT OF MATRIMONY. Answered by the Rev. J. M. Phelan of the Diocese of Green Bay. Second Edition. Green Bay, Wis.: F. Kaster Co. 1909. Pp. 64. Price, $0.10.

VERTUS ET DOCTRINE SPIRITUELLE DE SAINT VINCENT DE PAUL. Par Abbé Maynard. Dixième édition. Paris: P. Téqui. 1910. Pp. xiii-432. Prix, 3 *fr.* 50.

LA RÉSURRECTION DE JÉSUS. Suivie de deux Appendices sur la Crucifixion et l'Ascension. Par l'Abbé E. Mangenot, Professeur d'Écriture Sainte á l'Institut Catholique de Paris. Paris: Gabriel Beauchesne & Cie. 1910. Pp. 404. Prix, 3 *fr.* 50.

COMMENTARIUS IN ACTUS APOSTOLORUM. Editio sexta denuo emendata et notabiliter adaucta. Opera A. Camerlynck, Can. Hon. Eccl. Cath. Brug., S. T. Doct. in Univ. Cath. Lovan., et S. Script. Profess. in Semin. Brugensi. (Commentarii Brugenses in S. Scripturam. A. R. Adm. D. J. A. Van Steenkiste primum editi.) Brugis: Sumptibus Car. Beyaert. 1910. Pp. 459. Pret. 5 *fr.*

PHILOSOPHICAL.

GESAMMELTE APOLOGETISCHE VOLKSBIBLIOTHEK. Erster Band. Volksvereins-Verlag Gmb. H. M. Gladbach. 1910. 484 Seiten. Preis gebunden 2.40 M.

AKADEMISCHE VORTRÄGE. Die Exerzitienwahrheiten von Heinrich Bruders S.J., Dr. phil. u. theol., Privatdozent für Dogmengeschichte an der Universität Innsbruck. Innsbruck: Druck und Verlag von Fel. Rauch. 1910. Pp. x-483. Preis, K 3.60.

HISTORICAL.

HISTORY OF THE CATHOLIC CHURCH IN WESTERN CANADA from Lake Superior to the Pacific. By the Rev. A. G. Morice, O.M.I. With Maps and Illustrations. Two Volumes. Toronto: Musson Book Co. 1910. Pp.: Vol. I, xxiv-362; Vol. II, xi-414.

THE STORY OF W. J. E. BENNETT, Founder of S. Barnabas', Pimlico, and Vicar of Froome-Selwood and of his Part in the Oxford Church Movement of the Nineteenth Century. By F. Bennett, M.A., Formerly Rector of Farleigh, Surrey. With Portrait. New York, London: Longmans, Green & Co. 1909. Pp. xvi-304.

A MARRIED PRIEST. By Albert Houtin. Translated from the French by John Richard Slattery. Boston: Sherman, French & Co. 1910. Pp. 100. Price, $0.70 *net.*

BLESSED MARY OF THE ANGELS, Discalced Carmelite (1661-1717). A Biography of the Rev. George O'Neill, S.J., M.A., Fellow of the Royal University of Ireland. New York, Cincinnati, Chicago: Benziger Bros. 1909. Pp. xiv-184.

DOM GUÈRANGER, ABBÉ DE SOLESMES. Par un Moine Bénédictin de la Congrégation de France. Tome deuxième. Avec un portrait en héliogravure. Deuxième édition. Paris: Plon-Nourrit & Cie. et G. Oudin & Cie. 1910. Prix, 8 *fr.*

LOUIS XVI. Étude Historique. Par Marius Sepet. Paris: P. Téqui. 1910. Pp. 494. Prix, 3 *fr.* 50.

MISCELLANEOUS.

CAPTAIN TED. By Mary T. Waggaman. New York, Cincinnati, Chicago: Benziger Bros. 1910. Pp. 199. Price, $0.60.

ALLELUIA. An Easter Booklet. By the Rev. T. J. O'Mahony, D.D., D.C.L., All Hallows' College, Dublin. Second Edition. Dublin: Browne & Nolan. 1910. Pp. viii-47. Price, 6 d.

A RED-HANDED SAINT. By Olive Katharine Parr. London: R. & T. Washbourne; New York, Cincinnati, Chicago: Benziger Bros. 1909. Pp. xiii-306.

DAS KREUZ IN GEFAHR. Deutsches Kulturbild aus dem achten Jahrhundert. Von Conrad von Bolanden. Regensburg, Rom, New York und Cincinnati: Fr. Pustet & Co. Pp. 244. Price, $0.50.

THE CATHOLIC ENCYCLOPEDIA. An International Work of Reference on the Constitution, Doctrine, Discipline, and History of the Catholic Church. Edited by Charles J. Herbermann, Ph.D., LL.D., Edward Pace, Ph.D., D.D., Condé B. Pallen, Ph.D., LL.D., Thomas Shahan, D.D., John J. Wynne, S.J., assisted by numerous Collaborators. In fifteen volumes. Vol. VII: Gregory—Infallibility. Pp. 800.

THE
ECCLESIASTICAL REVIEW

FIFTH SERIES.—VOL. II.—(XLII).—MAY, 1910.—No. 5.

THE GIFT OF TONGUES IN THE EARLY CHURCH.

G LOSSOLALY (γλωσσολαλία) or the gift of tongues is the
most perplexing of the " charismata " or spiritual gifts
which were a prominent feature in the Apostolic Church. The
subject has been much debated by scholars in recent times, and
the present state of the question may be summed up in the statement that there are now two views as to the nature of the gift
—the ancient and the modern. The ancient view regards the
gift of tongues as a supernatural faculty, conferred by the
Holy Ghost, of speaking in foreign languages previously
unknown to the speaker. The modern view, which has been
pretty generally adopted by non-Catholic scholars, maintains
that the " tongues " were not languages, but ecstatic, ejaculatory, and generally incoherent utterances prompted by powerful religious emotion and bearing a close resemblance to, if
they are not altogether identical with, the phenomena which
may be witnessed in our own day in many a Protestant " revival " meeting. This theory is subject to different modifications in the hands of different exponents: some advocates preserve the divine character of the gift by admitting that the
phenomena were ultimately due to the influence of the Holy
Spirit; whilst others reject the notion of a Divine principle
and assign as the cause pure and simple hysteria. In the latter
form the modern theory has been maintained by a recent
writer in an American review,[1] who rises from the study of
modern " revival " movements convinced that the glossolaly

[1] *American Journal of Theology*, April, 1909.

of the early Church was identical in form and origin with the phenomena which he has seen at Protestant meetings in Chicago and elsewhere.

From the theological point of view there would seem to be no reason why the modern theory, in its modified form, should not be admitted by Catholics if there were sufficient evidence in its favor. The student of mystical theology is aware that the psychological and physical abnormalities which accompany such a state as that of ecstacy are not in themselves an infallible index of the nature of the underlying operating principle: they are, considered alone, quite neutral, and other evidences have to be carefully examined before it can be certainly ascertained whether the external phenomena are the effect of a divine or of some other agency. There would seem therefore to be no intrinsic reason why the scenes witnessed at Pentecost and in the churches of St. Paul should not have been similar, so far as external phenomena are concerned, to those that occur in modern Protestant sects, and why we should not employ the latter to assist us in forming a conception of the glossolaly of the Apostolic age. Everything depends upon the evidence—upon whether the data of our historical documents justify us in adopting the modern view.

Our authorities are unfortunately very scanty—a few passages in the Acts of the Apostles and a couple of chapters (13 and 14) in St. Paul's First Epistle to the Corinthians. In the appendix to St. Mark's Gospel (16:17) our Lord promises His disciples that they shall speak in " new tongues " (γλώσσαις καιναῖς); but since the word καιναῖς is of doubtful authenticity, the passage does not afford us any assistance. Nor do we derive any help from the early Fathers. St. Irenæus indeed says that in his own day there were Christians who spoke with " all manner of tongues " (παντοδαπαῖς γλώσσαις),[2] but he tells us nothing as to the nature of the phenomenon. By the time of St. John Chrysostom the gift was defunct in the Church.

Turning to our sole authorities, there is no sufficient reason for supposing with some commentators that the " tongues " of the Acts are in any way inconsistent with those mentioned by St. Paul. Many modern critics, taking their stand upon

I Cor. as being the earlier document, find it difficult, if not impossible, to reconcile St. Luke's account with St. Paul's, because while St. Luke gives us the impression that the tongues were foreign languages, St. Paul's description seems to accord with the view that they were mere ecstatic ejaculations. Consequently, it is said, we have to suppose that St. Luke's account, written later, is either " colored by the thought of the gift of the spirit as bringing a reversal of the curse of Babel ",[3] or that it is hopelessly unhistorical, or that it refers to some different phenomenon from that referred to by St. Paul.

(1.) The first of these hypotheses is utterly gratuitous, since there is not the slightest reason for supposing that St. Luke in writing his account even so much as thought of the confusion of Babel. (2.) With regard to the second suggestion, it is important to remember how marked has been the reversion of critical opinion in recent years to the traditional view of the Lucan authorship of the Acts and to the recognition of their historcial value. Prof. Harnack now supports that position, and no sane criticism on our present day evidence claims to be able to overthrow it. It is difficult to imagine how anyone approaching the question with a mind free from *a priori* assumptions can fail to note the literary qualifications of the author of the Acts and how conspicuous in his work are the diligence and painstaking observation which are necessary to the true historian. (3.) It is quite unjustifiable to assert that St. Luke's gift of tongues differs from that of St. Paul. Luke was a disciple and, for a considerable time, a close companion of the Apostle, and consequently he could hardly be unacquainted with the nature of as prominent a phenomenon as the glossolaly which was current in the Pauline churches. And when we find both writers speaking of a gift of tongues and applying to it the same terminology ($\lambda\alpha\lambda\epsilon\tilde{\iota}\nu$ $\gamma\lambda\acute{\omega}\sigma\sigma\alpha\iota\varsigma$), it seems only reasonable to suppose that they are referring to one and the same thing.

The three opinions to which we have just referred are at any rate valuable in this, that they afford testimony to the strong impression given by the Acts that the gift conferred at Pentecost upon the disciples was a faculty of speaking foreign

---

[3] Soudge, *Comment. on I Cor.* (Westminster Commentaries), p. 134.

languages. This really is the only way in which the account in Acts 2 can be interpreted. When St. Luke describes how people from " every nation under heaven " hear the disciples speak in the tongues in which they were born, it seems absurd to torture the passage into meaning incoherent and senseless ejaculations. And, moreover, we have no reason for doubting that Luke takes the tongues in the same sense in the other passages in which he refers to them (10: 44-46, the case of Cornelius; and 19: 6, the case of the converts at Ephesus); and in fact St. Peter expressly identifies the gift conferred upon Cornelius with that which the Apostles themselves had received at Pentecost (11: 15). Clearly then the gift of tongues in St. Luke's mind meant one thing alone, viz., an infused power of declaring the praises of God in foreign languages.

Here we meet an objection. Though undoubtedly the *prima facie* impression given by the Acts favors the traditional theory of glossolaly, are there not intrinsic evidences that this impression is not correct? St. Luke gives a list of fifteen " nationalities " (2: 9 ff.); but when we examine the catalogue we find that the people whom he enumerates are all Jews of the Dispersion (with the exception apparently of a few proselytes among the " sojourners from Rome "). And we observe that in this list there is no room for a multiplicity of languages, since those spoken by all these " nations " may be reduced to two—Greek and Aramaic. Thus " Parthians and Medes and Elamites and the dwellers in Mesopotamia " represented the Babylonian group of Jews, who used the east Aramaic dialect; the " Judeans " and probably also the " Arabians " would use western Aramaic; and all the others would speak Greek, which was universally understood and spoken in the Græco-Roman world at that time, and was adopted by the Jews of the Dispersion themselves, as is shown by their inscriptions. What then can St. Luke mean?[4]

It does not seem impossible to discern the lines along which an explanation is to be sought. We have seen that, on the most obvious interpretation, St. Luke supposes, whether rightly or wrongly, that his catalogue is representative—at least roughly—of the languages of "every nation under heaven". Now whatever be the source from which he drew the history of the early chapters of the Acts, it is hard to imagine that a writer so careful and so observant as St. Luke, who had had personal and wide acquaintance with the Jews of the Dispersion, should have failed to notice the inconsistency, if such it really be, which recent scholars have discovered in his narrative. Strange as it may sound to some critical ears, it may not be temerarious to suggest that St. Luke knew what he was writing about a great deal better than we, with our scanty information, can ever expect to know. It is indeed true that Greek was the universal language of the Græco-Roman world, and the evidence which we possess seems to show that the dispersed Jews resident in Græco-Roman environments used the same tongue. But does it follow from this that *no other* language than Greek was spoken in the Hellenized world of the Apostolic age? It were surely rash to deny the probability that there may have been multitudes of native languages employed among themselves by the peoples who had succumbed in other respects to the all-prevailing Hellenism. In the case of Asia Minor, which included five of the countries mentioned in St. Luke's catalogue, there were a number of autochthonous tongues which survived among the people, though Latin and Greek became the language of government, of literature, and of polite society. St. Luke himself attests that the Lycaonian language, for example, was actually spoken in Lystra when St. Paul went there on his first missionary journey (Acts 13:11). Sir William M. Ramsay, than whom no living scholar possesses a profounder knowledge of Asia Minor in early Christian times, tells us that Greek was not the popular language of those countries, and that even as late as the third century the mass of the people still used their own native speech, although those who wrote books wrote Greek and those who governed spoke Latin.[5] Prof. C. Holl, of Berlin,[6] has shown that such languages as Isaurian, Cappadocian, Phrygian, Lycian, etc, were spoken for centuries after Christ. If then St. Luke is correct

legitimately presume that he is 'correct also in regard to the other nations that he enumerates? [7]   There is no need to suppose that the Jews themselves adopted the autochthonous languages: their inscriptions would seem to show that they did not.   But St. Luke's obvious meaning is that the " devout Jews " present at Pentecost regarded the speech of their habitual neighbors as the " language in which they were born ", and it would be hypercritical indeed to assert that the phrase is anything but reasonable and natural.

From this it follows that it is unnecessary to have recourse to the somewhat lame expedient, often suggested, of supposing the varieties of language at Pentecost to have been mere differences of dialect.   The word διάλεκτος in itself may have either meaning, but " language " is clearly the only signification that is admissible in the present case.

We conclude then from examination of St. Luke that the modern theory of glossolaly is thus far untenable.   We now turn to St. Paul, and ask whether—as is often asserted—there is anything in his account that is at all inconsistent with what is told us by St. Luke.   In view of what has been already said concerning the connexion between the two writers, I venture to think that the particulars given by St. Paul which are not found in St. Luke are not of the nature of inconsistencies, but rather additional details which enable us to complete the conception formed from a perusal of the Acts.   The circumstances at Corinth which led St. Paul to treat of the question of glossolaly are too familiar to need recapitulation here.   We must observe, however, that since the Apostle is seeking to wean his correspondents from an inordinate esteem of the gift of tongues based upon its ostentatious character, it is natural that he should emphasize those aspects of the gift which betray its inferiority to the other charismata; and consequently there is no call for surprise if the picture which he draws seems at times to indicate a low form of religious excitement not unlike certain modern phenomena.   Glossolaly, as he describes it, is clearly a kind of ecstacy, in which the subject behaves in a very abnormal manner.   The exercise of the gift is accom-

[7] The objection, however, which we have just answered seems to die hard. It is found in quite recent commentaries (e. g. Rackham on Acts), and it still stares us in the face from the pages of Hastings' new (one volume) *Bible Dict.*

panied by a grave danger to order and decorum, so that if an
unbeliever or an ἰδιώτης, or person who is unaccustomed to such
strange manifestations, happens to stray into a church where
everybody is simultaneously ventilating his own particular
tongue, he is amazed at the unruly babel and not unnaturally
concludes that the whole assembly is mad (I Cor. 14: 23). It
is to check such disorders that St. Paul lays down stringent
rules for the regulation of glossolaly (vv. 26-33). Moreover,
the Apostle compares the utterances spoken in a "tongue"
to a "pipe or harp that give not a distinction of sounds" (v.
7), or to a trumpet that gives an "uncertain note" (v. 8).
The speaker addresses himself not to men but to God (v. 2),
and does not seem himself to understand what he is saying (v.
14),[8] unless indeed—as sometimes happened—he possessed
also the complementary gift of "interpretation" (v. 13). To
the general audience the tongue was unintelligible, and therefore St. Paul rejoins that it is not to be spoken unless there be
present some person who is competent to "interpret" (v. 28).
For these reasons the gift of tongues in comparison with other
charismata is of inferior value, since it does not benefit the
congregation at large or tend unto their "edification".

It must be admitted that this sketch of the Corinthian
tongue-speaking does not seem to exhibit parallels to the
modern phenomena. In many "revival" meetings the congregation, under the influence (as they imagine) of the Spirit,
are frequently seized with an extraordinary frenzy; arms
move frantically, heads jerk violently, and "speaking in
tongues" is heard, varying from a mere rapid repetition of
a few syllables to a complex combination of euphonious sounds,
to which some sort of spiritual meaning is given by someone
who possesses the gift of "interpretation".[9]

But St. Paul says other things than those we have just cited
—things which seem to connect his glossolaly with that of the
Acts. In his great hymn to Charity (13), he tells his correspondents that without virtue "all the tongues of men and of
angels" are of no more value than "sounding brass or a

clanging cymbal ". Here he is obviously speaking καθ' ὑπερβολήν, and the very purpose of his sentence requires that the tongues should not be only of the greatest possible variety but also of the *highest possible order*—a condition which is scarcely satisfied by the senseless and incoherent sounds cited by the American writer whose view we are criticizing. He can therefore be using "tongue" only of rational speech, and the presumption is that he intends the same meaning of the word throughout. Again, when the Apostle wants to show that the gift of tongues is given as a sign " not to them that believe but to the unbelieving " (14: 21, 22), he quotes Is. 28: 11 ff.: " By men of strange tongues and by the lips of strangers will I speak unto this people ". Here there is no point in the quotation unless St. Paul intends to place the charismatic tongues in the same category as the foreign language of the Assyrian whose invasion of Ephraim Isaiah was foretelling. And lastly, when he asks how a stranger who hears a blessing being given in a tongue can be expected to answer Amen to the blessing, surely this implies that the blessing must have been something which the listener would have understood if it were only uttered in a language with which he was familiar.

These data, taken in conjunction with St. Luke's (which we have seen cannot reasonably be divorced from St. Paul's), seem to furnish the key to the somewhat ambiguous passages (I Cor. 14: 7 ff.) which are claimed in favor of the modern theory. Just (says St. Paul) as the notes of pipe or harp cannot be understood as music " when time is broke and no proportion kept ",[10] so speech which is not clear for him to comprehend will seem to the listener no better than a jangle of inharmonious sounds. The sounds of the human voice are of many kinds, differing in various parts of the world; but unless I employ the kind with which my listener is familiar, I shall seem to him to be an empty babbler.

We may claim then that, in spite of certain ambiguities, St. Paul's account seems to support the traditional rather than the modern view of glossolaly. This applies of course to the essential character of the gift—the faculty of speaking in foreign tongues. We may readily admit that in accidental fea-

---

[10] διαστολή, pause or interval in music.

tures there may have been a strong resemblance to the phenomena of the Protestant sects, for ecstatic states have much in common with various religions all the world over, and hence, to a great extent, probably have their root in other than supernatural causes. St. Paul recognizes this when he enjoins due care in the " discernment " of the gifts (14: 29), and in fact the " discerning of spirits " was one of the charismata given to the early Church by the Holy Spirit (12: 10). Its use would be especially necessary at a place like Corinth, where the gifts which (like glossolaly) were more ostentatious than the rest, were often sought from vain and unworthy motives.

Many further questions arise at this point. Some writers have pointed to a class of phenomena which have occurred at various times—notably among the Protestants of the Cevennes at the end of the seventeenth and beginning of the eighteenth century—where adult persons and even little children normally scarce able to talk have delivered long and fluent discourses in languages which under ordinary circumstances they were quite unable to speak. Psychical research, I believe, has brought similar cases to light in our own day. The usual explanation seems to be that such phenomena are due to a freak of memory which recalls what has once fallen uncomprehended upon the ear and then lain dormant until it has been excited and called forth in moments of strong emotion. Whether this explanation can be legitimately applied—as it is applied by some critics [11]—to the tongues of the New Testament is a question which would require more space than can be afforded here.

Whichever theory of glossolaly we adopt it cannot be denied that difficulties remain. The modern view, both in its rationalistic and its modified form, conflicts with the data of the New Testament; the traditional view does not seem to supply an adequate *raison d'être* of the miracle. It requires little effort to realize the utility of gifts like prophesy, " healings ", " helps ", " governments ", and the rest. Glossolaly no doubt, as St. Paul shows, was a gift which might stimulate

vine Love and drawing him into closer union with God; but why the gift should take the particular form of speaking in a strange language which under normal circumstances scarce anyone present would understand, must remain for us an insoluble enigma. Most of the Fathers (e. g. Origen, St. John Chrysostom, St. Gregory Nazianzen, St. Gregory of Nyssa) seem to regard the gift as conferred for evangelistic purposes. We cannot however maintain this view, because (1) there is not the slightest indication that the gift was ever used for purposes of preaching;[12] (2) this use would in most cases be rendered unnecessary, at any rate in the Græco-Roman world, by the fact that, owing to the providential disposition of things, Greek was practically universally understood, whilst among the Jews Aramaic would generally suffice; and (3) St. Paul expressly tells us that the " tongues " were addressed not to men but to God.[13] Some commentators have thought that the miracle of Pentecost consisted in a power given to hearers of various nationalities enabling them to understand what was spoken by the speakers in their (the speakers') own tongue, as happened in the well-known case of St. Vincent Ferrer. But the evidence makes it perfectly clear that the miracle was one not of *hearing* but of *speaking*. If we must inquire why the Holy Spirit chose to manifest His operations in the extraordinary manner described in the New Testament, we can only suggest that the gift, apart from its profit to the possessor, had a symbolic significance, typifying the universality of the Church of Christ, which was destined to spread over all the world and to draw to its embrace men and women of every tongue and nation under heaven.

W. T. CELESTINE SHEPPARD, O.S.B.

Oxford, England.

---

[12] Note that at Pentecost the disciples were not preaching, but simply proclaiming the " magnalia Dei ". It was only by accident that a crowd of foreigners happened to hear and understand them.

[13] I Cor. 14:2; cf. Acts 2:11.

CONDITION OF THE EASTERN ORTHODOX CHURCH IN AMERICA.

IN the two former articles [1] on the Eastern Orthodox Chur we saw that the majority of its members are under jurisdiction of the Czar of Russia, while the greater part the minority is to be found in the Ottoman Empire, Kingdom of Greece and the Balkan States. These tions constituted that ancient Greek empire which once tained perfection in every form of civilization and held leading place in European history. This was centuries ago when, as St. Gregory Nazianzen says, " her cities are full mechanics and slaves, who are all of them profound th logians and preach in the shops and in the streets." This tellectual and moral progress was stifled by political and sp itual despotism when the seat of empire was established Constantinople and the Church came under the immedi protection of the State. Delight in discussion and dialec controversy, which was the glory of the Greek mind, led the development of those inherent weaknesses of Greek ch acter—insincerity, fickleness, and disregard of truth. In ke but unscrupulous emulation, sophistry became a justifia weapon when reason failed; falsehood and deception w practised without hesitation to compass success, and amid general degradation manly virtues disappeared from amc the people. The Church in common with the community s fered from those debasing influences and sank into spirit apathy; religion stiffened into formalism; external holiness placed sincere and heartfelt devotion, until the ignora blindly following their teachers, plunged into the grossest a most superstitious practises, for there seems to be scarc any limit to the folly or foulness of the superstitions to wh men become victims when they mistake the compass of ti religion directed by an infallible guide.

Those religious peculiarities that designate the Greek ch acter at the present day are equally applicable to the Slavo nations. While aptitude for organization and religious dev

planation of their religious beliefs; even those who have come to this country, with Oriental dislike of strangers, evade every attempt at inquiry.

Although the inhabitants of those countries were never prone to Western emigration, the last twenty years have witnessed a great exodus, and westward the trend of emigration takes its way. It is from Italy, Greece, Hungary, and Slavonic Europe that the tide now flows in abundance. As I write, the Hamburg American liner " President Grant " is landing 3,000 steerage passengers on our shores, principally Hungarians, Greeks, Poles, and Russians. Driven by militarism, with its demands upon the best years of a man's life, and by the strain of taxation, they seek a home where they find life worth living and where every man can worship God according to the dictates of his own conscience. It is this freedom of worship that has made the United States the lodestone for many an exile and has welded its heterogeneous members into one homogeneous whole. They come to this country with their religion, their prejudices, and their preferences; and many with a superstitious tenacity cling to them, whilst others known as radicals deem them obstacles in their path of progress. Permeated with the spirit of mammon, and mistaking liberty for license, the watchword of these latter is " no serf, no priest, no master." They despise religion and authority and drift into socialism and anarchy.

Eastern Orthodox churches have practically come into existence in the United States since 1890; before then they were not reckoned in the religious statistics of our nation. The year 1894 showed an estimate in America and Canada of 35,000 Orthodox Christians, with 58 churches and 60 clergymen. The United States religious census for 1906 gave the number as 129,606 communicants, having 80 churches and 108 clergymen. The number at the present moment (1910) can be reckoned in round numbers as 350,000 members, with 120 churches and 160 clergymen. Nearly every city of considerable size from the Atlantic to the Pacific has one or more churches of the various nationalities belonging to the Orthodox communion. There is very little unity amongst them and they generally look to the Synods of their home countries for advice and direction.

While they preserve the language and discipline of the Byzantine rite they lack exterior bonds and concentration of action. As a consequence they are in a continual storm of various unpropitious, religious, and even political currents. The majority of them are uninformed and follow the politics of their native land as keenly as if they were still on the other side of the Atlantic. This fact sometimes gives their respective governments an excuse for interference here, and the result is the stirring up of dissensions which cause no inconsiderable trouble. Speak to them of spiritual unity, and they reply that it is the conscious communion of the believer with the Divine life. The Rev. A. Libedett in " Differences in the Church Doctrines of the Orthodox and the Romanists," now appearing in English, in the semi-monthly supplement to the *Amerikansky Pravoslavny Viestnik* (American Orthodox Messenger), published at St. Nicholas's Cathedral, New York, writes: " Uniting in Christ as their invisible Head, all the believers necessarily unite amongst themselves, composing one bond, one unity, one Church. Not to fall out from this spiritual union, they have one creed, one doctrine, one divine service and one prayer, one church canon and one hierarchical order. Therefore the creed, the divine service, and the church canon are the triple wall which guards the one Ecumenical, or Universal, Holy Apostolic Church. Whoever breaks down this wall though but in part, goes out of the Church union. He who breaks the creed is a heretic; he who breaks the divine service or the canons is a dissenter or a sectarian." And he continues: " However we enlarge this wall, however great the number of those forming separate, independent local churches, so long as they are within the wall, all the believers are conscious of their unity, because they always remain in the communion of prayer and sacraments."

In the United States, while they use the Slavonic, the Greek, the Arabic, and Roumanian, as their liturgical languages, there is a certain unity in the practice of their ancient

extended cross-arm and the foot-board placed obliquely to distinguish it from the head-board. They adhere tenaciously to the appellation Orthodox, and strongly resent the title Schismatic, which is synonymous and used by nearly everybody. If one would avoid hurting the feelings of those whose friendship is sought after, however, it is more expedient to use the title Orthodox.

To the Orthodox immigrant whose mind is still imbued with the reminiscences of his ancestral worship, form and ceremony generally constitute religion, and his attachment to outward observances, his fidelity to rites established by ancient usage, has made him very observant of what is accidental but heedless of what is essential. His religion is based more on sentiment and tradition than on intellectual conviction. He celebrates with much display the feast of a saint and neglects the sacraments. The sacrament of Penance in Oriental countries as well as in America among these immigrants has degenerated into mere formal and external celebration and has lost much of its vivifying influence. It is restricted to sins of a grave and serious nature, and takes no account of matters of thought or conscience. A few general questions and the stereotyped reply, " I am a sinner ", comprise all that is usually necessary for absolution. There is no confessional or privacy, for the priest and penitent stand face to face and not always separated from the congregation. To the piously inclined the Sacrament is full of solemn meaning, but to the multitude it is simply an observance ordained by law to be performed at stated intervals. Hence in this country, delivered from the Erastian yoke of the State, they are less observant of the sacraments of Penance and Holy Eucharist and of other precepts vital to their faith.

Of the many nationalities that constitute the Eastern Orthodox Church in the United States, the Russian is the oldest, the best organized, and the most solidly established. It is subsidized by the home government and many wealthy Russians in Europe assist it with liberal contributions. Its financial status is better than that of other nationalities and so its ceremonies are performed in more stately churches and with great pomp and magnificence. Its first foothold in America was secured over a century ago when missionaries were sent from St. Petersburg to Alaska, then a Russian territory. Jossaph was consecrated its first bishop in 1798, and in 1804 he established his see at Sitka where many Indians and Esquimo were afterwards converted. Orthodox Christians migrated along the coast of the Pacific and in 1872 the cathedral see was moved from Sitka to San Francisco. About this time a Russian Orthodox church was built in New York under the care of the Rev. Nicholas Bjerring, who after a few years closed it and joined the Presbyterians. He finally became a priest of the Catholic Church.

Russian immigration to the eastern cities caused churches to spring up along the Atlantic coast and a beautiful cathedral was erected in 1902 in the city of New York, whither the see of San Francisco was transferred in 1905, under the jurisdiction of Bishop Tykhon, who was raised to the dignity of archbishop, with two suffragan sees, one in Brooklyn and the other at Sitka, Alaska. The present incumbent in Brooklyn is the Right Rev. Raphael Hawawaeni, born in Damascus, Syria, and educated in Russia. In 1901 he came to America and was consecrated in Brooklyn, February, 1904, the first and up to the present time the only Orthodox bishop consecrated in the New World. His appointment was the cause of much rejoicing among the Syrio-Arabians, as the Schismatics of that nationality prefer to be called. These latter are under the quasi-jurisdiction of the Russian church and for this and other reasons the Rev. Raphael Hawawaeni was promoted. His influence is the cause of no little dissension among the Syrian Catholics. The see of Sitka is ruled by the Right Rev. Alexio Innocent, a Russian by birth and education, who for many years was a strenuous missionary in the United States.

In 1907 Archbishop Tykhon was called back to Russia and was succeeded by the present Archbishop Platon, once a member of the Russian Duma. It must be remembered that Archbishop Tykhon was the man who in October, 1905, received a

Orthodox movement was put under the direction of the " Orthodox Missionary Society of all Russia ", which attends to its financial wants and supplies priests for its development. In March, 1909, a code of local laws, subject to the Holy Synod, was signed and drawn up by Archbishop Platon, a copy of which lies before me as I write. It is a little pamphlet of about five thousand words defining the rights of the clergy and laity, regulating the finances of the churches and schools, determining the qualifications of converts, and even specifying the construction of the priest's house, as we see in section IX. It is a complete local canon law and betokens much religious activity.

The press of the Eastern Orthodox Church in America is active and ably edited, but its tone toward Greek Catholics in union with Rome is bitter. A semi-weekly magazine, *Amerikansky Pravoslavny Viestnik* (The American Orthodox Messenger), edited by the Very Rev. A. A. Hotovitzky, of New York City, in Great Russian, has the largest circulation, while a weekly, *Svit* (Light), printed in Ruthenian, wields great influence. The former also issues a monthly supplement in English, but scarcity of funds, as the manager informs the writer, prevents its regular appearance. For the past two years it has been completely taken up with a biased account of the doctrinal differences between the Orthodox and the Catholic Church. These discussions are eagerly read by Orthodox members and in many Uniate parishes excite much controversy. In fact, *The Messenger* publishes now and then lists of the " reunited ", as evidence of the activity of the Orthodox in bringing back to their fold some of those united with the Catholic Church.

A great impetus in this direction was given in 1892, when the Rev. Alexis Toth, a Greek Catholic priest in Minneapolis, Minnesota, joined the Orthodox Church. When disciplined by Archbishop Ireland he left the diocese and submitted himself to the Orthodox bishop, then living in San Francisco. Returning afterwards to Minneapolis, he persuaded his former congregation to secede from Rome, and, not satisfied with this, he undertook in 1894 to take over the congregation and church property of St. Mary's, Wilkes-Barre, Pennsylvania. Much litigation followed, but failure attended his efforts relative to the property, the courts deciding against him. But the priest in charge and half the congregation seceded. Through his exertions and bitter opposition to the Catholic Church, it is estimated that about 12,000 Uniates joined the Orthodox Church, and his efforts were duly appreciated by the "Holy Governing Synod of Russia", for in 1895 he was elevated to the dignity of an archpriest. Two others, the Rev. Demetrius Gebe, now in Russia, and the Rev. John Olshevsky, now pastor of the Orthodox church at Mayfield, Pa., followed the example of Father Toth; but their efforts to get their parishioners to secede had but little effect. I am pleased to state that these defections are liberally conpensated for by sincere converts, priests and laymen, from the Orthodox Church to Catholicity.

In the past priests were supplied from Russia, but in 1905 a strenuous effort was made to establish an ecclesiastical seminary in Cleveland, Ohio. The movement met with failure, but now the nucleus of a seminary has been started in Minneapolis, and it is expected thereby to facilitate the re-union of the Uniates; because a seminary in this country would prepare priests who might meet the wants of those Uniates who long for Slavic ideals independent of Russian control. The latest figures for the Russian Orthodox Church in America, including Alaska, are: one archbishop, two bishops, 97 priests, 77 churches, and 37,000 members.

Closely allied with the Russian Orthodox Church is the Syrio-Arabian, which uses the Arabian language in its liturgy. They are said to be about 55,000 in the United States, and are assisted in the construction of their churches and in the support of their missions by the Russians. The majority of them lead a nomadic form of life, and seek employment as factory hands, traveling salesmen, peddlers, and the like. The elevation of a man of their nationality to the Orthodox bishopric of Brooklyn by the Russians draws them closer to the latter, and appeals strongly to the religious sentiments of these imaginative Orientals.

The Servian Orthodox Church is found in the greater part of the Balkan States in Hungary and in Transylvania. They all speak the southern Slavonic language. Numerous emigrants from these districts have come to America in the past decade of years and settled in Pennsylvania and the West. Those from Servia, while not recognizing the jurisdiction of the Russian archbishop, have a friendly feeling for his church, and now number about 85,000, with twelve priests and fourteen churches, two of them imposing structures at Pittsburg, Pa., and St. Louis, Missouri. The Roumanians, like the Servians, incline toward the Russians and number about 27,000, with five priests and seven churches, the largest, at Cleveland, Ohio, having been built a few years since. The Bulgarians, probably on account of their status in Europe, will associate neither with the Russians nor the Greeks, but claim the Exarch of Bulgaria as their lawful spiritual adviser. With the Macedonians they number about 25,000 and have five priests to attend to their spiritual needs.

According to the religious census of 1906, in the Servian Orthodox Church the males formed 85.8 per cent of all communicants; in the Russian Orthodox, 67.6 per cent; and in the Syrian Orthodox, 60.5 per cent. The number of male adults without families so far exceeds the number of females that it will be only a short time before these peoples shall have doubled their number. These able-bodied men are the advance guard sent to this country to make a home. By their thrift and industry they soon succeed, and no sooner have they got a foothold in the land than they send for their parents, sisters, and brothers.

Nor must we overlook the Greeks, who in the past twenty years have grown in numbers to 135,000. They of all nationalities showed the largest percentage of males in the census of 1906. They publish twenty newspapers, of which two are dailies, and many of their churches are temples of art, that of Holy Trinity, New York, holding first place for size and attractiveness. Thirty-six priests attend to their spiritual wants, half of whom are subject to the Patriarch of Constantinople and the remainder to the Synod of Athens. Following the custom of the Eusabia Society established in Smyrna, Asia Minor, in 1893, laymen preach in their churches. Then, too, for sometime after coming to this country, they do not distinguish between religion and nationality owing to the teaching of their clergy; and hence an Orthodox Greek will refuse to become a Catholic lest he should cease to become a

Greek, but the language, manners, and customs of the country in a short time bring about a better spirit of understanding and sympathy. The Russians have made many fruitless advances toward them, yet they are on terms of union arising from a common faith and a common orthodoxy.

For the past five years they have earnestly endeavored to get a Greek bishop of their own nationality, but the jealousy existing between the Patriarch of Constantinople and the Synod of Athens, neither being willing to grant the prerogative to the other, has thwarted their efforts. Although not affiliated with Russian Orthodoxy, they took pride in the fact that Eastern Orthodox Christians had bishops here in America and Greek Uniates had none, and they used this as a potent argument to induce the latter to secede from Rome. They slighted the idea of being ruled by Latin bishops, or, as they disdainfully called them, " Irish " bishops. Now that Rome has appointed a bishop of the Greek rite over the Uniates, their only consolation is that he has at present no diocesan power or authority, being only an auxiliary to the Latin bishops.

All the Orthodox churches of the Byzantine rite that we have mentioned, no matter of what nationality, have a corresponding Greek Catholic Church in communion with Rome. That is what we call the Uniate, whether they are by race or speech Greek or Slav, Servian or Syrian. In the United States they number about 400,000, the majority of whom belong to the Ruthenian race. To those Uniates Rome sent a bishop in the person of the Right Rev. Stephen Soter Ortynski, a native of Galicia, in September, 1907, who was to exercise vicarious jurisdiction and safeguard their ecclesiastical rights. His efforts in establishing churches and encouraging the Ruthenians to hold their Catholic faith and become good American citizens have met with unprecedented success. The first Uniate Church in America was established at Shenandoah, Pa., in 1886, and the first Uniate priest, the Rev. Ivan Volanski, came to this country in 1885. To-day the Uniates have 126 priests and 146 churches. There are many converts from the Orthodox church influenced by strong, well-organized, helpful societies, established on a mutual benefit basis, and by pamphlets_issued for the information of members on various national and religious subjects.

The Apostolic Letter, *Ea Semper,* issued by Pius X under date of 14 June, 1907, the feast of St. Basil the Great, Patriarch of the Eastern Church, defining certain rules for Catholics of the Ruthenian (Greek) rite, resident in the United States, is simply an extension of the regulations issued by Benedict XIV, in 1743, for the Greek Melchites of the Turkish dominion. These rules are set forth in thirty-six articles grouped under four heads—Position of the Ruthenian Bishop; Functions of the Ruthenian Clergy; Relations of the Ruthenian Laity to the Clergy and *vice versa;* Intermarriage of Ruthenians and Latin Catholics.[2] Its first appearance created much dissatisfaction amongst the Uniate clergy and laity, who saw in it an attack upon their Slavic nationality and the Eastern rite. Urged on by the Russian Orthodox Church, they imagined it was an attempt to Latinize their ancient rites and customs. The result was that about 12,000 defected from the Ruthenian and joined the Orthodox Church. But after the first bewilderment was over, matters adjusted themselves, reaction set in, and many are already coming back.

It is a problem presented to the Catholic Church of America to keep them in the faith, educate them into good citizens, and do this with as little friction as possible. They are progressing in ability and wealth and are becoming American citizens in ever-increasing numbers. Their clergy are gradually taking a more active part in making them good Americans. The noble work of Father Philip Salomone, the Uniate Syrian priest of La Crosse, Wisconsin, has received conspicuous notice from the secular newspapers, because of his leading part in the amicable settlement with our government on the question of citizenship rights to his countrymen of Syria. His efforts were ably seconded by Father Benedict Bullama, Uniate Syrian priest of Minneapolis, Minnesota.

When Greek Catholics established their rite in America a feeling of distrust and even dislike was entertained toward them by Roman Catholics accustomed to the Roman rite. The formation of their churches, their strange liturgy, their married clergy, Communion under both kinds, their curious manner of making the sign of the cross, the segregation of the

---

[2] ECCLESIASTICAL REVIEW, November, 1907.

sexes in church—all these customs offended the Latin Catholics and caused an unpleasant feeling, that in no way contributed to attract their Uniate brethren, but on the contrary was a means of driving them into Orthodoxy. The Pastoral Letter of Bishop Canevin of Pittsburg, issued in 1904, was the first official statement made to clarify the situation. It anticipated in many things the Apostolic Letter of Pius X. It was an extremely interesting and valuable Pastoral, a compendious statement of the theology of the matter for priests, and an inestimable guide to the people at large. Its influence for good amongst the Uniates, who are numerous in his diocese, was soon felt; it created a healthy atmosphere, and drew closer together in the bonds of charity the children of the One Holy Catholic Church exercising different rites and customs.

Since the fatal day when Greek schismatics cut themselves off from the True Vine, many unsuccessful attempts have been made at reunion. I fancy that if there is any hope for reunion with Rome, the elements are riper for it in America, owing to the common interests, language, and association, than in Europe, where prejudice is both national and bitter. While the Russian Orthodox Church has little respect for European Anglicanism, yet in September, 1903, when the astute Bishop C. Grafton of the Protestant Episcopal diocese of Fond du Lac, Wisconsin, went to Russia purposely to arrange a union between the Russian Orthodox and the American Episcopal churches, he was received with great urbanity by the Metropolitans of St. Petersburg and Moscow, and his case was laid before the Synod and submitted to various theological bodies in order to reach some basis of understanding. Of course, it must be admitted that the American branch of Anglicanism approaches nearer to the Orthodox Church than does the European. This may be seen from the fact that in the American book of Common Prayer there is added the Epiklesis, which is not found in the European; and the black rubric containing the expression against transubstantiation is omitted from the American manual. Yet while nothing good came out of the Anglican's visit to Russia, it showed the kindly feelings of the Orthodox Church in Europe toward Anglicans who are citizens of America. Likewise we find the Old Catholics of America and Europe, a rather unimportant body, coquetting with the Orthodox, and advances were made by the latter to bring about a union at the recent congress held in Vienna. By order of the Holy Synod his most high holiness Anthony, Metropolitan of St. Petersburg, sent a letter to the Old-Catholic bishops conveying to them the congratulations of the Synod and praising their enthusiasm for truth. He further stated that he hoped in the near future to see the Orthodox and the Old-Catholic churches united. At the same time considerable interest was manifested at St. Petersburg in the congress and one of the influential papers devoted a long article to the *rapprochement.*

These movements on the part of the Russian Church show that the prejudices and jealousies, which for centuries have been fossilizing into principles, are vanishing before the trend of latter-day civilization. Nevertheless so long as Orthodoxy is the slave, the tool, the dupe of the State, so long will there be no hope or prospect of reunion with the Bride of Christ. We can firmly assert that there is no sympathy with Protestantism in the Orthodox church even amongst the immigrants in our country. If it ever seek unity, it will be within the fold of Christ, for it has still within it the germ of divine grace. It is not heretical, but only schismatic. It has the body of divine truth and the grace of the sacraments. But whilst the State continues to wield absolute power in spirituals and temporals, we can entertain no hope of a Church so subjected being able to consider any vital proposition from an independent standpoint.

But a rift is seen on the horizon. The past two years have seen a mighty change come over the semi-barbaric East. Orthodoxy in Europe is rising from its slough of ignorance and prejudice; freedom of worship is tolerated in bureaucratic Russia; thousands are seeking rest in the Catholic Church, and a better feeling of mutual charity unites Catholics and Schismatics. Foreign influence and education have brought liberty of thought and freedom of speech to the benighted inhabitants of the Ottoman Empire. Young Turkey is rejoicing in her regeneration, and all forms of religion are so far tolerated that one is considered as good as another, except by some hardened Moslems. This regeneration of the East affects

Looking at this great religious change that has been wrought, there is ample encouragement for us to do all that lies in our power to hasten the day of reunion. Orthodox immigrants to our country in future will be more enlightened and less bigoted. Freedom from Erastian government and that inborn instinct against Protestantism will draw them closer to Catholicity. Affinity of blood and belief, as well as the common lot of being immigrants, is naturally drawing Uniates and Schismatics closer together in spiritual matters. The education of more Uniates for the ministry would certainly attract more Schismatics to Catholicity. For the latter practically nothing is wrong but the schism. In case of other sects one sees so much to be changed—false doctrine and headstrong mutilation of the faith; but the Orthodox Church has kept practically all the faith. The question of the *Filioque* and Infallibility are the main points at issue, and we know and they know that their forefathers at Chalcedon (451) all cried out, " This is the faith of the Fathers; this is the faith of the Apostles. . . . Peter has spoken by Leo."

Greeks have sat on St. Peter's throne. No one would think of asking them to accept our technical ideas and philosophy. No one would dream of touching their ancient liturgies, their magnificent ritual, their time-honored canon law, or any of those customs endeared to their hearts. Priests and people of the United States must extend the hand of friendship not only to the 400,000 Uniates, but also to the 350,000 Orthodox in our midst. We must persuade the latter that reunion means only going back to the state of things before the ninth century. We do not want them to break up their pictured *Ikonostases* or deny the deacon the pleasure of waving his repidon over the Holy Gifts. Communion under one kind, celibacy, and azyme bread are Latin customs, and Rome would easily arrange such matters of discipline.

The great obstacle to the Orthodox is their fear of being Latinized or having to give up rites which they love. Their discipline and liturgy, except in so far as it is contrary to faith, would be left undisturbed. Their common interests and associations with Catholics in this country have established a better feeling of love and unity. It then behooves us priests to manifest a deeper interest in our Orthodox brethren. More Pastorals like that of Bishop Canevin and more striving after unity on the part of the Catholic priests and laity will help to blot out the embittered feelings of a thousand years. The Apostolic Letter of Pius X to the Ruthenians of the United States is working untold good. With that Christian spirit of " restoring all things in Christ ", he invites the faithful to unite again in prayer for the enlightenment of all who bear the Christian name, that they may be guided by the Holy Spirit to a true knowledge of Christ's saving Faith, and be re-united in the bonds of Christian charity, that the scattered and wandering sheep of the Saviour may be again gathered into one Fold, under one Shepherd.

WILLIAM LEEN.

Walker, Iowa.

GLIMPSES OF DEVOTION TO THE BLESSED VIRGIN MARY IN ANCIENT IRELAND.

EVEN a cursory glance into the history of early Christianity in Ireland suffices to show that foundations in honor of Our Lady are coeval with the very beginnings of the Christian religion in the Isle of Saints. There is good authority for saying that the Abbey of Canons Regular at Trim, dedicated to Christ's Immaculate Mother, was founded by St. Patrick himself, as early as the year 432. Of St. Brendan, the son of Findloga, we read that he founded an abbey at Clonard, A. D. 553, or 562, which he placed under the patronage of Our Lady. Kells, in County Meath, is said to have been the gift of Dermod, the son of Fergus Kervail, to St. Columban, who founded a monastery there, sometime about the year 550; it also was dedicated to the Blessed Virgin. These instances of the dedication of religious houses and their churches to Our Lady—one of them, and that the earliest, by the great Apostle of Ireland; and the last, not later than the middle of the fifth century—give ample proof that in Ireland devotion to Our Lady was co-existent with the dawn of the Christian faith.

Trim, or Ath Truim, has been called by some the most celebrated sanctuary " of the Blessed Virgin in Ireland "; and to it pilgrimages were made from all parts of the country, Irish and Anglo-Irish alike emulating each other in reverencing and enriching it with costly gifts and votive offerings. Numerous and wonderful were the miracles wrought there. We read that Hugh MacMahon in 1397 " recovered his eyesight fasting in honor of the Holy Cross at Raphoe, and of the Blessed Virgin Mary at Ath Trim." In 1444, " a great miraculous cure was wrought by the image of the Blessed Virgin Mary at Trim; it restored sight to a blind man, speech to a dumb man, and the use of his feet to a cripple, and stretched out the hand of a person which had been fastened to his side."

We are not surprised to learn that a shrine so famous attracted the greed of Henry VIII; " that the gifts of the pilgrimes were taken away from thence ", and the celebrated image consigned to the flames. " In 1537," we read, " they [the Saxons] burned the images, shrines, and relics of the Saints of Ireland and England." " And there was not," laments another chronicler, " in Erinn a holy cross or a figure of Mary, or an illustrious image over which their power reached, that was not burned."

The ancient Franciscan Abbey of Muckross, with its greatly venerated image of the Blessed Mother of God, is too well known to need mention here. In the Abbey Church of Navan, too, was an image of Our Lady which was held in such high repute that persons of all grades of society, from the highest to the lowest, and from every part of Ireland, were in the habit of journeying thither, in order to offer their gifts, and make their petitions. Indeed, so much esteemed was this image that in the Dublin Parliament in the year 1454, it was decreed that " letters patent of the King be made . . . for taking into protection all people, whether rebels or others, who shall go in pilgrimage to the Convent of the Blessed Virgin of Navan ".

The mention of pilgrimages brings us to a noteworthy fact in this connexion, namely, that the Irish, from the earliest days of Christianity, were conspicuous to a quite extraordinary degree for their love for this particular form of devotion.

were by no means unusual in Ireland, for the ancient history of that country tells of the expedition of the sons of Corra, and the wandering pilgrimage of Snedhgns and MacRiaghla, in the seventh or early in the eighth century. Full of strong faith and ardent devotion, the pure-hearted love of the Celt, to whom heaven and heavenly things are more real than the earth upon which he moves and the objects he sees around him, they started on these pious journeyings, taking no thought for the morrow, intent only upon performing a religious duty which they held to be sacred.

It must be confessed, however, that occasionally their fervor prompted them to undertake pilgrimages in a somewhat imprudent manner; and sometimes even without any definite object, save that of being—as the old chronicler calls it—" in a state of pilgrimage for the love of God ". It is most interesting in this connexion to find that, in 892, " Three Scots came to King Alfred in a boat *without any oars from Ireland,* whence they had stolen away, *because they desired, for the love of God, to be in a state of pilgrimage, they recked not where.* The boat in which they came, was wrought of two and a half hides, and they took with them food for seven nights, and on the seventh night they came to land in Cornwall, and they went straightway to King Alfred. Thus were they named Dubslane, Macbetha, and Maclinmum." Immense numbers of pilgrims, both from Great Britain and Ireland, were in the habit of crossing the Channel, in order to visit such famous French sanctuaries as those of Our Lady of Boulogne, Puy, Chartres, Roc-Amadour, and many others.

Some of these pilgrimages were made in person; some by deputy; and old constitutions prove how universal was the custom. For example, according to a regulation made in 1268, the Canons of Senlis were allowed fifteen days of non-residence to go on pilgrimage to Our Lady of Boulogne; whilst in Ireland, " the law protected from distress " a member of a tribe who had gone on pilgrimage, or to obtain Holy Communion, or to summon a physician for a person seriously ill.

It is not surprising that the Irish, who have ever been fore-

in visiting different shrines and sanctuaries, realizing that
" very often "—as St. John of the Cross says—" our Lord
grants His graces by means of images in remote and solitary
places. In remote places, that the pilgrimage to them may
stir up our devotion, and make it the more intense. In solitary places, that we may retire from the noise and concourse
of men to pray in solitude, like our Lord Himself."

Another point connected with the deep love of Ireland for
God's most holy Mother should be noted here. We refer to
the reverence, carried to quite an extraordinary extent, in
which was held her sacred name. Although, later on, custom changed in this respect, it is certain that during the earlier
ages of Christianity in that land, Irish men and women, influenced by the profoundest feelings of humility and respect,
never gave to their children the name of Mary—nor indeed
the names of the saints; instead, with a charmingly ingenious
self-effacement and pious abjection, they adopted the prefix
Mael, or *Maol.* This prefix, so constantly familiar in Irish
names, signifies servant. For example, Maelisa means servant
of Jesus; Maelmuire, servant of Mary; Maelpadraic, servant
of Patrick.

A reference to ancient documents proves beyond doubt that
the name Maelmuire was given indiscriminately to children
of either sex. But as a learned authority on this subject has
truly said, " No translation can give the full beauty of this
unique and happy combination; and few would guess that the
real name of the celebrated monk of Ratisbon, known under
the Latinized form of Marianus Scotus, was in reality Maelmuire."

Again, the prefix Giolla, or Gilla, which also means a servant, and whence the term gilly is derived, is found in the
name of Gillamuire; for instance, we find mention in an old
document of Gillamuire, an anchorite of Ard-Macha, who died
in the year A. D. 1159; and it will be remembered that this
prefix still survives in the family names of Gilchrist, servant
of Christ; and Gilmurray, servant of Mary.

Many centuries elapsed before the name of God's Blessed

veneration for it; so much, indeed, that women, although of royal birth, were not allowed to bear it, as if the dignity of this holy name would be compromised by being conferred upon women, even though they were queens."

Erin, the Island of Saints, whose hierarchy represents an unbroken line from her great Apostle, St. Patrick, and whose national religion is the faith of Christ, which has only burned the brighter through centuries of persecution and difficulty, has shown her love for Our Lady in yet another direction— the wide domain of literature. The poetry and hymnology of Ireland, even at an early date, bear witness to this. Cœlius Sedulius, whose reputation spread wide and far, and St. Cuchumneus and others, toward the close of the sixth century, composed hymns which enlarge on the special dignity, privileges, and graces of the ever Blessed Virgin. An old Irish hymn, believed to have been written in the eleventh century, and entitled, " The Protecting Corselet of Mary," consists of twenty-four stanzas, of which the first begins thus:

> Direct me how to praise thee,
> Though I am not a master of Poetry. . . .

and continues:

> I offer myself under thy protection,
> O loving Mother of the Only Son,
> And under thy protecting shield I place my body,
> My heart, my will, and my understanding.

To Ireland again is due the honor of having composed the first Litany of Our Lady. This litany, which, according to the learned Professor O'Curry, is at least as old as the middle of the eighth century, differs in many respects from early litanies of Our Lady in other languages, thus proving that it is not a translation. Indeed, the most careful research has brought to light no similar form of supplication at that period; and in England there is no trace of any litany of Our Lady in Anglo-Saxon times. In the Litany of the Saints used by the Anglo-Saxons, the name of the Blessed Virgin stands indeed before that of any angel or saint, and is repeated three times;

ginity," " Inextinguishable Lamp," etc. Yet in all these homilies we find merely the suggestion of a litany such as was actually composed by the Irish—that is, a prayer to Our Lady in the shape of what is now understood by the word litany, which, as Cardinal Wiseman tells us, " is not a studied prayer, intended to have logical connexion of parts," but " a hymn, a song of affectionate admiration, and at the same time of earnest entreaty." [1]

M. Nesbitt.

THE ROMAN CURIA.

Offices (Continued).

THE SECRETARIATE OF STATE.

THIS Office of the Roman Curia is of less ancient origin than any of those we have considered. It does not date farther back than the fifteenth century; indeed some writers hold that the first Papal Secretary of State was St. Charles Borromeo, who was appointed to the position by Pius IV in 1560.[1] The institution of this Office was contemporary with the introduction of diplomatic embassies at royal Courts. At first it was generally some near relative of the Pope enjoying his special confidence, who was appointed to take charge of diplomatic business with civil governments; hence he was called " Cardinalis Nepos." [2] He had a considerable number of Secretaries under him to assist in performing the necessary functions. The custom of appointing a relative of the Pope as head of the Secretariate of State was discontinued by Innocent XII, who issued (22 June, 1692) the Bull *Romanum decet,* against nepotism.

SECRETARIATE OF STATE IN RECENT TIMES.

In recent times, before the Roman Pontiff was despoiled of his temporal dominions, the Cardinal Secretary of State was required to preside at meetings of the Ministerial Council,

---

[1] To the ancient Irish litany is attached an indulgence of one hundred days, granted by Pope Pius IX of happy memory, for all who receive it. It is to be found in the *Leabhar-Mor,* which is now preserved in the Royal Irish Academy.

which consisted of the Ministers of Justice, Finances, Commerce, Industry, War; he was also required to carry on diplomatic affairs with foreign governments; but after the annexation of 1870, his duties in this respect were diminished. However, even since the spoliation of the temporal dominions of the Holy See, the Cardinal Secretary of State has had charge of many weighty and responsible functions. There have been some civil governments with which the Holy See has carried on diplomatic relations; for instance, Austria-Hungary, Spain, and Portugal continue to send their ambassadors. There are other governments which without having an embassy at the Vatican appoint a minister, such as Prussia, Bavaria, Belgium, etc. Hilling (p. 112) mentions eighteen countries which still hold diplomatic relations with the Holy See. Then there are Nunciatures established by the Holy See in various countries, for instance, in each of those having an ambassador to the Holy See; there are other nunciatures of less importance, being called nunciatures of the second class, such as those in Bavaria, Belgium, and Brazil. Besides conducting diplomatic affairs with various governments, the Cardinal Secretary of State has given directions to Apostolic Nuncios, and by special command of the Pope has been employed to transmit instructions to Ordinaries; he has also been appointed to expedite pontifical appointments in the Roman Curia. In all these functions he has been the chief agent and representative of the Holy See.

THE SECRETARIATE OF STATE UNDER THE NEW CONSTITUTION.

According to the Constitution, *Sapienti consilio,* there are three sections or branches in the Secretariate of State. The first of these relates to extraordinary ecclesiastical affairs; it pertains to the duties of this section to transmit to the Congregation for Extraordinary Ecclesiastical Affairs those matters which the Roman Pontiff has ordered to be examined by this Congregation; while the matters which appertain to the province of each of the other Congregations are to be remitted to these Congregations respectively according to the character of the business. The second section relates to the ordinary affairs which have been handled by the Secretariate of State in recent times, as was stated above. It likewise be-

longs to this section to confer dignities both civil and ecclesiastical, except those reserved to the prelate placed over the
papal household. The third section or branch of the Secretariate of State has charge of the expedition of these Briefs
committed to it by the various Congregations; the Secretariate
of Briefs which hitherto existed has been abolished and its
functions are now discharged by this third section of the Secretariate of State.

THE PERSONNEL OF THE PRESENT SECRETARIATE OF STATE.

The Cardinal Secretary of State is supreme moderator of
the whole Office, while in each of the three sections just referred to there is a special president. The Secretary of the
Congregation of Extraordinary Affairs presides over the first
section; the Substitute for Ordinary Affairs presides over the
second; and the Chancellor of Apostolic Briefs is the president of the third section. In each section there is a number
of officials appointed, a list of whom the reader will find in
the *Acta Apostolicae Sedis* for January, 1909 (p. 134).

THE SECRETARIATES OF BRIEFS TO PRINCES AND OF LATIN LETTERS.

The fifth and last of the Offices named in the Constitution,
Sapienti consilio, bears the title *Secretariae Brevium ad Prin-
cipes et Epistolarum Latinarum.* Heretofore there were three
distinct Secretariates in the Roman Curia, the Secretariate of
Briefs, the Secretariate of Briefs to Princes, and the Secretariate of Latin Letters.

ORIGIN OF THE SECRETARIATE OF BRIEFS.

The Apostolic Chancery, which has already been considered
in the present series of articles was for a long period the only
Office for the expedition of Apostolic Letters; but by degrees
a distinct department was formed to expedite matters of less
importance. This was the Secretariate of Briefs dating back
to the fifteenth century. This Office acquired exclusive authority to expedite Briefs strictly so-called, which by common
law or by special ordination of the Roman Pontiffs were required for certain matters. Moreover it was empowered to
grant various favors, as is clear from the Bull, *Gravissimum*

of favors and privileges which this Secretariate could confer either exclusively, or cumulatively along with the Dataria. Thus it could grant dispensation from the canonical age for ordination, the privilege of keeping the Blessed Sacrament in a private chapel, as well as that of a private oratory for the celebration of Mass. Besides, this Secretariate could grant to the clergy the faculty of blessing rosaries with the Apostolic Indulgences attached thereto, as also the faculty of a privileged altar. Furthermore, there were petitions sent to the Holy See, which could not be directly granted by the Secretariate, but which the latter had authority to examine and, if deemed proper, could recommend the Holy See to grant. This Secretariate was employed by the late Sovereign Pontiff Leo XIII to make grants of Indulgences, after the power had been withdrawn from the Congregation of Indulgences by the Motu Proprio, *Christianae reipublicae;* but this last-named power is now reserved exclusively to the Congregation of the Holy Office.

The second Secretariate of the Roman Curia was called the Secretariate of Briefs to Princes. It was separated from the Secretariate of Briefs by the Bull, *Romanus Pontifex,* in April, 1678. As its name implies, its chief purpose was to expedite Apostolic Letters to persons of exalted position.

The Secretariate of Latin Letters was instituted for the composition of Latin Briefs which were not expedited by either of the two preceding Secretariates. It has had a Secretary and an Assistant.

THE THREE SECRETARIATES UNDER THE NEW REGIME.

The Secretariate of Briefs is no longer a separate Office of the Curia; it is now, as has been observed, a section or department of the Secretariate of State, which is set down in the Constitution, *Sapienti consilio,* as the fourth Office of the Curia. The other two, the Secretariate of Briefs to Princes and the Secretariate of Latin Letters, form a twofold office, and their functions continue as heretofore. The former has at present a Secretary and two Assistants; the latter (the Secretariate of Latin Letters) has a Secretary and one Assistant.[3] Among the " Normae Peculiares " it is stated that a special Commission of three Cardinals, one of whom is the Cardinal

[3] Cf. *Acta Apost. Sed.,* Vol. I, p. 135.

Secretary of State, is charged with the preparation of new formularies for the issuance of Apostolic Briefs.[4]

We have now completed our study of the three departments of the Roman Curia as reorganized by the Constitution, *Sapienti consilio.* In treating of the Sacred Congregations it has been our purpose to point out the competency of each of them as determined by that Constitution and to show in what respects the new legislation differs from what preceded it. When considering the other two branches of the Roman Curia, the Sacred Tribunals and the Offices, we followed a similar method. In this commentary upon the new Constitution it has been our endeavor to collect the proper interpretation of each portion from the terms in which the legislation has been expressed, and to make use of the pontifical pronouncements and the opinions of various writers for the same purpose. In some particulars it is not unlikely that doubts will arise concerning the competence of the several Congregations, Tribunals, and Offices of the Curia. These will be solved by the Consistorial Congregation, to whose province it belongs to solve such doubts.[5]

It has been suggested that it would be well to present here a summary of the functions appertaining to each of the Congregations, Tribunals, and Offices of the Roman Curia, so that one may see at a glance their precise competence. This may be done as follows:

THE SACRED CONGREGATIONS.

HOLY OFFICE — Defence of doctrine; judgment of heresy and of other crimes which excite suspicion of heresy; doctrine and use of Indulgences; Pauline privilege, *disparitas cultus,* and *mixta religio;* doctrine of the Sacraments.

CONGREGATION ON THE DISCIPLINE OF THE SACRAMENTS	Discipline of the Sacraments; matrimonial dispensations *in foro externo, sanatio in radice,* dispensation *super rato,* legitimation of offspring; dispensation of seculars for ordination; dispensation regarding the time, place, and conditions for receiving Holy Communion, saying Mass, and reserving the Blessed Sacrament.
CONGREGATION OF THE COUNCIL	Universal discipline of the secular clergy and faithful; observance of the precepts of the Church, such as fasting (not the Eucharistic fast), abstinence, feasts; regulations for parish priests and canons; Sodalities, pious legacies, stipends for Masses, benefices, ecclesiastical goods; celebration and recognition of Councils.
CONGREGATION FOR RELIGIOUS	Affairs of religious of either sex with simple or solemn vows; others living in common like Religious; secular Third Orders; regulation of matters of religious between themselves and with others; dispensations from vows and precepts.
CONGREGATION DE PROPAGANDA FIDE	For countries subject to its jurisdiction " Ceteras Congregationes habet in ventre "; not however in matters relating to faith, matrimony, discipline of Sacred Rites, or to Religious *as Religious.*
CONGREGATION OF THE INDEX	Examination of books brought under its notice, and, if advisable, their condemnation; dispensations for prohibited books; investigation concerning the circulation of writings deserving condemnation; reminding Ordinaries to condemn and denounce pernicious works.
CONGREGATION OF SACRED RITES	Rites and ceremonies of the Latin Church, especially for Mass, administration of the Sacraments, divine Office; dispensations therein; insignia and privileges in relation to Sacred Rites; beatification and canonization of Saints; Sacred Relics.
CEREMONIAL CONGREGATION	Ceremonies to be observed in the Pontifical Chapel and Court; sacred functions of Cardinals outside the Pontifical Chapel; precedence of Cardinals and representatives sent to the Holy See.
CONGREGATION FOR EXTRA. ECC. AFFAIRS	Matters submitted for its examination by the R. Pontiff through the Cardinal Secretary of State, especially those relating to civil laws and to pacts made with different States.

CONGREGATION OF STUDIES	Regulation of the studies in universities depending on the authority of the Church; approval of new institutions; faculty for conferring academic degrees.

TRIBUNALS.

SACRED PENITENTIARY	Jurisdiction for the *forum internum* alone, in which absolution, dispensations, etc., are granted.
S. ROTA.	All contentious cases, civil or criminal, not major ones.
APOST. SEGNATURA	Particular cases concerning Rotal sentences and Auditors of the Rota.

OFFICES.

APOSTOLIC CHANCERY	Expedition of Apostolic Letters *sub plumbo* concerning the provision of consistorial benefices, erection of new dioceses, and other important affairs of the Church.
APOSTOLIC DATARY	Apostolic Letters regarding non-consistorial benefices reserved to the Holy See; dispensations from conditions required for these benefices; pensions and charges imposed.
APOSTOLIC CAMERA	Administration of the property and temporal rights of the Holy See, especially during a vacancy.
SECRETARIATE OF STATE	Extraordinary affairs submitted for examination to the Congregation for Extra. Affairs; ordinary affairs, especially the right of conferring honors, civil and ecclesiastical; despatch of Apostolic Briefs from the S. Congregations.
SECRET. OF BRIEFS TO PRINCES AND OF LAT. LET.	The expedition of Apostolic Letters to persons of exalted position; composition of Latin Letters.

In the concluding portion of the Constitution, *Sapienti consilio,* the Sovereign Pontiff sets forth various enactments, some of which have been referred to in previous articles in this REVIEW; there are others which have not yet been touched upon, such as certain regulations for the transaction of business in the Departments of the Roman Curia, as well as the authority of these Departments during a vacancy of the Holy See. On some future occasion these latter topics will form matter for the closing article of this series.

THE STORY OF A MODERN CAPUCHIN.

ON Saturday, 21 September, 1850, Mgr. Mioland, Coadjutor of Cardinal d'Astros, conferred the priesthood upon Leo Francis Clergue in the chapel of the Grand Séminaire. On the next morning the young priest celebrated his first Mass at Lavaur, assisted by the venerable archpriest of Toulouse, in the old cathedral of St. Alain in which he had been baptized. "What tears," he writes, recalling this event, "when for the first time I raised in my trembling hand the Sacred Victim and fed my happy parents with the Bread of Life! What happiness and what transports of love!"

Appointed *vicaire* or curate at Saint-Gaudens, a distant part of the country unknown to him, where the people spoke a dialect he had never heard, the first fruits of his missionary zeal were an association for youth, a congregation for servants and country girls, a branch of the Society of St. Vincent de Paul, and the restoration in 1854 of the Chapel of La Caone, dedicated to the saint who gave the town its name, erected at the extremity of a hill in view of the beautiful plain of the Garonne, near the very spot where the shepherd saint was martyred by the Saracens. He not only restored this sanctuary with the unpurchased aid of forty willing workers, to whom bread and wine were gratuitously given by the townsfolk, but also restored the pilgrimages thereto which had ceased. He was at the end of his resources when he undertook it, the poor of the parish and mountains of the Ariège having absorbed all his savings. "I had then," he says, "to confide in my Mother in heaven: I multiplied my pilgrimages to Notre Dame du Bout-du-Puy, and had many prayers offered, particularly by the poor, those great friends of heaven, and the shepherds, my little brethren. Since my arrival at Saint-Gaudens, they were the chosen portion in the work of parochial catechism classes. The sight of their little bare feet and their cheerful faces contributed not a little to give me the seraphic vocation."

His acceptance of this country curacy, despite the opposition of his family, was the more meritorious as he stood a great chance of a vacant curacy at Saint Exupère in Toulouse. "It was providential," observes a biographer. "What was a parish to him? Such a great heart needed for its fiery zeal a whole city, a whole district, and soon a whole world!"

The Abbé Clergue was not one of those French priests who shut themselves up in their presbyteries, throw all the blame upon the Revolution for the evils that exist and all the responsibility of remedying those evils on Providence, a species of religiose fatalism which seems until recently to have stricken the Church in France with a moral paralysis. "He thinks of everything and provides for everything," writes Père Ernest-Marie.[1] "He works unceasingly, he multiplies himself, and although this impetuous zeal draws out of their quietude venerable priests long attached to the service of the parish, no one thinks of taking umbrage at it and each one tries to second his efforts. He is bringing about an appreciation, in view of the material and spiritual ruins which the Revolution has heaped up, that the priest ought to be something more than the pious supervisor of his church, receiving there the faithful and only emerging from it with circumspection to administer the sacraments. When the Church was mistress and queen, this method perhaps sufficed; it suffices no longer nowadays, for its rights are contested, it is combated from without, its children are snatched from it, and it must arm for its defence, go to the people and become a conqueror. It is now understood, and the pretence that impiety sets up to confine the priest to the sacristy contributes not a little to open people's eyes. But toward the middle of the last century, an epoch of transition, there were still many blind and indolent who, palliating their inaction under a pretext of wisdom, hesitated to adopt new methods, not even knowing how to defend the flock confided to them. The Abbé Clergue, in going in quest of the tradesmen at Toulouse and in establishing organizations for men at Saint-Gaudens was truly a precursor in this work."

He brought the classes and the masses into close contact. As he got young ladies of the wealthiest families to join the Congregation of the Children of Mary, so he brought the

active workers. Wishing to initiate them early in the good work, he insisted on parents taking their children with them into the garrets when they visited the poor. He himself continually traversed the lanes of the little town, particularly the most out-of-the-way and wretched quarters, penetrated into hovels, mounted miserable stairs to reach the attics and shapeless recesses in which were hidden secret destitution and heartrending sorrows. In the country all round the hill on which the town was built he saw many sad scenes. But the spiritual indigence far surpassed the material penury. These people of the fields, since the Revolution, had given up going to church. Absorbed in earthly cares, they wallowed in ignorance and were drifting into complete paganism. He soon became popular in the faubourgs where, smiling and busy, they saw him pass by in quest of some misery to be assuaged, his hands full of alms. One night he was seen laden with a mattress on his shoulders which he was carrying to a sick Spanish woman who was without resources and without a bed, and a bundle of wood which he distributed to the poor to warm themselves in winter. The mattress had been taken off his own bed, and when his father, noting its absence, replaced it, the new one quickly went the way of the first; an incident which reminds one of the Curé of Ars. And when, observing that his son never warmed himself, the father bought him some fuel: "Good windfall for the poor," thought the Abbé, who continued to find warmth in the sunlight and in the love of God. He wanted wood, but not for his own use. Counting beforehand on the charity of one of his friends, he went at night and took some, without saying anything about it. The owner, seeing his provision of fuel diminishing and thinking he was the victim of some robbery, watched and was astonished to see the priest thus secretly transform himself into a porter for the poor. This is another Franciscan trait, reminding one of St. Francis making free with Pietro Bernardone's merchandise and, in his father's absence, loading the table with bread to be given to the poor. The Abbé Clergue, the Saint of Toulouse, followed closely in the footsteps of the Saint of Assisi. The three curates in Saint-Gaudens took their meals together. It often happened that the Abbé Clergue was late and in his hurry would leave his portion of meat untouched, so that he might later come and take it to some poor man. The good he did was incalculable. The number of communicants rose to fourteen hundred, which was considered enormous for that small locality.

He was then in the full flush of youthful vigor and of a robust constitution, but such fatiguing and multiplied labors told on him, and by medical advice he had to suspend his work and go to the celebrated thermal establishment in Cauterets for treatment of a throat malady. While there he sustained a fracture of the left arm through a fall from a horse at the base of the hill of Luz where, seventy-four years before that (1778), was buried the celebrated French Capuchin of the eighteenth century, Père Ambroise de Lombez, "the hammer of the Jansenists," whom the Church, it is hoped, will one day raise to the honors of its altars. He attributed the saving of his life to the Blessed Virgin, whom he invoked at the moment the accident occurred, and dated his vocation from it, feeling convinced that God had preserved him in order that he might give himself more perfectly to His service. He attributed also to Our Lady his preservation from the cholera which about that time ravaged the South of France. Being then senior curate, he arranged with his confrères to go to the succor of the neighboring parishes where the epidemic was severest. The district of Soneich, where the population was decimated, fell to his lot. Upon his arrival he found the curé worn out and exhausted from fatigue, lying on a sick bed. People were dying in every house, so that for a fortnight he had to go from the bedside of the sick and from the confessional to the cemetery, having hardly time to eat, sleep, or say Mass; hearing nothing, day or night, but the painful cries of the dying and their relatives, the dull sound of the gravedigger's spade, and the death-bell.

The first thought of the religious life, the still, small voice of grace making itself heard in the innermost depths of heart or soul, to which he often refers in his notes, goes back to the beginning of his ministry at Saint-Gaudens, if not to the Seminary where he joined the Third Order. The accident during his sojourn at Cauterets decided his choice of his future

purchase from an Italian hawker of religious images of a statue of St. Anthony of Padua holding the Divine Infant in his arms was one of these. It had a directing influence in the life of one who was destined to bear that Saint's name and propagate devotion to him. " A compact was made between them," says his biographer; " a sweet and intimate familiarity henceforward regulated their mutual relations, and St. Anthony began his marvels by heaping favors on his new protégé." Most decisive of all in shaping his course of life was what he calls " the most precious grace he received in this world ". It was near one of Our Lady's sanctuaries, Notre Dame du Bout-du-Puy, on a hill-top opposite the town of Saint-Gaudens—the extremity of the Pyrenees, below which flows the tumultuous Garonne—where he heard the voice of God speaking to his soul as it had spoken of yore to Moses from out of the burning bush. He thus records the incident: " It was a Saturday during the month of Mary (it was always in this blessed month the greatest graces have come to me from heaven) in the second year of my curacy. As usual, I made my pilgrimage to Bout-du-Puy, to visit the good Mother and hear the confessions of two hermits who guard her sanctuary. I was performing my regular devotion of the way of the Cross, the stations of which were erected on the side of the mountain. At the ninth station I suddenly heard a voice which spoke to my soul, but a very distinct voice, ' Thou wilt be a Capuchin '. It was like a violent blow at my heart. It made me tremble, and I was so vividly impressed by it, that on reaching the chapel with my eyes turned toward Mary, ' Oh! my good Mother,' I said to her, ' if that voice comes from heaven, give me to understand, for it terrifies me: although the sacrifice may be terrible, crushing, I am ready. May the will of God be done! But if that voice does not come from heaven, deliver me as soon as possible from it.' "

Far from being delivered from it, it became more persistent. Seeking more light, he made a pilgrimage on foot to Garaison, walking for six hours, setting out at midnight and reaching his destination about seven o'clock in the morning, when he sought the counsel of Mgr. Laurence, Bishop of Tarbes, the future founder of the world-famed sanctuary of Lourdes, to whom he opened his mind in confession. That experienced

prelate, after silently listening to him, replied: " My so
is serious, very serious; let us not go too quickly. Ret
Saint-Gaudens; continue to do the great good God has e
you to do there; always love the Blessed Virgin, and
back next year during the month of Mary: I shall expe
and we'll see what is to be done." In the May follow
went again to Garaison, but Mgr. Laurence had left for '
on diocesan business. " My friend," he said to the Su
before leaving, " I am going with one regret. At thi
last year I made an appointment here with a curate
Saint-Gaudens; he will certainly come. Listen attentiv
what he will tell you, and do not decide too quickly.
case is grave; the decision to be taken is too important t
cipitate anything." The Superior repeated the bishop
vice of the previous year. " The Blessed Virgin had sp
he says; " I obeyed and applied myself to prayer to he
ing the ensuing year, 1855. In the month of Mary a
spoke to my heart. ' Now is the decisive hour!' M
was more than ever full of the great thought of the rel
life; the impression it made was sometimes sweet, but o
painful, so painful that it made my heart bleed. It w
agony, and for three years this agony was a martyrdom.
Lady of Garaison, who held her immolated Son in her
visibly desired to associate me with her sorrows. To
the sacrifice of everything and of myself was indeed a
trial, but nothing as compared with the pain I felt at
ing my father." He was prompted during prayer t
Lady to consult an experienced Jesuit in Toulouse and
the decision to him, and he accordingly opened his min
heart to Père Delage, a former Provincial of the Society.
latter, without a moment's hesitation, said: " God wishe
to be a Capuchin." He asked him to repeat it thrice, wh
did. Then the Abbé Clergue recognized that " Goc
spoken!"

Formidable obstacles to this extraordinary vocation
" The demon," says Père Ernest-Marie, " as if he had fo
the war this new son of St. Francis was going to wage a
him, unfalteringly, for more than fifty years, did every
to thwart his projects. What a victory for Satan, if he

world!" The obstacles were.overcome, but not without a keen struggle, and on 2 March, 1855, the Capuchin Provincial, Père Laurent of Aosta, sent him to Marseilles to make his novitiate. On 13 June, the feast of St. Anthony of Padua, he was given the habit and name of Marie-Antoine. " God, in giving me these two names," he says, " wishes me to remember all my life that it was to Mary and St. Anthony of Padua I owed the grace of my seraphic vocation." He was not the first of his family who received such a vocation and such a name; for his granduncle, who died at Lavaur, was also a Capuchin and bore the name of Anthony. He was known as Father John Anthony of Lavaur. Expelled from his convent by the Revolution, he was for some time administrator of the parish of Fiac.

The novitiate was no interruption of his apostolate. His novice-master was Father Archangel. The chapel of the novitiate was dedicated to Our Lady of Angels, and each novice, on entering, received an initiator who took the name of " guardian angel ". After some months of probation, Père Marie-Antoine became the " guardian angel " of a novice who exercised his patience and his zeal. This was a venerable *curé-doyen* of the diocese of Tulle, who gave up an important parish to become a Capuchin. Sorely tempted to discouragement and on the point of drawing back, he had his trunk packed three times and asked for his soutane; but Père Marie-Antoine, although his junior, dissuaded him, helped him to overcome his temptations and to presevere until he made his profession. It was a victory over the evil one, a prelude to many others. The novice was Father Cyprian of Mosel, one of Père Marie-Antoine's future coöperators as guardian of the Toulouse convent.

Some time after taking the habit, he received from St. Anthony what he designates as a signal favor. " I envied him," he says, " the happiness of seeing and contemplating Jesus and begged him to make me participate in that happiness, not in receiving Him into my arms like him—I knew too well that I was unworthy of such a grace—but in rendering His presence visible and sensible to my soul. And I then heard as it were an interior voice say to me: ' What thou askest of me is easy;

step by step, all that I have done and all that the priest says during holy Mass, and thou wilt see Jesus live again therein; thou wilt always have Him before thine eyes and retain the happiness of His presence.' All at once, the Divine plan of the Sacrifice of the Mass became luminous and unfolded itself before my enraptured gaze. I saw Jesus living and filling all the ages, coming from eternity and returning to eternity, as the priest comes from the sacristy and returns thereto, after accomplishing before our eyes the great work of Redemption which occupies all the ages. I have preached that everywhere, to the great satisfaction of my hearers. For more than forty years I have propagated it under this title ' Marvelous method of hearing Holy Mass—Jesus living under our eyes '."

Novices are rarely sent to preach, but he was one of the exceptions. It was a distinction which was at the same time a humiliation. "The Pyrenean mountaineer singers," he relates, " being on their way to Marseilles, and learning that a curate from the Pyrenees was in the Capuchin convent, offered to sing their best pieces. The Father Guardian fixed the feast of All Saints for it. On this occasion he sent out a large number of invitations anouncing that a grand and beautiful sermon would be preached by a new Father. I was this Father. He called me and said, ' Prepare a grand sermon.'—' Customarily,' I replied, ' I content myself with thinking out my subject well and taking notes which I develop.'—' No, don't do that. It must be a grand sermon, written and learnt by heart, word for word.'—I had to obey. The sermon was written and found perfect by him. It was learnt literally. But as soon as I entered the pulpit, there was a total eclipse of memory, and I could not recall a word. I had to be resigned and content myself with the only thought that occurred to me at that moment. ' My brethren,' I said, ' despite my good will, unable to praise the saints as they deserve, may I at least, by the humiliation God sends me, begin to imitate them. Pray for me that this humiliation may inure to my sanctification.' It seems that grace accompanied these words, for they made a greater impression than the finest sermon could have done; hardened sinners were touched and converted. So, from that

He notes that these humiliations ran counter to all his reckonings and all his merits; that when he was most unworthy of it and made every effort to be glorified, God humiliated him. He lays down these two rules for his guidance in preaching: " (1) to draw all my inspirations for the direction of my soul or for sermons rather from meditation and prayer than from study, which I shall do without anxiety and continually raising my heart to God; (2) to meditate on my subject and be deeply impressed with it, putting myself always as it were in the presence of my hearers, after making a well-ordered plan of all the points, in the dogmatic, moral, and ascetical order, and always using by way of illustration Gospel parables and examples."

On Friday, 13 June, 1856, he made his profession. Then began an uninterrupted external apostolate which occupied his whole life. Marvelous results, which remind us of what we read of the thirteenth-century Friars when the Franciscan Order was in its first fervor, attended it from the start. We may give here a few incidents illustrative of it. He was preaching during the Octave of All Souls at St. Louis in Toulon and giving a retreat to the Third Order in that city. " Great conversions, particularly among men," he relates, " consoled my apostolate. I content myself with recording the most remarkable. One of the wealthiest citizens, who had dissipated his fortune, was seized with despair. He had writen a final farewell to his wife and children, left it on his desk, and went out to throw himself into the sea. Seeing the crowd thronging into the Church of St. Louis, he entered. I was in the pulpit. I do not remember what the Lord inspired me to say, but he was so touched by it, that he waited for me at the foot of the pulpit, and threw himself at my feet. He broke out into sobs and told me his woes, while he accused himself of his faults. I clasped him in my arms, revived his courage, and led him back to his weeping family. They all thought he was at the bottom of the sea. What a joyful returning! His brother immediately undertook to regulate his affairs, and everything was restored to order. The next day the two brothers, the mother, and children received Communion in thanksgiving at my Mass. On the closing day of the Octave I announced to him my departure. ' No, no,

Father,' he cried, seizing my arm, ' no, no, I'll not thus separate from you. My work must be finished: you've rescued me from the demon, but that is not enough; I must be confirmed in good. If you absolutely wish to go, I'll go with you.'—' But, my friend, I am going on foot; I have no money, and I beg all along the way! '—' I shall take no money with me, and I'll beg like you. No, no, it will count nothing to me if I am with you.' We set out then, contenting ourselves, at the different stages, with eating the bread they gave us dipped in water."

Another companion wanted to make the long journey from Toulon to Marseilles on foot, *à la franciscaine*. This was M. Paulin de Montety, a fervent Tertiary of St. Francis, formerly marine engineer on the " Aigle ", a yacht belonging to Napoleon III. A boiler explosion, which severely wounded him, obliged him to renounce his brilliant future. He then devoted to God and good works his premature retirement. At Toulon, where he married, he was the soul of every work and the edification of the city. After his wife's death he went to live in the Marseilles convent, putting on the habit of the Order, and assisting at all the exercises day and night. It was in this capacity he accompanied Père Marie-Antoine to the mission at Toulon.

All this is quite medieval in the best sense of a much-misunderstood word. It recalls the mysterious attraction exercised by St. Francis, drawing all hearts toward him, like the Divine Model he so closely copied. With all the anti-Christianism and Modernism of these later ages, there is not, after all, such a wide, impassable moral gulf between the nineteenth and twentieth centuries and the thirteenth, as some think.

R. F. O'CONNOR.

Cork, Ireland.

[To be continued.]

ECCLESIASTICAL HERALDRY.

III.

5. ESSENTIALS OF ECCLESIASTICAL HERALDRY (CONTINUED).
THE TINCTURES.

AFTER considering the field itself of the escutcheon, namely its various shapes, its nine points, and its possible divisions, we now pass to the tinctures which may be put on the same; and by tinctures are understood the metals, colors, and furs. This heraldic device is the most primitive means of distinguishing one escutcheon from another; in fact, from earliest times, colors have been the most common of symbols. Thus, for instance, the factions of the circus in Rome and later in Constantinople were designated by their colors, the White and the Red, or the Blue and the Green, just as we have "the Blue and the Gray". Among the Irish and Caledonians the king had the privilege of wearing seven colors, the druid six, and the noblemen four. Spain is credited with having been the first of all nations to use black for mourning; and from medieval times the knights and doctors dressed in red or scarlet, as distinguished from others by their learning or valor. But of this symbolism we shall speak later on.

The most common tinctures in heraldry are: two metals—gold and silver; five colors—blue, red, black, green, and purple (intermediate color); two furs—ermine (silver and black spots) and vair (*various color,* silver and blue bells). Two other colors were sometimes used, but they are no longer retained in English heraldry, viz. orange or tawney, and sanguine or murrey. Lastly, there is also a third fur called potent (silver and blue crutches). Animated beings and all objects represented in their natural aspect and coloring are blazoned proper. In blazon, the metals always take precedence of the colors, unless the contrary be specified.

The tinctures, when the coat of arms is found in black print, engravings, or sculptures, are conventionally indicated by dots and lines—an ingenious system introduced about 1630 by an Italian, Fr. Silvestro di Petrasanta, who no doubt took his idea from the divisions of the shield: the blue is represented

Aurum puncta notant, *argentum* absentia signi;
Linea stans *rubeum, cœruleumque* jacens;
Descendit *virida* in lœram, quâ *purpura* surgit,
Cumque jacens stanti linea mixta *nigrum* est.

ILLUSTRATION 4.—TINCTURES—METALS, COLORS, AND FURS.

METALS.

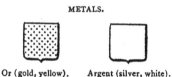

Or (gold, yellow).   Argent (silver, white).

COLORS.

Azure (blue).   Gules (red).   Sable (black).   Vert (green).   Purpure (purple).

FURS.

Ermine.   Vair.

This conventional system must necessarily be used when a coat of arms is given without tinctures in print; else it is impossible, even for a heraldist, to know the colors of the armorial bearings, and consequently to read and describe or blazon the same. Engravers who furnish the etchings of their coats of arms to our bishops should know of this. The M. H. Wiltzius Company, the editors of our official *Catholic Directory,* publish what is sent to them and are not to blame for the blurred and ugly shape of most of our episcopal coats of arms: these, then, should be somewhat larger in dimension, and faithfully give the colors according to the Petrasanta system.

metal be not on metal, nor color, on color. When an exception is admitted, such arms are called *à enquerre,* to be inquired into, viz. for the reason of the exception granted by the sovereign. A remarkable transgression of this law is found in the arms of the Crusader kings of Jerusalem, showing " a *silver* shield upon which five golden crosses are charged ". The motive for this exception is to use the richest tinctures and cause this shield to be unlike that of any other sovereign. So also Leo XIII's coat of arms shows " a *green* poplar tree on a *blue* field ". This rule is modified in the case of varied fields, upon which may be charged a bearing of either a metal or a color. Likewise, a charge in natural color, or proper, may be borne on a metal or a color: instance, the stag proper of the O'Connells is found on a silver and green field. Minor details of a charge are not included in this law: thus a silver lion having a red tongue may be charged on a blue shield. Marks of cadency, denoting different branches of a family, chiefs, cantons, and bordures, are also occasionally exempted from the general rule, being not laid on the shield but *cousus* or sewed to it.

A remarkable arrangement is counterchanging, that is, dividing the field of an escutcheon in such a manner that it is partly a metal and partly a color, and then disposing the charges so that they are reciprocally of the same color and metal: thus, on Bishop Fenwick's family coat of arms the field is red in chief and silver in base; and of the martlets (six martins), the three on the red field are silver and the three on the silver field are red; another example is the conjoined half rose and half fleur-de-lis, *counterchanged.* (Illustration 5.)

ILLUSTRATION 5.—COUNTERCHANGED.

" (Party) per pale, argent and gules, a half rose and a half fleur-de-lis conjoined in the centre, counterchanged." [A patrician family of Augsburg, fl. A. D. 1300.]

Counterchanged.

SYMBOLISM OF THE TINCTURES.

An entire volume might be written on this subject, for, no-withstanding the venerable adage " De coloribus non est dis-putandum! " heraldists have enlarged upon this matter more than upon any other. But we shall not abuse our readers' patience. Let us notice, first of all, the strange denominations of *sable, argent, azure, gueules.* They have their explanation in the condition of physics and chemistry in the eleventh cen-tury, and hence correspond to the four natural elements then admitted by the School, earth, water, air, and fire, with their respective primary properties of cold, dampness, dryness, and heat; thus, by adaptation of these colors and the corresponding elements to heraldry, their names were changed, and sable was used for black and the cold earth, argent for white and the damp water, azure for blue and the dry air or sky, and gules (from *gueule,* lion's mouth) for red and hot fire. Now, for the sake of brevity, we here append in tabulated form the symbolic meaning of the nine principal tinctures—only men-tioning the " extravagant " nomenclature taken from the *planets* for princes' heraldry and from the *gems* or precious stones for peers' heraldry (the latter possibly being of some interest in the choice of the gem in the episcopal ring) :

METALS : *or—gold,* yellow, Sun, topaz,
   expresses riches, strength, faith, purity, con-stancy.

argent—silver, white, Moon, pearl,
   expresses innocence, candor, virginity; (ec cles.) glory of Heaven.

COLORS : *gules—red,* Mars, ruby,
   expresses valor, boldness, intrepidity; (eccles.) martyrdom.

azure—blue, Jupiter, sapphire,
   expresses royalty, majesty, beauty, serenity.

sable—black, Saturn, diamond,
   expresses science, modesty, affliction; (eccles.) mourning.

vert—green, Venus, emerald,

FURS : *ermine* (silver and black), duchy of Brittany (King
Arthur).

vair (silver and blue), from the fur lining of the
scarlet cloak of noblemen, *varii coloris.*

The clerical reader will have no doubt observed that these
meanings of the colors coincide with the symbolism attributed
to them by the Church, for instance in her liturgical vestments.[1]

THE CHARGES OR HERALDIC FIGURES.

We have now reached the central point, as it were, of our
essentials; for it is in the selecting and disposition of these
armorial bearings of the shield that the greatest care is to be
taken. And it is here likewise that the most glaring blunders
are committed.

Charges are various figures or devices on the field of the
shield or escutcheon, distinguishing it from other shields.
These charges are divided into *proper* (which are either *honorary ordinaries* or *subordinaries*), and *common* charges, comprising everything else, whether animate, inanimate, or chimerical.

Proper Charges.

1. The *Honorary Ordinaries* are certain old and very frequent heraldic bearings, " which always have been held in the
highest esteem ",[2] and may be considered as representations
of the wooden or metal strengthenings of the ancient shields,
the Cross among them always having a definite symbolism of
its own. They are variously given as about ten or twelve in
number, and follow in shape and direction the Divisions of the
shield already explained.[3] They are: the Chief, the Champagne or Base, the Fess, the Pale, the Cross, the Bend, the
Barre or Bend Sinister, the Saltire, the Chevron, the Pall, and
the Pile. (Illustration 6.)

The Chief is the upper third of the shield; its diminutive,
the *fillet,* is the lower fourth part of the Chief. Example,
Archbishop Falconio's Chief, showing the Franciscan arms.[4]

---

[1] See ECCLES. REVIEW, February, 1910, pp. 148 ff.

[2] Boutell, *English Heraldry.*

[3] ECCL. REVIEW, February, 1910, pp. 197, 198.

[4] ECCL. REVIEW, March, 1910, p. 337.

The Champagne or Base is the lower third of the shield.

The Fess (Latin, *fascia*) is the central third of the shield; its diminutives are the bar, one-fifth of the shield, and the barrulets, in pairs, one-fourth of the bar. Example, Bishop de Goesbriand's arms, " azure, a fess or ". (Illustration 6.)

ILLUSTRATION 6.—THE HONORABLE ORDINARIES.

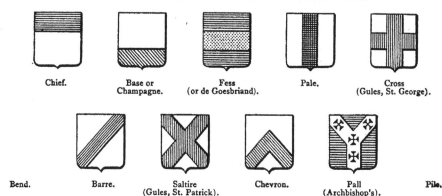

Chief.	Base or Champagne.	Fess (or de Goesbriand).	Pale.	Cross (Gules, St. George).

Bend.	Barre.	Saltire (Gules, St. Patrick).	Chevron.	Pall (Archbishop's).	Pile.

The Pale (Latin, *palus*) takes also one-third of the shield; its diminutives are the pallets, one-half of the pale, and the *indorse,* one-fourth.

The Cross occupies likewise one-third of the shield in all directions. No heraldic device has more varieties than this. They are over a hundred in number, of which some forty are of great beauty and in frequent use. Example, cross of St. George, " argent, a cross gules ". (Illustration 6.)

The Bend (French, *bande*), when not charged, is one-fifth or one-third of the shield; its diminutives are the bendlet, or garter one-half, the cotise one-fourth, and the riband one-eighth of the bend:

The Barre or Bend Sinister, is same size as the Bend; its diminutives are *scarpe* one-half, and the *baton* one-fourth. (When cut short at both ends it is a mark of illegitimacy.)

The Saltire (French, *sautoir*) or Cross of St. Andrew, is one-fifth of the shield's dimensions. Example: Cross or saltire of St. Patrick, " argent, a saltire gules " (Illustration 6) ; the one of St. Andrew being " azure, a saltire argent ".

The Chevron, which is rather more than the lower part of a saltire, has as diminutives the chevronel, one-half, and the couple close, one-fourth in pairs.

The Pall (Latin, *pallium*) is the insignia of an archbishop. Only one-half of it is shown in heraldry, and it resembles a Y: it is borne in the arms of the Sees of Canterbury, Armagh, and Dublin (Anglican), and with us by right could be found in those of Baltimore.

The Pile (French, *pile*), when uncharged, is one-third of the shield; its reverse is called the Point.

Some Rules of the Ordinaries. These Ordinaries may be formed by any of the border lines mentioned above (when treating of the Divisions of the Shield), that is, instead of consisting of right lines, they may be made engrailed, indented, wavy, etc. Occasionally they are borne alone; but more generally they are associated with other bearings, or they have various figures and devices charged upon them. When they are multiplied, several of these figures become diminutives, as stated above.

Paly, bendy, barry, barry-bendy, etc., is said of the field when it is divided by lines in the directions of pale, bend, barre, etc.; instance, the United States national ensign, " a barry of thirteen argent and gules ". In chief, in fess, etc., or fesswise, bendwise, etc., mean in the shape or direction of a chief, a fess, etc.—and should not be confounded with *on,* v. g. on a chief, etc.

Charges displayed on a bend slope with it, and if on a saltire or chevron they slope with its limbs, the central charge being erect (see Illustration 6, *the Pall*). Lastly, following the rule of tinctures, charges must in all cases differ in tincture from the field.

Symbolism of the Ordinaries. As the heraldists have referred the principal points of the shield [5] to the different parts of the human body, so also these first and primary heraldic bearings find their meaning, in being applied to a knight whom we imagine to be represented on the shield, and thus the pale is his lance, the bend and bend sinister his shoulder belt, the fess his scarf, the cross and saltire his sword, the chevron his boots, the bordure and orle his coat of mail.

2. The *Subordinaries* are another group of devices, second in rank to the Ordinaries. The following are more commonly

ILLUSTRATION 7.—THE SUBORDINARIES.

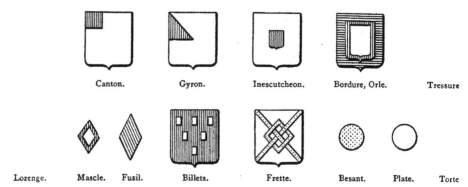

Canton.	Gyron.	Inescutcheon.	Bordure, Orle.	Tressure

Lozenge.	Mascle.	Fusil.	Billets.	Frette.	Besant.	Plate.	Torte

The Quarter (French, *franc-quartier*), when charged, takes one-fourth of the shield, and overlies the charges; its diminutive is the Canton; and the Gyron is its half diagonally divided. A rare instance of the canton is met with in the ecclesiastical heraldry of France, 1808, when Napoleon made all his Concordat archbishops and bishops, counts, barons, and senators of the Empire, with for the archbishops a dexter canton of the chief " azure, a cross pattee or ", for the bishops a sinister canton, " gules, a cross couped or ", and for the senators also a sinister canton, " azure, a mirror in pale or over against a serpent argent ". But all these cantons vanished at the Restauration.

The Inescutcheon is displayed " in pretense " upon another shield larger than itself, and usually placed " en cœur " or on the centre point *over all*. Instances, the king of Spain bears for inescutcheon the three fleur-de-lis of the Bourbons; a titular bishop may thus show the arms of his titular see.

The Roundels, in constant use at all times, are called be-
sants when or, plates when argent, torteaux when gules, etc.,
a reminiscence of the Byzantine coins of the Crusaders.

An Annulet, or a plain ring, was sometimes blazoned as a
false roundel.

When a field is covered or semee with some of the above
devices it is respectively called gyronny, lozengy, fretty, be-
santee, etc.

Marks of cadency (French, *brisures*) are figures and devices
introduced to distinguish the different members and branches
of the same family. Sometimes it was done by the use of a
bordure or other difference. Sometimes, especially in English
heraldry, it was by the use of the following figures, overlying
the original coat of arms: the label, crescent, mullet, martlet,
annulet, fleur-de-lis, rose, cross moline, octofoil, to designate
the eldest, second, third, etc., down to the ninth son and his
descendants—a device, however, which cannot consistently be
carried through all the ramifications of a family for a succession of generations.

Common Charges.

Besides the *honorable ordinaries.* and the *subordinaries,*
which are purely heraldic figures connected in their origin
with the shield itself, there are the *common* charges: for these,
the knights in the early days of heraldry ransacked the animal,
the vegetable, and the mineral kingdom, as well as the range
of things natural and artificial, for cognizances which would
be distinctive, and at the same time emblematically suggestive
(*armes parlantes*) of the name or title of the bearer of them.
Of these common charges, Guillim, in his *Display of Heraldry*
(A. D. 1611), gives the following quaint enumeration: " The
formes of pure celestiall bodies mixt with grosse terrestrials;
earthly animals with watery; savage beasts with tame; fowls
of prey with home-bred; these again with river fowles; reptiles with things gressible; aery insecta with earthly; also
things natural with artificiall." And in this again heraldry
has but followed in the footsteps of antiquity. Æschylus, in
his Seven Chiefs before Thebes, minutely describes their
shields with the emblems engraved on them and the chosen
mottoes. Homer's description of the shield of Achilles is a

classical masterpiece. Virgil and Ovid depict their heroes bearing on their shields and helmets figures by which they are easily recognized during battle. Hence also, to strike their foes with terror or at least to keep alive ancient traditions, all nations have had figured symbols or national emblems: the Athenians an owl, the Carthaginians a horse's head, the Saxons a bounding steed, the chief of the druids several stags, the Romans the she-wolf, a raven, and later an eagle; the Gauls, auxiliaries of Cæsar, a lark, the hieroglyphic of vigilance; the Germans, according to Tacitus, had similar emblems; the Celtic races of Caledonia had the thistle, still to be found in Scotland's coat of arms, as also the druidical harp, in the one of Ireland.

By natural figures are meant angels, man (human figure and some limbs), animals, birds, and fish, trees, and plants, celestial objects, and devices from the elements; artificial ones are drawn from instruments used in sacred or common life: war, the arts and sciences, and various trades; chimerical figures and monsters are taken from imagination.

Angels, winged and vested, are occasionally introduced in heraldry, their office however being rather to act as "supporters" to armorial shields.

Human beings are of very rare occurrence in heraldry, except also as supporters. "Moors' heads" and "Saracens' heads" appear in some coats; arms also (*cubit arms*) right and left, blazoned dextrochere and senestrochere. We all know of the "red *hand* of Ulster", and of the "*heart* of the Bruce" still emblazoned with a royal crown in the shield of the descendants of "good Sir James Douglas". And lastly there is that strange heraldic freak, the three *legs* conjoined, carried in the escutcheon of the Isle of Man, which led a Poursuivant of Arms to remark that "the arms of Man are legs"; this curiosity is likewise found on the coins of ancient Sicily (Trinairia), and the medieval family of Tremaine bears three human arms united in the same manner.

Among animals, the lion, "the king of beasts", has always occupied the first place; hence many sovereigns have borne lions upon their royal shields: witness England, from the time

" the king of birds ", the eagle. In more recent heraldry the lion is a favorite supporter. There is moreover the demi-lion rampant, the lion's head, the lion's face, the lion's jambe (or paw), which are frequent charges. Their tincture may be or, argent, azure, gules, and sable. When not rampant (in the erect attitude), they are rather blazoned leopards, as also lioncels, when multiplied or diminutive. Deer, stags, the horse, the greyhound, boars, bulls, calves, rams, the wolf, and the lamb shared heraldic service and honors with the lion, and many others in modern armory. Not a few animals, besides, appear as *armes parlantes:* the bear is borne by Fitz Urse, the ram by Ramsey, the lamb by Lambert, etc. It should be remarked, moreover, that these animals generally look to dexter, and in blazoning are technically described: a lion, as rampant (erect), passant (walking), statant (standing), rampant gardant (looking), sejant (sitting), couchant (at rest), coward (looking back), etc.; a deer, as lodged, at gaze, tripping, at speed; a stag, as attired of his antlers; others, as armed, hoofed, unguled, langued, vorant, etc.

Next to the king of beast in popularity appears, as we said, " the king of birds ", the eagle, especially in German heraldry. As far back as A. D. 1275, the shield of the Emperor of Germany or Emperor of the Romans shows on a field of gold a black eagle displayed having two heads (a feature preserved in the Austrian and Russian escutcheons), to represent the Western and Eastern Empire; whilst Imperial France, Prussia, and our own United States show but a single head. The eagles of the Duchy of Lorraine-Hapsburg are blazoned as alerions,[6] and small eagles as eaglets. In a later period, after a few other birds, the eagle was joined by the following: falcon, ostrich, raven, cock, parrot (blazoned popinjay), crane (with a pebble blazoned vigilance in paw dexter), swan (blazoned proper, i. e. white with red beak and legs), peacock (blazoned in his pride when with tail expanded), pelican (said in its piety when feeding its young), etc. The favorite bird, however, of early heralds was the martlet or heraldic martin, which is still with us. In blazonry, birds are said to be rising, volant, soaring, and birds of prey armed, beaked, and membered (beak and talons of a different tincture).

[6] Alerion is the anagram of Loraine.

Almost all the then known fish have been made use of in early heraldry, but nearly always as the symbol of a name: the barbel, the luce (or pike), the herring, the roach, etc. A favorite is the dolphin (the Dauphin, the eldest son of the King of France, had it for his arms, since the conquest of Dauphine, A. D. 1364). Let us mention also the escallop-shell (the badge of the pious pilgrims to Jerusalem *outre mer,* or Compostella, or the Mt. St. Michel). In blazoning, fish are described as finned, naiant, hauriant, etc., and the dolphin sometimes as embowed or bent.

Reptiles and insects occur but rarely; bees and bee-hives, flies, butterflies, snails, and even bats are sometimes found in later periods. Insects are blazoned volant when flying; reptiles, gliding, nowed (twined into knots).

The chapter of trees, plants, and flowers is a rich and interesting part of heraldry. Among the trees are distinguished in particular the palm tree, the pine or poplar tree, the olive tree, the oak, etc. From among the plants, we have already mentioned the thistle of Scotland; there is also the trefoil, the quatrefoil or primrose, the shamrock, etc. Fruits are found in use occasionally, sheaves (blazoned garbs) and ears of corn, leaves, and chaplets (instance, the crancelin, German *Kränzlein,* that crosses the shield of Saxony, an augmentation conferred, it is said, with the Duchy of Saxony on Bernard of Ascania by the Emperor Barbarossa, who took from his head his own chaplet of rue and threw it across the Duke's shield: *Se non è vero,* etc.). There remains something to be said about the two flowers of England and of France, the rose and the lily or fleur-de-lis (see Illustration 5). The heraldic *rose,* the " white rose " of York as well as the " red rose " of Lancaster, has five leaves of the respective color, but the five smaller leaves of the calyx, blazoned *barbs,* are green, and the seeds in the centre are golden. Both roses are at times surrounded with rays, and each is then termed *rose en soleil:* this is the meaning of the " sun of York ", mentioned by Shakespeare after the " winter of discontent ". The heraldic

the lily iris and showing the head of a spear, was first adopted as his royal ensign by Louis VII, A. D. 1137, and charged on his shield of arms, " azure, semee of fleur-de-lis or ", that is, the fleur-de-lis freely scattered over the field, which is *France Ancient.* About A. D. 1365, Charles V of France reduced the number of the fleur-de-lis to three, and this shield is now known as *France Modern.* The fleur-de-lis is also borne on many shields in all countries.

As celestial objects there is the sun, with rays or, termed in glory or eclipsed; the moon, blazoned crescent, increscent or decrescent; the stars, termed estoiles when with six or more wavy rays or points, and *mullets* when with five, and sometimes more, points formed by right lines; comets; clouds; the rainbow, generally per fess or rounded bend, with four barrulets or, gules, vert, and argent, when proper. Let us add also: fire (flames, a pyre, torches) ; water (waves, or a fountain) ; earth (mountains, hills, rocks).

Of artificial devices we shall give simply an enumeration: sceptre, crown, globe or orb; castles, turrets, bridges; helmets, hatches, buckles, arrows, trumpets, spurs, stirrups, swords, spears, hunters' horns, horse shoes; sickles, cornucopia, scales, keys, knots, annulets, gems, cups; bells, churches, pilgrim's staff, ships or galleys, beacon or lighthouse; lyre; letters of the alphabet, initials, etc.

Lastly, there are a few imaginary and fabulous beings admitted in heraldry: griffin or gryphon, dragon, hydra, sphinx, centaur or sagittary (supposed to be a badge of King Stephen of England, A. D. 1066), harpy, medusa, mermaid (more frequently as a crest), salamander, phœnix, unicorn (generally as a supporter), etc.

Rules of the common charge. Charges may be placed either simply on the field, or on one of the ordinaries. Sometimes, one of the ordinaries is placed over a charge, in which case the charge is said to be debruised by the ordinary. Three charges of one kind are placed two above and one below, unless blazoned in fess or in pale.

ALOYSIUS BRUCKER, S.J.

[To be continued.]   •

Analecta.

S. CONGREGATIO RITUUM.

I.

DE "POSTCOMMUNIONE" IN MISSA SS PERPETUAE ET FELICITATIS MM. ET "COMMUNIONE" IN MISSA S. AGNETIS SECUNDO.

Fridericus Pustet, S. Sedis Apostolicae necnon Sacrorum Rituum Congregationis Typographus, novas parans Missalis Romani editiones, eidem Sacrae Congregationi sequentia dubia pro opportuna solutione humiliter proposuit, nimirum:

I. Decreto diei 25 Augusti 1909, Festum Ss. Perpetuae et Felicitatis Martyrum e simplici ritu ad duplicem minorem evectum, die sextae Martii assignatum cum Officio et Missa propriis atque ad universam Ecclesiam extensum est. Iamvero de Communi non, cum desit littera *N.* Quaeritur quid sit eligendum?

II. In Communione Festi S. Agnetis secundo, die 28 Ianuarii, inter diversas Missalis Romani editiones antiquiores, recentiores et recentissimas aliud parvum extat discrimen. Nempe post illa verba: *quaerenti bonas margaritas, inventa* in quibusdam editionibus additum est verbum *autem,* in quibusdam deest. Quaeritur utrum in futuris editionibus Missalis Romani addendum sit verbum *autem,* vel non?

Et Sacra Rituum Congregatio, exquisito Commissionis Liturgicae suffragio, reque accurate perpensa, ita rescribere rata est:

Ad I. In Missa *Me expectaverunt,* si fuerint plures Martyres, sive Virgines sive non Virgines "*Postcommunio*" post verba *Martyribus tuis* addantur *N. et N.,* uti in Orationibus praecedentibus.

Ad II. Stetur editioni Gradualis Romani nuperrime approbatae, typisque Vaticanis evulgatae, in qua verbum *autem* non habetur.

Atque ita rescripsit, die 3 Decembris 1909.

> Fr. S. Card. MARTINELLI, *Praefectus.*

L. * S.

> PH. CAN. DI FAVA, *Substitutus.*

II.

DE FESTO SANCTARUM MARTYRUM PERPETUAE ET FELICITATIS IN ECCLESIA PROPRIA.

Rmus Dnus Willibrordus Benzler, Episcopus Metensis, exposuit quae sequuntur:

Decreto Sacrorum Rituum Congregationis, diei 25 Augusti 1909, festum Sanctarum Martyrum Perpetuae et Felicitatis, ad ritum duplicem minorem evectum est pro tota Ecclesia, ipsique adsignata est, ut dies quasi-natalitia, sexta Martii. Quaeritur: Utrum in Ecclesia propria, Festum harum Ss. Martyrum Titulare, quod hucusque celebrabatur die septima Martii, translato Festo S. Thomae Aquinatis, amodo recoli debeat die sexta Martii, an potius relinquendum sit in die natalitio?

Et Sacra eadem Congregatio, exquisito Commissionis Liturgicae suffragio, re sedulo perpensa, ita respondendum censuit: *Affirmative* ad primam partem; *Negative* ad secundam, iuxta Decretum n.° 3876 *Quebecen.* 13 Decembris 1895, ad III.

Atque ita rescripsit, die 28 Ianuarii 1910.

Fr. S. Card. MARTINELLI, *Praefectus.*

L. * S.

PH. CAN. DI FAVA, *Substitutus.*

III.

DE QUIBUSDAM PECULIARIBUS CONSUETUDINIBUS IN OFFICIO, IN MISSA, ALIISQUE SACRIS FUNCTIONIBUS.

Hodiernus Rmus Episcopus Dioecesis Cephaludensis a Sacra Rituum Congregatione insequentium dubiorum solutionem humillime postulavit, nimirum:

I. Utrum tolerari possit longaeva consuetudo adhibendi in expositione insignis Reliquiae S. Crucis D. N. C. I. nonnullus ritus qui servari debent coram SSmo Sacramento solemniter exposito, scilicet genuflectendi utroque genu ante eam transeundo, illam incensandi a celebrante genuflexo et illam obtegendi velo violaceo si concio habeatur; vel potius standum sit decretis iam latis N. 2324 *Brixien,* 15 Septembris 1736 et N. *2727 Lucionen.,* 23 Maii 1835?

II. Et quatenus negative ad primam partem, an consuetudo illa servari possit saltem in Feria VI Parasceve, non obstante decreto N. 3201 *Montis Regalis,* 20 Martii 1869, ad VII?

III. In choro adest consuetudo recitandi flexis genibus quocunque anni, tempore Antiph. *Salve Regina* cum versiculis et oratione *Omnipotens sempiterne Deus,* post antiphonam finalem de tempore, expleta hora prima, vel, si chorus non interrumpitur, expleta hora tertia ante Missam conventualem. Petitur, utrum servari ista consuetudo etiam quando Antiphona finalis de tempore est *Salve Regina,* ita ut bis repetatur; et quatenus affirmative, an semper dicenda flexis genibus etiam diebus Dominicis et tempore paschali?

tini in Officio Defunctorum et in Missa pro Defunctis, quando chorus silet?

VI. Utrum in Missa solemni *Benedictus* cani possit ante elevationem, vel standum sit praescriptioni Caeremonialis Episc. Lib. II, cap. VIII, 70-71?

VII. Utrum in benedictione quae datur cum Reliquiis Sanctorum genuflectendum sit in choro vel standum? Et quatenus affirmative ad primam partem, utrum etiam a Canonicis?

VIII. Missam solemnem in Cathedrali celebrans, quando est Canonicus, induit paramenta in aula capitulari et ministri sumunt vestimenta in sacristia. Quid de hoc? Standumne consuetudini, an decretis N. 2703 *Recineten.*, 16 Martii 1833 et N. 3937 *Urgellen.*, 11 Decembris 1896?

Et Sacra eadem Congregatio, exquisito Commissionis Liturgicae suffragio, propositis dubiis ita respondendum censuit:

Ad I et II. Standum decretis.

Ad III. Negative ad utrumque.

Ad IV. Negative.

Ad V. Negative ad primam partem; et Negative ad secundam, iuxta Caeremoniale Episcoporum Lib. I, cap. XXVIII, N. 13.

Ad VI. Standum Caeremoniali Episcoporum.

Ad VII. Genuflectendum est ab omnibus.

Ad VIII. Standum Decretis.

Atque ita rescripsit, die 16 Decembris 1909.

Fr. S. Card. Martinelli, *Praefectus.*

L. * S.

Ph. Can. di Fava, *Substitutus.*

IV.

Dubia circa Ecclesiae et Altarium Consecrationem.

Rmus Dnus Paulus Huyn, Episcopus Brunensis, Sacrorum Rituum Congregationi ea quae sequuntur reverenter exposuit:

I. In Consecratione Ecclesiae consecratum fuit Altare, cuius

cruces, at cum sacris oleis tantum primae quatuor et sexta, omissa quinta. Quid in casu faciendum? Hinc quaeritur:

II. An signandae et ungendae sint primae quinque cruces, an primae quatuor et sexta?

III. An responsum huic quaestioni valeat etiam pro Altaribus portatilibus?

IV. An in Consecratione Altarium portatilium Episcopus consecrans debeat ipse omnes cruces propria manu ex incenso formare et candelas imponere; an his in actionibus a sacerdotibus adiuvari possit?

Et Sacra Rituum Congregatio, exquisito Commissionis Liturgicae suffragio, omnibus perpensis, ita rescribendum censuit:

Ad I. Orator seu consecrans in casu acquiescat.

Ad II. *Affirmative* ad primam partem; *negative* ad secundam.

Ad III. *Affirmative.*

Ad IV. Episcopum consecrantem in praedictis actionibus posse adiuvari a sacerdotibus.

Atque ita rescripsit, die 14 Ianuarii 1910.

Fr. S. Card. MARTINELLI, *Praefectus.*

L. * S.

PH. CAN. DI FAVA, *Substitutus.*

V.

DE BENEDICTIONE PARTIS TANTUM SACRORUM OLEORUM.

Postulato Rmae Curiae Episcopalis Mantuanae ad Sacram Rituum Congregationem pro opportuna declaratione transmissum sub die 24 Ianuarii 1910 circa consuetudinem antiquam etiam immemorialem benedicendi Feria V in Coena

VI.

De machina " Grammofono " in Sacris Functionibus.

R. D. Bellarminus Ruggiero, Archipresbyter Curatus Vallis-fioritae, Squillacensis Dioeceseos, de consensu sui Rmi Epis-copi Administratoris Apostolici, a Sacra Rituum Congrega-tione sequentis dubii solutionem humillime expostulavit; ni-mirum :

An in Missa solemni et aliis functionibus, in Ecclesiis, qui-bus est carentia magistri organi vel cantorum, etiam laicorum, liceat uti machina vulgo dicta *Grammofono* pro cantu, stricte liturgico gregoriano, partium variabilium Missae solemnis, hymnorum et aliorum canticorum?

Et Sacra eadem Congregatio, exquisito Commissionis Li-turgicae suffragio, proposito dubio respondendum censuit: *Negative.*

Atque ita rescripsit, die 11 Februarii 1910.

Fr. S. Card. Martinelli, *Praefectus.*

L. * S.

Ph. Can. di Fava, *Substitutus.*

VII.

De usu Kalendarii Regularium, quibusdam in casibus.

Rmus P. D. Ioseph Sailer, Moderator Generalis Canoni-corum Regularium Lateranensium, Congregationis Austriacae, Praepositus et Abbas S. Floriani, Sacrorum Rituum Congre-gationi ea quae sequuntur pro opportuna declaratione humil-lime exposuit; nimirum:

I. Ab ultimo ante tres annos defuncto Parocho perinsignis Ecclesiae Abbatialis S. Floriani, praedictae Congregationis, extructum fuit in ipso oppido S. Floriani nosocomium, cuius administratio, iuxta statuta suae fundationis, penes Parochum pro tempore supradictae Ecclesiae residere debet. Iamvero in capella seu sacello dicti nosocomii, in quo quotidie Missa celebratur ab uno ex Canonicis supramemoratae Abbatiae, usu venit ad Divina peragenda Directorium seu Kalendarium Canonicorum Regularium.

II. Iisdem Canonicis Reg. S. Floriani, in parva Civitate

peratoris Iosephi II adnexa fuit municipalis Ecclesia, in qua pariter usu venit Kalendarium Canonicorum Regularium.

III. In eadem Civitate *Wochlabruch* est domus Sororum scholis addictarum (*Schulschwestern*) apud quas multae puellae bonis litteris instituendae degunt. In domo hac duo habentur sacella, in quibus Sacrum peragitur et quae a duobus Canonicis Regularibus supradictae Abbatiae S. Floriani inserviuntur, cum ipsis demandata fuerit ab Episcopo Linciensi cura spiritualis tam sororum quam puellarum.

Hisce expositis, quaeritur: An in primo, secundo et tertio casu adhibere valeat Directorium seu Kalendarium proprium Canonicorum Regularium Lateranensium praefatae Congregationis?

Et Sacra eadem Congregatio, exquisito Commissionis Liturgicae suffragio, omnibus sedulo perpensis, ita rescribere rata est:

Ad I. *Negative.*

Ad II. *Affirmative,* dummodo Ecclesia sit filialis Ecclesiae Parochialis, vel praefatae Congregationi Canonicorum Regularium Lateranensium concredita.

Ad III. In sacello principali publico vel semipublico *negative;* in altero sacello, utpote privato, *affirmative;* iuxta decreta n.° 3862 *Urbis et Orbis* 9 Decembris 1895, et n.° 3910 *Ruthenen.* 22 Maii 1896.

Atque ita rescripsit, die 11 Februarii 1910.

Fr. S. Card. MARTINELLI, *Praefectus.*

L. * S.

PH. CAN. DI FAVA, *Substitutus.*

S. CONGREGATIO CONSISTORIALIS.

DE RELATIONIBUS DIOECESANIS ET VISITATIONE SS. LIMINUM. (*Continued.*)

ORDO SERVANDUS IN RELATIONE DE STATU ECCLESIARUM.

quo modo sustententur: quae sit eorum fama: utrum aliqui in maioribus ordinibus constituti adsint in dioecesi a suis Praepositis eiecti vel dimissi; et quaenam sit eorum agendi ratio.

103. Quibusnam muneribus obeundis se addicant in dioecesi: quo fructu, qua fama: an eorum hospitalia, orphanotrophia, scholae, etc. iuxta canonicas praescriptiones Ordinarii vigilantiae subsint.

Qui curam animarum in parochiis sibi addictis exercent, an in omnibus, quae ad istam curam spectant, ab Ordinario dependeant.

104. Si religiosi adsint quaestuantes, utrum opportuna S. Sedis decreta hac de re edita ab eis serventur, et an aliquid inconveniens in his acciderit.

105. Utrum aliquod habeat Episcopus cum regularibus offendiculum in exercitio iurisdictionis sive suae, sive sibi a iure delegatae.

106. Si congregatio aliqua dioecesana adsit, dicatur in quem finem fuerit instituta, an fini suo respondeat, et quo fructu. An in alias dioeceses se diffuderit, et quo vinculo domus extradioecesanae cum dioecesanis nectantur.

CAP. X.

De institutis religiosis mulierum.

107. Utrum generatim ita religiose vivant ut fidelium exemplo sint: an forte aliqui abusus irrepserint, praesertim post ultimam relationem, et quinam.

Utrum in monasteriis monialium, Praelatis regularibus subiectis, omnia prout de iure procedant, an aliter; et hoc in casu quomodo provisum fuerit.

108. Utrum circa clausuram serventur leges canonicae.

109. Utrum monasteriorum reditus fideliter administrentur: an monialium dotes fuerint persolutae et investitae, et quomodo administrentur.

An ipsae quoque moniales exemptae Ordinario rationem reddant de bonorum administratione iuxta canonicas leges.

110. Utrum pro confessione monialium constitutiones et decreta apostolica serventur.

111. Quae *vitae activae* addictae sunt, quibus operibus incumbant, quo spiritu, qua fidelium utilitate et Ecclesiae aedi-

112. Si adsint quae infirmis in privatorum domiciliis inserviant, aut rem domesticam in hospitalibus aliisque virorum domibus gerant, quomodo caveatur ne quid inconveniens accidat: an cautelae ipsae rite custodiantur; an aliquid hac in re deplorandum sit.

Si religiosae adsint quaestuantes, utrum opportuna S. Sedis decreta hac de re edita ab eis serventur, et an aliquid inconveniens in his acciderit.

113. Si instituta mere dioecesana habeantur, an haec cohaerenter ad canonicas leges regantur, in quem finem fundata sint, quo fructu vivant, an etiam extra dioecesim diffusa sint, et an variae domus ab invicem independentes sint, an non.

Cap. XI.

De populo generatim.

114. Quinam in universum sint populi mores, et an specialia vitia in eo invalescant, et quaenam.

115. Utrum dominicis et festis diebus fideles generatim abstineant ab operibus servilibus, missam audiant, et hos dies, prout christianos decet, sanctificent.

Si inter varia dioecesis loca differentiae notabiles adsint, hae notentur.

116. Eodem modo referatur quae sit observantia legum abstinentiae et ieiunii, et Paschalis praecepti.

117. Pariter indicetur quae sit frequentia ad sacramentalem confessionem et ad S. Communionem in variis dioecesis locis pro diverso personarum sexu, conditione, aetate.

118. Utrum parentes solliciti generatim sint, ut recens nati saltem intra hebdomadam baptismo abluantur: an sint qui nimium differant, aut forte negligant, vel prohibeant baptismum ministrari.

119. Utrum matrimonia mere civilia sive concubinatus habeantur, et qua frequentia. An alii speciales vigeant abusus contra sanctitatem matrimonii.

121. Utrum parentes generatim curent filios suos non solummodo in sinu familiae sed etiam extra, et maxime in scholis, christianis moribus instituere.

122. Utrum fideles qui graviter decumbent generatim extrema sacramenta deposcant.

An, quo numero et quibusnam de causis funera civilia contingant.

123. Utrum in exercitio iurium politicorum et civilium curent fideles ita agere, vel tales eligere, quo religioni et libertati Ecclesiae plene consulatur.

124. Utrum adsint in dioecesi sectae secretae, praesertim massonicae.

An socialismus aliaeque societates ab Ecclesia damnatae in dioecesi radicem fixerint et propagentur.

An *spiritismi* praxis habeatur.

Quid fiat ut fideles ab his omnibus avertantur, et quo profectu.

CAP. XII.

De iuventutis institutione et educatione.

125. Referatur in primis ac generatim quae sit ratio institutionis et educationis filiorum in dioecesi iuxta usum legesque civiles.

Utrum contra sacrum Ecclesiae et parentum catholicorum ius opponantur christianae iuventutis educationi obstacula; et quid fiat ut haec amoveantur.

Utrum scholae distinctae iuxta sexum sint, an utrique sexui communes: quae mala inde sequantur: et quaenam remedia adhibeantur.

126. Si agatur de dioecesi in catholica natione constituta, dicatur utrum ibi scholae publicae primordiorum, vulgo *elementares,* bonae vel innoxiae generatim sint, et an ibidem per ecclesiasticos viros aut idoneos magistros christiana doctrina digne tradatur: an potius noxiae sint.

Et in hoc casu an scholae liberae habeantur: quomodo sustententur: a quot alumnis frequententur: an Ordinarii vigilantiae et inspectioni subsint.

127. Si agatur de dioecesi ubi catholici cum acatholicis

Et si scholas proprias non habeant, et frequentare cogantur scholas publicas mixtas, an saltem catholica fides ibi non offendatur, et catholicis alumnis iusta libertas relinquatur ut in fide per ecclesiasticos viros vel idoneos magistros instituantur.

128. Quod si pueri et puellae scholas publicas primordiorum adire cogantur, quae noxiae sint, quid fiat ut iuventus a perversione et corruptione immunis fiat.

129. Utrum scholae mediae vel superiores quae in dioecesi habentur, vel ad quas dioecesani confluere solent, hostiles sint, vel non, catholicis veritatibus et doctrinis.

Et si sint hostiles, quid fiat ut adolescentes ab erroribus et vitiis praeserventur. An habeantur scholae mediae vel superiores catholicis propriae: et quinam sit earum status.

130. Utrum opera quae *post-scholaria* dicuntur, ut recreatoria, circuli, scholae catecheticae, oratoria serotina et festiva, ad sanam christianae iuventutis institutionem et praeservationem in dioecesi habeantur; quaenam, et quo fructu.

Cap. XIII.

De piis sodalitatibus aliisque religiosis consociationibus.

131. Utrum adsint piae sodalitates aliaeque religiosae consociationes rite institutae: quot et cuius nominis: an habeantur eae quae a S. Sede potissimum commendatae sunt, ceu illae a SSmo Sacramento, a Rosario, a christiana doctrina, aliaeque pro pueris et puellis in fide, pietate, morumque puritate excolendis.

132. Utrum erectae sint in ecclesiis paroecialibus et religiosorum, vel habeantur etiam quae in propriis et distinctis ecclesiis exsistant.

An in ecclesiis monialium sodalitates virorum adsint, et qua facultate.

133. Utrum ab auctoritate ecclesiastica iuxta canonicae legis praescripta dependeant: quem fructum afferant: an forte aliquod gignant incommodum.

134. Utrum adsint tertiarii in saeculo viventes, cuius ordinis, quo fructu: an saepe congregentur, et an sint exemplo fidelibus.

CAP. XIV.

De piis legatis et eleemosynarum collectionibus.

136. Utrum habeantur in dioecesi pia legata missarum, aliorumve religiosorum onerum, et an de iisdem Curia dioecesana indicem habeat cum recensione onerum et indicatione redituum.

137. A quibus generatim administrentur, an fideliter et fructuose.

138. Utrum missis legatorum aliisque obligationibus intra praescriptum tempus regulariter satisfiat: et si hoc nequeat fieri, an reditus praesertim missarum fundatarum Ordinario tradantur: an adsint qui hac de re ad officium revocari mereantur, aut revocati iam sint, et quo fructu.

139. Utrum et quo fructu fiant in dioecesi piae collectiones eleemosynarum a S. Sede praescripta vel commendatae pro communi Ecclesiae bono, ut, pro Fidei propagatione, pro sancta Infantia, pro redemptione captivorum, pro obolo S. Petri, pro Terra sancta.

140. Utrum fiant collectiones, speciales pro ipsius dioecesis necessitatibus, ut, pro fidei conservatione, pro praeservatione ab erroribus et cleri pro sustentatione, si opus sit.

141. An et quaenam aliae collectiones eleemosynarum in dioecesi usuveniant.

Si religiosi vel religiosae quaeritantes habeantur, an tot sint numero ut nimium gravamen fidelibus afferri videatur.

CAP. XV.

De operibus piis et socialibus.

142. Utrum hospitalia, orphanotrophia, brephotrophia aliaque similia caritatis instituta in dioecesi fundata sint; et an dependeant ab auctoritate ecclesiastica iuxta S. Concilii Tridentini praescripta. Et nisi dependeant, referatur an in iis quae a materna Ecclesiae protectione et directione subtracta sunt, catholici spirituali adsistentia frui saltem libere possint.

143. Utrum adsint in dioecesi opera illa quae *socialia* dicuntur quibus dum consulitur bono morali et religioso fidelium, prospicitur etiam eorum temporali utilitati vel necessitati, ut, asyli pro infantibus, patronatus pro iuvenibus utriusque sexus, circuli pro iuventute catholica, aut pro studiis peragendis, con-

sociationes operariorum, agricolarum, mulierum in hunc vel alium pium finem vel mutuum subsidium, arcae nummariae aliaque similia.

144. Utrum consociationes et opera haec socialia, et potissimum qui eis praesunt, debitam in omnibus Ordinario et Summo Pontifici reverentiam praestent, et in iis quae fidem, mores et iustitiae leges attingunt, S. Sedis directioni et moderationi omnino subsint.

145. Cura ne sit ut hisce consociationibus et operibus praeficiantur qui non nomine tenus, sed corde et opere catholici sint. Et an caveatur, quatenus opus sit, ut qui hisce consociationibus et operibus adscripti sunt, aut beneficia et subsidia ab iis nanciscuntur, a vitiis recedant, in fidei doctrina instituantur, et christianam vitam ducant.

146. Utrum caveatur ne in hisce catholicis consociationibus connumerentur sectis secretis adscripti, increduli, impii vel religioni adversi, qui consociationes ipsas vel earum opera a recto fidei et iustitiae tramite deducere possint.

Cap. XVI.

De editione et lectione librorum et diariorum.

147. Utrum in dioecesi edantur libri, ephemerides, illustrationes, diaria obscena vel impia, vel utcumque religioni noxia; a quibus, et quali cum diffusione et detrimento.

148. Utrum libri et diaria impia vel obscena aliarum civitatum dioecesim ingrediantur, ibique diffusa sint, et quaenam potissimum sint.

149. Utrum strenue a catholicis agatur et praesertim a parochis et a sacerdotibus, ut libri et diaria obscena vel impia a dioecesi removeantur, adhibita etiam, si fieri potest, civilis auctoritatis opera.

An cleri et maxime confessariorum cura sit ut libri et diaria obscena vel impia a catholicis familiis arceantur, et a fidelibus non legantur.

150. Utrum libris et diariis noxiis alia opponantur religiosa et honesta: quot sint, quomodo diffusa et quo fructu.

Datum Romae, die 31 mensis decembris anno 1909.

C. Card. De Lai, *S. C. Consistorialis Secretarius.*

E SACRA CONGREGATIONE INDICIS.

DAMNANTUR VARIA OPERA.

JOSEPH TURMEL. Histoire de la théologie positive, depuis l'origine jusqu'au Concile de Trente. Paris, Gabriel Beauchesne et C.ie.

— Tertullien. Paris, Bloud et C.ie.

— Saint Jérôme. Ibid.

ANGEL PULIDO FERNANDEZ. Espanoles sin patria y la raza sefardí. Madrid, E. Teodoro, 1905.

LUIS GAMBARA. La sociología; manual para estudiantes de derecho, de filosofía y de bachillerato y de cultura general. Barcelona, casa editorial, 1909.

— Sociología criminal; manual para abogados, médicos forenses estudiantes de derecho y de medicina y de cultura general. Ibid., 1909.

— Antropología criminal; especial para abogados, médicos, estudiantes de derecho y de medicina y de cultura general. Ibid., 1909.

— Psicología y antropología criminal; curso dado en el salón doctoral de la universitad de Barcelona. Ibid., 1909.

Itaque nemo cuiuscumque gradus et conditionis praedicta opera damnata atque proscripta, quocumque loco et quocumque idiomate, aut in posterum edere, aut edita legere vel retinere audeat, sub poenis in Indice librorum vetitorum indictis.

IOSEPHUS TURMEL et FORTUNATUS RUSSO. Decreto S. Congregationis, edito die 5 Iulii 1909, quo quidam libri ab eis conscripti notati et in Indicem librorum prohibitorum inserti sunt, laudabiliter se subiecerunt.

Quibus Sanctissimo Domino Nostro Pio Papae X per me infrascriptum Secretarium relatis, Sanctitas Sua decretum probavit, et promulgari praecepit. In quorum fidem etc.

Datum Romae die 9 Martii 1910.

FRANCISCUS Card. SEGNA, *Praefectus.*

L. * S.

THOMAS ESSER, O.P., *Secretarius.*

ROMAN CURIA.

PONTIFICAL APPOINTMENTS AND NOMINATIONS.

The Holy Father through the Secretary of State nominates by Brief of—

15 January, 1910.—The Rev. Henry A. Brann, D.D., Rector of the Church of St. Agnes, New York, Domestic Prelate.

25 January, 1910.—James McAdam, Esq., of London (England), Knight of the Order of St. Gregory.

1 February, 1910.— The Rev. Thomas Kennedy, Rector of the English College at Valladolid (Spain), Domestic Prelate.

17 February, 1910.— Mgr. Joseph Hendrick, of the Diocese of Rochester, Secret Chamberlain of the Pope, Domestic Prelate.

The Holy Father through his Major-domo nominates by billet of—

11 February, 1910.—Mr. Helier R. H. Goselin, of Errwood Hall, in the Diocese of Shrewsbury, England, Secret Chamberlain of Sword and Cape.

3 March, 1910.—Mr. David S. Kenny, of the Diocese of Trenton, U. S. America, Secret Chamberlain of Sword and Cape.

The S. Congregation of Consistory nominates by Decree of—

17 February, 1910.—The Rev. John Joseph Nilan, of the Archdiocese of Boston, to the Episcopal See of Hartford, U. S. America.

4 March, 1910.—The Rev. Patrick Richard Heffron, rector of the Archiepiscopal Seminary of St. Paul, Minnesota, to the Episcopal See of Winona, U. S. America.

Studies and Conferences.

OUR ANALECTA.

The Roman documents for the month are:

S. CONGREGATION OF RITES:

1. At the instance of Fr. Pustet, certain corrections are made in the new edition of the Roman Missal for the feast of SS. Felicitas and Perpetua, and of St. Agnes (Secundo).

2. The celebration of the feast of the Holy Martys, SS. Felicitas and Perpetua, *in ecclesia propria*.

3. Certain customs which have crept into the liturgy of the Office and Mass are censured and corrected.

4. Solves some doubts regarding the consecration of a church and altars.

5. The blessing of a part only of the Sacred Oils.

6. Forbids the use of the " Graphophone " at liturgical services.

7. The use of the Ordo of Regulars.

CONSISTORIAL CONGREGATION: Conclusion of the *Normae Communes* laid down for bishops in making their diocesan report and visitation *ad limina*.

S. CONGREGATION OF THE INDEX publishes list of recently condemned books.

ROMAN CURIA: List of recent Pontifical appointments and nominations.

RECENT ADDITIONS TO THE MARRIAGE LAWS OF THE UNITED STATES.

In the current issue of the ECCLESIASTICAL REVIEW YEAR BOOK there is given (pp. 180-211) a collection of the State matrimonial laws in so far as they affect the class and condition of parties to a marriage, the prohibited degrees of kindred, the marriage license, and the duties of the solemnizing clergymen. Since the collation of these marriage statutes

existing law are given below so as to bring up-to-date the information in this regard contained in the YEAR BOOK for 1910.

ARIZONA.

" Males under 18 and females under 14 shall not marry."

ILLINOIS.

Common-law marriages are by statute void in this State unless a license has been obtained, " and the marriage solemnized " as provided by law, i. e., celebrated before a minister of the gospel, or certain public officials. This will practically prohibit common-law marriages.

IOWA.

The marriage of first cousins is now prohibited by statute.

MAINE.

" Every ordained minister of the gospel, clergymen engaged in the service of the religious body to which he belongs, or person licensed to preach by an association of ministers, religious seminary or ecclesiastical body, whether a resident or non-resident of this State, and of either sex, may solemnize marriages therein, after being duly licensed for that purpose." The definition of the solemnizing minister has thus undergone a slight change. And licenses to solemnize marriages must now be applied for to the Secretary of State on blanks furnished for that purpose, to be signed by the applicant and certified to by any municipal officer of the town wherein the applicant resides, or where the marriage ceremony is to take place. This license to solemnize marriages shall continue in force until revoked, for cause, after notice and opportunity to appear and be heard.

MINNESOTA.

The marriage certificate must now be returned to the clerk of the district court who issued the license.

MISSOURI.

White persons are now by law forbidden to intermarry with

negroes, Chinese or Japanese. Persons who shall solemnize
any such marriage are liable to a fine of $500, imprisonment
for one month, or both.

New Mexico.

An Act of 1909 validates marriages otherwise legally contracted, which were celebrated during the year 1905 without
a license.

North Carolina.

The class of persons allowed by statute to solemnize marriages is further enlarged by the addition of the words " or
minister authorized by his church ".

Rhode Island.

" Any non-resident minister or elder who is pastor of any
church in this State which has no other pastor competent to
act or any bishop or any other similar officer who is the official head of the religious work of his denomination in this
State may obtain a license from the Secretary of the State
Board of Health." These licenses to solemnize marriages are
valid until " such time as the holder thereof shall be domiciled
outside this State ". Notice of removal from one place in the
State to another within the State must be given to the town
registrar.

If the woman to be married is not a resident of the State,
she must obtain a marriage license at least five days before
the marriage.

The overseer of the poor of the town or city wherein any
minor resides may give consent in writing to that minor's
marriage.

South Dakota.

Intermarriage between persons of the African and persons
of the Caucasian race is now prohibited.

Wisconsin.

A certificate of marriage is now given to the parties about
to be married, completely filled out as far as possible from the

within three days to the local registrar of vital statistics. The marriage license is kept by the solemnizing clergyman as *prima facie* evidence of his authority to perform the ceremony.

THE MERITS OF FATHER BOARMAN'S CATECHISM ONCE MORE.

To the Editor, The Ecclesiastical Review.

With regard to Father Boarman's reasons for the things objected to by me, I am very much pleased at the spirit in which he takes criticism of his little Catechism.

It seems to be much better than many catechisms that have been put on the market to worry the minds of our children and confuse our teachers; and, as he admits, there is much room for improvement.

I still hold to most of the criticisms made by me in the issue of Nov., 1909, p. 632, viz.—

1. I do not think it at all advisable to treat of the reasons why St. Joseph is the *foster-father* of our Lord. That is certainly going too deep for *children;* I think most instructors in catechetics would not treat of such subjects even before adults.

2. Christ saved us by His *life* more than by His sufferings and death, i. e. if He had become man only for an instant, He would have redeemed the world, even without any suffering or death. I believe this is a teaching in the schools, and it is not condemned by authority. It seems to have been the general practise of certain writers to insist too much on the more prominent parts of Christ's life and to forget some other truths that are not insisted on enough in our teaching in the school and in the pulpit. And this is one of the points, viz., the greatest work done for our Redemption was the fact of God becoming man, i. e. by His *life,* more than His sufferings and death.

3. Facts are facts, and should be enumerated when the question asks for facts. Are *miracles* among the chief works of Christ or not? I believe the miracles are used in theology as an argument to prove some truths that are "abiding", e. g. the divinity of Christ, the foundation of the Church, etc., etc.

4. "Tradition" should have a better definition than that of the catechism. It is quite difficult to prove that the *Apostles* taught many doctrines of the Church that are not contained in the Bible.

the Church is the true Church which Christ founded, is beyond me. Some of the Popes did not believe explicitly that they were infallible; some did not believe that the line was unbroken. It seems to me that the *teaching* of the Popes through the centuries may be regarded as an indication of the truth that the Papacy is an argument in favor of the truth that the Church is that of Christ.

6. Of course *cannot* implies no moral guilt—in ignorance; but the question in the catechism asks for a fact as an answer, and *do not* expresses a fact and not *cannot*. Most educated Protestants *can,* but as a matter of fact *do not,* get a knowledge of the true faith, etc.

7. Pledges, I always understood, bound one in conscience, according to the intention of the one making the resolution, or accord to the nature of the obligation one is under. Else what is the use of ever taking any resolutions either in the tribunal of Penance or out of it?

8. In this country holidays of obligation *are not* kept as Sundays, and therefore no obligation should be expressed in a catechism. The general law is suspended in this case by the general consent (tacit or otherwise) of our bishops, etc. People accuse themselves of this sin, and I do not think they ought to be led by catechisms or prayer-books to see sin where our lawful superiors see no reason for them to be disquieted, e. g. when they work on such holidays.

9. With regard to the six sins against the Holy Ghost, it is well to quote St. Matthew 12:31-32: "Therefore I say to you: every sin and blasphemy shall be forgiven men, but the blasphemy of the Spirit shall not be forgiven." Father Maas (*Com. on St. Matt.,* p. 148) says: "We may consider the *sin* against the Holy Ghost as consisting in a resistance of evident truth, the *blasphemy* of the Spirit consists in ascribing the signs wrought in proof of divine truth, to the power of the devil." He then shows that the six special sins enumerated in our catechism were thought out by St. Augustine. There is no agreement among the Fathers or Scripture writers as to the meaning of the text in question; it still seems to me better to omit this answer from our catechisms.

10. Hell—what it is and where it is—has always been a favorite question among the writers in the Church. At the present day, theologians seem to consider Hell more as a *state* than as a *place.* It seems to my mind, that it makes little difference in what *place* the soul is, so long as its state is all right, i. e. in the *state* of sanctifying grace, and not in the *state* of mortal sin. For instance, Father R. Moss, O.P., in his *Oxford Conferences* "On Grace", (1899-1900),

Ravignan, "has no need of changing 'anything in the state of the sinner's soul in order to punish him. He abandons him to his sin, and in that the reprobate finds his everlasting hell." It is a thought the importance of which cannot be overestimated. (P. 112, "Hell, the Failure of Grace.")

Bishop Hedley, in his Retreat, says it is not God who is "angry", it is the sinner who places a barrier between himself and that Being who alone is his happiness. The sinner, therefore, damns himself. A soul in mortal sin only requires the dissolution of its mortal frame to be, by that very fact, in Hell.

Most modern theologians, it seems to me, teach very little about the *place* where Hell is and insist more on the two ideas of the loss of the beatific vision and the *poena sensus*.

11. Baptism of Desire is, to my mind, in most cases no *wish* at all. Most Mohammedans, savages, Chinese, etc., who die in the perfect love of God never *wished* for Baptism, because they never knew in any way about Christ and His ordinances; "nil volitum, nisi prius cognitum" is the principle. Father Maher (*Psychology*) says: "Desire may be defined as a mental state of longing or want aroused by the representation of some absent good." An "implicit" desire, it seems to me, is no desire at all.

I may here add some more criticisms and suggestions in regard to Father Boarman's little book.

On page 7: "God made all things for His own honor and glory;" add: *and* for our use and salvation.

P. 12 (end) : To open the gates of heaven for all.

Pp. 14, 15 : Put the dates March 25th and December 25th after the word "celebrated"; because these are disputed.

P. 20: This would be more complete: the Church of Christ is the union of all the faithful in doctrines of faith and morals, under one visible head.

P. 20 :In sending the Apostles, Christ used some other words; use them.

prove that the Church has the right to give commandments. Is this correct? " He that hears you, hears Me," etc., would be better.

Pp. 33, 40: Sacrilege may be here defined. It is referred to several times, but I have noticed no definition of it.

In the question " When does one receive a sacrament unworthily? " there seems to be something wrong with the answer; "when he receives in mortal sin any sacrament *but* Baptism and Penance." How about Extreme Unction when the person is unconscious? Then, when Baptim *is* received, is there any mortal sin left on the soul of the individual?

In the following question there must be a correction of the construction of the sentence—to read: because they imprint on the soul a character that lasts forever, instead of, they imprint a character on the soul that lasts forever.

P. 43: It seems to be the teaching of most theologians nowadays that it is not mortal sin to neglect Confirmation, except it be out of contempt for the sacrament.

P. 53: It seems beter to say that the penance should be performed as soon as *possible,* instead of as soon as convenient, as in the text.

SCRUTATOR.

TWO ODES OF FRAY LUIS DE LEON.

As a foreword to these first versions in English of two odes of Fray Luis de Leon, it may not be out of place to note that, since Meléndez y Pelayo—whom many consider the greatest critic of contemporary Europe—proclaims this gentlest of authors as the glory of Spanish religious lyric poetry, he has assumed an importance to the literatures of the world at large, such as is extraordinary after the long neglect in which his poems have been suffered to remain.

Luis de Leon — he is sometimes, although without real warrant, called Luis Ponce de Leon—was born in 1527 at Belmonte, Cuenca, or, according to lesser authorities, at Granada, Andalusia; he was the son of Iñes de Valera and Don Lope de Leon, Seigneur of Port-Lope and Councillor of Castile. His death occurred at Madrigal, Old Castile, 23 August, 1591.

When fourteen years of age he was sent to the University

he gradually attained such eminence that the supreme honor of the chair of theology in the University was conferred on him at an early age. It is also known that he lectured in the courses on Saint Thomas and Durandus and was consultor in many of the important questions of his time.

Such brilliant qualities, as well as his growing fame in literature, were not long in arousing bitter rivalry; he was denounced before the Holy Office for having made without permission a Spanish version of the Canticle of Canticles, together with annotations savoring of Judaism and Lutheranism. Pending these charges he was held in the prison of the Inquisition for five years, and only after appearing twenty times before the tribunal was he formally acquitted, 13 August, 1577.

The University of Salamanca went out *en fête* to welcome and lead him back to his class-room, which is still preserved in its original simplicity. Professors, noblemen, doctors, and students acclaimed him in their brilliant ceremonial of robes and torches. When they had brought him to his desk and gathered in throngs to hear his statement, he merely took up his old lecture with the words, now passed into a Spanish proverb, " *Como deciamos ayer* "—"As we were saying yesterday."

The prose of Fray Luis is esteemed for its purity among sixteenth-century models of style, for besides a number of treatises in Latin he has left several much-appreciated works in Spanish, such as *La Perfecta Casada* " The Christian Home " and a mystical commentary on " The Names of Christ."

in the art of his transitions, in the greatness of line, in lyric movement.   None has risen so high, nor so infused, as he has done, the classic forms with modern spirit.   The marble of Pentelicon under his hands becomes Christian statuary, and across the wealth of his reminiscences of Greek, Latin, and Italian authors, of Horace, Pindar, Petrarch, Virgil, and the Hymn of Aristotle to Hermias, there stirs a breath of life that transfigures and rejuvenates them all.   It is an error to think that originality in poetry consists in the ideas.   A poet so scholarly and cultivated, so devoted to antiquity, and filled with such erudition and doctrine as was Fray Luis de Leon, can be also as simple in expression, and as candid and ingenuous as is possible to any poet—and not through artifice or study but because in conjunction with the idea there sprang from his soul the pure, perfect, and simple form, such as they whose ears have been accustomed from infancy to the clamor and violence of odes written after the manner of Quintana, can neither understand nor appreciate."

THE HEAVENS AT NIGHT.

When I contemplate o'er me
  The heaven of stars profound,
And mark the earth before me
  In darkness swathed around,—
  In careless slumber and oblivion bound;

Then love and longing waken
  The anguish of my soul;
Mine eyes with tears are taken
  Like founts beyond control,—
  My tongue sighs forth at last its voice of dole:—

O Temple-Seat of Glory,
  Of Beauteousness and Light,
To thy calm promontory
  My soul was born!   What blight
  Holds it endungeoned here from such a height?

What mortal aberration
  Hath so estranged mankind

No thought amid his slumber
  He grants impending fate,
The while heaven's dawns keep number
  In step apportionate,
  And life is filched away, his poor estate.

Alas! awake, sad mortals,
  And measure all your loss!
Statured for deathless portals,
  Can souls such birthright toss
  Away, and live for shadows vain and dross:

Alas! let eyes beholding
  Yon pure celestial sphere
Unmask the wiles enfolding
  The life that flatters here—
  The little day of mingled hope and fear.

What more is earth than giver
  Of some brief moment's pause,
Compared to Time's vast river
  Where all is swept like straws,
  Yea, all that is, that shall be, and that was?

Who to that throng of splendors
  Eternal can set gaze,
The order it engenders,—
  Its majesty of ways,—
  The concord and the wisdom it displays,—

How through her silvered arches
  The moon encircles; squired
By Learning's star she marches,
  While Love's fond planet, fired
  In beauty, follows her so long desired.

How down his outer spaces
  Red Mars is rolled aflame;—
How Jupiter retraces
  The horizon's tranquil frame,
  And soothes the heavens amorous of his name;—

Beyond swings Saturn, Father

Who can behold such vision
  And still earth's baubles prize?
Nor sob one last decision
  To rend the bond that ties
  His soul a captive from such blissful skies?

There hath Content her dwelling;
  Peace, her bright realm; and there
Enthronéd fair past telling
  Love-Sacred hath repair,
  With joys and glories cent'ring round her chair!

A Beauteousness unmeasured
  Shows cloudless there, and Light
Of perfect ray is treasured
  Through days where comes no night;
  There Spring Eternal flowers without a blight.

O fields of Truth-Abiding!
  O pastures green with rills!
Mines where are treasures hiding!
  O joyous-breasted hills!
  Re-echoing vales where endless balm distils!—

TO A LATE REPENTANT MAGDALENE.

See, Lisa, how the wealth of gold
  That once thy haughty brows adorned
With rifts of snow proclaims thee old;
  Alas, how often have I warned,
  Time flies; withdraw ere thou are scorned?

See how already all are gone
  Who vowed thee service in thy youth,
So they no more may look upon—
  They whose eternal vows seemed truth!—
  Thy furrowed cheek and blackened tooth.

From all thy past what dost thou keep
  Save bitterness? What is the fruit
Of thine endeavor but to weep

What pledge to thy vain cause hast made
 To hold thee thus in hostile ranks
Against thy sovereign good arrayed?
 What evil-boding shackle clanks
 Upon thee in the galley-banks—

Where thy soul joyless lies? For whom
 Dost watch, for whom these jealousies,
These wearying plaints, the ceaseless fume,
 And sighs and importunities,
 Ignoring thy true maladies?

Yea, see with life's poor shreds endowed,
 Lighter than bird did ever press
'Gainst Leda's heart its bosom proud
 For adoration and caress,
 Thou claspst to thee thy bitterness!

O happier had thy beauty been
 That gift high heaven itself bestows
In sign whereof the robe serene
 Of sanctity is given to those
 Unstainéd by earth's joys or woes.

But swiftly die the hours away,—
 For merciful the heavens can be
That fix duration to the day;
 Full soon the fevered breast is free
 Of grief, and sleep is liberty.

Lo, how the gentle Magdalene,
 For all the squalor of her state,
Could with sweet fervor intervene
 And quench the threatened flames of fate
 With breast contrite and conflagrate!

The fires of her misguided love,
 Consumed in her devotion pure,
She found herself preferred above
 The guest who deemed himself secure
 Of virtue, whereof none is sure.

Prone there before His feet divine
  In her abandonment she lay,
And made an offering more fine
  Than e'en His chosen thought to pay
  With hands, and lips, and eyes, that day.

She bathed them in such flood of tears,
  Her own deep stain was cleanséd too ;
The gold unloosed about her ears
  Dried at His feet to beauty new ;
  And peace to her own peace she drew,

With sighs : " O solitary door
  Where grief may knock, last remedy
To save me, hospice to restore
  My frame diseased, incline to me
  The countenance of Thy divinity !

" Alas, what can I offer now
  Who hath lost all ?—these hands so used
To wound Thee—these vain eyes, O how
  Raise them to Thine ?—these lips so bruised,
  How plead with them so self-accused ?

" My very love is an offence,
  My service soils, my very prayer
From evil takes its eloquence ;
  Mine eyes so baleful in their snare,—
  May they be tearful founts fore'er !

" O let them bathe Thy holy feet,
  My tresses dry Thee ! let the seal
Of my lips dolorous entreat
  Their pity on me where I kneel
  And risk condemning for my zeal !

" To Thee as most accords, I bring
  One languishing of wounds so sore
As claim supreme physicianing,—
  Awaiting from Thy perfect lore
  The word that heals to echo evermore."

THOMAS WALSH.

DE LICEITATE VASECTOMIAE.

The Rev. Fr. Stephen M. Donovan's Rejoinder to Mgr. J. De Becker.

Responsa R. P. De Becker ad solutionem dubiorum de liceitate vasectomiae a me propositam, necnon sententia RR. PP.
Collegii Maximi, S.J., Lovanii, duas praecipue continent ob-
jectiones contra doctrinam ibi allatam. Negant, imprimis, hi
theologi mutilationem de qua in casu, levem esse; ut opinatus
sum ego, quum scripsi: " Quod si fit, quum mutilatio omnino
levis dicenda sit, vix veniale peccatum excedet, nisi fortasse
ratione motivi graviter mali aliarumque circumstantiarum
lethalis culpa habeatur." Dicit praeterea P. De Becker: " Ad
auctoritatem civilem quod attinet, ea nullum jus habet relate
ad vitam et libertatem innocentium et consequenter ea prorsus
excluditur a jure mutilandi innocentem etiam sub praetextu
boni communis." Negat ergo potestatem civilem ullum jus
habere praescribendi operationem de qua in casu. Quibus
difficultatibus in sequentibus satisfacere conabor.

1. Mutilatio definiri potest: cutis, musculorum, aliarumque
corporis partium integritatis solutio subitanea violentiâ cau-
sata. Quae enormis esse potest quando, videlicet, " impedit
ex toto actum humanum aliquem qui competeret homini secundum illam partem amputatam, ut in manus dextrae ampu-
tatione, ubi aufertur omnino actus humanus, natus competere
secundum illam manum; vel non enormis, id est, non impedi-
ens actum humanum, ut amputatio digiti, vel alicujus partis
digiti." [1] Quum vero peccaminositas mutilationis eo funda-
mentaliter sit petenda quod homo actum dominii usurpat qui
soli Deo competit;—solus enim Deus vitae ac membrorum con-
ditor et conservator eorumque dominus absolutus est [2]—sequitur, quod pro ratione injuriae Deo irrogatae, mutilatio vel
levis erit vel gravis: ideoque mutilatio gravis, grave, mutilatio
vero levis, leve peccatum constituet. Fieri vero nonnunquam
potest, ut ea mutilatio quae physice loquendo levis est, mora-
liter sumpta gravis evadat: et hoc dupliciter. Vel quia apta
est quae mortem directe causet; vel quia aut necessario aut in
intentione agentis effectus habet secum junctos qui citra rea-
tum peccati mortalis intendi nequeant. Mutilationem, ergo,

---

[1] Cf. Scotum, 4 Sent., dis. XV, qu. 3, n. 4.
[2] Sporer, Tract. V, n. 396.

quae operatione vasectomiae indúcitur, si in se spectetur, adhuc levem esse censeo; nec video cur gravis malitia statui
possit praecise ob functionem, qua operatio hominem privat.
Id enim verum esset, ut opinor, si obligatio speciem propa-
gandi et ideo functionem conservandi organorum ad hoc a
Creatore destinatorum, personalis esset seu in individuum ca-
deret. Hoc vero, nemo est, quod norim, qui dixerit. Caeterum, ad praxim quod attinet, non facile fingi potest ratio
qua haec operatio cohonestaretur; immo, circumstantia aliqua
gravem malitiam. inducens saepe aderit: ideoque non raro
erit graviter peccaminosa.

Huc spectat alia ejusdem generis operatio, castrationem
dico; quae privata omnino auctoritate in pueros fieri solebat,
ut vox suavis et acuta ad canendum eis conservaretur. Porro
certum est, non defuisse theologos gravitate et doctrina con-
spicuos, quos citat S. Alphonsus,[3] qui eam licitam statuebant.
Scimus quidem, Benedictum XIV[4] hanc praxim condemnasse
ac sententiam negantem approbasse. Est tamen opinio P. Ballerini, sententiam illorum theologorum qui liceitatem evira-
tionis affirmabant, sua probabilitate adhuc gaudere.[5]

Age nunc, negari non potest castrationem simplici vasectomia multo graviorem esse, non solum ob mutilationem ipsam
physicam verum etiam quia eviratis potentia generandi ita
adimitur ut ne minima quidem spes effulgeat eam amplius
recuperandi. Quod de illis, qui per vasectomiam steriles efficiuntur, non verificatur. His enim, juxta artis medicae peri-
tos, integritas vasis divisi per subsequentem operationem restitui potest; et ita organorum functio illaesa habebitur, acsi
prima operatio nunquam facta fuisset.

Quae omnia cum ita sint, aliquantula forsan probabilitas
doctrinae a me propositae tribui potest: ideoque immerito, ut
mihi videtur, rotunde rejicitur tanquam " plane improbabilis
et damnosa ".

2. Quo melius satisfiat difficultati secundae, fusius declarare
juvat, quinam sint aegroti de quibus in priore articulo age-
batur. Non de aegrotis quibuscumque, igitur, sermo est; sed
de istis quorum aegritudo rationem quasi criminis habet; in

---

[3] Lib. 4, Tract. 4, n. 374.
[4] De Syn. Dioec. Lib. XI, Cap. VII, n. IV et V.
[5] Vide Ballerini, Opus Morale, Tom. II, Tract. VI, Sect. V, n. 47.

quos, aliis verbis, sive abusu potuum alcoholicorum, mor-
phinii, aliorumque ejusdem generis medicamentorum, sive
venereis aliisque in vivendo excessibus, conditio quaedam
pathologica atque systematis nervosi mala dispositio inducta
est; ex qua provenit innata reapse et fere beluina propensitas
ad furtum faciendum, mortem aliis vel sibimetipsis infer-
endam, raptum perpetrandum, id genus alia.

Porro notandum est, nocentem intelligi eum, qui sciens et
volens legem justam violaverit. Is pro gravitate delicti vel
capitis vel alius poenae minoris juste condemnari potest, uti
communissime tenent theologi. Si vero hujus potestatis quam
habet gubernium civile, reum videlicet puniendi, ratio quae-
ratur, ea peti nequit ab admissa culpa theologica seu peccato
formali;—de existentia enim peccati non est auctoritatis civilis
judicare—nec ex eo quod republica jus directum habeat in
vitam et bona temporalia hominis nocentis; sed potius ex eo
quod potestas illa est a Deo concessa ad tuendam ordinis socialis et moralis stabilitatem ac firmitatem, cui non satis cautum
esset nisi sanctiones poenales adessent. Quousque autem se
extendat haec puniendi facultas, praesertim si de poena mortis agatur, non unica est theologorum sententia. Etenim,
juxta nonnullos, inter quos citatur S. Thomas, homo omnino
innocens, qui tamen in judicio externo tanquam reus apparet,
et potest et debet capitis condemnari, etiamsi judex privata
scientia certo eum innocentem esse cognoscat.[6] Cujus rei alia
sufficiens ratio non habetur nisi quia " bonum publicum ex-
poscit, ne juris ordo pervertatur ".[7] Eadem res, mutatis mu-
tandis, sustineri potest, quum de poenis ipsa morte minus gravibus agatur. Immo vero mente capti libertate privantur atque
in custodias includuntur; et leprosi a communitate segregati
tenentur. Ad propositum nostrum ea quoque faciunt quae
communiter, quamvis non unanimiter, a theologis statuuntur
circa obligationem resarciendi damnum ex sola culpa juridica
ortum.

Concludendum est, igitur, duas requiri conditiones ut puni-
tio aliqua a lege civili juste statui possit: (1) ut ea certe et
directe cedat in bonum commune; et (2) ut in punitione seu
poena infligenda rectus servetur ordo juridicus. Quae con-

---

[6] Vide Sporer, Tract. V, n. 182.
[7] Sporer, l. c.

ditiones satis, ni fallor, verificantur in casu nostro. Prima quidem manifesta est omnibus qui in re sociali et morali apprime sunt versati. Ad secundum quod attinet, sufficit notare, cautissime omnino procedi, juxta tenorem legum in pluribus statibus hujus regionis nunc vigentium, priusquam ad vasectomiam veluti ad extremum denique remedium deveniatur.

Quod ultimo loco adducitur de impotentia auctoritatis civilis impedimenta matrimonialia statuendi, ultro conceditur; quamvis admitti debeat: " sacramentum matrimonii cum ad conservationem quoque et incrementum societatis humana dirigatur, cognationem et necessitudinem habere cum rebus ipsis humanis, quae matrimonium quidem consequuntur, sed in genere civili versantur: de quibus rebus jure decernunt et cognoscunt qui rei publicae praesunt." [8] At de vasectomia dubitari potest utrum simplicem sterilitatem an potius impotentiam ideoque verum impedimentum dirimens inducat. Qua de re nihil certi statui potest. Pro impotentia stare fortasse dixeris P. Gasparri, qui ait: " Idem (adest non mera sterilitas, sed impotentia) dicas si testes adsunt, sed non resident in loco debito aut non habent cum membro virili debitam conjunctionem, ita ut seminis vel praeparatio vel conductio fieri nequeat." [9] Utrum vero haec verba casui nostro applicari possint, equidem nescio. Caeterum, quum res sit dubia et juxta superius dicta impotentia, si quae est, rationem habeat impedimenti temporanei potius quam perpetui, validitas legum quae vasectomiam spectant quaeque his ultimis annis hac in regione latae sunt, infitianda non videtur ex defectu potestatis rei publicae constituendi impedimenta matrimonialia pro baptizatis.

THE QUESTION OF GRAVE MUTILATION.

To the Editor, THE ECCLESIASTICAL REVIEW.

In his very brief, though very positive, reply to Father Donovan's questions regarding the lawfulness of " vasectomy " under certain grave conditions, Monsignor de Becker says (April number, p. 475) that " a grave mutilation is permissible only in so far as it is necessary for the conservation of life. Therefore the motive given is plainly inadequate to justify the performing of the operation in question."

---

[8] Leo XIII, Encycl. Arcanum.

[9] Tract. Canon. de Matrimonio, edit. altera, Vol. II, p. 356, n. 528.

In proposing the difficulty for discussion Father Donovan stated (March number, pp. 272-3) that many physicians had found among the good effects of the operation of vasectomy on inveterate offenders against the Sixth Commandment, the following—" they begin as it were a new life; they refrain from their bad habits, and they are made stronger against temptation."

Now if it is quite lawful for one whose physical health is threatened, to undergo a surgical operation for his body's sake only, and suffer " grave mutilation " in this case at the surgeon's hands, e. g., the amputation of an arm, or the excision of other more important members of the body, would not the spiritual good that is said to follow the operation of vasectomy, justify it in those serious cases mentioned by Father Donovan? In other words, an operation that it is quite proper to perform for the cure of a merely physical ailment, may surely be undertaken when there is a reasonable expectation that it will tend to remove a moral malady. It may be that there is some fallacy lurking in this argument, or that the principle may take us too far afield. Be that as it may, the question here is whether it is fairly applicable to the particular case in point. For it is more than a mere assumption that the special class of persons above proposed for the operation of vasectomy are in effect suffering from a local physical disease or irritation which is lessened by the operation. Thus there is a twofold motive for the performance of the operation, and good grounds for saying that both moral and physical good results from it.

PERPLEXUS.

RUSSIA AND THE UNITY OF THE CHURCH.

To the Editor, THE ECCLESIASTICAL REVIEW.

I have read with much pleasure Father Leen's admirable article upon " The Russian Orthodox Church " in the April number, but there are just two statements in it to which I would like to call attention.

magnificent office to him in the *Menaea* on his feast day, 6 December, will testify.[1]

The facts involved are even more effective in showing the unity of the Russians with the Holy See at that period. At the dawn of the Crusades and over thirty years after the break between the East and the West, Pope Urban II caused the body of St. Nicholas to be removed from Myra in order to prevent it from being desecrated by the Mohammedan invaders of Asia Minor and had it transported to Bari, near Brindisi, in Italy, where it was solemnly reïnterred in a special shrine (the church of St. Nicholas built specially for that purpose) on 9 May, 1089. The Pope thereupon instituted the Feast of the Translation of St. Nicholas.[2] The Greeks, still smarting over their excommunication in 1054, and notwithstanding their great veneration for St. Nicholas, absolutely refused to acknowledge the new feast, taking the position that the Pope was a schismatic if not actually a heretic. The Russians, however, joyfully received the new feast and composed a special office for it and still celebrate it 9 May, many of them even going to Bari nowadays to venerate the relics of the Saint.[3] This shows that the Russians at that time took quite a different view of the Pope from the Greeks, considering him as the centre of unity and following his prescriptions.

The second statement is Father Leen's exact translation of a phrase in the oath taken by the members of the Holy Synod of Russia, which is given literally exact and not by way of summary as in Silbernagel quoted under the article " Holy Synod " in the *Catholic Encyclopedia.* He might well have given the paragraphs from the oath introducing that phrase whereby the members bind themselves to carry out the will of the Czar, defend his sovereignty and support his supremacy even with their lives, if need be. It is true that the particular phrase cited by Father Leen was suppressed in 1901, perhaps owing to Catholic criticism of it, and is no longer to be found in the oath taken by the later members of the Holy Synod. But the liturgical forms of the Russian church have not been changed ; and they are as positive on this point as the oath was.

In the " Order for Election and Consecration of a Bishop " (St. Petersburg, 1901), the bishop-elect is summoned to the Synod and the ceremony begins: " Honored Father N., our Sovereign Lord

---

[1] See the Orthodox Euchologion, Venice, 1898, p. 629. " Feast of our Father among the Saints, Nicholas, Bishop of Myra in Lycia, the Wonderworker."

[2] See letter of Urban II, 9 October, 1089; Migne, *Pat. Lat.*, Vol. 151, pp. 307-309.

[3] See Maltzew, *Die Nachtwache*, Berlin, 1902, pp. 700-702, where the various *troparia* and *kontakia* are given in Slavonic and German; also the Sluzhebnik (missal), St. Petersburg, 1901, p. 391.

Nicholas Alexandrovitch, Autocrat of All the Russias, by an edict signed by his Majesty's name commandeth (*povelêvaet*) and the Most Holy Synod of Russia assenteth thereto, that your Reverence shall be the Bishop of the godly cities of N. and N." And the Bishop-elect answers: "Seeing that our Sovereign Lord Nicholas Alexandrovitch, Autocrat of All the Russias, hath commanded my elevation and the Most Holy Synod of All the Russias hath deemed me worthy of such ministry, I return thanks and accept, and say nothing contrary thereto."

In the very consecration service itself, after the bishop-elect has recited the Nicene Creed and later a second Russian Creed, he takes the oath by means of a third Creed or profession of faith in the course of which he says: "that I will in all things follow and always obey the Most Holy Governing Synod of All the Russias," and "that I have received it (the episcopate) by the election of the Most Holy Governing Synod of All the Russias and by the election of our Most God-fearing Emperor, Nicholas Alexandrovitch, Autocrat of All the Russias."

In the Russian Mass, to give the Great Entrance as a familiar example,[4] the priest bearing the Holy Gifts prays: "May our Lord God remember in his kingdom our most honored Autocrat, our Sovereign Lord and Emperor, Nicholas Alexandrovitch, of All the Russias, always, now and forever, world without end." Then he prays for the Empress, the Empress Dowager, the Crown Prince, and other members of the Imperial family, and then finally: "May our Lord God remember in his kingdom the Most Holy Governing Synod, his Lordship the Most Reverend Metropolitan N., (or the Archbishop N., or the Bishop N., as the case may be) always, now and forever, world without end," and after that the other clergy.

Let us compare this with the same prayer of the Great Entrance in the Greek Catholic Mass [5] where the priest prays according to the ancient Eastern form: "May our Lord God remember in his kingdom our Most Holy Ecumenical Bishop, Pius, Pope of Rome, our Most Reverend Metropolitan N., our God-loving Bishop N., and all the priesthood, diaconate, and the monastic ranks of the clergy; our faithful and God-protected Emperor N., and all his orthodox army; and all the blessed founders and benefactors of this temple, for eternal memory; and all you orthodox Christians, always, now and forever, world without end."

A NOTE ON BIBLICAL INERRANCY.

To the Editor, THE ECCLESIASTICAL REVIEW.

A very cheering statement has just come from the Eternal City. Early last month, the Very Reverend President of the Biblical Institute, Fr. Fonck, S.J., delivered a most entertaining lecture on the pretended conflict between the Bible and Science, in the presence of "one of the keenest, most critical, and most cultured audiences that any city in the world can furnish". *The Catholic Standard and Times,* of Philadelphia, 9 April, is our informant.

Among other things, Fr. Fonck made in substance the following enlightened remarks relative to "the general concept of the universe according to the expression of the Bible": "The opposition between this concept and the real constitution of the universe is easily explained by means of the well-known distinction between fact and phenomenon. The sacred writer has no other intention than to describe the perception of the senses, and in this evidently there can be no falsity. Nor is there any, because the author describes precisely what the senses really know. It is quite true that in his mind there is corresponding to that perception a judgment of identity with the reality which is absolutely in error; but this judgment is the element proper to man and does not touch that which is common to God and man in the act of inspiration."

Some years ago Fr. Lagrange, in treating the same subject, expressed a similar view in language more scholastic. In a case like the one under discussion, he says, I may be told that "if a proposition is not true, it must be false. What then becomes of the veracity of the Bible? The reply is very simple. A proposition is indeed either true or false, but there is no proposition here. . . . When we treat only of appearances, our judgment does not go to the bottom of things. Now where there is no judgment there is neither affirmation nor negation. But truth and error are found only in formal judgments. This is elementary logic." [1]

Fr. Delattre, S.J., could not grasp the subject so deeply, and replied: "Elementary logic? Not even that: far from it. In the first place the Biblical author is represented as expressing himself *in a way to make known his opinion* about the vault of heaven; then, his judgment *does not go to the bottom of things.* But, by expressing himself in a way to make known his opinion as to the nature of a thing, does he not wish to express himself thoroughly and unreservedly? . . . And then, if the Biblical author, despite his good faith, has failed to grasp the bottom-truth, are not his utterances, when taken objectively, real falsehoods?" [2]

It is needless to give Fr. Lagrange's reply. Fr. Fonck has answered his confrère far more effectively by going back part way to Fr. Lagrange's " elementary logic ".

Yet the learned Dominican's view may be even more correct in a very important detail than the version of Fr. Fonck's just cited. The latter admits positive error in the mind of the sacred writer who wrongly identifies what his senses perceive with the reality of things. But this so-called " judgment of identity " is excluded by Fr. Lagrange. According to him the sacred writer, like all his contemporaries, simply took the identity for granted. He never thought of questioning it. To do so would have been absurd at that remote epoch. Consequently he passes no judgment on it, as Fr. Fonck permits him to do, thereby putting him " absolutely in error ". The head of the Jerusalem school gains by the comparison, unless it be shown on good authority that the *Standard and Times'* report of Fr. Fonck's address is at fault.

THOMAS À K. REILLY, O.P., S.T.L., S.S.L.
Immaculate Conception College, Washington, D. C.

FREQUENT COMMUNION WITHOUT FASTING.

To the Editor, THE ECCLESIASTICAL REVIEW.

In answer to an unsigned communication in your February issue you state as your opinion that an invalid priest might be allowed to say Mass when not fasting, should fasting be forbidden by his medical advisers. In the March issue a letter from the Rev. Andrew Byrne contains an opposite opinion.

But, while authorities may differ with regard to the right to *celebrate Mass,* neither you nor Father Byrne has stated that the priest might not be allowed to *receive Holy Communion* when not fasting, even when his physical condition allows him to be up and about, attending in a limited way to the duties of his calling. This question is of deep importance to the laity. There are hundreds of persons, particularly those on whom old age is advancing, who are able to get around in some way and even perform a certain amount of useful work, but who cannot endure the exertion and exposure involved in frequently going abroad in the early morning hours. Could the leniency of the Church be extended to these, and thus avoid the necessity of withdrawing the light of God's Real Presence from the last years of a life worn out in His service?

At the risk of a slight digression, may I say a few words on the subject of abuses, though not exactly in the sense in which you allude to them?

For something like a year previous to my first appearance in your columns, I had been engaged in a study of this subject of the Eucharistic fast. Rather to my surprise, I have found the almost universal opinion of theologians to be that relaxation of the law would be undesirable on account of the possibility of abuse. Our dear Saviour Himself shows no disposition to withdraw from His children for fear of personal disrespect or annoyance.[1] Furthermore, St. Paul, in his remonstrances to the Corinthians, does not even hint at the introduction of *fasting* as a means to cure the abuses of which he complains.[2] However, as the authority of the Church is the tribunal which must decide these points, may I respectfully ask the opinion of theologians as to this view of the question: Could not abuses be entirely prevented by allowing the law to stand as it is —merely putting the dispensing power in the hands of the local diocesan authorities, who could readily distinguish between the lambs and the goats of their several flocks?

S. C. B.

THE "PROPOSITUM NON PECCANDI DE FUTURO" IN CONFESSION.

To the Editor, THE ECCLESIASTICAL REVIEW.

It is held by some theologians that the *propositum non peccandi de futuro* in the sacrament of Penance must of necessity be explicit. Many text-books of theology, after giving the three opinions of theologians on this question concerning the explicit *propositum,* append the advice of St. Alphonsus, viz.: since the opinion which holds that the explicit *propositum* is necessary *absolute,* does not lack probability, in practice *ante factum* it is safer to follow it, and the confessor ought to take care that the penitent have an explicit *propositum;* but *post factum* the penitent ought not to be disturbed if in good faith he has confessed with an implicit *propositum* only, since the confession is probably valid.

In practice many wise confessors give themselves no concern in this matter, acting on the principle *ex communiter contingentibus* that the penitent is sufficiently instructed. They argue on this point in the same way as does the confessor who does not take care to know that each individual penitent has a knowledge of the mysteries of the Blessed Trinity and of the Incarnation, or that he has at least attrition for his sins. This too in spite of the fact that many penitents, either from ignorance, as in the case of children, or from nervousness or inadvertence, sometimes say the Confiteor, the Creed, or a conglomeration of the other acts, instead of the Act of Contrition. An expression of the judgment of the Reverend editor upon this matter will be appreciated.

A READER.

Resp. Theologians now practically agree that the integrity of the Sacrament of Penance is sufficiently safeguarded by a disposition on the part of the penitent which excludes the positive wish to commit in future the sin confessed.

The doubt as to the necessity of making an explicit purpose not to commit in future the sin confessed arises apparently from the disposition of a person who, while confessing a sin with real regret (from a supernatural motive), nevertheless foresees that on certain occasions over which he has no absolute control, he is likely to commit the sin again. He dreads the offence against God, but is drawn to, and partly controlled by, the circumstances which are apt to bring it about. He confesses the sin because he feels the restraint of a guilty conscience and the danger of eternal punishment, but he lacks the moral and perhaps the physical courage to cut loose from the surroundings or offices which present the temptation to which he has found himself yielding in the past.

Must a person in such a state of mind—apart from avoiding the immediate or direct occasion of such sin—explicitly purpose not to commit the offence? We would answer: Since he is not bound to avoid the merely remote occasion of sin— because that is practically impossible—he satisfies the requirements of due sorrow for his sin by a desire (not an explicit purpose) to avoid the sin. But the desire not to commit sin, although sufficient for the integrity of the confession, since it excludes the wish to sin, is always included in a sincere confession. Prayer and the sacramental grace furnish a legitimate hope that God will render efficacious the penitent's desire to be preserved from falling into the sin he fears his weakness will lead him to commit.

to the opinion, cited by St. Alphonsus, that the *propositum virtuale* suffices only when the penitent does not reflect at all about the future, he writes: " At haec posterior vix a nostra sententia discrepat; nam dum statuit valere confessionem cum proposito virtuali quando homo de futuro non cogitat, concedit propositum formale non pertinere ad essentialia sacramenti; hypothesis autem quam facit hominis efficaciter dolentis et tamen, etiam ubi de futuro cogitat, non elicientis propositum vitandi peccata, chimaerica est." (Génicot, *Theol. Moral.,* Tract. XV, Sect. II, n. 280.)

ROSECOLOR IN THE LITURGY.

The question of the proper colors of the vestments to be worn during the liturgical services has given rise to the query: What is meant by the *color rosaceus* to which the *Cæremoniale Episcoporum* refers in speaking of " Gaudete " (third) Sunday in Advent (Lib. II, Cap. xiii, n. 11)? Rubricists explain the use of this color as indicating the note of joyous expectancy, in the midst of the penitential preparation during Advent and Lent as introductory to the great festivals of Christmas and Easter. On " Gaudete " and " Laetare " Sundays, the initial exclamations of joy in the liturgy of the Mass are suggestive of this hope, and the service is made more festive by the admission of musical accompaniment and of flowers on the altar.

In harmony with the gleam of expectant joy thus manifested in the external rites the penitential purple of the vestment takes on a brighter coloring, not indeed without the suggestion of penance, but indicative also of the heightened hope which sustains the pilgrim on his way to the heavenly Jerusalem for the great feast, by a sight, amid the Judean hills, of the pinnacles of the temple gleaming beautifully from afar, and brightening the final stage of his journey.

The expression in color of this sentiment of joyous hope during the penitential journey corresponds to a brightening or tempering of the sombre purple so as to approach to the color of the rose (" rosaceus qui est violaceo clarior et quodammodo tendit in rubrum "). The precise shade is not neces-

stronger the blue is in the mixture the more sombre and dark will be the purple; whereas the more the clear red predomi_nates in the combination, all the brighter and more festive will be the purple. It is the predominance of red therefore that lends its characteristic to the symbolism of the special color used on the two Sundays of Advent and Lent on which we chant " Gaudete " and " Laetare ". But the red, though it predominates in the purple, must not make it too closely re-semble the red used on feasts of martyrs; for it does not indi-cate bloody martyrdom or sacrifice, but joy. Hence the tint to be chosen is a light, pale rose red, since white is the sym-bolic color of joy in the liturgy. The term " rosaceus " stands therefore not for a purple crimson or pink, but rather for the brighter rose color approaching the tints of the " rosa albina " or flower known by horticulturists as " La France ", with the suggestion of blue in its tone. That would differentiate the color of " Gaudete " and " Laetare " from that of the martyrs and of the fiery red of the Pentecostal flame. A still brighter rose color is admitted in some liturgies for the octave of Holy Innocents, in order to give full significance to the symbolism of innocence (white) mingled with the crimson of their blood; since they are virgins who shed their blood without the volun-tary confession of faith which distinguishes the martyr of Christ.

When we say bright, we do not of course mean the garish rose tint that is produced by the dilution of coal-tar colors in commercial use. These are not found in nature. Vegetable dyes, such as archil and madder, subdued by an admixture of white, would give a natural and becoming *rosaceum*.

WHEN THE "ORATIO IMPERATA" IS TO BE OMITTED.

private or solemn (*cantatae*), unless the rubrics expressly exclude commemorations of any kind.

Accordingly the *imperata* is to be omitted—

(1) On doubles of the *first class,* both in low and solemn Masses. This includes also solemn votive Masses, such as at the Forty Hours, etc.

(2) On doubles of the *second class,* in solemn Masses only. (In low Masses the *imperata* is said *ad libitum.*)

(3) On days when the special rubric of the Mass prescribes *only one oration,* i. e. on Palm Sunday, Holy Thursday, Holy Saturday, the Vigil of Christmas and of Pentecost.

(4) Whenever the *imperata* is the same as one of the orations prescribed in the Mass by the general rubrics.

(5) In Requiem Masses, unless the *imperata* is for the dead. In this case the *imperata* is omitted only in Requiem Masses in which one oration is prescribed, as *in die obitus,* etc.

THE POPES AND TOBACCO.

Qu. On reading the article " Tobacco " in the *New International Encyclopedia* (ed. 1904), I came upon the following statement (p. 775) : " The popes Urban VIII and Innocent XI fulminated against it the thunders of the Church." Is this statement true?

M. A.

Resp. The statement, if intended to mean that the Popes above-mentioned condemned, by the exercise of their spiritual authority, the use of tobacco, is quite untrue and savors of bigotry.

What was in the mind of the author of the article on " Tobacco " in the *New International Encyclopedia,* or rather in the older English and German encyclopedias, from which the writer has copied, is a document of Pope Urban VIII (*Cum ecclesiae,* 30 January, 1642) addressed to the Dean and Chapter of the Metropolitan Church of Spain, in answer to a request by that body that the Pontiff should use his influence to put a stop to the abuses, incident to the wholesale introduction of

tended the service. A similar constitution is cited by Ferraris [1] as having been issued by Pope Innocent X,[2] who wished to safeguard the cleanliness of the Vatican Basilica. Of this document we find no mention in the *Bullarium;* but Benedict XIII subsequently refers to it in a letter to Cardinal Annibal of Albano, archpriest of the Roman Basilica, in which he expressed the wish that the censure on the use of tobacco in church be abrogated, and that other measures be taken to keep the edifice clean and free from the abuses which seem to have obtained in the previous century.

To say therefore that the Popes fulminated the censures of the Church against the use of tobacco, is on a par with the statement of one who should say that the President of the United States extorts fines from and visits imprisonment on persons who use tobacco, referring to the fact that spitting tobacco juice on the floor of the White House, or smoking in certain parts of it, would render the contumacious offender subject to punishment.

Readers interested in the controversy will find much light thrown on the matter by the Rev. Dr. Hugh T. Henry, in a review of a volume by Charles Carleton Coffin (Harper & Bros., 1881). The erudite president of the Catholic High School, Philadelphia, lays bare the prejudice of Mr. Coffin, whose book had been recommended to teachers by Dr. Edward Brooks, the then Superintendent of the Public Schools of Philadelphia, as a useful work in the study of Language and General Reading. Doctor Henry's critique of the volume was published in the *Records of the American Catholic Historical Society* (1901), and subsequently appeared as a separate brochure in the series of " Educational Briefs " (No. 7, July, 1904) under the title of " Old Times in the Colonies ". We understand that later on Dr. Brooks withdrew his recommendation of Mr. Coffin's volume—a result, no doubt, of the critique. Prospective purchasers of popular encyclopedias and histories would do wisely to turn to such topics as the one here mentioned and make a test of the accuracy and true scholarship of the work, before putting it in their libraries.

---

[1] *Bibliotheca,* ad art. Tabaccum.

[2] The fact that different popular encyclopedias mention Innocent XI, which appears to have been a misprint originally, instead of Innocent X, indicates how one copies the lie of the other without any examination of sources.

Ecclesiastical Library Table.

SOME MODERN ERRORS IN THE STUDY OF THE LIFE OF CHRIST.

G. Stosch[1] feels convinced that Gospel criticism does not exhibit an honorable page in the annals of the history of human errors. Probably it attained its lowest degradation in the shameful way in which it has treated the chosen witnesses of Jesus Christ. No historical documents have been treated as frivolously and unjustly as the Gospels. If any scientific process stands self-convicted, it is the so-called critical method which has torn the Gospels to pieces; some of these it has rejected; others it has acknowledged as genuine with a patronizing air. In other cases it has compared fragment with fragment and estimated their value with a proud self-sufficiency and an incredible lack of penetration, treating their authors as school-boys convicted of cheating, or ridiculed and humbled as imbeciles. Sincere observers cannot pass these monuments of scientific degradation without a blush. The initiated know how blunted the axe has become which tried to cut down the old vigorous trees of the Gospels. They are convinced that the trees are as fully alive as ever, that at worst their bark is a little scratched, while the axe has slipped off without being able to penetrate. And what are the principal conclusions reached by these critical students of the life of Christ?

1. *Jesus Christ never existed.* An American Professor of Mathematics, William Benjamin Smith, published his work on *Jesus Prior to Christianity*[2] in Germany. He endeavors to show that Jesus Christ is nothing but an idea, an abstract being, who never had any personal existence.—This work may have influenced *Die Christusmythe*[3] of A. Drews. The writer treats his subject wholly according to the principles of Comparative Religion. Pointing to the Messianic faith of the Parsees, to the Hellenistic idea of a mediator, and to the Jew-

---

[1] *Die Augenzeugen des Lebens Jesu;* Gütersloh, 1895.

ish conception of a pre-Christian Jesus, he believes himself to be justified in his denial of the historicity of a personal Jesus.—The English writer John Robertson argues in the same strain: Jesus is only a mythical personality; Christianity has been formed to a great extent out of elements furnished by Mithraism, Krischnaism, and other pagan worships. The triumphal entrance of Jesus into Jerusalem, for instance, is a reminiscence of the myth of Bacchus riding on an ass to the temple of Dodona. Bacchus is said to symbolize the sun in the zenith; the entrance of Jesus into Jerusalem, therefore, signifies that the sun-god Jesus has reached the height of his glory. Similarly, the crown of thorns is nothing but the nimbus surrounding the sun.[4]—The theory of Bruno Bauer was adopted in Holland by A. D. Loman who denied the historical existence of Jesus Christ in the *Revue Theologisch Tijdschrift* for 1882 and 1883 and in his work *Symbol en Werkelijkheit in de evang. Geschiedenis.*[5]—The same opinion is defended by the pseudonymous writer "Verus" [P. van Dyk] in his popular publication entitled *Vergleichende Uebersicht der vier Evangelien* which appeared in Leipzig, 1897.— Albert Kalthoff delivered in 1880 a course of Conferences on the life of our Lord in which he accepted the results generally admitted by contemporaneous theologians.[6] But since then he has become an enthusiastic follower of Bruno Bauer, and has published three pamphlets in defence of his position.[7] Jesus cannot be the founder of Christianity, the writer contends, since he never existed. In the Gospels, the Epistles of St. Paul, and the other books of the New Testament everything is allegory, or legend, or falsehood. Christianity is the result of the grand popular and social movements which rose simultaneously among the Jews, the Greeks, and the Romans about the time of the reputed birth of Christ. Jesus is therefore a fictitious person, an eponymic hero, who was credited with the foundation of the Church after the fact had been accomplished.—C. L. Fillion has studied the problem of the his-

---

[4] *Christianity and Mythology*—Pagan Christs; London, 1903.

[5] Amsterdam, 1884.

[6] *Das Leben Jesu*, Reden gehalten im protestantischen Reformverein zu Berlin; Berlin, 1880.

[7] *Das Christus-Problem;* Leipzig, 1902. *Die Entstehung des Christentums;* neve Beiträge zum Christus-Problem, Leipzig, 1904. *Was wissen wir von Jesus?* Berlin, 1904.

torical existence of Jesus Christ from a Catholic point of view. The reader will find an article on the subject in the *Revue des Questions Historiques.*[8] A special volume entitled *L'Existence Historique de Jésus et le Rationalisme Contemporain*[9] develops the question at greater length. L. Schulze too has treated the question from a conservative Protestant point of view;[10] he first considers the non-Biblical, then the Biblical sources of the life of Jesus.

2. *The Historicity of Jesus minimized.* Charles T. Gorham has come to the conclusion in his *Transformation of Christianity* (pp. 14-15) that one cannot trust the Gospels in the least. He appears to ask with modern criticism: Is there anything in the Gospels that can be believed?—Dr. F. C. Conybeare has written a book on Christ and the Gospels which he has called by the name *Myth, Magic, and Morals.*[11] The title of the work is apt to make the reader impatient, but the author pleads to be heard out. He feels quite convinced that most Christians can allege no better reason for the faith they profess than they can for the color of their hair being what it is. Here then is Dr. Conybeare's theory: The New Testament is occupied with two distinct persons, the one real, the other fictitious. The real person he calls Jesus, the fictitious Christ. Of the real Jesus we know so little that the writer is not surprised at those who deny his existence. He was born in Nazareth, of Joseph and Mary; he was circumcized and named Jesus. Christian tradition tells us that in course of time he was baptized by John in the Jordan; moreover, he was a successful exorcist, and his enthusiastic followers thrust upon him the belief that he was the Messias. After this he began to say that he would return after death and inaugurate the reign of God upon earth. This is a summary of what we know of the real Jesus; Dr. Conybeare tells us so. But whence comes the fictitious Christ? who invented him? The Christ of the Gospels and of Christianity was invented by Saul of Tarsus. Paul was an idealist; hence his large and liberal teaching. He was an epileptic; hence he dreamt dreams and saw visions.

it had not been for the Christ of Paul's creation, Jesus would have remained a mere human Messias of the Jews. Christianity would have vanished as it began, an obscure sect in Galilee. Paul must have been a man of extraordinary range of imagination. For when he said, " to me to live is Christ," or " yet not I, but Christ liveth in me," the Christ of whom he said these things was evolved out of his own ecstatic consciousness.

J. Estlin Carpenter, Professor in Manchester College, Oxford, has written two conferences on " The Gospels according to Modern Criticism " in which he communicates the historical residue left of the Gospels after a severe critical examination. First we find Jesus among the audience of John; next, He begins His own public ministry, His doctrine tending to a religion without priests, without sacramental mediation. The exorcisms of the Gospels prove to Prof. Carpenter that the evangelists constantly follow the ancient beliefs in magic, and that they are intimately related to the medical rites of African fetichism and of Singhalese sorcery. Finally, the power of the Christian religion flows not from the historical life of Jesus, but from another life which is hidden in the sanctuary of the souls of his disciples.

We need not speak of the character of the articles bearing on the Life of Christ which appeared in the *Encyclopædia Biblica*. The reader remembers Prof. Schmiedel's pillar-passages and his allied views as stated in the articles on the Gospels and on John the son of Zebedee; similar opinions may be met with in the articles " Judas ", " John the Baptist ", " Joseph ".—It is rather painful to notice the change in the views of Professor Bruce. In several publications [12] he had shown himself as a defender of the conservative Protestant position. But in his contribution to the *Encyclopædia Biblica* [13] and in his catechetical appendix to his book entitled *With Open Face, or Jesus Mirrored in Matthew, Mark, and Luke* [14] the writer is swept away by the critical current. The Resurrection of Jesus and his life in glory are summed up in the brief statement that Jesus is now in the house of his

Father in heaven where he prepares a place for his followers. The story of the Passion as contained in the Gospels is, according to Prof. Bruce, not the pure truth, but truth mixed with doubtful legends.—The works of J. A. Crooker,[15] C. A. Briggs,[16] E. P. Gould,[17] and W. C. Allen [18] did not shock their Christian readers as much as some of the foregoing publications, but they are of a decidedly liberal trend.—Prof. James Moffatt belongs to a more advanced type of critics. In his work entitled *Historical New Testament* he does not clearly define his attitude toward the Incarnation and the Resurrection of Jesus; but Mt. 28: 16-20 is a mere appendix. Besides, the Gospels do not give us an exact and faithful picture of Jesus. Words are placed on the lips of Jesus which He never spoke, but which were supposed to agree with His interior sentiments; the Church has lent Him her own thoughts and her own experiences, so that Jesus is lost in the Church, just as the Church is lost in Christianity, and Christianity in humanity.—Prof. F. C. Burkitt is again of a more moderate type; but the party-tendencies which he admits in the Church for a century and a half, his liberal views on the fourth Gospel, his theory as to the pretended repetitions in the Gospels make him reject the historicity of many a passage. The title of his work is *The Gospel History and its Transmission.*[19] —Similar views seem to have found their way into the writings of less professional authors. Matthew Arnold, for instance, believes that our popular religion considers the birth, the ministry, and the death of Christ as wholly plunged into the miraculous; but, then, miracles have not happened.—T. H. Green is of opinion that about two generations after the death of St. Paul a certain disciple gave to the person of Jesus that spiritual interpretation which has removed it forever from the realm of history.—Hastings's *Dictionary of the Bible* and *Dictionary of Christ* are rightly considered as representing,

---

[15] *The Supremacy of Jesus,* Boston, 1904.

[16] *Messianic Prophecy,* New York, 1886; *The Messiah of the Gospels,* Edinburgh, 1894; *The Messiah of the Apostles,* Edinburgh, 1895; *New Light on the Life of Jesus,* 1904.

[17] *Critical and Exegetical Commentary on the Gospel according to St. Mark,* Edinburgh, 1897.

on the whole, the views of conservative Protestants; still in this latter work the cursing of the fig-tree is regarded as only a concrete form of the parable of the barren fig-tree.—Prof. Sanday appears to doubt the historicity of the miracles related in the fourth Gospel.[20]—Even Dr. Salmon, for many years the pillar of orthodoxy, appears to have surrendered the resuscitation of Lazarus.

Thus far we have spoken only of English and American writers who are as a rule more conservative than their colleagues on the Continent. A full list of German and French scholars would lengthen this paper beyond its proper limits. Dr. Brandt, for instance, applies the critical method of Strauss to the Passion of Jesus Christ.[21]—Dr. Havet has been almost from his childhood filled with the spirit of Voltaire. He is an ardent admirer of Renan, but regrets that the ex-seminarian has not gone far enough. He is convinced that we are never quite certain that an event related in the Gospel is authentic. Only one fact appears to be incontestable to the writer, that Jesus was crucified under Tiberius, by order of the procurator Pontius Pilate. But even this fact is not certain on the authority of the Gospels, but because it is mentioned in the Annals of Tacitus.—A more complete list of these rationalistic writers and their refutation may be seen in Fillion's series of articles entitled " Ce que les Rationalistes daignent nous laisser de la vie de Jésus." [22]

3. *The Human Dignity of Jesus impeached.* Prof. Weinel does not hesitate to write of those who take exception to the moral dignity of Jesus: " In reading such writings one asks oneself, where the lack of intelligence ends, and where hatred and a voluntary misunderstanding begin." Still the moral rectitude of Jesus, which had been *doubted* by Reimarus, Strauss, Renan, etc., has been openly attacked in our own day. Theodore Parker [23] is convinced that if Christianity is true, it would not be less so, if Herod, or Catiline were its founder; what is more, that the religious doctrine of Jesus is not af-

---

[20] *The Criticism of the Fourth Gospel,* London, 1905.

[21] *Die evangelische Geschichte und der Ursprung des Christentums auf Grund einer Kritik der Berichte über das Leiden und die Auferstehung Jesu,* Leipzig, 1893.

[22] *Revue du Clergé Français,* LV,. 5-23, 257-283, 641-665.

[23] Cf. Nicoll, *The Church's one Foundation,* p. 11.

fected by whatever moral inperfections there may be in him.
—As long as thirty years ago, Jules Soury [24] contended that
the picture of Jesus as contained in the Gospels presents Him
as a madman. Like most of the great men, Jesus is to-day
nothing but a problem of morbid psychology. Jesus' belief
in His Messianic character is a raving conception.—E. von
Hartmann was at first a firm believer in Jesus; but a journey
to Palestine turned him into an enemy of Christianity. And
what was the reason? He found the roads in Palestine badly
kept, and this lack of having provided durable means of communication for his country convinced the traveler that Jesus
was not an eminent man. But the traveler soon sank deeper
still in his appreciation of Jesus. He is scandalized by the
moral teaching of Jesus; Jesus despised work, the rights of
property, and family duties; he exhibits signs of a Semitic
grossness; Christian dogma has made a mistake in considering
Jesus as an ideal of morality; Jesus was not able to evade the
narcotic influence of honor and glory; he allowed himself to
be inebriated by the pride of the Messianic dignity.[25]—An
anonymous writer charges Jesus with being vain and brutal;[26]
Wolfang Kirchbach finds that Jesus taught pantheism.[27]
Similar blasphemies may be seen in the publications of G.
Tschirn, Moritz von Egidy,[28] and of the Social Democrats.—
Jülicher [29] believed that Jesus not only deceived himself, but
led others too into error; in his answer to the question, *Was
Jesus an Ecstatic?* [30] Oscar Holtzmann represents our Lord
not only as an eccentric dreamer, but as a common fool.[31]—
George Lomer, director of an asylum in Holstein, has pub-
lished a work under the pseudonym of Dr. de Loosten [32] in
which he attempts the scientific proof for the thesis that
Jesus was a madman. A similar work was published by the

---

[24] *Jésus et les Évangiles*, Paris, 1878.

[25] *Das Christentum des Neuen Testamentes*, Sachsa, 1905.

[26] *Finsternisse: die Lehre Jesu im Lichte der Kritik*, Zürich, 1899.

[27] Cf. Weinel, *Jesus, im 19 Jahrhundert*, second edit., pp. 142-151.

[28] *Jesus ein Mensch, nicht Gottessohn; Fehdebrief gegen das falsche Kir-
chenchristentum.*

[29] *Die Gleichnissreden Jesu*, Tübingen, 1899.

[30] *War Jesus Ekstatiker?* Tübingen, 1903.

Danish theologian E. Rasmussen.[33]—These works were answered by Prof. Phillip Kneib, of Würtzburg,[34] and by the Protestant theologian Hermann Werner.[35]—J. Warschaver protests indeed against the liberal view of the life of Jesus, but grants at the same time that Jesus was certainly limited in his knowledge and his power; that there were things he did not know and he could not do.[36]—Alexander Robinson too rather emphasizes the " Man-Jesus " in whom there were human weaknesses and earthly bounds, who hesitated a long time about his religious plan and made a mistake in his predictions of the future.[37]—We might add to this list of books, but what has been said sufficiently illustrates how modern writers impeach the human dignity of Jesus.

4. *The Divinity of Jesus is denied.* The general leaning of writers on the life of Jesus with regard to his Divinity may be learned from an occurrence of the past year. The *Hibbert Journal* for January, 1909, published an article entitled " Jesus or Christ ". According to the opinion of a competent critic, it was a bad article, and it was badly printed. But within a week of the publication of the article, replies and criticisms, eulogies and condemnations, began to pour in to the editor from all quarters. Hence he conceived the idea that a certain number of men should be invited to express themselves on the alternative, " Jesus or Christ ". Seventeen men responded to his invitation, and their contributions together with an amended edition of the original article have been issued in a volume. Its title is still " Jesus or Christ ".

The writer of the original article had signed himself as " Congregational Minister ". It was soon made clear that the Rev. R. Roberts had not been a Congregational minister for eleven years. The article was written from a Unitarian point of view, and the title seemed to invite the future contributors to take sides either with the Unitarians or the Trinitarians. All the writers agreed that Jesus was a perfect man;

---

[33] *Jesus; eine vergleichende psychopathologische Studie,* Leipzig, 1905.

[34] *Moderne Leben-Jesu-Forschung unter dem Einflusse der Psychiatrie,* Mainz, 1908.

[35] *Die psychische Gesundheit Jesu,* Berlin, 1909.

[36] *Jesus or Christ,* London, 1909.

[37] *A study on the Saviour in the newer Light, or a Present-Day Study of Jesus Christ,* 1895 and 1898.

but the question was asked whether he was more than man.
Dr. Garvie, one of the contributors, calls it the most important
and urgent question with which the Christian theologian is
to-day called to deal.   But perhaps we have anticipated the
answer of most readers by identifying Jesus with man, and
Christ with more than man.   Prof. Schmeidel is most particular about keeping the alternative clearly before us.   " I
maintain," he says, " a clear distinction between the terms
Jesus and Christ in my own practice, and demand that it shall
be maintained in the intercourse of theologians with one another."   But the majority of writers in the new volume do not
accept the alternative.   They accept Jesus and Christ, just as
the Catholic theologian accepts both Jesus and Christ.

But there is this difference between the Catholic writer and
the contributors to the new volume. The Catholic theologian
will not admit that Jesus is a mere man; he identifies Jesus
with Christ, because Jesus is as highly elevated above mere
humanity as the term Christ implies. The contributors to the
new volume identify Jesus with Christ, because they lower
Christ to the level of the merely human.   The Rev. R. J.
Campbell, for instance, says expressly that " the greatness of
Jesus consists in the fact that he has made the word Christ a
synonym for the best and highest that can truly be called
human."

It cannot be denied that some of the writers speak most
beautifully of Christ.   Dr. James Drummond so wholly ab-
sorbs the title Christ that one should have been unable to tell
from his paper that the writer is not a believer in the Divinity
of Christ; yet he tells us in so many words that he is a Unitarian.   Neither is Prof. Gardner a believer in the Divinity of
Christ; yet he claims for Jesus almost all that Professor
Schmiedel would reserve for Christ.   The reader may have
known men who refused to call themselves Christians, but
still appropriated the blessings of Christianity to themselves;
but now we have the curious spectacle of men to whom Jesus
is a mere man, and who claim for themselves all the blessings
derived from the faith in Jesus Christ the God-Man.   And
the proportion of the Unitarian writers in this volume to the

Criticisms and Notes.

AN ESSAY ON THE BEGINNINGS OF THE IMMACULATE CON-
CEPTION IN ART. Francia's Masterpiece. By Montgomery Carmichael, author of " In Tuscany ", " The Life of John Wm. Walshe ",
etc. New York: Dutton & Co. 1909. Pp. 67.

Readers interested in Italian types—and who that seeks culture
or loves the beautiful in art or nature is not?—are likely to be
familiar with Mr. Carmichael's literary excursions along Tuscan
and Umbrian by-ways. His recitals are never merely descriptive:
they are often interwoven with allegory, illumined by a touch of
spiritual romanticism, and always have an agreeable religious bias
that gives a quasi-controversial character to his exposition of facts
and indicates that the author labors from conviction and with love
for his truth.

In the present volume the discussion turns upon a painting—an
altarpiece in the old Lombard Basilica of San Frediano at Lucca—
by the Bolognese painter, Francesco Raibolini, more commonly
known under the name of Francia. Francia was hardly the inferior
of Raphael, who loved him as a father, for the former was thirty
years the senior of the Umbrian master; and the two are closely
allied, even as they were for a time by friendly association during
their lives, in the technical perfection, the delicate intelligence of
their symbolic construction, and the grace of their figuring. If in
these things Raphael reaches higher, it must be allowed that the
elder master, Francia, outdoes him in the pure elevation of sentiment
which excludes all that is spiritually gross or simply human in his
sacred art.

and his reviser Antonio Mazzarosa, Cavalcaselle, Symonds, Hare, and Baedeker tell us, nor an " Assumption ", as the editors of Vasari and Murray's *Traveller's Handbook* assure us, but the " Immaculate Conception ", as suggested first by Michele Ridolfi,[1] and in a manner by Mrs. Jameson who speaks of it as a representation of " the election or predestination of Mary as the immaculate vehicle or tabernacle of human redemption ". Mr. Carmichael suggests that it is probably the first picture of this subject among the masterpieces of art that have been preserved to us. He justly criticizes Mrs. Jameson's statement that the Immaculate Conception does not distinctly appear in art until the seventeenth century, and adds " without question the doctrine was pictorially represented above altars at least from 1479 onwards ".

As a matter of fact, the subject appears in pictures much earlier than Mr. Carmichael assumes, though he finds no trace of it in the writers on Marian Iconography which he has consulted. The *Biblia Pauperum,* which were in many cases merely altar decorations, of fully a century earlier, present unmistakable illustrations of the Immaculate Conception; and the *Speculum Humanae Salvationis,* commonly attributed to Ludolf of Saxony, the Carthusian who died in 1377, depicts a complete series of the Life of Our Blessed Lady in which the Immaculate Conception is placed before the scene of the Nativity of Our Blessed Lady by the triple image shown to Blessed Joachim, of King Astyages's dream, of the " hortus conclusus ", the " fons signatus ", and of the prophetic image of Balaam's star. The picture refers plainly to the Immaculate Conception of the Virgin who was to be the Mother of Christ.

But this fact does not weaken the force of Mr. Carmichael's argument nor lessen the interest of his inquiry. The proof that Francia's picture represents neither the Assumption nor the Coronation of Our Lady, but her Immaculate Conception, is rightly found by him in the image of the rod, the touch of the life-saving sceptre of the Eternal Father upon the head of the Virgin, above the admiring and worshipping gaze of Solomon and David, Anselm and Augustine, each with a significant reference to the *Immaculata* upon the scrolls in their hands. Between them, kneeling, is the figure of a son of St. Francis, taken by some to be St. Anthony of Padua, by others to be Petrus Igneus. In reality the figure is that of Duns Scotus who may be justly called the champion of the Immaculate Conception, even as he has earned the titles of *Doctor Marianus* and *Doctor Subtilis.* The cumulative force of the evidence which Mr. Car-

ing sources of its composition, its locality, adjuncts, and general history, make an excellent plea for the thesis he has undertaken to prove. The volume is not only a charmingly executed contribution to Marian literature, but is also serviceable as opening a field of study in the interpretation of Christian art, a study which must become most attractive to priests as well as to cultured lay Catholics who enter upon it.

OÙ MÈNE L'ÉCOLE SANS DIEU: aveo une lettre d' introduction de Mgr. Baudrillart, Recteur de l' Institut Catholique de Paris. I. Criminalité croissante. II. Decadence intellectuelle. III. Instituteurs sans foi et sans patrie. IV. Faillite de la morale laique. Par Fénelon Gibon. Paris: Pierre Téqui. 1909. Pp. viii–169.

Upwards of twenty-five years ago, there used to be displayed along some of the public squares of Paris, and maybe with intensified malignity down the southeastward precincts of Boulevard St. Germain, several blasphemous posters whose object was to vilify the Incarnation. They were a scurrilous travesty, in short, of the Gospel record as especially presented in the opening chapters of the Evangelist Luke. The volume before us describes what progress free speech and untrammeled education have since then made in Republican France. Under the watchword of " Every open school means a prison closed ", the Republican liberality of creed and morals has wrought manifold significant advancements in social science.

" All principal crimes in France to-day are perpetrated by adolescents."

" This appalling increase in criminal adeptness goes hand-in-hand with the innovations effective in organized public instruction."

" In 1894, a given tabulation of 40,000 delinquent and criminal minors, disclosed 32,849 from sixteen to twenty-one years old."

" We have organized schools by the thousand, but we have forgotten education. Everything is designed to put forth diplomas; whereas neither the schools, nor the colleges, nor even, at a pinch, the teaching forces, are moral factors. . . . Suicide, even worse than the delinquencies proper, attests a growing collapse in the morals of vouth."

cal causes are also charged, besides the " free " schools, with the pro-
vocative incentives: namely, the congestion of unsettled multitudes
in great cities, migration from the country to industrial centres,
dissolution of the marriage bond in family life, decline of appren-
ticeships, with their sometime approximation to household decorum.
But the schools, in particular, are charged with demoralizing influence, in so far as they provide nothing equivalent to religious teaching and its moral reaction.

That the free schools, as now " emancipated " from all religious
control, even fail in a school's primary object of imparting knowledge, in a school's requisite condition of attendance by the taught,
brings our author to the second of his main contentions, " Intellectual
Decline ". Here, again, he offers tabulated official statistics: but
we shall dwell chiefly on the picturesque apologetics of Monsieur
the Deputy Steeg, sometime Protestant pastor. On facing some
rather evasive returns of comparative illiteracy at one of the Seine
recruiting stations, where the avowed percentage was compromised
by wholesale absences, or absentees whose degree of illiteracy could
not be checked, the Deputy is frank to own: " It is permitted to
believe that these nomads, these intangible vagabonds do not altogether compose an intellectual *élite;* but that they rather include
no few illiterates." And as touching what locally amounts to practical contempt of compulsory attendance laws, Monsieur Steeg thus
gracefully relieves the ordinary tedium of statistical discussion by
pictures of rural France. " The school is, occasionally, very remote; the roads impassable, months at a time; the children lack
shoes and clothing. Yet again, they are positively useful at home:
they gather grass for the rabbits, tend the geese, the cow, the little
brother or sister. The parents, in turn, are the more easily persuaded that the children lose nothing by knowing nothing beyond
the parental standard, because this itself is ignorance total. In a
word, school attendance is peculiarly difficult to enforce in the very
districts that need it most." In " rugged Périgord "—famed for those
epicure truffles which, by stuffing (or " farcing ") enhance a turkey
to eighty francs, or so—we learn, from an Academic report, that
even the chestnut culling is apt to curtail the school attendance. The
author's remedial suggestion is to beget in the parents themselves
that respect for the schools which only the Church can radically
supply, where education becomes instilled through religious channels.

Monsieur Steeg, however, advances one cogent, and everything but
equivocal reason, for poor attendance in certain districts: " There
is no school there! We insist on this point, because the remedy
comes under the *budgetary* head." In like manner, he would have
the State inform itself more minutely concerning the aggregate of

children both entitled and bound to school attendance. "The State knows the number of horses, dogs, *wheels;* it follows a bottle of brandy all the way from the still to the table, yet fails to know the exact account of children fit for school."

We are not prepared to second the author's more or less recurrent opinion that the present godless régime of public instruction in France is directly inspired, aggressively contrived, by Freemasonry in France; although the detail that the French Freemasons are nowadays " excommunicated " by British and American lodges, for overt atheism, speaks loudly enough on the score of the French lodges' irreligion. Among quoted utterances to this effect, in the volume before us, here is a notably explicit specimen, formulated A. D. 1898 by the Lodge of Grenoble: "Let us broadly propagate the futility and the dogmatic harmfulness of all religions. We, like our progenitors the Sans-Culottes of the great Revolution, will not leave intact, not even as monuments of art and value whatsoever, the cathedrals, churches, convents; nay more, and with no thought of actual sacrilege, we will apply to them torch and flame. We will pulverize all these nests of vermin, these keeps of obscurantism. Neither, to speak with Ranc, shall we find any gallows high enough to accommodate the base tools of all that canting clerical rabble ! " And one or two individual French Masons, who are also said to represent present French statecraft, have said: " The struggle between Catholicism and Freemasonry is a *fight to the death,* no truce nor quarter: wherever the *man in black* appears, let Freemasonry step forward." " We must crush the infamous one; only the infamous one is not the clerical caste, but God ! " Quoth, furthermore, at *Orleans,* she, the Citizeness Pajaud: " God must be crushed, seeing that he prevents us from eating the fruit of science." In short, the very ravings of these " emancipated " atheists but corroborate one of the Gospel's profoundest analyses of human passion: " He who is not for us is against us." The Freethinkers' first step was to *neutralize* the schools; but next in order, neutrality meant aggressive partisanship, and " the school *without* God becomes the school *against* God." Witness the ungloved discourse of *Mr. Minister of Labor* Viviani: " So they prate to you of school neutrality ! Time to tell you that school neutrality was never anything but a diplomatic lie and politic bit of cant. We trumped it up to lull the scrupulous, appease the scary. Now that all this is done and gone, cards in sight ! We never had any other design than to create an *anti-religious* university [which signifies, in France, the whole *corpus* of public instruction]. And that, too, on active militant, war-whoop lines." " Catholicism or anarchy," says our conservative author, will be the residual dilemma confronting French family heads, for their children's education. It was, we are told, Deputy Maurice Allard who declared in *La Lanterne:* "Expelling God from school is not sufficient, by any means; but he must be antagonized there through the institution of genuine scientific instruction." On the other hand, a distinguished "liberal" more cautiously pauses: "This one thing alone disturbs me: having eliminated God, how shall we proceed to find a new base for the moral law?" Especially, since even though Sinai and the Ten Commandments, in the phrase of a sensational "free lance" of our own times in America, too, were "blasted with the exploded Rock of Ages"; yet Mr. Economist Le Play reminds us gravely, "the Ten Commandments are inscribed by the Creator in the conscience of all the world." Indeed, on the morally destructive side of declared atheism, our author goes so far as to tax the irreligious extremists in France with destroying all *patriotic* sentiment, as well; under cover of a fantastic internationalism. "Our laic youth [and in the liberal vocabulary, *laic* is nowadays defined as equivalent to creedless] should explain to the people that the *national* idea, as hitherto evolved, is changing from day to day, and must ultimately, *fatally* disappear, giving way to universal love between all 'nations' that shall once have learned the lesson of world-wide labor union. . . . For then the slogan will be: *Humans* of every country, join hands!" Almost a grotesque instance of "extremes meet", this atheistic apostrophe for universal brotherhood *without* the Church, and the Catholic ideal of ecumenical comprehension *within* the Church; yet not as obliterating, in one sole house of faith, the "many mansions", even here below. The parallel is then drawn: "Some little while ago, God, though remnantly honored, was *suspected* of being *clerical*. It is now the country's turn, though still in honor, to be under suspicion of Chauvinism!"

Possibly the following examples of the atheistic fad in public instructors will escape the ordinary damnation they might seem to challenge, by fact of unaccountable mania, to say the least. "If I offered Father *bon Dieu* 50,000 francs to blow out the sun, could he earn 50,000 francs? You see, then, clearly enough, that God is not." "The intelligence is in the brain. But the brain rots after death: *ergo,* when one is dead, one dies all over." A Masonic examiner, *lycée* "professor" to boot, thus puts the question: "Could you not tell me something of one Jesus, who attempted to found a religion, once of a time?" There are further gross insults mentioned by the author, and ostensibly with due accountability for what he says, on

to the category of rational irreverence. A schoolmaster to his pupils in the Department of Loiret: " There is no God. The priests have taught that there is a God. But I teach the contrary. Besides, everything can come about quite by itself, the earth, the trees. One can well blaspheme God, even in the face of thunder. When it thunders very hard, come, look for me, and I will show you how one may blaspheme God with impunity." Even dismal old Malthus would appear to be " resurrected " (in a derivative atheistic fashion), to supply certain of the recent moralists in French education with a philosophic tenet for decreasing society, on prudential grounds of selfishness.

For sophistical impudence, note this " liberal " apology: " Who speaks of preaching atheism in the schools? We say simply that our bounden explanation of the universe excludes every notion of Providence. There is no use in saying, and neither shall we do so in our teaching at all, that there is no God. But the *consequence,* indeed; and I do not say, the *object,* of this identical instruction will be to invalidate, to render impossible, the belief in God." A volume published by the *Société de propagande par l'éducation laïque:* to wit, an illustrated " Republican, Popular, Scientific *Catechism ":* declares more positive warfare. " In order to diffuse and establish social happiness in our midst, in order to liberate the people, we must not only beat down the Church, we must kill God." The author sagaciously observes: " God does not die."

Meanwhile, what is *Catholic* France to do in the teeth of such Satanic irreligion? A generally defensive policy, at least, would seem to be not unseasonably outlined, in a pastoral to his own people, by Monseigneur Delamaire, Suffragan Bishop of Cambrai: " If the neutral school became impious (he wrote this in 1907), we should not hesitate to remind parents that they are charged with souls in the sight of God, and that no temporal consideration, however weighty, may be laid in the balance against the souls of their children. To leave their sons and daughters in schools polluted by impiety, as though under color of prudential expediency, or security of advancement, would be selling these poor children's souls to the enemy: traffic unworthy of a noble heart; discreditable to a noble Christian." Several of the French Bishops, indeed, have expressly disallowed Christian parents to patronize atheistic schools, under pain of exclusion from Catholic prerogatives. There would also appear to be some encouragement for French Catholics in the measure of success achieved by Catholics in Belgium, against " impious " legislation. " There is yet enough latent faith, in our Christian France, to promise our country's revival and resurrection." It is not the first time, certainly, when the Church has had to recall prophecy's assuring challenge: *Quare fremuerunt gentes, et populi ima-ginati sunt inania?* leaving God to act for its renewed fulfilment.

W. P.

TRUE DEVOTION TO THE BLESSED VIRGIN. A Treatise by the Blessed Louis Marie, Grignon de Montfort. Translated from the original French by Frederic William Faber, D.D., Priest of the Oratory. With a Preface by Cardinal Vaughan, Archbishop of Westminster. New York, Philadelphia: P. J. Kenedy & Sons. Pp. xix-198.

Blessed Grignon de Montfort, who was beatified during the pontificate of Leo XIII, died in 1716, and the above treatise was found by accident by one of the priests of his Congregation in 1842. Father Faber published a translation of it in 1862, and he tells us that, after having studied the life and spirit of the Venerable Grignon for more than fifteen years, he has come to the conclusion that "those who take him for their master will hardly be able to name a saint or ascetical writer to whose grace and spirit their mind will be more subject than to his". Such an expression from an authority like Father Faber is enough to commend a treatise on Our Blessed Lady. The writer divides his theme into two parts. The first speaks of the excellence of devotion to the Blessed Virgin, and points out the fundamental truths which serve as tests for discerning true from false devotion to the Virgin Mother of Christ; for that there is a false devotion which leads to superstition and dishonor he would not have us ignore. In the second part of his treatise the author explains the different ways of honoring Our Blessed Lady by a perfect consecration of ourselves to Jesus and Mary, and certain interior and exterior practices. There is at the end of the volume a formula of consecration which is very beautiful and most suitable for celebrations in honor of Our Lady.—We are not aware that there has ever been published a similar American edition of the volume, although Father Faber's version has been repeatedly reprinted in England, and Cardinal Vaughan wrote his preface to the fifth edition.

GESCHICHTE DER VEREHRUNG MARIAS IN DEUTSCHLAND während des Mittelalters. Ein Beitrag zur Religionswissenschaft und Kunstgeschichte. Von Stephan Beissel, S.J. Mit 292 Abbildungen. Freiburg im Breisg.; St. Louis, Mo.: B. Herder. 1909. Pp. 678.

Few writers of our day have made more valuable contributions to

owe the above volume. Many of his works are of particular value as illustrating the social relations of the artisan and laboring classes employed in the great architectural enterprises of pre-Reformation times. A notable instance of this study is furnished by the Church of St. Victor in Xanten, which presents a typical specimen of the methods adopted by the guild to regulate the value of labor, to determine the compensation, the number of working hours, the rights and privileges as well as the duties of the individual members of the builders' union. Other kindred studies by Father Beissel, covering the period from the thirteenth to the sixteenth century, are helpful to the understanding of decorative art in glass, vestments, miniatures, illumination, as well as of architectural detail.

This latest work, the History of the *cultus hyperduliae* paid to Our Blessed Lady in Germany during the Middle Ages, is of exceptional interest, since, apart from its apologetic worth, it offers a delightful survey of many curious inventions of love which the devotion to the Virgin Mother of Christ inspired in our Teuton forefathers.

The first part of the volume deals with the time when the fortunes of France and Germany were determined by the same ecclesiastical authority, the Carlovingian period, during which devotion to Our Blessed Lady established the chief festivals and inspired a liturgy out of which grew noble masterpieces of poesy, painting, and architecture. At the end of the thirteenth century pictorial art had greatly developed, and in the fifteenth and sixteenth centuries, owing to the activity of the monastic institutions, first the Cistercians and Premonstratensians, then the Dominicans and the Franciscans, and finally the smaller congregations whose origin was largely due to the inspirations that come from the devotion to the Mother of Christ, it had attained a high degree of perfection. A chapter rich in the exposition of the fostering elements of piety and art is the one that deals with the " Rosary " and the " Ave Maria ". The sections treating of the " revelations ", " relics ", and " reliquaries " of the twelfth and two succeeding centuries are instructive. They show that the alleged exaggerations which claim the honor paid to the Madonna was something more than hyperdulia, were much more rare than is assumed by historians who write of this period. Likewise they prove that the Church never endorsed any extravagances of devotion which might tend to give to the Mother of Christ a worship that belongs only to God. The subject of pilgrimages and shrines in honor of Our Lady under the various titles indicating the mysteries of her life, forms a conspicuous feature of the exposition. Throughout the volume there are evidences of critical care and exactness in pointing out sources and references. Whilst the work is not intended to be a controversial history, it serves as an excellent apology for the devotion of Catholics to the Mother of Christ. The illustrations are in most cases original and unfamiliar, but apposite and well-executed. We trust the author, who did much of the work under the stress of severe illness, will be able to complete a task which he mentions as being under way, namely a history of the devotion to the Blessed Virgin from the end of the Middle Ages down to our own time.

HISTOIRE DE L'ÉGLISE DU IIIᵉ AU XIᵉ SIÈCLE. LE CHRISTIAN-ISME ET L'EMPIRE. Par Albert Dufourcq, Professeur a l'Université de Bordeaux. Paris: Bloud & Cie. 1910. Pp. 356.

HISTOIRE GÉNÉRALE DE L'ÉGLISE. Par Ferdinand Mourret, Professeur au Séminaire de Saint-Sulpice. Paris: Bloud & Cie. 1910. Pp. 495.

Having in the first volume of his work discussed the providential preparation for Christianity through paganism and Judaism, and in the second and third volumes having treated of the foundation of the Church and its early development, in the present, the fourth, volume Professor Dufourcq unfolds the history of the Church from the third to the eleventh century. He reduces the events of this period to their geographical unity. They all gather within the Mediterranean borderlands, moving first politically inward and then religiously outward. The period opens with the barbarian invasions. The Persians appear on the Euphrates; the Goths on the Danube; the Germans and Franks on the Rhine; and the onslaught begins, which during the fifth and sixth and seventh centuries shatters the walls of the old empire. The political rule of the army with the despotism of the military emperor succeeds to the authority of the Senate and for a time dominates the outlying provinces which it presently is unable longer to control. The prestige of Rome slowly sinks; the unity of the empire dissolves; the juridical laws and customs of the provinces flow into the city without blending with its legal code; the old conquered nations regain their youth, and the ancient empire yields in its political and moral decrepitude to their vigorous onslaught. Over this scene of growth and decay the drama of history as described by Professor Dufourcq moves in three acts. During the first period—" the Roman period " (the third

centuries. Christianity, driven out where Islam takes possession, spreads throughout Byzantium and establishes herself amongst the Barbarians. But the revolution advances apace and the imperial is almost buried in the national and political upheavals. The Church, after transforming the civilization of the Barbarians, is shamefully betrayed and maltreated by the Germans whom she had most benefited, and the whole religious as well as social fabric seems about to collapse as the tenth century reaches its close. It is this eventful and disastrous period ending in " une époque de l'histoire du monde qui finit "—as he picturesquely calls it—which is surveyed by Professor Dufourcq in the present volume. Surveyed, when regarded from the vastness of the territory covered, but made the personal property of the reader when viewed from the side of the art and manner of the writer. Professor Dufourcq has the happy power of bringing a multiplicity of events under certain focal ideas that illuminate their far-reaching and many-sided significance. The period with which he deals is that in which the Christian Fathers lived and labored. Not the least, perhaps the most, instructive and attractive parts of his book are those which are devoted to the great doctors and Saints of the time, notably Origen, St. Athanasius, and St. Augustine. These personalities are well portrayed, their writings analyzed, and their influence on their times made manifest. In these as well as in the other parts of the volume the general student finds in the text the information he requires, while the abundant annotations with bibliographical references point the special student of history, profane or religious, to the sources of fuller knowledge.

"age of iron" (867-962). The field covered is thus seen to be almost coextensive with that of Professor Dufourcq's volume, but the purpose which determines the method and style of the work is to tell the history of the Church in its onward progress rather than to reduce it to certain typical ideas. Centralizing ideas there are of course and must be, but in M. Dufourcq's work they stand out as dominating the events, while in the present book they rather guide and direct than control. The two works are therefore mutually supplementary. Both are scholarly productions, the works of experienced professors. Of the two, perhaps the second is the most graphic and easy in style, narrative as it is in purpose. Moreover, besides the copious documentary apparatus and the analytical table of contents—which features it shares in common with the preceding work—it contains a good index of proper names, a convenience which Continental authors have not always the considerateness to provide for the student.

Literary Chat.

Referring to Father Sheahan's article on "The Three Days", in the April number of the REVIEW, Dr. Charles F. Aiken of the Catholic University offers the following criticism: "In the illustration of Jesus in the rock-tomb, the sacred body is represented as lying on the rocky floor. In most Jewish tombs cut out of the rock, either niches were made for the reception of the dead, or else longitudinal shelves. On such a shelf the body of Jesus seems to have been laid, for we read in John 20:12, 'And she saw two angels in white, sitting, one at the head, and one at the feet, where the body of Jesus had been laid.' Less l appy still is the representation of the Jewish priests and Pharisees exploring the interior of the tomb after the body of Jesus had been laid within. In the Mosaic Law, the defilement incurred by contact with a corpse or tomb was of the grossest kind, segregating the transgressor as unclean for seven days, and necessitating an elaborate purification described in the nineteenth chapter of Numbers. That the priests and Pharisees would deliberately expose themselves to such defilement is absolutely improbable." While Dr. Aiken's argument regarding the niches or shelves and the law of cleanliness is based on what was customary in Jewish times, the passage from St. John is hardly conclusive, and the question of defilement by mere entrance into the tomb without touching the corpse appears to be also an open one.

In an article entitled "Rhythmic Hymns in Metrical Forge", Father Cl. Blume, S.J., discusses the reform which was undertaken by the censors of the Roman Breviary at the beginning of the seventeenth century, and which subjected the hymns of our sacred poets incorporated in the Catholic liturgy to corrections according to the standard of the Roman classics. Father Blume divides the "thesaurus hymnorum" of the Breviary into three groups—1. metric hymns which conform to the laws of prosody; 2. rhythmic hymns of the period between the fifth and tenth centuries which take no account of prosody but cultivate rhythm and accent; 3. rhythmic hymns of the twelfth and thirteenth centuries which constitute the golden period of rhythmic

Latin poetry, fully equal in merit to the classic productions of a Hilary, Ambrose, Prudentius, Paulinus of Nola, Sedulius, Ennodius, Fortunatus, although not conforming to the laws of syllabic quantities. It was of course to the second group that the "corrections" were chiefly applied.

The change of the metrically defective lines in which the writers had chiefly aimed to express dogmatic and devotional sentiments in rhythmic forms, was not always happy, since the classic measures were introduced often at the expense of the original sense. Father Blume instances the initial strophe of the old trochaic hymn:

> "Urbs beata Hierusalem, dicta pacis visio,
> Quae construitur in coelis, vivis ex lapidibus
> Et angelis coornata ut sponsata comite."

This was altered into iambics. The change unfortunately destroyed also the beautifully suggestive idea of the heavenly origin of the new Jerusalem:

> "Coelestis urbs Jerusalem, beata pacis visio,
> Quae celsa de viventibus saxis ad astra tolleris
> Sponsaque ritu cingeris mille angelorum millibus."

The "corrections" made in this fashion amount to 952; but, as Father Blume shows, they touched few of the really excellent hymns, whether metric or rhythmic. Hence the charge often made that the revisers barbarously forced beautiful and rhythmic hymns into classic forms, thereby destroying the musical quality and the sense of the medieval hymns, is somewhat exaggerated. What the "reformers" so-called may be charged with is simply that they frequently turned poor rhythm and good sense into good metre and poor sense. (*Stimmen aus Maria Laach*—III, 1910. B. Herder, agent.)

Professor Alfons Schulz in *Biblische Zeitschrift*, (Vol. VIII, n. 1,) makes a survey of the status of opinions touching the question of the "Noachian Deluge". Was it anthropologically as well as geographically universal? The consensus of opinion among recent Catholic exegetes is against the assumption of a universal inundation of all the countries of the earth, not only because such an event is impossible by the laws of nature, but also because the words of Sacred Scripture allow us to read "all the land", where hitherto the understanding was "all the earth". But the question whether all human creatures were embraced in the destruction has been generally answered in the affirmative, upon the authority of St. Peter (I Ep. 3:20, and II Ep. 2:5) as commonly interpreted. There are nevertheless Biblical scholars who dissent from the opinion that this interpretation is *de fide*, and Dr. Schulz, despite the fact that he belongs to the conservative school of exegetes, frankly recognizes that there are difficulties of a serious character against the assumption of the anthropological universality of the Deluge, and these difficulties justify one in withholding his judgment until the facts are more clearly defined.

Dr. G. Périés has written an instructive pamphlet touching the school question in France, *La Lutte Scolaire—Rôle du clergé et des fidèles*, in which he discusses the means which the clergy are advised to employ to give practical effect to the *Lettre collective* issued by the French hierarchy toward the end of last year. (Questions Ecclesiastiques, 15 rue d'Angleterre, Lille.)

Among the publishing firms which from the outset have taken generous and rightly-directed interest in the promotion of the *Motu proprio* regarding the reform of Church music, is the Düsseldorf house of L. Schwann, known for its artistic presswork. It has recently published *Cantus Graduales*, a collection of twenty versicles suited to the different feasts of the liturgical year, set to the music of the psalm tones in *falsi bordoni* style. It has just issued also a "Missa in honorem S. Antonii de Padua" for three unequal voices, with organ accompaniment by Joseph Scheel; a "Te Deum" for three male voices by Ant. Chlondowski; two Litanies in honor of St. Joseph, one for two voices by Sinzig, and the other for three male or female voices by A. Müller. For organ playing they issue *Organum comitans* after the Graduale by Wiltberger (edit. Schwann 2) and *24 Kurze Orgelstücke* by Erlemann. In this connexion we may also mention August Weil's *Neunzig Vor und Nachspiele* recently published by Fr. Pustet; and a Gregorian Requiem Mass according to the Vatican Edition by Eduardo Marzo, published by Oliver Ditson of Boston. The agents for the Schwann firm are the Fischer Brothers of New York.

It appears that the discussion as to whether the liturgical chant as it is edited by authority of the Holy See was intended to embody a special form of rhythm or to leave to the individual choir-director the right to apply to the series of notes in act any rhythm he might deem appropriate to them, has been settled by a letter of Cardinal Martinelli to Professor Haberl of Ratisbon. We have stood for the defined rhythm, and there has been much adverse criticism of our position from men otherwise able and zealous in the cause of Church music. Now the discussion is decided in our favor. But we shall print the document with comment in our next number.

The Rev. F. G. Holweck, theological censor of the Archdiocese of St. Louis, whose archeological studies, applied especially to liturgical and pastoral topics, give evidence of deep erudition and a wide classical scholarship, has issued in German a brief history of the liturgico-dogmatical aspects of the Catholic tradition regarding the bodily Assumption of the Blessed Virgin into heaven. We hope to have Father Holweck discuss the subject in the Review at some early date in order that our readers may have a survey of the arguments and their force relative to the prospective definition of the Assumption as a dogma of faith.

The Benziger Brothers have succeeded in establishing a unique depot for a variety and choice of healthy and entertaining Catholic literature. Their monthly magazine appears to have been wisely instituted as a means to enable them to stir up literary talent among the native force of Catholic writers. It supplies them with a divining-rod by which the hidden springs of literary genius are more readily discovered. Thus they are at length enabled to offer our Catholic public such a collection such as *The Best Stories by the Foremost Catholic Authors* at a price accessible to all classes of readers. Among the writers included in this series we have Fathers Benson and Finn, the two Mulhollands, Christian Reid, Eleanor C. Donnelly, Canon Sheehan, Lady Kerr, Catherine Conway, Fathers Bearne and Copus, Anna Sadlier, Mary Waggaman, and others of like merit. The size and typography of the volumes are an additional commendation of their worth.

The April number of the *Irish Theological Quarterly* contains an article by the Rev. Dr. J. Slattery on "The Sacrificial Idea". The author advocates the theory that the essential element of the sacrificial notion is not the offering in itself nor the destruction in itself, but rather "the offering to God of a

REVIEW, Sept., 1905, p. 269) : " On the banquet theory, then, the case stands thus: The Cross and the Last Supper are not two forms of sacrifice of different orders, . . . but they are two distinct parts of one and the same complex operation. Each requires the other in order to the completion of the whole. The death of Jesus is not a ritual sacrifice without the Last Supper; the Supper would only be an empty memorial of the last evening before the Passion if it did not consist of the flesh and blood immolated on Calvary. The Cross and the Supper are two parts of the one sacrifice." Surely, whether we accept the Bishop's theory that the essential feature of the sacrifice of the Mass was the banquet, or whether we argue that the act on consecration (including the act of oblation before and after), together with the Communion, constitutes the essence of the Eucharistic Sacrifice, we are not forced to read the above words as implying that the Last Supper was a sacrifice complete in essence and perfect in rite, apart and distinct from the sacrificial death of the Cross. Such a construction of Bishop Bellord's words is certainly misleading.

A reader interested in the movement to restore the old Roman chasuble in our solemn liturgical worship suggests the republication of the late Father William Lockhart's treatise, printed by Burns and Oates in 1891, under the title of *The Chasuble: Its Genuine Form and Size.* Father Lockhart had published the substance of his paper in the *Irish Ecclesiastical Record* (December, 1890, pp. 1079-1091), taking occasion to discuss the subject from a previous article by Mr. Gilliat Smith, in which the latter had referred to the adoption of the older and ampler form in certain churches of France and Belgium, such as the Cathedral of Nîmes, and the abbey church of Maredsous, as being in reality more conformable to the approved Roman pattern. The latter "when made of the regulation size, according to the brass plate kept in the sacristy in St. Peter's, is larger than any other variety, and has an orphrey of a pillar-like form on the back instead of a cross, and a cross in front" (*Irish Ecclesiastical Record*, April, 1890, p. 302).

"The chasuble," writes Mr. Gilliat Smith, "usually worn in France and Belgium differs from the Roman in that it is considerably smaller." It is true, many priests in Rome now wear the French chasubles. "France," says Father Lockhart, "is apt to set the fashions in dress to the rest of the world, and so French fashions in vestments followed much the same law. Moreover, as Italy is very apt to be influenced by French fashions, so French fashions in vestments penetrated and have produced the more modern Roman vestments, which are little different from French vestments, except that the cross is on the front instead of behind" (*Irish Ecclesiastical Record*, l. c.).

speaker and an incisive writer on all topics of modern interest which demand thoughtful treatment. In his outline of the needs in seminary training he lays great stress on the virtues of retirement and silence as if these were the fundamental habits from which energy and pastoral influences are generated. Father J. M. O'Kavanagh's translation is excellent (Benziger Brothers).

H. L. Kilner and Co. publish *The Life of Blessed Gabriel of Our Lady of Sorrows* (Gabriel Possenti) of the Congregation of the Passion. Cardinal Gibbons, who writes an Introduction to the volume, says of the work of Fr. Nicholas Ward, the editor: "This little volume is a new departure in hagiography and one to be commended." The new departure is given in the "Plan of Work", which deals with the biography in distinct sections, following the psychical development rather than the historical continuity of the Saint's career. This plan makes it well suited for habitual reading, since the growth of virtue, apart from the life of the hero which illustrates the same, is dwelt upon as it is in meditation books.

Practical Hints on Education to Parents and Teachers by Elise Flury (Benziger Brothers) is the result of many years' experience as a Catholic governess. It is replete with practical suggestions based upon a careful analysis of character and disposition; a book particularly helpful to parents who are anxious to give their children proper home training.

Books Received.

THEOLOGICAL AND DEVOTIONAL.

OUR FAITH IS A REASONABLE FAITH. A Word to combat Unbelief and to defend the Faith. Translated from the German of E. Huch by M. Bachur. Techny, Illinois: Society of the Divine Word. Pp. 261. Price, $0.50.

THE CATHOLIC DOCTRINE IN ONE HUNDRED SENTENCES. A Guide to the Oral Introduction of Adults of Limited Time and Education. By the Rev. Peter Geiermann, C.SS.R. St. Louis, Mo.: B. Herder. 1910. Pp. 23. Price, $0.05.

MAXIMS AND COUNSELS FOR RELIGIOUS. Collected from the Letters of St. Alphonsus and arranged for every day in the year. By the Rev. Peter Geiermann, C.SS.R. St. Louis, Mo.: B. Herder. 1910. Pp. 33. Price, $0.05.

FIRST COMMUNION FOR CHILDREN AND ITS CONDITIONS. Translated from the French of Père H. Mazure, O.M.I., by F. M. de Zulueta, S.J. London and Edinburgh: Sands & Co.; St. Louis, Mo.: B. Herder. 1910. Pp. 45. Price, $0.10.

MEDITATIONES VEN. P. LUDOV. DE PONTE, S.J., de praecipuis fidei nostrae mysteriis, de Hispanico in Latinum translatae a Melchiore Trevinnio, S.J., de novo in lucem datae cura P. Lehmkuhl, S.J. Editio altera recognita. Pars V. Friburgi Brisg., et St. Louis, Mo.: B. Herder. 1910. Pp. 376. Price, $1.25.

JESUS, DIR LEBE ICH! Kommunionbuch für Welt und Ordensleute. Zweite Auflage von P. Regalat Trenkwalder, O.F.M. Innsbruck: Fel. Rauch. 1910. Pp. 360.

THE CHIEF SOURCES OF SIN. Seven Discourses on Pride, Covetousness, Lust, Anger, Gluttony, Envy, and Sloth. By the Rev. M. V. McDonough. Baltimore, New York: John Murphy Co. 1910. Pp. 114. Price, $0.75.

THE SUBLIMITY OF THE HOLY EUCHARIST. Also a Visit to the Seven Churches in Rome on the occasion of the Jubilee. Five essays by Father Moritz Meschler, S.J. Translation by A. C. Clarke. St. Louis, Mo.: B. Herder; London, Edinburgh: Sands & Co. 1910. Pp. 174. Price, $0.75.

THE YOUNG MAN'S GUIDE. Counsels, Reflections, and Prayers for Catholic Young Men. By the Rev. F. X. Lasance. New York, Cincinnati, Chicago: Benziger Bros. 1910. Pp. 782. Price: cloth, $0.75; Levant, gold edges, $1.00; American seal, limp, gold edges, $1.25.

THE SERMONS, EPISTLES, AND APOCALYPSES OF ISRAEL'S PROPHETS. From the Beginning of the Assyrian Period to the End of the Maccabean Struggle. By Chas. Foster Kent, Ph.D., Woolsey Professor of Biblical Literature in Yale University. (*The Student's Old Testament.*) With Maps and Chronological Charts. New York: Chas. Scribner's Sons. 1910. Pp. xxv-516. Price, $2.75 *net.*

CARDINAL MERCIER'S CONFERENCES. Delivered to his Seminarists at Mechlin in 1907. Translated from the French by J. M. O'Kavanagh. With an Introduction by the Very Rev. P. A. Canon Sheehan, D.D. New York, Cincinnati, Chicago: Benziger Bros. 1910. Pp. xvii-206. Price, $1.50 *net.*

HEROES OF THE FAITH. New Conferences on the English Martyrs delivered at Tyburn Convent by Dom Bede Camm, O.S.B., Editor of the St. Nicholas Series. New York, Cincinnati, Chicago: Benziger Bros. 1910. Pp. xxvi-149. Price, $0.80 *net.*

LITURGICAL.

OFFICIUM PRO DEFUNCTIS cum Missa et Absolutione nec non Exsequiarum Ordine quod juxta editionem Vaticanam hodiernae musicae signis tradidit Dr. Fr. X. Mathias Regens Seminarii Episcopalis Argentinensis. Ratisbonae, Romae, Neo Eboraci et Cincinnati: sumptibus et typis Friderici Pustet. MCMX. Pp. 104. Price, $0.30.

HANDBOOK OF THE DIVINE LITURGY. A Brief Study of the Historical Development of the Mass. By Charles Cowley Clarke, Priest. With an Introduction by the Right Rev. George Ambrose Burton, D.D., Lord Bishop of Clifton. London: Kegan Paul, Trench, Trübner & Co.; St. Louis, Mo.: B. Herder. 1910. Pp. 180. Price, $0.90.

A HANDBOOK OF CHURCH MUSIC. A Practical Guide for all those having the Charge of Schools and Choirs, and others who desire to restore Plainsong to its Proper Place in the Services of the Church. By F. Clement C. Egerton. With a Preface by H. G. Worth, M.A., Member of the Pontifical Commission. New York, Cincinnati, Chicago: Benziger Bros. 1909. Pp. xiv-218. Price, $1.15 *net.*

HISTORICAL.

BRIEFE DER DIENERIN GOTTES MUTTER MARIA VON JESUS, Maria Deluil Martiny, Stifterin der Gesellschaft der " Töchter des Herzens Jesu ". Aus dem Französischen übersetzt mit bishöfl. Erlaubniss. Regensburg, Rom, New York, Cincinnati: Fr. Pustet & Co. 1910. Pp. 255. Price, $0.75.

HISTORY OF THE SOCIETY OF JESUS IN AMERICA, COLONIAL AND FEDERAL. By Thomas Hughes, S.J. Documents. Vol. I, Part II. Nos. 141-224 (1605-1838). Cleveland: The Burrows Bros. Co.; London, New York: Longmans, Green & Co. 1910. Pp. 1222. Price, $4.50.

LA LUTTE SCOLAIRE. Rôle du Clergé et des Fidèles. Par le Rev. D. C. Périès. Lille: Administration des Editions des Questions Ecclesiastiques. 1910. Pp. 25.

REPORT OF THE COMMISSIONERS OF EDUCATION for the Year ending June 30, 1909. Vol. II. Washington: Government Printing Office. Pp. v and 599 to 1373.

HISTORY OF THE CHRISTIAN CHURCH. By Philip Schaff. Vol. V, Part II: The Middle Ages. From Boniface VIII, 1294, to the Protestant Reformation, 1517. By David S. Schaff, D.D., Professor of Church History in the Western Theological Seminary, Pittsburg. New York: Chas. Scribner's Sons. 1910. Pp. xi-795. Price, $3.25 *net*.

THE LIFE OF BLESSED GABRIEL OF OUR LADY OF SORROWS, Gabriel Possenti, of the Congregation of the Passion. Begun by the Rev. Hyacinth Hage, C.P., rewritten and enlarged by the Rev. Nicholas Ward, C.P. With an Introduction by Cardinal Gibbons. Superiorum Permissu. Philadelphia: H. L. Kilner & Co. 1910. Pp. 295. Price, cloth, $0.50; paper, $0.25.

MISCELLANEOUS.

AMES EN PRISON. L'Ecole française des Sourdes-Muettes-Aveugles et leurs Sœurs des Deux Mondes. Par Louis Arnould, Professeur à l'Université de Poitiers. Quatrième édition, mise à jour et doublée. Illustrée de 13 gravures hors texte. Précédée d'une Lettre de M. Georges Picot, Secrétaire perpétuel de l'Académie des Sciences morales et politiques. Paris: G. Oudin & Cie. 1910. Pp. xix-479.

WHAT TIMES! WHAT MORALS! WHERE ON EARTH ARE WE? By the Rev. Henry Churchill Semple, S.J., Moderator of the Theological Conferences of the Archdiocese of New York, author of *Anglican Ordinations*, etc. New York, Cincinnati, Chicago: Benziger Bros. 1910. Pp. 76. Price, $0.35.

WHERE MISTS HAVE GATHERED. By Mrs. MacDonald of Skeabost. St. Louis, Mo.: B. Herder; London, Edinburgh: Sands & Co. 1910. Pp. 236. Price, $1.00.

THE PURPOSE OF THE PAPACY. By the Right Rev. John S. Vaughan, D.D., Bishop of Sebastopol. St. Louis, Mo.: B. Herder; London, Edinburgh: Sands & Co. 1910. Pp. 158. Price, $0.45.

JEAN AND HER FRIENDS. By Evelyn Mary Buckenham. Illustrated. St. Louis, Mo.: B. Herder; London, Edinburgh: Sands & Co. 1910. Pp. 123. Price, $0.50.

THE MARRYING OF BRIAN, AND OTHER STORIES. By Alice Dease. With colored illustration. St. Louis, Mo.: B. Herder; London, Edinburgh: Sands & Co. 1910. Pp. 83. Price, $0.50.

A BUNCH OF GIRLS AND WAYSIDE FLOWERS. By "Shan". With colored illustration. St. Louis, Mo.: B. Herder; London, Edinburgh: Sands & Co. 1910. Pp. 108. Price, $0.50.

PRINCE IZON. A Romance of the Grand Canyon. By James Paul Kelly. Five Illustrations in Color by Harold H. and Edwin Betts. Chicago: A. C. McClurg & Co. 1910. Pp. 399. Price, $1.50.

THE LIGHT OF HIS COUNTENANCE. A Tale of Rome in the Second Century after Christ. By Jerome Harte. New York, Cincinnati, Chicago: Benziger Bros. 1910. Pp. 276. Price, $1.25.

THE BEST STORIES BY THE FOREMOST CATHOLIC AUTHORS. With an Introduction by Maurice Francis Egan, LL.D. In Ten Volumes. New York, Cincinnati, Chicago: Benziger Bros. 1910. Pp., each volume, 255.

PRACTICAL HINTS ON EDUCATION TO PARENTS AND TEACHERS. A Translation from her original German work by Elise Flury. New York, Cincinnati, Chicago: Benziger Bros. 1910. Pp. viii-206. Price, $0.75 *net*.

THE
ECCLESIASTICAL REVIEW

FIFTH SERIES.—VOL. II.—(XLII).—JUNE, 1910.—No. 6.

THE BIBLICAL COMMISSION AND THE DEGREES IT CONFERS.

II.[1]

ORAL EXAMINATION.

IN the previous paper we gave some account of the origin of the Biblical Commission and of the object for which it was created; we also gave the program of the examinations held by the same Commission for the purpose of conferring the Degrees of Licentiate and Doctor in Sacred Scripture. In that paper we were able to touch upon the written portion only of the examination for the Licentiate; in this we will examine at some length the oral portion of the same examination, and the Doctorate examination.

For convenience sake we repeat the program as given in the preceding paper.

AD PROLYTATUM.

IN EXPERIMENTO QUOD SCRIPTO FIT.

(A) Exegesis (*i. e. expositio doctrinalis, critica et philologica*) quattuor Evangeliorum et Actuum Apostolorum. *Pericope ex his, a iudicibus eligenda, exponetur nullo praeter textus et concordantias adhibito libro; de qua verbis quoque periculum fiet.*

(B) Dissertatio de historia biblica *iuxta materiam infra sub n. III assignatam.*

(C) Dissertatio de Introductione generali aut speciali *iuxta materiam infra positam sub nn. IV et V.*

IN EXPERIMENTO VERBALI.

IV. Introductio specialis in singulos libros utriusque Testamenti (*i. e. au-
    thenticitas, integritas, compositionis circumstantiae, scopus, divisiones
    generales*).
V. Introductionis generalis quaestiones selectae, nimirum:
    1. *De Bibliorum Sacrorum inspiratione.*
    2. *De sensu litterali et de sensu typico.*
    3. *De legibus Hermeneuticae.*
    4. *De antiquis Hebraeorum Synagogis.*
    5. *De variis Iudaeorum sectis circa tempora Christi.*
    6. *De gentibus Palaestinam tempore Christi incolentibus.*
    7. *Geographia Palaestinae temporibus Regum.*
    8. *Palaestinae divisio et Hierusalem topographia tempore Christi.*
    9. *Itinera Sancti Pauli.*
    10. *Inscriptiones Palaestinenses antiquissimae.*
    11. *De kalendario et praecipuis ritibus sacris Hebraeorum.*
    12. *De ponderibus, mensuris et nummis in Sancta Scriptura memoratis.*

The first item is the " Four Gospels and the Acts of the
Apostles in the Greek text." This examination lasts half-an-
hour. The candidate presents himself before the appointed
examiner, who does not form part of a board, but sits at a table
apart. The examination is, however, public, and students
from the various Colleges in the City throng around. It is
sometimes amusing to witness a candidate being escorted by
his companions from the Greek examiner to the Hebrew examiner, and thence, if time permits, to the board of three or
more who preside over the other portions of the oral examination. First, then, for the Greek. It is not an examination in
exegesis, though the examiner may, if he think fit, take up
points in the candidate's written paper—" de qua verbis quoque periculum fiet ". The object is to test the candidate's
knowledge of New Testament Greek. He must be able to
read, to parse, to construe; he must show that he is aware of
the force of the various tenses—he must not, for instance, take
aorists as presents or vice-versa—similarly, he must bring out
the full significance of the different prepositions, especially in
compound verbs. In short, the candidate is expected to give
proof of a competent knowledge of the Greek text; he must be
able to use it not merely as something subsidiary to exegesis,
but as its basis. Thus the examination is not only on the
grammar; it turns on the philology as well; peculiar New Testament usages should be known and some of the characteristics
of the different New Testament writers should have been
grasped.

All this evidently demands work, and it is not precisely the
kind of work that can be done in class, though of course the

assistance of a professor will be of the greatest advantage, but the real work must be done by the student himself. It might seem idle to insist on this, yet every professor will endorse the statement that there is a tendency nowadays to regard the professor as a kind of "coach" whose duty it is to cram the student—at least his note-book. And the royal road to an adequate knowledge of the Greek Testament is assiduous reading of it. There is no other. It will not avail to read the latest idiosyncracies "from Germany", nor to be the proud possessor of the most recent *Einleitung*. The best of all Introductions is the book itself. Of course a commentary will be needed, but it need not be an erudite one, and, though we say it with shame, there is nothing to equal the Cambridge Bible for Schools—that is, the Greek Testament portion of it. We are not afraid of avowing this, for, though there may be a deal of incidental heresy in these editions, they are not written with an heretical bias. Moreover we are dealing with students, be it remembered, who have already taken their Doctorate in Theology and who are capable of detecting heresy when it is thrust upon them.

The text, then, a simple commentary, a handy concordance to the Greek text, and an elementary Grammar of New Testament Greek—these are the tools the student requires; and, next to the text, the concordance is, perhaps, the most essential of all; for a man who can use a concordance well has at hand most of the materials for a good commentary.

The next item on the Program is the Hebrew. It must be confessed that it is a formidable one. The four Books of Kings comprise one hundred and two chapters, and the tyro who has with difficulty waded through a solitary chapter of the Hebrew Bible will gasp at the idea of reading and deciphering this large amount of Hebrew. Certain chapters, too, contain a good deal of technical matter involving a proportionate amount of dictionary-work. On the other hand, the Hebrew narrative style is exceedingly simple; the same words, the same constructions, and the same ideas, repeat themselves again and again; moreover, there are no poetical portions except the Canticle of Anna and the Lament of David over Saul and Jonathan. As for the amount of knowledge required, it would appear that, as in the case of the Greek

New Testament, the student must be able to read aloud with a fair degree of fluency; he must be able to parse the various forms, and he must thoroughly possess the different Hebrew conjugations. He is not supposed to be a Semitic scholar, but he is supposed to have a thoroughly good working knowledge of the language so as to be able to make practical use of it when he comes to teach Sacred Scripture.

A student will, of course, have to work hard to attain the requisite knowledge, but there are ways and ways of working. A boy who has to construe a page of Xenophon takes each word as it comes and, probably without a moment's reflection, looks it out in his dictionary. His work is essentially laborious and, it must be confessed, generally unprofitable. Similarly, a boy has had a long spell of pure grammar-work before he approaches an author, and he has been made familiar with a multitude of forms and rules with their exceptions. Whether the boy-mind requires such formation is open to question; for our part we decline to believe it; but we are certain that this is not the way in which a man should approach the study of an Oriental language. The first step must, of course, be an elementary knowledge of the principles of the Grammar. And we would emphasize the word " principles ", for the details can only be learnt by practice and by familiarity with their concrete application. In other words, assiduous reading of the original is the golden method. It should be read without a dictionary, but with the help of a good translation and for this purpose the Revised Version is the best since it undertakes to give the meaning of the Hebrew text itself. Thus a student who has a sufficient knowledge of the Grammar to be able to distinguish, at least roughly, between a verb and a noun should take the first Book of Kings and steadily plough his way through it with the assistance of the Revised Version. Again and again he will find himself pulled up short and will be unable to see how a particular sense is to be wrung from the Hebrew he sees before him; he may, and probably will, attach the wrong meaning to many words, but what matter? He is gradually getting accustomed to a multitude of forms merely by seeing them day after day. He has not had to waste hours in turning over the pages of his dictionary. Occasionally he should look up a form in the Grammar, but if he cannot identify it let him not waste time over it. When he has waded through the first book he will have read thirty-one chapters of Hebrew. It is true that he will feel that his knowledge is very shaky and somewhat chaotic. But let him now take up his grammar: we venture to say that it will have lost half its terrors, and this for the simple reason that the forms are now familiar and not the bugbears they were before.

If he will now devote two or three weeks to a steady examination of the Hebrew conjugations, he will readily master them and will never have any real difficulty with them again. At the same time there are certain points which demand sheer hard wrestling, for instance the chapter on the permutation of vowels, for principles are there involved which are alien to all the student has ever had to learn before, and this because it is an arbitrary system—not one which has developed according to the rules of language. It has to be learnt, and after its principles have been mastered let the student take a Hebrew Bible without points; two or three chapters of this, read aloud and slowly, will serve to crystallize his knowledge. Indeed the present writer may be allowed to remark that he has found that the best results were secured when, after reading two or three books of the Bible, the student was taken outside the Bible and introduced to such a book as Cooke's *North-Semitic Inscriptions.* The interest is at once aroused by the historical character of the materials there collected; to read them at all a student must have mastered the question of vocalization; to understand them he must work systematically and by the application of principles. We would guarantee the accuracy of the knowledge of any student if he had read carefully the Moabite Stone, for example, or the Siloam inscription. Facsimiles of these are easily obtainable and the decipherment of the archaic forms serves to stimulate the student's interest besides serving as an invaluable introduction to epigraphy.

And with Hebrew, as with any other language, the student plods wearily but perseveringly on, feeling his way as he goes, often discouraged by his apparently slow progress, when suddenly he awakes to the fact that he *possesses* the language. This may sound ridiculous, but we are confident that any one who so possesses a language will endorse what we say. And when this moment arrives there are no more difficulties; words will of course have to be learnt, but there will be no more doubt about principles. It should not be forgotten, however, by the student who is preparing himself for the Licentiate that he will have to translate the Hebrew into Latin; hence he should practise himself in reading aloud in Hebrew and in rendering it, also aloud, into Latin. Nothing will so help a student to acquire the necessary familiarity with the two languages as the use of a Polyglot, and he can also " kill two birds ", or rather three, " with one stone " if he keeps an eye upon the Septuagint translation in his Polyglot at the same time. Patient work alone will bring about the desired result; it is amazing how much ground the daily chapter will cover.

Finally, it is universally acknowledged, in theory at least, that we know no language till we can speak it and write it. Now no student can be expected to speak or write Hebrew with fluency, but he can do something in this way. He can learn small portions by heart, and if he does so he will be astonished at the command of the forms and of the turns of expression this will give him. It would be almost enough to commit to memory the " De Profundis ". And it is the same with the Greek of the New Testament; a student who gets off by rote the Ave Maria or one of the Canticles, will know a great deal of New Testament Greek and, what is more to the point, will be able to use his knowledge. It is of interest in this connexion to note how St. Jerome learnt Hebrew; there were no Grammars in those days. Probably if the Saint had had access to one he would never have attained to the wonderful knowledge of the language which he constantly displays. In default of a Grammar, then, he induced a Jew, for a very considerable sum, to teach him. " I remember," he says almost pathetically, " that in order to understand this volume (Job), I paid a not inconsiderable sum for the services of a teacher, a native of Lydda, who was among the Hebrews reckoned to be in the front rank." [2] And he describes, almost

language, the expenditure of much time and energy barely enabled me to utter the puffing and hissing words; I seemed to be walking in a sort of underground chamber with a few scattered rays of light shining down upon me; and when at last I met with Daniel, such a sense of weariness came over me, that, in a fit of despair, I could have counted all my former toil as useless. But there was a certain Hebrew who encouraged me, and was for ever quoting for my benefit the saying 'Persistent labor conquers all things'; and so, conscious that among Hebrews I was only a smatterer, I once more began to study Chaldee. And to confess the truth, to this day I can read and understand Chaldee better than I can pronounce it." These words show us how important a thing St. Jerome conceived it to be able to speak the language; and though he sometimes, as here, speaks in a disparaging way of his powers, he at other times insists that he has a really good knowledge of it. "We have," he says in the above-quoted Preface, "some slight knowledge of Hebrew"—words which of course are to be taken in an ironical sense. Nothing, however, better shows the supreme command over the language which he possessed than the account he has left us of his mode of procedure when translating the Books of Tobias and Judith: "Inasmuch," he says, "as the Chaldee is closely allied to the Hebrew, I procured the help of the most skilful speaker of both languages I could find, and gave to the subject one day's hasty labor; my method was to express in Latin, with the aid of a secretary, whatever an interpreter expressed to me in Hebrew words." Surely this was a stupendous psychological feat!

Practice in writing Hebrew, too, will be of advantage. The student will find that if he will now and again take the pains to translate a few verses from the Revised Version into Hebrew he will probably improve his knowledge of the language. It was to the practice of translating classical English into classical Latin that Cardinal Newman attributed his power of writing both languages so well.

The next item on the Program is "the History of the Hebrews from Samuel to the Babylonian Captivity; also the Gospel-History and that of the Apostles down to the Roman Captivity of St. Paul."

We have already adverted to this portion of the Program
when treating of the written examination.   But it should be
noted that it is one thing to write a paper on any particular
period of Biblical History when one has time to think and has
a Bible at hand and also a good concordance; it is quite
another thing when you find yourself in the presence of an
examining board, are naturally " dimidium tui ipsius " at such
a moment, and, more than all, have no Bible to turn to for a
hint.   A great deal of memory-work is, then, required for
the oral examination in Biblical History.   The contents of
the Books must be thoroughly known, precis of their historical
data must be made, the history of the Kings must have been
read in the light of the Prophets, both Major and Minor, and
the chronological question must have been clearly grasped.
We have known such questions to be asked, for instance, as
the following: " Sketch the relations between Egypt and the
Kings of Judah from David to the Captivity "; and the unhappy candidate was not allowed to give any merely general
answer: he was pinned down to the precise dynasty and the
precise period as far as it was known.   It does not follow, of
course, that he would have been rejected had he not known
these details; but he was certainly expected to know a good
deal about them.   And though this may seem at first sight excessive, it is not really so.   Such knowledge is imparted in our
Board-Schools!   Moreover, there are Manuals of Biblical
History which cover all the ground, though here once more
we must perforce lament the want of Catholic Manuals of the
requisite kind.   Two of the most useful books are now unfortunately out of date, viz. Geikie, *Hours with the Bible;* and
Stanley, *The History of the Jewish Church.*   They are out of
date now simply because so much has been discovered since
they were written.

With regard to the New Testament History, it may be said
that it is question of a thorough knowledge of the text of the
Gospels and the Acts.   The life of our Lord, the journeys
He made to and from the Holy City, the dates generally accepted for the commencement of His Ministry and for its close
—these and similar self-evident points must be thoroughly
got up.   It is the same for the life of St. Paul; a student must
be able to trace his missionary journeys, discuss his visits to

Jerusalem, know the probable dates assigned to the Epistles, their order and their contents. And as the student works away at these questions he will notice with joy that to master one question he has to study several and is thus covering a great deal of ground. He cannot, for instance, prepare his Special Introduction to the Acts without going into the question of St. Paul's journeys, but this latter point is one of the set questions in the Program, and, moreover, may almost be termed the key to the History of the Apostles which, as we have seen, is another set question. And it is the same all through the Program—one question thoroughly done means that several more are thereby at least half done.

The next feature in the Program is the oral examination on the Special Introduction to every book of the Bible. What we have said above concerning the oral examination in history may be applied here. The student has no book before him and hence must trust to his memory. He has not the least idea what Book may be set him. But whatever it is, he is supposed to be able to give its main divisions, discuss its authenticity, its date, and any other points which the particular Book may bring forward. Thus we have heard students asked to analyze the Book of Job and to discuss its authenticity, etc. And this, too, without a text! Yet it is not so hard as it might seem if only we have accustomed ourselves to read the Bible itself rather than books upon the Bible! The Introduction to Esdras and Nehemias is not an uncommon question, and it is certainly not an easy one; Professor Van Hoonacker, unfortunately for students, has excogitated a theory which the student is expected to know, at least in its broad lines. This question of the Special Introduction is undoubtedly the most heart-breaking of all those in the Program, and the student will often feel as St. Jerome felt with regard to the Chaldaic of the Book of Daniel. But it is also true that the labor involved in committing this mass of material to memory will amply repay the student in after years. He will find when he comes to sit in the Professor's chair that he has a grasp of the Bible, and a practical knowledge of its contents, which will stand him in good stead; it will enable him to illustrate one part of the Bible by another in a most felicitous way; and, after all, what is meant by " commenting " but bringing out the harmony and unity of the Book of Books?

There remains but one question more and it is a large one, for it embraces twelve " Select Questions of General Introduction ". But nearly every one of these questions will have forced itself upon the attention of the student in his work of preparing the rest of the examination. With the exception of the first question, that namely on Inspiration, they are all straightforward and can be studied in numberless " Aids to the Bible " and also, if need be, in more profound treatises. But the question of Inspiration is a bugbear! There has been so much controversy on the subject, and a student so often has the feeling that he is treading on the very edge of the pit of heresy! The " Locus Classicus " is, of course, the Encyclical *Providentissimus Deus.* This the student must know thoroughly and he must be able to defend it. He must be prepared to give a definition of Inspiration and to analyze it. He is, of course, perfectly free to hold any view he likes on the point—any view, that is, which has not been condemned. It would be invidious here to mention particular treatises on the question, but the writer himself often wonders how any but an out-and-out " Thomist " can possibly explain the Encyclical.

The Examination for the Doctorate.

Candidates who have passed the Licentiate successfully may present themselves for the Doctorate after the lapse of at least one year from that date. The Program for the Doctorate examination is as follows :

Ad Lauream.

de scripto.

Amplior quaedam dissertatio circa thesim aliquam graviorem ab ipso candidato de Commissionis assensu eligendam.

coram.

I. Dissertationis a Censoribus impugnandae defensio.
II. Exegesis unius ex sequentibus Novi Testamenti partibus a candidato deligendae atque pro arbitrio iudicum exponendae :
1. *Epistolae ad Romanos.*
2. *Epistolarum I et II ad Corinthios.*
3. *Epistolarum ad Thessalonicenses I et II et ad Galatas.*

III. Exegesis ut supra alicuius ex infrascriptis Veteris Testamenti partibus:
    1. *Genesis.*
    2. *Exodi, Levitici et Numerorum.*
    3. *Deuteronomii.*
    4. *Iosue.*
    5. *Iudicum et Ruth.*
    6. *Librorum Paralipomenon, Esdrae et Nehemiae.*
    7. *Iob.*
    8. *Psalmorum.*
    9. *Proverbiorum.*
    10. *Ecclesiastae et Sapientiae.*
    11. *Cantici Canticorum et Ecclesiastici.*
    12. *Esther, Tobiae et Iudith.*
    13. *Isaiae.*
    14. *Ieremiae cum Lamentationibus et Baruch.*
    15. *Ezechielis.*
    16. *Danielis cum libris Machabaeorum.*
    17. *Prophetarum minorum.*
IV.
    1. *De Scholis exegeticis Alexandrina et Antiochena, ac de exegesi celebriorum Patrum Graecorum saec. IV et V.*
    2. *De operibus exegeticis S. Hieronymi ceterorumque Patrum Latinorum saec. IV et V.*
    3. *De origine et auctoritate textus Massoretici.*
    4. *De versione Septuagintavirali et de aliis versionibus Vulgata antiquioribus, in crisi textuum adhibendis.*
    5. *Vulgatae historia usque ad initium saec. VII, deque eiusdem authenticitate a Concilio Tridentino declarata.*
  V. Peritia praeterea probanda erit in aliqua alia ex linguis praeter Hebraicam et Chaldaicam orientalibus, quarum usus in disciplinis biblicis maior est.

The most important feature in the examination is the Thesis which the candidate presents and which he has to defend publicly. When deciding to present himself for the Degree he must propose some subject upon which he feels that he can write a practical thesis. No suggestions are made as to the kind of subject which should be presented, but each candidate will have his own predilections. It is generally agreed that it is not well to present any of the essentially controverted themes, e. g. a candidate who proposed to write a thesis on the vexed question of Inspiration would probably be advised to take another subject. If, indeed, he were allowed to present it he would probably draw down upon his devoted head a most unenviable storm at the examination! A candidate will do well, then, to take the advice of the examiners on the subject of his thesis immediately after passing his Licentiate examination. The following theses have been presented by the four candidates who have up to now taken the Doctorate. " The Messianic Character of the Parables in the Book of Enoch ";

" A Critical Study of the Alexandrian Additions to the Book of Proverbs "; " An Examination of the Apologetic Writings of St. Irenæus "; " The Date of the Composition of the Book of Deuteronomy ".

This list may, perhaps, serve as a guide to other aspirants. The thesis must be printed, or at least type-written. Copies must be sent to the five members of the jury, and the candidate is advised to have other copies ready for any members of the Commission who may be in Rome at the time of the examination and who may wish to attend or to propose difficulties. According to the edition of the Program in French, the thesis as a general rule is to be written in Latin, but if a candidate wishes he can easily obtain leave to write it in some modern language.

At the same time that he proposes the subject of his thesis he must also state what Book or group of Books of the Old as well as of the New Testament he wishes to take up; a glance at the Program will show how the Books of the two Testaments are grouped. The examination is essentially on the original text of each book, and though he has already proved his competence with regard to Hebrew and Greek at the examination for the Licentiate, the examinee must expect to be asked grammatical and philological questions arising from the text proposed to him. The examination, however, is essentially an exegetical one and the candidate is expected to have a very full knowledge of his subject; he cannot complain if very difficult questions are put to him—provided always that they can fairly be said to arise from the text.

The next point in the Program, viz. No. IV, may be divided into two parts. Divisions 1 and 2 are concerned with Patrology, Nos. 3-5 deal with historical and textual criticism. Under the heading " Patrology " comes first of all the question of the exegetical schools of Alexandria and Antioch, and the student is expected to know something about the exegetical methods of the better-known Greek Fathers of the fourth and fifth centuries. In the second place come the Latin Fathers of the same period, and especially the exegetical work of St. Jerome. No. 3 is concerned with the existing Hebrew text of

sions anterior, in point of time, to the Vulgate, which are of importance in textual criticism; these are the Coptic, Syriac, and Old Latin versions. No. 5 is concerned with the history of the Vulgate version down to the beginning of the seventh century, and also with the Tridentine declaration of its authenticity.

The last point in the Program is perhaps somewhat ambiguously worded; at any rate the student must not take the words "Peritia probanda erit" as though they meant that only a smattering of some other Oriental language besides Hebrew and Chaldaic was required. A good sound knowledge, though not a specialist's knowledge, is called for. The languages admissible are Old Egyptian, Coptic, Assyrian, Syriac, Arabic, and Ethiopic. Some definite book or books in the language chosen must be presented—a notable portion, for example, of some version of the Bible, e. g. the Pentateuch or the Gospels and Acts.

The actual examination is a serious matter. It is divided into two distinct parts, the preliminary and the solemn. The preliminary portion takes place in the morning and lasts from two hours and a half to three hours. Proceedings open with the examination in the Oriental language which the candidate has chosen. This may continue for half an hour or thereabouts. The examinee is expected to be able to read the language fluently, to translate it into Latin, to parse the forms, and to discuss syntactical questions. Then follows the examination on the Old Testament Book or Group of Books. This also lasts half hour or a little more. A quarter of an hour's rest is then given, followed by half-an-hour's examination of the New Testament Book. Both these examinations are searching and a candidate must be really well up in his subject. Then follow the Patrology and the history of the Versions as indicated above. Of course all is in Latin and a candidate must try to perfect himself in speaking this language, for if he stumbles for words and is guilty of repeated solecisms he gives a bad impression and also hampers himself. Talking Latin aloud to oneself will often prove a real aid to acquiring a tolerable proficiency; better still if two can talk it together.

If the result of the preliminary examination is satisfactory, the examinee is told that he is to present himself again at the

Vatican—all the examinations take place in the rooms off the Cortile di San Damaso—at a specified hour in the afternoon when he will be informed as to the subject on which he is to give a lecture or class. For this he is allowed one hour's preparation. The subject of this lecture is chosen either from the Old Testament or New Testament Books presented by the candidate, or from the section of the Program numbered IV, but not from the thesis which the candidate has sent in nor from the Oriental language which he has taken up. His lecture is supposed to last about fifteen or twenty minutes; he should try to make it as much as possible like a formal lecture such as he would give in class. It must not be oratorical, but should consist of a brief exposé of the question at issue, with an examination—necessarily very brief—of the difficulties occurring in the matter. Questions are then put which are meant to test the reality of the knowledge shown, and the candidate should try to answer these much as he would do if students were putting difficulties to him in class. For the preparation of this lecture it appears usual to allow the use of any notes which the student may have; it would, presumably, not be permitted to have commentaries and such-like at hand.

On the following afternoon comes the second portion of the solemn examination, viz. the defence of the Thesis sent in by the candidate. This is a very formal function. The Cardinal President of the Biblical Commission attends in state and the Commissioners wear their official robes. There is usually an immense crowd of students from the various Colleges and the examinee may well be excused if he feels nervous. When all are seated he reads aloud a résumé in Latin of his thesis; this should not take long, some twenty minutes at the most. Three of the examiners then proceed in turn to attack the doctrine exposed. The examinee should, for clearness sake, repeat the arguments briefly and then analyze them as shortly as possible. There seems to be no definite time assigned during which these objections can be put, but it is hardly likely that they would be continued beyond two hours.

The Cardinal President then retires with the body of Com-

suspect that he has not done too well he feels in an unenviable frame of mind. However the President soon sweeps into the Hall once more and all doubts, whether for good or for ill, are set at rest.

These examinations, then, are really serious. They demand solid work from those who would gain the coveted Degrees. No mere tyro need attempt them; nor need anyone think that because he has been a professor he can therefore " sail through " the Licentiate and the Doctorate. We have endeavored to put before our readers a just picture of what is required; we have not minimized the difficulties, nor, on the other hand, have we exaggerated them. Our object throughout these two papers has been twofold. In the first place there are many, both in the Church and outside it, who are inclined to ridicule the examinations, the members of the Commission, and the two Écoles Bibliques. To such cavilers we would say: Try the examination yourselves, and if you " sail through it " without difficulty, we shall be much surprised. And in the second place there are many Biblical students— and it is especially for these we have written—who would like to present themselves for examination but—" omne ignotum pro magnifico ". Such students will, we trust, gather from the foregoing pages two things: first that the examination will require serious preparation, and secondly that the preparation demanded will prove an invaluable asset to them as future Biblical professors. How often we are told that the Biblical courses in our Seminaries are neglected and that fully equipped Professors are hard to find! The remedy is at hand. Encourage students to prepare themselves for these Degrees, and in order to fit them for the work send them to one of the Écoles Bibliques where alone they can obtain adequate training.

HUGH POPE, O.P.

Rome, Italy.

A POET-BISHOP OF PORTO RICO.

A T the period of the discovery of America, Spain was advancing rapidly toward the golden age of her literature. The influence of the Italian Renaissance was beginning to make itself felt in letters, if not in the arts, and, though the old Castilian school still existed in history and poetry, there was a change in the air. The medieval chronicle was soon to surrender its rights to a new form of history, more worthy of the name, under the auspices of such writers as Zurita, Mendoza, and Mariana, and, though not without a struggle, the old style of Castilian versification was to yield to the Italian metre, through the influence of Boseau, and Garcilaso de la Vega. With Garcilaso the brilliant period of Castilian literature began that was to culminate in the glorious triumvirate of Cervantes, Lope de Vega, and Calderon.

When Garcilaso was born, eleven years had passed since the landing of Columbus in America, and when he died, the wonderful races of Mexico and Peru had been met and conquered. It was a period of great excitement, when a horde of adventurers were crossing the ocean in quest of gold. Yet in the midst of fierce passions, men and women found time to cultivate the muses. The first strains of the American lyre come to us with the feeble and indistinct sounds of the dawn. We hear them in the West Indies, in the songs of a consecrated virgin of Santo Domingo, Sister Leonora de Ovando, the first female poet of America, and of Francisco Tortado, and Doña Elvira de Mendoza in the same island. In the heart of the Cordilleras, when Santa Fé de Bogotá was in its cradle, the *conquistador,* Quesada, employed his leisure moments in discussing the merits of the Castilian metre, and the one-time soldier, Castellanos, now a priest in remote Tunja, might relate in verse the exploits of his countrymen. It was especially in Mexico that the muses flourished, in that Mexico where works had been printed since 1535, and where a few years later a university arose with such brilliant professors as Fray Alfonso de Vera Cruz of the Augustinian Order, and the secular priest, Cervantes Lalazar. The *Dialogues* of Lalazar, give us a splendid idea of the culture and of the literary society of the Mexico of those days, more than half a century before the Pilgrims landed on Plymouth Rock.

Certamenes or poetical competitions were the order of the day, and many a writer struggled for the laurel wreath. In one of these, held in 1585, in the presence of the Archbishop, Don Pedro Moya y Contreras, and of six bishops who had gathered from other dioceses to attend the third Mexican Council, the prize was won by a youth of seventeen. This youth was destined to rank as one of the foremost poets of the New World, to become, according to the estimate of Menendez y Pelayo, the most American of American poetic writers, though a native of Spain, and to occupy an honorable position in the history of Spanish literature. His name was Bernardo de Valbuena. The Spanish Academy deplores the fact that so little is known of his life. Although every detail is written concerning those boisterous conquerors who were frequently more injurious than beneficial to humanity, obscurity is too often the fate of literary men. Born at Valdepeñas in Spain in 1568, Valbuena must have come early to America, for we find him pursuing his studies in a Mexican college. There he soon felt the literary influence of his day. Remember that the youth of Valbuena falls into the most brilliant period of literature in the Peninsula. Diego Hurtado de Mendoza, the author of *Lazarillo de Tormes,* was still alive, and Cervantes and Lope de Vega were mounting to fame. Their works were eagerly read in Mexico and in Peru, and their influence was strongly felt. Not only were the works of the Spanish poets brought to America, but some of the great writers paid a visit to the New World. It was in America, on a long and difficult journey from Peru to Mexico, that Diego Mejia began and finished amid many difficulties his translation of the *Heroidas* of Ovid, the best translation of that poet in the Spanish language. Juan de la Cueva also visited Mexico, leaving in verse a description of the capital city as he found it. The author of the *Picaroon Guzman de Alfarache,* one of the most typical of the Spanish picaresque novels, Lucas Alaman, died in Mexico. The great dramatist, Ruiz de Alarcon y Mendoza, who soon transferred his labors to Spain, was also a contemporary of Valbuena. It was amid such influences that Ber-

nardo de Valbuena spent his youth in Mexico, and it is therefore no wonder that a man of his poetic temperament and
genius should, at an early period of his life, have succumbed
to the charms of the muse. Yet his studies in a lighter vein
did not hinder his studies in theology in which he took the degree of Bachelor, and later that of Doctor at Siguenza in his
native land. At what precise period he entered the ecclesiastical state I am unable to affirm with certainty, but at the
age of thirty-nine we find him a priest in Jamaica.

There were at that time many influences for good in Spanish America. Religious men of various orders, such as the
Franciscans, Dominicans, Augustinians, and Jesuits, were
giving great edification by their virtues and by their writings,
and the churches of New Spain had been edified by zealous
bishops like Marroquin of Guatemala, who was a secular ecclesiastic. A considerable number of men, like Cervantes,
Lalazar, Juan de Castellanos, and Archbishop Ugarte of Lima,
had embraced the priesthood late in life, after distinguishing
themselves as laymen in war, in letters, or in the law. Some
of these, like Ugarte, acquired great fame for virtue. In
the absence of more accurate data, it is safe to assume that
the talents and the reputation for virtue in Bernardo de Valbuena must have influenced the authorities when they promoted him to the episcopal dignity.

The see of San Juan de Puerto Rico is one of the oldest in
America. It had been established shortly after the discovery
of the New World, and its early history may be gathered from
such works as those of Las Casas and Juan Diez de la Callé.
The latter in his *Memorial y Noticias Sacras* gives the list of
the bishops of Porto Rico from Alonso Manso, the first to occupy the see, to the Trinitarian Friar, Damian Lopez de Aro
who became bishop in 1643. The immediate predecessor of
Valbuena was Domingo Cano, a Dominican, who resigned in
1619, even before he had received his bull of appointment.
The see of Puerto Rico was more than a century old when
our poet ascended its pontifical throne in 1620. He was then
over fifty years of age, and his career was drawing to a close,
for he lived only seven years longer. These seven years fell
in troubled times, for during the period of his administration
the island was attacked by a combined English and Dutch

fleet, great suffering being thereby occasioned. During these few years the good bishop distinguished himself as a zealous pastor, visiting the various parts of his diocese and convening a synod in 1624, the second that had been held in Porto Rico. One or two years previously, he had taken part in the provincial council of Santo Domingo. Bishop Valbuena died at five o'clock in the afternoon of 11 October, 1627.

The last years of his life belong to the ecclesiastical history of Porto Rico, but his whole life is the common property of Spain and of the world. He must have continued his labors to the end, for his last work *El Bernardo* was published while he lived in Porto Rico. He wrote a large number of works, many of which have disappeared. When we take into consideration the fact that at that early date printing in America was only in its infancy, it is a wonder that so many works have been preserved. The art was introduced into Mexico in 1535, and fifty years passed before another typographical centre was established in America, when the press began operations in Lima. Hence it was that most authors were obliged to take their works to Europe for printing, that a large number of writings remained for centuries in manuscript, and that many of them have vanished completely.

Among the published works of Valbuena, three are best known. The first, *La Grandeza Mexicana*—the Greatness of Mexico—composed in eight cantos, serves to increase our knowledge of Mexico as it existed in the first century of Spanish colonization in America. This poem must be read with the historians, and with the dialogues of Lalazar. It was written as a letter to Doña Isabel de Tobar y Guzman, and at her request that she might be better acquainted with the capital she expected soon to visit. This illustrious lady, whom the author praises very highly in the prologue of his work, became a nun in the Convent of San Lorenzo.

The second work of Valbuena is characteristic of a form of literature then in vogue in the Peninsula, the Pastoral, and it is the most prominent, if not the only one, of its kind in Spanish America. Unlike the *Grandeza Mexicana,* it drew its inspiration from across the seas. Written several years before the author was raised to the episcopal dignity, it first appeared in print at Madrid in 1608. At the time when Valbuena wrote, a form of poetic composition, which was to obtain a certain popularity, had been introduced into Spain from Italy, through Portugal. I refer to the Pastoral in which prose and poetry alternate. The name was borrowed from the principal personages, shepherds and shepherdesses figuring in it. It is evident that such poetry was suggested by peoms like Virgil's Eclogues and Bucolics, at a time when everything classical was in vogue. The personages are thoroughly idealized, as their conversation rises above what one might naturally expect from their station in life. In the Pastorals, pagan mythology is strangely mingled with Christianity, while contemporary adventures often figure under the forms of ancient pastoral life. The *Arcadia* of Sannazaro, translated into Spanish in 1547, is one of the most prominent examples of this species of verse. Prose Pastorals were introduced from Portugal into Spain by George of Montemayor, the author of *Diana enamorada,* a favorite work of Cervantes, who also tried his hand at this kind of verse in his famous *Galatea.* Lope de Vega, the most prolific and versatile poet of ancient or modern times, has also given us a pastoral in his *Arcadia,* choosing the same title as Sannazaro. Valbuena's work must be traced to the same sources as those of Cervantes and Lope. It bears the title *Siglo de Oro en las Selvas de Erifile,* or " The Golden Age in the Woods of Erifile." Erifile, the scene of this pastoral fiction, is a natural fountain on the banks of the Guadiana. There the characters in the work, in which prose succeeds alternately to poetry, hold their discourses in a series of eclogues. The *Siglo de Oro,* like most compositions of the time, breathes the spirit of the Renaissance and of mythology.

The third poem of our author and the last published, bears the title *El Bernardo,* or " The Victory of Roncesvalles ". As the title indicates, the poet again turned for his inspiration to the Old World, and this time to the early days of Castilian chivalry, when the reconstruction of the Spanish monarchies had begun, and Christian knights were forcing back the waves of a Moorish invasion that had threatened to submerge Christianity. This poem has been regarded as Valbuena's best.

to a poet famous in the history of Spanish American literature, who also wore the mitre in a Western island that has passed from Spain to the United States, and whose last successor is an American, I will content myself with this sketch and make no attempt to analyze his poems.

To those desirous of further acquaintance with Bishop Valbuena, I will say that outside of the few current histories of Spanish literature that we have in our language, like George Ticknor's monumental work and a more recent one by Fitzmaurice Kelley, little will be found in English regarding Valbuena. One must look for more information in this regard to the introduction to his *Siglo de Oro,* reprinted in the early part of the last century by the Spanish Academy, and to such writings as the introduction by Menendez y Pelayo to the *Antologia de Poetas Hispano-Americanos.* With the Academia, we regret that so little is known of the writer; but the works that have survived him will immortalize the name of Bernardo de Valbuena, the Poet-Bishop of Porto Rico.

CHARLES WARREN CURRIER.

Washington, D. C.

BELFRY, VANE, AND STEEPLE.

ONE has to be acquainted with England to know that there alone has bell ringing attained to an art. To those who hear the swell and cadence of the bells—as it floats across moor and meadow, hill and dale—the music has a hallowing influence. It at once puts the hearers into a reflective train of thought. It is a call to prayer or praise. But the history of church-bell ringing has both its bright and sordid side; and we shall have occasion to refer to this twofold aspect of the subject.

" ringing chamber ". As we enter, a loud, sharp, metallic, creaking noise arrests our attention; and the heavy, hoary works of the clock are discerned in the dim light. The great tower clock is about to strike, and for some minutes is preparing itself for the alarming event. Dangling from the ceiling are the ropes from the belfry. On the floor stands an aged carved oak settle for the use of the ringers; and an ancient, iron-bound, highly-ornamented chest. Opening the latter, we find it full of old, cobwebbed, dusty, and disused parish-rate, tenure, and other books, with old banners (of St. George and the Union Jack) rolled up and laid on top.

Affixed to the walls of the ringing chamber are the " peal boards ", recording the achievements of former ringers, and the rules (in rhyme) relating to ringers:

> He that a bell doth overthrow,
> Shall twopence pay before he go;
> And he that rings with spur or hat
> Shall fourpence pay, be sure of that :
> And if these orders he refuse,
> No less than sixpence will excuse.

THE BELFRY.

In the corner of the ringing chamber is a well-worn ladder, ascending which, and passing through the trap-door—the wind whistling through the louvres and well-nigh taking our hat and breath away—we reach the belfry. A sudden and loud dong alarms us, but our nerves regain their equilibrium as we realize that it is only:

> The crazy old church clock
> And the bewildered chimes.

RINGERS' PITCHERS.

It is not altogether surprising that the ringers sometimes conducted themselves in a somewhat free and easy manner

(never in too complimentary a style!) on the boards and walls, wrote scurrilous verses on the screen, played practical jokes on each other; and sometimes even introduced buffoonery and games.

The old-time belfry laws were a fruitful source of fines; and the money so obtained was generally spent in ale. The ringers' pitchers were by no means uncommon, and some were curious examples of the potters' art. These ale-jugs still remain in some of the old English parishes and are forcible evidence that the ringers regaled themselves in the ringing chamber—not, let us hope, always unwisely, even if well!

Hadleigh, in Suffolk, still retains such a pitcher. It is made of brown-glazed earthenware and holds sixteen quarts. The inscription—rudely indented, apparently with a chisel when the clay was soft—bears the names of the eight ringers and these lines:

> If you love me, doe not lend me;
> Euse me often and keep me clenly;
> Fill me full, or not at all,
> If it be 'Strong', and not with 'Small'.

At Hinderclay, also in Suffolk, a ringers' pitcher is still preserved in the church tower. In form and size it is similar to that at Hadleigh. It is thus inscribed:

> From London I was sent,
>   As plainly doth appear:
> It was with this intent—
>   To be filled with "Strong-beer".
> Pray remember the pitcher when empty!

" Clare Ringers, 1729 ". At the base there is a tap to draw off the beer, as there is no spout or lip. The jug holds seventeen quarts, and on special ringing days it was carried about by the ringers, who asked for contributions to fill it. When it had completed its century in 1829, the landlord of the Bell Inn gratuitously filled it as a treat to the ringers, who at that time made the inn their place of meeting. It was the custom to exhibit this jug in the town on special ringing days, but this usage has since been discontinued. This jug has now found a resting-place in a very handsome oak-case with glass sides, presented by the Lady Malcolm of Polttalloch, of Barnadiston Hall, Haverhill, in Suffolk.

RINGERS' RULES.

Reference has already been made to the peal-boards which adorned the walls of the ringing-chamber and contained the rules. As these ringers' rules were both quaint and stringent we will mention them in detail. The three following versions are from three different parts of England and must suffice as representative of those once so general all over the country.

At Hathersage, Derbyshire, the ringers' rules (or laws of the belfry) date back to 1660, when the accession of Charles II brought in the much-welcomed Restoration:

> You gentlemen that here wish to ring,
> See that these Laws you keep in everything;
> Or else be sure you must without delay,
> The penalty thereof to the Ringers pay.
>
> First, when you do into the bell-house come,
> Look if the Ringers have convenient room;
> For if you do be an hindrance unto them,
> Fourpence you forfeit unto these gentlemen.
>
> Next, if you do here intend to "ring",
> With hat or spur, do not touch a string;
> For if you do, your forfeit is for that,
> Just fourpence down to pay, or lose your hat.
>
> If you a bell turn over, without delay,
> Fourpence unto the Ringers you must pay;
> Or if you strike, misscall, or do abuse,
> You must pay fourpence for the Ringer's use.

But whoso doth these orders disobey,
Unto the stocks we will take him straightway,
There to remain until he be willing
To pay his forfeit and the clerk a shilling.

The next instance is that of the ringers' rules at St. Peter's, Shaftesbury, Dorset. They are of interest as showing in what high regard the ringers held both their bells and their art:

What music is there that compar'd may be
To well-tuned bells' enchanting melody?
Breaking with their sweet sounds the willing air,
They, in the list'ning ear, the soul ensnare,
When bells ring round, and in order be,
They do denote how neighbours should agree;
But if they "clam", the harsh sound spoils the sport,
And 'tis like women keeping Dover Court.
Of all the music that is played, or sung,
There's none like bells, if they are well rung.
Then ring your bell—well if you can,
Silence is best for every man;
In your "ringing" make no demur,
Pull off your hat, your belt, and spur;
And if your bell you "overset",
The ringers' fee you must expect!
Fourpence you are to pay for that.
But that if you do swear or curse,
Twelvepence is due; pull out your purse;
Our laws are old, they are not new;
Both Clerk and Ringers claim their due.

Whereas the belfry laws in prose or verse were for regulating the conduct of the ringer and visitor, we find that some of these rules—many of which are extremely curious—appear framed as a ready means of obtaining money (in fines) to be spent in beer. In bygone times there would seem to have been in some cases a close connexion between the belfry and the cellar. One can scarcely be surprised at this, if we realize what prolonged, arduous, and precise work good bell-ringing involves. The following lines are but too conclusive evidence that in some instances the belfry did witness occasional scenes of Bacchanalian festivity: they are from the belfry of Dunster parish church, in Somerset:

If anyone shall curse or swear
  When come within the door,
He then shall forfeit for that fault
  As mentioned before.

If anyone shall wear his hat
  When he is ringing here,
He straightway then shall sixpence pay
  In cyder or in· beer.

If anyone these Articles
  Refuseth to obey,
Let him have nine strokes of the rope,
  And so depart away.

INSCRIPTIONS ON BELLS.

Inscriptions on church bells are very common. Often they are in English, but a Latin inscription is more general on the older bells. At Alkborough a bell which is believed to belong to the early part of the fourteenth century bears the inscription:

Jesu For Yi Moder Sake Save All
Ye Sauls That Me Gart Make.
  Amen.

An early sixteenth century bell at Semperingham carries the following very useful advice: " Be Not Ouer Busie ".

Benniworth possesses a bell that merely records the year in which it was made: " Anno Domini 1577 ". It is by no means an uncommon thing to find only a date upon the bell. Not a few of them bear the names of the churchwardens for the time being, or the name of the donor of the bell or bells. Medieval bells have many curious inscriptions, recording the name of the donor and the founder, together with heraldic and other devices. The inscriptions are often in the first person, the bell being supposed to utter the sentiment as it sends forth its sound.

A study of the inscriptions on bells is full of interest. The earliest are simple dedications of the bell to our Lord, or to some saint. The principal inscriptions of this class are:

Names of benefactors often find a permanent memorial on the bells they gave. There is an instance of this at Binstead, Hampshire, where a bell records:

> Doctor Nicholas gave five pound
> To help cast this peal tuneable and sound.

Another bell in the same tower immortalizes the name of the famous Berkshire bell founders, the Knight family:

> Samuel Knight made this ring
> In Binstead steeple for to ding.

At Badgworth, Gloucestershire, a bell that has been recast eulogizes its new founder at the expense of its original maker:

> Badgworth ringers they are mad,
> Because Rigbe made me bad;
> But Abel Rudhall you may see
> Hath made me better than Rigbe.

Some bells are very self-complacent in their inscriptions. One makes the declaration:

> If you have a judicious ear,
> You'll own my voice is sweet and clear.

Another asserts:

> My treble voice
> Makes hearts rejoice.

Not a few bells moralize in their inscriptions. Bakewell, Derbyshire, has a peal of eight bells, and each bears a very different kind of inscription:

used for various secular purposes. It is not to be wondered at then that the bells also took after the character of their church. Overwhelming evidence of this is to be met with in the old church accounts and church-bell inscriptions. Was there cause for national rejoicing? The bells sounded forth the sentiments of the people; were it for national loyalty, victory, or safety. The church bells were always rung on joyous occasions; hence inscriptions expressive of thankfulness and praise were appropriate and are often to be met with, as: " Laus et Gloria Deo ", " Laus Deo : Gratia Benefactoribus ", " Alleluja ", " Praise God ". Of Victory, as in the case of the sixth bell at Bakewell:

> When vict'ry crowns the public weal
> With glee we give the merry peal.

The bell at Ashover, Derbyshire, was recast with this inscription: " This old bell rung the downfall of Buonaparte and broke, April 1814." In some parts of England the bells were rung on the fifth of August to commemorate the escape of James I from the Gowrie plot.

Not merely at seasons of national rejoicing did the church bells sound forth their merry peal, but also on occasion of local thanksgiving or interest, such as the birth of an heir to the local estate; the completion of the ingathering of the fruits of the earth, and the " Harvest Home "; the annual fair; or a local cock-fight, when a "long-main " had been won. Indeed, church bells were sometimes rung even for successful race horses as is shown by the accounts of St. Edmund's, Salisbury: " 1646. Ringing the race-day, that the Earl of Pembroke his horse winne the cuppe—Vsh."

Church bells were often rung in honor of winning cocks. Kings frequently attended these battles. Henry VIII encouraged this form of sport, and James I much enjoyed it. Cromwell prohibited it in 1658. But no sooner had Charles II ascended the throne than it was revived and under royal patron-

—namely Thos. Middleton, of Cliff, John Coats, Ed. Wid-house, and John Batley."

Repeated attempts were made to put down this barbarous pastime, but it was not successfully prohibited until the year 1849.

In fact, multitudinous were the offices of the old English church bells. They were not confined to ecclesiastical functions; but did duty as alarms, business clocks, calendars, advertisements, and sign-posts. They aroused the slumbering swain to his early employment, guided the wayfarer toward his destination, warned tradesmen it was time to close their shops, summoned merchants to market, sounded the outbreak of a fire, and reminded housewives it was time to prepare the mid-day meal. In short, they entered heart and tongue into the interests and feelings of the people. A bell at Coventry, dated 1675, states:

> I ring at Six to let men know
> When to and fro' their work to go.

At St. Ives a bell bears the inscription: " Arise, and go about your business." At Epworth a bell is rung at 6 A. M., 12 noon, and 6 P. M., to call the laborers to work, to dinner, and to rest. At a period when clocks had not become general and anterior to the invention of steam " hooters ", it was a matter of consequence that the steady sequence of the morning bell should not be broken, and the hour of its ringing regular. To guard against such a mishap the Articles of Faversham directed the sexton to " lye in the church steeple ", so as to be at his post at the proper time. And who will deny that the sound of the church bell is not preferable to the shrill shriek of the steam whistle, or howl of the hooter?

At Culworth the tenor bell is sounded in the case of a fire. This was the general custom of summoning neighbors to help in extinguishing the outbreak of fire. A bell at Sherbourne bears the inscription:

has made Bow Bells sufficiently familiar.   But it is not generally known that in 1469 (Edward IV's reign) an order was
given by the Court of the Common Council for Bow Bell to
be rung nightly at 9 P. M.   Nine was the recognized hour for
tradesmen to shut their shops.   The clerk whose duty it was to
ring this bell, being unpunctual in his habits, the irregular
performance of this duty disappointed the toil-worn apprentices, who thus addressed him:

> Clerk of Bow bell,
>   With thy yellow locks,
> For thy late ringing
>   Thy head shall have knocks.

The clerk's reply was:

> Children of Cheape,
>   Hold you all still,
> For you shall hear Bow bell
>   Ring at your will.

Much is now said and written about " physical salvation ".
How to keep " fit " never becomes a serious problem until a
man begins to " read-up " the subject.   Left to his own devices he often does keep " fit " by direct and simple methods,
and bothers no more about it; but when he takes up the matter
scientifically the position becomes more complex, and he grows
fat and flaccid while studying it.   There is in the North of
England a rector who does not read about " fitness ", but
simply secures it.   One Sunday morning, not half a dozen
years ago, a man and his family were driving from a distance
to church and saw a dark figure bobbing along ahead.   On
overtaking it, they found to their surprise that it was the
rector, posting along the road as if he were catching a train.
The man with the phaeton pulled up, invited his clergyman
to jump in, and expostulated with him for hurrying so.   " Not
for worlds, thank you, my kind friend," answered the rector.
" This is my only way of keeping fit.   I am inclined to put
on flesh ! "   So saying, he hopped over a five-barred gate and

STEEPLES.

It has been sometimes stated that the shape of the steeple has an ethical origin and meaning, the idea being that it should emulate the beholder to look and aspire toward heaven. There may be some truth in this theory; for, when one beholds the steeples of the churches in our great cities towering over the tops of all the other high buildings, or views the spire of some country church losing itself in the clouds as one looks over the intervening meadows and the distant village, the thoughts are involuntarily transported to the realm beyond space and to subjects and things heavenly. Another theory that the writer would diffidently suggest as a possible origin of the fashion in steeples is that the early architects of the spire were moved by a recollection of that passage: " Ye are the light of the world: a city set on a hill cannot be hid." It is certainly significant that in most cases where there is an eminence near, the church has been built on the hill, even when often the village was in the valley.

A comparison of the heights of various spires and of spires compared with the principal monuments of the world is of interest. The cathedral of Cologne has the highest spire, 511 feet; whereas the Eiffel Tower, France, 984 feet, is the loftiest building in the world; and the Washington Monument is said to come next with 550 feet. So that the loftiest ecclesiastical building—the spire of Cologne—is the third highest structure in the world. Rouen Cathedral is 482 feet; St. Stephen's Cathedral, Vienna, 470 feet; Strasbourg Cathedral, 468 feet; the great pyramid, 450 feet; St. Peter's, Rome, 448. The tallest spire in England is that of Salisbury Cathedral, 404 feet. St. Paul's, London, is 365 feet; St. Patrick's Cathedral, New York, but 328 feet; and Canterbury Cathedral, England, only 235 feet.

STEEPLE RHYMES.

Quite a fair proportion of parishes in the British Isles possess steeple rhymes. These are not very poetical and often are far from complimentary to places and people. They are, at all events, not a little. curious. A rhyme respecting the parish of Kinkell-Statheam, runs as follows:

Was there e'er sic a parish, a parish, a parish,
Was there e'er sic a parish as that o' Kinkell?
They've hangit the minister, drowned the precentor,
Dang down the steeple, and drucken the bell.

The circumstances that gave birth to this rhyme were that the minister had been hanged, the precentor drowned in attempting to cross the Earn from the neighboring parish of Trinity Gask, the steeple had been taken down, and the bell sold to the parish of Cockpen, near Edinburgh.

The Carlow rhyme is of interest, as it refers to two branches of local trade that have long disappeared:

Low town and high steeple,
Proud folk, beggarly people,
Carlow spurs and Tullow garters.

Respecting Boston, Lincolnshire, the question is put and answered thus:

Boston! Boston!
What hast thou to boast on?
High steeple, proud people,
And shoals that souls are lost on.

The following refers to four churches in the same county (Lincolnshire):

Gosberton church is very high;
Surfleet church is all awry;
Pinchbeck church is in a hole,
And Spalding church is big with foal.

The parish church of Paull, Yorkshire, is situated on a commanding eminence and stands by itself, about a quarter of a mile from the village; which circumstance has given rise to the following distich:

High Paull, and Low Paull, and Paull Holme,
There was never a fair maid married at Paull Town.

VANES.

How few, when studying the architecture of old churches, castles, and houses, think to give careful attention to the vane;

On the stately towers of the castles (and mansions) of the titled and great, the vane is frequently in the shape of a banner. On the towers and steeples of churches the cock is the most familiar form; hence the synonym " weather-cock ". It is believed that the male of the barn-door fowl was first employed for this purpose as a representation of vigilance to be emulated by the clergy. But may it not equally have been employed to remind parishioners of the dreadful denial and bitter repentance of St. Peter; and to impress upon them the danger of self-complacency and over-assuredness; to bring home to them the words of St. Paul to the Corinthians: " Wherefore let him that thinketh he standeth take heed lest he fall "?

The cock is not, however, by any means the only form of vane that surmounts the towers and steeples of our churches. Most churches are dedicated to some particular saint; and we should expect the emblem of that especial patron saint to be alike the most natural and fitting form for the vane. Hence we find the vane of St. Peter's, Cornhill, London, is in the form of a golden key; that of St. Laurence, Bishopstone, Herefordshire, was in the form of a gridiron; while that at St. Laurence, Norwich, is also a gridiron, but with the holy martyr across its bars; at Filey, Yorkshire—once a small fishing village—the vane of the parish church is the model of a fish.

who possibly held their meetings there. According to the local legend of the arrow (vane) was placed in its position to commemorate a shot made by Robin Hood from the Old Field —a mile distant—which hit the steeple. St. Mary-le-Bow (" Bow Church "), Cheapside, is one of the best known of all the London churches. Its vane is a dragon—the emblem of the city.

The church of Great Ponton, near Grantham, in Lincolnshire, has a tower which is surmounted with a steeple on the summit of which floats a vane of singular design—a bow and fiddle. Quite a history is attached to this vane. At Great Ponton, long years ago, there lived a laborer who increased his meagre wages by playing the fiddle at fairs, feasts, and other places. Being of very frugal habits, he saved enough money to enable him to emigrate to America. Hard work, careful living, and sound judgment enabled him to become a rich man. Unlike many, he did not forget his old and humble Lincolnshire home, and in his days of prosperity was anxious to show in a worthy manner his gratitude to the Almighty for his good fortune. Consequently, he provided money for the erection of a handsome church in the parish of his birthplace; and in doing this he made one condition—that a model in copper of his cherished fiddle be placed on the summit of Great Ponton church. The vane of an old parish church is then a matter of some importance. From it we can often learn who is the patronal saint of the parish, what the original industry of the place, or some item of local historical or legendary interest.

J. R. FRYAR.

Canterbury, England.

THE ETHICS OF FOETICIDE.

THE subject for practical discussion is reducible to this question: Is it ever justifiable to remove from the maternal pelvic cavity a living but not viable fœtus? A fœtus six months old is not viable; one seven months old sometimes is saved by expert care, and such a fœtus is technically called

tion has only an indirect connexion with religion as such. Some physicians are under the erroneous opinion that the prohibition of abortion is a regulation emanating from ecclesiastical authority, like the prescription of a liturgical procedure. The question, however, is older than the visible Church. It is a matter of the natural law altogether, of pure reason, prescinding from creed.

The question is also very practical, because there are many physical conditions in pregnancy wherein the premature removal of a living fœtus is apparently the sole means the physician has of saving a woman's life, and commonly this fœtus is not viable. This condition may exist in ectopic gestation, in some cases where a degenerating fibroid tumor of the womb complicates pregnancy, in diseases of the maternal heart where compensation has failed, in certain degrees of purulent nephritis, in some forms of eclampsia, in pernicious vomiting, and in premature separation of the placenta causing intrauterine hemorrhage. Again, in cases where the maternal pelvis is too narrow for natural delivery some physicians think they are justified in performing embryotomy or craniotomy. Besides these conditions, there is the ordinary criminal abortion, where the fœtus is artificially removed to prevent maternal disgrace or inconvenience.

priates and adapts to its own use surrounding nutritive matter. It thus grows and divides into two distinct though connected cells. Each of these subdivides, and by a repetition of the process the cells multiply, until from the inherent qualities, forces, or material, call it what you will, of the centrosomes in the pronuclei, the vegetative principle rapidly shapes a specialized embryo. From the germ-cells the vegetative principle makes its own organism, by nutritive assimilation; the maternal ovum and uterus are a mere residence.

Now, this vegetative principle which started to work at the very first cell-fission in the ovum, after the germ-nuclei fused, is evidently, as any amateur in embryology knows, identical with the principle found in the human being after birth, and unto the end of life, because the operations are exactly the same, and we can judge the nature of anything only from its operations.

Secondly, the ultimate principle of vegetative life is identical with the ultimate principle of sensitive life, and these two are identical with the ultimate rational principle. One and the same vital principle is simultaneously at the bottom of our cognitive, sensitive, and vegetative life, just as the same mind thinks, wills, and remembers. We have the testimony of consciousness that the same mind thinks and feels. This assertion is so evident that it needs no proof.

The vegetative life is also identical with the sensitive and rational ultimate principle. Organic and vegetative changes and sensations arise simultaneously: inhibit, exercise, or destroy a vegetative function and the result is simultaneous pain, pleasure, sensation, or death of the sensitive principle. Destroy the sensory apparatus or injure it and you correspondently destroy or injure the vegetative life, whilst acting on the sensory and intellectual life.

We are not always exercising the three phases of life, but they are always present. In sleep, or whilst under the influence of a narcotic, we vegetate solely; even when we are awake often we do little more; in our highest mental activity we

When we began to vegetate, our life began; we were human beings; we had a soul; and this as soon as the pronucleus of the spermatozoön fused with the pronucleus of the ovum, and made the first segmentation-nucleus. Before the first fission of that segmentation-nucleus was completed into two distinct cells the soul was present, for that fission was independent life; and any life is impossible without a soul, or, what is the same thing, a vital principle. Since, moreover, the soul with the body is the man, and the process of vegetation in our present state is identical with that first cell-fission, this splitting primordial cell is a human being. The active primordial cell in this stage is as much a complete phase of human life as are the body and soul of a person at puberty, or at adult age. Indeed, that cell with its vital principle at this stage of the process of human life is the only normal, possible, condition of the human body beginning life. This splitting cell has an absolutely independent life; it is feeding itself from the ovum, as later it will feed itself from the placental blood, and later still from the maternal milk, and yet later with a knife and fork. The ovum is only a necessary container, as the womb will be later; essential but extraneous.

If the soul is not present in this starting body, when does it enter? After, say, the seventy-sixth cell has been set into place? after the *primordial streak* has been laid down? By no means. The falling into line of the seventy-sixth cell, or of the third cell, is as much a vital process as the appearance of the beard, or of senile palsy.

We are to bear in mind then, that the human embryo in the womb, no matter how young it may be, is as much a child as the week-old babe; and, because it is a human being, it has all the rights of a human being to its life. The opinion formerly followed in the civil law that life begins with quickening is utterly unscientific and immoral. At quickening the child is four or five months old. In the human fœtus three days old examined by Peters there were already thousands of cells in one cross-section, and millions in the whole embryo.

In any case, therefore, there is no period during pregnancy, capable of diagnosis as such, where we have not a new human life to deal with. This conclusion would be very evident if the entire development of the embryo is understood, but the de-

scription of this development is so technical that it is not advisable to attempt it here.[1]

Granting, as we must, that the youngest human embryo is
a living human individual, are there no conditions in which
this new person may be at least indirectly deprived of its life
in defence of the maternal life?

The ultimate necessary tendency of man is toward happiness, and, of course, happiness, or any other perfection, is impossible without existence; hence the instinctive recoil from
the destruction of our life, which is the requisite condition of
happiness. Even those that abnormally destroy their own life
do so with horror for the destruction itself, and act thus unreasonably to escape evil, not to escape life; or they seek what
they think will be a fuller life.

We can do no other injury to a man so great as the depriving him of his life, for that deprivation destroys every right
and possession he has. He can recover from all other evil, or
hold his soul above every other evil, but death is the absolute
conqueror. No matter how debased or how diseased a man's
body may be, no one may disassociate that body from its soul,
except in defence of individual or social life under peculiarly
abnormal conditions; but even such defence is permissible
only whilst the man respects other human life and the social
life; whilst he is innocent; has done no harm to society commensurate with the loss of his own life.

Existence, no matter how debased, is immeasurably better
than non-existence, for non-existence is nothing; and when
we consider eternal life after the decay of the body, even as a
probability that fact raises existence to infinite possibility
above the void of non-existence. A human life, even in an
Australian Bushman, in a tuberculous pauper, in the vilest
criminal, is in itself so stupendously noble a thing that the
whole universe exists for its upholding toward betterment.
The uplifting of human life to a better condition has been the

[1] Fecundatio intra tubam Fallopianam normaliter accidit. Henle autem
spermatozoon sese movere posse centimetrum tribus partibus horae sexagesi-
mis patefecit. Si ovulatio tempore mensium perficiatur, ovaque in tuba Fallo-
piana adsint, spermatozoa quindecim centimetra inter cervicem uteri et medium

sole tendency of all the magnificent charity, sacrifice, patriot-
ism, and heroism, the best men and women of the world since
time began have striven in. The necessary First Cause Itself
is life, and life is by far the most sacred thing possible for this
First Cause to effect.

It is not permissible, under any possible circumstances, *directly* to kill an innocent human being. By killing directly
is meant, (1) either as an end desirable in itself, as when a
man is killed for revenge; or, (2) as a means to an end. By
an innocent human being is meant a person that has not by
any voluntary act of his own done harm commensurate with
the loss of his own life.

To kill a human being is to destroy human nature; to destroy anything is to subordinate and sacrifice that thing absolutely to the purposes of the slayer. But no one has a right so
to subordinate another human being, because this other human
being is a person, an intelligent nature, and consequently independent, free, referring rightfully its operations solely to
itself as to their centre. This very freedom differentiates
man from brutes and inanimate things. These are not free,
not independent; they are rightfully possessed by man; but
man may be possessed by no one. Even external human slavery is abhorrent to us as a corollary to the intrinsic freedom of
man, which is absolute. This intrinsic freedom is such that
we may not under any circumstances lawfully resign it to
another's possession. All morality depends on that freedom,
all civilization, and social life.

struction would ensue—hence the baseness in cynicism, and the selfish cowardice in the expression " What's the use? " As there is nothing greater and nobler than liberty, the freedom of the sons of God to do what they have a right to do, and as every human being has a right to that liberty, so there is nothing baser than its contrary, the destruction of that liberty; and no destruction is so final as that of killing the man, no usurpation so abhorrent to man or God as that annihilation of human nature. Abhorrence for such a death is the primal instinct of all living things.

Now, a fœtus in the womb, as we have already shown, is as much a human being as a man fifty years of age, since it has a soul and body, and therefore is as free intrinsically; consequently, no other human being may presume so to usurp the freedom, all the rights, of the fœtus as to destroy it by killing it.

Justice, order, must finally prevail; this is the first law of the universe; all else is subordinate to that law. Justice, moreover, is a moral equation, and whenever one right transcends another it must be superior to the right it holds in abeyance. The right an innocent human being has to its life, however, is so great that no other human right can be superior to it, whilst he remains innocent; even the State may not kill directly an innocent man, although in certain grave conditions it may, to save itself, indirectly permit such a death; the individual also indirectly may permit such a death in another whilst striving to save his own life. However, even in defence of his own life against an unjust aggressor, so sacred and important is all human life, he may not destroy the unjust aggressor if wounding will suffice.

Morality is from the intention or volition: if I accidentally, unintentionally, stumble against a man, knock him into a river, and drown him, there is no question of morality; if I intentionally stumble against him with a like result, I am a murderer. There is no question of morality when an insane person kills a man, because the insane are not capable of volitional intention. An act from an intention to be good or permissible must, among other essential requisites, have this quality that

not kill him. This law, however, is not to be stretched to a sentimental extent. If there is a grave doubt about your ability to maim, you need not hesitate to kill in self-defence; still the law remains that human life even in an unjust aggressor is a very sacred thing. So great an authority in ethics as De Lugo, however, holds that we may directly kill an unjust aggressor; but he argues from the extreme value of the attacked life.

Means to any end may be good, bad, indifferent, or excusable. Excusable means are such as have an element of evil, but become justifiable by circumstances. Thoroughly bad means are never justifiable; an end in itself, however good, does not justify evil means. To succeed in a certain operation may be so important as to favorably affect one's whole life, and an act of perjury may be the means to insure success; but you may not perjure yourself, because perjury is essentially and always so gravely evil to society in general that no circumstance justifies it. Hence also you may not kill a human being that good may come of the deed.

The injury to social order which makes perjury so grievous an offence against morality is found in a higher degree in homicide. Murder of the individual is a direct attack on the ultimate end of all civil society, which is the protection of the individual in his rights. Murder with impunity makes society impossible, and a single murder of an innocent human being is an offence against the stability of society so great that nothing can condone it, nothing justify it—there is no question of self-defence in dealing with an innocent human being; self-defence supposes a *nocent* human being.

A further argument against the killing of the innocent is drawn from an analysis of the offence such a deed is to the First Cause; but this argument would take too much space in the developing. A man that needs any argument to keep him from homicide, believes vaguely if at all in the very existence of God; he knows nothing of the relation between Creator and creature, and so on.

cumstance to the end or the means. The means help to the end; the circumstances here do not. For example, two swimmers, A and B, are trying to save C, who dies in the water, and, as he dies, C grips A and B so tightly that they can not shake the corpse off. A is weak, and he will soon sink and drown, owing to this weakness and the weight of the corpse; B also will go down later owing to the weight of A and C. A, however, cuts his own clothing loose from the grip of the corpse, and is saved; but thus immediately B is drowned, owing to the fact that the full weight of the corpse comes upon him. Is A justified in cutting himself loose? Certainly he is. That is an example of indirect killing. A intends to save his own life by cutting himself loose from the corpse, C; he does not directly intend to kill B; he has great repugnance even to permitting the death of B; nor does he use the means (the cutting loose) to kill B, but to save himself. The killing of B is a circumstance attached to the means.

Suppose, again, the same condition of A, B, and C; but A is not able to cut himself loose. D, a fourth party, can cut A loose and save him, but can do no more; he must let B go down with the corpse of C. May D cut A lose? Certainly he may; and the incidental death of B is an indirect killing.

In a craniotomy on a living child, however, done to save a mother's life, the killing of the child is direct, not indirect. The removal of the child is solely a means to the end, which is to save the mother's life. The physician is not like D in the last example, cutting A, the mother, loose from C and B; he is D braining B to save A, whilst B has the same right to life as A.

Take another example: B is a swimmer disabled by cramps and about to drown; A, going to save B, is seized by B, and both will be drowned; D goes to help A and B. He can not get B loose, and he finds he can save only one. May D knock B senseless to save A, bring in A and so leave B to drown? Certainly he may; but he is thus permitting the death of a materially unjust aggressor (of which, presently), a case altogether different from craniotomy, where the child is not an aggressor at all. D is saving A as if he were pushing away a maniac who was about to shoot A. The child in

In an abortion done to save a mother's life whilst the child is alive but not yet viable, the removal of the child is a means to the end, which is to save the mother's life. This removal is also a direct killing, not indirect.

In an ectopic gestation where the living but not viable fœtus has ruptured the Fallopian tube, and the mother is in certain danger of death from hemorrhage, if the surgeon ligates the torn vessels of the tube to save the mother's life, he by the same act shuts off the blood-supply of the fœtus and leaves it to die, or rather slightly hastens its death. That would be an indirect killing, not a killing as an end or a means, but this indirection makes it altogether different from a craniotomy or abortion.

If in ectopic gestation the tube is yet unruptured, and the surgeon, *as a precaution,* ligates the vessels and removes the tube together with the living fœtus, the killing of the fœtus here, in the opinion of practical moralists, is a direct killing, as direct as an abortion; and the Church has forbidden such intervention. In an article I wrote in *Essays in Pastoral Medicine* (New York, 1906), I argued in favor of this surgical intervention; but my position is now untenable. Apparently also my tentative argument in that same book in favor of surgical intervention when a degenerating fibroid tumor of the uterus complicates pregnancy, is not " safe ", because it was based on the same principles largely as my argument concerning ectopic gestation.

Craniotomy is never justifiable. It is first a direct killing by a private individual; secondly, apart from the morality of the action, craniotomy and embryotomy are very rarely indicated, owing to the possibility of substituting the Cæsarean section. Sometimes an aftercoming head may be so jammed that it can not be delivered even by Cæsarean section: in such

where two or more competent physicians have come to the decision in a given case of pregnancy, where the fœtus is not viable, that if the woman's womb is not emptied at once she will die, and if it is emptied she will very probably recover. If the womb is emptied, the fœtus will be killed by the physi · cian; if the womb is not emptied, both the mother and the fœtus will almost certainly be killed by the disease—there is very little chance for the fœtus in any event. The abortion often does little more than to hasten its death.

It is not, however, certain even in a bad case of eclampsia that the woman will die if she is not delivered at once. The maternal mortality is about twenty-eight per cent; the fœtal mortality is from thirty-three to fifty per cent. Emptying the uterus reduces the maternal mortality to eleven per cent, but does not save every case. The fact that about seventy per cent of eclamptic women recover without emptying the uterus, evidently makes the condition different from what it would be if all eclamptic women were certainly doomed. Let us suppose, however, an extreme case where competent men have decided that a particular woman will surely die if her womb is not emptied, and she has a chance of recovery if it is emptied (no one can be certain that such a case will surely recover). At best she has eighty-nine chances in 100 for recovery, since the mortality even after artificial abortion is still eleven per cent for all stages of pregnancy. When eclampsia occurs in early pregnancy, as is supposed in our case, the disease is extremely fatal, even if the uterus is emptied. The abortion will surely kill the child, and it will probably save the mother. May the physician empty the uterus?

He certainly may not. To hasten even an inevitable death is homicide, and that quality of merely hastening adds nothing for extenuation: every murder is merely a hastening of inevitable death. To give a dying man a fatal dose of morphia " to put him out of misery ", is as criminal a murder as to blow out his brain whilst he would be walking the streets in health; to ease pain is not commensurate, by any means, with taking a human life. This subversion of the moral or natural law for the sake of sentimentality is culpable ignorance, and always does grave damage to human society. Physicians are constantly mistaking inclination, or the mental vagaries of the women that influenced their childhood, for rules of moral conduct. A physician is not a public executioner, not a judge with the power of life and death: his business is solely to save life, not to destroy it.

I have already shown that murder as such is not permissible; but an objector says, in the case of the supposed abortion, you are opposing the life of a useless fœtus to that of a useful mother of a family. If that objection were true—and it is not, because the real fact is that we are opposing one human life to another without the only sufficient reason—what has that to do with the matter? If there were anything in that argument, where would it stop? If it held for the taking of life in an unpleasant condition, it would hold *a fortiori* in every other less unpleasant condition where a life would not be at stake. You incur a legitimate debt, say, $10,000, and you give your note for the money. When the note falls due it is decidedly inconvenient to pay it, it would even bankrupt you to pay it. Does that let you out of the obligation under the moral law, or even the civil law? The eclamptic mother conceived the child, got into the difficulty, and she and her physician have no right to tear up the note, especially when such a tearing implies homicide. Suppose, again, a woman has done a deed for which she has in due process of just law been condemned to death; suppose also there is only one man available to put her to death, and if this man were killed she could escape. Would her physician be permitted to shoot that executioner to let her out of the difficulty? Certainly not. That, however, is what the physician does who empties an eclamptic uterus. You may not do essential evil that good may come of it, or that anything may come of it. This is not a case of indirectly permitting evil; it is a case of directly doing evil, and that evil is the destruction of a human life, one of the most heinous crimes possible; furthermore, this very destruction may be so futile as to fail of its end.

If I may kill a so-called "useless fœtus" to save a useful mother, do gross evil to effect great good, why should I stop there? Why may I not rob a bank to make my children rich, murder a useless miser to employ his money in founding orphanages, reject all my most sacred promises whenever their observance makes me suffer? Where will the sentimental

moralist draw a line? That the civil law may permit thera-
peutic abortion is no excuse whatever. The civil law permits
many things which morality forbids; it takes no cognizance
of evil thought unless its expression disturbs peace; it ab-
solves bankrupts even if they afterward become solvent; it
permits the marriage of divorced persons, and so on indefinitely.

Suppose a lady, in every sense of the term, marries in good
faith a man she deemed a gentleman, but who turns out to be
a syphilitic sot, who disgraces her and makes her life a perpetual misery, immeasurably worse than the condition of any
eclamptic woman. No greater blessing could come to her than
his death. Would she therefore be justified before any tribunal of God or man in murdering him to get rid of her trouble?
No; she must bear with her evil for the sake of social order.
So must the eclamptic woman.

Nothing whatever justifies an individual, like a physician,
in taking human life, except the defence of his own or another's life against an unjust aggressor; and no fœtus in the
womb can possibly be an unjust aggressor. The ethical foundation for killing in self-defence is this: It is a primary law
of nature that every human being should and will strive to
resist destruction, and in certain conditions, which I shall explain, a man may kill another to preserve his own or another's
existence. Justice, as was said before, requires a moral equation, and if the right prevails it must be superior to the right
it supersedes. At the outset both the aggressor and the intended victim have equal rights to life, but the fact that the
aggressor uses his own life for the destruction of a fellow man
sets him in a condition of juridic inferiority with regard to
the latter. The moral power of the aggressor is equal to his
inborn right to life, *less* the unrighteous use he makes of it;
whilst the moral power of the intended victim remains in its
integrity, and has consequently a higher juridic value.

The right of self-defence is not annulled by the fact that the
aggressor is irresponsible. The absence of knowledge saves
him from moral guilt, but it does not alter the character of the
act, considered objectively; it is yet an unjust aggression; and
in the conflict, the life assailed has still a superior juridic
value. In any case the right of killing in self-defence is not

based on the ill-will of the aggressor, but on the illegitimate character of the aggression. An insane or other irresponsible aggressor is called a materially unjust aggressor; a sane aggressor is formally unjust.

A fœtus in the womb of an eclamptic mother is not a formally unjust aggressor, nor is it even a materially unjust aggressor. The child has a natural right to be where it is; it did not put itself where it is—the mother put it there; its natural presence in the womb is not in any sense of the term an unjust aggression. If any one is an aggressor the mother is, but there is no question of killing her.

You object, the fœtus is as *materially* unjust as the irresponsible lunatic who is about to attack me with a knife; I may kill this irresponsible lunatic; therefore I may kill the fœtus. I deny the parity. The lunatic is an active aggressor, actually attacking my life; the fœtus is altogether passive; it is attending solely to its own business of growing, not attacking anything. You can not even prove that the fœtus itself causes eclampsia; you know little about this disease except its symptoms, and the fact that it occurs in pregnancy. If eclampsia were caused by pregnancy solely, every pregnant woman should be eclamptic. The pregnancy starts into action a pathological diathesis, and the fœtus may not be deprived of life for that fact.

more, the fœtus is utterly innocent of any aggression whatever. If it is murder to kill a child outside the womb, and mere therapeutics to kill it inside the womb, then it is murder to shoot a man on the street, and mere good markmanship to shoot him to death inside his house, especially if he is an undesirable citizen.

Would it not be better that the fœtus should be killed than that the mother should die? By no means. It might be better that the fœtus should *die* rather than that the mother should die (apart from the question of baptism); but that is very different from killing the fœtus. The first fact in the world is that justice, law, order, should be observed no matter what the cost; better that ten thousand mothers should die than that one fœtus should be unjustly killed.

When ectopic gestation is considered, and some of the tumors that complicate pregnancy, conditions arise which differ in part from those in craniotomy and abortion, but it is impossible to discuss these in the space of a single article.

What is the conclusion from all this argumentation? What is the physician to do who meets a case that imperatively calls for abortion according to the common medical practice? The answer is clear enough: if he has any regard for the natural law, upon which all morality and all social order rest, he unfortunately can do nothing; if he has no regard for this law, he will kill the fœtus. The law seems to be hard, but nearly all law is hard to the loser; yet that fact does not abrogate the law, nor make it bad.

Life is too cheap with us in America, and the physician should be the first, with the clergyman and lawyer, to place safeguards about it; not seek to destroy it. We are by far the most homicidal nation on the face of the earth. We have committed 8,813 murders annually for the past twelve years; we have in that time murdered 112,892 human beings, or 2,812 more than all the men lost in battle and by wounds in the Federal armies throughout our Civil War. We killed one human being every sixty minutes of the day and night

Northwestern Europe would require one thousand million inhabitants to raise its present murder-rate up to ours; and all this excludes the slaughter by the professional abortionists and the preventable homicides of commerce and the Fourth of July—last Fourth of July we killed 217 children. It is estimated that there are 100,000 abortions in the State of New York alone in a single year; but I do not know the value of this estimate. We have three times the number of inhabitants that England and Wales have, and from twenty-seven to thirty times the number of annual murders. Our lynchings run as high as 241 in a single year, and in England, Ireland, and Scotland together there has not been a single lynching for the past seventy-five years. For the past twenty years our lynchings have exceeded the legal executions. In 1908 there were 257 murders in Chicago and St. Louis, yet only *two* of the murderers were executed. For the past twenty-one years in the State of New York out of every 500 murderers five were executed, ninety were sent to prison, and 405 were let go scot-free. If you kill a quail in the United States out of season, you will get into trouble; if you kill a man, you will only get your picture in the yellow journals. We are the Cain of the human family, drenched with our brother's blood, a stench in the nostrils of God, but we boast like Apaches of our " glorious Republic ". It is high time for a change, and we may as well begin with the physicians who practise abortion as with any other class of murderers—before the patience of God gives out.

AUSTIN O'MALLEY, M.D., PH.D., LL.D.

Philadelphia, Pa.

A PLEA FOR A NEW METHOD OF INSTRUCTION IN CHRISTIAN DOCTRINE:

THE NEED OF CHANGE.

we forget that times had completely changed. The children of this generation have neither the same dangers nor the same incentives as those even of that immediately preceding. Then an aggressive Protestantism, supported at times by racial prejudice, furnished a stimulus to the study of religion that is wanting now. The combative instinct was aroused by the " felt " atmosphere, and the study of Christian Doctrine became for the most part a course in polemics. The practical part was secured by the thoroughly Catholic influence of the home, wherein the Church was the dominant factor, first and last in all arrangements, domestic and social. It is not too much to say that a subtle change has crept into our Catholic homes, at least in congested urban districts, and religious interests have been relegated to a position quite subordinate in comparison with that formerly occupied. The regulations of the Church are no longer dominant and prominent. Unfortunately too those regulations are in many cases framed to meet family convenience or worldly comfort, in an effort, that is out of harmony with the spirit of the Catholic faith, to attract worshipers by pandering to their selfish and sensual instincts. The fundamental mistake, in our judgment, is committed in not making religious instruction attractive, and at the same time thorough, on the profound principles enunciated in the prayer to the Holy Ghost: *Corda fidelium Sancti Spiritus illustratione docere;* so that they may *in eodem spiritu recta sapere.* St. Paul in one of his *fervorinos* on the Resurrection appropriately used in the Easter liturgy emphasizes the same thought when he urges the Colossians *quae sursum sunt sapere.* Contemporary pedagogics make use of precisely the same principle, because its chief canons insist on the awakening and sustaining of interest, and, therefore, on the need of making subjects attractive. Now, while it is of revealed truth that faith cometh by hearing, it is experimentally true that one of the very best aids to hearing is sight. The really universal language is not Esperanto but gesticulation. When words fail, gesture comes to the rescue; so the illustration makes clear the printed word. What a boon it would have

useless labor if the text-books of an earlier day could have made clear to us by carefully precise illustrations the arrangements of *biremes* and *triremes* that caused so much puzzling perplexity in the uncompromisingly correct text! The change in methods that has produced the profusely illustrated text-books of the schools, has also been responsible for the improvements whereby Geography and History can be made intensely interesting even to Shakespeare's school-boy, who is fascinated by the wonderful and beautiful pictures thrown on a screen by a stereopticon. Classes in Botany, Physiology, etc., can now have the material objects in their natural colors and proper form enlarged by the reflectoscope. One has only to view with envy the splendid collection of glass flower models in the museum at Harvard to realize the immense strides that have been made in visual instruction as well as its very great possibilities. And, finally, any teacher of the biological sciences can testify that the projection of microscopical specimens has rendered comparatively easy a very difficult study.

VISUAL INSTRUCTION.

The Department of Education in the State of New York has recognized this fact by establishing a special bureau of Visual Instruction which contains lantern slides by the tens of thousands illustrating every branch of knowledge, and at the service gratuitously of all institutions registered by the University of the State. The Board of Education in the City of New York has also recognized it by its extensive and wonderfully comprehensive series of free public illustrated lectures.

It was inevitable, therefore, that in spite of the badly misunderstood and unreasonably overworked *nil innovetur,* the methods of Visual Instruction should be introduced into the teaching of Christian Doctrine. The study of religion is historically the most fascinating of all study for the human mind. But austere methods had quite succeeded in making it, at least for the youthful mind, the most tiresome. I think it must be admitted that our Protestant friends were the first in this field. By means of models, maps, charts, and gradually the whole paraphernalia of the modern classroom, and notably through the well-organized International Sunday School Lessons, they long since demonstrated how up-to-date methods might successfully be used in inparting religious information. The Sunday-school lecture illustrated by lantern slides became quite an American institution, and by degrees found its way into Catholic circles. Zealous priests saw great possibilities in such methods: but in almost every case were finally discouraged by the absence of illustrations suitable for Catholic teaching, or by the crudity of such views as were obtainable, or by the expense entailed in procuring those that were both artistic and apposite. Another element that discouraged many was the practical impossibility of getting co-ordinated illustrations of a high standard. By degrees several successful illustrated lectures on the " Life of Christ " and the " Blessed Virgin in Art " were achieved: but even in the best of these there was an occasional blur owing to a crude conception or to a lack of knowledge of the rich treasures of art. One ardent apostle of this visual method of religous instruction went to a very considerable expense in having made a series of paintings of American History from the Catholic point of view so as to illustrate properly for his children their class study. Naturally, the result, while good, was not within the reach of every pastor. While the fortunate possessor was only too willing to lend his slides, he had no means of communicating that fact to the number of priests and teachers who would be eager to avail themselves of his kindness: and then, too, delicate considerations about breakage, remuneration, inconvenience, etc., deterred the comparatively few who did know. Another discouraging cause arose from the consciousness of awkwardness and inferiority. What chance would the bungling manipulation of a lantern by an unfamiliar hand, and the exhibition of views, sometimes crude to the extent of absurdity, stand of holding the interest of even a youthful audience accustomed to the technical perfection of the ubiquitous dime moving-picture show with its marvelous films and its striking illustrations of popular songs? Then, too, there was the dampening criticism of superior brethren who were only too ready to point out shortcomings of which the zealot was keenly conscious, but who were not so eager to help remedy the defects or so successful in suggesting better things. And, above all, was that appalling calamity for the wide-awake, ardent neophyte, the acquiescence of the

chief of the parish in his schemes provided they
irried out without any expense—the old contract of
icks without straw.

: spasmodic efforts have been made, and are making
lividuals, and while in some cases the results have
: successful considering the difficulties and reid while in a few instances these efforts have been
ʒ, they have not been general nor have they tended
an established and permanent factor. The excellent
iia *Manual of Religious Instruction* was a long step
it direction. Results from its use are prominent at
tions of Confraternities of Christian Doctrine, and
:n in the admirable work done in the higher grades
if our parochial schools. Father Yorke's series of
s, and latterly Dr. Shields's series, seem to show that
ds are working at the problem, and evidently have
eading ideas. The present widespread endeavor to
:atechisms, familiar to all who follow the letters
ip so frequently in the pages of THE ECCLESIASTI-
w, and particularly to those who have taken note
rement in many important dioceses in France; and,
: recent appearance of several collections of Cate-
:xamples, for instance, Father Chisholm's in Eng-
ow the translation of Father Scherer's monumental
1 under the title, *Dictionnaire d'Exemples,* all in-
perhaps the time is ripe for a general movement
e the most improved and modern methods into our
classes. To help to that desirable end it may not
) call attention to an organization that has most
· used the method of visual instruction—probably
all : and to point out that we in the United States
ourselves largely of its achievements to help our-

THE WORK OF " LA BONNE PRESSE ".

cause of religion. Its history is a recital of heroic work in the apostolate of the press that would make us American Catholics realize how inert we have been in this direction. But what now appeals to the inquirer is the *finesse* apparent in this special department of its work. Careful organization, judicious economy, sound business principles, thorough scholarship, wide knowledge of what constitutes *actualité,* are what commend it most.

It is now more than ten years since under the leadership of *La Bonne Presse* a *Société Catholique des Projections* was formed. Branches were soon established in many dioceses. The object was to prepare suitable *Conférences* or lectures on religious topics to be illustrated by well-chosen views. The association was to be able to rent not only these views, but, if needed, a complete stereopticon outfit together with the text of the *Conférence*. The headquarters was at the *Maison de La Bonne Presse,* 5, Rue Bayard, Paris. The printed lecture texts ultimately resulted in the establishment of a weekly magazine entitled *Les Conférences* issued at the subscription price of 6 francs for France, and 8 francs for the Postal Union. As stated in the official catalogue the aim of *Les Conférences* is to help lecturers by furnishing texts and material on all subjects that may be of service to the apostolate of the press. It proposed to publish religious and apologetic lectures on questions of acute present interest, to refute the objections made against faith by false science, and to offer a serious and solid defence of religion. It would present careful historical studies calculated to protect the Church against the lies circulated by its enemies. It was to treat social and economic questions, and bring into communication lecturers and men of action, heads of reading circles, chiefs of those organizations which aim at improving the condition of the poor and the workingman. It would likewise furnish illustrated lectures of travel, written from the Catholic point of view, while at the same time promising to keep its readers abreast of current industrial and scientific questions in physics, chemistry, mechanics, astronomy, recent inventions, etc. Each month it would detail what has been achieved in the way of

in their special work. In connexion with the *Fascinateur* it is the official organ of the Federation of diocesan associations whose object is to spread the apostolate of the press by means of lectures and illustrated conferences. The *Fascinateur,* it should be noted, is a magazine devoted to the technical side of stereopticon work, publishing interesting articles on the manner of "running" a lantern, as we say, giving valuable instruction on the different kinds of apparatus, the improvements continually making, new methods of photographing, of making lantern slides, suggestions for preparing interesting and amusing séances. It also has quite a valuable column devoted to bargains or exchanges, through which correspondents can procure, at a very considerable reduction from the original prices, lantern slides or stereopticon apparatus that their owners for one reason or another desire to dispose of. It also fully records the proceedings of the different committee meetings held from time to time, and of the conventions that occur either annually or semi-annually in different dioceses. The discussions so reported are of great interest and of considerable importance for any priest on the mission, as a surprisingly large number of excellent suggestions are made, and many of the ideas proposed can easily be adapted to local circumstances. Moreover, the directions given for the mechanical part of the stereopticon exhibition should be of great practical benefit to the priest in places where the facilities for acquiring such information are meagre. Any intelligent man could learn with slight difficulty to become an expert operator even of a complicated moving-picture apparatus from a careful study of this publication, which since its foundation in 1903 has under a carefully chosen editorial staff been of considerable assistance in furthering this form of the apostolate of the press.

It must not be supposed that the work which in France has now grown to remarkable size was unattended by difficulties. There were objectors and many of them. Some of the objections were delightfully French. One good soul was very much disturbed at what might happen in the *Salles des Conférences* whilst the lights were out, the audience being a "mixed" one. Others frowned upon the introduction of such worldly methods. But the work went on just the same,

bishop after bishop taking an active interest in it and forming
a diocesan association in charge of some zealous priests, until
at the annual congress a fairly national representation is gathered.

TOPICS OF INSTRUCTION.

Our interest, however, is mainly in the details of practical
working. First as to how the brilliant program outlined in
the prospectus of *Les Conférences* has been carried out. A
glance through the table of contents during the present year
is reassuring. In the issue of 6 January, Abbé Eyraud has
a lecture on " Masonic Toleration " in which he contrasts the
pretended intolerance of the Church with the real intolerance
of Freemasonry. He shows how tolerant was the French Revolution, and compares the conduct of Catholics in power with
the actual behavior of the present masonic administration in
France in every department, the army, education, justice,.
charity, etc. A Professor of History continues a minute examination of the historical text-books condemned by the
French Bishops. For the benefit of Reading Circles or Study
Clubs the Ferrer affair is discussed. The issue of 13 January
gives another idea of the completeness of this program. A
distinguished agricultural chemist lectures on " The Stable ",
a title that is quite a poser for us until we read the analysis
which tells us of the value of cattle on the farm, and the importance of housing and feeding them properly and profitably.
This conference is illustrated with views among which we note
slides showing the well-known types of bulls and cows, the
cattle which have been raised in various countries and introduced into France, etc.

There is also a conference on the " Church and the School ".
The list of views is significant and suggestive: 1. Jesus among
the Doctors; 2. Saint Peter preaching; 3. The Four Evangelists; 4. St. John writing the Apocalypse; 5. St. Paul at the
Areopagus; 6. St. Justin and the Old Man; 7. St. Justin and
Triphon; 8. St. Catherine of Alexandria confuses the Doctors;.
9. St. Athanasius; 10. St. Augustine teaching; 11. St. Augustine and the Mystery of the Blessed Trinity; 12. St. Bene--

atinate School; 16. Charlemagne and the School; 17. Education of St. Louis by Blanche of Castille; 18. St. Louis founds the Sorbonne; 19. St. Thomas Aquinas and St. Bonaventure; 20. St. Bruno teaches Theology at Reims; 21. St. Bruno persuades his Disciples to renounce the World; 22. St. Ignatius at 32 a Pupil; 23. The Royal College of *La Flèche;* 24. The Class of Students; 25. The Council of Trent establishes Seminaries; 26. St. John Baptist de La Salle offers the Rule of the Christian Brothers to the Blessed Virgin; 27. Ven. Louis Marie Bandouin amongst his Pupils; 28. The Blessed de Montfort; 29. Ven. Elizabeth des Ages, Foundress of the Holy Cross Sisters; 30. Ven. Mme. Barat; 31. Julie Billiart, Foundress of the Notre Dame Nuns; 32. Père Lacordaire; 33. Père d'Alzon; 34. Montalembert; 35. Christian Brothers; 36. The War against the Sisters; 37. Archbishop Amette.

The mere reading of these titles shows how complete the treatment and how wonderfully suggestive. Then for study clubs we have answers to the objections of atheists, particularly to the agnosticism of Herbert Spencer and the atheism of Le Dantec.

The number of 20 January extends the variety of topics. The leading place is given to a conference on " First Aid to Sick Children " while awaiting the coming of the doctor. The rights of the fathers of families are considered in the second lecture—a subject that is surely up-to-the-minute in France. And so it goes. We note splendidly suggestive illustrated conferences on " The Cultus of the Blessed Virgin in the East and West "; and discussions on " St. Bartholomew's Massacre "; the action of the Lord Mayor of London in sending a Mansion House Fund to Abp. Amette instead of to M. Fallières; the repression of strikes in history; the question of the housing of the poor in Paris; the history of public charity or assistance among the first Christians—surely an appetizing collection of titles. As for contemporaneous interests, what more actual than the illustrated lecture on the Paris Floods

THE FURNISHING OF ILLUSTRATIONS.

Any priest who has endeavored to get up a lecture such as that on the cultus of the Blessed Virgin will acknowledge 1. the difficulty of getting a proper collection of photographs in this country; 2. the expense of making these special slides; 3. the almost insuperable obstacle of getting an intelligent colorist.[1] Observe how these difficulties are overcome by the French association. In the first place *La Bonne Presse* puts at your disposal a fine assortment of slides made from the great pictures of the world, as we shall see later. In the second place, without the need of much labor on the part of the lecturer he can secure an able exposition of almost any desirable theme. The advantage of this can not be overestimated. Our experience has been that, even where we have the great libraries of this country at our service, the books we most need are to seek in our American collections, and unless one is a student and a buyer of books it is well-nigh impossible to obtain the proper information for correctly illustrating the subjects that are important for our purpose. Thirdly, one need not buy the apparatus or the slides but can rent them at what are to us rates ridiculous in their cheapness.[2]

The most recent catalogue shows a collection of 600 slides on religious subjects made from the great masterpieces; then there are 270 made from the treasures of museums, engrav-

---

[1] The writer recalls a series of illustrated lectures prepared by him on the "Iconography of the Mass". The initial expense of Rohault de Fleury's book was $263. The slides, uncolored, cost 60 cents a piece, or $120. It was simply impossible to find any one in this country competent to color them properly, and the expense of time and money to have them done properly was prohibitive. Again, during the past winter being desirous of teaching the children effectively how to make the Stations, he sought for suitable lantern slides among the stock dealers. Despite all efforts he found himself obliged to use some made after very common-place models of art. Unable to endure the contrast with the really fine ones made from old masters and modern artists of renown, he attempted to obtain substitutes. In the first place he could secure only two photographs of paintings of repute, although search was made in the best shops of New York. All the others he wanted would have to be imported. As time was the vital 'factor, he had to purchase these two at a cost of $10, then pay $1.60 a piece for making and coloring the slides, and finally found when they were delivered that the colorist was ignorant of the exact tints of the originals, and in making a duplicate had colored our Lord's robe red, whereas, in the other it was blue! These are only samples of what one has to expect in this country if he wants to do anything that is genuinely worth while.

[2] Here is a specimen: For a loan of 8 days the rental is 6 francs for a lamp, 2 cents each for uncolored, 4 cents for colored views. Such rates certainly place this method of teaching within the reach of the poorest parish.

ings, ivories, illuminations, etc. To run hastily through this interesting and suggestive catalogue, we find 160 slides illustrating the Old Testament, and 80 the New; 153 illustrating the Gospels, the slides of each Sunday being especially marked so as to be used for that Sunday. Then there are the stock Doré illustrations; " The Life of Christ " by German artists (49 views); " The Holy Childhood " (46 views); " Christmas " as depicted by the great painters (26 views); the " Public Life of Jesus " (31 views); " The Teaching of Jesus " (30 views); " The Apostolic Journeys of Jesus " (30 views).

The analysis of the Conferences on " The Divinity of Jesus Christ " will be illuminating to all who have tried that difficult theme. It is partly as follows, and is based on Freppel's *Conférences sur la Divinité de Jésus Christ:*

Jesus Christ the Central Fact of History: 1. the Promises of His Coming. *Illustrations*—(1) the Holy Family (Murillo), (2) the Sacrifice of Abraham (Rembrandt), (3) Moses (Michael Angelo).

2. The determination of the time of His coming by Jacob, Daniel, Aggeus, Malachias. *Illustrations*—(1) Ezekiel's Vision (Raphael), (2) the Temple of Jerusalem, (3) the Wall of Wailing at Jerusalem.

3. The personal characteristics of Christ as foretold by David, Isaias, Jeremias, and Zachary. *Illustrations*—(1) the Annunciation (Fra Angelico), (2) the Virgin in Adoration (Filippo Lippi), (3) Ecce Homo (Guido Reni), and so on through nine headings each containing nine illustrations, making a total of 81 views.

Very interesting are the iconographical series made from the Ravenna mosaics, and the story of the Cross reproduced from French engravings of the fifteenth century. It will be remembered that references are given to the texts from which the teacher, who need not be an art connoisseur, can derive all necessary information. Nor is there any danger of tedious repetition. There are series illustrating—1. the Life of our Lord and the Blessed Virgin from the Frescoes of Aubert at Notre-Dame-des-Champs; 2. the Life of the Blessed Virgin after the great masters; 3. the Mysteries of the Rosary; 4. the Great Pilgrimages to Our Lady in France; 5. Lourdes (a splendid collection of 152 views); 6. a separate lecture on the cures at Lourdes (36 views); 7. a special conference on The Miracle, illustrated with 23 views taken partly from the Scriptures, partly from Lourdes.

Omitting other collections from famous art galleries, let us note a conference on " Sacrifice in the Economy of Religion " (50 views); " The Great Truths of Religion " (21 views); " Catholic Liturgy ", a complete course in liturgy covering five conferences and embracing 135 views. Some of the titles are illuminating: Altar, Tabernacle, Ciborium, Chalice, etc.; Catafalque, Baptism, the Exorcism, Profession of Faith, Ablution; Penance: the Confessional, the Accusation, the Absolution; Orders: the Prostration, Tonsure, Minor Orders, Subdiaconate, Diaconate, Priesthood. There is a series of 37 views on the " Ceremonies of Holy Mass " that we have found most instructive for children. Another on the relation of the Mass to the Passion of Jesus Christ will enable the teacher to fix this important idea most firmly in the youthful mind. Other objects beautifully treated are the Eucharist (31 views); Prayer (52 views); the Sacred Heart and France (50 views). There are 434 views on the Lives of the Saints. The early history of the Church is well presented by conferences on St. Peter and St. Paul. An interesting historical course is given in " The Religious Movement in France during the Nineteenth Century " and " Learned Christians in the Nineteenth Century ". Science is not neglected. We have conferences on " Instinct and Intelligence " (35 views); "Does Man come from the Ape? " (30 views). Nor are philosophy

Existence of God" (36 views); "The Existence and {
ituality of the Soul" (24 views). Social questions are pr
nent: "The Church and the Poor" (35 views); "The Ch
and Woman" (40 views); "The Church and Labor"
views). There are also the usual collection of views histo
artistic, geographical, etc. But of more interest is the s
entitled "Calvary through the Centuries".

Enough has been quoted from this interesting catalog
justify the adjectives by which we qualified the work of
excellent organization. Its success has excited compet
from purely commercial houses. As I write I have befor
an enormous catalogue from a leading Parisian firm, the
Part of which is given up to "Religion". Its sections emb
—1. "Set Lectures"; 2. "Old Testament Views"; 3. ".
Testament Scenes", embracing five series on the Blessed
gin and no less than twelve on our Lord; 4. "The Histor
the Church", comprising six series; 5. "Catechism", div.
into Dogma, Moral, Sacraments, Prayer, and Liturgy
"Allegories"; 7. "Illustrated Hymns". The study of
catalogue is most instructive as showing how quickly busi
instincts appreciate a good thing: because a comparison '
that of *La Bonne Presse* gives indications that much o
thunder has been stolen. But the many new and good th
introduced emphasize likewise the benefits of competition.
factor evidently resulting from this is that a marked re
tion in the cost of slides is apparent. It is interesting als
note that not only motion pictures of religious subjects are
sidered, but also the very latest development of projection,
reproduction of stereoscopic effects, certainly the most effec
and attractive method of presentation.

It is encouraging also to know that intelligent efforts
making in England to extend this manner of teaching relig
As we write, a circular comes from London detailing the
mation of a company for the exploitation of motion-pic
films dealing with Catholic religious subjects. The first
the list is Lourdes, which we suspect to be identical with

more hopeful than the characteristically American enterprise which is announced almost by the same mail and which offers the same film on the same subject but without the added value of a name like Father Vaughan's to cover the text, the prime object apparently being the gathering of funds, the lion's share of course to the proprietor, the crumbs to the soft-hearted pastor. The terms of the English concern are rather high, but would no doubt be very much reduced if the work spread.

Practical Method of Introducing the Work Among Ourselves.

It remains now to consider the matter of practical and efficient organization possible for the introduction and development of such a work in our country. The main difficulties are dissipated by the wealth of material and the thoroughness achieved by the French society. The greatest difficulties to be overcome here would be in our judgment to find or establish a suitable central depot or managing committee. No one who has not engaged in works of this character can estimate the narrow-mindedness and petty jealousies that are encountered. It is usually sufficient for a work to have originated in Oshkosh to have it poohpoohed and condemned in Weehawken, no matter how excellent it may be *per se*. That is bad enough, but when Weehawken calmly proceeds to appropriate the ideas and methods of Oshkosh without so much as asking " by your leave ", the situation becomes aggravating. The worst feature of it is that division means failure either absolute or comparative. But there appears to be at least one business-like, thoroughly capable and remarkably efficient organization already established that could, if it would, take up a work of this character and successfully carry it on, " The Catholic Church Extension Society." Its avowed missionary character would enable it to bring in free of duty, and therefore at a comparatively small cost, a sufficient quantity of the material above described to serve as a *fond* for lending out purposes. The splendid editorial department of its magazine *Extension* could

contributions in English.   Its capably managed business and
shipping departments could easily conduct the somewhat complicated details attending purchase, sale, renting, etc.   Its
recently acquired printing plant, together with its already established magazine, could undoubtedly handle at a minimum
of expense the otherwise almost insuperable obstacles of publication and publicity.   The field is not preëmpted, and hence
no vested rights are involved.   The Society has proved its
unselfishness and disinterested zeal, and therefore the friction
of individual conceit would be avoided.   Its thoroughly business methods would assure financial stability.   We trust the
officers of the Society both here and in Canada will see their
way to take up the matter, and, if they do, it is certain to be
carried to a successful issue.

We hope to be permitted in a succeeding article to describe
the details of the French diocesan organizations.

JOSEPH H. McMAHON.

New York City.

DIOCESAN REPORTS AND EPISCOPAL VISITS TO ROME.

THE S. Consistorial Congregation has recently published
a series of regulations to be hereafter observed by the
Ordinaries of dioceses not directly subject to the S. Congregation of Propaganda, regarding the canonical reports upon the
status of the churches under their jurisdiction.   Since these
regulations apply to the hierarchy of the United States as well
as to England, it will be of service to study them and to note
the chief points of the obligations they impose.

Before Sixtus V issued his Constitution *Romanus Pontifex*
in 1585, there existed no definite law binding the bishops of
the Universal Church to pay a periodical visit *ad limina* for
the purpose of making a report concerning the affairs of their
dioceses.   It was this pope who organized the Roman Congregations, and it became the office of the latter to make inquiry
into the affairs of the different departments of ecclesiastical
administration in order the better to supervise and direct their
activity.   To the eminent canonist Prospero Fagnani may be
ascribed the first effort to outline a scheme or questionary,

which, as subsequently amended by Benedict XIII, was to be
sent to the bishops, with instructions as to the manner of
drawing up their reports for the examination of the S. Congregation of the Council.   Missionary countries, subject to
the S. C. Propaganda, were to make their reports to the latter
Congregation.   By the new regulations the Bishops of the
United States have ceased to be subject to the Propaganda,
and henceforth all American matters ecclesiastical are to be
transacted through the regular officials who represent the general interests of the Church.

The recent legislation, which, we understand, is part of the
reformed universal *Jus Canonicum* to be published hereafter
and at present in the hands of a special Commission in Rome,
consists of two parts.   The first embodies a number of canons
imposing upon Ordinaries the obligation of making a report
to the Holy See regarding the condition of their dioceses every
five years and of visiting Rome every five years (for Ordinaries of European dioceses), or every ten years (for Ordinaries of other dioceses).

1.

Heretofore the period allowed for the visit *ad limina* varied
according to the distance of the different sees from Rome.
The bishops of Italy had to report every three years; those of
Germany, every four years; other European countries, every
five years, whilst for American bishops the limit extended to
ten years.   The date on which the visit became due was to be in
all cases determined by calculation from the 20 December,
1585.

Whilst the Ordinaries of the United States were not bound
to make their visits *ad limina* before the expiration of the
tenth year of their term of office, and, owing to the peculiar
mode of calculation, sometimes not earlier than the nineteenth
year, the Third Plenary Council of Baltimore (Tit. II, *de
Episcopis,* n. 14) had enjoined upon them the obligation of
transmitting a written report of the status of their dioceses to

ad limina is likewise restricted to a term of five years for the Ordinaries of sees in Europe. Those outside of Europe are bound to visit Rome every ten years. Thus far the law remains practically unchanged for the United States. But the date on which the term of the twofold obligation of visit and report begins is altered for us in the United States. The time for making reports and visits is now fixed as follows: For Italy it begins on the first day of January, 1911. Then the other sees of Latin Europe and those of the British Isles make their reports in 1912. The Austrian, German, and Northern sees report in 1913. All the American Ordinaries of both North and South America will send their reports to the S. Congregation during 1914, and make their visit in 1919. The Ordinaries in Australia and Africa and Asia are to send in their reports in 1915 and make their visit *ad limina* in 1920.

The obligation of the visit *ad limina* may be fulfilled by the coadjutor or the auxiliary bishop. If any other priest is sent as substitute for the Ordinary, he must be chosen from those' who permanently reside in the diocese; and permission is required from the Holy See in order that any one, except the coadjutor or auxiliary bishop, be commissioned to make the visit *ad limina* and the report.

The visits *ad limina*, due, under the old regime, during the present year 1910, are suspended, and no diocesan reports will be required. The bishops of the British Isles who made their reports in 1909 (according to the old law) are exempt from making a report or visit during the years 1911 and 1912. A bishop who has been in office for only two years or less need not make his report at the first term.

As to the manner of making the report the Holy See sends out a schema which contains a detailed set of questions to be answered. The first time this schema is to filled out, it will be necessary to answer a number of questions which are calculated to furnish a complete survey of the general conditions, economic, civil, religious and moral, in the diocese. Through the information thus furnished the authorities in Rome are enabled to adapt their legislation and decisions to local circumstances and to make apposite inquiries concerning the pastoral needs of the churches of any district.

All subsequent reports will be based upon the information

furnished by the first report. Accordingly they admit of certain assumptions about conditions which it will not be necessary to report in future, unless definite changes occur to give them new value.

The reports are to be signed, not only by the Ordinary, but by some priest who has acted as diocesan visitor and is familiar with the conditions of the diocese. He may be called to testify concerning local customs, abuses, and other matters relative to the status of the diocese.

II

The second part of the document gives the detailed topics upon which the diocesan report is to be made. It consists of six chapters, dealing respectively with the material and economical, the religious and devotional, the administrative and canonical, aspects of diocesan government.

1. The preamble of the first report will contain, if properly filled out, a complete history of the diocese: its origin, title, and prerogatives. Next follows a description of its geographical, climatic, national position; of the episcopal residence, its access by railway, also telegraph and postal communication; of the population, its religious complexion, the relative proportion of Catholic and non-Catholic inhabitants; characteristics of sectarian activity. In the third place, it will give an account of the ecclesiastical body engaged in pastoral work under the direction of the bishop—the clergy, the various divisions, ranks, consultative and administrative offices; the different religious communities of men and women, seminarists. Finally, the number of Catholics in the diocese, their distribution in parishes, local vicariates, churches, and chapels.

2. The second chapter calls for information about the freedom of worship, the obstacles to the progress of religion, and the means employed to supply the religious needs of the faithful. Inquiry is made into the condition of the churches, their fitness for worship, their maintenance and methods of conservation, the provisions made against alienation by violence or fraud.

and without being harrassed for money. The question directly put is: Whether the churches are free of access to the poorest so that all may attend without discrimination or being humiliated and inconvenienced. This clause appears to be a direct censure of the now almost universal custom of placing collectors at the church doors to exact a fee for attending the service, whether under pretext of thus supplying them with a seat or of excluding them from special worship.

The report also requires a clear statement regarding the use which may have been made of churches for secular and profane entertainments, such as academical, musical, and kindred diversions unbecoming the holy place.

The remaining items of the *questiones* in this chapter turn about the liturgical observances, the furniture, and personnel of the churches, the abuses and local customs in vogue, etc.

3. The Ordinary is required to give likewise an account of his own personal status: his sources of income, debts; his relations to the civil government; his residence and domestic arrangements, and the personnel of his household. His ecclesiastical privileges, titles, and faculties are likewise to be described. In truth, the inquiry into the exercise of the episcopal functions of the Ordinary is very minute. The Holy See wants an account of the frequency of: (a) his actual attendance at sacred functions in the Cathedral or elsewhere; (b) his pastoral letters and addresses to the clergy; (c) his use of faculties for reserved cases; (d) the method observed in the diocese of administering Confirmation, Sacred Orders; (e) his methods of promoting priests, and in particular whether he has promoted men who are not fitted or disposed to perform the duties which the Church requires of them; (f) stress is laid upon the obligation of the bishop's making a visitation of the churches in such a way as to give him accurate knowledge of the condition of each parish, of each priest and his daily and pastoral life, his activity in instructing the children in school, his administering the temporal as well as spiritual affairs in a way which will not only prevent scandal and confusion but give edification; (g) an account of diocesan or provincial synods, conferences, and canonical enactments held in the diocese during the five years covered by the report.

4. The next three sections deal with the personnel of the clerical body, the vicar general, chapters, and counselors, and the methods employed to inform and to govern the clergy. There are inquiries about idle and delinquent priests, about the reading habits of priests, and what means the bishop has taken to direct or to check the same.

5. One of the most searching chapters is that regarding the manner of governing parishes. First of all: how are parish priests appointed? Is due provision made for all the established parishes? How are the clergy supported? What are their regular income and their perquisites? Regarding perquisites the inquiry reads: Are there any methods which give rise to complaint on account of the exorbitant fees demanded at marriages and funerals, or on account of the rigor with which such fees are exacted?

The methods of bookkeeping and registration, of parochial administration, of liturgical observance, are minutely examined. Whether the people have Mass regularly, whether they are taught by sermons and instructions; and whether this duty of preaching and regular catechizing is anywhere neglected, the Holy See wishes to be informed.

The question is asked whether the bishop has noted any complaint about priests being slow to attend sick-calls, shirking the confessional or the giving of Holy Communion, administering Baptism, or assisting at other offices. These and the familiar topics of pastoral life are examined with an evident perception of the true needs of the Church in every part and under varying circumstances.

6. Chapter VIII treats of the Diocesan Seminary. This subject has an importance of its own and needs to be discussed separately in the course of our readings. It is followed by an inquiry, in two chapters, into the various religious institutes of men and women, their particular spheres of action, observance, and their relation to the Ordinary and the secular clergy.

7. A further chapter examines the moral, religious, and social conditions of the faithful, touching the subject of church

Separate chapters are devoted respectively to inquiry into the methods of instructing and educating the young, into the establishment of unions, sodalities, conferences for promoting religious life; into the administration of funds for the preservation and propagation of faith and of charity; into the efforts made to interest the faithful in what are known as social works for the uplifting spiritually and materially of the ignorant and destitute.

8. The concluding chapter constitutes a series of questions on the spread of literature, the work done in the diocese through books, periodicals, prints; the good and the harm done by the press.

Such is the character of the vigilant supervision the Head of the Church wishes the bishops to exercise. The members of the priesthood are not only intimately interested, but they are capable of coöperating with the leaders in the episcopate, so that the battle-cry of the Chief Pastor, the noble and meek Pontiff Pius X may be verified:

Instaurentur omnia in Christo!

Analecta.

S. CONGREGATIO DE SACRAMENTIS.

I.

DUBIORUM CIRCA DECRETUM DE SPONSALIBUS ET MATRIMONIO.

In plenariis comitiis a S. Congregatione de disciplina Sacramentorum habitis, die 12 martii 1910, sequentia proposita fuerunt dirimenda dubia nimirum:

I. Quid intelligendum sit nomine " regionis ", seu in qua distantia debeant versari contrahentes a loco in quo est sacerdos competens ad assistendum matrimonio, ut hoc possit valide et licite iniri coram solis testibus ad normam art. VIII decr. " Ne temere ".

II. Accidit non raro ut ob sacerdotum inopiam plures paroeciae ab uno tantum parocho regantur, qui easdem omnes singulis mensibus invisere nequit. Sunt pariter quaedam amplae paroeciae, vicos etiam cum sacello publico valde dissitos continentes, qui infra mensem, tum ob viarum asperitatem, tum ob fluminum impetum lustrari a parocho nequeunt omnino,

coram duobus testibus tantum, iuxta art. VIII; (*b*) Quilibet vicus, in secundo casu possitne tamquam " regio " haberi, ita ut ibi degentes facultate praefati art. VIII uti valeant.

III. Utrum valide matrimonium coram solis testibus ineat qui in " regionem ", de qua art. VIII *in fraudem legis* se conferat.

IV. An possint adhiberi ut testes mali christiani atque adeo pagani in ordine ad observandas praescriptiones art. II, III, VII et VIII.

V. Quoad menstruam commorationem et vagos quaeritur: (*a*) Utrum commoratio menstrua, de qua in art. V, § 2, sit accipienda *sensu relativo,* i. e., quoad eos qui alibi habent domicilium aut quasi-domicilium, an *sensu absoluto,* seu quoad illos qui nullibi praedictum domicilium aut quasi-domicilium habent: (*b*) Utrum parochus vel Ordinarius proprius, de quo eodem art. V, § 3, sit parochus vel Ordinarius commorationis menstruae sensu absoluto acceptae; (*c*) Utrum nomine vagorum, de quibus art. V, § 4, ii omnes veniant qui destituuntur domicilio et quasi-domicilio, an ii tantum qui, domicilio et quasi-domicilio destituti, praeterea nullibi habent parochum vel Ordinarium commoratione saltem menstrua acquisitum.

VI. Accidit ut parochorum coadiutores ab Episcopis nominentur, et quidem ex iure particulari facultate assistendi coniugiis non sint instructi; tamen usuvenit ut, ab incepto officii exercitio, parochis non contradicentibus, sed irrequisita eorum licentia, matrimonii adsistant, in libris etiam matrimoniorum adhibentes solam sui ipsorum subscriptionem; imo praesertim in maioribus paroeciis semper vel fere semper matrimoniis adsistant. Quaeritur in casu: (*a*) An matrimonia coram coadiutoribus hucusque inita, tacentibus parochis, sint valida; (*b*) Quatenus affirmative, an licite coadiutores se gerant in assistentia connubiis praestanda ab incepto officio exercitio, absque expressa parochorum delegatione; (*c*) Utrum tolerari possit mos ut coadiutores omnibus vel fere omnibus matrimoniis in paroecia adsistant, an potius parochi urgeri debeant ad hanc adsistentiam ut plurimum et ordinarie per seipsos explendam, nisi legitima et gravi causa, onerata ipsorum conscientia, impediti fuerint, quo in casu deputationem coadiutoribus conferant et ita solitus verbis connubia in libris matrimoniorum describantur.

VII. Utrum per art. I decreti maneant abrogatum ius speciale ante illud decretum in Hispania vigens, et ad Americam Latinam extensum, vi cuius ad valorem sponsalium requirebatur scriptura publica *a notario* subscripta.

VIII. Utrum Ecclesiae regulares exemptae ad tenorem decreti existimari possint et valeant tamquam territorium parochi seu Ordinarii, in quorum territoriali districtu sunt sitae, ad effectum adsistentiae matrimonii.

IX. An et quomodo annuendum sit petitionibus quorundam Ordinariorum, nimirum: 1.° Episcopi Rosensis postulantis dispensationem ab obligatione imposita per art. IX, § 2, adnotandi in libro baptizatorum coniuges tali die in sua paroecia matrimonium contraxisse; 2.° Vicarii Apostolici Kiam-Si Orientalis postulantis dispensationem non solum ab obligatione adnotandi matrimonium contractum in libro baptizatorum, sed etiam in libro matrimoniorum; 3.° quorundam Ordinariorum Sinensium qui quaerunt: Utrum responsum S. C. C. diei 27 Iulii 1908, ad VII, restringatur ad solos duos casus tunc in quaesito proposito; et, *quatenus affirmative,* postulant ut responsum extendatur ad alios casus verae necessitatis; 4.° Episcopi Mangalorensis qui postulat ut sibi facultas detur permittendi ut matrimonium celebratum in libro matrimoniorum describi possit a Sacerdote qui ex delegatione parochi matrimoniorum adstitit, quando parochus sit absens.

Et Emi Patres ad huiusmodi dubia ita respondendum censuerunt:

R. Ad 1.um Matrimonium potest valide et licite contrahi coram solis testibus sine praesentia Sacerdotis competentis ad assistendum semper ac, elapso iam mense, Sacerdos competens absque gravi incommodo haberi vel adiri nequeat.

Ad 2.um Provisum in primo.

Ad 3.um Affirmative.

Ad 4.um Quoad qualitates testium a decreto " *Ne temere* " nihil esse immutatum.

Quoad 5.um Ad *a* et *b*. Provisum per responsum ad quintum datum a S. C. Concilii die 28 Martii 1908.

Ad *c:* Nomine vagorum, de quibus art. V, § 4, veniunt omnes et soli qui nullibi habent parochum vel Ordinarium proprium ratione domicilii vel menstruae commorationis.

Quoad 6.um Ad *a:* acquiescant, facto verbo cum SSmo; ad

b: serventur de iure servanda; ad *c:* quoad assistentiam matrimoniis a parochis personaliter praestandam Archiepiscopus pro suo iure urgeat si quae sunt de ea re leges Concilii Provincialis. Quoad descriptionem matrimonii celebrati servetur art. IX Decreti *"Ne temere"* et praescriptum Ritualis Romani.

Ad 7.um Affirmative.

Ad 8.um Affirmative.

Quoad 9.um Ad 1.um Non expedire et ad mentem. Mens, est ut Ordinarius aliique ipsius cooperatores quantum in Domino possunt, satagant illam perniciosam superstitionem ab animis fidelium avertere, qua ab usurpandis Sanctorum nominibus in baptismo receptis deterrentur. Doceant ipsos frequenter, idcirco nomina eis imponi Sanctorum, ut eorum exemplis ad pie vivendum excitentur et patrociniis protegantur. Parochis vero aliisque animarum curae praepositis sacerdotibus commendent, ut quamdiu illa perniciosa superstitio eradicari non possit, omni, qua valeant, diligentia libros parochiales conscribant, etiam adhibita opera aliorum, quorum industria ea in re iuvari posse credant. Quodsi in casu particulari verum nomen coniugati scire non poterunt, stante morali impossibilitate legem observandi, ea non obligantur.

Ad 2.um Non expedire quoad utrumque et ad mentem. Mens est: Ordinarios curare debere, ut a Missionariis regesta celebratorum matrimoniorum diligenter conficiantur et conserventur, eisque pro suo prudenti arbitrio praescribere cautiones ad vitanda incommoda exposita, adhibitis etiam, si opus fuerit, signis conventionalibus.

Ad 3.um Quoad 1.um Negative; quoad 2.um Provisum in primo.

Ad 4.um Pro gratia prudenti arbitrio et conscientiae Episcopi.

Die autem 13 eiusdem mensis et anni SSmus Dominus

II.

Instructio Supremae Sacrae Congregationis ad probandum Obitum alicuius Coniugis, an. 1868.

Matrimonii vinculo duos tantummodo " Christo ita decente, copulari, et coniungi posse, alterutro vero coniuge vita functo, secundas, imo et ulteriores nuptias licitas esse, dogmatica Ecclesiae Catholicae doctrina est ".

Verum ad secundas, et ulteriores nuptias quod attinet, cum de re agatur, quae difficultatibus, ac fraudibus haud raro est obnoxia, hinc Sancta Sedes sedulo curavit modo Constitutionibus generalibus, saepius autem responsis in casibus particularibus datis, ut libertas novas nuptias ineundi ita cuique salva esset, ut praedicta matrimonii unitas in discrimen non adduceretur.

Inde constituta Sacrorum Canonum quibus, ut quis possit licite ad alia vota transire, exigitur quod de morte coniugis certo constet, uti Cap. *Dominus, de secundis nuptiis,* vel quod de ipsa morte recipiatur *certum nuncium* uti Cap. *In praesentia, De sponsalibus et matrimoniis.* Inde etiam ea quae explanatius traduntur in Instructione *Cum alias, 21 Augusti 1670* a Clemente X sancita, et in Bullario Romano inserta super examine testium pro matrimoniis contrahendis in Curia Emi Vicarii Urbis, et coeterorum Ordinariorum. Maxime vero quae propius ad rem facientia ibi habentur NN. 12 et 13.

Et haec quidem abunde sufficerent si in eiusmodi causis peragendis omnimoda et absoluta certitudo de alterius Coniugis obitu haberi semper posset; sed cum id non sinant casuum propemodum infinitae vices (quod sapienter animadversum est in laudata Instructione his verbis: *Si tamen huiusmodi testimonia haberi non possunt, Sacra Congregatio non intendit excludere alias probationes, quae de iure communi possunt admitti, dummodo legitimae sint, et sufficientes*) sequitur, quod stantibus licet principiis generalibus praestitutis, haud raro casus eveniunt, in quibus Ecclesiasticorum Praesidum iudicia haerere solent in vera iustaque probatione dignoscenda

premam hanc Congregationem habeantur recursus, non sine porro partium incommodo, quibus inter informationes atque instructiones, quas pro re nata, ut aiunt, peti mittique necesse est, plurimum defluit temporis, quin possint ad optata vota convolare.

Quapropter Sacra eadem Congregatio huiusmodi necessitatibus occurrere percupiens, simulque perpendens in dissitis praesertim Missionum locis, Ecclesiasticos Praesides opportunis destitui subsidiis, quibus ex gravibus difficultatibus extricare se valeant, e re esse censuit, uberiorem edere Instructionem in qua, iis, quae iam tradita sunt, nullo pacto abrogatis, regulae indigitentur, quas in eiusmodi casibus haec ipsa S. Congregatio sequi solet, ut illarum ope, vel absque necessitate recursus ad Sanctam Sedem, possint iudicia ferri, vel certe, si recurrendum sit, status quaestionis ita dilucide exponatur, ut impediri longiori mora sententia non debeat. Itaque:

1. Cum de coniugis morte quaestio instituitur, notandum primo loco, quod argumentum a sola ipsius absentia quantacumque (licet a legibus civilibus fere ubique admittatur) a Sacris Canonibus minime sufficiens ad iustam probationem habetur. Unde sa. me. Pius VI ad Archiepiscopum Pragensem die 11 Iulii 1789 rescripsit, solam coniugis absentiam atque omnimodum eiusdem silentium *satis argumentum non esse ad mortem comprobandam,* ne tum quidem cum edicto regio coniux absens evocatus (idemque porro dicendum est, si per publicas ephemerides id factum sit) nullum suimet indicium dederit. *Quod enim non comparuerit,* idem ait Pontifex, *non magis mors in causa esse potuit, quam eius contumacia.*

2. Hinc ad praescriptum eorumdem Sacrorum Canonum, documentum authenticum obitus diligenti studio exquiri omnino debet; exaratum scilicet ex regestis paroeciae, vel xenodichii, vel militiae, vel etiam, si haberi nequeat ab auctoritate ecclesiastica, a gubernio civili loci in quo, ut supponitur, persona obierit.

stantias. Qui insuper, si defuncti propinqui sint, aut socii itineris, industriae, vel etiam militiae, eo magis plurimi faciendum erit illorum testimonium.

4. Interdum unus tantum testis examinandus reperitur, et licet ab omni iure testimonium unius ad plene probandum non admittatur, attamen ne coniux alias nuptias inire peroptans, vitam coelibem agere cogatur, etiam unius testimonium absolute non respuit Suprema Congregatio in dirimendis huiusmodi casibus, dummodo ille testis recensitis conditionibus sit praeditus, nulli exceptioni obnoxius, ac praeterea eius depositio aliis gravibusque adminiculis fulciatur; sique alia extrinseca adminicula colligi omnino nequeant, hoc tamen certum sit, nihil in eius testimonio reperiri quod non sit congruum atque omnino verisimile.

5. Contigit etiam ut testes omnimoda fide digni testificentur se tempore non suspecto mortem coniugis ex aliorum attestatione audivisse, isti autem vel quia absentes, vel quia obierint, vel aliam ob quamcumque rationabilem causam examinari nequeunt; tunc dicta ex alieno ore, quatenus omnibus aliis in casu concurrentibus circumstantiis, aut saltem urgentioribus respondeant, satis esse censentur pro secutae mortis prudenti iudicio.

6. Verum, haud semel experientia compertum habetur, quod nec unus quidem reperiatur testis qualis supra adstruitur. Hoc in casu probatio obitus ex coniecturis, praesumptionibus, indiciis et adiunctis quibuscumque, sedula certe et admodum cauta investigatione curanda erit, ita nimirum ut pluribus hinc inde collectis, eorumque natura perpensa, prout scilicet urgentiora, vel leviora sunt, seu propriore vel remotiore nexu cum veritate mortis coniunguntur, inde prudentis viri iudicium ad eamdem mortem affirmandam probabilitate maxima, seu morali certitudine promoveri possit. Quapropter quandonam in singulis casibus habeatur ex huiusmodi coniecturis simul coniunctis iusta probatio, id prudenti relinquendum est iudicis arbitrio; heic tamen non abs re erit plures indicare fontes ex quibus illae sive urgentiores, sive etiam leviores colligi et haberi possint.

quoquo modo notis utriusque coniugis. In quorum examine requiratur *ex. gr.:*

An ille, de cuius obitu est sermo, bonis moribus imbutus esset; pie, religioseque viveret; uxoremque diligeret; nullam sese occultandi causam haberet; utrum bona stabilia possideret, vel alia a suis propinquis, aut aliunde sperare posset.

An discesserit annuentibus uxore et coniunctis; quae tunc eius, aetas, et valetudo esset.

An aliquando, et quo loco, scripserit, et num suam voluntatem quamprimum redeundi aperuerit, aliaque huius generis indicia colligantur.

Alia ex rerum adiunctis pro varia absentiae causa colligi indicia sic potuerunt:

Si ob militiam abierit, a duce militum requiratur quid de eo sciat; utrum alicui pugnae interfuerit; utrum ab hostibus fuerit captus; num castra deseruerit, aut destinationes periculosas habuerit *etc.*

Si negotiationis causa iter susceperit inquiratur, utrum tempore itineris gravia pericula fuerint ipsi superanda: num solus profectus fuerit, vel pluribus comitatus: utrum in regionem ad quam se contulit supervenerint seditiones, bella, fames, et pestilentiae *etc., etc.*

Si maritimum iter fuerit aggressus, sedula investigatio fiat a quo portu discesserit; quinam fuerint itineris socii; quo se contulerit; quod nomen navis quam conscendit; quis eiusdem navis gubernator; an naufragium fecerit; an societas quae navis cautionem forsan dedit, pretium eius solverit: aliaeque circumstantiae, si quae sint, diligenter perpendantur.

8. Fama quoque aliis adiuta adminiculis argumentum de obitu constituit, hisce tamen conditionibus, nimirum: quod a duobus saltem testibus fide dignis et iuratis comprobetur, qui deponant de rationabili causa ipsius famae: an eam acceperint a maiori et saniore parte populi, et an ipsi de eadem fama recte sentiant; nec sit dubium illam fuisse concitatam ab illis, in

gregatio diligenter expendere solet; cumque de re gravissima agatur, cunctis aequa lance libratis, atque insuper auditis plurium theologorum, et iurisprudentum suffragiis, denique suum iudicium pronunciat, an de tali obitu satis constet, et nihil obstet quominus petenti transitus ad alias nuptias concedi possit.

11. Ex his omnibus Ecclesiastici Praesides certam desumere possunt normam quam in huiusmodi iudiciis sequantur. Quod si, non obstantibus regulis hucusque notatis, res adhuc incerta et implexa illis videatur, ad Sanctam Sedem recurrere debebunt, actis omnibus cum ipso recursu transmissis, aut saltem diligenter expositis.

S. CONGREGATIO CONSISTORIALIS.

DECRETUM DE SECRETO SERVANDO IN DESIGNANDIS AD SEDES EPISCOPALES IN FOEDERATIS STATIBUS AMERICAE SEPTENTRIONALIS.

Recta ecclesiasticae disciplinae ratio postulat, ut nomina eorum qui ad provisionem sedium episcopalium in *Foederatis statibus* Americae Septentrionalis a cleri consiliis, iuxta leges ibi vigentes, S. Sedi proponuntur, secreta omnino serventur. Hoc exigit decus ecclesiasticae electionis et gravitas negotii, reverentia erga supremum Romani Pontificis iudicium quod invocatur, ipsaque iustitia candidatis debita. Nam cum horum nomina, ut saepe accidit, patefiunt, hoc ipso publicae discussioni exhibentur, quae pro varia hominum ac diariorum acceptione aliquando aequa est, saepius iniusta et iniqua. Quod, quum honori candidati, et aliquando absque facili plenaque reparatione, detrahit, tum etiam sereno S. Sedis iudicio et iustae electionis liberati impedimentum affert. Unde fit ut optimi plures ne in candidatorum album referantur totis viribus refragentur, non solum ob iustissimum tanti officii timorem, sed etiam ne in vulgi ore versentur, et in varias vituperationes incurrant.

cognosceret quae iusta quae opportuna statui possent, omnes et singulos *statuum Foederatorum* Americae Antistites audiri iussit.

Modo vero, de consulto Emorum Patrum S. C. Consistorialis, iuxta vota ferme concordia omnium illius regionis Antistitum, ea quae sequuntur statuit, et ut ab omnibus ad quos spectat ad amussim serventur mandavit.

1. Convenientibus dioecesanis consultoribus et parochis qui ius habent suffragium ferendi pro prima candidatorum propositione, vulgo *terna,* ab initio sessionis omnes et singuli coram Praesule praesidente iusiurandum dabunt de secreto servando circa nomina quae in discussionem veniunt, et circa ea quae ex maiore suffragiorum numero probata manent, ut Episcoporum iudicio subiiciantur.

2. Si quis consultor, quod Deus avertat, iuramento desit, praeter alias poenas quibus obnoxius evadere potest, statim a consultoris officio removendus erit; si parochus, poena erit perpetua privatio iuris ad suffragium ferendum.

3. Episcopi idem secretum servare *sub gravi* obligantur: et ab initio sessionis in qua de candidatorum scrutinio agitur, Praeses de hac obligatione eos opportune admonebit.

4. Ad idem secretum *sub gravi* tenentur apostolicae Delegationis administri, iuxta iuramentum quod ab iisdem praestari solet; et ii quoque ad quos forte apostolicus Delegatus se diriget ut opportunas notitias de candidatis habeat: qua de re sive verbis, sive litteris aliquem interpellet, ipse tenetur de gravi hac obligatione interpellatum docere.

5. Exemplar huius decreti in singulis curiis episcopalibus servetur, ut omni tempore singulis ad quos spectat norma et regula sit.

Praesentibus valituris contrariis quibuslibet minime obstantibus.

Datum Romae, die 30 Martii 1910.

C. Card. DE LAI, *Secretarius.*

L. * S.

S. TECCHI, *Adsessor.*

S. CONGREGATIO RITUUM.

I.

MONITUM AD EDITORES LIBRORUM LITURGICORUM.

I. In rubricis Generalibus Breviarii Romani tit. IX, n. 6, post Festum Nativitatis B. M. V. inseri debet *Septem Dolorum, Dominica tertia Septembris.*

II. In parte hyemali Breviarii Romani in Festo S. Thomae Aquinatis, die 7 Martii, ubi legitur: " *Lectio IX, de Homilia etc.",* substituantur verba: " *In Quadragesima, lectio IX, de Homilia et comm. Feriae ".*

III. In Rubrica Breviarii et Diurnalis quae invenitur die 16 Septembris in Festo Ss. Cornelii et Cypriani Mm. et quae incipit: " Si Festum Ss. Cornelii et Cypriani occurrerit Dominica, etc. . . ." et concluditur *in I Vesp. et Laud. tantum,* verba *I Vesp. et* deleantur.

IV. In Missali Romano, tum in Festo Ss. VII Fundatorum, tum in Missa *Intret* de Communi plurium. Mart. 1 loco, ad Graduale legendum; " *in generationem et generationem",* prouti legitur in textu S. Scripturae, Eccl. 44, 14.

V. In Rituali Romano, Benedictio novae Campanae, quae ad usum Ecclesiae, sive Sacelli, inserviat, adprobata per Decretum S. R. C. 22 Ianuarii 1908, ponatur inter benedictiones reservatas in appendice, ante benedictionem simplicem novae Campanae, quae tamen ad usum Ecclesiae non inservit, nuper reformatam.

VI. Item in Rituali Romano, Benedictio Officinae Librariae et Machinae Typographicae nuper adprobata Decreto 12 Maii 1909, inseratur inter benedictiones non reservatas, in appendice, ante benedictionem Domus Scholaris noviter erectae.

DECRETUM.

Sanctissimus Dominus Noster Pius Papa X, referente infrascripto Cardinali Sacrorum Rituum Congregationi Praefecto, suprascriptas variationes Brevario, Missali ac Rituali Romano respective inserendas decrevit. Die 9 Martii 1910.

II.

OFFICIUM, MISSA AC ELOGIUM DE S. PAULINO, EPISCOPO NOLANO
CONFESSORE, PRO UNIVERSA ECCLESIA.

IN BREVIARIO ROMANO.

Die 22 Junii

In Festo S. Paulini Episcopi Confessoris.

Duplex.

Omnia de Communi Confessoris Pontificis, praeter sequentia:

ORATIO.

Deus, qui omnia pro te in hoc saeculo relinquentibus, centuplum
in futuro et vitam aeternam promisisti: Concede propitius; ut, Sancti
Pontificis Paulini vestigiis inhaerentes, valeamus terrena despicere,
et sola coelestia desiderare: Qui vivis et regnas.

———

IN I. NOCTURNO.

Lectiones de Scriptura occurrente.

IN II. NOCTURNO.

(*Ex Brevi Pii Papae X, diei 18 Sept., 1908*).

Lectio IV.

Pontius Meropius Anicius Paulinus, anno reparatae salutis trecen-
tesimo quinquagesimo tertio, a clarissima civium Romanorum familia,
Burdigalae in Aquitania natus, acri fuit ingenio ac moribus suavibus.
Ausonio magistro, eloquentia ac poeseos laude excelluit.   Praeno-
bilis ac ditissimus, honorum cursum ingressus, florenti aetate, senatoria dignitate potitus est.   Dein Italiam petiit consul, et Campa-
niam provinciam nactus, sedem Nolae statuit.   Hic divino lumine
tactus, ob coelestia signa, quae Felicis presbyteri martyris sepulchrum illustrabant, verae Christi fidei, quam iam animo cogitabat,
impensius adhaerere coepit.   Fasces igitur ac securim nulla caede
maculatam deposuit, et reversus in Galliam, variis aerumnis ac
magnis terra marique laboribus iactatus, oculo capitur, sed a beato
Martino Turonensi Episcopo sanitati restitutus, lustralibus baptis-
matis aquis a beato Delphino Burdigalensi Antistite abluitur.

admiratae plebis tumultu correptus, ac frustra reluctans, a Lampidio Episcopo presbyter ordinatur. Inde redit in Italiam, et Nolae, quo sancti Felicis religione ductus fuerat, penes illius sepulchrum monasterium condidit, et adscitis sociis, coenobiticam vitam aggreditur. Hic vir iam senatoria et consulari dignitate praeclarus, stultitiam crucis amplexus, toto fere orbe admirante, vili indutus tunica, vigilias inter ac ieiunia, in assidue coelestium rerum contemplatione dies noctesque defixus manebat. Sed, percrescente sanctimoniae fama, ad Nolanum Episcopatum evehitur, atque eodem in pastorali munere obeundo, miranda pietatis, sapientia, ac potissimum caritatis exempla reliquit.

Lectio VI.

Haec inter, sapientia referta, de religione ac fide pertractantia, ediderat scripta, saepe etiam, numeris indulgens, concinnis carminibus sanctorum acta concelebraverat, summam christiani poetae famam adeptus. Quotquot sanctitate ac doctrina praestantissimi viri eo tempore erant, tot sibi amicitia atque admiratione devinxit. Quamplurimi ad eum, ceu ad christianae perfectionis magistrum, undecumque confluebant. Vastata a Gothis Campania, facultatem omnem, relictis quidem sibi rebus ad vitam necessariis, in alendos pauperes et captivos redimendos contulit. Postea vero Vandalis easdem regiones infestantibus, cum ab eo posceret vidua ut filium sibi redimeret ab hostibus captum, consumptis bonis omnibus in officio pietatis, se ipsum pro illo tradit in servitutem, atque in vincula coniectus in Africam rapitur. Tandem, non sine praesenti Dei ope, libertate donatus et Nolam reversus, dilectum ovile bonus pastor revisit: ibique annum agens septuagesimum octavum aetatis suae, placidissimo exitu obdormivit in Domino. Corpus, prope sancti Felicis sepulchrum conditum, postea, Longobardorum tempore, Beneventum, atque, Othone tertio Imperatore, Romam ad Basilicam sancti Bartholomaei ad insulam Tiberinam translatum fuit. Pius vero Papa decimus iussit sacras Paulini exuvias Nolae restitui, et festum ipsius ad ritum duplicem pro universa Ecclesia evexit.

IN III. NOCTURNO.

Lectio VII.

Lectio sancti Evangelii secundum Lucam (*cap. 12*).

In illo tempore, dixit Iesus discipulis suit: Nolite timere, pusillus grex, quia complacuit Patri vestro dare vobis regnum. Et reliqua.

Homilia sancti Paulini Episcopi.

tes facere, ut nemo indigeret altero; sed infinitae bonitatis consilio sic paravit misericors et miserator Dominus, ut tuam in illis mentem probet. Fecit miserum, ut agnosceret misericordem; fecit inopem, ut exerceret opulentum. Materia divitiarum tibi est fraterna paupértas, si intelligas super egenum et pauperem, nec tibi tantum habeas quod accepisti, quia ideo et illius partem tibi in hoc saeculo contulit Deus, ut tibi deberet, quod de suis donis tuo voluntario affectu indigentibus obtulisses, ac te vicissim in aeterna die de illius parte ditaret. Per ipsos enim nunc accipit Christus, et tunc pro ipsis rependet.

Lectio VIII.

Refice esurientem animam, et non timebis in die mala ab ira superventura. Beatus enim (inquit), qui intelligit super egenum et pauperem, in die mala liberabit eum Dominus. Operare igitur et excole hanc regionem terrae tuae, frater, ut germinet tibi frugem fertilem, plenam adipe frumenti, magno cum foenore centesimum tibi fructum multiplicati seminis afferentem. In huius vel possessionis vel negotiationis appetitum et studium sancta et salutaris est avaritia; nam talis cupiditas, quae regnum coeleste meretur et bonum perenne desiderat, radix bonorum est. Tales igitur divitias concupiscite, et huiusmodi possidete patrimonium, quod in centenos fructus vobis creditor pensitet, ut vestros quoque vobiscum bonis perennibus augeatis haeredes. Possessio enim haec vere magna et pretiosa est, quae possessorem suum non cumulo saeculari onerat, sed reditu ditat aeterno.

Lectio IX.

Verum, dilectissimi, non solum ut bona aeterna quaeratis, sed ut mala innumera vitare mereamini, praesenti sollicitudine et sedula operatione iustitiae providete. Magno enim adiutorio teque praesidio nobis opus est, et multarum atque indeficientium orationum patrociniis indigemus. Adversarius enim noster non quiescit, et in nostrum pervigil hostis interitum obsidet omnes vias nostras. Multae

IN MISSALI ROMANO.

Missa Sacerdotes, *ut in Missali romano, cum Epistola et Evangelio propriis* (*22 Iunii*), *et cum Orationibus sequentibus:*

Oratio.

Deus, qui omnia pro te in hoc saeculo relinquentibus, centuplum in futuro et vitam aeternam promisisti: concede propitius; ut sancti Pontificis Paulini vestigiis inhaerentes, valeamus terrena despicere, et sola coelestia desiderare: Qui vivis et regnas.

Secreta.

Da nobis, Domine, perfectae caritatis sacrificium, exemplo sancti Pontificis Paulini, cum altaris oblatione coniungere: et beneficentiae studio sempiternam misericordiam promereri. Per Dominum.

Postcommunio.

Tribue nobis, per haec Sancta, Domine, illum pietatis et humilitatis affectum, quem ex hoc divino fonte hausit sanctus Pontifex tuus Paulinus: et ipsius intercessione, in omnes, qui te deprecantur, gratiae tuae divitias benignus effunde. Per Dominum.

IN MARTYROLOGIO ROMANO.

Die 22 Iunii.

Apud Nolam, Campaniae urbem, natalis beati Paulini, Episcopi et confessoris, qui ex nobilissimo et opulentissimo factus est pro Christo pauper et humilis, et quod supererat, seipsum, pro redimendo viduae filio, quem Vandali, Campania devastata, captivum in Africam abduxerant, in servitutem dedit. Claruit autem, non solum eruditione et copiosa vitae sanctitate, sed etiam potentia adversus daemones: cuius praeclaras laudes sancti Ambrosius, Hieronymus, Augustinus et Gregorius scriptis suis celebrarunt. *Eius corpus Beneventum, inde Romam translatum, iussu Pii Papae decimi Nolae restitutum fuit.*

DECRETUM.

SSmus Dnus noster Pius Papa X, ex sacrorum Rituum Congregationis consulto, ac referente infrascripto Cardinali eidem sacro Coetui Praefecto, suprascriptum Officium itemque Orationes proprias, Missae de S. Paulino Episcopo confessore inserendas, necnon verba emendanda in elogio Martyrologii romani, iuxta litteras apostolicas in forma Brevis datas, sub die 18 Septembris anno superiore, in posterum universim adhiberi mandavit. Contrariis non obstantibus quibuscumque. Die 9 Iunii, 1909.

Fr. S. Card. MARTINELLI, *Praefectus.*

SECRETARIA STATUS.

I.

EPISTOLA AD ARCHIEPISCOPOS, EPISCOPOS ALIOSQUE LOCORUM ORDINARIOS IN AMERICA LATINA ET INSULIS PHILIPPINIS.

Illme ac Rme Domine,

Sanctissimus Dominus Noster Americae Latinae et Philippinis Insulis, per Rescriptum die 1ª Ianuarii huius anni datum, quod typis impressum praesentibus litteris apponitur, amplissimum Indultum super ieiunio et abstinentia, ad decem annos valiturum, concedere dignatus est.

Ut Amplitudini Tuae videre est, gratiae, quas per Indultum hoc generale in re ieiunii et abstinentiae Sanctitas Sua universis praefatarum regionum Dioecesibus est elargita, tanti sunt momenti eamque praeseferunt benignitatem in conscientiis fidelium expediendis a conditionibus praescriptisque onerosis Indulti anni 1899, ut superare sane dicas quantum elapsis temporibus hac de re concessum fuerit, ipsis in locis ubi Bulla *Cruciatae,* quae dicitur, vigebat. Cum autem haec Bulla et Indulta sive *Summaria* quadragesimalia aliave id genus Rescripta, quae dari una cum memorata Bulla consueverunt, iamdiu in pluribus Americae Latinae regionibus vim amplius non obtinerent, atque, ubi vigebant, eleemosynae quae hoc titulo solvendae erant, potius ex hodie remisso passim fidei Christianae fervore quam ex vero Ecclesiae legum contemptu, a paucioribus, pro fidelium numero, in dies praestarentur; idem Pontifex sapientissime desiderans ne id, quod initio ad ani-

nignitas in elargiendis, tum generali tum peculiari forma, Indulgentiis plenariis vel partialibus, compertum quidem erit
nunc harum omnium, partem abunde compensari, partem alio
de capite, sed pari profusione concedi; quare ex hac Bullae
Cruciatae cessatione, regionum earum fideles nil prorsus de-
trimenti neque spiritualium Ecclesiae beneficiorum imminu-
tionem esse passuros iam praevidere fas est. Nam:

1.° Spirituali indulgentiarum lucro per relatam Bullam
concessarum, tam vivis quam defunctis, satis superque per tot
pietatis opera vel preces, quae nunc exstant, ab Ecclesia indulgentiis locupletatas, facile suppleri potest.

2.° Facultatibus, quae pro interdicti tempore tribuebantur,
vix unquam, in hodierna Ecclesiae praxi, opus esse videtur;
quod, si casus huiusmodi forte contingat, ita, ad agendi rationem quod attinet, interdicti applicatio mitigata evadet, ut
vetera Indulta expetendi necessitas fere non habeatur.

3.° Votorum ac iuramentorum commutationibus aliunde
aditus plane patet, propter Apostolicas facultates, quae, ad
tempus non ita breve, a S. Sede Episcopis communicantur
atque propter tot tantaque privilegia ac particularia indulta,
quibus plurimi ex utroque clero confessarii gaudere solent.

4.° Eaedem facultates satis consulere videntur etiam casibus
canonicarum inhabilitatum, aeque ac difficultatibus, quae oriri
solent ex poenis incursis a Beneficiariis in acquisitione et usu
sui beneficii.

5.° Idem dicendum de absolutione a censuris, de dispensa-
tione super canonicis irregularitatibus et matrimonialibus impedimentis quibusdam, atque de celebrandi licentia per horam
ante lucem et per horam post meridiem; quibus omnibus a S.
Sede optime provisum est per facultates quam amplissime
earum regionum Episcopi collatas, quae longe excedunt quotquot Bulla *Cruciatae* continebantur.

Hisce compositum litteris, item Rescriptum Amplitudo tua
reperiet, quo facultates quaedam, Dioecesibus Americae Latinae anno 1900 a Leone PP. XIII f. r. ad decennium tum per
Rescriptum a S. Congregatione Negotiis Ecclesiasticis Extra-
ordinariis praeposita datum die 1ª Ianuarii sub nn. 1, 2, 3,
4, 6, 7 et 8, tum per Rescriptum S. Congregationis Concilii
diei 4ae Maii concessas, ad aliud decennium confirmantur, et
ad Insulas Philippinas item ad decennium extenduntur.

Haec omnia patefacere atque consideranda Tibi proponere
tenebar; iamque superest ut Tibi sensus exprimam plenissimae
existimationis meae ex animo.

Amplitudinis Tuae

Romae, die 1ª Martii 1910.   Addictissimus

R. Card. MERRY DEL VAL.

II.

INDULTUM CIRCA ABSTINENTIAM ET IEIUNIUM PRO AMERICA LATINA ET INSULIS PHILIPPINIS.

Ex Audientia SSmi die 1ª Ianuarii 1910.

Archiepiscopi et Episcopi Americae Latinae, in Urbe, anno
MDCCCXCIX, in plenarium Concilium congregati, Leoni PP.
XIII f. r. exposuerunt maximam difficultatem in qua, ob speciales regionum conditiones, versantur fideles suarum dioece-
sium servandi ecclesiasticas leges de ieiunio et abstinentia non
obstantibus amplissimis indultis a S. Sede iam concessis. Supplices proinde dederunt preces ut Sanctitas Sua ampliorem
et generalem pro America Latina dispensationem concedere
dignaretur.

Porro idem Pontifex, re mature perpensa atque praehabito
voto nonnullorum S. R. E. Cardinalium, attentis gravissimis
causis allatis, referente me infrascripto Cardinali a Secretis
Status, volens animarum necessitatibus atque anxietatibus occurrere, servata ecclesiastica lege ieiunii et abstinentiae ac
salvis permanentibus excusationibus ab eadem lege iure communi, iuxta regulas probatorum auctorum, admissis, amplius
indultum et generale concessit, quibusdam conditionibus cir-
cumscriptum.

est; novum indultum de speciale benignitate concedendum
duxit ad decennium, et concessit, singulis annis ab omnibus
et singulis Americae Latinae et Insularum Philippinarum Ordinariis, facta mentione apostolicae delegationis, simpliciter
et ad litteram prout iacet promulgandum, cuius virtute:

I. *Lex ieiunii sine abstinentia* a carnibus servetur feriis VI
adventus et feriis IV quadragesimae.

II. *Lex ieiunii et abstinentiae* a carnibus servetur feria IV
cinerum, feriis VI quadragesimae et feria V maioris hebdo-
madae.

Sed diebus ieiunii semper licebit omnibus, etiam regularibus,
quamvis specialem dispensationem non petierint, in collatione
serotina, uti ovis ac lacticiniis.   In refectiuncula autem matutina permittuntur lacticinia, salva lege parvitatis et exclusis
ovis.

III. *Abstinentia a carnibus* sine ieiunio servetur in quatuor
pervigiliis festorum Nativitatis D. N. I. C., Pentecostes, As-
sumptionis in coelum B. M. V. et Sanctorum Apostolorum
Petri et Pauli.

Circa usum huius indulti, Sanctissimus haec quae sequuntur
statuere dignatus est:

1.° Firma remanent privilegia in Const. Leonis XIII *Trans
Oceanum,* die 18ª Aprilis 1897 Americae Latinae concessa,
et per aliud Indultum, hac ipsa die datum, ad Insulas Philippinas extensa.

2.° Omnia alia indulta circa ieiunium et abstinentiam, etiam
sub titulo Bullae *Cruciatae* et Summariorum, quae eidem Bullae adnectebantur, hucusque in usu, quamvis Apostolicis Litteris confirmata, penitus et totaliter in universa America
Latina et in Insulis Philippinis abrogata declarantur.

3.° Nulla omnino taxa pecuniaria nullaque eleemosyna quocumque titulo deinceps imponi poterit pro usu indulti; nec
petitio eiusdem indulti a singulis fidelibus vel familiarum
capitibus facienda amplius requiritur.

4.° Quamvis ex capite dispensationis circa ieiunia et abstinentiam vel ex titulo indultorum Bullae *Cruciatae* et Summariorum, quae huic adnectebantur, nulla taxa nullaque eleemosyna imponi possit, tamen Sanctitas Sua hortatur fideles
qui id possint, ut, per spontaneas eleemosynas, sumptibus
cultus divini, christianae institutionis iuventutis, beneficentiae

et missionum concurrere non omittant: ad quod, singulis annis, in quatuor diebus festis de praecepto, uniformi ratione in unaquaque Provincia Ecclesiastica seu regione Americae Latinae et Insularum Philippinarum a respectivis Ordinariis praescribenda, in omnibus parochialibus ecclesiis et in omnibus ecclesiis et sacellis iurisdictioni Episcoporum subiectis fiant collectae eleemosynarum extraordinariae (omnino tamen voluntariae seu non praeceptivae) ad hunc finem destinatae, et respectivo Ordinario tradendae; cuius prudentiae et conscientiae earumdem eleemosynarum distributio committitur. Et omnes fideles speciali diligentia curent, non tamen sub praecepto, hanc S. Sedis benignam indulgentiam piis precibus, praesertim per Rosarii Marialis recitationem, compensare.

5.° Religiosi utriusque sexus, speciali voto non obstricti, quamvis sint ex Ordinis Minorum Familiis, de consensu suorum Superiorum uti possunt praesenti indulto, etiam quoad abstinentias et ieiunia in propria regula sive statutis praescripta. Hortandi tamen sunt Superiores Regulares, praesertim Provinciales et quasi Provinciales, ut pro viribus abstinere curent ab usu huiusmodi indulti intra claustra; subditi vero stent iudicio suorum Superiorum.

Contrariis quibuscumque, etiam specialissima mentione dignis, non obstantibus.

Datum Romae, die, mense et anno praedictis.

R. Card. MERRY DEL VAL, a Secretis Status.

III.

FACULTATES DECENNALES EPISCOPIS AMERICAE LATINAE ET INSULARUM PHILIPPINARUM CONCESSAE.

Ex Audientia SSmi die 1^a Ianuarii 1910.

II. Ut ubi necessarium sit ob paucitatem sacerdotum, audito Capitulo, et ubi Capitulum non adsit, habito voto Consultorum dioecesanorum, Episcopi ad Synodum dioecesanam singulis vicibus aut dimidiam partem Parochorum vel Rectorum, aut illos vocare possint, quos opportunius vocandos in Domino iudicaverint.

III. Ut in Missis vivorum quae celebrantur cum cantu, in duplicibus primae et secundae classis, in dominicis aliisque diebus sollemnibus, et quoties SS. Eucharistiae Sacramentum publicae fidelium venerationi patet expositum, quamvis haberi non possint ministri sacri, liceat thurificationes peragere.

IV. Ut " *Memoriale Rituum* " a Benedicto XIII editum pro parochiis ruralibus adhiberi possit etiam in ecclesiis non parochialibus, in quibus verificentur conditiones *parvarum ecclesiarum.*

V. Ut attentis specialibus circumstantiis praedictarum regionum clerici etiam simpliciter tonsurati, ultra triennium ab omni officio et beneficio suspensi, elapso suspensionis triennio, privati ipso facto habendi sint iure deferendi habitum talarem et tonsuram, nisi obtineant specialem licentiam in scriptis a proprio Ordinario.

VI. Ut tuto admitti possint tamquam causae speciales privationis ab officio et beneficio parochiali, praevia legitima seu trina monitione, eae quae habentur in articulo 820 decretorum Concilii Plenarii Americae Latinae, idest:

1.° Publica, perdurans graviterque culpabilis infamatio quoad mores sacerdotales, etiam post legitimas admonitionem non correctos, qua cura animarum grave damnum patiatur:

2.° Temeraria et post legitimam monitionem contumaciter repetita ad matrimonium admissio eorum, qui publicis impedimentis rite non dispensatis detinentur:

3.° Omissio temeraria instructionis catecheticae, diebus saltem dominicis et festis solemnibus, per maiorem anni partem et post legitimam monitionem pertinaciter continuata. Item temeraria et post legitimam monitionem iterata negligentia, in administratione sacramentorum fidelibus in articulo mortis constitutis, etiam ex sola causa distantiae ab ecclesia parochiali admissa;

4.° Gravis, publica et post legitimam monitionem repetita iniustitia et inobedientia in exigendis taxis, praesertim occasione matrimoniorum contrahendorum aut funerum, contra leges dioecesanas de taxis latas;

5.° Gravis, publica, per maiorem anni partem temere protracta, atque post legitimam monitionem pertinaciter continuata negligentia spiritualis curae et institutionis christianae Indis et Nigritis paroeciae impendendae secundum normas in legibus dioecesanis praescriptas.

VII. Ut attentis specialibus circumstantiis dictarum regionum circa bona ecclesiastica, Episcopi, praevio Capituli vel Consultorum dioecesanorum consensu, facultatem habeant:

1.° Locandi bona ecclesiastica ultra consuetum triennium, usque ad novem vel duodecim annos, dummodo iuxta leges civiles periculum non adsit quod locatio transeat in emphyteusim;

2.° Libere alienandi bona ecclesiastica, ubi summa pecuniae non excedat valorem viginti millium libellarum monetae propriae nationis, si necessitas vel evidens utilitas id postulent, et pretium inde obveniens investiatur loco honesto tuto et fructifero, favore Ecclesiae seu causae ad quam bona pertinebant.

VIII. Ut designatis, ubicumque fieri poterit a singulis Ordinariis in propria dioecesi nonnullus paroeciis principalioribus, quae Sacerdotibus maturae aetatis, probatae vitae, non communi scientia et pietate praeditis, in titulum ad tramitem iuris de regula ordinaria conferantur, ceterae omnes paroeciae, imo et superius recensitae, si adiuncta (prudenti Ordinarii iudicio aestimanda) id exigant, conferri possint absque concursu et ad nutum, salvis tamen privilegiis ab Apostolica Sede concessis, et cauto ut facultate transferendi aut removendi paroeciarum rectores, Episcopi nonnisi moderate et ex iusta causa utantur; onerata super hoc eorumdem Episcoporum conscientia.

IX. Ut Episcopi conferre possint absque concursu omnes Canonicatus de officio, quoties expedire iudicaverint.

Contrariis quibuscumque, etiam speciali mentione dignis, non obstantibus.

Datum Romae, die, mense et anno praedictis.

R. Card. MERRY DEL VAL, *a Secretis Status.*

IV.

INDULTUM EXTENSIONIS LITTERARUM APOSTOLICARUM
" TRANS OCEANUM " ET CONSTITUTIONIS " ROMANOS PON-
TIFICES " AD INSULAS PHILIPPINAS.

Ex Audientia SSmi die 1ª Ianuarii 1910.

SSmus D. N. Pius Div. Prov. Papa X, referente me infrascripto Cardinali a Secretis Status, de speciali benevolentia,
ad Provinciam Ecclesiasticam Manilensem seu ad universam
regionem Insularum Philippinarum extendere dignatus est
privilegia Americae Latinae, per Litt. Apost. *Trans Oceanum,*
die 17ª Aprilis 1897, a sa. me. Leonis Papae XIII ad triginta
annos concessa; ita tamen ut, quousque dicta privilegia pro
America Latina perdurent, eodem tempore pro Insulis Philippinis vigeant, ut tum in America Latina tum in praefatis Insulis eadem sit privilegiorum duratio.

Insuper in perpetuum ad easdem Insulas Philippinas ex-
tendit Constitutionem *Romanos Pontifices* ab eodem Leone
XIII octavo Idus Maii 1881 editam.

Contrariis quibuscumque, etiam speciali mentione dignis,
non obstantibus.

Datum Romae, die, mense et anno praedictis.

R. Card. MERRY DEL VAL, *a Secretis Status.*

ROMAN CURIA.

PONTIFICAL APPOINTMENTS.

By decree of the S. Congregation of Consistory:

2 April, 1910: The Rev. John Bapt. Gorordo, Titular
Bishop of Nilopolis, to the See of Cebú.

The Rev. John Bernard MacGinley, of Philadelphia, to the
See of Nueva Caceres.

9 April, 1910: The Rev. Timothy Corbett, of Duluth, to
the See of Crookston.

The Rev. Vincent Wehrle, O.S.B., Abbot of St. Mary's,
Richardton, to the See of Bismarck.

The Rev. Joseph F. Busch, head of the mission band of St.

Studies and Conferences.

OUR ANALEOTA.

The Roman documents for the month are:

I. S. Congregation of the Sacraments:

1. Solves a number of *Dubia* regarding the Decree *Ne temere*. Among others, (a) decides that parties may marry validly and licitly without the attendance of a competent priest, whenever such priest cannot be had without grave inconvenience and after a delay of one month. The requisite number of witnesses to the marriage may not in such cases be dispensed with, however; (b) decides that the term *vagi* applies to all parties who have no recognized parish priest or Ordinary where they live; (c) directs the Ordinaries to insist on the prescribed entry of newly-married persons in the Baptismal Register.

2. Gives certain directions concerning the method to be observed in proving the death of a married person before admitting the surviving party to a new marriage.

II. S. Consistorial Congregation publishes a decree enjoining secrecy under oath upon the electors of the *terna* by which candidates are proposed for bishoprics in the United States.

III. S. Congregation of Rites:

1. Makes certain corrections and additions in the text of the liturgical books.

AUTHENTIC INTERPRETATION REGARDING THE RHYTHM OF THE LITURGICAL CHANT ACCORDING TO THE VATICAN EDITION.

We give below a translation of the letter of Cardinal Martinelli to Dr. Haberl, the president of the German Cecilienverein. The original was published in *Musica Sacra* for March, 1910. It affords us an occasion to point out how unwarranted were the persistent efforts of those who sought to discredit the views we advocated for the promotion of the liturgical chant upon the lines prescribed by the Holy See. On account of the bearing of this letter upon the articles which Father Bonvin, S.J., is publishing in several papers and magazines the letter will no doubt be of great interest to many of our readers. A commentary on the important document is also given below.

LETTER OF CARDINAL MARTINELLI, PREFECT OF THE CONGREGATION OF RITES TO MONSIGNOR FRANCIS XAVIER HABERL, DOMESTIC PRELATE AND PRESIDENT OF THE ASSOCIATION OF ST. CECILIA IN GERMANY, RATISBON, BAVARIA.

His Holiness has learned that, particularly in Germany and among the Germans of the United States, a view concerning the Vatican edition of the liturgical chant is being spread which is absolutely false in itself and very prejudicial to the uniform restoration of the said chant in the whole Church. It is insinuated that the Holy Father in publishing the aforesaid edition did not intend to embody in it a special form of rhythm, but to leave to the individual music directors the right to apply to the series of notes, taken materially, any rhythm they deem most appropriate.

How erroneous this opinion is may be deduced from a simple examination of the Vatican edition in which the melodies are evidently arranged according to the system of the so-called free rhythm, for which also the principal rules of execution are laid down and inculcated in the preface to the Roman Gradual in order that all may abide by them and that the chant of the Church be executed uniformly in every respect. Moreover, it is well known that the Pontifical Commission, charged with compiling the liturgical Gregorian books, had expressly intended from the beginning and with the

Gradual by order of the Holy Father extends not only to all the particular rules by which the Vatican edition has been made up, but includes also the rhythmical form of the melodies, which, consequently, is inseparable from the edition itself. Therefore, in the present Gregorian reform it has always been and still is absolutely foreign to the mind of the Holy Father and of the Sacred Congregation of Rites to leave to the discretion of the individuals such an important and essential element as the rhythm of the melodies of the Church is.

By reason of the great authority which your Reverence enjoys as President General of the worthy Association of St. Cecile, you are requested to make the present communication known to all the members of the aforesaid Association, exhorting at the same time the patrons of Church Music to desist from all attempts, which in the present state of archeological, literary, and historical studies, cannot have a serious and gratifying result. They only serve to confuse the minds of the less experienced and to alienate the hearts from the Gregorian reform, as it was intended by the Holy Father and which, also with regard to the rhythm, has not only been accepted and more and more elucidated through new and useful researches by the most renowned Gregorian theorists, but is now actually rendered with complete and consoling success by innumerable schools in all parts of the world.

It was my duty to communicate this to you by special commission of His Holiness.

With sentiments of sincere esteem and devotedness,

CARDINAL FR. SEBASTIAN MARTINELLI.

Rome, 18 February, 1910.

To this letter, which he publishes in the original Italian text and in German translation in *Musica Sacra,* March, 1910, Dr. Haberl adds the following note:

The undersigned declares that he yields perfectly to the will and wish of His Holiness and the Cardinal Prefect of the Congregation of Rites. He has given orders that the many contributions which are sent in concerning the rhythm, and the essays which have been composed by various authors in purely scientific form regarding this subject, will no longer be published either in the *Musica Sacra* or in the official organ of the " Caecilienverein " (*Fliegende Blaetter*). And he urgently admonishes the members of the " Caecilienverein " to submit obediently to the wish and declaration of the Holy Father.

F. X. HABERL.

in the above-translated letter of Cardinal Martinelli, will be but vaguely and insecurely appreciated by those who, trained in the method of rendering the Chant by the *Magister Choralis* of Haberl, have not followed the discussions which have signalized the recent reform movement in the Sacred Chant. The "Ratisbon" edition, commended so heartily by Pius IX and Leo XIII, found acceptance and enthusiastic adoption especially in Germany and America, where its practical use was fostered by the great Cecilienverein. Dr. Haberl composed, for the better training in the Chant thus popularized, his *Magister Choralis,* which became the prominent guide to the interpretation of the Chant.[1]

The fundamental rule for the rhythm advocated by Dr. Haberl and the Cecilienverein generally, was the now famous statement: "Sing the words with notes, as you would speak them without notes." This rule will depend for its application on the proper method of speaking Latin—and here the question of the real value of the Latin accent comes into prominence. Roughly speaking, Haberl looked on the accented syllable as one which was longer in duration and stronger in emphasis than the unaccented syllables of a word. He said, for example: "We often find in such words as *Dominus,* quite a group of notes over the short syllable *mi,* and but one or two perhaps over the accented syllable *Do.* In this and similar instances the group of notes over the short syllable, should be sung quickly but smoothly and with a depression of the voice; while the single note (if there be but one) over the syllable *Do,* should be delivered with emphasis and power." The names given to the plainchant notes (*nota longa, nota brevis, nota semibrevis*) further insinuated a distinction of time-value based on the form of the note.

Recent paleographic studies in the Chant, however, appeared to contradict this view of the function of the notes and of the value of the accent, and to demonstrate that the various forms (*virga, punctum*) of the notes bore no relation even to relative time-values, the same melody appearing in various MSS. indifferently noted with *virgae* or *puncta.* Other indications from the MSS., which it would be tedious further to illustrate here, showed that the rhythm adopted by Haberl had not the sanction of the ancient usage of those who composed and embellished the chants. Haberl entitled his Rhythm "*even* measure", and represented it as opposed both to the measure of modern music (which he properly styled "*mathematically equal* measure ") and to the rough approximation to equality of all the notes of plainchant (which he styled " equal time-value "). Haberl's view of rhythm in plainchant was thus different from the view entertained by the Vatican Commission which has produced the Vatican edition (a rhythm styled in Cardinal Martinelli's Letter " free rhythm "), and was also different from the view of those who advocated a mathematically proportioned value for the notes (and who are now styled " mensuralists ", while their system is styled " mensuralism ").

Shortly before (and ever since) the appearance of the first issue (the *Kyriale*) of the Vatican Edition, the question of the proper rhythm for the Chant was hotly debated by specialists in the Chant. The fact that, when the *Kyriale* appeared, it gave no clear intimation of the view which the Commission had (as later appeared) determined as the correct one concerning rhythm, seemed to give a " right of way " to any school of opinion. In a pamphlet reviewing Dom Molitor's *Die Nach-Tridentinische Choralreform,* Professor Riemann wrote: " The problem of the restoration of the Gregorian Chant is far from being cleared up with the recovery of the original versions of the melodies, and a new papal brief will be needed to decide between the rhythmical views of Houdard, Dechevrens, Mocquereau, and the rest. In what sense this decision will be made cannot now be seen." [2]

The " mensuralists," while comparatively few in number, were represented by several able disputants, and finally the Rev. Father Dechevrens, S.J., established his magazine, the *Voix de St.-Gall,* as an organ for the propagation and explication of their views. It suspended publication at the end of two years, however; but hospitality was extended by Mgr. Haberl, in the pages of his own magazine, to the exposition of that " mensuralism " which was a contradiction of his own previous (and possibly present) view of plainchant rhythm. While Father Dechevrens had given pretty copious illustrations of mensuralism, as applied to the melodies of the Chant, in his *Voix de St.-Gall,* the question became of insistent practical importance by the publication of the plainchant Requiem, transcribed mensurally, by the Rev. Ludwig Bonvin, S.J. (Pustet). This publication was reviewed, and the system of mensuralism adopted in it assailed, by the Rev. Gregory Huegle, O.S.B., in *Church Music* (May, 1909, p. 154), and the Rev. Dominic Waedenschwiler, O.S.B. (*ibid.,* p. 171). Father Bonvin replied to the criticisms in the same publication (July, p. 223), while in the September issue Mr. Joseph Otten pointed to the prominence of some of those who advocated

---

[2] Cf. *Church Music,* March, 1906, p. 279.

mensuralism, and the Rev. Father Huegle wrote a rejoinder to the Rev. Father Bonvin.

The questions in dispute are now authoritatively settled by the Letter of Cardinal Martinelli. This should be a great gain to the cause of a uniform restoration of the Chant. Throughout the long controversy over the matter in foreign lands and recently in America, *Church Music* maintained its advocacy of the "oratorical" or "free" rhythm. Its position is now vindicated by the authoritative Letter of the Cardinal Prefect of the Congregation of Rites.

The Letter indicates clearly, therefore, that it is no longer allowed to the choirmaster to have the chant sung according to his own fancy, which would result in having as many kinds of rhythmic rendition as there are tastes (or minds) of choirmasters. The vague method adopted by Haberl and his followers obviously left much to the taste and caprice of each director of a choir. The direction of Haberl, that "the group of notes over the short syllable should be sung quickly but smoothly and with a depression of the voice", which had not the countenance of the MSS., has not any longer the tolerance of ecclesiastical authority. It was, from an artistic stand-point, vague and indecisive, however satisfactorily it might appear to work in the case of any one, single choir. On the other hand, the extreme mathematical exactness indicated by a mensuralistic tran-scription of a plainchant melody is similarly placed under the ban of competent ecclesiastical authority. Much has been written—and much might still be written—about the meaning of certain medieval theorists in their theoretical works. Mgr. Haberl, in a spirit of filial submission, promises to omit such discussions from the pages of his magazine; and doubtless the same course will be pursued everywhere. They can serve no other practical purpose than to darken counsel, to hold minds in suspense, to place obstacles in the way of the realization of the devout hope of the Holy Father in respect of Gregorian Chant.

H. T. HENRY.

Overbrook Seminary, Pa.

THE SETTLING OF MISUNDERSTANDINGS AMONG ECCLESIASTICS.

To the Editor, THE ECCLESIASTICAL REVIEW.

The suggestion of B. M. O. in your last issue for settling parish

it will have little or no beneficial effect unless it be imposed on some-one as a legal duty to put it into force. About this time the new code of Canon Law is being sent in sections to the different Curias of Christendom inviting just such beneficial suggestions before the code is cast in its final form. Hence it would be a splendid idea to have the suggestion of B. M. O. recommended to the Commission in charge of the new code for enactment into law.

Another suggestion, kindred to it and much more necessary, ought to be made to the same authority for adjusting *diocesan* misunder-standings, the evils of which are much more dreadful and deep-seated than *parish* ones. Though the extreme delicacy of this ques-tion makes one shrink from referring to it in print, its overpowering importance claims ventilation for it in the fresh air of a healthy public opinion rather than letting it stagnate and produce a crop of most deplorable results later. After all, when there is a mis-understanding between a pastor and his people, they have easy ac-cess, generally speaking, to other priests who attend to their wants. But an estrangement between a bishop and some of his priests leaves no such remedy.

The writer happens to know several dioceses where open and covert antagonisms, between the bishop and one or more of his priests, constitute a corroding sore in the Christian life of that portion of the Lord's vineyard. On both sides the principals are ordinarily good men, as the world goes, imbued perhaps more with human than super-natural motives on one side or the other, if not on both. Antipa-thies have gradually grown up between them. They have locked horns, metaphorically speaking, on close-knit issues. Their actual daily attitude toward each other constitutes a mutually self-destruc-tive warfare that is a stumbling-block and a scandal to the faithful and a by-word to the unfaithful. With regret it must be owned that this internecine strife is carried on with an unscrupulousness and a refinement of ill-will unknown to the laity. It is beside the gravity of the question to attempt to estimate which side deserves the more blame. The writer has heard time and time again from scandalized lay people this remark: " Well, if that is the way bishops and priests can spite one another, what can you expect from us poor sinners? "

Is there no resourceful remedy for such a cankering pestilence? Why cannot the law provide some swift and sure enactment along the lines of compulsory arbitration for stamping out at once this deadly evil? Two priests of tact, good judgment, and charity could, *in the space of one hour,* devise an honorable compromise on which these two men, bishop and priest, could compose their differences and live in peace the rest of their lives. Now suppose a simple law were made, not only empowering, but making it incumbent upon, the Apostolic Delegate, for example, to write to both bishop and priest notifying them that unless they settled amicably their differences *within one month* they are hereby requested to name two arbiters, one each. These two arbiters, with the aid of a third whom they should mutually choose in case of disagreement, should be empowered and obliged to render a decision, *within one month, absolutely binding on both sides.* As to when the Apostolic Delegate could and would be bound to institute such a tribunal some provision should be made in the law. For instance, whenever at least three parish priests of the diocese should in their discretion write him a joint letter notifying him that such an irreconcilable condition existed between the bishop and any of his priests. *Hoc vel alio meliore modo.*

It is now, while the final definite form of the new laws is still under consideration, the time for making suggestions for any rule which experience has taught to be necessary and which the *bonum commune* demands.

P. J.

THE HOLY SEPULCHRE.

To the Editor, THE ECCLESIASTICAL REVIEW.

I have read with very great interest the excellent article in your April number by the Rev. Jos. F. Sheahan, Poughkeepsie; and while fully appreciating the clearness and accuracy of the information conveyed, I would wish to be permitted to make a few remarks upon the illustrations so ingeniously designed by the Reverend author of the article.

There are a few points which appear to me to require modification. Thus:

BURIAL OF JESUS.

PLATE I.

1. The three Crosses are represented in the *left*-hand upper corner

of Calvary and the Holy Sepulchre. The entrance to the great Basilica of St. Helena whose vast dome covers both sites, is at the south side, the position from which the spectator views Father Sheahan's picture. Calvary with the three holes in the rock for the Crosses, is to the right (east), while the Holy Sepulchre is to the left (west). These relative positions are correctly shown in Tissot's *Life of Christ* (Vol. IV, p. 237), where the Crosses are at the right-hand side.

2. The Crosses in the picture are represented as being on the top of a hill at a considerable distance, whereas the two sites, Calvary and the Sepulchre, are quite near each other, scarcely twenty yards apart, "not a stone's throw off," [1] and are, as I said above, both included within the walls of the Church of St. Helena or Constantine. These two errors are repeated in all the other illustrations.

This conception of Calvary, making it appear as a great craggy mountain, arduous of ascent, is perpetuated by the painters of the Middle Ages, and has given a somewhat erroneous opinion to the world concerning the nature of the whole site. It is not a *mountain;* scarcely a hill. It is nowhere in the Scripture called a *mount,* or mountain, but simply the *place* of Calvary, *calvariae locus.* There is indeed an ascent to it from the east or city side, from the valley of the Tyropœum, but on the west side there was only a slight elevation above the road.

PLATE II.

This illustration shows the double cave quite correctly, and the large stone "lapis . . . *quippe valde magnus*" μέγας σφόδρα. But the stone has apparently the form of a *ball* or globe, like a huge snow-ball. This is not correct. The Scripture does not anywhere say that it is a *round* stone. The idea of its being round has no doubt arisen from the word *roll* (*advolvere—revolvere*). Thus we read (Mark 15:46): "Joseph rolled a stone to the door of the Sepulchre".[2] Again (Mark 16:3): "Who will roll us back the stone?"[3] And (*ib.,* vers. 4): "They saw the stone rolled back."[4] It may be remarked that this method of speaking is used for the placing or removing of a stone in a general way, as we use it to-day, of the stone placed at the mouth of tombs. Thus in St. John (11: 38) the tomb of Lazarus at Bethany is described: " It was a cave, and a stone was *laid over it."* [5] Now although interiorly there is a considerable difference between the tomb of Lazarus, at Bethany—at least as it is shown to the pilgrim to-day—and that of our Lord, the former being considerably beneath the surface of the earth, to be reached by a flight of stairs; whereas our Lord's tomb is cut in the side of a hill, and on a level with the ground outside. *Exter-*

ENTRANCE TO TOMB
showing closing rock half rolled away.

iorly, however, that is to say as regards the entrance or door-way, they are the same.

To confirm what has been said above, we find the identical expression of taken or moved away, applied to the stone at the mouth of the tomb of Jesus: "And she [Magdalen] saw the stone taken away." [6]

From this then I argue that there is nothing in the Gospel narrative to indicate that the stone was round, like a ball. There is, however, a sense in which it was round, namely as a disk or cylinder, or in plainer words as a grindstone or a mill-stone, and this is admirably expressed by the Greek word ἀπεκύλισε from κυλίνδω hence κυλίνδρος, a cylinder. Tissot, who spent ten years studying the topography, customs, and monuments of the Holy Land, and restored and reproduced many of them in a most realistic manner in his drawings, gives several sketches of the typical tombs still existing, near Jerusalem. He says (Vol. IV, p. 236) : " The tomb, hewn in the living rock, is reached through a second rock-cut chamber. . . . The opening giving access to the Sepulchre is low, and those who have to enter it have to stoop. . . . It is closed on the outside by a *rounded* stone not unlike a mill-stone running in a groove. This stone, heavy and difficult to move as it was, would engross the thoughts of the holy women when they came to visit the Sepulchre on the morning of the Resurrection. Levers were generally used for moving stones of this kind, and once in place they were kept firmly in their grooves by wedges. An example of' the method of closing tombs in the time of our Saviour can still be seen in the so-called Tomb of the Kings on the North of Jerusalem."

CHRIST IN THE TOMB.

Fr. Sheahan represents the swathed body of the Lord lying on the ground in the inner cave. This is not correct. The body was laid in a sort of sarcophagus or stone coffin, or, as Tissot says, " a kind of trough ". At the present day there is no coffin there; but there is a sort of shelf or ledge of rock on which the coffin rested; it rises about a foot from the ground. Above it is placed the table of the Altar, on which I had the unspeakable privilege of offering up the Holy Sacrifice of the Mass.

PLATES IV AND V.

These illustrations show an attempt to depict the Resurrection, but as that most glorious event was not seen, indeed could not possibly be seen by mortal or corporal eyes, it seems to me that any attempt to depict or even to explain it in descriptive fashion must prove futile. One runs the risk of giving to the whole scene a touch of irreverence, as when the writer says that the Body of Christ, " like an X-ray ", passed through the rock. Again we read (p. 390) : " In what direction Jesus left the Sepulchre we cannot tell, whether through the rocky roof, the side walls, or through the great stone which filled the entrance." Any conjectures in this matter would

informs it, it manifests itself; it appears visible or ceases to be visible in this or that place. Hence with regard to the appearance of our Lord in the Cenacle, the Gospel states that Jesus stood in the midst of them, the " doorway being closed ". This is said to signify that He did not enter through the doors; but it does not follow, as is generally interpreted, that therefore He *did* come through the walls. He simply stood in the midst of them, and that is all we know or may say about it. But apart from these strictures I wish to acknowledge the decided merits of Fr. Sheahan's article and the very great interest I experienced in the reading of it.

✠ M. F. HOWLEY,
Archbishop of St. John's, Newfoundland.

DEFILEMENT ACCORDING TO THE JEWISH LAW.

To the Editor, THE ECCLESIASTICAL REVIEW.

While not wishing to appear contentious, I should like respectfully to express my insistence on the utter improbability of the invasion of Christ's tomb by the priests and Pharisees, as represented in the April issue of the REVIEW, because of the grave defilement that would thereby be incurred. In the May number, the answer is made that the question of defilement by mere entrance into the tomb without touching the corpse appears to be an open one. As far as I have been able to learn, this dreaded defilement was incurred, not simply by contact with a corpse, but by entering the room where it lay, or by touching a grave or tomb.

In the nineteenth chapter of Numbers, it is laid down in verse fourteen that when a man dies in a tent, " all that go into his tent and all the vessels that are there shall be unclean seven days." Again in verse sixteen we read: " If any man in the field touch the corpse of a man that was slain, or that dieth of himself, or his bone, or his grave, he shall be unclean seven days." In likening the Pharisees to whitened sepulchres, He alluded, as you know, to the custom of making graves and tombs conspicuous so as to save unwitting trespassers from defilement. This law of not approaching the dead is especially emphasized for priests in Ezekiel 44:25, which reads: " And they shall come near no dead person, lest they be defiled, only their father and mother, and son and daughter, and brother and sister that hath not had another husband: for whom they may become unclean."

MASSES CELEBRATED "JUXTA INTENTIONEM DANTIUM."

A definite intention, arising from justice, should be formed in the application of Masses for which a stipend has been received. We have a practical case in the United States that offers difficulty. *Missae manuales* and Masses in such number as require six months or a year for their celebration are given to our priests. The number frequently exceeds that which the individual can personally satisfy. These "intentions" may have been received from different persons, or several parties may have given five or ten stipends each, which stipends may have been determined for different intentions by the parties making the offering. A priest finding that he has too many intentions, sends a bank check to a brother priest and a note to this effect: "Thirty intentions *ad intentionem dantium.*" In turn the priest who receives these may find that he too has more "intentions" than he can satisfy and he sends them to some one else with the request that they be celebrated *ad intentionem dantium.*

Is this method to be approved of, and may this application of Masses be considered licit? No, this method of sending Masses is not to be approved of, and the application may be illicit.

In writing or sending "intentions" to a brother priest, a few extra words or lines will enable the sender to specify the definite intention.[1] If the intentions sent from one priest to another were received from thirty different persons successively, the application may be sufficiently specified according to the axiom *qui prior est tempore potior est jure.* If the thirty Masses were given by six different persons, each person giving five dollars, and having a different intention for each Mass, it may be questioned whether these Masses applied *ad intentionem dantium* would be clearly enough determined, on the principle *qui prior est tempore potior est jure.*

Is there no way, then, of applying these intentions received

tion of giving one-thirtieth of each Mass to the parties who
gave the stipends. As the fruit of the Mass is divisible, each
of the six parties who requested the Masses to be said will receive a just proportion of the fruit of the Holy Sacrifice.
Bishops or superiors of religious communities may sometimes
have a number of Masses, received from various sources, to be
distributed in order to have them celebrated within the time
specified by the *Vigilanti studio* and *Ut debita.* Supposing
there be a thousand Masses to be celebrated, and the specified
intention for each Mass be not known. The better method for
the bishop or religious superior to follow is to state before giving out the thousand Masses that one thousandth-part of the
fruit of the Holy Sacrifice in each Mass is to be applied according to the intention of the person or persons who gave the
stipends.

Many may have scruples in consequence of these statements,
owing to the confused manner in which they have been applying Masses. If, after careful examination and consultation
with those whose judgment in such matters can be followed,
some priests decide that they have not had a determined intention in the Holy Sacrifice for stipends received, there are
two courses open to them. First, to celebrate these Masses
again with a specified intention. If this be impossible or not
feasible, recourse can be had to the Sacred Congregation of
the Council. The Supreme Pontiff from the treasury of the
Church can make up for the deficit.

INDULGENCES "A CULPA ET A POENA."

To the Editor, THE ECCLESIASTICAL REVIEW.

In his article on Indulgences in the *Catholic Encyclopedia* (Vol.
VII), Father Kent writes: " (2) Some writs of indulgence—none
of them, however, issued by any pope or council (Pesch, *Tr. Dogm.,*
VII, 196, § 464)—contain the expression, 'indulgentia a culpa et
a poena', i. e. release from guilt and punishment; and this has occasioned considerable misunderstanding (cf. Lea, *History* etc., III, 54
sqq.). The real meaning of the formula is that, indulgences presup-
posing the Sacrament of Penance, the penitent, after receiving sacramental absolution from the guilt of sin, is afterwards freed from

obliterated, only when complete reparation, and consequently release from penalty as well as from guilt, has been made " (page 783). Having thus vindicated the theological correctness of this formula, or at least vindicated it from the charge of theological error, one wonders at what immediately follows in the article, namely: " *Hence* Clement V (1305-1314) *condemned* the practice of those purveyors of indulgences who pretended to absolve ' a culpa et a poena ' (Clement, I, v, tit. 9, c. ii) ; the *Council of Constance (1418) revoked* (Sess. XLII, n. 14) *all indulgences containing the said formula; Benedict XIV (1740-1758) treats them as spurious indulgences* granted in this form, which he ascribes to the illicit practices of the ' quaestores ' or purveyors (De Syn. dioeces., VIII, viii, 7)." The italics I have placed call attention to the character of my difficulty. If the phrase " a culpa et a poena " is theologically explicable and defensible, why so much pother in condemning the writs containing this phrase? why should Benedict XIV call them spurious? why should the Council of Constance revoke them? Further on in the article (page 787), under the head of " Abuses ", some additional light appears to be thrown on my difficulty, but not enough, I think, to clear away all obscurity: " In 1450 Cardinal Nicholas of Cusa, Apostolic Legate to Germany, found some preachers asserting that indulgences released from the guilt of sin as well as from the punishment. This error, due to a misunderstanding of the words ' a culpa et a poena ', the cardinal condemned at the Council of Magdeburg." While Cardinal Nicholas condemned the error of the preachers, the Council of Constance had condemned also the formula, by revoking all indulgences containing it, and Benedict XIV afterward treated them as " spurious ". Also, Father Kent is careful to say that such indulgences had never been issued by any pope or council, and surely seems to intimate, by this parenthesis, that the phrase was so questionable in character as not to be chargeable to either of the highest authorities in the Church. May it then be critically assumed that those who actually did issue indulgences with this queer phrase meant something else than did the preachers, the purveyors, of them? Or, if facts (and not theological afterthoughts of subsequent apologists) really warrant a correct explanation of the phrase as occurring in the writs of indulgence, would it

natural) meaning of the phrase as interpreted by Bellarmine? If popes and councils never employed the phrase, but revoked and considered spurious the writs containing it, is there not at least *prima facie* evidence that the phrase was itself incorrect? I am asking these questions, as Protestants might ask them; and I should feel very grateful to Father Kent for more light, or for a good answer to give to such Protestant questioners.

PERPLEXED.

VIATICUM TO DYING CHILDREN.

At what age may Viaticum be given to dying children? Should only those who have made their First Communion receive the Viaticum? The age for First Communion is disputed by moralists and the practice in the United States is not at all uniform. If it were to be insisted on that only dying children who have made their First Communion are to receive Viaticum, we would set up a very unsatisfactory principle. It must be borne in mind that there is a divine precept to receive, if possible, Holy Communion, when in danger of death, imposed on all who have the use of reason; that is, those who know good from bad and who are capable of sinning. Moralists agree on this, that dying children who have sufficient use of reason to distinguish between good and evil, and who consequently can be guilty of sin, are not only permitted but are obliged to receive Viaticum and Extreme Unction. Thus a child, whether he be seven, eight, or nine years of age, in whom is verified the above condition should be prepared for death by the reception of Viaticum and Extreme Unction.

The objection often made that the child is innocent and does not need the Sacrament, should not be considered. How many, without a second thought, acting on the principle that *sacramenta sunt propter homines,* give the sacraments to those dying who are only doubtfully disposed. This causes no anxiety. Why then be so fearful of giving Viaticum to one whose little innocent life is so pleasing to God. If the dying child, whether seven or eight years of age, etc., who has the use of reason, is innocent, we must be thankful and feel that

was, with the sinner and penitent, even with those who are only doubtfully penitent; yet we must not be ungenerous and positively stingy with the good and innocent.

PAPAL HONORS AND "CANDIDUS AMERICANUS".

To the Editor, THE ECCLESIASTICAL REVIEW.

Since my former paper there has appeared in THE ECCLESIASTICAL REVIEW what was intended to be a strong criticism of Roman honors in general and Ecclesiastical Heraldry in particular. "Candidus Americanus," I suspect, must have read my two first articles on the latter subject in a rather desultory way; for, being an American citizen myself, I had whilst writing at least one eye wide open to local conditions. Hence, I venture to think that our Rev. "Candidus Americanus" unwittingly wrote down a few mistakes.

1. I think it a mistake to "assume" that the present Pope "really does not sympathize with all this show, but merely yields to pressure from the outside by according such honors, at the request of influential persons whom he does not want to offend". To say that the Pope "yields to pressure" is to say exactly the opposite to what is meant by *Motu proprio,* and it was by a *Motu proprio,* i. e. *on his own accord,* that the Pope recently (1905) regulated the minutest details of those *prelatic* honors, as well as a few days later, still minuter details of merely *civic* honors.[1] As to these honors being granted "at the request", etc., "Candidus Americanus" has perhaps forgotten what Father Nainfa, in his text-book of Roman etiquette, *Costume of Prelates,* writes on page 22: "The Roman Court wishes the precept retained, 'Ask and you shall receive,' etc."—a very different explanation from the one of "Candidus Americanus."

2. The Rev. gentleman seems rather light-hearted about "giving up" the temporal power of the Pope, for he asks, "whether these honors belong to the temporal power or to the spiritual". I answer, "To both," as the Pope himself shows by the fact in the two *Motu*

Broadway in a Prince Albert coat; nor are there many now, let us hope, who would care to see our present Holy Father treated, or treating, if that were possible for him, *à la Rough Rider* (as a New Mexico paper very pointedly puts it). Clearly, the recent deplorable occurrence, more perhaps than anything else, shows the false and "intolerable position of the Holy See and proves more peremptorily the necessity for Papal independence ". [2]

3. " Candidus Americanus " thinks it is " the wrong thing to publish such honors ". Why should it be the wrong thing to *publish* them, if it is not the wrong thing to *grant* them? Now surely, as a general rule, the granting of them conforms to the beautiful motto of the Order of Pius IX, " Virtuti et Merito !" Far from being a danger to " the democratic spirit and the popular ideals of our government," it seems to me the Roman way would precisely be the deathblow to corruption and graft, which too evidently enjoy a scandalous prominence among us.

4. Lastly, " Candidus Americanus " would banish " Ecclesiastical heraldry from our democratic land," coats-of-arms, seals, and all— not unlike Plato, who would have banished poets and all poetry from his Republic. If it were question only of banishing *bad* heraldry, I would be with " C. A." *toto corde;* but his declaration is too sweeping. And strange, here again, our own " American Republican " Department of State is in direct opposition to " C. A.", for it officially published, last year (1909), an extremely neat pamphlet, illustrated, and entitled, *The History of the Seal of the United States;* there, " C. A." will find very interesting reading anent the official Coat-of-Arms (sic) and the Great Seal of the United States, which " wrong thing " all the other States of the Union have since imitated, including the Benjamin among the States, Oklahoma. And to say that such eminent men as Franklin, John Adams, Jefferson, Charles Thomson, Daniel Webster, Frelinghuysen and John Hay busied themselves with such trifles! But to return to our ecclesiastical heraldry, " Candidus Americanus " concludes that " priests and bishops can afford to do without escutcheons ", etc. This I most emphatically deny, and even go far beyond the mere contradictory, once more quoting the text-book of Roman etiquette.[3] " When a privilege is granted to a class of dignitaries, each one of them is considered as *bound to make use of the privilege;* otherwise he wrongs the body of which he is a member. Moreover, *he has no right to refuse a privilege* the concession of which has been ' made

rather to the body than to him individually." I think this is sound *jus canonicum.* Now, let my Rev. friend settle the matter with these authorities, for I am, personally, too much interested to be deemed impartial.

AL. B.

THE PRAYER OF THE MASS ON THE FEAST OF ST. PAULINUS (22 JUNE).

We would direct attention to a difference of the *oratio* assigned in various missals for the feast of St. Paulinus of Nola, whose Office and Mass are to be celebrated in an altered form from the one given under 22 June in the older editions of the missal. According to the official version the Mass is *Sacerdotes tui,* second in the order of the " Commune Confessoris Pontificis " at the end of the missal. The Epistle and Gospel are proper as found under the date of the feast in the body of the missal. The Prayer, Secret, and Postcommunion are new. (The Lessons proper for Matins of this feast will be found in our YEAR BOOK under the proper date.)

ORATIO.

Deus, qui omnia pro te in hoc saeculo relinquentibus, centuplum in futuro et vitam aeternam promisisti: concede propitius: ut sancti Pontificis Paulini vestigiis inhaerentes, valeamus terrena despicere, et sola coelestia desiderare: Qui vivis et regnas.

SECRETA.

Da nobis, Domine, perfectae charitatis sacrificium, exemplo sancti Pontificis Paulini, cum altaris oblatione coniungere: et beneficentiae studio sempiternam misericordiam promereri. Per Dominum.

POSTCOMMUNIO.

Tribue nobis, per haec Sancta, Domine, illum pietatis et humilitatis affectum, quem ex hoc divino fonte hausit sanctus Pontifex tuus Paulinus: et ipsius intercessione, in omnes, qui te deprecantur, gratiae tuae divitias benignus effunde. Per Dominum.

A MEDAL AS SUBSTITUTE FOR THE SCAPULARS.

A number of our readers have been inquiring about a supposed decree which authorizes the wearing of, for the sake of convenience, a small medal instead of the scapulars.

There is no such decree; nor is there any authorization to indicate that the Holy See approves in general the substitution of a medal for the scapulars. The Sovereign Pontiff has simply permitted the change as a privileged concession, called for by exceptional circumstances, and to be used at the discretion of local pastors who may obtain the faculty.

This fact becomes evident when we read the original petition and the manner of its concession. It appears that the Procurator of the Belgian missions in Africa had applied to the Holy Father for the favor of allowing the natives (who, having been baptized, were enrolled in the pious confraternities so that they might share in the communion of graces and indulgences with other Christians throughout the world) to wear a medal, after they had been duly invested with the scapulars, instead of the regular cloth strips, since the latter, owing to the outdoor habits of the semi-savage people who wear only a cloth about their loins, soon became soiled with dust, grease, and perspiration, making the emblem by which they are commonly recognized as Christians, repulsive.[1]

The Holy Father granted the request, and the fact was communicated to the Vicar Apostolic of the Belgian Congo. But as there soon arose the question how far the concession might be applied to other Christians in the same region, or to those who migrating might find themselves amid wholly civilized conditions where the original reasons assigned might be supposed not to exist, the Procurator applied to the Holy Father once more, proposing the question: "An solius munditiae vel commoditatis causa omnes fideles possunt illa numismata loco scapularium assumere, quin unusquisque, cum animi anxietate, inquirat de propriis motivis?" To this the Holy

---

[1] Nam scapularia ex panno confecta, post breve tempus, pulvere, oleo et sudore sordidi panniculi fiant; et siquidem super nuda pectora miserrimi nigritae illa gerere soleant, eo modo se christianos confitentes, insignis distinctio christianorum inter paganos non est nisi linteolum omnino decorum. (Letter of the Very Rev. Albert Misonne, procurator of the Belgian Missions, to the Holy Father.)

Father, through Monsignor John Bressan, replied: *"Affirma-tive."*

Thus the privilege granted to the Christians in Africa in-dicated that the Sovereign Pontiff was willing to make the same concession to those who might apply for the faculty, in order to obviate similar conditions of uncleanliness and in-convenience. And in this spirit the privilege will be granted to any pastor who applies for it.

But it is in no sense a general concession indicating that the scapulars may be discarded after being used as emblems of investiture. It would be a distinct loss to Catholic devo-tion if the custom of substituting for the scapulars a medal which may be worn around the neck or attached to the beads or kept in the pocket, should be generally adopted. It would, as the Abbé Boudinhon points out,[2] soon cause us to lose sight of the origin and history of the scapulars which repre-sent the religious habit of the Carmelites, Trinitarians, and the monastic institutes to which the wearer becomes affiliated. And although, as Father Vermeersch, commenting on the subject, points out, this feature has not been respected in many cases, nor is it exclusively a part of the scapulars as now generally worn, it certainly has its effect in arousing the con-scious obligation of observing the spirit of the evangelical counsels, which is not often suggested by the wearing of a medal.

The privilege, when obtained by addressing the Holy Father, is communicated through the Prefect of the S. Congregation of Rites for a limited period only (five years). There is no special formula for the blessing. A simple sign of the cross made upon any medal of the Blessed Virgin by the priest having the faculties, is sufficient authorization for replacing the scapular.

We subjoin both the formula of petition and the form of concession usually adopted in the request and grant of the faculty.

(APPLICATIO.)

Beatissime Pater,

N. N., parochus ecclesiae *N. N.,* ad pedes S. V. humillime provolutus, implorat facultatem benedicendi sacra Numismata, quae Beatae Mariae Virginis Imaginem praeseferant, substituenda uni vel pluribus e quinque Scapularibus, nempe Ssmae Trinitatis, Passionis D.N.I.C., et Beatae Mariae Virginis sub respectivo titulo Immaculatae Conceptionis, Septem Dolorum et Montis Carmeli, ac gestanda a fidelibus, qui maluerint, rite pridem adscriptis.

Et Deus, etc.

(RESPONSUM.)

Sacra Rituum Congregatio, utendo facultatibus sibi specialiter a Sanctissimo Domino Nostro Pio Papa X tributis, R. Oratori benigne ad proximum *quinquennium* potestatem fecit benedicendi unico signo Crucis Numismata B.M.V., juxta preces Scapularibus substituenda, absque ullo Indulgentiarum et privilegiorum, quibus respective adscripti fideles perfruuntur, detrimento. Contrariis non obstantibus quibuscumque. Die ——, anno ——.

N. N. Card. *N. N., Praef.*

There is usually a small fee for notary costs added to the petition.

Criticisms and Notes.

TEXTES ET DOCUMENTS POUR L'ETUDE HISTORIQUE DU CHRIS-
TIANISME. Par H. Hemmer et P. Lejay. Picard, 82 Rue Bona-
parte, Paris.

This admirable series supplies a want which was up to this keenly
felt by students. For many of them until quite recently it has been
difficult and sometimes impossible to find such works of the Fathers
as they desired to read. The same may be said in reference to the
decrees of early councils, liturgical texts, etc. And though of late
years owing to the unwearied efforts of scholars several most important documents have been brought to light and published, e. g.
the *Didache,* the fragments of Priscillian, the *Logia,* and so on, yet
they were out of the reach of many of the earnest-minded inquirers
who resolve to consult sources of information for themselves and to
get their knowledge of Christian antiquity at first-hand. Persons
who live in remote villages, or in parts of the country at a long distance from universities and colleges and cities, cannot as a rule
have access to great libraries. Copies of the Benedictine or of the
Migne editions of the Fathers are not to be found everywhere, neither
are the books which give the latest discoveries or the publications of
learned societies. As regards the works of the Fathers, we may
add that the very size and appearance they present in the editions
just mentioned may have deterred some persons from reading them,
for after all the courage necessary to get through a folio or a quarto
volume is not possessed by everyone. Indeed we cannot help thinking that if Horace and Virgil, Homer and Demosthenes, were to be
had only in these ponderous forms, very few would know much about
them. Instead of a hundred good classical scholars, there would
perhaps not be five. At the present day, authors must be well
dressed if they are to make many acquaintances. The fact that the
new series by Hemmer and Lejay possesses this attractive quality,
is a reason and not one of the least reasons for its recommendation
in these pages.

required. And, not to speak of the invaluable collection of Apocryphal Gospels, Epistles, etc., so far the only three-volume issue that is announced is that which contains the Ecclesiastical History of Eusebius. For this work no doubt all real students will be grateful, as, we venture to say, very few of them possess a copy of the Church's first historian. In this new edition each work has been entrusted to a competent scholar. The various introductions we have examined are excellent and the notes all that can be desired. What a student needs in order to understand the early writer, is given to him here. Comparisons are proverbially odious; but if we are able to form a correct judgment they are sometimes unavoidable. So let us take some of the modern pocket editions, those namely by Hurter, Krüger, Vizzini, and the Delegates of the Clarendon Press. One has no notes except in Latin, another no translation, and so on. In certain respects therefore we prefer Hemmer and Lejay's edition to any of them. No doubt a great deal of historical and grammatical lore is contained in the Clarendon Press series, and though non-Catholic it is free from Protestant bias or prejudice. We gladly indeed acknowledge our many obligations to it. With obvious limitations we must say that it is one of our favorites. In many respects it is admirable, worthy to be put by the side of that " Library of the Fathers " which Newman and his Oxford compeers edited long ago. And to illustrate this, we think that a Patristic scholar who intends to read the Catechetical Discourse of St. Gregory of Nyssa could not do better than to take up Srawley's edition (*Clarendon Press*) and Meridier's (*Hemmer & Lejay*). It may be added in passing that the text of the Paris edition is confessedly a reprint of the Oxford one.

As we implicitly observed above, one of the advantages bestowed on the ordinary reader by the edition we are reviewing, is that the text is accompanied by a translation. They are printed on opposite pages. The translation is accurate, clear, and elegant. The delicate shades of thought often concealed from the multitude by the mere fact of their being expressed in Latin or Greek are here, so to speak, made visible and intelligible by being put into French. Few ecclesiastics have time or taste to keep up the knowledge, whatever it amounted to, that they acquired of Greek in their school-days, and few ecclesiastical students have time to spare from more important and imperative duties for the perusal of the heathen classics. We have to bear in mind also that a class of Patrology, for instance, is not a grammar or a rhetoric class, though from time to time grammatical remarks, etc., may of necessity have to be made by the pro-

Father's teaching are being verified in class by quotations and references, it is no small advantage if the student have before him both text and translation.

Then there is a wider circle of readers for whose needs provision is hereby made. We allude to those for whose benefit the Catholic summer schools are primarily intended. But indeed on further consideration we may add to them many others, such as nuns, etc. To all these persons, with few exceptions, a work by a Latin or a Greek Father is a sealed book. Though they may often have heard, for example, that St. Augustine wrote *The City of God,* what the work contains they cannot of themselves know. This and countless other treasures of Christian literature are hidden from them. They feel a very reasonable aversion to non-Catholic translations, they know they can hardly trust them, and so never open them. But in this new French translation, made mostly by priests, they have a thoroughly reliable one and at the same time a first-class piece of literary work. Of course there are many who do not fall into the class here designated as ordinary readers. Among the clergy there are many Greek scholars, some of them known to the present writer, who dislike to be obliged to trust a translation and prefer to read the text for themselves. They find a pleasure in examining the original.

Of the advantages of reading the Fathers nothing needs to be said. Their writings possess a special charm for us. It would be unreasonable to compare their claims on our attention with that which the pagan classical authors have. No one would put, for instance, St. Gregory Nazianzen and St. Augustine on the same level as Sophocles or Tacitus. Apart from the artistic perfection of the style in certain of their works, what the Christian writers have to say is immeasurably superior to anything that was ever uttered in pagan Greece or Rome. Many of the Fathers as, for instance, the two mentioned above and Minucius Felix were, it is said, skilled rhetoricians. But in forming our estimate of them, even though we were to confine our attention to mere matters of style, we should find that beautiful as their language undoubtedly is, it was not on language that their chief care was bestowed. Though their sermons show them to have been great orators and their essays prove them to have been great writers, it was to the matter under consideration rather than to the mode of expression, to the thought rather than to the words, that their attention was devoted.

Before concluding this brief notice of an excellent and up-to-date edition, it may be as well to mention those volumes of the series which have already been published and some of those which will appear. In the first class there are St. Justin's Apologies and his Dialogue with Tryphon; Tertullian's *De Poenitentia, De Pudicitia,* and *De Praescriptione Haereticorum;* the Apostolic Fathers (Doctrine of the Apostles, Epistle of Barnabas, St. Clement's Epistle, and the so-called Second Epistle; The Epistle of St. Ignatius, and the Epistle of St. Polycarp, etc.) ; Eusebius's Ecclesiastical History, (Books, I.-VIII) ; St. Gregory of Nazianzen, Funeral Discourses on his brother Caesarius, and on St. Basil of Caesarea; St. Gregory of Nyssa, Catechetical Discourse; Philo's Allegorical Commentary on the Law; The Apocrypha of the New Testament: (1st vol. Proto-Evangelium of James, etc). Among the works we are promised, the following may be mentioned: St. Cyprian's Letters ; Greek Councils; African Councils; Minucius Felix's Octavianus; Clement of Alexandria's Protrepticus; the Apostolic Constitutions; St. Ambrose's *De mysteriis,* etc. ; St. Augustine's *The City of God;* etc., etc. ; St. Chrysostom's Select Works. We are far from exhausting the list; but what we have said will suffice to give our readers a clear idea of the nature of the collection. The aim of the editors is, as they say themselves, to put the best books in the hands of all. Such a noble enterprise deserves our warmest gratitude.

REGINALD WALSH, O.P.

Collegio Angelico, Rome.

LETTERS TO HIS HOLINESS POPE PIUS X. By a Modernist. Chicago: The Open Court Publishing Co.; London: Kegan Paul, Trench, Trübner & Co. 1910. Pp. 280.

There is an Introduction to these "Letters" which is signed " P. C.," presumably the initials of Dr. Paul Carus, editor of the *Open Court* magazine. "Judging from what I know," he writes, "the author is a devout Christian in the broad sense of the word. He has been an active priest for many years, and is devoted to his pastoral work." The author himself, in setting forth his motives, seems to confirm P. C.'s high estimate of his devotion to duty when applied to the task of producing this book. " I can say in very solemn truth that before setting to work on the ' Letters ' I examined my conscience. All the thought that I could bring to the decision (of writing these Letters) as well as all the counsel I could get, preceded the determination to go ahead with the work. So far as I can read the process of mind and conscience that issued in the decision to write the book, these two considerations were foremost. First to do a work of education among the priests of the Church. I

substitute a new spirit, a new belief and discipline conformable to the times, under the name of Christian Catholicism, for that which prevails at present. " Should the Roman Catholic Church," says P. C. in concluding his appreciation of the author's purpose, " not conform to the demands of the time, should the Curia continue to prevent a reformation so much needed, it is quite probable that many pious souls will break away from Rome and originate a genuine Catholic church " (Introd., p. x).

Now there are twenty-one " Letters," and there are, besides, six chapters and an epilogue dealing with the attitude of the Roman authorities toward their subjects. The Inquisition, Italian Absolutism, Roman Legates and Fathers General, The Present Discipline of Celibacy, The Jesuits and Intellectual Tyrany, are topics which would naturally rouse the suspicion that the book was nothing more than a repetition of those vulgar tirades against established institutions altogether misconceived by the ignorant or maliciously misrepresented by those who have felt the sting of rebuke from those same authorities and seek to vent their spleen by writing against them. But we should prefer to take our author in good faith even on these subjects which partiality only as a rule selects because they appeal to certain set prejudices and thus create an atmosphere favorable to specious reasonings of a more subtle kind against Catholic truth.

If his sole aim is to reform the external regime of the Catholic Church, to eliminate abuses in practice and superstitions in doctrine, there may be room for his labors and a hearing due to his pleadings in the sense in which there was room for the reforms of the Council of Trent or of St. Charles Borromeo or of Pius X.

But what does he plead for in his proposal to modernize things and to bring the Church of the Ages into harmony with the spirit of the times? This—that we abandon the belief in the Divinity of Christ. This is the burden and ultimate climax of the appeal of "A Modernist " to Pius X, head of the Catholic Church and the supreme interpreter of the Apostolic doctrine. Of Christ the author speaks in these words at the very end of his volume (pp. 272-273) : " God was His life, His love, His enthusiasm. . . . But that He was God, that awful Infinite beyond the space of the stars,

have their humors as had the disciples at the Council of Antioch and the Pauline evangelists in Crete and Philippi. But what distinguishes the Church of Christ everywhere from the temples of Baal is the belief in the Messianic mission of the Man-God.

And even if it could be otherwise, even if the Catholic Church could abdicate her fundamental principles, (which she never can), and accept that extreme Protestantism of the new rationalist forms of belief inaugurated by Baur and Strauss and refurbished by Loisy after half a century, how far could we trust this writer who styles himself "A Modernist" and withholds his name whilst he claims to be "an active priest for many years who is devoted to his pastoral work"? What sort of Catholic piety is it that makes this "active priest" play the part of being "devoted to pastoral work", which in the Catholic Church means the celebration of the Holy Sacrifice, the imparting of the Sacraments, and the preaching of the Divinity of Christ on every Sunday and holiday of the year? The lesson of hypocrisy thus confessed is not of the doctrine of Him who said: "He that shall confess Me before men, Him shall I also confess before my Father who is in heaven." If we take the author at his word, his works denounce him as an impostor notwithstanding the fact that he could make the editor of the *Open Court* believe in his sincerity.

THE LIFE OF ST. CLARE, ascribed to Fr. Thomas of Celano of the Order of Friars Minor (A. D. 1255–1261); translated and edited from the earliest MSS. by Fr. Paschal Robinson, of the same Order. With an Appendix containing the Rule of Saint Clare. Published by the Dolphin Press at Philadelphia. MCMX. Pp. xliii–169.

Strange indeed that there should have been up to this time no English biography of "the chief rival of the Blessed Francis in the observance of Gospel Perfection"! Next to the Umbrian *Poverello* she was the prime mover in that great religious revolution which brought a new spirit into the ascetical observance of monastic life, sweet and musical, so as to charm by the echoes of its otherworldly wisdom the philosophers and geniuses who had hitherto known the expression of highest truth only in the scholastic precepts of Aristotle or the ascetical rules of Benedict of Nursia. Yet so it is—

spirit opens its beautiful chalice, and sends forth the exquisite aroma of a unique devotion and affiliation to the Franciscan rule of life.

No better guide could have been found than Father Robinson, whose familiarity with everything relating to St. Francis, whether hidden in the recesses of Assisian and other archives, or published in the thousand and one commentaries love and scholarship have gathered around this theme, gives security that we have here the best and most authentic record of what is known about St. Clare. Nor is it simply a story of early devotion to a great cause, of self-abnegation and prayer, and of the sublime Christian heroism of a virgin who represents a perfect type of the valiant woman eulogized by the Hebrew seer. There runs through this interesting biography something of the chaste charm of medieval romance. The friendship of St. Francis and St. Clare, unlike any other in the history of the Saints—although we have records of many a noble companionship from the days of St. Jerome and Paula to those of St. Francis de Sales and Chantal—appeals to the reader of this chronicle with a force begotten of the simplicity and holiness which breathe from Celano's account. With this account it is not our purpose to make our readers acquainted. Let them go to the book, and they will get the value of a beautiful image which urges virtue upon the reader without wearying him with didactic forms.

The Rule of St. Clare, which is added in the Appendix, too, has its special worth; for it is a first copy of a long-lost document, which was found after centuries in the sleeve of the Saint's habit, kept as a relic untouched for many a day, until an accident brought it to light.

But aside from an accurate and charmingly readable translation of an ancient document that draws for us a true picture of St. Clare, we have here a valuable contribution to modern Franciscan literature in the Introduction, which covers some forty pages of this exquisite volume. Father Robinson traces the sources of the History of St. Clare, discusses their character, authenticity, and critical worth. Celano's biography is examined as to the details of date and authorship. From the Introductory Letter prefaced to it, it is evident that it must have been written within eight years after the Saint's death. As to the author there is no direct clue. The spirit of the age which cultivated a communism in things that referred to the honor of God, no less than the modest self-abnegation which the rule of St. Francis inspired, prevented the writer from giving us his name. For a long time St. Bonaventure was credited with the work, and some manuscript copies actually bear his name. The Bollandists hesitated to accept the tradition; they saw intrinsic evidence against this attribution. The Fathers of the Franciscan

"Scriptorium magnum" at Quaracchi have on critical grounds decided the question for us by attributing the work to Thomas of Celano; and whilst there is no extrinsic or absolute evidence to this effect, the common consent of Franciscan scholarship has sanctioned the conclusion as most probable. Pope Alexander IV who canonized St. Clare and who had known her personally, is said to have commissioned Friar Thomas to write her Life, and the assumption is confirmed by a document published by Cozza-Luzzi and by the earlier testimony of the great Conventual critic Papini, which Father Paschal Robinson had occasion to examine critically in 1909.

Incidentally our author throws the light of judicious interpretation upon the belief and prejudices of the ages of faith. Whilst he is hardly so outspoken in his capacity of objective historian as are recent writers like the erudite Bollandist Delahaye or the German historian Grisar, both of the Society of Jesus, he wisely discriminates between the supernatural faith which accepts the miraculous as part of the Divine economy of salvation, and the tendency "to believe that God continually interfered with the course of nature", as we find it expressed in popular briefs and legends innumerable of that age. This temper of the time in which St. Francis and St. Clare lived and Celano wrote must be kept in mind if we are to understand aright certain exaggerations into which the innocently credulous and yet nobly enthusiastic temper of the writer led him when describing the gifts and virtues of his heroine. To have pointed it out is rather a decided merit of Father Robinson's volume, and one is nettled as well as surprised to find that this very excellence has been made the subject of criticism in a recent notice of the book by some critic in a reputable Catholic journal, who evidently did not understand the purpose of Father Paschal's expression and had the rash grace forthwith to offer a correction of it.

But we must leave the reader to satisfy himself with a careful perusal of the volume, beautifully illustrated and enriched with a critical bibliography of MSS., editions, and translations, to which Father Robinson refers us in his learned Introduction.

EACH FOR ALL, AND ALL FOR EACH. By John Parsons, D. D. Sturtis and Walton Company: New York. 1910. Pp. viii–390.

LA VALEUR SOCIALE DE L'EVANGILE. Par L. Garriguet. Bloud et Cie: Paris. 1910. Pp. 313.

improve the social system. Each of these manifest streams has of course numerous inlets and outlets, but the one is fully differentiated from the other. The two books here introduced are typical examples of the dual tendency just instanced. *Each for All, and All for Each* contains a theory of society determining the interrelations of the individual to the State. The *Social Value of the Gospel* is a summary of Christ's doctrine on social welfare and duty.

Dr. Parsons in the first place gives a brief analysis of " the social system " in order to bring out the mutual interdependence of the individual and society—the former by his very nature, not by choice or in virtue of any original compact, being dependent on the latter for economic subsidy, for companionship, for direction; while society depends on the individual for initiatives, leadership, and ideals. The conception of society as an " organism " is then developed, the limitations of the concept being clearly determined. After a chapter on " individual initiative ", the various ways in which the individual extends his influence to the social system are set forth in turn under the captions—Diffusion, Succession, Convergence, Germination, and Correlation. Analogical expressions these are of course, but not arbitrary inventions; they spring out of the general structure of life as unfolded in the social system. They represent the provision in the human constitution for a developed and personal life (49). The permanency of these methods of individual influence, the harm to society which their abnormal operation entails, the cure of such harm, the progress of individualism through social evolution—these topics likewise receive a just measure of consideration. Into none of these subjects does the author penetrate very deeply. He has essayed no technical work on " social psychology ". Possibly for this very reason his book will be found all the more useful by at least general readers. It serves to arouse and strengthen " social consciousness ", to make the reader more actually aware of the invisible process of the inter-human world, of the currents of subtle reciprocity between himself and his social surroundings. The work is sensible and clear. It contains none of the strained technicalities which mystify so much of the current writing on sociology. Here and there one notices a lack of accuracy in statement. For instance, where it is said that " the sociality of human beings is of a higher grade than that of the brutes " (p. 6). *Grade,* of course, here means *kind.* Again " the law of existence " in an oak " implies " very much more than " the perfection of the tree " (p. 15). Other such *naevi* might easily be noticed, but they make nothing against the substance of a book in which there is so much sane and solid thought, so much from a non-Catholic author which the Catholic reader is glad to be able to **endorse.**

The author of *La Valeur Sociale de l'Evangile* is widely known through his *Traité de Sociologie* (3 vols. Paris, Bloud & Cie.) and a number of shorter esays on economic subjects. In the work at hand he first outlines the various opinions maintained by different schools concerning the social teachings of the Gospel. He then points out what Catholic writers have done in the way of educing those teachings. Having next determined what one may reasonably look for in our Lord's social doctrines, he goes on to establish the thesis " that the Gospel has exercised an immense influence on even the material destinies of humanity, that its efficiency is not exhausted, and that now as heretofore it affords most precious helps for establishing in the midst of a society so sadly divided and diseased the reign of order, justice, union, and peace " (p. 7). All this sounds familiar enough, platitudinous indeed it may seem. It is only in the development of the thought implicit in the generality that the definiteness of the truth and the range of its application stand out with something of actuality. When the Gospel teaching respecting the perfection of the individual, the restoration of the family, personal rights, the new spirit which it introduced into humanity, the social evolution which it inaugurated, its relation to democracy—when the explicit truths and their valid implications in these directions are unfolded as they are in the work at hand, they reveal their value and their wealth of practical application. They show themselves to be not simply the seeds from which social regeneration sprang nineteen centuries ago, but the perennial fruit from which the nations of to-day can best derive both nutriment and healing. All this M. Garriguet makes definite and evident. At the same time he does not ignore the objections that have been urged against his thesis on the ground of " the otherworldness " of the Gospel principles. These he fairly states and justly answers. Both for its' constructive and its critical perfections the book deserves praise and recommendation.

Literary Chat.

A new monthly Review has just been started in Paris. As its title, *L'Eucharistie*, suggests, it is devoted to the Blessed Sacrament. Doctrinal

The little brochure entitled *Practical Socialism* by the Right Rev. J. M. Lucy, V.G., has within a month passed into a second edition ·(10,000). This may be taken as an indication that, notwithstanding the many other booklets and fracts already in the field, it is found to be a serviceable ally in the anti-Socialistic campaign. It is a practical brief on the impracticability of practical Socialism. Its price is no less practical—twenty-five cents per hundred (Catholic Publication Society, Little Rock, Arkansas).

Damien of Molokai, a recent addition to the charming *St. Nicholas Series,* should meet with a warm welcome from all who admire heroism and desire to read the story of one of its noblest personal embodiments. To say that the present life is from the graceful pen of May Quinlan is to attest its literary perfection (Benziger Bros.).

The Divine Story, a short Life of our Lord written especially for young people by the Rev. Cornelius Holland, S.T.L., has recently appeared in "a popular price edition", which places the book within easy reach of the impecunious and facilitates a wider circulation by priests amongst the youth under their charge. Notwithstanding the small price (fifty cents), the book is very well made and presentable (Tally, Providence).

Prince Izon by James Paul Kelly (Chicago: McClurg) is a unique sort of a novel—unique certainly in its location, in some at least of its characters, nor less so in its action. In the heart of the Grand Cañon of the Colorado two wonderful cities are mysteriously discovered by an archeologist and his fair daughter and niece, under the guidance of Black Eagle, a friendly Indian chief—Red City, founded and inhabited by pagan descendants of the ancient Aztecs; and Pearl City, established by Christian descendants of the same race. The exploring party is rescued from imminent perils by Prince Izon, the mighty and beautiful ruler of Pearl City and the last descendant of Montezuma. Both he and they are shortly afterwards suddenly captured by marauders from Red City. The story then centres on the life of the prisoners in the Red City, where unbounded luxury and pagan orgies run riot. Love, intrigue, plots, counterplots, secret communications, telepathic and subterraneous, between the captives and the Christian Aztecs, hair-breadth escapes, preternatural feats, weird things succeed one another with marvellous rapidity. Pagan villians are destroyed. Christians and heroes triumph. The marriages of Prince Izon and Mariam, Black Eagle and Isabel, are left to the reader's easy inference. The story reflects a great but an undisciplined imagination. The impossibility of two magnificent cities being hidden away in a cañon exceeds all bounds except such as are set by Gulliver or Münchausen. Then, too, some of the voluptuous details are needlessly minute. They mar the story and unfit it for pure eyes. Mr. Kelly, it may be inferred from some liturgical descriptions here and there—beautiful, too, by the way they are—is a Catholic. He will do good fictional work when he brings his imagination under the discipline of healthy, temperate art. *Ne quid nimis.*

The unforeseen crowding of official documents and other matter pre
arranged to appear in the present number of the REVIEW, together with the
added Index of Volume XLII, obliges us to hold over some important papers
among which is an article on Fr. Stephen Donovan's argument *De operatione
chirurgica Vasectomiae* by the Roman Professor Ethelbert Rigby, of the Dominican Seminary, Collegio Angelico.

An unprejudiced exposition of the view St. Jerome took of Biblical inspiration forms the subject of the last number of *Biblische Studien*. It is a topic
which, like the Christological studies that have recently appeared in the great
series of monographs under the direction of Dr. Bardenhewer, demands the
careful consideration of our teachers of Scripture and dogma in the Seminary.
The air is full of Modernism in the sense in which Loisy represents it, and
we cannot afford to exaggerate the orthodox teaching in the opposite direction
and in the name of the Church, without being charged with narrowness where
the charge is just.

Many priests will read with a sense of satisfaction the arguments advanced
by Dr. O'Malley on the immorality, from the medical standpoint, of interfering with the life of the unborn child. Whilst we have the stereotyped plea
of our moral theologians and the concessions on similar grounds of the older
medical ethicians, it has become a general principle of action among surgeons
who otherwise hold to sound doctrines of Christianity, that in the domain of
rights to existence the maternal life has a claim superior to that of the undeveloped offspring. Dr. O'Malley, who unites the advantages of a thorough
familiarity with theological ethics to the opportunities of observation and
practice during a number of years as chief surgeon in one of the best city
hospitals, addresses himself to surgeons chiefly. Hence his defence of the
rights of the unborn child will serve to relieve pastors from the necessity of
arguing with the physician who may follow the popular view. Let them
simply place a copy of Dr. O'Malley's article in the hands of the medical
men in the parish. THE ECCLESIASTICAL REVIEW has kept a number of separate
reprints for this purpose to be had at the publishing office.

The Rev. M. Lepin's *Jésus, Messie et Fils de Dieu* has just been translated
into English and is published under the title *Christ and the Gospel* (John
Jos. McVey, Philadelphia). The book deals chiefly with the proofs of the
Divine Messiahship demonstrated from the Synoptic Gospels, and is an admirable answer to the critique of Loisy and the Modernist school of exegetes.
The Introduction on the authorship and historicity of the Synoptic Gospels
forms an essential part of the study of the great problem of Christ's manifestation of Himself as the Man-God.

A neatly-printed little volume by the Rev. Dr. John F. Mullany adds to the
copious but ever-welcome devotional literature on the Blessed Sacrament. *The
Holy Eucharist, the Bread of Angels* is a series of twenty meditations discussing the characteristics, fruits, and manifold relations of the Holy Eucharist.
Each brief reflection is followed by a practical indication of fruits to be
gathered from the thoughts presented. As the English is good, it would have
been a graceful thing to indicate in the Preface the sources of the translations from the French mentioned on the title-page.

Books Received.

BIBLICAL.

CONFÉRENCES DE SAINT-ÉTIENNE (École Pratique d'Études Bibliques), 1909-1910. (*Études palestiniennes et orientales.*) Paris: J. Gabalda & Cie. 1910. Pp. x-321. Prix, 3 *fr.* 50.

L'ÉVANGILE EN FACE DU SYNCRÉTISME PAÏEN. Par Bernard Allo, O.P., professeur à l'Université de Fribourg. (*Études de Philosophie et de Critique Religieuse.*) Paris. Bloud et Cie. 1910. Pp. xxi-205. Prix, 3 *fr.*

THE CHILDHOOD OF JESUS CHRIST ACCORDING TO THE CANONICAL GOSPELS. With an Historical Essay on the Brethren of the Lord. By A. Durand, S.J. An authorized translation from the French. Edited by the Rev. Joseph Bruneau, S.S., D.D. Philadelphia: John Joseph McVey. 1910. Pp. xxv-316. Price, $1.50 *net.*

THE DIVINE STORY. A Short Life of our Blessed Lord written especially for young people. By the Rev. Cornelius Joseph Holland, S.T.L. Illustrated. Providence, R. I.: Joseph M. Tally. 1909. Pp. ix-223. Price, $0.50.

BUCH DES PROPHETEN SOPHONIAS. Erklärt von Dr. Joseph Lippl. (Biblische Studien. Bd. XV, n. 3.) Freiburg, Brisg., St. Louis, Mo.: B. Herder. Pp. 140. Price, $1.20.

SONNENKRAFT: Der Philipperbrief des hl. Paulus, in Homilien für denkende Christen dargelegt. Von Dr. Franz Keller. Approb. Erzb. Freiburg. Freiburg, Brisg., St. Louis, Mo.: B. Herder. 1910. Pp. 128. Price, $0.55.

THEOLOGICAL AND DEVOTIONAL.

DIRECTION PRATIQUE ET MORALE POUR VIVRE CHRÉTIENNEMENT. Par le R. P. Quadrupani. Traduction nouvelle par le P. V. H., S.J. Sixième édition. Paris: P. Téqui. 1910. Pp. xvi-179. Prix, 1 *fr.*

DIRECTION POUR RASSURER DANS LEURS DOUTES LES AMES TIMORÉES. Par le R. P. Quadrupani. Traduction nouvelle par le P. V. H., S.J. Sixième édition. Paris: P. Téqui. 1910. Pp. xvii-158. Prix, 1 *fr.*

NEWMAN MEMORIAL SERMONS. By the Rev. Joseph Rickaby, S.J., and the Very Rev. Canon McIntyre, Professor of Scripture at St. Mary's College, Oscott. New York, London: Longmans, Green & Co. 1910. Pp. 44. Price, $0.36 *net.*

TRAITÉ DES SCRUPULES. Instructions pour éclairer, diriger, consoler et guérir les personnes scrupuleuses. Par M. l'Abbé Grimes, auteur de *L'Esprit des Saints.* Nouvelle édition augmentée d'un chapitre sur les Scrupules par le R. P. Faber. Paris: P. Téqui. 1910. Pp. iv-266. Prix, 1 *fr.*

LA SAINTE VIÈRGE. Exercice en trente méditations. Par L'Abbé P. Feige, Chanoine honoraire, Directeur de l'Œuvre de Marie-Immaculée, Missionaire diocésain de Paris. (*Aux âmes pieuses*) Deuxième édition. Paris: P. Téqui. 1910. Pp. xv-244. Prix, 1 *fr.*

JEANNE D'ARC ET L'ÉGLISE DEVANT LA LIBRE-PENSÉE. Conférence. Par Auguste Texier. Paris: P. Téqui. 1910. Pp. 34. Prix, 0 *fr.* 50.

THE HOLY EUCHARIST. The Bread of Angels. Translated from the French by the Rev. John F. Mullany, LL.D. Syracuse, N. Y.: 1408 Park St. 1909. Pp. xiv-169.

THE RACCOLTA, or Collection of Indulgences, Prayers and Good Works. By Ambrose T. St. John, of the Oratory of St. Philip Neri, Birmingham. New York, Cincinnati, Chicago: Benziger Brothers; London: Burns and Oates. 1910. Pp. xv-428. Price, $1.00.

BUDS AND BLOSSOMS. By the Right Rev. Charles H. Colton, D.D., Bishop of Buffalo. New York, Cincinnati, Chicago: Benziger Brothers. 1910. Pp. 296. Price, $1.25.

DIE GNADE. Sechs Fastenvorträge von Pfarrer Heinrich Hansjacob. Mit Approb. Erzb. von Freiburg. Freiburg, Brisg.; St. Louis, Mo.: B. Herder. 1910. Pp. 64. Price, $0.85.

GOD AND HIS CREATURES. Annotated translation of the "Summa contra Gentiles" of St. Thomas Aquinas. By the Rev. Joseph Rickaby, S.J., author of *Aquinas Ethicus*. St. Louis, Mo.: B. Herder; London: Burns & Oates. 1905. Pp. 423.

JENSEITSRELIGION. Erwägungen über brennende Fragen der Gegenwart. Von Dr. Georg Grupp. Freiburg, Brisg., St. Louis, Mo.: B. Herder. 1910. Pp. 202. Price, $1.00.

DAS GOTTESBEDÜRFNIS. Als Gottesbeweis den Gebildeten dargelegt von Otto Zimmermann, S.J. Freiburg, St. Louis, Mo.: B. Herder. 1910. Pp. xiii-192. Price, $0.70.

THE MONTH OF MARY. Short Meditations, Applications, and Prayers in honor of the Blessed Virgin Mary for every day of the month of May. By the Rev. Bonaventure Hammer, O.F.M. Ratisbon, Rome, New York, Cincinnati: Fr. Pustet & Co. Pp. 104. Price, $0.10.

DIE EXERZITIENWAHRHEITEN. Akademische Vorträge von Heinrich Bruders, S.J. Privatdozent für Dogmengeschichte a. d. Universität Innsbruck. Innsbruck: Felix Rauch. 1910. Pp. 483. Price, $1.00.

HISTORICAL.

DAMIEN OF MOLOKAI. By May Quinlan. Together with Father Damien, an open letter to the Rev. Dr. Hyde of Honolulu, by R. L. Stevenson. New York, Cincinnati, Chicago: Benziger Brothers. 1909. Pp. vii-183. Price, $0.80.

L'AME DE JEANNE D'ARC. Deuxième Edition. Recueil de Panégyriques et Conférences. Par l'Abbé Stephen Coubé. Paris: P. Lethielleux. 1910. Pp. 439. Prix, 4 *francs*.

THE BASILICA OF S. CLEMENTE IN ROME. By Louis Nolan, O.P., B.A. With 53 illustrations. Rome: Fr. Pustet. 1910. Pp. xxix-238. Price, *Lire* 7.50.

HISTORY OF THE HOLY EUCHARIST IN GREAT BRITAIN. By T. E. Bridgett, C.SS.R. With Notes by the Rev. Herbert Thurston, S.J. St. Louis, Mo.: B. Herder; London: Burns & Oates. 1908. Pp. 325.

LIVES OF THE POPES IN THE MIDDLE AGES. By the Rev. Horace K. Mann, St. Cuthbert's, Newcastle-on-Tyne. The Popes in the Days of Feudal Anarchy. Formosus to Damasus II. 891-1048. Vol. IV. St. Louis, Mo.: B. Herder; London: Kegan Paul, Trench, Trübner & Co. 1910. Pp. 453. Price, $3.00.

ANALECTA.